ADDITIONAL COOKBOOKS AND DVD SETS AVAILABLE FROM THE PUBLISHERS OF *COOK'S COUNTRY* INCLUDE:

The *America's Test Kitchen* Library Series

The *America's Test Kitchen* Do-It-Yourself Cookbook

Slow Cooker Revolution

The Best Simple Recipes

Slow Cooker Revolution Volume 2: The Easy-Prep Edition

The Six-Ingredient Solution

Comfort Food Makeovers

Cook's Country Blue Ribbon Desserts

From Our Grandmothers' Kitchens

Cook's Country Best Potluck Recipes

Cook's Country Best Grilling Recipes

Cook's Country Annual Editions
from each year of publication (2005–2013)

From the Editors of *Cook's Illustrated*

The *Cook's Illustrated* Baking Book

The Science of Good Cooking

Cook's Illustrated Cookbook

The Best One-Dish Suppers

The *America's Test Kitchen* Menu Cookbook

Soups, Stews & Chilis

The New Best Recipe

The Best Skillet Recipes

The Best Slow and Easy Recipes

The Best Chicken Recipes

The Best International Recipe

The Best Make-Ahead Recipe

The Best 30-Minute Recipe

The Best Light Recipe

The *Cook's Illustrated* Guide to
Grilling and Barbecue

Best American Side Dishes

Cover & Bake

Steaks, Chops, Roasts, and Ribs

Baking Illustrated

Perfect Vegetables

Italian Classics

The Best American Classics

1993–2013 *Cook's Illustrated* Master Index

Cook's Illustrated Annual Editions
from each year of publication (1993–2013)

America's Test Kitchen

The *America's Test Kitchen* Cooking School Cookbook

The Best of *America's Test Kitchen* (2007–2014 Editions)

Cooking for Two (2009–2013 Editions)

The *America's Test Kitchen* Family Baking Book

The *America's Test Kitchen* Family Cookbook

The *America's Test Kitchen* Healthy Family Cookbook

The *America's Test Kitchen* Quick Family Cookbook

The *America's Test Kitchen* Series Companion Cookbooks

America's Test Kitchen: The TV Companion Cookbook (2013)

America's Test Kitchen: The TV Companion Cookbook (2012)

America's Test Kitchen: The TV Companion Cookbook (2011)

The Complete *America's Test Kitchen* TV Show Cookbook (2010)

America's Test Kitchen: The TV Companion Cookbook (2009)

Behind the Scenes with *America's Test Kitchen* (2008)

Test Kitchen Favorites (2007)

Cooking at Home with *America's Test Kitchen* (2006)

America's Test Kitchen Live! (2005)

Inside *America's Test Kitchen* (2004)

Here in *America's Test Kitchen* (2003)

The *America's Test Kitchen* Cookbook (2002)

The *America's Test Kitchen* Series DVD Sets
(featuring each season's episodes from our hit
public television series)

The *America's Test Kitchen* 4-DVD Set (2002–2013 Seasons)

The *America's Test Kitchen* 2-DVD Set (2001 Season)

The *Cook's Country* TV Series Cookbooks and DVD Sets
(featuring each season's episodes from our hit
public television series)

The Complete *Cook's Country* TV Show Cookbook

The *Cook's Country* 2-DVD Set (Seasons 1–6)

Visit our online bookstore at CooksCountry.com to order any of our cookbooks and DVDs listed above. You can also order subscriptions, gift subscriptions, and any of our cookbooks and DVDs by calling 800-611-0759 inside the U.S., or 515-246-6911 if calling from outside the U.S.

$35.00

Published by America's Test Kitchen, 17 Station Street, Brookline, MA 02445
ISBN-13: 978-1-936493-67-8   ISSN: 1552-1990

To get home delivery of *Cook's Country*, call 800-526-8447 inside the U.S., or 515-247-7571 if calling from outside the U.S.,
or subscribe online at CooksCountry.com.

2013 Recipe Index

Cook's Country

FEBRUARY/MARCH 2013

New Orleans Beignets

Honey-Roasted Baby Back Ribs

Best Chicken and Stuffing

"Impossible" Quiche
The Crust Makes Itself

Roast Beef with Gravy
Step-by-Step Cooking Class

Chocolate Angel Pie
Crisp Meringue Pie Shell

Five Easy Tomato Sauces
15 Minutes to Deep Flavor

Slow-Cooker Meatloaf
Surprise Secret Ingredient

Low-Fat Tiramisù
Still Silky and Decadent

Testing Cookie Sheets
50 Percent Fail Completely

Broiled Pork Chops
Crusty but Tender

Tasting Chili Powders
How Much Heat Is Good?

CooksCountry.com
$4.95 U.S./$6.95 CANADA

The famous beignets of New Orleans are a varied lot. The very best we found there were tender, delicately sweet, and pleasantly yeasty. After weeks in the test kitchen, we figured out how to make them just like that. PAGE 6

Cook's Country

Dear Country Cook,

Every fall I stop by Saratoga Apple and visit with Nate Darrow, whose family has been in the apple-growing business for five generations. He shares information about growing apples (I have my own small orchard), including the benefits of adding stone dust and kelp to enhance the soil. Since folks buy fewer apples these days—they used to buy a couple of bushels; now they pick up just a handful—Nate offers hay rides, hot chocolate, jams and jellies, baked goods, and, my favorite, homemade cider doughnuts. These orbs of happiness are cranked out of a Rube Goldberg machine, dumped off of a long conveyer belt into a pile, and then sugared. I buy a half-dozen for my ride home, and the white, crinkled bag is empty before I turn into the driveway.

I grew up on Marie Brigg's nutmeg doughnuts—huge country-style fistfuls of fried dough, crisp on the outside and moist in the center. For years, I made them for coffee hour at the Methodist Church, my stack of mahogany rings flanked by leftover birthday cake, yellow plastic coffee mugs, and a half-box of Entenmann's cookies. It doesn't pay to outdo the neighbors (no pancakes made to order please!), but nutmeg doughnuts are always welcome.

During World War II, the American Red Cross was ordered by the Secretary of War to start charging soldiers for doughnuts after the British complained that since they charged for their food, they looked cheap by comparison. That left hard feelings on the part of many veterans and with good reason. Coffee and free doughnuts are reminders of a nation's generosity.

That makes me wonder—if we just handed out free doughnuts, maybe we could change the world!

Christopher Kimball
Founder and Editor, Cook's Country

Doughnuts for Doughboys: During World War II, American-style doughnuts cheered the spirits of many North American soldiers who were stationed in England.

Cook's Country

Founder and Editor Christopher Kimball
Editorial Director Jack Bishop
Editorial Director, Magazines John Willoughby
Executive Editor Peggy Grodinsky
Managing Editor Scott Kathan
Senior Editors Lisa McManus, Bryan Roof, Diane Unger
Test Kitchen Director Erin McMurrer
Associate Editors Chris Dudley, Amy Graves, Rebeccah Marsters
Test Cooks Sarah Gabriel, Nick Iverson, Carolynn Purpura MacKay, Cristin Walsh
Assistant Editors Hannah Crowley, Shannon Friedmann Hatch, Taizeth Sierra
Copy Editors Nell Beram, Megan Chromik
Executive Assistant Christine Gordon
Test Kitchen Manager Leah Rovner
Senior Kitchen Assistant Meryl MacCormack
Kitchen Assistants Maria Elena Delgado, Ena Gudiel, Andrew Straaberg Finfrock
Executive Producer Melissa Baldino
Associate Producer Stephanie Stender
Production Assistant Kaitlin Hammond

Contributing Editors Erika Bruce, Eva Katz, Jeremy Sauer
Consulting Editors Anne Mendelson, Meg Ragland
Science Editor Guy Crosby, Ph.D.
Executive Food Editor, TV, Radio & Media Bridget Lancaster

Managing Editor, Web Christine Liu
Associate Editors, Web Eric Grzymkowski, Mari Levine, Roger Metcalf
Senior Video Editor Nick Dakoulas

Design Director Amy Klee
Art Director Julie Cote
Deputy Art Director Susan Levin
Associate Art Director Lindsey Timko
Staff Photographer Daniel J. van Ackere
Color Food Photography Keller + Keller
Styling Catrine Kelty
Designer, Marketing/Web Mariah Tarvainen
Photo Editor Steve Klise

Vice President, Marketing David Mack
Circulation Director Doug Wicinski
Circulation & Fulfillment Manager Carrie Fethe
Partnership Marketing Manager Pamela Putprush
Marketing Assistant Joyce Liao
Customer Service Manager Jacqueline Valerio
Customer Service Representatives Megan Hamner, Jessica Haskin

Chief Operating Officer David Dinnage
Production Director Guy Rochford
Senior Project Manager Alice Carpenter
Workflow & Digital Asset Manager Andrew Mannone
Production & Traffic Coordinator Brittany Allen
Production & Imaging Specialists Heather Dube, Lauren Pettapiece, Lauren Robbins
Systems Administrator Marcus Walser
Helpdesk Support Technician Brianna Brothers
Senior Business Analyst Wendy Tseng
Web Developer Chris Candelora
Human Resources Manager Adele Shapiro

VP New Media Product Development Barry Kelly
Assistant Editor, New Media Amy Scheuerman
Chief Financial Officer Sharyn Chabot
Director of Sponsorship Sales Anne Traficante
Retail Sales & Marketing Manager Emily Logan
Client Services Associate Kate May
Sponsorship Sales Representative Morgan Ryan
Publicity Deborah Broide

ON THE COVER:
Beignets
Keller + Keller, Catrine Kelty
ILLUSTRATION: Greg Stevenson

Cook's Country magazine (ISSN 1552-1990), number 49, published bimonthly by Boston Common Press Limited Partnership, 17 Station St., Brookline, MA 02445. Copyright 2013 Boston Common Press Limited Partnership. Periodicals postage paid at Boston, Mass., and additional mailing offices. USPS #023453. Publications Mail Agreement No. 40778.Return undeliverable Canadian addresses to P.O. Box 875, Station A, Windsor, ON N9A 6P2. POSTMASTER: Send address changes to Cook's Country, P.O. Box 6018, Harlan, IA 51593-1518. For subscription and gift subscription orders, subscription inquiries, or change-of-address notices, visit AmericasTestKitchen.com/customerservice, call 800-526-8442 in the U.S. or 515-248-7684 from outside the U.S., or write to Cook's Country, P.O. Box 6018, Harlan, IA 51593-1518. PRINTED IN THE USA

Contents

FEBRUARY/MARCH 2013

BUTTERY BRAISED VEGETABLES, 5

CHICKEN AND RICE SOUP, 17

CHOCOLATE ANGEL PIE, 22

Features

Departments

Calling All Adventurous Cooks

With a good recipe guiding the way, homemade is always better. So why stop at dinner? In our latest cookbook, *The America's Test Kitchen Do-It-Yourself Cookbook* ($26.95), our editors and test cooks walk you through more than 100 of our favorite DIY kitchen projects, showing you why everything from ketchup and corn chips to goat cheese and prosciutto tastes better when you do it yourself. You'll find plenty of good things to eat, drink, and make, whether you're a seasoned pro or simply a curious cook.

America's Test Kitchen is a very real 2,500 square-foot kitchen located just outside Boston. It is the home of *Cook's Country* and *Cook's Illustrated* magazines and is the workday destination of more than three dozen test cooks, editors, and cookware specialists. Our mission is to test recipes over and over again until we understand how and why they work and until we arrive at the best version. We also test kitchen equipment and supermarket ingredients in search of brands that offer the best value and performance. You can watch us work by tuning in to *Cook's Country from America's Test Kitchen* (CooksCountryTV.com) and *America's Test Kitchen* (AmericasTestKitchenTV.com) on public television.

RECIPES THAT WORK®

Ask Cook's Country

BY SARAH GABRIEL

I was shopping for a spiral-sliced ham, and I noticed that some were labeled "shank end" and others "butt end." What's the difference? Which one should I buy?
Cole Tucker, Northampton, Mass.

A whole ham is the entire rear leg of a pig. Hams are often split into the "butt" (sometimes called "sirloin") portion, which is closest to the haunch, and the "shank" portion, which is lower down the leg, yielding two half hams of more manageable proportions (about 7 to 10 pounds each). Most of the time, they are labeled, but if not, they are clearly distinguishable in that the butt is more domed, while the shank end is more conical. The butt end is meatier and less fatty than the shank end but it has odd-shaped bones, making it trickier to free the slices. The shank end is slightly fattier but, with a simpler bone structure, is much easier to carve. To see exactly how we carve a shank-end, spiral-sliced ham, go to **CooksCountry.com/mapleglazedham.**
THE BOTTOM LINE: For easy carving, buy a shank-end, spiral-sliced half ham, heat, and simply slice the meat off the bone. The butt (or sirloin) end requires the carver to remove blocks of meat from around the T-shaped bone structure.

BUTT END
Domed shape, trickier to carve.

SHANK END
Pointed shape, a breeze to carve.

I've stashed spent vanilla beans in white sugar to make vanilla sugar. Does this work with brown sugar?
Sally Witherspoon, Mobile, Ala.

When we're using the seeds from a fresh vanilla pod to flavor custard or panna cotta, say, we save the spent (halved lengthwise) pods to make vanilla sugar: We simply stick the spent pods in an airtight container of sugar and wait. Be sure to dry the pods first, if they are wet, and try rubbing sugar into them to extract extra flavor. To see whether brown sugar, which is more assertive and moister than granulated white sugar, would pick up vanilla flavor in the same manner, we made two batches of vanilla sugar: one with light brown sugar and one with the usual granulated sugar. We let them sit for two weeks so the vanilla flavor could fully infuse.

Tasted straight out of the container, the vanilla granulated sugar had significant vanilla aroma and flavor, while the vanilla brown sugar had only a slight aroma and very little vanilla flavor. When baked into cookies, the results tracked: The sugar cookies made with vanilla granulated sugar were redolent of vanilla, while it was hard to detect any vanilla flavor at all in the brown sugar cookies made with vanilla brown sugar.
THE BOTTOM LINE: Because brown sugar has strong flavors to begin with, don't bother storing it with vanilla bean pods: You won't taste the vanilla. Save your spent vanilla pods for making vanilla sugar with white granulated sugar.

I've heard that applesauce can be a healthier substitute for oil when making box-mix brownies. Really?
Rachel Miller-Munzer, Boston, Mass.

Most brownie mixes—including our taste test winner, Ghirardelli Chocolate Supreme—require the baker to add oil, water, and eggs. Some of these box mixes recommend applesauce as a substitution for the oil to cut fat. To test the idea, we made two batches of the Ghirardelli mix and of mixes from industry giants Duncan Hines and Betty Crocker. We made one batch of each mix according to the package instructions and another swapping an equal volume of applesauce for the oil.

The verdict was mixed. At best, several tasters found the applesauce versions "acceptable for a low-fat brownie" (hardly a ringing endorsement). It was the texture that suffered. The brownies made with oil were chewy and fudgy, while the applesauce versions were cakey in the best cases ("Like a snack cake," tasters said of the Ghirardelli mix) and spongy and dry in the worst (the mixes from Duncan Hines and Betty Crocker). These applesauce brownies didn't look right, either. Their tops were dull and pockmarked.

Not thrilled with the results, we wondered whether other common baking substitutes intended to reduce fat would fare better in brownie mix. Using the same three brands, we made six more batches of brownies, substituting, in turn, prune baby food and fat-free mayonnaise for the oil. The results were similar to those of the applesauce tests. Some of these brownies tasted like tolerable chocolate cake (they weren't rich and fudgy like brownies, but they weren't awful, either). Others were gummy, tough, spongy, and entirely unacceptable.
THE BOTTOM LINE: Skip applesauce, prune baby food, or fat-free mayonnaise in place of oil in brownie mixes. In fact, skip the mix altogether and make our recipe for Fudgy Low-Fat Brownies (**CooksCountry.com/lowfatbrownies**). Granted, it's more work, but the texture and taste are spot on.

BROWNIE BUMMERS
Using nonfat mayonnaise, prune baby food, or applesauce in brownie mix is a bad idea.

My wooden cutting board is starting to look dull and dry. How can I keep it lustrous and prevent it from cracking?
Lou Spezzaferro, Wewoka, Okla.

Wooden cutting boards need to be washed in hot soapy water to keep them clean and safe (some people use a diluted bleach solution, but we've found that isn't necessary), but over time this treatment takes a toll. Repeated wetting and drying can make wood fibers rough and dry, and eventually the wood may warp or even split. You could use a plastic board, but we prefer the feel of wood.

To keep wooden cutting boards in great shape, we recommend rubbing them with food-grade mineral oil (available at most drugstores and hardware stores) every few months. The wood soaks up the mineral oil, creating a barrier to water. Most wooden cutting boards require oiling six or seven times a year (depending on how frequently they are used and washed). Don't use olive or vegetable oil, which can become rancid and can make the food that comes into contact with the board taste bad. Our favorite cutting board, the Proteak Edge Grain Teak Cutting Board, requires less oiling because teak (a tropical wood often used in shipbuilding) contains compounds that are naturally resistant to moisture.
THE BOTTOM LINE: Give your wooden cutting boards a moisture-blocking coat of food-grade mineral oil when they're new and every month after that. Or pick up the Proteak Edge Grain Teak Cutting Board ($85), which is naturally moisture-resistant and should require oiling only once or twice per year.

FOOD-GRADE MINERAL OIL
Prevents the moisture damage that can eventually make wooden boards crack.

PROTEAK EDGE GRAIN TEAK CUTTING BOARD
At $85, our favorite cutting board is a hefty investment, but you won't have to oil it that frequently.

When frying chicken cutlets, I use beaten whole eggs to help the bread crumbs adhere. Some recipes use egg whites. Is that better?
Adam French, Bend, Ore.

To answer your question, we made two batches of fried chicken cutlets: one using beaten whole egg and one using egg whites between the flour and bread-crumb dredges. Both batches of pan-fried cutlets offered big crunch and held on to the bread crumbs perfectly. A few tasters noticed that the cutlets breaded with whole egg had a richer, fuller flavor, but the difference was minimal.
THE BOTTOM LINE: Either beaten whole eggs or whites will work for breaded cutlets. Whole eggs will give the cutlets a slightly fuller flavor—and you won't be stuck with a leftover yolk. On the other hand, using just whites will shave some fat and calories.

▶ To ask us a cooking question, visit **CooksCountry.com/askcookscountry**. Or write to Ask Cook's Country, P.O. Box 47073, Brookline, MA 02447. Just try to stump us!

Illustration: Jay Layman

Kitchen Shortcuts

COMPILED BY NICK IVERSON

TIDY TIP **No-Mess Breakfast**
Norma Dudley, Saratoga Springs, N.Y.

My kids love to make waffles on the weekends, but they usually make a mess of the kitchen—batter oozes out the sides of the iron and gunks up the counter. I know it sounds obvious, but I've found that setting the waffle iron on top of a sheet of aluminum foil makes cleanup easy; a disposable aluminum foil baking sheet works, too, if your kids are world-class mess makers.

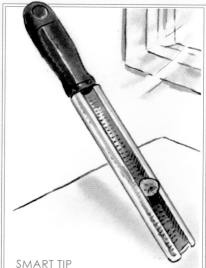

SMART TIP
Shelter from the Storm
Sandy Wilson, Eureka, Calif.

My kitchen has a lot of windows, so I often have a pretty good breeze blowing through. This was a problem after I had used my rasp-style grater to grate fresh nutmeg: Sometimes the wind would wreak havoc on my neatly grated piles of the spice. Now I grate nutmeg (and small amounts of chocolate) with the grater's plastic protective sleeve on; the sleeve is meant to cover the grating side, but it's easy to flip it. The sleeve catches the nutmeg and protects it from blowing away.

DOUBLE DUTY **Instant Thickener**
Ron Sopp, via E-mail

When I need to quickly thicken a gravy or stew, I grab a box of instant mashed potatoes. Just a sprinkle of the dehydrated flakes helps me achieve the desired consistency in seconds without changing how the dish tastes.

Submit a tip online at **CooksCountry.com/kitchenshortcuts** or send a letter to Kitchen Shortcuts, *Cook's Country*, P.O. Box 470739, Brookline, MA 02447. Include your name, address, and phone number. If we publish your tip, you will receive a free one-year subscription to *Cook's Country*. Letters may be edited for clarity and length.

NEAT TRICK
Ending Butter Blast
Paula Sullivan, Minnetonka, Minn.

When I used to melt butter in the microwave, it was always a delicate balance between not quite melted and so hot it splattered all over. A neighbor recently showed me a trick that can help: Put a small bowl of water in the microwave along with the dish of butter. The water absorbs the brunt of the microwave's energy, so the butter melts gently instead of splattering.

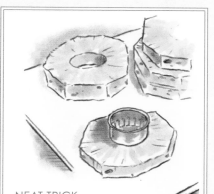

NEAT TRICK
Perfect Pineapple
Sena Lauritsen, Wood, S.D.

TV chefs always seem to peel, core, and dice pineapple in seconds, but prepping pineapple is a chore for me. After a lot of trial and error, I've come up with a simple, efficient method. I cut off the top and bottom and then cut away the peel (and eyes) before slicing the pineapple into rounds. Then I use a small cookie cutter to cut out the core. It's easy and it works great.

SMART TIP **Lid Leverage**
Meggan Rice, Tucson, Ariz.

If you've ever tried to remove the second plastic lid (the one with the holes, beneath the screw cap) from a spice bottle so you can get your measuring spoon inside, you know it can be one of those tougher-than-it-should-be tasks. I broke many a fingernail wrestling with those lids until I hit upon a better way. I take a bottle opener and pop off the second lid. It comes off nice and easy.

DOUBLE DUTY **Jiffy Lube**
Mark Collins, Omaha, Neb.

A friend recently showed me a great way to grease muffin tins. Instead of throwing out the wrapper after finishing a stick of butter, I use the residual butter left on the wrapper to grease the muffin tins. There's no mess and no waste.

Weeknight Roast Chicken with Stuffing

We wanted to make this homey, classic dinner easy enough to enjoy on any night of the week.

BY CAROLYNN PURPURA MACKAY

Roast chicken is fairly simple to make, but add stuffing (or "dressing") on the side, and suddenly dinner gets a lot more complicated. And don't get me started on all the pots and pans required to prepare it: a baking sheet (to toast or stale the cubed bread), a skillet (to sauté the onion, celery, and herbs), a bowl and wooden spoon (to mix everything together), and a roasting pan (for the chicken itself). Chicken with stuffing is doable as a weekend project, but what if you want it on a Tuesday? I vowed to streamline the recipe.

First, though, why cook the stuffing on the side and not inside the bird? In the test kitchen, we're not fans of stuffed chickens: By the time the stuffing reaches a safe 165 degrees inside the bird, the breast meat is seriously overcooked, stringy, and dry. On top of that, the cavity of a chicken can't fit enough stuffing to feed four diners. But there's a drawback to cooking the stuffing separately, too: It can't absorb the delicious chicken juices. We've learned to live with that, but only reluctantly.

I didn't have to look too far for great recipes for roast chicken or tasty stuffing; the test kitchen has plenty of each. I began with a stovetop stuffing recipe (I'd still have to toast the bread in advance) and a recipe for chicken that calls for brushing the bird with herb butter (I figured that would echo the flavors in the stuffing) and then roasting it at 325 degrees in a roasting pan, starting breast side down and flipping it partway through. Since the oven was already on, I'd toast the bread cubes on a baking sheet underneath the chicken. As bread and bird cooked, I sautéed onions, celery, thyme, and

There's no need to toast the bread (or wait for it to stale): Our recipe uses fresh cubed bread and takes only about an hour to cook.

sage for the stuffing. Ninety minutes later, the chicken was ready, but in this comparatively slow oven, the bread had staled (good) but not browned (bad, since color translates into flavor). While the chicken rested so the juices could redistribute, I combined the toasted bread cubes, sautéed aromatics, and some chicken stock that I'd warmed up (what? Another pot?) and let the mixture sit, covered, for several minutes to moisten.

This chicken was moist, nicely flavored, and buttery, but 90 minutes was a long wait. Also, the stuffing was merely fine; not unexpectedly, it lacked good toasty flavor. I didn't need to be a rocket scientist to solve these problems. I increased the oven temperature to 375 degrees. Now the bread browned properly and the chicken was ready in 1 hour.

But my kitchen sink was still full of dishes. Could I cook the vegetables with the chicken? I tried roasting the

chicken over a bed of raw onions, celery, and herbs. The vegetables picked up extra flavor from the chicken juice, but that gain was negated by their failure to brown. Since cooking the aromatics in the roasting pan hadn't worked out, how about roasting the chicken in the skillet? After sautéing the vegetables in the skillet, I plopped the raw bird on top and moved the entire setup to the oven, where . . . the delicate breast meat overcooked.

Why? I'd followed normal test kitchen procedure, roasting the chicken breast side down to shield it and slow its cooking (white meat is ready at 160 degrees, dark meat at 175). But wait—this skillet was hot before it ever entered the oven, so the breast meat, in direct contact with the hot skillet, actually cooked quicker—the last thing I needed. The next time, I cooked the chicken breast side up for the entire time, letting the hot pan jump-start the cooking of the dark-meat thighs and putting light and dark meat on a compatible schedule.

After weeks of roasting chickens, it suddenly occurred to me to scatter the bread cubes in the skillet around the raw chicken instead of toasting them in a separate pan, as I'd been doing. If this worked, I would be able to cook my entire meal in one dish and at one time (plus, now the bread could absorb the chicken juice after all). The chicken baked, the bread cubes browned, and the kitchen smelled fantastic. When the bird was done, I let it rest on a plate, added a splash of chicken broth to the vegetables and bread cubes still in the skillet, and warmed the stuffing through. Now I can eat my favorite Sunday supper any night of the week.

SKILLET-ROASTED CHICKEN AND STUFFING Serves 4

You can find Italian bread in the bakery section of your grocery store. Take care when stirring the contents of the skillet in steps 4 and 5, as the skillet handle will be very hot.

- 1 (4-pound) whole chicken, giblets discarded
- 6 tablespoons unsalted butter
- 2 tablespoons minced fresh sage
- 2 tablespoons minced fresh thyme
  Salt and pepper
- 2 onions, chopped fine
- 2 celery ribs, minced
- 7 ounces Italian bread, cut into ½-inch cubes (6 cups)
- ⅓ cup low-sodium chicken broth

1. Adjust oven rack to lower-middle position and heat oven to 375 degrees. Pat chicken dry with paper towels. Melt 4 tablespoons butter in small bowl in microwave, about 45 seconds. Stir in 1 tablespoon sage, 1 tablespoon thyme, 1 teaspoon salt, and ½ teaspoon pepper. Brush chicken with herb butter.

2. Melt remaining 2 tablespoons butter in 12-inch ovensafe skillet over medium heat. Add onions, celery, ½ teaspoon salt, and ½ teaspoon pepper and cook until softened, about 5 minutes. Add remaining 1 tablespoon sage and remaining 1 tablespoon thyme and cook until fragrant, about 1 minute. Off heat, place chicken, breast side up, on top of vegetables. Arrange bread cubes around chicken in bottom of skillet.

▶ Want something green on the plate? Visit CooksCountry.com/amandine for our recipe for Green Beans Amandine.

3. Transfer skillet to oven and roast until breasts register 160 degrees and thighs register 175 degrees, about 1 hour, rotating skillet halfway through roasting.

4. Carefully transfer chicken to plate and tent loosely with aluminum foil. Holding skillet handle with potholder (handle will be hot), stir bread and vegetables to combine, cover, and let stand for 10 minutes.

5. Add broth and any accumulated chicken juice from plate and cavity to skillet and stir to combine. Warm stuffing, uncovered, over low heat until heated through, about 3 minutes. Remove from heat, cover, and let sit while carving chicken. Transfer chicken to carving board, carve, and serve with stuffing.

TEST KITCHEN TECHNIQUE **Layering Skillet-Roasted Chicken and Stuffing**
With our method, you can roast a chicken and make stuffing with hardly any hands-on time—or dishes.

BUTTER ON BIRD
Brush chicken with seasoned herb butter.

BUILD FLAVOR BASE
Sauté celery and onion in butter with more herbs, salt, and pepper.

BIRD ON VEGETABLES
Place chicken in center of skillet on top of sautéed vegetables.

BREAD AROUND BIRD
Surround chicken with untoasted bread cubes and bake.

Buttery Braised Vegetables

Two sticks of butter and 45 minutes' cooking time? Give us a break. We'd make this dish faster, slimmer, and better. BY CAROLYNN PURPURA MACKAY

SINCE I'M ALWAYS on the hunt for simple vegetable side dishes, I was excited recently when I came across a recipe that called for slowly braising carrots, Brussels sprouts, and radishes in butter. It sounded delicious, and it was. The tender vegetables were infused with and coated in sweet, salty, savory butter—the braised radishes, especially, were a revelation. Unfortunately, this recipe used two sticks of butter and took close to 45 minutes to make—deal breakers for me. After all, this is just a simple vegetable side (and one that I'd prefer didn't clog my arteries). I headed into the test kitchen to try to reduce both the cooking time and the amount of butter.

My first thought was to cook the vegetables in just 8 tablespoons of butter whisked into a few cups of water to form a stable emulsion. This worked well. It worked so well, in fact, that I repeated the test seven more times, lopping off a tablespoon of butter each time. By the time I got down to a single tablespoon of butter (for 2 cups of water), I was shocked (and pleased) that my tasters and I could still register some butter flavor in the vegetables. For faster cooking, I cut the vegetables into smaller pieces, slicing the carrots on the bias and quartering the radishes and Brussels sprouts. Then I cooked them, covered, until they were tender, about 15 minutes.

Now, how best to deliver a final blast of butter? Tossing the drained vegetables with 3 tablespoons of melted butter added nice flavor but made the dish a little greasy. In my next test I strained the vegetables and reserved the braising liquid. Then I made a fast sauce by whisking that same 3 tablespoons of butter into ¼ cup of the butter-and-vegetable-infused cooking liquid. This made an emulsified sauce that was much better. To boost the flavor even more, I switched to chicken broth for braising instead of the water I had been using. It more than worked. With a final flourish of a sprinkling of chives, I had a rich—but not deadly—dish of buttery braised vegetables that took only about 15 minutes to cook. This dish will definitely become a regular in my repertoire.

Our vegetable mix includes radishes, which soften and sweeten when braised.

BUTTER-BRAISED VEGETABLES
Serves 6
Look for Brussels sprouts slightly smaller than golf balls; if using smaller sprouts, you may want to halve them.

- 2 cups low-sodium chicken broth
- 4 tablespoons unsalted butter
- 1 pound carrots, peeled and sliced ¼ inch thick on bias
- 1 pound radishes, trimmed and quartered
- 12 ounces Brussels sprouts, trimmed and quartered
  Salt and pepper
- 2 tablespoons minced fresh chives

1. Bring broth to simmer in Dutch oven over medium-low heat. Whisk in 1 tablespoon butter until melted. Add carrots, radishes, Brussels sprouts, 1 teaspoon salt, and ½ teaspoon pepper to pot. Cover and cook, stirring occasionally, until vegetables are tender, 11 to 14 minutes. Using slotted spoon, transfer vegetables to serving dish.

2. Remove all but ¼ cup broth from pot. Whisk remaining 3 tablespoons butter into remaining ¼ cup broth in pot until melted and slightly thickened and pour over vegetables. Season with salt and pepper to taste. Sprinkle with chives. Serve.

New Orleans Beignets

The city's legendary doughnuts are light, airy, and delicate. If only we could make them at home . . .

BY REBECCAH MARSTERS

Europe*an cooks have been frying bits of sweet dough since the Middle Ages, and naturally the French were in on it. Beignets (ben-YEYS), as the French call these fritters, reached Louisiana in the 18th century with French settlers, or French Canadians, or then again it could have been the nuns; culinary historians can't say for sure. What is certain is that once these golden doughnuts came, they conquered. Today, beignets are the object of desire of every tourist in New Orleans and even the barometer of the city's recovery from Hurricane Katrina—it began when the city's fabled beignet cafés reopened. I can state for a fact that when my beignet order at the Morning Call café reached my table, things were definitely looking up.*

They didn't taste like ordinary doughnuts. They were delicate, lightly sweet, and yeasty—almost tangy. Their structure, a gossamer honeycomb of holes, reminded me of ciabatta bread. And the "chew" was good, with the slightest of tugs to the bite. Although the café's recipe is an old and closely guarded secret (make that really old; the place opened in 1870), Morning Call's manager kindly let me watch the dough get mixed, rolled, cut into squares, and deep-fried. The really interesting part? The baker incorporated dough scraps from the previous day into this new batch. I was beginning to understand where these beignets got their fabulous and complex flavor.

Some travelers to New Orleans bring

Fry, dust with confectioners' sugar, and eat. Don't let them sit on the cooling rack long—beignets wait for no one.

home T-shirts; others carry Mardi Gras masks. I wanted a memento of a different sort: a recipe for beignets like these.

I had plenty of recipes to choose from, with plenty of variables—although I didn't find any calling for old dough scraps. All beignets are made from flour, eggs, fat, liquid, and leavener; sugar is a common addition. The leavener is traditionally yeast but occasionally baking powder; the fat may be butter, shortening, or oil; and the liquid options are water, fresh or evaporated milk, or a

combination. The techniques range, too. Sometimes, the ingredients are stirred together to form a soft dough that rises for up to 2 hours, after which it's rolled out and cut. Other recipes produce a batter, which is simply dropped into the hot oil to form fritters.

Following a selection of these recipes, I produced cakey, sweet, dense beignets; squishy, gummy beignets; and beignets that disintegrated into flakes before I could get them off the plate and into my mouth. None matched the Morning

Call beignets. I'd tailor my recipe accordingly, but it would have to be easy enough for a home cook to make, and obviously, she wouldn't have dough scraps at her disposal, either.

This test had clarified two points, though: I'd use yeast, and to streamline, I would limit myself to 1 hour of rising time. The recipe that had come nearest the mark called for yeast, fresh milk, and oil (along with flour, sugar, and egg). I let the dough rise for just 1 hour, rolled it out, cut beignets, and fried them.

But my self-imposed fast rise meant I'd given the dough less time than ever to develop flavor. To get around that, first I went up on yeast (from 2¼ teaspoons to 1 tablespoon); the flavor of the beignets improved somewhat. Next, I tried warming the milk before combining it with the yeast and a little sugar, which yeast converts into flavor molecules. I let this mixture sit for a few minutes. Although instant yeast doesn't require warm liquid to proof, heat does jump-start the fermentation process. I hoped that it would jump-start the flavors, too. With these two fixes in place, I fried a new batch of beignets. Amazingly, this batch was full-flavored, with that slightly sour yeastiness.

My beignets still lacked the right chew, though. Chewiness in baked goods comes from gluten development, which occurs both when flour gets wet and when it is kneaded vigorously. To keep my recipe simple, I ruled out kneading. I scanned my recipe looking for other ideas. I got it: milk. Milk contains fat and a gluten-weakening peptide called glutathione, both of which make for tender baked goods—the opposite of what I wanted. I replaced the milk with water and, just like that, got chewier beignets. No one even noticed the swap (frying covers up all manner of sins).

But the crumb was still even and cakey instead of airy. A co-worker who is a whiz at bread baking advised me to build a wetter dough. More water means more steam, he explained. As bread bakes, the carbon dioxide in yeast creates holes, the steam enlarges these holes, and the holes set. Although beignets are fried, not baked, he thought the same principle might apply. I gradually added water, until I had a very sticky dough—which made the best beignets to date. Since wet dough is tricky to roll and chilled dough easier, I stuck it in the refrigerator to rise. Luckily, 1 hour's chilling time curbed the stickiness without slowing down the yeast.

These beignets—light and delicately chewy, with a simultaneously sweet yet slightly tangy yeast flavor—disappeared faster than a Sazerac on Mardi Gras. But now that I could make them, I'd need a new excuse to visit New Orleans. So . . . how do you make jambalaya?

BEIGNETS Makes about 2 dozen beignets

This dough is very wet and sticky, so flour the counter and baking sheet generously. You'll need a Dutch oven with a capacity of at least 6 quarts.

- 1 cup water, heated to 110 degrees
- 3 tablespoons granulated sugar
- 1 tablespoon instant or rapid-rise yeast
- 3 cups (15 ounces) all-purpose flour
- ¾ teaspoon salt
- 2 large eggs
- 2 tablespoons plus 2 quarts vegetable oil Confectioners' sugar

1. Combine water, 1 tablespoon granulated sugar, and yeast in large bowl and let sit until foamy, about 5 minutes. Combine flour, remaining 2 tablespoons granulated sugar, and salt in second bowl. Whisk eggs and 2 tablespoons oil into yeast mixture. Add flour mixture and stir vigorously with rubber spatula until dough comes together. Cover bowl with plastic wrap and refrigerate until nearly doubled in size, about 1 hour.

2. Set wire rack inside rimmed baking sheet. Line second sheet with parchment paper and dust heavily with flour. Place half of dough on well-floured counter and pat into rough rectangle with floured hands, flipping to coat with flour. Roll dough into ¼-inch-thick rectangle (roughly 12 by 9 inches). Using pizza wheel, cut dough into twelve 3-inch squares and transfer to floured sheet. Repeat with remaining dough.

3. Add enough of remaining 2 quarts oil to large Dutch oven to measure about 1½ inches deep and heat over medium-high heat to 350 degrees. Place 6 beignets in oil and fry until golden brown, about 3 minutes, flipping halfway through frying. Adjust burner, if necessary, to maintain oil temperature between 325 and 350 degrees. Using slotted spoon or tongs, transfer beignets to prepared wire rack. Return oil to 350 degrees and repeat with remaining beignets. Dust beignets with confectioners' sugar. Serve immediately.

TEST KITCHEN TECHNIQUE **Forming Beignets**

Our dough is very wet, a quality that allows a network of delicate holes to develop in the beignets. However, wet dough can be tricky to work with. Here's how to easily shape and cut the beignets.

STOP STICKING Dust the counter and rolling pin heavily with flour before you roll out the chilled beignet dough.

CUT INTO SQUARES Traditionally, beignets are measured by the size of the cook's hands: four fingers by four fingers. We cut 3-inch squares with a pizza wheel.

TESTING CONFECTIONERS' SUGAR SHAKERS

Nothing finishes a dessert more quickly or elegantly than a dusting of powdered sugar. We usually turn to a fine-mesh strainer for this task, but sugar shakers promise convenience and portability. We tested five models. The top performers featured miniature fine-mesh strainers, and we liked the models that could also store sugar. However, shakers rely on steadiness of hand to achieve an even appearance; we prefer the effortless results of a fine-mesh strainer. That said, frequent bakers may find the recommended shakers handy, especially when taking a cake to a bake sale or party. –SARAH SEITZ

KEY **Good ★★★   Fair ★★   Poor ★**

RECOMMENDED

		CRITERIA		TESTERS' NOTES
ATECO Stainless Steel Fine Mesh Shaker **Model:** 1347 **Price:** $3.88 **Source:** instawares.com		Ease of Use ★★★ Performance ★★★		The narrow cylinder of this metal shaker nestled snugly in testers' hands while its mesh head produced a fine, even dusting that could be layered as needed. It doesn't come with a cap, so it's not ideal for storage.
CUISINOX Stainless Steel Mesh Top Dispenser **Model:** DIS20 **Price:** $7.50 **Source:** MyCuisina.com		Ease of Use ★★ Performance ★★★		This metal shaker produced the same neat sugar coating as our top choice, but its wider shape made it slightly less comfortable to hold. If you're assembling a dessert at a picnic or party or wish to store confectioners' sugar in the shaker, you'll appreciate its plastic storage cap (which takes a little practice to remove).

RECOMMENDED WITH RESERVATIONS

		CRITERIA		TESTERS' NOTES
PROGRESSIVE INTERNATIONAL Powdered Sugar Keeper **Model:** DKS-300 **Price:** $12.95		Ease of Use ★★ Performance ★★		If storage and convenience are a priority, this plastic canister-style shaker takes the cake. It holds a pound of confectioners' sugar and sports a locking lid with hidden mesh for shaking and a straight edge for leveling off a measured amount. However, it was cumbersome to shake, and sugar fell unevenly, so forget about decorating fancy desserts.

NOT RECOMMENDED

		CRITERIA		TESTERS' NOTES
FOX RUN All-Purpose Plastic Shaker **Model:** 4647 **Price:** $1.19		Ease of Use ★★ Performance ★		This model's thick plastic head regularly clogged with sugar, making us tap it against the counter to dislodge clogs after a few shakes. Sugar fell in inconsistent, spotty patterns, and it was nearly impossible to target small areas.
WINWARE BY WINCO Stainless Steel 10-Ounce Dredge with Handle **Model:** DRG-10 **Price:** $5.20		Ease of Use ★★ Performance ★		Confectioners' sugar plummeted through the large holes of this stainless steel shaker, landing in heavy, uneven piles. The thin metal handle had sharp, unfinished edges that rubbed against our fingers as we shook out the sugar.

"Impossible" Ham-and-Cheese Pie

Bisquick popularized these pies more than 25 years ago, using one easy batter to make both filling and crust. After tasting a few, we knew it was possible to improve the "impossible." BY DIANE UNGER

WHAT DO YOU remember about the 1970s? Watergate? The Bicentennial? Call us kitchen geeks, but we remember "impossible" pies. A Bisquick-based batter is poured over ingredients (diced vegetables, diced cooked meats, grated cheese, fruit, etc.) that are scattered over a pie plate. The selling point? A pie without the bother of a pie shell: no mixing dough, no rolling, no shaping, no chilling, and no parbaking. General Mills popularized these pies by printing recipes on the Bisquick box throughout the 1970s, transforming all manner of ingredients into easy pies for dinner or dessert. Impossible? Impossibly great, said the pies' many fans.

These recipes have made their way into many a newspaper and community cookbook, and they're all more or less the same: the basic batter of Bisquick, milk, and eggs is poured over ingredients in a pie plate. I wanted to make a savory version, so I grabbed a classic recipe that called for crumbled bacon, sautéed onions, and cheese. Then I baked a pie and called the tasting team. We were underwhelmed. The "pie" was very bland. Its pale, soft bottom didn't even remotely suggest pie crust, and most of it stuck to the pie plate anyhow. We didn't see the need for the Bisquick (it merely combines flour, shortening, leavener, and sugar—we can do that ourselves, thank you very much). Also, we were expecting something with a custardy center, like quiche, but this recipe produced a pie that was cakey and not very rich.

To fix it, I'd start with the (so-called) crust. I buttered three pie plates—a no-brainer antisticking strategy. Then I mulled over ingredients that could give the crust texture and color without giving the cook (me) added work. I sprinkled one pie plate generously with Parmesan cheese, the second with crunchy panko bread crumbs, and a third with ordinary bread crumbs. I filled the shells with bacon, onion, Gruyère cheese, and the classic Bisquick batter (for now; I'd get to that next). To give the crusts a better shot at browning, I baked the pies on the lowest oven rack, nearest the heating element, for about 30 minutes, until they were golden brown. All three pies released without a hitch, but the attractively browned, slightly crispy, nutty-flavored Parmesan crust was our undisputed favorite.

This savory pie is somewhere between a quiche and a strata. Whatever you call it, it's delicious.

Admittedly, it wasn't a real, honest-to-goodness pastry pie crust, but it was crisp and brown on the bottom, with a distinct textural contrast from the filling.

Now for the filling: Impossible pies are meant to be easy. For that reason, I replaced the sautéed onions with mince-and-go scallions. Likewise, I skipped the bacon and opted for diced deli ham instead. We've adapted recipes that require Bisquick before, so I made a homemade mix using our usual ratio of flour, baking powder, and shortening, and then I scaled it down so that I had just enough for one impossible pie. I assembled and baked a new pie to reevaluate. The improvement was marked, but my pie was still bland and cakey. To make it creamier, I doubled

the number of eggs to four, and I switched from milk to half-and half. To improve the flavor of the pie, I swapped out the shortening for butter (which tastes much better), and I experimented with adding hot sauce (nope), white wine (nope), and mustard (yes, indeed) to the batter, ideas that I borrowed from other recipes. Specifically, Dijon mustard gave the pie a nice, tangy shot in the arm. After more testing, I also added a little nutmeg (a classic quiche ingredient), and I learned to scatter the cheese, ham, and scallions evenly on the pie plate bottom and pour the custard over them gently so they didn't get piled up in one spot.

I baked a pie, cut it into wedges, and called the tasters to the table. We

all agreed that the name was a bit of a gimmick: This wasn't exactly a pie. Maybe more like a frittata or a quiche? We all agreed on something else, too: Our impossible pie was incredibly easy and totally delicious.

"IMPOSSIBLE" HAM-AND-CHEESE PIE
Serves 8

Use a rasp-style grater or the smallest holes on a box grater for the Parmesan.

- 1 tablespoon unsalted butter, softened plus 2 tablespoons melted
- 3 tablespoons finely grated Parmesan cheese
- 8 ounces Gruyère cheese, shredded (2 cups)
- 4 ounces thickly sliced deli ham, chopped
- 4 scallions, minced
- ½ cup (2½ ounces) all-purpose flour
- ¾ teaspoon baking powder
- ½ teaspoon pepper
- ¼ teaspoon salt
- 1 cup half-and-half
- 4 large eggs, lightly beaten
- 2 teaspoons Dijon mustard
- ⅛ teaspoon ground nutmeg

1. Adjust oven rack to lowest position and heat oven to 350 degrees. Grease 9-inch pie plate with softened butter, then coat plate evenly with Parmesan.

2. Combine Gruyère, ham, and scallions in bowl. Sprinkle cheese-and-ham mixture evenly in bottom of prepared pie dish. Combine flour, baking powder, pepper, and salt in now-empty bowl. Whisk in half-and-half, eggs, melted butter, mustard, and nutmeg until smooth. Slowly pour batter over cheese-and-ham mixture in pie dish.

3. Bake until pie is light golden brown and filling is set, 30 to 35 minutes. Let cool on wire rack for 15 minutes. Slice into wedges. Serve warm.

Finger Food
To serve our "Impossible" Ham-and-Cheese Pie as an hors d'oeuvre at your next party, forgo the pie plate and instead bake it in an 8-inch square baking dish. Slice it into 1-inch squares and serve warm or at room temperature.

Guinness Beef Stew

Both Guinness and beef stew have deep, roasted, delicious flavor. So why should putting them together lead to bitter disappointment? BY SARAH GABRIEL

BEING A LOVER of both beef stew and dark beers, it would stand to reason that I'd go nuts over Guinness beef stew. Unfortunately, I always find that this staple of Irish pubs and St. Patty's Day get-togethers is somehow less than the sum of its parts. Guinness beef stew rarely tastes much of beer, and when it does, it captures only the bitterness and none of the deep, roasted flavors of the brew. In theory, toasty, malty flavor with a hint of bitterness should improve beef stew. Would reality track with theory?

I cooked half a dozen batches of stew from existing recipes, and while none was what I had in mind, I established some ground rules: I'd keep the vegetable selection simple (carrots and potatoes), use a combination of beer and chicken broth (beer alone yielded bitter sauce), and cut the meat from a chuck roast (precut stew chunks were inconsistent). Most recipes followed a standard stew method, searing the meat in batches, browning the onions, sprinkling in flour, whisking in beer and broth, adding the vegetables, and then cooking it all, covered, either in the oven or on the stove. But one recipe called for just tossing everything in a Dutch oven, covering, and cooking until the meat was tender. The sauce came out thin in terms of both flavor and consistency, but the prospect of skipping the sear (and the resulting splatter) was enticing.

I remembered a test kitchen recipe for Spanish-style beef stew that didn't call for searing the meat; it simply required browning the onions, tomato paste, and garlic and then cooking the stew uncovered. I gave this method a try, browning the onions, garlic, and paste and cooking my stew uncovered in a 325-degree oven. The sauce and meat took on a more robust, roasted flavor (uncovered, the sauce reduced and concentrated, making up for the lack of fond) and the meat that stuck up above the liquid even browned, but the vegetables were practically baby food. To fix that, I simply let the meat cook for 90 minutes before stirring the vegetables into the pot. Tasters were impressed with the simple method but weren't ready to sign off: "Where's the beer flavor?" Back to the kitchen.

Naturally, I thought more beer would give me more potent beer flavor, so I upped the Guinness from 1 cup to 1½ cups. Bad move—50 percent more beer just made the stew 50 percent more bitter. Trying to amp up toasty flavors in other ways, I tested batches of stew with molasses, brown sugar, espresso powder, ground-up toasted barley (it's an ingredient in the beer so I figured it would help; it didn't), various spices, and even bittersweet chocolate. Most additions didn't make a difference—or made too much of a difference—but we liked brown sugar's toasty complexity and extra sweetness, which balanced the bitterness of the beer. It was a good, easy-to-put-together stew, but it still didn't exactly scream Guinness.

Most beef stew recipes called for adding all of the beer at the beginning, but a few called for adding most or all at the end. Maybe the key wasn't quantity but timing. I made several more batches, adding beer at the start, at the end, and splitting the difference. Eventually, I determined that ¾ cup of Guinness poured in along with the broth and ½ cup more added after cooking yielded the best balance of bitterness, hefty roasted taste, and beer flavor. With good timing and a streamlined method, I'd harnessed the roasty, complex flavor of Guinness.

GUINNESS BEEF STEW Serves 6 to 8

Use Guinness Draught, not Guinness Extra Stout, which is too bitter.

- 1 (3½- to 4-pound) boneless beef chuck-eye roast, pulled apart at seams, trimmed, and cut into 1½-inch pieces
  Salt and pepper
- 3 tablespoons vegetable oil
- 2 onions, chopped fine
- 1 tablespoon tomato paste
- 2 garlic cloves, minced
- ¼ cup all-purpose flour
- 3 cups low-sodium chicken broth
- 1¼ cups Guinness Draught
- 1½ tablespoons packed dark brown sugar
- 1 teaspoon minced fresh thyme
- 1½ pounds Yukon Gold potatoes, unpeeled, cut into 1-inch pieces
- 1 pound carrots, peeled and cut into 1-inch pieces
- 2 tablespoons minced fresh parsley

1. Adjust oven rack to lower-middle position and heat oven to 325 degrees. Season beef with salt and pepper. Heat oil in Dutch oven over medium-high heat until shimmering. Add onions and ¼ teaspoon salt and cook, stirring occasionally, until well browned, 8 to 10 minutes.

2. Add tomato paste and garlic and cook until rust-colored and fragrant, about 2 minutes. Stir in flour and cook for 1 minute. Whisk in broth, ¾ cup Guinness, sugar, and thyme, scraping up any browned bits. Bring to simmer and cook until slightly thickened, about 3 minutes. Stir in beef and return to simmer. Transfer to oven and cook, uncovered, for 90 minutes, stirring halfway through cooking.

3. Stir in potatoes and carrots and continue cooking until beef and vegetables are tender, about 1 hour, stirring halfway through cooking. Stir in remaining ½ cup Guinness and parsley. Season with salt and pepper to taste, and serve.

For bold beer flavor, we add some Guinness to the stewing liquid and stir in a bit more to finish.

TEST KITCHEN DISCOVERY Cook It Uncovered

Most stew recipes start by searing meat in batches on the stovetop. We avoid that messy task by cooking the stew uncovered in the oven; the open pot allows the meat on top to take on flavorful browning. In addition, the liquid reduces, concentrating in flavor and texture, while the meat cooks.

The beef browns in the oven.

Brown Irish Soda Bread

Homemade bread for dinner after just 10 minutes' work? It can be done.
We wanted a wholesome loaf that was hearty, not heavy. BY REBECCAH MARSTERS

Robust, moist, and permeated with a delicious wheaty sweetness, brown Irish soda bread is very easy to like, very easy to make, and—unlike yeast breads—doesn't require much waiting around. This bread adds coarse, whole-meal flour to the all-purpose flour used in the more familiar Irish soda bread. In the most basic versions, the flours are simply stirred together with baking soda and buttermilk, briefly kneaded, patted into a round, and baked. (Eggs, sugar, and butter are American additions.) It sounded great to me.

I rounded up recipes for brown soda bread. A few called for the traditional whole-meal flour. But that's hard to find in the United States. Most recipes substituted ordinary whole-wheat flour. The second group skips the white flour and combines the whole-wheat flour with practically the complete contents of a natural foods store (bran, ground oatmeal, etc.). Predictably, the former produced loaves with scarcely any wheat flavor, while the latter made loaves with great wheaty taste but heavy, gummy, crumbly textures.

To get the flavor correct, I tried the most basic recipe from my first round of testing with varying ratios of all-purpose and whole-wheat flours. Eventually, I opted for 2 cups of white flour combined with 1½ cups of whole-wheat for a loaf with nice wheat flavor and mild sweetness. To round out that flavor and play up the toasty, nutty aspects, I added by turns wheat germ (the embryo of the wheat berry), wheat bran (the outer layer of the grain that's removed to make white flour), and oatmeal (which I toasted and ground to make oat flour). My tasters and I liked them all, but the bran required a trip to a specialty store,

Whole-wheat flour and toasted wheat germ give this easy bread nutty sweetness and depth of flavor.

while the oats demanded both toasting and processing. Toasted wheat germ is sold in jars at the supermarket, so that's what I'd use.

The wheaty taste was now spot-on, but just like many of the loaves in my initial test, my loaf was dense and crumbly. I knew why: The extra bran and germ in whole-wheat products means less gluten formation, and gluten is what gives bread its chew and elastic structure. To fix that, I swapped out the all-purpose flour in my recipe for bread

flour, which can form stronger gluten. But the loaf was denser and more compact than ever. What was going on? Our science editor explained that while bread flour is capable of developing more gluten than all-purpose is, it needs time to do so. With quick bread, it doesn't get that. I went back to all-purpose flour and tried more baking soda. Instead of lightening the loaf, it imparted a chemical, soapy flavor. What about baking powder? Though it's not traditional in soda bread, I found that equal amounts

of the two leaveners lightened the bread without changing its flavor.

I called over tasters to get their take. They approved the earthy flavor and hearty texture, but they complained that I'd gone all-or-nothing on them: Just because it's healthier brown soda bread, they said, doesn't mean it can't have any butter or sugar. I added them in, tentatively and gradually to stay away from scone territory. Ultimately, decided that 3 tablespoons of sugar an 2 tablespoons of melted butter added sweetness, tenderness, and a delicate richness without crossing the line. When the bread came out of the oven, I brushed it with extra melted butter. Wholesome and wholly delicious, this loaf was as good warm from the oven as it was sliced, toasted, and slathered with jam the next morning.

BROWN SODA BREAD   Makes 1 loaf

2	cups (10 ounces) all-purpose flour
1½	cups (8¼ ounces) whole-wheat flour
½	cup toasted wheat germ
3	tablespoons sugar
1½	teaspoons salt
1	teaspoon baking powder
1	teaspoon baking soda
1¾	cups buttermilk
3	tablespoons unsalted butter, melted

1. Adjust oven rack to lower-middle position and heat oven to 400 degrees. Line rimmed baking sheet with parchment paper. Whisk all-purpose flour, whole-wheat flour, wheat germ, sugar, salt, baking powder, and baking soda together in large bowl. Combine buttermilk and 2 tablespoons melted butter in 2-cup liquid measuring cup.

2. Add wet ingredients to dry ingredients and stir with rubber spatula until dough just comes together. Turn out dough onto lightly floured counter and knead until cohesive mass forms, about 8 turns. Pat dough into 7-inch round and transfer to prepared sheet. Using sharp serrated knife, make ¼-inch-deep cross about 5 inches long on top of loaf. Bake until skewer inserted in center comes out clean and loaf registers 195 degrees, 45 to 50 minutes, rotating sheet halfway through baking.

3. Remove bread from oven. Brush with remaining 1 tablespoon melted butter. Transfer loaf to wire rack and let cool for at least 1 hour. Serve.

Fastest. Bread. Ever.

No yeast, no rise time, and almost no kneading or shaping.

Measure and whisk dry ingredients	5 minutes
Measure and combine wet ingredients	2 minutes
Stir wet into dry	1 minute
Knead briefly	1 minute
Shape simply	1 minute

Total work time	**10 minutes**

BROWN SODA BREAD WITH CURRANTS AND CARAWAY

Add 1 cup dried currants and 1 tablespoon caraway seeds to dry ingredients in step 1.

Black-Eyed Peas with Greens

It may not sound like much, but when we got into the kitchen, this classic Southern dish won over the skeptics. BY NICK IVERSON

A BIG, LUSTY pot of black-eyed peas and greens is quintessential Southern food, right up there with fried green tomatoes and candied yams. There are probably as many versions of this comforting, easygoing dish as there are Southern cooks. Recipes use various greens; fresh, frozen, or canned peas; and pork (and there's always pork) in all manner of forms. Likewise, the liquid may be pork or chicken stock or just water, and add-ins run the gamut.

Despite the jumble of ingredients, recipe methods are fairly constant—put the ingredients in a pot, cover, and simmer for anywhere from 30 minutes to several hours—except that some recipes require sautéing the onion first. After a few hours in the kitchen, I lined up six pots of peas and solicited opinions. Everyone agreed that bacon was a great shortcut to smoky flavor, and better flavor justified the extra step of browning the onion. Among the add-ins, only tomatoes made the cut.

But what about the peas? Black-eyed "peas" are actually beans, the most well-known in a family of legumes that Southerners call field peas. Fresh black-eyed peas are delicious, but outside the South, they're hard to come by. Frozen peas weren't so easy to find either, and I lacked the patience to wait for dried beans to soften and cook. So I opted for canned. Unfortunately, in the 30-some minutes that the dish needed to simmer, they disintegrated into near mush. I was able to fix that by taking a few precautions: I added the canned black-eyed peas for only the last 15 minutes of cooking, and I stirred them in very gently. Next I turned to side-by-side tests of greens, chopping them up to go into the pot with the water. All were tasty, but in a poll of my coworkers, collard greens won by a nose.

Since my black-eyed peas were cooking in just half an hour—no time for a ham bone to add much flavor—I swapped the water for stronger stuff: chicken broth. To boost the flavor further, I added lots of garlic, red pepper flakes, and cumin (unorthodox, but good) with the softened onion.

I made a new pot with the added seasonings. Once the beans were warm, the greens silken and porky, and the kicked-up, rustic flavors had melded, I removed the lid and cranked the heat to let the cooking liquid reduce and

concentrate. At the end, I stirred in vinegar (for brightness) and a little sugar, sprinkled on the bacon, and dipped in my fork. Southerners say that black-eyed peas are lucky. I can see why.

BLACK-EYED PEAS AND GREENS
Serves 6 to 8

Don't crush the peas—stir gently.

6	slices bacon, cut into ½-inch pieces
1	onion, halved and sliced thin
1¼	teaspoons salt
4	garlic cloves, minced
½	teaspoon ground cumin
½	teaspoon pepper
¼	teaspoon red pepper flakes
1	(14.5-ounce) can diced tomatoes
1½	cups low-sodium chicken broth
1	pound collard greens, stemmed and chopped
2	(15.5-ounce) cans black-eyed peas, rinsed
1	tablespoon cider vinegar
1	teaspoon sugar

1. Cook bacon in Dutch oven over medium heat until crisp, 5 to 7 minutes. Transfer bacon to paper towel–lined plate; set aside.

2. Remove all but 2 tablespoons bacon fat from pot. Add onion and salt and cook, stirring frequently, until golden brown, about 10 minutes. Add garlic, cumin, pepper, and pepper flakes and cook until fragrant, about 30 seconds.

3. Add tomatoes and their juice. Stir in broth and bring to boil. Add greens, cover, and reduce heat to medium-low. Simmer until greens are tender, about 15 minutes.

4. Add black-eyed peas to pot and cook, covered, stirring occasionally, until greens are silky and completely tender, about 15 minutes. Remove lid, increase heat to medium-high, and cook until liquid is reduced by one-fourth, about 5 minutes. Stir in vinegar and sugar. Top with reserved bacon. Serve.

Who says collards need to cook for hours? Ours spend only 35 minutes in the pot.

Steamed Cheeseburgers

Most burgers dry out if you cook them beyond medium-rare. Not these. Steamed burgers stay incredibly juicy and moist even when cooked to medium-well. BY SARAH GABRIEL

"You make cheeseburgers how?" Never having heard of steamed cheeseburgers, I thought this sounded like a ridiculous—and bad—idea when I was first told about them. A burger without a tasty seared crust? But it turns out that steamed cheeseburgers have been the specialty of a few beloved diners and lunch counters in central Connecticut for more than 50 years. They're said to descend from steamed beef-and-cheese sandwiches sold from horse-drawn carts to area construction workers in the 1920s. From what I read, their appeal is not only the meat, which is incredibly juicy despite being cooked to medium-well, but also the gooey, molten cheddar that smothers the burger.

With many a scary story in the news about food-borne illness these days, cooking burgers to medium-well (which kills most of the pathogens that can cause illness) is increasingly appealing. Despite my initial skepticism, I was getting excited about giving these burgers a shot.

There are dozens of videos online showing how the Connecticut diners steam their burgers: The cooks press the meat and cheese into separate shallow metal molds and put them into a custom-made steam cabinet to cook and melt, respectively; the cheese is poured onto the meat before serving. This moist, steamy environment is one reason these burgers stay juicy. The second is that they aren't subject to the good, hard sear of a pan or grill so

It may sound crazy, but we were quick converts. We steam our cheeseburgers (and warm the buns) in a steamer basket set in a Dutch oven.

there's no risk the meat near the outside will be gray, dry, and overcooked.

I don't know about you, but my home kitchen doesn't have specialty molds or a steam cabinet. Hoping to make this recipe work with equipment that most of us already own, I dropped a metal steamer basket into a Dutch oven with a few cups of water, fired up the burner, and shaped four 6-ounce burgers while the water came to a boil. I seasoned the patties with salt and pepper, arranged them on the open steamer

basket, and put the lid on. There wasn't room in the pot for melting the cheese separately, so after 5 minutes I plopped a slice of cheddar on each patty and re-covered the pot. After 10 minutes, the burgers were cooked through to medium-well. Tasters were impressed with the amount of juice running out of these medium-well burgers (no small feat), but there were a couple of problems. First, the meat was woefully underseasoned. And second, the cheese had run off the edges of the burgers,

nestling in a gooey mess at the bottom of the steamer basket.

I was puzzled that the meat was underseasoned because I had been generous with salt and pepper. But without the crusty sear you get from direct exposure to dry heat (in a pan, on a grill, or under a broiler), these steamed burgers obviously needed a boost. I turned to two of the test kitchen's go-to ingredients for savory, meaty seasoning: soy sauce and tomato paste. I made several batches of burgers, mixing arying amounts of each ingredient into he meat. In the end, 2 teaspoons of oy sauce, 1 teaspoon of tomato paste, nd the same amount of onion powder nade the burgers deeply flavorful—even ithout a sear. To keep the burgers from nounding up as they cooked, I used a est kitchen trick: I made a divot in each atty before placing it in the steamer.

My next order of business was getting the cheese to melt properly— and stay put on the patties. The steamed burgers in Connecticut are famously heesy, so my first step was to ditch the uny slices and hand-cut a healthy slab f cheddar for the top of each burger. found that if I added the cheese too oon, it melted off the edges, but if added the cheese too late, the very enter of the slab remained chalky and nmelted. I turned to shredded cheese. I as able to pile a full ¼ cup of shredded heddar on each burger, but even when added the cheese in the last minute of ooking, it ran off.

Maybe gentler heat was the answer. made another batch of patties and put n a pot of water. This time, I cooked ne burgers for 8 minutes, until they ere just short of done, and then shut ff the burner, added the cheese, and eplaced the lid. In the 2 minutes that it ook for the burgers to finish cooking, ne cheese melted to gooey perfection. I nought I was done when one taster said, Wouldn't this be awesome with a soft, eamed bun?" I had to agree. It took a w tests, but I figured out that I needed nly 30 seconds to steam the buns: I aited until the cheese had melted, put ne top bun in place on top of the cheese, nd dropped the bottom bun, cut side p, on top of it for a quick steam. Then I emoved the bottom buns, dressed them ith condiments, and used a spatula o drop the burger (with the top bun ready in place) on top.

Want some fries with your burgers? Visit ooksCountry.com/ arlicfries for our recipe r Garlicky Oven Fries.

I had had my doubts at the start—and so did most of my tasters—but after scarfing down the last round of impossibly juicy burgers completely coated in gooey melted cheddar, we were all steamed-burger believers.

CONNECTICUT STEAMED CHEESEBURGERS Serves 4
The test kitchen's favorite steamer basket is the Progressive Easy Reach Steamer Basket. We prefer these burgers cooked medium-well, but for medium burgers, steam them for 7 minutes before shutting off the heat and adding the cheese. Serve these burgers with the usual array of garnishes and condiments: lettuce, tomato, onion, ketchup, mayonnaise, and mustard.

- 1½   pounds 85 percent lean ground beef
- 2   teaspoons soy sauce
- 1   teaspoon onion powder
- 1   teaspoon tomato paste
- ¾   teaspoon salt
- ¾   teaspoon pepper
- 4   ounces sharp cheddar cheese, shredded (1 cup)
- 4   hamburger buns

1. Combine beef, soy sauce, onion powder, tomato paste, salt, and pepper in bowl. Divide beef into 4 balls. Gently flatten into patties ¾ inch thick and 4 inches wide. Press shallow divot in center of each patty. Bring 4 cups water to boil in covered Dutch oven over medium-high heat (water should not touch bottom of steamer basket).

2. Arrange patties in steamer basket. Set steamer basket inside Dutch oven, cover, and cook for 8 minutes. Remove Dutch oven from heat and divide cheese evenly among burgers, cover, and let sit until cheese melts, about 2 minutes. Place top buns on burgers and bottom buns, cut side up, on top of top buns. Cover and let sit until buns soften, about 30 seconds. Transfer bottom buns to cutting board, add condiments, and top with burgers and top buns. Serve.

TEST KITCHEN TECHNIQUE
Steamer Setup
We devised a homemade steam cabinet and a stacking system for juicy burgers, gooey cheese, and warm buns.

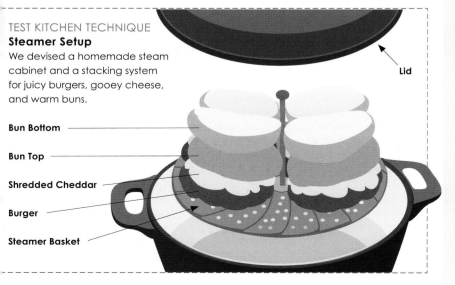

Lid
Bun Bottom
Bun Top
Shredded Cheddar
Burger
Steamer Basket

French Onion Dip

Made with instant soup mix, this dip is no work but tastes salty and fake. Real onions add great flavor but take time to prep. How to reconcile?

BY CRISTIN WALSH

Caramelized onions and balsamic vinegar give this dip an upgrade.

ADD SOUR CREAM to a packet of instant onion soup mix and *voilà*, French onion dip. It's been a party favorite for decades, and it takes just seconds to make. But compare this dip with from-scratch versions and, well, there *is* no comparison. Homemade French onion dip, which typically calls for stirring (long-cooking) caramelized sliced onions into sour cream, is sweet, tangy, and rich. I wanted the best of both: convenience and the deep flavor of real onions.

Caramelizing onions normally requires cooking them in butter over the lowest possible flame for up to 90 minutes. The slow heat releases the onions' sugars, which then caramelize, turning the slices soft and sweet. When I tried shortchanging this step, the onions were bland and crunchy. To streamline their cooking, I chopped them instead of slicing. The extra surface area releases more sugars, which means faster caramelization. A bonus: The onions weren't stringy, so it was easier to scoop up the dip. To further hurry things along, I turned the heat to medium, but the onions started to burn. Eventually, I learned to start them at medium, reduce the heat to medium-low after 10 minutes, and add water in increments toward the end of cooking. With these adjustments, the onions browned (but didn't burn) and developed deep, rich flavor in 30 minutes. The work was mostly hands-off and the payoff was high.

I stirred the cooled onions into 1½ cups of sour cream. For my next test, to soften the sour cream's tang, I replaced ½ cup of it with mayonnaise, and to cut the dip's cloying creaminess, I stirred in some balsamic vinegar. Its sweetness echoed that of the caramelized onions, while its acid tempered the dip. A pinch of cayenne added a bit of heat. Time for a beer and a bag of chips.

FRENCH ONION DIP
Serves 4 to 6
You can make this dip up to 24 hours in advance.

- 3   tablespoons unsalted butter
- 2   pounds onions, chopped fine
    Salt and pepper
- ⅛   teaspoon cayenne pepper
- ¼   cup water
- 2½   teaspoons balsamic vinegar
- 1   cup sour cream
- ½   cup mayonnaise

1. Melt butter in 12-inch skillet over medium heat. Add onions, ½ teaspoon salt, ½ teaspoon pepper, and cayenne and cook, stirring occasionally, until onions are translucent, about 10 minutes. Reduce heat to medium-low and continue cooking until onions are golden, about 10 minutes.

2. Add 2 tablespoons water to skillet and cook, scraping up any browned bits, until water is evaporated, about 5 minutes. Add remaining 2 tablespoons water and cook until onions are caramelized and water is evaporated, about 5 minutes longer. Remove from heat and stir in vinegar. Transfer onions to medium bowl and let cool for 10 minutes.

3. Add sour cream and mayonnaise to onions and stir to combine. Season with salt and pepper to taste. Refrigerate for at least 30 minutes to allow flavors to blend. Serve.

Honey-Roasted Baby Back Ribs

On paper, honey-glazed baby back ribs make perfect sense. But somewhere between paper and plate, the pork turns bland and the glaze saccharine. We knew we could do better. BY JEREMY SAUER

Honey-slathered ribs roasted to tenderness is one of those dishes that sound incredible but rarely rank above "decent" on the taste-o-meter. This defies logic, really. How can savory baby back ribs and floral honey end up tasting so, well, ordinary? With a fridge full of baby backs and a cupboard full of honey, I set out to unlock the secrets to extraordinary honey-roasted ribs. My goals: perfectly tender meat and a crusty, sticky, honey glaze so good it makes you lick your fingers and reach for another rib.

When I researched recipes, I was taken aback by their diversity. Some recipes called for marinating the ribs, others for brining. Still others required employing a spice rub, while some instructed to season the ribs with nothing but salt and honey. I tried each method and it quickly became apparent that marinating was key. Unlike grilling, during which ribs pick up a pleasant smokiness over the fire, oven roasting seems to sap the pork of its flavor; a marinade was an easy way to add back some taste. Since I wanted honey to be the star of the show, I cobbled together a honey-based marinade using a bit of onion and garlic for a savory edge, a little vinegar and a dose of pepper to balance the honey's sweetness, and soy sauce for its proven marinating powers. (Not only does soy sauce add "meaty" flavor, but its sodium content keeps the meat moist, too, as with a brine.)

With a working marinade in hand, I was ready to cook. I was surprised to find that many recipes for so-called roasted ribs actually call for braising the ribs on the stovetop before finishing them under the broiler. This technique promises moist, tender meat and a

The sheen from the honey glaze gives our ribs a lacquered look.

nice char, but my tasters repeatedly tagged the braised ribs "spongy," with a "boiled" flavor even after broiling. I attempted to simply roast the ribs (trying almost every increment between 225 and 400 degrees), but no matter the temperature the ribs were dried out by the time they were fully cooked. Thankfully, the solution was simple: I cooked the ribs elevated on a wire rack and loosely covered with foil for 1 hour and 15 minutes at 325 degrees. The foil trapped the steam that rose from

the ribs, both accelerating the cooking process and preventing the ribs from drying out. Then I removed the foil and roasted the ribs uncovered for another hour so that they could fully tenderize and develop appealing color and flavor.

Next up: the glaze. Many recipes tell you to simply brush honey over the ribs as they cook, but this method resulted in ribs that were better suited for dessert than for dinner. As I was thinking about what to put together for the ideal glaze, I realized that the ingredients were going

to be almost exactly the same as those in the marinade. Why not combine the two? With a little tweaking—a heavy shake of cayenne here, a big squirt of Dijon mustard there—I had an efficient and effective marinade that, after it was cooked down for a few minutes, also made an excellent glaze.

I figured I'd start brushing the ribs with the glaze as soon as I uncovered them, but the drippings from the glaze scorched on the bottom of the pan and smoked out my kitchen. Thankfully, I found a simple fix: I added water to the bottom of the pan. Better still, the water gave off extra steam that helped keep the ribs moist and juicy even after I removed the foil. Even so, I quickly realized that the glaze adhered best if it was added in the last half-hour or so of cooking.

When I pulled the final batch of ribs out of the oven, I knew that I was nearing my goal. The glaze—loaded with honey flavor—had bubbled and browned into a lip-stickin', finger-lickin' good time. For a finishing touch, I scattered sliced scallion greens over the ribs (I'd use the scallion whites in the marinade instead of onion). Then I sprinkled a little kosher salt on top to add a salty crunch. Mission accomplished.

Can't get enough honey? Serve these ribs with our **Honey Cornbread**. Find the recipe at CooksCountry.com/honeycornbread.

HONEY-ROASTED RIBS
Serves 4

Cutting the racks into thirds allows them to fit into the plastic bags to marinate. The used marinade is boiled and transformed into a glaze for the ribs.

- 2 (2½- to 3-pound) racks baby back ribs, trimmed, membranes removed, each rack cut into 3 equal pieces
- 1 cup honey
- 5 tablespoons soy sauce
- ¼ cup cider vinegar
- ¼ cup Dijon mustard
- 4 scallions, white parts minced, green parts sliced thin
- 4 garlic cloves, crushed
  Kosher salt and pepper
- ¼ teaspoon cayenne pepper

1. Divide ribs between two 1-gallon zipper-lock bags. Whisk honey, soy sauce, vinegar, mustard, scallion whites, garlic, 1 teaspoon salt, 1 teaspoon pepper, and cayenne together in bowl. Divide marinade between bags, seal, and turn to coat ribs evenly with marinade. Refrigerate for at least 1 hour or up to 24 hours, turning bags occasionally.

TEST KITCHEN TIP
Use a Big Pot to Avoid Scary Boilovers
It's important to use a Dutch oven when you boil the marinade to turn it into the glaze and a sauce: The honey mixture will boil up and in a smaller pot could be a dangerous mess. The roomy Dutch oven also allows you to toss in the ribs at the end to coat.

2. Adjust oven rack to middle position and heat oven to 325 degrees. Line rimmed baking sheet with aluminum foil and set wire rack in sheet. Add enough warm tap water to cover entire bottom of sheet (about 2 cups). Transfer ribs, meaty side up, to prepared wire rack; reserve marinade in refrigerator. Tent ribs loosely with foil and bake for 1¼ hours. Uncover ribs and continue cooking until just tender, about 1 hour longer.

3. Bring reserved marinade to boil in Dutch oven over medium-high heat and cook until thickened to glaze consistency, about 5 minutes. Brush ribs with ⅓ cup glaze, return to oven, and continue to cook until glaze begins to bubble and ribs are brown, 15 to 30 minutes. Transfer ribs to cutting board (leave hot water and sheet in oven to cool), tent loosely with foil, and let rest for 10 minutes.

4. Cut ribs between bones, add to Dutch oven, and toss to coat with remaining glaze. Transfer to platter and sprinkle with scallion greens and ½ teaspoon salt. Serve.

TEST KITCHEN TECHNIQUE One Mixture, Three Uses

MARINADE
We marinate the ribs in the honey–soy sauce mixture, giving them deep flavor.

GLAZE
After boiling and concentrating the honey mixture, we use it to glaze the ribs.

SAUCE
We toss the individual ribs in the honey mixture to sauce them on all sides.

Fennel Salad

A right and a wrong way to slice fennel? Who knew? Technique down, we made a lively salad.

BY DIANE UNGER

Capers, almonds, and raisins enliven our fennel salad.

IF YOU DON'T know fresh fennel—its mild licorice flavor and celery-like crunch—you're in for a treat. A great way to get to know this underused (at least in the United States) vegetable is thinly sliced in salad. Since fennel is a classic Mediterranean ingredient, I decided I'd look there for inspiration. I rounded up and tested five fennel salad recipes, each with somewhat different ingredients and methods. After tasting them, I knew I wanted an assertive salad with a balance of sweet, salty, slightly sour, and bitter flavors. I also found myself wondering why the fennel was fibrous and stringy in some of these samples and pleasantly crunchy in others.

It turns out that there's a right way and a wrong way to cut fennel. As with meat, cutting fennel against the grain—or, in this case, fibers—shortens the fibers, which makes the slices less stringy.

For sweetness, I threw a handful of raisins into a salad bowl, and for the salty component, capers. Thinly sliced red onion added pungency while Italian flat-leaf parsley added an herbal note—especially if I treated it more like a vegetable, tossing in whole leaves instead of mincing it.

For the vinaigrette, olive oil was a given, and I liked fresh lemon juice for its bright, cheery flavor; I balanced the lemon with a little honey. Dijon mustard helped emulsify the vinaigrette and added bite. I mixed the fennel slices with the other salad ingredients and poured on the dressing. The onion came on way too strong. For my next batch, I'd try letting the onion slices macerate briefly with some vinaigrette to tame them—a method we like in the test kitchen. As I was about to toss the two together, it occurred to me to add the fennel as well, letting both vegetables sit in the vinaigrette for 30 minutes, which served to soften the onion's raw bite and to season the fennel. Just before I was ready to eat the salad, I stirred in the parsley and some almonds (for extra crunch). My salad, a mix of bright colors, lively flavors, and contrasting textures, was an edible advertisement for fennel.

FENNEL SALAD Serves 4 to 6

- ¼ cup extra-virgin olive oil
- 3 tablespoons lemon juice
- 2 teaspoons Dijon mustard
- 2 teaspoons honey
  Salt and pepper
- 2 fennel bulbs, stalks discarded, bulbs halved, cored, and sliced thin crosswise
- ½ red onion, halved through root end and sliced thin crosswise
- ½ cup golden raisins, chopped
- 3 tablespoons capers, rinsed and minced
- ½ cup fresh parsley leaves
- ½ cup sliced almonds, toasted

1. Whisk oil, lemon juice, mustard, honey, 1 teaspoon salt, and 1 teaspoon pepper together in large bowl. Add fennel, onion, raisins, and capers and toss to combine. Cover and refrigerate for 30 minutes to allow flavors to blend.

2. Stir in parsley and almonds. Season with salt and pepper to taste, and serve.

TEST KITCHEN DISCOVERY
Slice Against the Grain
Cutting fennel this way shortens the fibers, so the fennel won't be stringy in the salad.

Getting to Know Herb and Spice Blends

Most cuisines around the world, including our own, have characteristic spice mixes. Here's a look at 12 spice blends, old and new, home-grown and foreign. BY REBECCAH MARSTERS

Pumpkin Pie Spice
THANKSGIVING HELPMATE

Most Americans reach for pumpkin pie spice just once a year. But in the test kitchen, we don't limit its use to our pumpkin pie. We use it to flavor carrot cakes and spice cookies or as a shortcut to Moroccan chicken. No need to buy a jar—you can make your own: Combine ½ teaspoon cinnamon, ¼ teaspoon ginger, and ⅛ teaspoon each nutmeg and allspice for every teaspoon of pumpkin pie spice called for in a recipe.

Herbes de Provence
FLOWER POWER

An aromatic blend from the south of France, herbes de Provence combines dried lavender flowers with rosemary, sage, thyme, marjoram, and fennel, and sometimes chervil, basil, tarragon, or savory. A natural partner for poultry and pork, herbes de Provence is worth trying in an herb butter to brush under turkey or chicken skin before roasting the bird.

Curry Powder
ESSENCE OF INDIA

As many as 20 different spices are blended to make curry powder, among them coriander, cumin, cinnamon, clove, turmeric, and black and red peppers. Madras curry powder is a hotter version; sweet (or "mild") is more versatile. Curry powder adds flavor to recipes like curried spiced nuts (for a recipe, go to **CooksCountry.com/curryspicednuts**). Penzey's Sweet Curry powder is our top pick.

Blackening Spice
CAJUN COATING

In the 1980s, New Orleans chef Paul Prudhomme became famous for dipping fish fillets in melted butter, dredging them in spices, and cooking them in a searingly hot skillet, thereby igniting a national "blackening" obsession. Not long after the trend swept the nation, blackening spice mixes hit supermarkets, combining paprika, onion and garlic powders, coriander, and red and black peppers.

Za'atar
KEBAB SIDEKICK

In Arabic, *za'atar* can refer to a specific herb (*Thymbra spicata*); to several herbs that are related to thyme, savory, and oregano; or to a blend of spices that contain these herbs, along with sesame seeds, salt, and (tart, sour) sumac. Za'atar (the blend) is traditionally sprinkled on kebabs and vegetables. To get to know its earthy, pungent, floral flavors, dunk bread in olive oil and then dip it in za'atar.

Italian Seasoning
THE BOOT IN A BOTTLE

This blend tries to cram the flavors of Italy into a single jar. It's chock-full of the Italian mainstays oregano, marjoram, rosemary, basil, sage, thyme, and savory. Toss potato wedges with oil, Parmesan, and Italian seasoning for a fast Mediterranean take on steak fries, or add a few pinches to a slow-simmered tomato sauce for an all-in-one flavor boost.

Chinese Five-Spice Powder
BALANCED BLEND

This pungent, aromatic blend contains five ingredients, namely cinnamon, clove, fennel seeds, Sichuan peppercorn, and star anise. Chinese culture values the balance of flavors that these spices represent. In recent years, Americans have taken to the spice, too, using it for both sweet (five-spice panna cotta) and savory (grilled pork chops) dishes. Dean & DeLuca makes our favorite blend.

Ras el Hanout [RAHS L ha-newt]
MOROCCAN CURRY

This North African seasoning translates as "head of the shop" because traditionally each blend was a unique combination of some 25 spices, seeds, dried flowers, berries, and nuts determined by the spice shop's proprietor. Blends often include cumin, saffron, cinnamon, nutmeg, dried rose petals, galangal, and paprika. Use *ras el hanout* in tagines, rices, and hearty meat dishes such as braised lamb shanks.

Crab Boil
SEAFOOD SACHET

Boiling huge pots of seafood, potatoes, and other vegetables is a time-honored culinary tradition, be it crawfish boil in Louisiana, Frogmore stew in the Carolinas, or a clam bake in New England. What to season the pot with? Crab boil. Popular brands include Zatarain's, Rex's, and Old Bay. Crab boil usually contains mustard seeds, celery seeds, coriander, peppercorns, bay, and allspice.

Pickling Spice
CUKE CURE

Now that there's a pickling revival sweeping America, reacquaint yourself with this blend. Pickling spice is a fruity, tart mixture of whole and coarsely crushed spices like bay leaves, cardamom, cinnamon, allspice, mustard seeds, cloves, coriander, and ginger. Not a pickle maker? Try grinding the blend in a spice grinder and using it to season poultry.

Garam Masala
CURRY'S KISSING COUSIN

Like curry powder, garam masala (literally "hot spice blend") is an Indian seasoning made from warm spices like cloves, cinnamon, peppercorns, cardamom, and cumin. Add a little garam masala to couscous or use it to flavor our Easy Chicken Tagine (find the recipe at **CooksCountry.com/moroccanchicken**). The test kitchen prefers McCormick Collection Garam Masala for its "citrusy," "smoky" flavors.

Chili Powder
COWBOY RATIONS

Before chili powder became a commercial product in the early 20th century, cooks had to mix their own from ground dried chiles (usually about 80 percent of the blend), garlic powder, oregano, and cumin. The quality of store-bought chili powder depends on both the chiles used and its freshness; if your jar is more than six months old, replace it. (See our **Chili Powder Taste Test** on page 31.)

BALSAMIC-GLAZED PORK CUTLETS

STIR-FRIED BEEF AND RICE NOODLES

TURKEY CLUB SALAD

POTATO-CRUSTED CHICKEN WITH CAULIFLOWER

STIR-FRIED BEEF AND RICE NOODLES Serves 4

WHY THIS RECIPE WORKS: Chicken broth, soy sauce, and rice vinegar make a quick and tasty stir-fry sauce.

- ½ cup low-sodium chicken broth
- ¼ cup soy sauce
- 2 tablespoons rice vinegar
- 8 ounces (¼-inch-wide) rice noodles
- 3 tablespoons vegetable oil
- 1½ pounds beef flap meat, cut into 2-inch-wide strips with grain, then cut against grain into ⅛-inch-thick slices
- 2 red bell peppers, stemmed, seeded, and cut into ¼-inch-wide strips
- 3 shallots, sliced thin
- 1½ teaspoons Asian chili-garlic sauce
- ½ teaspoon five-spice powder

1. Whisk broth, soy sauce, and vinegar together in bowl; set aside. Bring 6 cups water to boil in large pot. Place noodles in large bowl. Pour boiling water over noodles and stir to separate noodles. Soak until noodles are almost tender, about 8 minutes, stirring once halfway through soaking. Drain and rinse with cold water. Drain well and toss with 2 teaspoons oil.

2. Heat 2 teaspoons oil in 12-inch nonstick skillet over medium-high heat until just smoking. Cook half of steak until browned on both sides, about 2 minutes per side. Transfer to plate and repeat with 2 teaspoons oil and remaining steak.

3. Heat remaining 1 tablespoon oil in now-empty skillet over medium-high heat until shimmering. Add bell peppers and shallots and cook until just softened, about 2 minutes. Add chili-garlic sauce and five-spice powder and cook until fragrant, about 1 minute. Add broth mixture, steak, and noodles and toss to combine. Cook until noodles are heated through, about 2 minutes. Serve.

BALSAMIC-GLAZED PORK CUTLETS Serves 4

WHY THIS RECIPE WORKS: Reducing supermarket balsamic vinegar concentrates its flavor and creates a sticky glaze.

- 8 (3-ounce) boneless pork cutlets, ¼ inch thick, trimmed
  Salt and pepper
- 2 tablespoons olive oil
- 1 garlic clove, minced
- 6 tablespoons balsamic vinegar
- 2 tablespoons packed brown sugar
- 2 tablespoons unsalted butter
- 1 tablespoon chopped fresh parsley
- 1 teaspoon Dijon mustard

1. Pat pork dry with paper towels and season with salt and pepper. Heat 1 tablespoon oil in 12-inch nonstick skillet over medium-high heat until just smoking. Cook 4 cutlets until golden brown on both sides and cooked through, about 2 minutes per side. Transfer to platter and tent loosely with aluminum foil. Repeat with remaining 1 tablespoon oil and remaining 4 cutlets.

2. Reduce heat to medium, add garlic to now-empty skillet, and cook until fragrant, about 30 seconds. Add vinegar and sugar and cook until slightly thickened, about 3 minutes. Off heat, whisk in butter, parsley, and mustard. Season with salt and pepper to taste. Pour sauce over cutlets and serve.

TEST KITCHEN NOTE: Serve with buttery mashed potatoes.

POTATO-CRUSTED CHICKEN WITH CAULIFLOWER Serves 4

WHY THIS RECIPE WORKS: We roast the cauliflower on one rack and cook the chicken on another in the same 450-degree oven.

- 1 head cauliflower (2 pounds), cored and cut into 2-inch florets
- ¼ cup olive oil
  Salt and pepper
- 1 cup (2½ ounces) crushed kettle-cooked potato chips
- 1 slice hearty white sandwich bread, torn into 1-inch pieces
- 1 tablespoon chopped fresh tarragon
- 2 tablespoons Dijon mustard
- 4 (6- to 8-ounce) boneless, skinless chicken breasts, trimmed

1. Adjust oven racks to upper-middle and lower-middle positions and heat oven to 450 degrees. Line 2 rimmed baking sheets with aluminum foil. Toss cauliflower, 3 tablespoons oil, 1 teaspoon salt, and ½ teaspoon pepper on 1 prepared sheet and bake on lower-middle rack until well browned and tender, about 25 minutes.

2. Meanwhile, pulse potato chips, bread, and tarragon in food processor until coarsely ground, about 10 pulses; transfer to shallow dish. Combine mustard and remaining 1 tablespoon oil in bowl. Pat chicken dry with paper towels and season with salt and pepper. Brush 1 side of chicken with mustard mixture. Press mustard-coated side of chicken into crumb mixture. Place on second prepared sheet and bake on upper-middle rack until golden brown and chicken registers 160 degrees, about 15 minutes. Serve chicken with cauliflower.

TEST KITCHEN NOTE: The test kitchen's favorite kettle-cooked potato chips are Lay's Kettle Cooked Original.

TURKEY CLUB SALAD Serves 4

WHY THIS RECIPE WORKS: The mayonnaise functions as seasoned oil in the making of the croutons.

- 4 (1-inch-thick) slices Italian bread
- ⅔ cup mayonnaise
- 8 slices bacon, chopped
- 3 tablespoons red wine vinegar
- 1 tablespoon Dijon mustard
- 12 ounces (¼-inch-thick) sliced deli turkey, halved lengthwise and sliced crosswise into ½-inch-wide strips
- 12 ounces cherry tomatoes, halved
- 1 (10-ounce) bag chopped romaine lettuce
  Salt and pepper

1. Adjust oven rack to middle position and heat oven to 475 degrees. Spread both sides of bread slices evenly with ¼ cup mayonnaise and arrange on baking sheet. Bake until golden brown, 8 to 10 minutes, flipping bread and rotating sheet halfway through baking. Let cool for 5 minutes, then cut into 1-inch cubes.

2. Cook bacon in 12-inch skillet over medium heat until crisp, 6 to 8 minutes. Transfer to paper towel–lined plate. Whisk vinegar, remaining mayonnaise, and mustard together in large bowl. Add turkey, tomatoes, lettuce, bacon, and bread cubes and toss to combine. Season with salt and pepper to taste. Serve.

TEST KITCHEN NOTE: The test kitchen's winning brand of mayonnaise is Blue Plate Real Mayonnaise.

30-MINUTE SUPPER

SKILLET CHICKEN WITH SPINACH ORZO

30-MINUTE SUPPER

STEAK TIPS WITH RED WINE SAUCE

30-MINUTE SUPPER

SWEET POTATO SOUP WITH BACON AND CHIVES

30-MINUTE SUPPER

PASTA WITH ROASTED ONIONS, RADICCHIO, AND BLUE CHEESE

STEAK TIPS WITH RED WINE SAUCE Serves 4

WHY THIS RECIPE WORKS: To build layers of flavor, we make the pan sauce in the skillet after cooking the steak tips. The browned bits left behind in the skillet add flavor to the sauce.

- 1½ pounds sirloin steak tips, trimmed and cut into 2-inch pieces
- Salt and pepper
- 1 tablespoon vegetable oil
- 4 tablespoons unsalted butter
- 1 shallot, minced
- ½ cup red wine
- 1 teaspoon packed brown sugar
- ½ cup beef broth
- ¼ teaspoon minced fresh thyme

1. Pat steak tips dry with paper towels and season with salt and pepper. Heat oil in 12-inch skillet over medium-high heat until just smoking. Add steak tips and cook until well browned all over and meat registers 125 degrees (for medium-rare), 5 to 7 minutes. Transfer to plate and tent loosely with aluminum foil.

2. Add 1 tablespoon butter to now-empty skillet and melt over medium heat. Add shallot and cook until softened, about 2 minutes. Add wine and sugar and simmer until nearly evaporated, about 3 minutes. Add broth and any accumulated steak juice from plate and simmer until liquid is reduced to ⅓ cup, about 3 minutes.

3. Off heat, whisk in remaining 3 tablespoons butter and thyme. Season with salt and pepper to taste. Return steak tips to skillet and toss with sauce. Serve.

TEST KITCHEN NOTE: Use a good-quality medium-bodied wine, such as a Côtes du Rhône or Pinot Noir.

SKILLET CHICKEN WITH SPINACH ORZO Serves 4

WHY THIS RECIPE WORKS: The heat from the pasta wilts the spinach.

- 1 cup orzo
- Salt and pepper
- 4 ounces (4 cups) baby spinach
- 3 tablespoons olive oil
- 3 tablespoons minced shallot
- ½ teaspoon grated lemon zest
- 8 (3- to 4-ounce) chicken cutlets, ½ inch thick, trimmed
- ¾ cup low-sodium chicken broth
- ½ cup dry white wine
- 3 tablespoons unsalted butter

1. Adjust oven rack to middle position and heat oven to 250 degrees. Bring 2 quarts water to boil in medium pot. Add orzo and 1½ teaspoons salt and cook, stirring often, until al dente. Reserve ¼ cup cooking water, then drain pasta and return it to pot. Add spinach, 1 tablespoon oil, 1 tablespoon shallot, and lemon zest and toss to combine, adding reserved cooking water as needed until spinach is wilted. Season with salt and pepper to taste. Cover and keep warm.

2. Meanwhile, pat chicken dry with paper towels and season with salt and pepper. Heat 2 teaspoons oil in 12-inch skillet over medium-high heat until shimmering. Cook half of chicken until browned on both sides and cooked through, about 3 minutes per side. Transfer to platter and tent loosely with aluminum foil. Repeat with 2 teaspoons oil and remaining chicken. Transfer platter to oven to keep warm. Reduce heat to medium. Add remaining 2 teaspoons oil and remaining 2 tablespoons shallot to now-empty skillet and cook until softened, about 30 seconds. Add broth and wine and bring to simmer, scraping up any browned bits. Simmer until reduced to ½ cup, about 8 minutes. Remove from heat and whisk in butter. Season with salt and pepper to taste. Pour sauce over chicken and serve with orzo.

PASTA WITH ROASTED ONIONS, RADICCHIO, AND BLUE CHEESE Serves 4

WHY THIS RECIPE WORKS: The cooking water and cheese merge to form a creamy sauce that softens the bitterness of the radicchio.

- 1 pound campanelle, fusilli, or penne
- Salt and pepper
- 2 tablespoons olive oil
- 2 onions, halved and sliced thin
- 1 head radicchio (10 ounces), cored and sliced thin
- 2 garlic cloves, minced
- 1 tablespoon balsamic vinegar
- 4 ounces blue cheese, crumbled (1 cup)
- ½ cup chopped fresh basil
- ½ cup walnuts, toasted and chopped coarse

1. Bring 4 quarts water to boil in large pot. Add pasta and 1 tablespoon salt and cook, stirring often, until al dente. Reserve 1 cup cooking water, then drain pasta and return it to pot.

2. Meanwhile, heat oil in 12-inch nonstick skillet over medium-high heat until shimmering. Add onions, radicchio, and 1 teaspoon salt and cook, covered, for 5 minutes. Uncover and continue to cook, stirring occasionally, until vegetables are soft and edges are browned, about 8 minutes. Add garlic and cook until fragrant, about 30 seconds. Off heat, stir in vinegar.

3. Add vegetables, blue cheese, basil, walnuts, and ¼ cup reserved pasta water to pasta and toss to combine. Add more cooking water to loosen sauce as needed. Season with salt and pepper to taste. Serve.

TEST KITCHEN NOTE: Serve with Parmesan cheese.

SWEET POTATO SOUP WITH BACON AND CHIVES
Serves 4

WHY THIS RECIPE WORKS: Slicing the sweet potatoes very thin allows them to cook very quickly. Add a salad and good bread to make a fast, easy supper.

- 6 slices bacon, chopped
- 1 onion, chopped fine
- 1 teaspoon packed brown sugar
- Salt and pepper
- 3 garlic cloves, minced
- 2 pounds sweet potatoes, peeled, quartered lengthwise, and sliced thin
- 4 cups low-sodium chicken broth
- 1 cup water
- 2 tablespoons minced fresh chives

1. Cook bacon in Dutch oven over medium heat until crisp, 6 to 8 minutes. Using slotted spoon, transfer bacon to paper towel–lined plate; set aside. Discard all but 2 tablespoons bacon fat from now-empty pot. Add onion, sugar, and 1 teaspoon salt and cook, stirring occasionally, until onion is softened, 5 to 7 minutes. Stir in garlic and cook until fragrant, about 30 seconds. Add potatoes, broth, and water and bring to boil. Reduce heat to medium-low and simmer until potatoes are tender, about 10 minutes.

2. Working in batches, process soup in blender until smooth, 1 to 2 minutes. Season with salt and pepper to taste. Serve soup, sprinkled with bacon and chives.

TEST KITCHEN NOTE: If after cooking the bacon you don't have quite 2 tablespoons of rendered fat in the pot, add olive oil to make up the difference. For a slightly spicy version of this soup, add ⅛ teaspoon cayenne pepper.

Chicken and Rice Soup

Too often, cutting corners in an effort to save time spoils the broth. Our version of chicken and rice soup cuts down on time but not on flavor. BY ERIKA BRUCE

AS WITH MOST other soups, the success of comforting, hearty chicken and rice soup depends on a strong foundation, namely a good homemade chicken stock. But nowadays few people (including me) have the time or the inclination to make homemade stock regularly. There are plenty of quick stock recipes that rely on canned broth and fast-cooking chicken breasts, but I was skeptical they'd suffice for this relatively plain, straightforward soup.

As I'd suspected, the recipes I tried had more chicken fragrance than flavor. Also, they contained lackluster onions, carrots, and celery, interspersed with little floating puff balls that I assume started their lives as grains of rice. A few recipes tried (unsuccessfully) to disguise their thin, watery flavor by thickening the broth with cornstarch or flour. I was determined to make an easy yet relatively fast soup that did justice to the old-fashioned, made-from-scratch original.

I knew that in order to extract the most flavor from raw chicken, I would need to use bone-in dark meat, brown the skin, and simmer it in water for a long time. Because it was starting to sound as though I'd be spending half a day waiting for a proper stock, I decided to cheat the clock by picking up a rotisserie chicken at the supermarket. I removed the meat (saving it for the soup), added the skin and bones (already rendered and nicely seasoned from roasting) to some browned onion and celery, and then stirred in bay leaves, thyme, and water. After just an hour, the broth had deep chicken flavor and the body to match. Happy with these results, I wondered if using commercial broth in place of the water could further speed the process. After several tests, I found that a mixture of water and broth resulted in the same deep flavor as before—in just half the time.

I was ready to focus on the vegetables and rice. Onion and celery were already flavoring the stock. Mushrooms made the broth murky. A leek, on the other hand, underlined my stock's savory quality, plus I could use the dark green top in the stock. Carrots and frozen peas contributed sweetness and color.

Adding the long-grain white rice to the simmering broth and cooking it until it was tender resulted in blown-out rice every time. A surefire solution was to steam the rice separately, but this meant more work and an extra pot to clean.

What about other types of rice? The aromatic qualities of basmati and jasmine didn't register in the soup, and brown rice was too chewy, but short-grain rice had a pleasant chew and held its shape fairly well. I borrowed a technique from another short-grain rice dish, risotto, and sautéed the rice in oil for a couple of minutes before adding the liquid. This firmed up the starches on the outside of the rice just enough to keep the grains intact while they cooked in the broth. Goodbye mystery puff balls.

This full-bodied soup took just over an hour to prepare. Sure, I relied on the supermarket to help me with some of the cooking, but those were shortcuts I could live with. The delicious end easily justified the means.

We base our quick stock on rotisserie chicken—a handy and speedy shortcut.

SHORT-GRAIN RICE

TEST KITCHEN TIP **Avoid a Blowout**
Short-grain rice, such as Arborio, holds its shape better than the long-grain rice usually used in chicken and rice soup. Sautéing the rice for a couple of minutes before adding the chicken stock causes the starches on the outside of the rice to firm up, so the grains don't blow out.

CHICKEN AND RICE SOUP
Serves 6
Wash the leek thoroughly after chopping.

- 2 tablespoons olive oil
- 1 onion, chopped
- 1 leek, white and light green parts halved lengthwise, sliced thin crosswise, and washed thoroughly; dark green part chopped coarse and washed thoroughly
- 2 celery ribs, chopped
- 1 (2½-pound) rotisserie chicken, skin and bones reserved for stock, meat shredded into bite-size pieces (3 cups)
- 6 cups low-sodium chicken broth
- 4 cups water
- 2 sprigs fresh thyme
- 2 bay leaves
- 2 carrots, peeled, quartered lengthwise, and sliced ¼ inch thick
- ½ cup short-grain white rice
  Salt and pepper
- 1 cup frozen peas
- 2 tablespoons minced fresh parsley

1. Heat 1 tablespoon oil in Dutch oven over medium-high heat until shimmering. Add onion, dark green leek part, and celery and cook until just beginning to brown, about 5 minutes. Add chicken skin and bones, broth, water, thyme, and bay leaves and bring to boil. Reduce heat to medium-low and simmer, loosely covered, for 30 minutes.

2. Strain stock through fine-mesh strainer into large bowl, pressing on solids to extract as much liquid as possible; discard solids and set stock aside. (You should have about 8 cups of stock. If you have less, add water to equal 8 cups.)

3. Wipe out now-empty Dutch oven with paper towels and heat remaining 1 tablespoon oil over medium-high heat until shimmering. Add white and light green leek parts and carrots and cook until softened, about 5 minutes. Add rice and cook, stirring frequently, until edges of rice become translucent, about 2 minutes. Add stock and 1 teaspoon salt and bring to boil. Reduce heat to medium-low and simmer, covered, stirring occasionally, until rice is tender, 12 to 14 minutes. Stir in chicken and peas and cook until heated through, about 5 minutes. Stir in parsley and season with salt and pepper to taste. Serve.

Potato-and-Onion Knishes

Portable, flaky, and satisfying, these stuffed pastries have been a popular street food in New York for 100 years. We hoped to bring them across state lines and into the home kitchen. BY DIANE UNGER

W hat's a knish, you ask? A flaky, handheld bun (cousin to a turnover) filled with beef, mushrooms, kasha (buckwheat groats), sauerkraut, cheese, or—my personal favorite—mashed potato and onion. These homey, filling pastries arrived in America in the early 1900s with Eastern European Jews. Barely settled in New York, the immigrants began to peddle knishes from pushcarts, as the pastries were portable and didn't require refrigeration. Why these hot and hefty snacks became so popular on hot summer days at the beach in Coney Island we can't explain. Or maybe we can: They're delicious anywhere and anytime. I hoped to learn to make them myself.

These savory knishes are hearty, satisfying, and fairly easy to make (plus they freeze well).

Following recipes from Jewish cookbooks, I mashed potatoes, rolled out dough, stuffed, sliced, shaped, crimped, and baked. Many hours later, I lined up dozens of knishes and assembled my team of noshers. The knishes were square or round, open-ended or sealed, small or hefty (Yonah Schimmel Knish Bakery, or knishery, which opened on the Lower East Side in 1910, sells a hulking ¾-pound version), thin or sturdy, plain (doughs made from oil, flour, and water) or rich (doughs with butter, eggs, margarine, or chicken fat). After eating the results of my survey of the field, we all settled in for a long nap. Just kidding. Actually, I summed up and jotted down what I wanted in my recipe: nicely seasoned potatoes; plenty

of onions; easy, tender, flaky dough; and a shaping method that didn't require a blueprint to figure out.

I'd get the easier part out of the way first: the filling. The test kitchen knows its way around mashed potatoes, so I knew to use high-starch russets for a fluffy mash, cubing and boiling them. I returned the drained, cooked spuds to the stove to dry briefly before mashing them and seasoning them liberally with salt and pepper. Not all potato knishes include onion, but if you ask

me, they should. Raw onion folded into the mashed potatoes tasted sour. Quickly sautéed onions (1½ pounds, double the amount called for in many recipes) weren't bad. But I hit pay dirt with really well-browned onions, which added sweet, deep flavor.

The plainest of the doughs I'd tried in my initial tests used nothing but flour, vegetable oil, salt, and water. This dough was difficult to roll out and crackerlike when baked, and the flavor was unexciting. Still, it was a good

starting point in that I could add the fats by turns and evaluate each. Schmaltz, Yiddish for rendered chicken fat, is traditional and it tasted as fabulous as you'd think, but who has that sitting around? Melted butter contributed delicious flavor—for about two bites. Given the dense, hefty filling, two bites were all most of us could manage. I wondered how olive oil in place of vegetable oil would fare. Incredibly well, it turned out. Plus, I could skip the step of melting the butter.

But I still had a couple of problems. To begin with, the dough tore when I rolled it out (it needs to be rolled very thin). I tried resting it on the counter instead of rolling it out immediately, allowing the gluten to relax. This definitely helped. Our science editor suggested that I add an egg (which I'd seen in some old recipes) to the dough for further insurance against tearing. The egg helps the water and olive oil blend together, he said, making the dough more supple. No more tears. Next up: dealing with the dense, heavy dough. I flipped through other recipes for ideas, and when I glanced at one recipe, "baking powder" practically leaped off the page. Baking powder should give the dough lift and tenderness, right? Right.

Even for an experienced cook, rolling out dough so thin that you can see the surface of a kitchen table beneath it is a little intimidating. Nor was I a fan of a recipe that had me rolling out tiny balls of dough into tiny circles to make many tiny knishes. To form mine, I turned to the easiest method I'd tried in my initial tests: I rolled the dough into a very thin square on a well-floured counter, formed the potato filling into a long rope along its length, rolled the dough around the filling, and sliced the roll into eight knishes. I repeated this procedure with the remaining dough. Then I stood each knish on its end, pressed down slightly, and baked the buns for about 40 minutes.

At this point, I'd worked for weeks on these knishes, yet tasters were still kvetching. What now? My version was neither light nor crispy enough, they complained. To make the knishes less dense, I brushed the dough with olive oil before filling it. As the slicked dough got rolled around the filling and then baked, the light film of oil kept the layers from sealing together into one mass. In the oven, steam was generated in the space between the layers, making for much lighter (and less dense) knishes. For crispier knishes, I brushed the parchment paper–lined baking sheet with oil, too, before setting the unbaked knishes on it.

Later that afternoon, I pulled one more batch from the oven. Admittedly, knishes are a project to make, but these were earthy, sweet, crispy, light, and peppery—worlds better than any I'd ever lugged home as a New York souvenir. I was so pleased that I experimented with some unconventional flavors, falling hard for a decidedly unkosher combination that added pastrami, Gruyère cheese, yellow mustard, caraway, and dill to my potato-onion filling. "My grandmother is turning over in her grave," a Jewish test cook said—but that didn't stop her from reaching for a second.

POTATO KNISHES Makes 16 knishes

A well-floured counter is essential here. To reheat baked knishes, place them in a 350-degree oven for 10 to 15 minutes.

FILLING
- 2¼ pounds russet potatoes, peeled and cut into 1-inch pieces
  Salt and pepper
- 1 tablespoon olive oil
- 3 onions, chopped fine

DOUGH
- 2 cups (10 ounces) all-purpose flour
- 1½ teaspoons baking powder
- ¾ cup olive oil
- ½ cup water
- 1 large egg, plus 1 large egg beaten with 1 tablespoon water
- 1 teaspoon salt

1. FOR THE FILLING: Combine potatoes and 1 tablespoon salt in Dutch oven and cover with water by 1 inch. Bring to boil over high heat. Reduce heat to medium and cook until potatoes are tender, 20 to 25 minutes. Drain potatoes and return to pot. Cook over low heat until potatoes are thoroughly dry, about 1 minute. Mash potatoes with potato masher until very few lumps remain. Transfer to large bowl and stir in ½ teaspoon salt and ½ teaspoon pepper.

2. Meanwhile, heat oil in 12-inch nonstick skillet over medium-high heat until shimmering. Add onions and ½ teaspoon salt and cook, stirring occasionally, until well browned, about 10 minutes. Transfer to bowl with mashed potatoes and stir to combine. Let filling cool completely. (Filling can be made up to 24 hours in advance, covered, and refrigerated.)

3. FOR THE DOUGH: Whisk flour and baking powder together in large bowl. Whisk 6 tablespoons oil, water, 1 egg, and salt together in separate bowl. Add wet ingredients to dry ingredients and stir with rubber spatula until dough forms. Transfer dough to floured counter and knead until smooth, about 1 minute. Wrap in plastic wrap and let rest on counter for 1 hour or refrigerate for up to 4 hours (let dough come to room temperature before rolling).

4. Adjust oven rack to middle position and heat oven to 350 degrees. Line rimmed baking sheet with parchment paper and brush parchment with 2 tablespoons oil. Divide dough in half and form each half into 4-inch square on well-floured counter. Working with 1 square at a time (keep remaining dough covered with plastic), roll dough into 16-inch square. Lightly brush dough with 2 tablespoons oil, leaving 1-inch border at farthest edge.

5. Form half of filling into 1-inch log along near edge of dough, leaving 1-inch border on sides. Brush far edge of dough with water. Roll dough around filling and seal edge. Trim knish log on each end so log measures 16 inches long. Cut log into 8 (2-inch) pieces. Stand each knish on end and press to 1-inch thickness. Space evenly apart on prepared sheet. Repeat with remaining dough, remaining 2 tablespoons oil, and remaining filling.

6. Brush tops and sides of knishes with egg-water mixture. Bake until golden brown, 35 to 40 minutes, rotating sheet halfway through baking. Transfer knishes to wire rack and let cool for 15 minutes. Serve.

TO MAKE AHEAD
Knishes can be made through step 5 and frozen for up to 1 month. If baking from frozen, increase baking time to 50 to 55 minutes.

POTATO, PASTRAMI, AND GRUYÈRE KNISHES
Omit ½ teaspoon salt from filling. Add 2 cups shredded Gruyère cheese, 8 ounces chopped deli pastrami, 2 tablespoons yellow mustard, 1 teaspoon crushed caraway seeds, and ½ teaspoon dried dill to filling with pepper in step 1.

STEP BY STEP **Easier Knish Construction**

ROLL OUT
Working with half of the dough at a time, roll it out into a 16-inch square so thin that you can see the counter through it.

FILL
After brushing the dough with oil, mound half of the filling evenly on it in a long rope, leaving about an inch clear at the nearest edge and at the ends.

ROLL UP AND CUT
Roll the dough around the filling and seal the seam. Trim the edges, place seam-side down, and cut the tube into pieces.

PRESS AND BAKE
Stand each knish on its end and lightly press. Place on an oiled, parchment paper–lined baking sheet; brush with egg wash; and bake.

Green Rice Casserole

To make this satisfying, flavorful oldie but goodie, you add spinach to rice and cheese and bake. Getting good flavor is easy. Avoiding oldie but gloppy requires some ingenuity. BY NICK IVERSON

I'M TOO YOUNG to remember green rice casserole myself, but a quick check of our cookbook library uncovered plenty of recipes, many from the 1960s and '70s. Cooked white rice, frozen spinach, sometimes canned condensed soup, and always cheese—cheddar, cream cheese, and/or cottage cheese— were combined and then often topped with bread crumbs. By all accounts, a big, satisfying dish.

But the recipes I tested badly needed an update. The casseroles came out stodgy and bland. The rice was mushy and the spinach stringy with barely noticeable flavor. Casseroles that included canned condensed soups were really salty and had that telltale canned taste. Still, I spied potential for a fortifying dish of perfectly cooked rice bound in a creamy, flavorful, spinach-flecked sauce and topped with crispy crumbs.

Most recipes call for cooked rice. But I figured that the double cooking of the rice was to blame for the blown-out grains. I'd start with raw rice instead, adding liquid so the rice could cook. Accordingly, I mixed raw rice with spinach, cheddar and cream cheese (our favorite combo from my first tests), and chicken broth, borrowing the rice-to-broth proportions from a test kitchen rice pilaf recipe. I put the mixture in a casserole, sealed it with foil so the rice would steam, and baked it. Mushy rice vanquished, I turned to the spinach.

I did a few tests with fresh spinach, but I needed so much that it was impractical; what starts as a huge pile cooks down to a piddly one. How else to boost spinach flavor? Use more. I worked my way up until I was using two 10-ounce boxes of thawed frozen spinach instead of one. I squeezed it very dry first so that it wouldn't add extra liquid to the casserole. And to prevent stringiness, I whizzed it in the food processor

A crumb topping adds crunch and contrast to our big, creamy casserole.

with the cream cheese.

Unfortunately, now the rice wasn't evenly cooked. The grains around the edges, top, and bottom of the casserole heated up first and cooked faster. If I preheated the broth, when the hot broth hit the other ingredients, hopefully they'd warm at the same rate. And as

long as I had a pan out to heat the broth, I'd improve its flavor by softening onion and garlic in the pan before the broth went in. So far, so good.

I also learned that the easiest, most efficient way to assemble the casserole was in layers: spinach mixture first and then rice, followed by cheddar cheese. I poured the hot broth over everything. After working through variables, I discovered that things turned out best if I baked the casserole, covered, at 350 degrees for 25 minutes. Then I chucked the foil, gave everything a stir (to help the rice cook evenly and distribute the cream cheese–spinach layer), and cranked the oven to 450. I let the casserole bake for another 15 minutes; sprinkled on a topping of fresh bread crumbs, butter, and Parmesan; and baked it 10 minutes longer. Tasters assembled, and

before I knew it, my baking dish was empty. Green rice casserole was back and it was better than ever.

GREEN RICE CASSEROLE
Serves 8 to 10 as a side dish

- 4 tablespoons unsalted butter
- 1 onion, chopped fine
  Salt and pepper
- 4 garlic cloves, minced
- ½ teaspoon minced fresh thyme
- 4 cups low-sodium chicken broth
- 2 slices hearty white sandwich bread, torn into quarters
- 1 ounce Parmesan cheese, grated (½ cup)
- 1¼ pounds frozen chopped spinach, thawed and squeezed dry
- 8 ounces cream cheese
- 2 cups long-grain white rice
- 8 ounces sharp cheddar cheese, shredded (2 cups)

1. Adjust oven rack to upper-middle position and heat oven to 350 degrees. Melt 2 tablespoons butter in medium saucepan over medium-low heat. Add onion and ½ teaspoon salt and cook until translucent, about 5 minutes. Add garlic and thyme and cook until fragrant, about 30 seconds. Add broth, increase heat to medium-high, and bring to boil. Cover and remove from heat.

2. Pulse bread, Parmesan, remaining 2 tablespoons butter, ½ teaspoon salt, and ½ teaspoon pepper in food processor until coarsely ground, 8 to 10 pulses; transfer to bowl and set aside. Combine spinach, cream cheese, ½ teaspoon salt, and ¼ teaspoon pepper in now-empty food processor and process until smooth, about 10 seconds.

3. Spread spinach mixture in even layer in 13 by 9-inch baking dish. Sprinkle rice evenly over spinach mixture. Sprinkle cheddar over rice. Pour broth mixture into baking dish, cover tightly with double layer of aluminum foil, and bake for 25 minutes.

4. Remove casserole from oven, remove foil, and stir to redistribute ingredients. Return casserole to oven, increase oven temperature to 450 degrees, and continue baking, uncovered, until all liquid is absorbed, about 15 minutes. Sprinkle bread-crumb mixture over top and bake until golden brown, 8 to 10 minutes. Let casserole cool for 20 minutes. Serve.

TEST KITCHEN TECHNIQUE **Casserole Construction**

Most recipes for green rice casserole call for mixing everything together and dumping it into a baking dish. Since we're using raw rice instead of the usual cooked, we found that layering was easier. We pour chicken broth over and bake, stirring once to distribute the ingredients evenly.

- Shredded cheddar
- Rice
- Spinach mixture

Broiled Thick-Cut Pork Chops

Straight from the grill, thick-cut chops can be fantastic—crusty, tender, and flavorful.
Could we get similar results under the broiler? BY JEREMY SAUER

THERE ARE PORK chops, and then there are thick-cut pork chops. I mean, if you're buying chops, why not go all out and buy big-boy bone-in loin (or rib) chops that stand 1½ inches tall? Big chops can be fantastic grilled or seared in a skillet and finished in the oven, but what about the broiler? Never afraid of a challenge, I bought a case of thick-cut chops, turned a row of test kitchen oven knobs to "broil," and got busy cooking.

A few dozen chops later, three problems were apparent: First, chops cooked close to the broiler element spattered and spit, making a greasy mess on the baking sheet that smoked out the kitchen. Second, thick chops are hard to cook perfectly. Depending on the method, they emerged from the broiler with some combination of leathery outsides, raw insides, and no crust. And third, these big chops were bland.

Tackling the cooking method first, I knew that the placement of the oven rack would be key. In my initial tests, chops cooked on the top rack had smoked out the kitchen by the time the inside was cooked, and I had red eyes, a choking cough, and a blaring smoke alarm to prove it. I dropped the oven rack to the upper-middle position, but trying to brown my chops this far from the heating element was like trying to get a suntan in Siberia.

Clearly, if I wanted any browning, I needed to get these chops as close to the broiler as possible yet somehow eliminate the smoke. I tried the upper oven rack again, this time arranging the chops on a wire (cooling) rack set inside a baking sheet in hopes that the fat would drain down and not smoke out the kitchen. No such luck. Once it dripped down onto the hot sheet, the fat still smoked. Then I remembered how a colleague had solved a similar problem. She'd broiled strip steaks over a bed of salt; the drippings fell harmlessly into the salt instead of burning on the hot pan. I tried it, and sure enough, this setup eliminated the smoke. After about 10 minutes per side, the chops were cooked to temperature (140 degrees) and actually had a solid char, especially around the edges. But my optimism faded when I took a bite. Twenty minutes of sitting directly under the broiler had left the exterior of the chops dry and leathery.

Fortunately, I had a plan. To keep the chops moist and to add seasoning at the same time, I'd try brining. The test kitchen has long championed this technique for lean meats such as pork chops and chicken breasts, which tend to dry out as they cook. I stirred together 3 tablespoons each of salt and sugar and 1½ quarts of water and soaked the chops for an hour. This drastically improved the juiciness and flavor inside the chops. But the exterior was still dry—almost desiccated. As my frustration was mounting, it occurred to me to use water instead of salt on the bottom of the baking sheet. I knew that the water would prevent the drippings from burning and smoking, and I hoped it would also create steam to keep the exterior of the chops moist. Happily, it did.

The brine had indeed boosted flavor, but tasters noted that these chops could use a spice rub, too. I wanted to keep things simple, so to a salt and pepper base I added sweet paprika for color and depth. This elicited yawns from tasters, so I threw in granulated garlic and swapped smoked paprika for the sweet stuff. What an improvement. The granulated garlic and smoked paprika lent a smoky savor that mimicked the rich, caramelized flavor of a grill-seared pork chop. For a final flourish, I stirred some of the rub mixture into softened butter to serve on top. These chops—flavorful, charred, and juicy inside and out—were so good that broiling just might become my go-to method, even during grilling season.

The water in the baking sheet prevents the rendered fat from scorching and smoking.

BROILED THICK-CUT PORK CHOPS Serves 4 to 6

The oven rack should be 5 inches from the broiler element. If your oven doesn't allow this, err on the side of distance: Place the rack slightly farther from the element. For chops that are less than 1½ inches thick, decrease the cooking time.

- Salt and pepper
- 3 tablespoons sugar
- 4 (12- to 14-ounce) bone-in pork rib or center-cut chops, 1½ inches thick
- 1½ teaspoons granulated garlic
- 1½ teaspoons smoked paprika
- 2 tablespoons unsalted butter, softened

1. Dissolve 3 tablespoons salt and sugar in 1½ quarts cold water in large bowl. Add chops, cover, and refrigerate for 1 hour. Combine 1 tablespoon pepper, garlic, paprika, and 1 teaspoon salt in small bowl. Combine butter and 1 teaspoon spice mixture in separate bowl; set aside.

2. Adjust oven rack 5 inches from broiler element and heat broiler. Set wire rack inside rimmed baking sheet. Remove chops from brine, pat dry with paper towels, and rub all over with remaining 2 tablespoons spice mixture. Arrange chops on wire rack, transfer sheet to oven rack, and add 1½ cups warm water to bottom of sheet.

3. Broil until chops are browned and register 140 degrees, 16 to 20 minutes, flipping once halfway through cooking. Transfer chops to platter (leave hot water and sheet in oven to cool). Divide spice butter among chops, tent loosely with aluminum foil, and let rest for 5 to 10 minutes. Serve.

TEST KITCHEN TIP **Water Safety**
Carrying a baking sheet filled with water and loaded with mammoth chops around your kitchen isn't a great idea. Instead, add the water after you've placed the sheet on the oven rack.

Chocolate Angel Pie

In our early experiments, this pie was no angel: The meringue crust stuck and the chocolate flavor was faint. BY CRISTIN WALSH

I f you think counting angels on the head of a pin is hard, try defining angel pie (aka heavenly pie). An assortment of recipes going by this name first appeared in print in the 1920s, but it was only after World War II that the name was used for a meringue pie shell filled with creamy mousse and topped with whipped cream. This version was an instant hit—and no wonder. Rationing was at an end, so eggs and sugar were in plentiful supply. A lavish dessert was in order. In my book, it still is. Ideally, chocolate angel pie should have a light, crisp meringue crust; a filling so chocolaty and satiny it could put a truffle to shame; and plenty of whipped cream. At the start of my testing, though, I got nowhere near this cosmic combination.

Pile a light, crunchy meringue crust full of luscious chocolate mousse and blanket it in whipped cream. What have you got? Angel pie.

Instead, the recipes I tested produced pies with chewy, brown meringue shells—so sticky and brittle that I couldn't cut slices without the crust shattering. The fillings typically called for whipping 1 cup of heavy cream and folding it into 2 to 4 ounces of melted semisweet chocolate (pastry chefs call this a quick mousse). How bad can whipped cream and chocolate ever taste? That said, these fillings were flat, with little chocolate punch.

I'd start with the meringue and work my way up to the pie layers. The meringue is made by whipping three egg whites with sugar, vanilla, and cream of tartar (for stability) until stiff. The mixture is spread into a pie plate and baked. Most recipes I found called for comparatively high oven temperatures and short bake times (325 degrees for 35 minutes). But this yielded sticky, dark tan meringues (the color indicates that the sugar is burning, so the shell will taste bitter). I unearthed a couple of recipes that called for longer baking times at lower temperatures: 1 hour at 250 degrees and then 3 hours to overnight in the turned-off oven. I liked the results of this technique—pale, crunchy, light meringues—but not the timetable.

To get a crisp meringue more quickly, I'd need to remove excess moisture faster. Hoping to do so, I added 1 tablespoon of cornstarch to the egg white mixture. It sped up the baking time somewhat. I fiddled with times and temperatures and eventually produced a crunchy shell on a more reasonable timetable. My solution was to bake the meringue shell (with added cornstarch) at 275 degrees for 1½ hours and then drop the temperature to 200 degrees

for an additional hour. Unfortunately, the pie shell still stuck to the pie plate. I greased the pie plate to no avail. Next, I greased the pie plate and dusted it with flour, as though I were baking a cake. The raw flour left a pasty film on our tongues. What if I dusted the pie plate with cornstarch instead? It worked. Now my meringue shell was delicate and crunchy, and it was easy to remove a slice intact.

I'd been using 4 ounces of bittersweet chocolate for the filling, but its normally strong, complex flavor was muted by all the whipped cream. Fine: I'd use more chocolate. After just a few extra ounces, though, the filling's appealing creaminess was ruined. I hit the cookbooks for ideas and found an old recipe that called for a cooked custard. A cooked custard, I realized excitedly, could handle extra chocolate. Following the recipe, I scalded half-and-half on the stovetop, slowly added it to three egg yolks and sugar, and poured this custard mixture over twice the chopped chocolate—a generous 8 ounces. I let the mixture cool a little and then folded in whipped cream.

The result spoke for itself: This chocolate filling was bold, smooth, and silky. It wasn't merely extra chocolate that accounted for the extra flavor, our science editor speculated; because of the yolks, the flavor molecules got pulled into the emulsified mixture of fat and water, where receptors in the mouth and nose can detect them more readily. He added that the yolks stabilized the emulsification between cream and chocolate, yielding that silken texture. As a bonus, I wasn't stuck with unused egg yolks.

Having unlocked the secret to great chocolate flavor, I pushed my luck by working my way up to nearly a pound. But now the bittersweet flavor came on too strong. I tested more pies (no complaints from eaters) with various ratios of milk chocolate to bittersweet. The filling achieved depth and balance at 9 ounces milk chocolate to 5 ounces bittersweet—more than three times the amount of chocolate I'd found in any other recipe. The airy, crisp meringue was its perfect counterpoint—plus my Chocolate Angel Pie could be cut into clean, neat slices. To finish, I slathered on lightly sweetened whipped cream. "It's like the chocolate is sitting on a cloud," one taster exclaimed. "Heavenly," sighed another.

CHOCOLATE ANGEL PIE

Serves 8 to 10
Serve the assembled pie within 3 hours of chilling.

FILLING
- 9 ounces milk chocolate, chopped fine
- 5 ounces bittersweet chocolate, chopped fine
- 3 large egg yolks
- 1½ tablespoons granulated sugar
- ½ teaspoon salt
- ½ cup half-and-half
- 1¼ cups heavy cream, chilled

MERINGUE CRUST
- 1 tablespoon cornstarch, plus extra for pie plate
- ½ cup (3½ ounces) granulated sugar
- 3 large egg whites
  Pinch cream of tartar
- ½ teaspoon vanilla extract

TOPPING
- 1⅓ cups heavy cream, chilled
- 2 tablespoons confectioners' sugar
  Unsweetened cocoa powder

1. FOR THE FILLING: Microwave milk chocolate and bittersweet chocolate in large bowl at 50 percent power, stirring occasionally, until melted, 2 to 4 minutes. Whisk egg yolks, sugar, and salt together in medium bowl until combined, about 1 minute. Bring half-and-half to simmer in small saucepan over medium heat. Whisking constantly, slowly add hot half-and-half to egg yolk mixture in 2 additions until incorporated. Return half-and-half mixture to now-empty saucepan and cook over low heat, whisking constantly, until thickened slightly, 30 seconds to 1 minute. Stir half-and-half mixture into melted chocolate until combined. Let cool slightly, about 8 minutes.

2. Using stand mixer fitted with whisk, whip cream on medium-low speed until foamy, about 1 minute. Increase speed to high and whip until soft peaks form, 1 to 3 minutes. Gently whisk one-third of whipped cream into cooled chocolate mixture. Fold in remaining whipped cream until no white streaks remain. Cover and refrigerate for at least 3 hours, or until ready to assemble pie. (Filling can be made up to 24 hours in advance.)

3. FOR THE MERINGUE CRUST: Adjust oven rack to lower-middle position and heat oven to 275 degrees. Grease 9-inch pie plate and dust well with extra cornstarch, using pastry brush to distribute evenly. Combine sugar and 1 tablespoon cornstarch in bowl. Using stand mixer fitted with whisk, whip egg whites and cream of tartar on medium-low speed until foamy, about 1 minute. Increase speed to medium-high and whip whites to soft, billowy mounds, 1 to 3 minutes. Gradually add sugar mixture and whip until glossy, stiff peaks form, 3 to 5 minutes. Add vanilla to meringue and whip until incorporated.

4. Spread meringue into prepared pie plate, following contours of plate to cover bottom, sides, and edges. Bake for 1½ hours. Rotate pie plate, reduce oven temperature to 200 degrees, and bake until completely dried out, about 1 hour longer. (Shell will rise above rim of pie plate; some cracking is OK.) Let cool completely, about 30 minutes.

5. FOR THE TOPPING: Spoon cooled chocolate filling into cavity of pie shell, distributing evenly. Using stand mixer fitted with whisk, whip cream and sugar on medium-low speed until foamy, about 1 minute. Increase speed to high and whip until stiff peaks form, 1 to 3 minutes. Spread whipped cream evenly over chocolate. Refrigerate until filling is set, about 1 hour. Dust with cocoa. Slice with sharp knife and serve.

DON'T MAKE THIS MISTAKE Busted Crust
The egg white crust is part of what distinguishes angel pie. To avoid a sticky, broken meringue shell, we added cornstarch to the whites, and we greased the pie plate and dusted it with more cornstarch. We also figured out the ideal baking time and temperatures to ensure that the interior and exterior of the meringue cooked properly.

MERINGUE MESS
Don't let this happen to you.

TASTING PROCESSED EGG WHITES

When you need a lot of egg whites for a recipe, it's tempting to grab a carton of egg whites sold in the supermarket dairy case or a canister of powdered egg whites in the baking aisle. But do these taste the same as fresh egg whites, and can you cook with them with comparable results? We bought four products (three liquid and one dehydrated) put out by national brands and made egg white omelets, meringue cookies, and angel food cakes, tasting them blind alongside samples made with egg whites from eggs that we cracked ourselves.

All four products were more or less acceptable in omelets (although the powdered whites were slightly grainy). But when it came to baking, fresh eggs produced taller angel food cakes and delicately crisp meringues, whereas egg white substitutes yielded shorter cakes and slightly harder, denser meringues.

Given that these products contain nothing but egg whites, what made the difference? The U.S. Department of Agriculture requires that liquid egg whites be pasteurized, a process that heats the whites enough to kill bacteria without cooking them. Powdered egg whites are made by evaporating water in a spray dryer. The substitutes can be safely added to uncooked frostings and drinks. But pasteurization changes the nature of the egg proteins enough to compromise their structure, especially in baked goods—a limitation that isn't always mentioned on product labels. The heating process prematurely links the proteins so that they unfold and stretch less readily when whipped. As a result, they cannot hold the same amount of air or achieve the same volume as fresh egg whites. That's why when we whipped the whites, one product needed 22 minutes to reach soft peaks, compared with just 6 minutes for fresh whites. Our top-ranked product, Eggology 100% Egg Whites, is a convenient substitute for fresh whites in omelets, scrambles, and frittatas, and it makes satisfactory baked goods. Just keep in mind that it costs more than fresh whole eggs. –SACHA MADADIAN

KEY Good ★★★   Fair ★★   Poor ★

RECOMMENDED		CRITERIA		TASTERS' NOTES
EGGOLOGY 100% Egg Whites **Price:** $5.99 for 16 egg whites ($0.37 per oz)		Omelet Baking Whipping	★★★ ★★½ ★★	This organic product looked like fresh egg whites and made an omelet that "tasted real" and an angel food cake that was "somewhat coarse but entirely acceptable." Meringue cookies were "hollow" and overly "crunchy," but their exteriors were "glossy and smooth."

RECOMMENDED WITH RESERVATIONS				
ORGANIC VALLEY Organic Pasteurized Egg Whites **Price:** $5.99 for 16 egg whites ($0.37 per oz)		Omelet Baking Whipping	★★½ ★★½ ★	The omelets tasted "very eggy," making this brand a good substitute when cooking an egg white omelet. We liked the taste of the cookies and the cake, too. But we had to wait 22 very long minutes for these whites to whip to soft peaks, so we don't recommend this product if you need to whip your whites.
DEB EL Just Whites 100% Dried Egg Whites **Price:** $9.29 for 21 egg whites ($3.10 per oz)		Omelet Baking Whipping	★½ ★★ ★★½	The meringue cookies tasted a little powdery, while the omelet was slightly grainy. Still, these whites were a dream to work with, whipping up even faster than fresh whites (although you do need to reconstitute them with water first).
EGG BEATERS All Natural 100% Egg Whites **Price:** $4.79 for 20 egg whites ($0.15 per oz)		Omelet Baking Whipping	★★½ ★ ★½	While they made an appealingly "fluffy, soft" omelet, these whites flopped—literally—when we tried to bake with them. We learned that they're twice pasteurized, making them unable to hold peaks when whipped or to rise properly in the oven when baked.

Cooking Class Roast Beef with Gravy

Who says a hearty roast beef and gravy dinner has to be expensive? We get fantastic results with an inexpensive cut and just one skillet. BY SCOTT KATHAN

Our technique produces rosy roast beef and minimizes the gray, overcooked edges.

ROAST BEEF WITH GRAVY
Serves 6 to 8

You can substitute top sirloin for the top round. Look for an evenly shaped roast with a fat cap. Be careful when cooking the vegetables in step 4, as the skillet handle will be hot when you begin making the gravy.

- 1 (4- to 5-pound) boneless top round roast, fat trimmed to ¼ inch
  Salt and pepper
- 1 tablespoon vegetable oil
- 4 tablespoons unsalted butter
- 2 carrots, peeled and cut into 2-inch pieces
- 1 onion, cut into ½-inch rounds
- 1 celery rib, cut into 2-inch pieces
- ½ cup all-purpose flour
- 1 teaspoon tomato paste
- 2 (10.5-ounce) cans beef consommé
- 1½ cups water

1. Tie kitchen twine around roast at 1-inch intervals. Sprinkle roast with 2 teaspoons salt and 2 teaspoons pepper. Wrap in plastic wrap and refrigerate for at least 1 hour or up to 24 hours.

2. Adjust oven rack to middle position and heat oven to 225 degrees. Heat oil in 12-inch ovensafe skillet over medium-high heat until just smoking. Pat roast dry with paper towels and brown all over, 8 to 12 minutes; transfer to plate.

3. Pour off all but 2 tablespoons fat from now-empty skillet. Reduce heat to medium and melt butter in skillet. Add carrots, onion, and celery and cook until lightly browned, 6 to 8 minutes. Add flour and tomato paste and cook until flour is golden and tomato paste begins to darken, about 2 minutes. Off heat, push vegetables to center of skillet. Place roast on top of vegetables and transfer skillet to oven. Cook until meat registers 125 degrees (for medium-rare), 2 to 3 hours. Transfer roast to carving board, tent loosely with aluminum foil, and let rest for 20 minutes.

4. Meanwhile, using potholder (skillet handle will be hot), return skillet with vegetables to medium-high heat and cook, stirring occasionally, until vegetables are deep golden brown, about 5 minutes. Slowly whisk in consommé and water, scraping up any browned bits. Bring to boil, then reduce heat to medium-low and simmer until thickened, 10 to 15 minutes. Strain gravy through fine-mesh strainer into 4-cup liquid measuring cup; discard vegetables. Season with salt and pepper to taste. Remove twine from roast. Thinly slice roast crosswise against grain. Serve with gravy.

Core Techniques

Season Early
Salting the meat at least 1 hour before cooking ensures well-seasoned meat. Here's why: Salt on the exterior of a piece of meat draws liquid from within the meat to the surface, where it mixes with the salt and then, through a process known as diffusion, penetrates back inside the meat. The longer a salted roast sits, the deeper the seasoning will go. Though even 1 hour works, 24 hours is optimal.

Get a Good Sear
We brown our salted, tied roast on all sides over medium-high heat. This has two benefits: First, when meat is seared, its amino acids and sugars react to form new flavor compounds—basically, good color means more flavor. (For the best browning, pat the roast dry before searing.) And second, some of these new flavor compounds invariably stick to the bottom of the skillet; they are called fond. After the meat is roasted, the fond helps enrich the gravy.

Roast Slowly
We cook our roast in a low 225-degree oven. The meat retains more of its juice, and we minimize the "gray band" of overcooked meat around the exterior of each slice. If we roasted the meat at a high temperature, its fibers would contract more forcefully and squeeze out precious flavorful juice. Slow roasting also decreases the chance of overcooking.

Deglaze the Pan
Searing the meat and browning the vegetables twice (before and after roasting) creates plenty of flavorful fond in the skillet. It's essential to deglaze the pan to unlock the fond's flavor. Deglazing simply means pouring in liquid (in this case beef consommé and water) and scraping the browned bits so they dissolve into the hot liquid as it cooks. Deglazing is a core technique for any gravy or pan sauce.

TEST KITCHEN TIP **Avoiding the Dreaded Gray Band**
Cooking meat at too high a temperature can result in an overcooked, dried-out gray-brown band around the perimeter of each slice. We roast at a low temperature (searing the meat first for a flavorful crust) for a juicy interior with a more uniform rosy-pink color.

BAD BEEF
When you cook a roast too fast (as shown here), the outside overcooks and dries out.

Roast Beef with Gravy Step by Step

1. PREP ROAST
Trim the fat, tie the roast with kitchen twine, and pat dry.
WHY? Tying the roast ensures even cooking. Patting dry helps the seasoning adhere.

2. SALT AND LET SIT
Season the roast with salt and pepper, wrap it in plastic wrap, and refrigerate it for 1 to 24 hours.
WHY? The longer the salted roast sits the more thoroughly seasoned and juicy the meat will be.

3. SEAR
Pat the roast dry and brown it on all sides in hot oil.
WHY? Dry meat sears more readily. A good sear creates extra flavor.

4. BUILD GRAVY BASE
Sauté the onion, carrots, and celery and then add flour and tomato paste.
WHY? We get the gravy base started early so it can cook with the roast and absorb meaty flavor.

5. RETURN ROAST TO PAN
Push the vegetable mixture to the center of the pan and place the seared roast on top.
WHY? Roasting the meat on a bed of vegetables elevates it for more even cooking and also maximizes flavor transfer between the meat and the vegetables.

6. SLOW-ROAST
Cook the roast to 125 degrees in a 225-degree oven, 2 to 3 hours.
WHY? Roasting at a relatively low temperature maximizes gentle, even cooking.

7. REST MEAT
Loosely tent the roast with aluminum foil and let rest.
WHY? The foil keeps some heat in (so your dinner won't be cold) while the juice redistributes throughout the roast.

8. BROWN VEGETABLES
Give the vegetables another 5 minutes over medium-high heat on the stovetop to take on more color (the skillet handle will be hot).
WHY? The deep browning will make the gravy even more flavorful.

9. ADD LIQUID
Whisk in the beef consommé and water and scrape the pan with a wooden spoon.
WHY? This is the liquid base of the gravy. Beef consommé adds more depth and richness than beef broth does.

10. BOIL, THEN SIMMER
Bring the gravy to a boil, then reduce the heat and simmer.
WHY? Any sauce thickened with flour needs to reach a boil to activate the flour's full thickening power. Simmer to meld the flavors and concentrate the gravy.

11. STRAIN
Pour the gravy through a fine-mesh strainer; discard the vegetables.
WHY? Gravy should be smooth, plus the vegetables have given up most of their flavor.

12. CARVE
Remove (and discard) the twine, carve the roast into thin slices, and serve with gravy.
WHY? Thin slices (carved against the grain) guarantee the most tender beef.

INGREDIENTS
The Right Roast
This recipe uses a top round roast, an inexpensive cut from the rump of the steer that's most commonly roasted and sliced for deli sandwiches. Since this cut is irregular, we tie it with kitchen twine to create a uniform shape that will cook evenly. And because it's relatively lean, we sear the roast quickly on the stovetop to build flavor before roasting it slowly so that it doesn't overcook and dry out.

TOP ROUND
Don't rush it and it'll make a fine roast.

Beef Consommé
Many gravy recipes call for beef broth to be added to the drippings. In search of more potent flavor, we cooked down the beef broth to half its original volume, and the gravy was much improved. To get the same concentrated beef flavor without the bother of dirtying another pan to reduce the beef broth, we turned to canned condensed beef consommé, to which we added

FLAVOR BUILDER
Fast path to beefy gravy.

only half of the water called for to reconstitute it. This gave our gravy big beefy flavor without requiring extra work.

EQUIPMENT Ovensafe Skillet
Our 12-inch ovensafe skillets are true workhorses in the test kitchen. We highly recommend the All-Clad Stainless 12-Inch Fry Pan ($155); it cooks food very evenly, with no hot spots. It's expensive but should last a lifetime. Our Best Buy skillet is the Tramontina 12-Inch Tri-Ply Clad Sauté Pan. This pan is very similar to the All-Clad pan but is a little heavier and a lot cheaper ($40). Both pans have aluminum cores (for efficient heating) "clad" with durable stainless-steel exteriors.

> **Our online cooking school** offers personalized instruction in roasting and dozens of other topics. Our program helps you master techniques, not just recipes. For details, visit **OnlineCookingSchool.com**.

Slow Cooker Meatloaf

Could we really make a tender, flavorful meatloaf in the slow cooker?

BY SARAH GABRIEL

MEATLOAF IS ONE of those recipes you find in every slow-cooker cookbook. If so many people are already making meatloaves in the slow cooker, what could be left to figure out? Plenty.

Some recipes call for just beef; others want a classic meatloaf mix of beef, pork, and veal. Some require sautéing onions and garlic first, while others instruct to just knead them into the meat raw. Most recipes include some kind of panade, or bread-milk mixture, to tenderize the loaf, relying on ingredients ranging from crackers to stuffing mix. Some call for vegetables. And seasonings are all over the map. I picked five quite different recipes and plugged in the slow cookers.

The loaves came out either mushy or dense and bricklike. And while there were differences in flavor (raw onions made the loaves sour, a few were too herby, and seasoned bread crumbs tasted stale), all of the loaves were similarly bland. Tasters demanded a tender yet meaty loaf with big, savory flavor . . . and, of course, a fuss-free recipe.

To isolate the particular effects of the slow cooker, I attempted to make a test kitchen favorite traditional meatloaf recipe in it. I browned onions and garlic on the stove; cooled the mix; and then combined it with eggs, 1 pound each of ground beef and pork, thyme, salt, pepper, and a panade made of saltines and milk. I formed the mixture into a loaf, put it in the cooker, set it on low, and left it for 4 hours. In the steamy slow cooker there was no browning, which

meant no deep, roasted flavors either. And despite the steam, 4 long hours in the cooker overcooked and dried out the meat. The advantage of using the slow cooker is the carefree hours afforded while supper cooks. I'd keep the 4-hour cooking time—I just had to boost flavor and maintain moisture.

Our science editor explained that, as meat cooks, the proteins shrink up, essentially wringing out the moisture. Panade interrupts the meat's protein network, preventing it from squeezing out so much liquid, and its starches form a gel that traps the moisture in the meat. Given that, I doubled the panade, but this made the meatloaf mushy, with a taste more of crackers than meat—I had overshot. I made three more loaves, decreasing the amount of crackers in each one, but the amount of panade I needed to amply tenderize the loaf diluted the meaty flavor. Before abandoning extra panade, I'd try boosting flavor. What if I replaced some of the milk with a more flavorful liquid? We often use Worcestershire sauce and soy sauce to boost meaty, savory flavors. I tested varying amounts of each and settled on replacing 1½ tablespoons of milk with Worcestershire (any more left a sour taste) and the 4 remaining teaspoons with soy sauce. At the same time, I switched from onion to milder shallot. Tasters deemed this meatloaf much improved but still not meaty enough. I'd have to lose the extra panade after all.

Two steps forward, one back: With

What's the secret to keeping meatloaf moist through 4 hours of cooking? Mushrooms.

less panade my meatloaf was meaty and flavorful, but the tough, dry texture had returned. What could I add that would stay tender, like panade, without muting flavor? One of the recipes from the first round had included ground carrots and celery. Tasters didn't like the vegetable flavor, but it *was* one of the more tender loaves. Just like panade, vegetables interrupt the protein network and keep the meat from wringing out its juice. Maybe mushrooms could help; their flavor might blend into the meat better.

I made another meatloaf, this time grinding up 6 ounces of mushrooms in the food processor with the crackers for the panade. I sautéed the mushrooms with the shallot and then cooled the mixture before combining it with the other ingredients. Now, instead of poking the meatloaf with their forks and frowning, the tasters were eating. Finally, my meatloaf was tender, moist, and meaty. To simplify the meatloaf-making procedure, I tried cooking the shallot in the microwave. It became sweet and mellow in just 90 seconds, and I was able to mix in the spices and

bloom them (which brings out their flavor) at the same time. Could I use raw mushrooms and save myself a step? Yes. Their flavor was less concentrated, so raw worked even better.

I had just one more task: a glaze. There was no way to get a browned, bubbly one in the slow cooker (believe me: I tried). So after removing the meatloaf from the slow cooker, I brushed it with some sweetened ketchup and set it under the broiler. The 5-minute broil was well worth it, but tussling with a hot meatloaf to remove it from the slow cooker wasn't my idea of a good time. To make the task easier and neater, I fashioned a foil sling. I formed the loaf right on the strip of foil, used the sling to lower the loaf into the slow cooker, and 4 hours later easily hoisted it out with the same sling. Then I glazed the meatloaf and put it in the oven.

With a little help from some flavor-boosting condiments and mushroom-enhanced panade, my slow-cooker meatloaf was just as beefy and tender as a traditional meatloaf . . . and even easier to make.

KEY TECHNIQUES **Making a Better Loaf**

MAKE A FOIL SLING
We fashioned an aluminum foil sling to neatly transport our meatloaf in and out of the slow cooker.

BROIL TO FINISH
In order to get a tasty, burnished crust, we brushed a simple glaze on the meatloaf and ran it under the broiler.

We wanted a from-scratch pasta sauce with depth and complexity—in just 15 minutes' time. BY NICK IVERSON

SLOW-COOKER MEATLOAF
Serves 6

Premium brand saltines now come in a round format; if you are using square saltines, go with 16 instead of 18.

18	saltines
4	ounces white mushrooms, trimmed
3	tablespoons milk
1½	tablespoons Worcestershire sauce
4	teaspoons soy sauce
1	teaspoon salt
¾	teaspoon pepper
1	shallot, minced
1	tablespoon vegetable oil
2	garlic cloves, minced
¼	teaspoon dried thyme
¼	teaspoon cayenne pepper
2	large eggs
1	pound ground pork
1	pound 85 percent lean ground beef
6	tablespoons ketchup
1	tablespoon packed brown sugar

1. Process saltines, mushrooms, milk, Worcestershire, soy sauce, salt, and pepper in food processor until paste forms, about 20 seconds, scraping down bowl as needed. Transfer to large bowl. Combine shallot, oil, garlic, thyme, and cayenne in small bowl and microwave until softened, about 90 seconds, stirring halfway through cooking. Whisk shallot mixture and eggs into saltine mixture.

2. Add pork to saltine mixture and mix until thoroughly combined. Add ground beef and knead until well combined. Fold 18-inch square of heavy-duty aluminum foil in half to make 18 by 9-inch strip. Form meat mixture into 9 by 4-inch loaf and place crosswise over center of strip. Using foil as sling, transfer meatloaf to slow cooker. Cover and cook until meatloaf registers 160 degrees, about 2 hours on low.

3. Adjust oven rack 5 inches from broiler element and heat broiler. Whisk ketchup and sugar together in bowl. Using sling, transfer meatloaf to rimmed baking sheet and brush with glaze. Broil until glaze is bubbly and spotty brown, 5 to 7 minutes. Transfer to serving dish (discard sling), tent loosely with foil, and let rest for 15 minutes. Slice and serve.

HOMEMADE TOMATO SAUCE is definitely better than the jarred stuff, but many recipes require a long cooking time to develop depth of flavor. They call for softening onions and garlic in oil; adding canned whole tomatoes, dried oregano, and red pepper flakes; and simmering for an hour or two. Fortunately, the test kitchen has a recipe for a quick, easy sauce that nonetheless has long-simmered taste. Flavor and speed, our recipe proves, don't have to be mutually exclusive.

To get started building flavor fast, we begin with butter, not olive oil. Butter can brown, and the depth of flavor that browning adds helps us produce a speedy yet fully flavored sauce. To speed things up further, we finely chop the onion instead of coarsely chopping it. The extra surface area from more finely diced onion releases more sugars (from the ruptured cells), allowing faster caramelization as the sugars heat up. Next, we add dried oregano to the butter and onion so that the fat and heat can draw out the herb's flavor. And it wouldn't be spaghetti sauce without minced garlic. To this solid base of flavor, we add crushed tomatoes. They require neither smashing nor pureeing, as canned whole or diced tomatoes would, so they save work and time. A touch of sugar rounds out the flavor of our quick sauce.

After a 10-minute simmer (you read that right—just 10 minutes), the sauce will have thickened and the flavors melded nicely. We finish it with a glug of extra-virgin olive oil and stir in fragrant chopped basil to bring out the kind of freshness you'll never find in jarred sauce. This tomato sauce comes together so quickly that I had plenty of time to hash out four equally fast and tasty variations on the theme: all'amatriciana, arrabbiata, puttanesca, and vodka cream.

TOMATO-BASIL SAUCE
Makes about 3 cups; enough for 1 pound pasta
Don't even think about using dried basil; the fresh herb adds flavor and brightness that dried can't.

2	tablespoons unsalted butter
¼	cup finely chopped onion
	Salt and pepper
¼	teaspoon dried oregano

Starting our sauce with butter—not oil—adds richness to this quick-cooked pasta sauce.

2	garlic cloves, minced
1	(28-ounce) can crushed tomatoes
¼	teaspoon sugar
2	tablespoons chopped fresh basil
1	tablespoon extra-virgin olive oil

Melt butter in medium saucepan over medium-low heat. Add onion, ½ teaspoon salt, and oregano and cook, stirring occasionally, until onions are golden brown, 3 to 5 minutes. Add garlic and cook until fragrant, about 30 seconds. Stir in tomatoes and sugar, increase heat to high, and bring to simmer. Reduce heat to medium-low and simmer until thickened slightly, about 10 minutes. Off heat, stir in basil and oil. Season with salt and pepper to taste, and serve.

ALL'AMATRICIANA SAUCE
Cook 4 ounces diced salt pork in melted butter until crispy, 7 to 10 minutes. Transfer pork to paper towel–lined plate. Remove all but 2 tablespoons fat from pot and cook onion mixture and garlic as directed. When garlic is fragrant, add ½ cup red wine to pot and reduce by half, about 2 minutes. Proceed with recipe, omitting basil and stirring in pork and ½ cup grated Pecorino Romano cheese at end along with oil.

ARRABBIATA SAUCE
Add ¾ teaspoon red pepper flakes to onion mixture. Increase garlic to 4 minced cloves. Substitute chopped fresh parsley for basil.

PUTTANESCA SAUCE
Add 4 rinsed and minced anchovy fillets and ½ teaspoon red pepper flakes to onion mixture. Substitute ¼ cup chopped kalamata olives and 3 tablespoons rinsed and minced capers for basil.

VODKA-CREAM SAUCE
Add ½ cup vodka along with tomatoes. Substitute chopped fresh parsley for basil and ¼ cup heavy cream for oil.

> What brand of crushed tomatoes is best? Get a (free) look at the winners in our taste test at CooksCountry.com/mar13.

Cooking for Two Chicken Cordon Bleu

Stuffing, breading, and frying chicken breasts is traditional, but a scaled-down version of chicken cordon bleu demanded an easier approach. BY REBECCAH MARSTERS

BACK IN THE 1960s, serving chicken cordon bleu at your dinner party was sure to impress; everyone knew that preparing this stuffed chicken dish was no easy task. When done right, the gooey cheese, salty ham, juicy chicken, and crunchy crust make it worth the effort. But I wanted an easier version of chicken cordon bleu for two, with all the appeal and none of the fuss of the original. Now *that* would be impressive.

Most of the "easy" recipes that I found were either gloppy casseroles or chicken breasts merely topped with ham and melted cheese. But without the standard ham-cheese core, these recipes had less allure. By contrast, traditional recipes require pounding out boneless chicken breasts and rolling them up with slices of ham and cheese or cutting pockets into the breasts and stuffing the ham and cheese inside. The filled breasts are dipped in flour, beaten eggs, and lastly bread crumbs and then fried in oil. Could I find an easier way?

My first decision was to cook my cordon bleu in the oven to avoid the messy frying. But should I pound and roll or cut a pocket and stuff? In my initial tests, the rolling technique was easier than stuffing (I ruined more than one breast by cutting the pocket too deep), but I still hoped to skip the step of pounding. When I rolled unpounded chicken breasts around slices of ham and cheese, however, the rolls were so

Breading just the top of each roll is easier and still provides plenty of crunchy coating.

fat that they needed more than an hour to cook in a 400-degree oven, plus the cheese oozed out. Thinner meat meant less baking time, which meant less time for the cheese to start flowing. Instead of pounding, I tried cutting each breast in half horizontally to form two thin cutlets (store-bought cutlets are often ragged and uneven). Making four smaller rolls let me slash the oven time by nearly half. And since I wasn't pounding out whole breasts into huge cutlets, I could snuggle four tidy rolls into a loaf pan (which helped contain any leaking cheese). But I wanted to minimize the escaping cheese.

If the chicken alone couldn't corral the cheese, maybe the ham could. For my next test, I cut fat sticks of Gruyère (instead of the slices of deli Swiss I had been using) and wrapped each tightly in a ham slice, folding in the sides. I rolled one cutlet around each ham-and-cheese bundle, first coating the chicken with mustard for extra flavor and sticking power. This method yielded cooked rolls with a cache of molten cheese in the center—perfect. On to the coating.

I knew that I needed a bread-crumb coating for crunch and egg for "glue," but I discovered I could skip the flour with minimal impact. For convenience, I switched from homemade bread crumbs to store-bought panko that I flavored with melted butter. Since the crumbs didn't brown in the time it took

the chicken rolls to cook through, I quickly toasted them in the oven (using the same loaf pan that would hold the breaded chicken). I further streamlined the method by breading just the top of each roll instead of the whole thing. With all the flavor of the dinner party classic and none of the hassle, I considered this 1960s dish successfully updated—and downsized.

CHICKEN CORDON BLEU FOR TWO

This recipe is best with ham slices with some heft. To prevent the cheese from oozing out, completely enclose it inside each ham slice.

- ⅔ cup panko bread crumbs
- 1 tablespoon unsalted butter, melted
  Salt and pepper
- 2 ounces Gruyère cheese, cut into four 2½ by ½-inch sticks
- 4 slices deli ham (4 ounces)
- 2 (6- to 8-ounce) boneless, skinless chicken breasts, trimmed
- 4 teaspoons Dijon mustard
- 1 large egg, lightly beaten

1. Adjust oven rack to upper-middle position and heat oven to 400 degrees. Toss panko with melted butter, ¼ teaspoon salt, and ¼ teaspoon pepper in 8½ by 4½-inch loaf pan until combined. Bake until golden brown, 5 to 7 minutes, stirring halfway through baking. Let cool completely.

2. Roll each piece of Gruyère in 1 slice of ham, folding edges of ham over so no cheese is exposed. Using sharp knife, cut each chicken breast in half horizontally into 2 equal-size cutlets. Season chicken with salt and pepper and spread 1 teaspoon mustard evenly on cut side of each cutlet. Working with 1 cutlet at a time, place 1 ham-and-Gruyère roll 1 inch from thick end of mustard side of cutlet and roll up tightly. Secure each chicken roll with toothpick and set aside, seam side down.

3. Brush tops of chicken rolls with egg and dip into panko mixture, pressing gently to adhere. Discard remaining panko mixture. Arrange chicken rolls, crumb side up, in now-empty loaf pan. Bake until chicken registers 160 degrees, 30 to 35 minutes, rotating pan halfway through cooking. Remove toothpicks and serve.

TEST KITCHEN TECHNIQUE **Roll 'em Up**
Instead of cutting pockets and stuffing each chicken breast, we use an easy rolling technique for our streamlined cordon bleu.

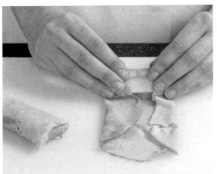

SEAL CHEESE
Enclosing the cheese stick within a slice of ham ensures that it stays put.

ROLL CHICKEN
Roll the mustard-coated chicken cutlet around the ham-and-cheese bundle.

Recipe Makeover Tiramisù

The name is Italian for "pick me up." We wanted a version that didn't weigh us down.

BY CAROLYNN PURPURA MACKAY

TIRAMISÙ APPEARS ON the menu of just about every Italian restaurant in America, and people love to make it at home, too. No wonder: Liqueur-and-coffee-soaked ladyfingers alternate with an ultra-creamy filling made from luscious mascarpone, billowy whipped cream, and rich, whipped egg yolks, all dusted with cocoa. Since the mascarpone alone has 60 calories and 6 grams of fat per tablespoon, I can't say I was surprised that a single serving of tiramisù weighed in at 530 calories and 36 grams of fat. But it did make me think twice about ordering it. Unwilling to give it up, though, I set out to create a lower-fat version.

Right away, I realized that the ladyfingers contributed few calories and little fat; to cut, I'd need to focus on the filling. I suspected that the mascarpone, whipped cream, and eggs would all have to go, so I dropped by the dairy counter to survey the field of potential substitutes. Although there's no such thing low-fat mascarpone, other fresh dairy cheeses do come in low-fat versions. The first one I reached for was part-skim ricotta. It's used to make cannoli, another classic Italian dessert, plus its lean, slight tang reminds me of mascarpone. Back in the test kitchen, I used the ricotta to replace both the mascarpone and the whipped cream. The taste was pretty good, but the texture? Not so much. Mascarpone is voluptuously smooth. Whipped cream is, um, creamy. But part-skim ricotta had a grittiness that was hard to mask, even when I tried whirling (and whirling and whirling) it in the food processor.

Reduced-fat cream cheese, low-fat cottage cheese, and nonfat Greek yogurt stand in for the traditional mascarpone cheese here. Result? Full flavor, 70 percent less fat.

Our science editor explained that the proteins in ricotta are highly cross-linked, which makes them resistant to breaking down. He suggested cottage cheese: Its more weakly linked proteins, he thought, would process to a nice creaminess. He was right. But the flavor was, well . . . I'll put it this way: Instead of a decadent dessert, this tiramisù tasted like cottage cheese. I tried again. I made one batch that combined cottage cheese with nonfat Greek yogurt (it has more body than ordinary yogurt) and a second batch using silken tofu processed with the cottage cheese. While the tofu wasn't awful, my tasters much preferred the smooth tang of the nonfat Greek yogurt, so I decided to go with that.

My tiramisù couldn't afford the fat that six egg yolks add to the classic version. (They are whipped, raw, with the sugar to start the filling.) Other than fat, though, did the yolks bring much? I didn't think so, so in one swift move I got rid of them. My tiramisù was loose and watery. Oops: It turns out that the emulsifiers in yolks help maintain

a strong, stable emulsion. Without the yolks in my tiramisù, the dairy was thinning and even separating. To bring the filling back together, I tried low-fat cream cheese (neufchatel), which I've used before to give low-fat desserts body and stability. It blended smoothly into the yogurt–cottage cheese mixture and restored the creamy texture.

Many full-fat recipes use as much as ½ cup of rum to flavor the filling, but to meet my self-imposed calorie limit, I restricted myself to just 2 tablespoons. Alas, we could barely taste it. How could I maximize the flavor from the smaller amount? Maybe the problem wasn't the amount but the distribution method. I made the tiramisù again, this time mixing rum (4 teaspoons) into the coffee soaking liquid for the ladyfingers, as usual, but then stirring the remaining 2 teaspoons into the filling. At the same time, I added 1 tablespoon of vanilla extract. Now the rum came forward, and the stepped-up flavors helped disguise the fact that I'd managed to cut a whopping 26 grams of fat and 180 calories—and still produce a delicious dessert.

The Numbers
Nutritional information is for one serving of tiramisù.

Traditional Tiramisù
CALORIES **530**
FAT **36 g** SATURATED FAT **19 g**

Cook's Country Reduced-Fat Tiramisù
CALORIES **350**
FAT **10 g** SATURATED FAT **5 g**

REDUCED-FAT TIRAMISÙ Serves 6

Be sure to use the crisp, firm ladyfingers found in the cookie or international aisle, not the fresh, cakelike ladyfingers found in the bakery department. Depending on the brand, 5 ounces is about 25 to 30 ladyfingers. You can substitute ¾ cup of strong brewed coffee for the hot water and espresso powder.

- ¾ cup hot water
- 1½ tablespoons instant espresso powder
- 2 tablespoons dark rum
- 8 ounces ⅓ less fat cream cheese (neufchatel), softened
- 8 ounces (1 cup) low-fat cottage cheese
- 1½ cups (6 ounces) confectioners' sugar
- ½ cup nonfat Greek yogurt
- 1 tablespoon vanilla extract
- 5 ounces dried ladyfingers (savoiardi)
- 1½ teaspoons cocoa

1. Combine hot water, espresso powder, and 4 teaspoons rum in 2-cup liquid measuring cup. Let cool for 5 minutes. Process cream cheese, cottage cheese, sugar, yogurt, vanilla, and remaining 2 teaspoons rum in food processor until completely smooth, about 20 seconds.

2. Place half of ladyfingers in single layer in bottom of 8-inch square baking dish (some small gaps are OK). Pour half of espresso mixture over ladyfingers. Let sit until most liquid has been absorbed, about 1 minute. Spread half of cream cheese mixture evenly over ladyfingers. Repeat with remaining ladyfingers, remaining espresso mixture, and remaining cream cheese mixture.

3. Cover with plastic wrap and refrigerate for at least 4 hours or up to 24 hours. Just before serving, dust with cocoa.

Equipment Review Cookie Sheets

Think your choice in cookie sheets doesn't matter? Think again. Most of the ones we tested ruined our cookies. BY TAIZETH SIERRA

IT'S JUST A flat piece of metal, so you'd think a cookie sheet couldn't fail. In fact, we've seen them bake unevenly and warp, not to mention let cookies burn, stick, or spread into blobs. Cookie sheets come in many materials, sizes, thicknesses, and finishes, insulated or not, with rims or not. What works best? Our previous favorite, the Vollrath Wear-Ever Cookie Sheet, bakes beautifully, but you have to buy it online or at restaurant supply stores. Is anybody making a quality cookie sheet for home bakers?

We gathered eight, including our previous winner, priced from $12 to $24, testing both single sheets and insulated versions. Manufacturers claim that insulated sheets heat more evenly and "allow virtually no chance of burning," as one puts it. The air pocket between two layers of metal is designed to buffer heat, preventing hot spots and warping.

To test them, we baked three types of cookies (spritz, lemon, and lace) on both unlined and parchment paper–lined sheets, blending batches of dough and using the same oven so that the only variable was the cookie sheet being tested. First, we looked at how evenly the sheets baked. Not very, it turned out. Many produced pale cookies and dark cookies within a single sheet. Surprisingly, one of the insulated sheets bombed this test, not only baking unevenly but nearly burning every batch, too. We got the best results from two single-layer sheets. One baked slightly faster than recipe times indicated, but it baked evenly, creating flavorful deep-golden bottoms and paler tops. Our previous winner produced perfectly even cookies with matched tops and bottoms. As for the nonstick sheets, the slick surfaces encouraged the batter to run and ooze before it set, so instead of tall, distinct edges, these cookies tapered to thin edges that overbaked.

Whether evenly browned or not,

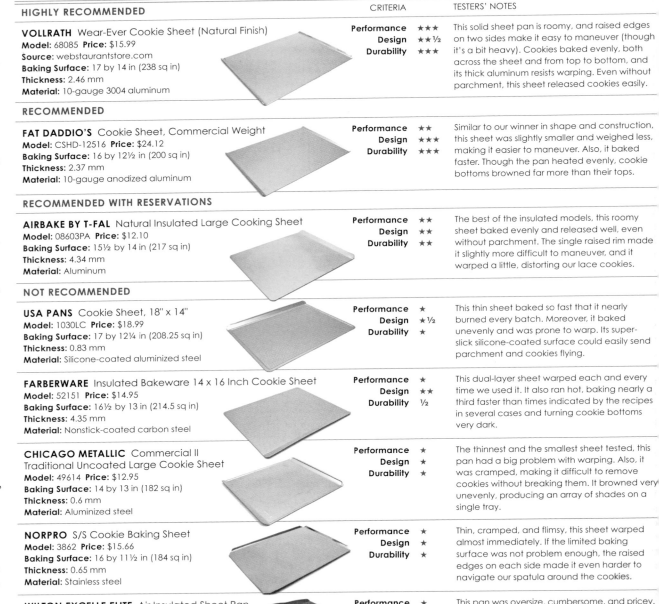

	CRITERIA		TESTERS' NOTES
HIGHLY RECOMMENDED			
VOLLRATH Wear-Ever Cookie Sheet (Natural Finish) **Model:** 68085 **Price:** $15.99 **Source:** webstaurantstore.com **Baking Surface:** 17 by 14 in (238 sq in) **Thickness:** 2.46 mm **Material:** 10-gauge 3004 aluminum	Performance ★★★ Design ★★½ Durability ★★★		This solid sheet pan is roomy, and raised edges on two sides make it easy to maneuver (though it's a bit heavy). Cookies baked evenly, both across the sheet and from top to bottom, and its thick aluminum resists warping. Even without parchment, this sheet released cookies easily.
RECOMMENDED			
FAT DADDIO'S Cookie Sheet, Commercial Weight **Model:** CSHD-12516 **Price:** $24.12 **Baking Surface:** 16 by 12½ in (200 sq in) **Thickness:** 2.37 mm **Material:** 10-gauge anodized aluminum	Performance ★★ Design ★★★ Durability ★★★		Similar to our winner in shape and construction, this sheet was slightly smaller and weighed less, making it easier to maneuver. Also, it baked faster. Though the pan heated evenly, cookie bottoms browned far more than their tops.
RECOMMENDED WITH RESERVATIONS			
AIRBAKE BY T-FAL Natural Insulated Large Cooking Sheet **Model:** 08603PA **Price:** $12.10 **Baking Surface:** 15½ by 14 in (217 sq in) **Thickness:** 4.34 mm **Material:** Aluminum	Performance ★★ Design ★★ Durability ★★		The best of the insulated models, this roomy sheet baked evenly and released well, even without parchment. The single raised rim made it slightly more difficult to maneuver, and it warped a little, distorting our lace cookies.
NOT RECOMMENDED			
USA PANS Cookie Sheet, 18" x 14" **Model:** 1030LC **Price:** $18.99 **Baking Surface:** 17 by 12¼ in (208.25 sq in) **Thickness:** 0.83 mm **Material:** Silicone-coated aluminized steel	Performance ★ Design ★½ Durability ★		This thin sheet baked so fast that it nearly burned every batch. Moreover, it baked unevenly and was prone to warp. Its super-slick silicone-coated surface could easily send parchment and cookies flying.
FARBERWARE Insulated Bakeware 14 x 16 Inch Cookie Sheet **Model:** 52151 **Price:** $14.95 **Baking Surface:** 16½ by 13 in (214.5 sq in) **Thickness:** 4.35 mm **Material:** Nonstick-coated carbon steel	Performance ★ Design ★★ Durability ½		This dual-layer sheet warped each and every time we used it. It also ran hot, baking nearly a third faster than times indicated by the recipes in several cases and turning cookie bottoms very dark.
CHICAGO METALLIC Commercial II Traditional Uncoated Large Cookie Sheet **Model:** 49614 **Price:** $12.95 **Baking Surface:** 14 by 13 in (182 sq in) **Thickness:** 0.6 mm **Material:** Aluminized steel	Performance ★ Design ★ Durability ★		The thinnest and the smallest sheet tested, this pan had a big problem with warping. Also, it was cramped, making it difficult to remove cookies without breaking them. It browned very unevenly, producing an array of shades on a single tray.
NORPRO S/S Cookie Baking Sheet **Model:** 3862 **Price:** $15.66 **Baking Surface:** 16 by 11½ in (184 sq in) **Thickness:** 0.65 mm **Material:** Stainless steel	Performance ★ Design ★ Durability ★		Thin, cramped, and flimsy, this sheet warped almost immediately. If the limited baking surface was not problem enough, the raised edges on each side made it even harder to navigate our spatula around the cookies.
WILTON EXCELLE ELITE Air Insulated Sheet Pan **Model:** 2105-422 **Price:** $23.89 **Baking Surface:** 18 by 14 in (252 sq in) **Thickness:** 6.4 mm **Material:** Nonstick-coated steel	Performance ★ Design ★ Durability ★		This pan was oversize, cumbersome, and pricey. It also baked unevenly, with dark cookies around the perimeter of the pan and underdone cookies in the center. Its nonstick surface scratched and looked beat-up by the end of testing.

all cookies should come off a baking sheet without sticking. To test how well sheets released cookies, we baked spritz cookies, which are so buttery they don't require parchment paper. It took a little more effort to remove cookies from sheets with traditional finishes, but in every case but one, we managed. (In that case, the anodized matte surface was to blame, we learned. Anodizing, which helps prevent scratching, is also used to prepare metal for pigments or coatings by making the surface rougher and more porous—and more likely to stick, explained Hugh Rushing of the Cookware Manufacturers Association.)

We turned to design. Lace cookies should spread into lovely lacy disks. But if your cookie sheet warps, the cookies run together or come out looking like amoebas. While any metal sheet can warp, we found that the thinnest, lightest pans were most likely to. We were disappointed that the insulated sheets

---

TESTING DISCOVERY Insulated Cookie Sheets Don't Deliver

What is an insulated cookie sheet? It's a sheet that consists of two layers of metal on either side of a hollow center (see illustration below); the idea is that the open space consistently buffers heat, so these sheets bake evenly with no hot spots. Is this true? In a word, no. With the exception of the AirBake by T-Fal, the insulated sheets we tested didn't bake evenly and all were prone to warp.

A cross-section of an insulated cookie sheet showing the hollow center.

Taste Test Chili Powder

Chili powder is essential for making perfect game-time chili, but many products fumble with weak, wan flavor. Do any score a touchdown? BY HANNAH CROWLEY

we tested warped, too. Even heating, which these promise, should prevent warping. Apparently not.

Next, could we easily maneuver a spatula between cookies? (This is especially important when you are baking without parchment paper, as you must move the cookies one by one to a wire rack to cool instead of simply transferring them en masse on a sheet of parchment.) Cookie sheets with less than 200 square inches of baking surface felt cramped. As for rims, while cookies can be misshapen if they hit a pan's rim, raised edges do provide a useful handhold. Pans with two raised edges on the short sides handled best. Single rims on the long side were out of reach after we rotated the pan (most of our cookie recipes call for rotating the sheets for even baking). Three rims was overkill.

Many dozens of cookies later, we tallied our findings: We like thick sheets; thin sheets baked unevenly, ran hot, and tended to warp. We don't, however, like insulated sheets; though some baked well, all warped to some extent. And light or dark finishes matter less than material: Aluminum sheets, we discovered, have better, more even heat transference than steel sheets. Of the eight cookie sheets we tested, there are five that we cannot recommend.

The good news? The Vollrath Wear-Ever Cookie Sheet, our once and future winner. With two raised edges for easy handling, plenty of space, and thick aluminum construction that resists warping and promotes even browning, this cookie sheet remains our favorite. And while you still have to buy it online, at least it'll be delivered to your door.

DID YOU KNOW? All products reviewed by America's Test Kitchen, home of *Cook's Country* and *Cook's Illustrated* magazines, are independently chosen, researched, and reviewed by our editors. We buy products for testing at retail locations and do not accept unsolicited samples for testing. We do not accept or receive payment or consideration from product manufacturers or retailers. Manufacturers and retailers are not told in advance of publication which products we have recommended. We list suggested sources for recommended products as a convenience to our readers but do not endorse specific retailers.

CHILI POWDER IS a seasoning blend made from ground dried chiles and an assortment of other ingredients. Much like curry powder, there is no single recipe, but cumin, garlic, and oregano are traditional additions. Chili powder is not to be confused with the lesser-known chile powder (also often spelled chili powder), made solely from chiles without additional seasonings. We use the blend to season batches of chili and in spice rubs and marinades.

But which brand is best? Wanting a bold, complex powder with a warming but not scorching heat, we chose seven widely available chili powders (including two from industry giant McCormick) and tasted them sprinkled over potatoes—to assess each uncooked on a neutral base—and cooked in beef-and-bean chili. What did we learn?

Top picks won praise for bold heat; those we liked less we faulted as "meek." Capsaicin is the chemical that gives chile peppers their heat; its strength is measured on the Scoville scale in Scoville heat units (SHU). We contacted each manufacturer to ask which peppers they use in their powders; three manufacturers deemed that information proprietary, but four were willing to share. Our top two products, which tasters liked for their "bold" heat, both use cayenne (30,000 to 50,000 SHU) in combination with milder peppers. The third- and fourth-place products use a single pepper named "6-4," developed at New Mexico State University (300 to 500 SHU). The 6-4 wasn't hot enough for our tasters. Manufacturers of the lowest-ranked products declined to reveal which peppers they use, but tasters found their heat levels lacking.

Yet a great chili powder is more than just heat. As we noted, our top two products used a combination of peppers to achieve complexity; both add paprika, which is made from dried sweet bell peppers (0 SHU), and one added ancho peppers (1,000 to 2,000 SHU). This layering of multiple peppers created depth that tasters preferred to the "flat" single-pepper powders.

Supporting spices also played a role. Manufacturers of two of the bottom three products also refused to share information about their "spices"; tasters found them sweet and not much else. Two less-preferred products branched off into Indian-influenced spice blends with coriander, cloves, and allspice.

RECOMMENDED

	TASTERS' NOTES
MORTON & BASSETT Chili Powder **Price:** $5.19 for 1.9 oz ($2.73 per oz) **Ingredients:** Paprika, cumin, cayenne pepper, garlic, parsley, oregano, black pepper.	This "smoky, sizzling, full-flavored" chili powder was "much more dimensional than others." "The flavor I've been waiting for!" one taster wrote. The "hot, smoky, herbaceous" powder was "balanced," "bright," and "lively," with "raisiny fruitiness" and a "nice building heat."
PENZEYS SPICES Medium Hot Chili Powder **Price:** $6.85 for 2.4 oz ($2.85 per oz) **Ingredients:** Sweet ancho chili pepper, cayenne red pepper, paprika, cumin, garlic, Mexican oregano.	Our second-place powder, Penzeys' best-selling chili powder, was similar to our winner, with "rich, round, balanced, roasted chili flavor [and] mild but perceptible heat." "Smokiness is tempered by sweetness," with "savory and bright" notes. The "nice kick" of heat was "low-lying."

RECOMMENDED WITH RESERVATIONS

SIMPLY ORGANIC Chili Powder **Price:** $5.08 for 2.89 oz ($1.76 per oz) **Ingredients:** Organic chili powder, organic cumin, organic oregano, organic coriander, organic garlic, silicon dioxide (an anticaking ingredient), organic allspice, organic cloves.	This "sweet" powder was "perfumy," "earthy," and "woodsy and fragrant," with "Indian flavors" (coriander, allspice, and cloves are included). Tasters found it "nice but not super-complex," with a "lingering sweetness" and "mild" heat: "I could go for something livelier," one taster wrote. "Frankly, it's kind of boring."

NOT RECOMMENDED

FRONTIER Chili Powder **Price:** $4.59 for 2.08 oz ($2.21 per oz) **Ingredients:** Chili peppers (may contain silicon dioxide), cumin, garlic, oregano, coriander, cloves, allspice.	This dark-hued powder had strong "roasted," "earthy" chili flavor, "like I ate a bag of anchos," one taster wrote. Some thought it less versatile than other products in our lineup: "Overt smokiness would prevent my using this as all-purpose." A common complaint was a "lack of heat" that made it "wimpy."
SPICE ISLANDS Chili Powder **Price:** $4.99 for 2.4 oz ($2.08 per oz) **Ingredients:** Chili pepper, spices, salt, garlic powder, silicon dioxide.	This powder was "so mild it was hard to taste," "super-boring and a little sweet, with no heat," said one taster. "Tastes like curry, cinnamon, or any of those warm spices," "not distinct chili." It had a "subtle" heat that was "bland and boring." "Doesn't taste of much."
MCCORMICK Hot Mexican-Style Chili Powder **Price:** $3.29 for 2.5 oz ($1.32 per oz) **Ingredients:** Chili peppers, cumin, salt, oregano, silicon dioxide, garlic.	Marketed as "hot," this product was hotter than the standard powder made by the same manufacturer but still "very mild" compared with others in our lineup. "Really one-dimensional," and "straight-up sweet," with "virtually no heat" and "little oomph." "Why bother?"
MCCORMICK Chili Powder **Price:** $2.99 for 2.5 oz ($1.20 per oz) **Ingredients:** Chili pepper, spices, salt, silicon dioxide, garlic.	This last-place powder was weak all around, making for "school-cafeteria chili, wan and bland, lacking complexity and heat." "Am I even eating chili?" asked one taster. At best it was "weak" and "oddly sweet." It was also "dusty," with a "metallic twang at the end."

Tasters found these products "muddled" and their flavor odd in a bowl of chili. Our top picks stuck with the classics: cumin, oregano, and garlic, with minor deviations, such as black pepper and parsley. The supporting spices rounded out flavor, complementing the peppers without dominating or distracting from them. Our two recommended products had something else in common: no added salt; the bottom three products all added it.

We cannot recommend four of the seven chili powders we tasted, but our winner, Morton & Bassett Chili Powder, had a deep, roasty, complex flavor; subtle sweetness; and just the right amount of heat. We used it on its own to season a batch of chili that was "bright," "sizzling," and "full-flavored."

Looking for a Recipe

Have you lost a recipe you treasure? Ask a reader. While you're at it, answer a reader. Post queries and finds at **CooksCountry.com/magazine**; click on **Looking for a Recipe** (or write to Looking for a Recipe, *Cook's Country*, P.O. Box 470739, Brookline, MA 02447). We'll share all of your submissions online and one recipe on this page; include your name and mailing address.

Smearcase
Bob Eppig, Rockledge, Fla.

I am from Baltimore but now live in Florida. I really miss an old-fashioned cheesecake that's sold in Baltimore called smearcase. It's baked in a sheet pan on a yeasted crust and is topped with a creamy cheese mixture. I'd love to be able to make it in my new home.

Chicken–Poppy Seed Casserole
Dylan Friedman, Queens, N.Y.

When I was growing up, we often ate chicken–poppy seed casserole at family gatherings, church functions, and Sunday dinners. The best part was the crunchy, buttery cracker topping. Now that I've moved away from Georgia, I miss the taste of home. Do you have the recipe for my favorite comfort food?

Goetta
Paula Wood, Aiken, S.C.

I grew up in northern Kentucky, where breakfast food is hearty and sticks to your ribs. My favorite was my mom's *goetta*. She cooked pork and whole pinhead oats [a type of steel-cut oats] together and then poured the mixture into a loaf pan. Once it firmed up, Mom would slice it and pan-fry the slices until they were brown and crispy. It was delicious with sorghum or maple syrup. I don't have her recipe, but I sure wish I did.

Breakfast Cookies
Charlene Moore, Holly Ridge, N.C.

For about 25 years, I have been trying to re-create a recipe that my home ec teacher used to make for us. She called them "breakfast cookies" because they were made from Raisin Bran, eggs, crumbled bacon, orange juice concentrate, oats, flour, brown sugar, and butter. They had a unique sweet-salty thing going on that was just wonderful. Does anyone else recall this cookie—and have the recipe?

COWBOY "BREAD" Serves 6 to 8
Marcella Lipp, Rapid City, S.D.

"I used to make this in the 1960s when I worked at Stevens High School in Rapid City. We served it with our chili, which the students loved." The "bread" is really more like coffee cake.

CAKE
2½   cups (12½ ounces) all-purpose flour
2½   cups packed (17½ ounces) brown sugar
 2   teaspoons ground cinnamon
 ½   teaspoon ground nutmeg
 ½   teaspoon baking soda
 ½   teaspoon salt
 6   tablespoons unsalted butter, cut into ½-inch pieces and chilled
 1   cup buttermilk
 2   large eggs, lightly beaten

TOPPING
 ¼   cup packed (1¾ ounces) brown sugar
 2   tablespoons unsalted butter, cut into ½-inch pieces and chilled

1. FOR THE CAKE: Adjust oven rack to middle position and heat oven to 375 degrees. Grease and flour 13 by 9-inch baking dish. Combine flour, sugar, cinnamon, nutmeg, baking soda, and salt in food processor and process until combined, about 3 seconds. Add butter and pulse until mixture resembles wet sand, about 8 pulses. Transfer to large bowl.

2. FOR THE TOPPING: Return ½ cup cake mixture to now-empty processor. Add sugar and butter and pulse until mixture resembles wet sand, about 4 pulses.

3. Whisk buttermilk and eggs into cake mixture until smooth. Pour mixture into prepared dish and sprinkle topping mixture over top. Bake until toothpick inserted in center comes out clean, 25 to 30 minutes. Let cake cool in dish on wire rack for at least 30 minutes. Slice and serve.

FIND THE ROOSTER!

A tiny version of this rooster has been hidden in the pages of this issue. Write us with its location and we'll enter you a random drawing. The first correct en drawn will win our top-rated cookie sh (see page 30), and each of the next f will receive a free one-year subscriptic to *Cook's Country*. To enter, visit **CooksCountry.com/rooster** by March 2013, or write to Rooster, *Cook's Coun* P.O. Box 470739, Brookline, MA 02447. Include your name and address. Lorili Johnson of Newport, Washington, foun the rooster in the October/November 2012 issue in the turkey photo on page and won our favorite grill pan.

WEB EXTRAS
Free for 4 months at CooksCountry.com
Basic Brownies
Beignets Travelogue
Crushed Tomato Taste Test
Curried Spiced Nuts
Easy Chicken Tagine
Fudgy Low-Fat Brownies
Garlicky Oven Fries
Green Beans Amandine
Honey Cornbread
Maple-Glazed Ham (with carving steps)

COOK'S COUNTRY IS NO ON iPAD!

Download the new *Cook's Country* app for iPad and start a free trial subscription or purchase a single issue of the magazine. All issues are enhanced with full-color Cooking Mode slide shows that provid step-by-step instructions for completin recipes and expanded reviews and ratings. Go to **CooksCountry.com/iPa** to download our app through iTunes.

Follow us on **Twitter**
twitter.com/TestKitchen

Find us on **Facebook**
facebook.com/CooksCountry

RC = Recipe Card

After Eight Cake

We reimagined the well-known after-dinner mint in grand-scale cake form.
If you're like us, you won't be able to wait until after eight to have a slice.

To make this cake you will need:

- 10 ounces bittersweet chocolate, chopped
- 1 cup plus 2 tablespoons heavy cream
- ¼ cup corn syrup
- Salt
- 16 tablespoons unsalted butter, softened
- 1¼ teaspoons mint extract
- 1½ cups (6 ounces) confectioners' sugar
- 2 recipes Basic Brownies*, uncut

FOR THE GLAZE: Place chocolate in large bowl. Bring 1 cup cream, corn syrup, and ⅛ teaspoon salt to simmer in medium saucepan over medium heat, stirring occasionally. Pour over chocolate and whisk until smooth. Whisk in 4 tablespoons butter and ½ teaspoon mint extract until glossy. Cover and refrigerate until glaze is firm but spreadable, about 1 hour.

FOR THE FILLING: Using stand mixer fitted with whisk, mix remaining 12 tablespoons butter, remaining 2 tablespoons cream, remaining ¾ teaspoon mint extract, and ⅛ teaspoon salt on medium-low speed until combined, about 1 minute. Slowly add sugar and continue mixing until smooth, about 2 minutes. Increase speed to medium-high and whip filling until light and fluffy, about 5 minutes.

TO ASSEMBLE: Set wire rack inside rimmed baking sheet. Place 1 brownie layer on wire rack. Spread filling in even layer over top. Place remaining brownie layer on top, bottom up. Spread top and sides of cake with about 1 cup glaze until smooth. Melt remaining glaze in microwave until pourable, stirring frequently, about 1 minute; reserve 2 tablespoons in small zipper-lock bag. Pour remaining glaze over cake to cover top and sides completely, spreading gently with spatula as needed. Cut ⅛ inch off corner of bag and decoratively pipe reserved glaze over top. Refrigerate until firm, about 30 minutes. Transfer to platter and serve.

▶ *Go to **CooksCountry.com/brownie** for our **Basic Brownies** recipe.

Inside This Issue

Cook's Country

APRIL/MAY 2013

Chocolate Sugar Cookies

Slow-Cooker Pulled Chicken

Crunchy French Toast

Yankee Pot Roast for Two
Deep Flavor Fast

Best Beef Burritos
No More Soggy Wraps

Milk-Can Supper
Heartland Favorite

Olive Oil Potato Gratin
High Flavor, Low Fat

Sheet Pan Pizza
Step-by-Step Instructions

Buttermilk Pie
Creamy Custard, Crackly Top

Crumb-Crusted Baked Ham
A New Holiday Classic

Testing Salad Spinners
Upstarts versus the Champ

Chicken Noodle Casserole
Fit for Grown-Ups

CooksCountry.com
$4.95 U.S./$6.95 CANADA

Though seemingly simple, sugar cookies are already hard to perfect. Then we upped the ante by adding chocolate. Twenty-four pounds of sugar later, we finally got our **Chocolate Sugar Cookies** *just right.* PAGE 23

Cook's Country

Dear Country Cook,

Thanksgiving and Easter are the two holidays that I love the most, since neither requires sending cards or buying presents. They also celebrate cooking and the advent of a new season—the coming of winter and the coming of spring.

One oddity in all of this is the Easter Bunny or hare, which has a long association with the Catholic Church. Hares, since they were considered virginal (an odd notion given their fecundity), were often scattered about paintings of the Virgin Mary. More to the point, the coming of spring has a close connection with fertility, and the colored eggs represented the blooming of flowers and the greening of trees. (More religious folk dyed their eggs red to represent the blood of Christ . . . think I prefer the bright, floral colors.)

Best of all, the rabbit is an odd, intriguing character in fiction. The Brothers Grimm recorded a rabbit's tale in which the rabbit tries to enslave young girls into marriage and domestic drudgery. "Come, maiden, sit on my tail and go with me to my rabbit hutch!" The maiden finally escapes, returning to her mother and freedom. The first feminist children's story?

Our family tradition was an Easter egg hunt, most years in the snow. I always left a few eggs white since this was perfect camouflage in a snow bank. And, of course, Lemon Layer Cake to celebrate spring. (Visit the website of our sister publication to get the recipe for free: **cooksillustrated. com/lemonlayercake**.)

Enjoy Easter, although a rabbit with a basket full of decorated eggs does seem strange. As one of my kids said about Santa Claus, "A guy dressed in red who breaks into our house at night is kind of freaky!" Well, that's the charm of holidays: Our kids ask the big questions, and we just follow traditions!

Christopher Kimball
Founder and Editor, Cook's Country

Yes, Virginia, there is an Easter bunny. Easter Wonderland at the Country Club Plaza shopping center, Kansas City, 1956.

Cook'sCountry

Founder and Editor Christopher Kimball
Editorial Director Jack Bishop
Editorial Director, Magazines John Willoughby
Executive Editor Peggy Grodinsky
Managing Editor Scott Kathan
Senior Editors Lisa McManus, Bryan Roof, Diane Unger
Test Kitchen Director Erin McMurrer
Associate Editors Amy Graves, Rebeccah Marsters
Test Cooks Sarah Gabriel, Nick Iverson,
Carolynn Purpura MacKay, Cristin Walsh
Assistant Editors Hannah Crowley,
Shannon Friedmann Hatch, Taizeth Sierra
Copy Editors Nell Beram, Megan Chromik
Executive Assistant Christine Gordon
Test Kitchen Manager Leah Rovner
Senior Kitchen Assistant Meryl MacCormack
Kitchen Assistants Maria Elena Delgado,
Ena Gudiel, Andrew Straaberg Finfrock
Executive Producer Melissa Baldino
Co-Executive Producer Stephanie Stender
Production Assistant Kaitlin Hammond

Contributing Editors Erika Bruce,
Eva Katz, Jeremy Sauer
Consulting Editors Anne Mendelson, Meg Ragland
Science Editor Guy Crosby, Ph.D.
Executive Food Editor, TV, Radio & Media
Bridget Lancaster

Managing Editor, Web Christine Liu
Senior Editor, Web Mari Levine
Associate Editors, Web Eric Grzymkowski, Roger Metcalf
Assistant Editors, Web Jill Fisher, Charlotte Wilder
Senior Video Editor Nick Dakoulas

Design Director Amy Klee
Art Director Julie Cote
Deputy Art Director Susan Levin
Associate Art Director Lindsey Timko
Deputy Art Director, Marketing/Web Jennifer Cox
Staff Photographer Daniel J. van Ackere
Color Food Photography Keller + Keller
Styling Catrine Kelty
Associate Art Director, Marketing/Web
Mariah Tarvainen
Production Designer, Marketing/Web Judy Blomquist
Photo Editor Steve Klise

Vice President, Marketing David Mack
Circulation Director Doug Wicinski
Circulation & Fulfillment Manager Carrie Fethe
Partnership Marketing Manager Pamela Putprush
Marketing Assistant Joyce Liao
Customer Service Manager Jacqueline Valerio
Customer Service Representatives Megan Hamner,
Jessica Haskin

Production Director Guy Rochford
Senior Project Manager Alice Carpenter
Workflow & Digital Asset Manager Andrew Mannone
Production & Traffic Coordinator Brittany Allen
Senior Color & Imaging Specialist Lauren Pettapiece
Production & Imaging Specialists
Heather Dube, Lauren Robbins
Systems Administrators Scott Norwood, Marcus Walser
Helpdesk Support Technician Brianna Brothers
Senior Business Analyst Wendy Tseng
Web Developer Chris Candelora
Human Resources Manager Adele Shapiro

VP New Media Product Development Barry Kelly
Development Manager Mike Serio
Developer Patrick Hereford
Chief Financial Officer Sharyn Chabot
Director of Sponsorship Sales Anne Traficante
Retail Sales & Marketing Manager Emily Logan
Client Services Associate Kate May
Sponsorship Sales Representative Morgan Ryan
Publicity Deborah Broide

ON THE COVER:
Chocolate Sugar Cookies
Keller + Keller, Catrine Kelty
ILLUSTRATION: Greg Stevenson

APRIL/MAY 2013

Contents

EASY ASPARAGUS TART, 13

CRUMB-COATED BAKED HAM, 4

BUTTERMILK PIE, 8

Features

Departments

Annual Holiday Cookie Contest

You needn't play Christmas music, string lights, or start shopping yet. But you do need to send us your original recipes for favorite holiday cookies. The due date for submissions is April 30, 2013. Find contest details at CooksCountry.com/cookiecontest. Our own celebration starts early as we mix, roll, stamp, and sprinkle, in accordance with your recipes, in order to choose one $1,000 grand prize winner and six $100 finalists.

America's TEST KITCHEN
RECIPES THAT WORK®

America's Test Kitchen is a very real 2,500-square-foot kitchen located just outside Boston. It is the home of *Cook's Country* and *Cook's Illustrated* magazines and is the workday destination of more than three dozen test cooks, editors, and cookware specialists. Our mission is to test recipes over and over again until we understand how and why they work and until we arrive at the best version. We also test kitchen equipment and supermarket ingredients in search of brands that offer the best value and performance. You can watch us work by tuning in to *Cook's Country from America's Test Kitchen* (CooksCountryTV.com) and *America's Test Kitchen* (AmericasTestKitchenTV.com) on public television.

Ask Cook's Country

BY SARAH GABRIEL

When using your recipes for brined chicken breasts, do I need to change the brine recipe if I add extra chicken to the brine bucket?
Eileen Carque, New Ashford, Mass.

We often call for brining to make chicken (and other lean meats) more flavorful and moist. Our standard recipe for four boneless, skinless chicken breasts is 2 quarts of water and ¼ cup of table salt. To answer your question, we set up two identical buckets, each with 2 quarts of water and ¼ cup of salt. We put four boneless, skinless chicken breasts in the first bucket and eight in the second, and then we let both batches soak for an hour. Next, we cooked both batches to 160 degrees on identical pans in identical ovens. In a side-by-side tasting, we determined that the batches were equally well seasoned and moist.
THE BOTTOM LINE: The ratio of salt to water is the important factor in brining, not the ratio of brine to chicken. It's OK to use extra meat as long as there's enough space in the container to keep all of the meat submerged.

Will carrot and celery sticks keep longer stored in water?
Billie Valentine Giannone, Dallas, Texas

To see if we could extend the life of carrot and celery sticks, we cut up two batches and stored one in a plastic container with a tight-fitting lid and the other in an identical container, covering the vegetables with cold water before putting on the lid. Both batches were crisp the next day, but after the second day, we began to see changes. As time went on, the dry-stored carrots looked parched but were still crunchy—even after five days. The carrots soaked in water looked fresher, but some tasters found them "slightly soggy" or "less sweet" than their less attractive counterparts. The appearance of the celery deteriorated less over time, whether stored in water or not, while the texture and flavor changes were similar to those that we observed with the carrots.
THE BOTTOM LINE: Prep celery and carrot sticks up to two days ahead; there's no need to store them in water. After that, they'll begin to very slowly deteriorate, whether stored dry or wet.

READY AND WAITING
The water isn't necessary. We store our carrots and celery sticks dry.

I made a lasagna, covered it with aluminum foil, and refrigerated it to bake later. The next day, there were holes in the foil. What happened?
Molly McMahon, Portland, Ore.

Aluminum is what is called an "active metal." That means that it's relatively easily transformed by outside influences. For instance, it dissolves when it comes into contact with acid, such as the tomato sauce in your lasagna. But tomato sauce couldn't dissolve enough aluminum foil overnight to result in holes, according to our science editor. The reaction you observed, he said, is not chemical but electrical.

We were intrigued. Aluminum atoms have a weaker hold on their electrons than do other metal atoms, like iron or steel (an alloy of iron and other elements), he continued. Given a conductive medium for electrons to travel across, electron-gripping iron atoms can steal aluminum's more weakly held electrons, converting them into electrically charged ions that are soluble in water (or tomato sauce). Acidic foods like tomato sauce, fruit juices, and wine reductions are conductive enough to provide such a pathway. So when you see holes in the foil covering a pan of tomato sauce, you are looking at areas where the pan has stolen electrons from the foil, converting the aluminum atoms into a substance that can dissolve in the sauce. The tomato sauce is serving as the getaway car in an electron heist masterminded by the steel pan. If you put acidic food in a glass, plastic, or aluminum container and cover it with foil, it won't develop holes because those materials don't have sticky fingers for electrons.

So was your lasagna safe to eat? Absolutely. The amount of aluminum that dissolved from the foil was just a few milligrams or less. People typically consume more than that amount every day from both aluminum pans and natural sources, like food.
THE BOTTOM LINE: If you are storing acidic foods in (nonaluminum) metal, wrap them in plastic wrap, not foil.

FOIL IS FINE
If the lasagna is in a Pyrex pan, the acid in the tomato sauce won't react with the foil.

USE PLASTIC
If you are storing lasagna or another acidic food in (nonaluminum) metal, such as stainless steel, wrap it in plastic to avoid holey aluminum foil.

I saw potato starch in the grocery store. Can I substitute it for cornstarch to thicken sauces?
Ahmir Thompson, Philadelphia, Pa.

Some sources, including the Argo cornstarch website, indicate that cornstarch and potato starch may be substituted for each other on a 1:1 ratio, while others say that potato starch has more thickening power (meaning it makes a thicker sauce than an equal quantity of cornstarch would). To see, we made a simple pan sauce using a recipe that called for thickening with cornstarch. We made the sauce a second time, substituting potato starch for the cornstarch, and tasted the two side by side. The potato starch made a thicker sauce. The reason, our science editor explained, is that potato starch granules are four to five times larger than cornstarch granules. When potato starch granules swell in hot liquids, they take up more space, restricting the liquid's flow more than smaller cornstarch granules, which results in a more viscous sauce. A few tasters found the potato starch sauce to be slightly "gooey-slimy" or "stringy," while others perceived it as more "velvety" than the cornstarch sauce. In the course of making the sauce, we also noticed that while cornstarch needed to be simmered in the sauce for a couple of minutes to achieve maximum thickness,

the potato starch thickened more quickly, even before the sauce came to a full simmer. We repeated this test with a blueberry Danish filling and got similar results.
THE BOTTOM LINE: Potato starch thickens at a lower temperature and to a greater extent than cornstarch. For every tablespoon of cornstarch, use 2 teaspoons of potato starch.

My grandmother used to put half of a peeled potato in the pot of cold oil when she fried doughnuts. She said it made them less greasy. True?
James Hamernick, via email

We've never heard that trick and we're always looking for an excuse to eat some doughnuts, so we mixed up two batches of batter for our Orange Drop Doughnuts and put 3 inches of oil in each of two Dutch ovens. We put half of a peeled potato into one pot and heated both pots over a medium flame until the oil reached the target temperature of 350 degrees. Then we fried doughnuts in each. Tasters detected no difference in greasiness in the finished doughnuts, though we did notice that by the time the oil reached the requisite 350 degrees, the potato had changed from white to golden brown. We contacted our science editor to see if he could think of a reason a potato

would minimize greasiness; he couldn't. We suspect that your grandmother was using the potato not to combat greasiness but rather to tell her when the oil was hot enough to start frying the doughnuts.
THE BOTTOM LINE: To monitor the temperature of frying oil, we recommend using an instant-read thermometer. If you don't have one, try a peeled potato, but don't expect precision.

WISDOM FROM GRANDMA
When the peeled potato is golden brown, your frying oil is hot enough.

TEST KITCHEN TECHNIQUE
For truly accurate temperature monitoring, use an instant-read thermometer. Our Best Buy is the Thermoworks Super-Fast Waterproof Pocket Thermometer ($24).

Kitchen Shortcuts

COMPILED BY NICK IVERSON

DOUBLE DUTY
Spice Mill
Martin Stills, Ann Arbor, Mich.

My family loves my "signature" spice blend—salt, pepper, dehydrated garlic and onion, coriander, and cumin—on chicken, steak, pork, or almost anything. I used to keep a coffee grinder dedicated to grinding spices for this task: I'd put the spices in, grind them, dump them into a bowl, and sprinkle them on whatever I was making. I found an easier way. Now I use a pepper mill for the same purpose (I mix everything together in a bowl before loading the grinder). In a few twists of the wrist, my spice blend goes right on the food and I'm ready to cook.

CLEVER TIP
Grate Solution
Eric Sullivan, Longmont, Colo.

Thanks, in part, to your magazines, my rasp-style grater is my new best friend in the kitchen, especially for grating ginger and garlic. My only gripe is that grated matter gets trapped in the corners of the grater's underside, where I can't easily scrape it out. A solution to this problem occurred to me when I was using a swivel peeler to peel potatoes recently: The pointed tip (meant for removing eyes from potatoes—almost all peelers have one) is the perfect size and shape for clearing the grated stuff from the corners of the grater. I just zip the pointed tip down the length of the grater on both sides, and whatever I've grated comes right out.

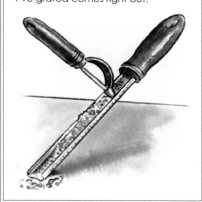

SPACE SAVER
Hang 'em Up
Miranda Lake, Hartford, Conn.

I cook recipes from every issue of *Cook's Country*, but I have a small kitchen and the magazine takes up valuable counter space. I've found that I can use a pants hanger (the kind with two clips, from the dry cleaner's) to clip the magazine and hang it from a cabinet knob near the stove. This way, the recipe is protected, doesn't take up counter space, and is right where I need it at eye level.

Submit a tip online at **CooksCountry.com/kitchenshortcuts** or send a letter to Kitchen Shortcuts, *Cook's Country*, P.O. Box 470739, Brookline, MA 02447. Include your name, address, and phone number. If we publish your tip, you will receive a free one-year subscription to *Cook's Country*. Letters may be edited for clarity and length.

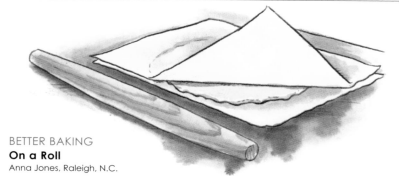

BETTER BAKING
On a Roll
Anna Jones, Raleigh, N.C.

I bake lots of pies for my grandchildren, so I know that using too much flour when rolling out the dough can make the crust tough (and is pretty messy, too). But if I don't use a lot of flour, the dough sticks to the pin and the counter. My solution? Rolling pie dough between pieces of parchment paper. This gives me tender crusts with no mess and no sticking.

DOUBLE DUTY
Fries in a Flash
Terry Wilson, Springfield, Mass.

My kids are nuts for oven fries—I must make them at least twice a week. I've found a simple trick that makes the prep go a lot faster. Instead of cutting the potatoes into wedges (I admit I'm not great with a knife, so my wedges were never very even), I use my apple corer/slicer to easily cut perfect wedges every time. Now all of the potato wedges are exactly the same size and cook at the same rate.

COOL TIP
Herb Cubes
Art Augustus, Manchester, N.H.

I like to cook with fresh herbs, but I rarely get through an entire bunch before it goes bad. Instead of letting the herbs rot in my refrigerator, I chop them and add a teaspoon to each well in an ice cube tray, pour in olive oil just to cover, and freeze. Once the cubes are frozen, I pop them out and store them in a labeled freezer bag. Now I turn to my freezer when a pasta dish, stew, or pan sauce needs a dose of fresh herb flavor.

COOL TRICK
Light My Fire
Liam O'Toole, Shaker Heights, Ohio

I read the newspaper online and grill over charcoal—so how am I supposed to light my chimney starter without newspaper on hand? I figured out that I can pour the charcoal I need into the chimney starter and then tear off the top portion of the charcoal bag and use that paper in lieu of newspaper. It works just as well as newspaper.

Crumb-Coated Baked Ham

We wanted a moist ham with crispy crumbs. But we kept getting dry ham and wet crumbs.
How could we reverse the two? BY DIANE UNGER

DURING MY YEARS in the test kitchen, I've crumb-coated fish fillets, chicken, baked tomatoes, macaroni and cheese, pork chops, beef tenderloin . . . the list goes on. But it had never occurred to me to apply this technique to ham. Then, I heard about crumb-coated baked ham from the mother of a friend of Scandinavian descent—apparently it's a common way to prepare the Christmas ham in Sweden. I immediately saw its potential.

I checked our library for recipes. They called for both spiral-cut and uncut hams; the crust might be made of fresh bread crumbs, dried bread crumbs, or crushed gingersnaps; and the crumbs were adhered to the ham with everything from mustard to melted butter, beaten raw egg yolks, brown sugar, sweet glazes, or some combination of these. A few recipes required pressing the crumbs onto the ham at the start, but most called for warming the ham without the crumbs, which were then applied toward the end of cooking. Following along, I baked six hams.

The results were dismaying: The bread crumbs were uniformly soggy, although definitely better when applied toward the end of cooking. Obviously, they were absorbing moisture from the ham. Likewise, the gingersnaps had lost their snap. When I tried to carve the uncut hams, the crumb coatings fell off. The spiral-cut hams fared better, but since they were not only precooked (like the uncut hams) but also presliced, they were prone to dry out. As one taster summed it up, "These taste like wet bread wrapped around dried-out ham."

Although the problem rather than the promise was in evidence, I still hadn't lost confidence in the concept. I just needed to figure out how to keep the ham moist and the crumbs dry. Meanwhile, I narrowed the scope of my recipe, deciding on bread crumbs and glaze (for now, a basic mix of brown sugar and mustard).

Also, since none of these test recipes had succeeded, I'd start instead with an easy test kitchen method for spiral-cut ham and then address the heart of the challenge: the crumbs. Here's how that recipe works: We enclose a sliced, room-temperature ham in an oven bag and bake it at a gentle 300 degrees. The

A sticky glaze made from brown sugar, mustard, vinegar, ginger, and cloves helps the seasoned bread crumbs adhere.

room-temperature ham heats up faster, with less time to dry out; the low temperature cooks the ham gently while the bag traps steam, guaranteeing a humid environment that keeps the ham moist. Once the ham was warm, I'd simply glaze and crumb-coat it and then return it to the oven to brown the crumbs.

A couple of hours later, I rolled back the oven bag to expose the hot ham and apply the crumbs. With the

bag scrunched up at the bottom of the roasting pan, it was awkward to reach in to try to press on the crumbs. The deep roasting pan compounded the problem. After trying out several contortions with hams and bags, I realized that rather than put the ham in the bag, I should put the bag over the ham. I did so, tucking the bag under the edges of the meat. To "seal" the bag at the bottom to create the closed, moist environment,

I set the ham on a square of aluminum foil. When it was time to remove the bag, it pulled off easily. As for pans, after trying out a few, I settled on a favorite test kitchen rig: a wire rack set inside a rimmed baking sheet. All parts of the ham were now easily accessible for coating with crumbs.

With the crumb-application mechanics worked out, I circled back to the coating itself. Since the bread crumbs

BAG IT Cover the ham with an oven bag, tucking it under the ham to prevent the meat from drying out. Bake the bagged ham for about 2 hours.

GLAZE IT Remove the ham from the oven, lift off the oven bag, and brush the warm ham with the brown sugar–mustard glaze.

CRUMB IT Sprinkle the seasoned crumbs on the ham and press them on to coat. Bake until golden.

I'd been using thus far turned mucky time after time, I tried panko, or super-crunchy Japanese-style bread crumbs. I tossed them with a little oil and some seasonings. Once the ham was warm, the bag came off and the glaze and crumbs went on (I was still using the brown sugar–mustard glaze for now). I cranked the heat to 400 degrees and browned the crumbs in about 25 minutes. The panko was a rousing success, but the glaze definitely needed fine-tuning in order to hold the crumbs in place. Hoping to turn it into the Krazy Glue of glazes, I cooked it down for some 15 minutes, until it was thick and ultrasticky. While I was at it, I added balsamic vinegar for mellow acidity and the classic ham flavorings of dry mustard, ginger, and cloves. Then I painted the glaze on the ham, pressed on the panko crumbs, and baked.

While the ham was in the oven, I took a few minutes to stir together ingredients for a slightly spicy no-cook mustard sauce. Half an hour later, I put several slices of ham on my plate—and was thrilled to see that the crumb coating stayed put. I took a bite: The ham was moist, the crumbs were crunchy, and the combination was everything I'd hoped for.

HOT MUSTARD SAUCE

The longer this sauce sits the milder it becomes.

- 3 tablespoons cold water
- 2 tablespoons dry mustard
- ½ teaspoon salt
- ½ cup Dijon mustard
- 2 tablespoons honey

Whisk water, dry mustard, and salt together in bowl until smooth; let sit for 15 minutes. Whisk in Dijon mustard and honey. Cover and let sit at room temperature for at least 2 hours. Use immediately or transfer sauce to glass jar with tight-fitting lid and refrigerate for up to 2 months.

CRUMB-COATED BAKED HAM

Serves 12 to 14

Our favorite spiral-sliced ham is Cook's Spiral Sliced Hickory Smoked Bone-In Honey Ham. This recipe requires a turkey-size oven bag. Serve the ham with Hot Mustard Sauce.

- 1 (8- to 9-pound) bone-in spiral-sliced ham
- 1 cup packed brown sugar
- ½ cup spicy brown mustard
- ½ cup balsamic vinegar
- 2 tablespoons dry mustard
- 2 teaspoons ground ginger
- ¼ teaspoon ground cloves
- 1½ cups panko bread crumbs
- ½ cup minced fresh parsley
- 3 tablespoons vegetable oil
- ¼ teaspoon salt
- ¼ teaspoon pepper

1. Line rimmed baking sheet with aluminum foil; set wire rack inside sheet. Place 12-inch square of foil in center of rack. Set ham on foil, flat side down, and cover with oven bag, tucking bag under ham to secure it. Let ham sit at room temperature for 1½ hours.

2. Adjust oven rack to lowest position and heat oven to 325 degrees. Bake ham until it registers 100 degrees, about 2 hours. (Lift bag to take temperature; do not puncture.)

3. Meanwhile, combine sugar, brown mustard, vinegar, dry mustard, ginger, and cloves in medium saucepan and bring to boil over medium-high heat. Reduce heat to medium-low and simmer until reduced to ¾ cup, 15 to 20 minutes. Let cool while ham cooks.

4. Combine panko, parsley, oil, salt, and pepper in bowl. Remove ham from oven, remove and discard oven bag, and let ham cool for 5 minutes. Increase oven temperature to 400 degrees.

5. Brush ham all over with brown sugar–mustard glaze. Press panko mixture against sides of ham to coat evenly. Bake until crumbs are deep golden brown, 20 to 30 minutes. Transfer ham, flat side down, to carving board and let rest for 30 minutes. Carve and serve.

WHAT TO DO WITH LEFTOVERS
Hawaiian Fried Rice

Crammed with ham and fresh pineapple, fried rice doesn't get any better (or easier) than this. BY DIANE UNGER

HAWAIIAN FRIED RICE—BASICALLY just highly seasoned fried rice studded with ham and pineapple—is one of those dishes that taste much better than they sound. If you're familiar with Hawaiian pizza (which stars the same two ingredients), you understand how well this particular salty-sweet flavor combination works. Many versions are made with Spam, but why use the can when you have leftover ham (or can buy thick-cut ham from any supermarket deli)?

I knew from experience that I needed leftover rice—cold leftover rice is best because it stays firmer than warm rice. Another classic problem? Greasy fried rice. I'd cook in a non-stick skillet so I could use less oil.

After testing a grab bag of add-ins, I settled on onion, garlic, ginger, red bell pepper, eggs, and scallions. To the usual soy sauce—not too much since ham is salty—I stirred in Sriracha sauce for a jolt of heat. I perfected my technique in a few practice runs: First, fry the vegetables and the ham to a light and flavorful brown and set them aside. Next, fry the rice in the same skillet, push it aside to cook the ginger and garlic, and incorporate them. Then push everything aside again to cook the lightly beaten eggs, return the vegetables and ham to the pan, stir, and pour on the seasoning. I stirred in the pineapple and scallion greens off heat. I made a new batch and was pleased at how quickly it came together—and how quickly this salty-sweet, spicy, and dangerously delicious fried rice disappeared.

HAWAIIAN FRIED RICE
Serves 4

Lee Kum Kee Tabletop Soy Sauce is our taste-test winner. You can use 6 ounces of chopped leftover ham, ham steak, or deli ham for this recipe.

- 3 tablespoons soy sauce
- 2 tablespoons toasted sesame oil
- 1 tablespoon Sriracha sauce
- 2 tablespoons plus 1 teaspoon peanut oil
- 1 cup (6 ounces) chopped ham

We add the pineapple and scallion greens last so they'll taste fresh and bright.

- 1 red bell pepper, stemmed, seeded, and cut into ½-inch pieces
- 6 scallions, white parts minced, green parts cut into ½-inch pieces
- 1 small onion, halved and sliced thin
- 3 garlic cloves, minced
- 1 tablespoon minced fresh ginger
- 4 cups cooked long-grain white rice, cold
- 2 large eggs, lightly beaten
- 1 cup ½-inch pineapple pieces

1. Combine soy sauce, sesame oil, and Sriracha in bowl and set aside. Heat 1 tablespoon peanut oil in 12-inch nonstick skillet over medium-high heat until just smoking. Add ham, bell pepper, scallion whites, and onion and cook, stirring occasionally, until lightly browned, 7 to 9 minutes. Stir in garlic and ginger and cook until fragrant, about 30 seconds. Transfer to plate.

2. Heat 1 tablespoon peanut oil in now-empty skillet over medium-high heat until shimmering. Add rice and cook, breaking up clumps with spoon, until heated through, about 3 minutes.

3. Push rice to 1 side of skillet; add remaining 1 teaspoon peanut oil to empty side of skillet. Add eggs to oiled side of skillet and cook, stirring, until set, about 30 seconds. Stir eggs and ham mixture into rice. Stir soy sauce mixture into rice until thoroughly combined. Off heat, stir in pineapple and scallion greens. Serve.

No leftover rice? Make your own. Get the recipe for **Faux Leftover Rice** from our sister magazine: CooksIllustrated.com/fauxleftoverrice.

Lighter, Brighter Potato Gratin

For a gratin with the focus on the potatoes, we had to create a satisfying dish that didn't rely on butter and cream. BY REBECCAH MARSTERS

POTATO GRATIN, a creamy casserole of thinly sliced potatoes with a crisp, golden crust, is usually more about gooey cheese and heavy cream than potatoes—most gratins are so rich I can barely manage to eat the main dish. I wanted a lighter potato gratin that actually tasted like potatoes.

My first stop was the test kitchen's cookbook library. For every dozen creamy, butter-laden potato gratin recipes I found in the stacks, there were one or two gratins that replaced the dairy with chicken or vegetable broth. Some of these broth-based recipes still called for topping the dish with cheese, but others simply let the potatoes stand alone. After preparing and tasting a sampling of these recipes, one thing became very clear: Gratins made without any fat at all tasted flat. One recipe, however, had promise: It used lots of extra-virgin olive oil to coat the potatoes. The bright, fruity olive oil heightened the flavor of the earthy potatoes without overpowering them.

My next step was to determine the best type of potato to use. Recipes called for all different varieties, with little

Caramelized onions and plenty of olive oil can be just as delicious as butter and cream.

explanation as to why, so I made three separate gratins, tossing sliced red potatoes, Yukon Golds, and russets with the oil; layering them in separate dishes; and pouring broth over the top. I covered the dishes with foil and cooked the potatoes in a 400-degree oven until the spuds were soft. The unanimous winner was Yukon Gold. Their rich flavor, dense texture, and modest starch content—which helped them hold their shape—were assets.

For the topping, grated Parmesan was a logical choice for flavor (most gratins use it), and since it needed to melt, I sprinkled some over the potatoes when they were almost tender and finished the cooking uncovered. But I wanted crunch, too. I tried adding a handful of panko bread crumbs to the cheese before topping the potatoes; rather than crispy, these crumbs were sandy and dry. To fix that, I moistened the crumbs with 3 tablespoons of olive oil before sprinkling the mixture on top. Wondering if I could add a little flair to the gratin, I tested grated Pecorino Romano against the Parmesan cheese. Tasters preferred the former's sharp, salty bite in the browned top.

But there was still room for improvement. One of the initial recipes I'd tried supplemented the potatoes with cooked onions. For my next gratin, I sautéed a pile of onion slices (using more extra-virgin olive oil, of course) and layered them with the potatoes in the dish. The browned onions added depth and a

welcome sweetness that set off the potato flavor even more. For background flavor, I added fresh thyme and garlic.

I'm usually not one to forgo the pleasures of lots of butter, cream, and gooey cheese, but the truth of the matter is that this gratin didn't need them. With the help of plenty of extra-virgin olive oil, I'd managed to put the "potato" back in potato gratin.

OLIVE OIL POTATO GRATIN
Serves 6 to 8
The test kitchen's favorite supermarket extra-virgin olive oil is Columela.

- 2 ounces Pecorino Romano cheese, grated (1 cup)
- ½ cup extra-virgin olive oil
- ¼ cup panko bread crumbs
  Salt and pepper
- 2 onions, halved and sliced thin
- 2 garlic cloves, minced
- 1 teaspoon minced fresh thyme
- 1 cup low-sodium chicken broth
- 3 pounds Yukon Gold potatoes, peeled and sliced ⅛ inch thick

1. Adjust oven rack to upper-middle position and heat oven to 400 degrees. Grease 13 by 9-inch baking dish. Combine Pecorino, 3 tablespoons oil, panko, and ½ teaspoon pepper in bowl; set aside.

2. Heat 2 tablespoons oil in 12-inch skillet over medium heat until shimmering. Add onions, ½ teaspoon salt, and ¼ teaspoon pepper and cook, stirring frequently, until browned, about 15 minutes. Add garlic and ½ teaspoon thyme and cook until fragrant, about 30 seconds. Add ¼ cup broth and cook until nearly evaporated, scraping up any browned bits, about 2 minutes. Remove from heat; set aside.

3. Toss potatoes, remaining 3 tablespoons oil, 1 teaspoon salt, ½ teaspoon pepper, and remaining ½ teaspoon thyme together in bowl. Arrange half of potatoes in prepared dish, spread onion mixture in even layer over potatoes, and distribute remaining potatoes over onions. Pour remaining ¾ cup broth over potatoes. Cover dish tightly with aluminum foil and bake for 1 hour.

4. Remove foil, top gratin with reserved Pecorino mixture, and continue to bake until top is golden brown and potatoes are completely tender, 15 to 20 minutes. Let cool for 15 minutes. Serve.

TEST KITCHEN TECHNIQUE
Two Ways to Slice

How to get 3 pounds of potatoes sliced quickly?

USE OUR WINNING MANDOLINE
OXO Good Grips V-Blade Mandoline Slicer.

Or if you don't own a mandoline, cut a slice off of one side of each potato to create a flat, stable surface for thin slicing.

Soft and Tender Biscuits

One of the oddest recipes we've ever heard of produced incredibly tender, fluffy biscuits. We just needed to open our minds—and our cupboards. BY NICK IVERSON

GREAT BISCUITS AND butter go hand in hand—or so I thought. In fact, until recently I believed that you couldn't have one without the other. But one day I came across an interesting recipe for something called secret ingredient biscuits; I've since learned that they go by the name mystery biscuits, too. The mystery? Mayonnaise in the dough instead of butter. Strange as that sounds, the recipe promised "really moist and tender biscuits." And it gets better: These were drop biscuits, which meant that the recipe promised ease, too—no tedious cutting in of butter, no rolling out of dough, no stamping. Just put together a few ingredients and drop the dough by spoonfuls onto a baking sheet. Still, *mayonnaise?* Skeptical but intrigued, I grabbed some jars and went into the kitchen.

All mayonnaise is not created equal. To find our favorite, read tasting story at ksCountry.com/mayo.

A coworker reminded me that of course a biscuit doesn't have to contain butter: Some biscuit recipes call for shortening, others for lard or even heavy cream. Still, I maintained that mayonnaise is a lot more "out there" than those alternatives—until I really thought about it, that is. Then I realized that it actually makes sense. Mayonnaise is, after all, an emulsion of oil and vinegar, plus salt, sugar, and eggs. The eggs would add fat and emulsifiers, which reduce gluten development and result in tender baked goods. On top of that, the mayonnaise, unlike fats that are hard at room temperature, would get thoroughly mixed into the dough, which also makes for especially tender (but not

flaky) biscuits. Put that way, mayo could be a veritable one-stop shop for tender, moist, flavorful biscuits.

The recipes that I found called for varying amounts of mayonnaise—anywhere from several tablespoons to a whole cup. After I got into the kitchen and baked several batches of biscuits, it was plain that there was a sweet spot: Too much mayonnaise and the biscuits were greasy, too little and they were dry and crumbly. After a few tests, I homed in on ¾ cup of mayonnaise for 2 cups of flour, plus 1 cup of whole milk, which also promotes tenderness. These ratios made a moist, tender, fluffy biscuit that wasn't greasy and didn't taste like mayonnaise.

With the most important part of the recipe settled, I turned to adjusting the flavor. Although mayonnaise already contains salt and sugar, I played up my biscuits' savory qualities by adding a little more of each. I turned on the oven, mixed the wet ingredients into the dry, scooped out the (very sticky) dough, and dropped it onto a baking sheet. Since this dough came together so quickly and effortlessly, I found that I could wait until the oven was fully preheated to 450 degrees before mixing everything together.

Less than 15 minutes later, the biscuits were an attractive golden brown. They looked scraggly, but in the most appealing, homey way possible. And they ate even better: moist, very tender, and slightly savory. "These are great," a former skeptic admitted. "You wouldn't even know that they have any mayo." I guess butter isn't always better.

These easy drop biscuits come together in minutes.

You Put *What* in Your Biscuits?!

You've probably heard of biscuits made with butter, with cream, and with lard. But have you ever tasted a biscuit made with mayonnaise? Granted, they sound pretty weird. But think about it: Mayonnaise is primarily an emulsification of oil and egg yolk, and these are fats that can make very tender biscuits. Plus the savory quality of mayonnaise comes through in these biscuits, making them perfect for eating with dinner.

MAYO CLINIC
Mayonnaise is made from oil, eggs, salt, and vinegar—all good things to put in biscuits.

SECRET INGREDIENT BISCUITS
Makes 12 biscuits
These biscuits are best with whole milk, but the recipe will work with reduced-fat milk. Don't use nonfat. Reduced-fat mayonnaise can be used, but the biscuits will be less tender and flavorful. Don't use fat-free mayonnaise.

2	cups (10 ounces) all-purpose flour
1	tablespoon sugar
2	teaspoons baking powder
½	teaspoon baking soda
¾	teaspoon salt
1	cup whole milk
¾	cup mayonnaise

1. Adjust oven rack to middle position and heat oven to 450 degrees. Line rimmed baking sheet with parchment paper. Combine flour, sugar, baking powder, baking soda, and salt in large bowl. Whisk milk and mayonnaise together in separate bowl. Stir milk mixture into flour mixture until just combined.

2. Using greased ¼-cup measure, drop 12 level scoops of dough onto prepared sheet, spacing them 1½ inches apart. Use small spoon, if necessary, to dislodge dough from measure. (This dough is sticky, and you may have to regrease your measure several times during portioning.) Bake until biscuit tops are golden brown, 12 to 14 minutes, rotating sheet halfway through baking. Transfer biscuits to wire rack and let cool for 5 minutes. Serve.

Buttermilk Pie

Buttermilk is a baker's secret—add it to just about anything for a moist, tender, tangy result. Now imagine how creamy and delicious it would be in a pie. BY CRISTIN WALSH

IN THE SOUTH, buttermilk pie is right up there with sweet potato, peach, and pecan pies—a classic, in other words. And making it is incredibly easy. You simply whisk together a few staples: granulated sugar, eggs, melted butter, flour or cornstarch, buttermilk (back in the day, buttermilk was a staple left over from churning butter), and lemon juice or vinegar. You pour this custard mixture into a standard pie shell and bake. Out comes a creamy, tangy, buttery pie with a crackly, lightly browned top.

That's what should happen, anyway. Southern cookbooks are full of recipes, all of which resemble one another closely, so I baked a representative sample. The results were pretty disappointing: The fillings were rubbery, pasty, and curdled. The butter (most recipes call for one stick) leached out of the filling and pooled on top. The pies with the best crackly tops used 2 cups of sugar, which was all you could taste. Even in the pies that weren't saccharine, the buttermilk flavor barely made a mark. To add insult to injury, the crusts were soggy. So far, buttermilk pie was seriously short on Southern charm.

The test kitchen knows how to prevent soggy pie crusts, so I'd begin there, deploying our arsenal of tricks. I baked the shell before filling it. When it was golden brown, I brushed it with lightly beaten egg white and let it bake a minute longer to help seal the crust. Using (for now) the best filling recipe from my first round of testing, I poured it into the hot shell. The eggs in the filling coagulate more quickly in a hot crust, speeding up the time it takes the filling to set, which, in turn, gives the crust less exposure to the wet ingredients and therefore a better chance of staying crisp.

The crust was in order, but I expected that the filling would be a tougher nut to crack. I was right. Since we could barely taste the buttermilk, I nearly doubled the wimpy 1 cup most recipes call for. With almost twice the liquid, my pie would never set, so I went up on the flour, too. The buttermilk in the resulting pie registered loud and clear, but all that flour translated to the stodgiest, starchiest, grainiest filling yet. I switched from flour to cornstarch. It's a stronger binder, so I could use just 3 tablespoons. That helped, but

This ultracreamy, tangy pie, with a slight sugar crunch up top, is a Southern classic of long standing.

my pie still had plenty of problems—namely, it was curdled, lumpy, and tasted thin.

I was making the pie one day and thinking about how buttermilk pie is basically a custard pie, meaning it's made from eggs, sugar, and dairy (in this case, buttermilk). The word "custard" suddenly hit me like a smack upside the head. Any pastry chef worth her sugar knows that custards do better

with gentle heat, so why did all the recipes for buttermilk pie call for a 350-degree oven? Was it any wonder that they curdled? I baked three more, one at the standard 350 degrees, another at 325, and the last at 300. As I'd anticipated, the last cooked most evenly.

Even at this gentle temperature, though, the pie wasn't creamy enough. It occurred to me that classic custards, like flans and *pots de crème*, have two

things that my buttermilk pie didn't: lots more egg (or just yolks) and heavy cream. If I treated my pie more like these, wouldn't it be that much smoother, creamier, and richer? I was using two whole eggs. I began to add yolks, and I didn't quit until I'd added, gulp, five. Next, I poured in ¼ cup of heavy cream, reducing the amount of butter I was using by ¼ cup. With so many egg yolks, which act as thickeners

Upping the Ante

Most recipes for buttermilk pie use just 1 cup of buttermilk—which is part of the reason the resulting pies don't taste like much. Our recipe calls for almost twice that much buttermilk, plus we add 2 teaspoons of white vinegar to underscore its tang. To keep the focus squarely on the buttermilk, we also cut way back on the sugar (Southern pies are very sweet).

FLAVOR BUILDERS
Much more buttermilk and a bit of vinegar.

'd need less cornstarch. A few tests howed that just 1 tablespoon of corntarch was enough to set my recalibrated illing to a delicate wobble. As a bonus, now that I was using less butter, it no longer separated out from the filling and pooled on top.

> This pie is delicious n its own, but if you vant to dress it up, our ecipe for **Strawberry** auce is available at ooksCountry.com/ trawberrysauce.

Now that the filling was xtravagantly creamy and rich, I'd ne-tune the flavor. I baked several pies vith a range of sugar measurements. We ound that just ¾ cup of sugar let the uttermilk flavor shine. In a side-by-side est, we picked vinegar ("subtle tang") ver lemon ("too strong"), and we pted for vanilla, which most modern uttermilk pie recipes call for.

One problem remained: I'd achieved he silky custard at the expense of the rackly top. Given the low oven temperture and the minimal amount of sugar, ow could I reinstate it? As a restaurant astry chef, I'd made hundreds of crème rûlées, using a blowtorch to caramelize ustings of granulated sugar. Could I et the same effect with a little sugar and very hot (450-degree) oven? When my uttermilk pie was nearly done, I sprinled it with sugar, cranked the heat, and noved it to the top oven rack, where I oped the reflective heat from the top of he oven would caramelize the sugar. It id, but in the time it took for the sugar o melt, the delicate custard overcooked. experimented until I had a foolproof nethod: I dusted the filling with sugar ıst 10 minutes into the baking time. Vhen I raised the oven rack and temperture at the end, as before, the sugar was ıready halfway melted, so it caramelized ı a quick 5 minutes.

At this point, I had spent several reeks in the kitchen and baked nearly 0 buttermilk pies. But the result spoke or itself: I'd made a gently tangy, barely t pie with a rich, creamy filling and a elicate, crackly sugar crust. The pie is lain, but in the way that really excellent anilla ice cream is plain. My buttermilk e had charm in spades.

BUTTERMILK PIE
Serves 8

All pies are best with homemade crust, and this one is no exception; find our recipe for Single-Crust Pie Dough at **CooksCountry.com/piedough**. But if you lack the time, our favorite store-bought crust is Wholly Wholesome 9" Certified Organic Traditional Bake at Home Rolled Pie Dough. Use commercial cultured buttermilk (avoid nonfat), as some locally produced, artisanal buttermilks that we tested were prone to curdle during baking.

CRUST
- 1 (9-inch) single-crust pie dough
- 1 large egg white, lightly beaten

FILLING
- ¾ cup (5¼ ounces) plus 2 teaspoons sugar
- 1 tablespoon cornstarch
- ¾ teaspoon salt
- 2 large eggs plus 5 large yolks
- 1¾ cups buttermilk
- ¼ cup heavy cream
- 4 tablespoons unsalted butter, melted
- 2 teaspoons distilled white vinegar
- 1½ teaspoons vanilla extract

1. FOR THE CRUST: Roll dough into 12-inch circle on lightly floured counter. Transfer to 9-inch pie plate. Fold overhanging dough under itself so edge of fold is flush with outer rim of plate, and crimp edge. Refrigerate for 40 minutes, then freeze for 20 minutes. Adjust oven racks to upper-middle and lower-middle positions and heat oven to 375 degrees.

2. Line chilled pie shell with 2 (12-inch) squares of parchment paper, letting parchment lie over edges of dough, and fill with pie weights. Place pie plate on rimmed baking sheet and bake on lower-middle oven rack until lightly golden around edges, 20 to 25 minutes. Carefully remove parchment and weights, rotate sheet, and continue to bake until golden brown, 5 to 7 minutes. Brush surface of hot crust with egg white (you won't need all of it to coat crust) and bake for 1 minute longer.

3. FOR THE FILLING: Meanwhile, whisk ¾ cup sugar, cornstarch, and salt together in large bowl. Whisk eggs and yolks into sugar mixture until well combined. Whisk buttermilk, cream, melted butter, vinegar, and vanilla into sugar-egg mixture until incorporated.

4. Reduce oven temperature to 300 degrees. Whisk buttermilk mixture to recombine and, leaving pie shell in oven, carefully pour buttermilk mixture into hot pie shell. Bake for 10 minutes.

5. Sprinkle remaining 2 teaspoons sugar evenly over top of pie. Continue to bake until center jiggles slightly when pie is shaken, 30 to 40 minutes. Remove pie from oven and increase oven temperature to 450 degrees. Once oven comes to temperature, place pie on upper-middle oven rack and bake until golden brown on top, 5 to 7 minutes. Let pie cool for 30 minutes on wire rack. Transfer to refrigerator to chill, about 3 hours. Serve.

TEST KITCHEN TECHNIQUE **Creating the Crackle**

Part of the appeal of this pie is the contrast between the velvety custard and the crackly, crisp sugar top. But it's easy to overcook the custard when you're trying to brown the sugar on top. Here's how to avoid that.

1. After the pie has baked for 10 minutes, sprinkle 2 teaspoons of granulated sugar over the filling; the sugar will melt and soften as the pie gently cooks.

2. When the pie is almost done, pull it from the oven, crank the heat, and place the pie back in the oven on a higher rack so the sugar can caramelize quickly.

Dale Evans and her horse, Buttermilk.

Stick the word "buttermilk" in front of a recipe today and it has an instant fresh-from-the-farm, nostalgic cachet: buttermilk biscuits, buttermilk pancakes, etc. But it wasn't always so. Beginning around the 18th century, buttermilk conjured up not wholesome milkmaids and happy cows but poverty. In Ireland, the (wealthier) English bought butter from the farmers, leaving the (poor) Irish with buttermilk—real buttermilk is the stuff left behind after butter is churned. (The Irish made do: If life gives you buttermilk, make soda bread.) On prosperous farms, buttermilk was fed to pigs and dogs, and poor folks in Appalachia and the South often supped on buttermilk mashed with cornbread and eaten with a spoon (Elvis Presley is said to have loved this). By the early 20th century, poor Scandinavian immigrants and Jews from eastern Europe drank glasses at the beach for refreshment, as today we'd enjoy ice cream cones. At some point, buttermilk's fortunes slowly began to change (as an ingredient, if not a stand-alone drink), not unlike pork belly and beef shins, cheap cuts of meat that now show up on many a trendy restaurant plate. In the 1940s and '50s, cheerful buttermilk references appeared in popular culture—composer Hoagy Carmichael's "Ole Buttermilk Sky" and cowgirl-actress Dale Evans's mount (named Buttermilk), to name two. It's also possible to track this shift in perception through a single 20th-century cookbook: Not one recipe with "buttermilk" in its title appears in the original 1931 *Joy of Cooking*, yet some 70 years later, an update of the classic had 15 such recipes. And just last year, *The New York Times* headlined its article on the subject "Buttermilk, Often Maligned, Begins to Get Its Due."

Beef-and-Bean Burritos

We were confident that we could make tasty burritos fast and easy enough for a weeknight.
But how would we solve the problem of doughy tortillas? BY NICK IVERSON

YOU KNOW HOW curry powder is more British than Indian and chop suey more American than Chinese? Well, burritos are like that. Although Mexicans have been eating food stuffed in tortillas (usually corn tortillas) for centuries, they probably wouldn't recognize the American-style, *grande*-size burritos, which are stuffed—overstuffed, some might say—with rice, beans, meat, and cheese. These American, supersize burritos have been mainstays in "Mexican" restaurants across California and Arizona for many years and more recently have become popular throughout the rest of the United States. No wonder—they're full of flavor and fun to eat.

Restaurants keep steam table pans of the components on hand so a burrito can be slapped together as soon as an order comes in. It's not that simple for the home cook. I wanted a quick, easy recipe that I could make on a busy weeknight. And along the way I hoped to fix a problem that's the scourge of restaurant burritos: soggy tortillas.

Traditional burrito recipes call for long-braised, shredded beef or pork, but even before I spent hours cooking, I knew that wouldn't fit my weeknight timetable. A simplified recipe that I tried called for ground beef, which made sense to me; it cooked to tenderness fast and had lots of surface area to soak up seasoning. Since I was streamlining, I nixed the idea of soaking and cooking the dried beans. I'd use a can—of pinto beans, which we found creamier than black beans.

Before I put together a rudimentary burrito incorporating these initial decisions, I figured out my basic technique: I would sauté an onion in oil along with the spices. "Blooming" spices in fat is a standard test kitchen technique to intensify flavors. Then I'd stir in the ground meat and, once that was cooked, add the (rinsed) beans and tomatoes. Lastly, I'd layer the meat filling with white rice and cheese inside the tortillas.

But which spices should I use? In a series of tests, we liked cumin and oregano but found chili powder and cayenne pepper lacking. For a smokier heat, I tried chipotle chile powder and got nods of approval. In a testing of tomato products, I landed on tomato paste; the filling benefited from its already concentrated flavor. I added it with the spices, so

A sprinkling of cheese on top and a quick turn under the broiler give these burritos extra texture—and fix the problem of soggy tortillas.

the quick sauté could deepen its flavor. Despite all my flavor-intensifying tricks, though, the filling tasted a little flat. Fortunately, it was nothing a squirt of lime juice couldn't fix.

But without the soft, succulent, long-braised meat and its juices, the filling wasn't cohesive. When I rolled it up in a tortilla with the rice, it tumbled out at first bite. A colleague suggested that I mash a portion of the beans into a paste to bind the filling. Good idea. I began again, this time mashing half of

the beans with some chicken broth at the start. Once the meat was cooked, I added the mashed bean mixture and let the filling cook down and meld. Then I stirred in the remaining (whole) beans and the lime juice. Delicious.

Now I turned to the rice. The white rice I'd been using so far was fine but unexciting. To boost its flavor, I made the rice with chicken broth instead of water, and I added some minced garlic to the pot. Much better. For a fresh, suitably Mexican herbal touch, I stirred

chopped cilantro into the cooked rice. Now it was good to go.

As the rice simmered, I made my quick filling, and I warmed six large flour tortillas in the microwave to softe them. I spooned on the rice, followed by the beef-and-bean filling, a little sou cream (which added richness, creaminess, and some extra cohesion insurance), and a sprinkling of grated sharp cheddar cheese (we preferred its flavor to mild Monterey Jack). I rolled up the burritos and passed them out to tasters

Um . . . you forgot to fix the problem of gummy tortillas, tasters said. Oops. And that wasn't all. The tortillas tasted raw and floury. Back to the kitchen, where I fretted awhile, until I thought of what I hoped would be a brilliant solution: I assembled the burritos once again, not changing my recipe one jot but this time arranging them, seam side down, on a baking sheet. Then I sprinkled on extra cheese and broiled them for several minutes. It was that simple. In less than 5 minutes, the broiler crisped the tortillas, eliminating the floury taste at the same time and producing a nice contrast with the soft burrito filling. Often, burritos are food to eat on the go—you just bite in. Mine were the knife-and-fork kind. But you know what? That didn't stop us from wolfing them down.

For salsa in a hurry, our recipe for e-Minute Salsa CooksCountry. n/1minutesalsa.

BEEF-AND-BEAN BURRITOS
Makes 6 burritos

RICE
- 1½ cups low-sodium chicken broth
- ¾ cup long-grain white rice
- 3 garlic cloves, minced
- ½ teaspoon salt
- ¼ cup minced fresh cilantro

BEEF-AND-BEAN FILLING
- ½ cup low-sodium chicken broth
- 1 (15-ounce) can pinto beans, rinsed
- 1 tablespoon vegetable oil
- 1 onion, chopped fine
- 3 tablespoons tomato paste
- 3 garlic cloves, minced
- 1 tablespoon ground cumin
- 1 teaspoon dried oregano
- 1 teaspoon chipotle chile powder
- 12 ounces 90 percent lean ground beef
- 1 tablespoon lime juice
- ¾ teaspoon salt
- 6 (10-inch) flour tortillas
- 10 ounces sharp cheddar cheese, shredded (2½ cups)
- 6 tablespoons sour cream

1. FOR THE RICE: Bring broth, rice, garlic, and salt to boil in small saucepan over medium-high heat. Reduce heat to low, cover, and cook until rice is tender and all liquid has been absorbed, about 20 minutes. Remove rice from heat and let sit, covered, for 10 minutes. Add cilantro, fluff rice with fork, cover, and set aside.

2. FOR THE BEEF-AND-BEAN FILLING: Meanwhile, combine broth and half of beans in medium bowl. Using potato masher, coarsely mash beans together with broth. Heat oil in 12-inch nonstick skillet over medium heat until shimmering. Add onion and cook until just beginning to brown, about 5 minutes. Stir in tomato paste, garlic, cumin, oregano, and chile powder and cook until fragrant, about 1 minute. Add beef, breaking up pieces with spoon, and cook until no longer pink, 8 to 10 minutes.

3. Stir mashed bean mixture into meat mixture. Cook, stirring constantly, until nearly all liquid has evaporated, about 3 minutes. Stir in remaining whole beans, lime juice, and salt. Remove from heat, cover, and set aside.

4. Adjust oven rack 3 inches from broiler element and heat broiler. Line rimmed baking sheet with aluminum foil. Wrap tortillas in clean dish towel and microwave until soft and pliable, about 90 seconds. Arrange tortillas on counter. Divide rice, beef-and-bean filling, and 1½ cups cheddar evenly among tortillas. Dollop each tortilla with 1 tablespoon sour cream. Fold sides of tortilla over filling, fold bottom of tortilla over sides and filling, and roll tightly. Transfer to prepared sheet, seam side down.

5. Sprinkle remaining 1 cup cheddar over burritos. Transfer to oven and broil until cheddar is melted and starting to brown, 3 to 5 minutes, rotating sheet halfway through broiling. Serve.

TO MAKE AHEAD
The rice and filling can be made and refrigerated up to 24 hours in advance. Microwave each until hot, about 2 minutes, stirring halfway through microwaving, before assembling burritos.

STEP BY STEP **It's a Wrap**

1. After you've filled the ortilla with the rice, beef-nd-bean mixture, and heese, fold two sides of he tortilla over the filling.

2. Next, fold a third side of the tortilla over the first two, as though you are wrapping a present.

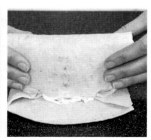

3. Roll up the burrito and place it seam side down on a baking sheet. To finish, sprinkle with more cheese and broil.

Mexican Street Corn

In Mexico, vendors sell this messy, cheesy, utterly delicious grilled corn from street carts. We wanted to duplicate it at home. BY NICK IVERSON

MY FIRST TASTE of Mexican street corn was not, I'm afraid, from a friendly vendor on a bustling Mexican street. Actually, I encountered it at a Mexican restaurant in Boston. Still, I was so blown away by the combination of flavors—smoky corn with a creamy garlic, chili, lime, and cheese coating—that I immediately ordered more. Back at work, I knew that I wanted to develop a recipe so that I could enjoy it in the comfort of my own kitchen.

First, I'd sort through the components. The traditional version features grilled corn on the cob dressed with mayonnaise or Mexican *crema* (which is similar to sour cream)—seasoned as I described above—and topped with crumbled Mexican cheese, usually Cotija or *queso fresco*. Since I wanted this to be a dish for all seasons—it works well with less-than-perfect corn—I decided I'd skip the grill and use the broiler. A few tests showed that about 20 minutes of broiling the corn 5 inches from the element and turning it halfway through nicely charred the corn without overcooking it. Brushing the raw ears of corn with olive oil beforehand protected them from drying out.

For the creamy coating, using mayonnaise was a no-brainer; most home cooks have a jar on hand (although if you have Mexican crema, by all means use it). I stirred in a little minced cilantro, lime juice, fresh minced garlic, chili powder, and salt. Then I topped the slathered corn with crumbled feta cheese, a common and more readily available substitute for salty, tangy Mexican cheeses. I called over tasters to render a verdict.

Fabulous, they said, fabulous. But they had a quibble: The cheese fell off as they ate the corn. Sure, this is street food, so a little mess is to be expected. Still, you want to eat the cheese with the corn, not decorate your clothing. Fortunately, I was able to fix the problem by stirring the cheese into the mayonnaise mixture, brushing the mixture on the charred corn, and then broiling the slathered corn for another minute or so to let the cheese start to melt. Now Mexican street corn is ready for American dining rooms.

The attached corn stalks make helpful handles when cooking and eating.

MEXICAN STREET CORN Serves 6

- 6 ears corn, husks and silk removed, stalks left intact
- 1 tablespoon olive oil
- ½ cup mayonnaise
- 1 ounce feta cheese, crumbled (¼ cup)
- 2 tablespoons minced fresh cilantro
- 1 tablespoon lime juice, plus lime wedges for serving
- 1 garlic clove, minced
- 1 teaspoon chili powder
  Salt and pepper

1. Adjust oven rack 5 inches from broiler element and heat broiler. Line rimmed baking sheet with aluminum foil. Brush corn all over with oil and transfer to prepared sheet. Broil corn until well browned on 1 side, about 10 minutes. Flip corn and broil until browned on opposite side, about 10 minutes longer.

2. Meanwhile, whisk mayonnaise, feta, cilantro, lime juice, garlic, chili powder, and ¼ teaspoon salt together in bowl until incorporated.

3. Remove corn from oven and brush evenly on all sides with mayonnaise mixture. (Reserve any extra mayonnaise mixture for serving.) Return corn to oven and broil, rotating frequently, until coating is lightly browned, about 2 minutes. Season with salt and pepper to taste. Serve corn with lime wedges and any extra reserved mayonnaise mixture.

Chicken with 40 Cloves of Garlic

It sounds almost inedible, but assuming you can get normally harsh-tasting garlic to turn mellow and sweet, you'll understand how this dish became a French classic. BY SARAH GABRIEL

FORTY CLOVES OF garlic? Seriously? This classic Provençal French dish may wield an extreme amount of garlic, but it's really just braised chicken with a sauce saved from probable blandness by that very garlic.

Scanning recipes from French and American sources, I teased out the major options: whole chicken or parts; covered Dutch ovens or skillets; peeled or unpeeled garlic; and, for serving, the braising liquid (usually broth) on its own or thickened into a sauce (bumped up with wine or sherry). I chose recipes representing each, grabbed a heap of garlic, and got to work.

This first round of testing showed that we preferred the crisp skin of chicken cooked in open skillets. We also liked chicken thighs, which were easier to brown on the stovetop and simpler to serve than whole chickens (and weren't as prone to overcook as breasts). And the sauce trounced the braising liquid.

This first test also crystallized my true challenge: how to foster garlic's sweet, mellow side. The traditional approach is to roast unpeeled cloves with the chicken. Although this yielded mild garlic, the unpeeled cloves didn't flavor the sauce. I started again with peeled garlic. After browning the thighs skin side down, I set them aside and browned the peeled cloves in the rendered fat. I poured in broth, sherry, and cream plus cornstarch to thicken; returned the chicken to the pan, skin side up; and cooked it in a 450-degree oven. The process was simple and quick (about 35 minutes total), and the chicken was perfectly cooked. But the garlic remained somewhat firm, with a pungent kick. I'd have to find a way to tame those 40 cloves. Luckily, I had a few ideas to try.

I tried smashing the raw cloves so they'd cook faster, but this made matters worse. Our science editor explained that

James Beard and Richard Olney popularized this classic French recipe in the United States some 40 years ago.

smashing raw garlic releases its harsh-tasting compounds, which my quicker-cooking recipe gave no time to mellow. Precooking looked like the only option. One recipe in my initial test had called for preroasting the garlic, but that step would double the cooking time.

What about microwaving? After a few tries, I found that 4 minutes in the microwave produced slightly soft cloves—a good start. To mimic the sweetness of long-roasted garlic, I tossed the cloves with a little sugar. Now when I added the garlic to the chicken fat, it needed only a minute or so of browning to develop its flavor. I added the sherry to the sautéed cloves, cooking it down to further deepen the sweetness.

Only then did I add the remaining liquid and proceed with the recipe. This time, the garlic was so soft and sweet that I wanted its flavor throughout the sauce, so I smashed half of the cloves into the sauce. Now, rather than cracking jokes about garlic breath, tasters were reaching for seconds.

CHICKEN WITH 40 CLOVES OF GARLIC Serves 4

You will need three or four heads of garlic to yield 40 cloves. You can substitute four bone-in, skin-on chicken breasts (halved crosswise) for the thighs, but reduce the cooking time in step 3 to 15 to 20 minutes.

- 40 garlic cloves, peeled
- 2 teaspoons vegetable oil
- ½ teaspoon sugar
- 8 (5- to 7-ounce) bone-in chicken thighs, trimmed
  Salt and pepper
- ½ cup dry sherry
- ¾ cup low-sodium chicken broth
- ½ cup heavy cream
- 2 teaspoons cornstarch dissolved in 1 tablespoon water
- 2 sprigs fresh thyme
- 1 bay leaf

1. Adjust oven rack to upper-middle position and heat oven to 450 degrees. Toss garlic in bowl with 1 teaspoon oil and sugar. Microwave garlic until slightly softened, with light brown spotting, about 4 minutes, stirring halfway through microwaving.

2. Pat chicken dry with paper towels and season with 1 teaspoon salt and ½ teaspoon pepper. Heat remaining 1 teaspoon oil in 12-inch ovensafe skillet over medium-high heat until just smoking. Place chicken in skillet, skin side down, and cook until skin is well browned, 7 to 10 minutes. Transfer to plate, skin side up. Pour off all but 1 tablespoon fat from skillet. Reduce heat to medium-low, add garlic, and cook until evenly browned, about 1 minute.

3. Off heat, add sherry to skillet. Return skillet to medium heat and bring sherry to simmer, scraping up any browned bits. Cook until sherry coats garlic and pan is nearly dry, about 4 minutes. Stir in broth, cream, cornstarch mixture, thyme, and bay leaf and simmer until slightly thickened, about 3 minutes. Return chicken to skillet, skin side up, with any accumulated juices. Transfer skillet to oven and bake until chicken registers 175 degrees, 18 to 22 minutes.

4. Transfer chicken and half of garlic to serving dish. Discard thyme and bay leaf. Using potato masher, mash remaining garlic into sauce, and season with salt and pepper to taste. Pour half of sauce around chicken. Serve, passing remaining sauce separately.

Easy Asparagus Tart

We set out to create a tart that would highlight the flavor of asparagus—
and wouldn't take all afternoon to make. BY CRISTIN WALSH

AN ASPARAGUS TART is like a crocus—a happy sign of spring. But most versions are either too much work or don't accentuate the asparagus. I set out to do better.

First I concentrated on the crust. I made various versions using a pie shell, a tart shell, and parbaked puff pastry. The first two crusts weren't bad, but they didn't stand a chance next to the buttery, flaky puff pastry.

I knew I'd use store-bought puff pastry, but how best to bake it? The problem is that if it is simply rolled out and baked, the center of the pastry puffs up. Most recipes deal with this by crushing the center of the shell flat after it's blind-baked. This approach worked, but it was messy. If I could keep the center from puffing in the first place, the tart would be much neater. I took out a new 9½ by 9-inch sheet of thawed puff pastry and placed it on a parchment paper–lined baking sheet. In a moment of inspiration, I grabbed an 8-inch square baking pan, greased the underside, threw baking weights into the dish to weigh it down, and centered it over the puff pastry, leaving a ½-inch border all around. I scored the puff pastry around the dish and baked it for 20 minutes. Then I removed the dish and baked the pastry for an additional 10 minutes to let the center brown. Problem solved.

I knew I wanted something easier and lighter than a quichelike custard filling. I opted instead for the pizzalike approach, which involves scattering asparagus and other ingredients over the puff-pastry base. I found that if I cut the asparagus spears into thin 1-inch pieces, rather than leaving them whole, the tart was easier to eat and the asparagus required no precooking. I just needed some sort of creamy base to "glue" the asparagus in place and add richness. Cream cheese tore the delicate pastry and ricotta was grainy and bland, but tangy, soft goat cheese nicely complemented the bright, grassy asparagus. To make the cheese more spreadable, I blended in a table-spoon of olive oil.

I dressed the tart up by tossing the asparagus with more olive oil, plus garlic, lemon zest, scallions, and olives. I sprinkled this mixture over the goat cheese, dolloped more cheese on top, and baked the tart. This tart, at last, was a springboard into spring.

Serve big pieces of this bright tart for lunch or a light supper, or cut it into smaller pieces for an impressive party appetizer.

TEST KITCHEN TECHNIQUE **Prebaking the Tart Shell**

1. Place a baking pan filled with pie weights (or pennies) over the puff pastry and trace around it with a paring knife.

2. Move the puff pastry, on its parchment paper–lined baking sheet, to the oven.

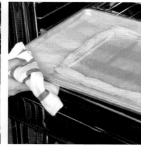

3. Return the parbaked puff pastry to the oven without the weighted pan so that the center can continue to bake and brown.

ASPARAGUS–GOAT CHEESE TART
Serves 4 as a main dish

To thaw frozen puff pastry, allow it to sit either in the refrigerator for 24 hours or on the counter for 30 minutes to 1 hour. Pennies work well in place of pie weights; if you use a Pyrex baking dish to weigh down the puff pastry, you can skip the pie weights altogether. Cutting the asparagus into thin pieces allows it to become tender without precooking.

- 1 (9½ by 9-inch) sheet puff pastry, thawed
- 6 ounces asparagus, trimmed and cut ¼ inch thick on bias into 1-inch lengths (1 cup)
- 2 scallions, sliced thin
- 3 tablespoons extra-virgin olive oil
- 2 tablespoons chopped pitted kalamata olives
- 1 garlic clove, minced
- ¼ teaspoon grated lemon zest
- ¼ teaspoon salt
- ¼ teaspoon pepper
- 4 ounces (1 cup) goat cheese, softened

1. Adjust oven racks to lower-middle and top positions and heat oven to 400 degrees. Line rimmed baking sheet with parchment paper and place puff pastry in center of sheet. Grease under-side of 8-inch square baking pan, place in center of puff pastry, and fill pan with pie weights. Using sharp paring knife, score puff pastry around perimeter of pan, ⅛ inch deep. (Do not cut through pastry.)

2. Leaving pan on pastry, bake on lower-middle oven rack for 20 minutes. Remove pan, rotate sheet, and continue to bake until pastry is golden brown, 5 to 10 minutes. Let cool for 30 minutes.

3. Meanwhile, combine asparagus, scallions, 1 tablespoon oil, olives, garlic, zest, salt, and pepper in bowl. In sepa-rate bowl, mix ¾ cup goat cheese and 1 tablespoon oil until smooth. Spread goat cheese mixture evenly over cooled puff pastry (avoiding raised border), then scatter asparagus mixture over top. Crumble remaining ¼ cup goat cheese over top of asparagus mixture.

4. Bake tart on top oven rack until asparagus is tender and tart shell has darkened slightly around edges, 10 to 15 minutes. Let cool for 15 minutes. Drizzle with remaining 1 tablespoon oil. Cut into 4 equal pieces and serve.

Really Crunchy French Toast

Adding crunch to this breakfast classic was easier said than done.

BY NICK IVERSON

A S THE VERY first thing I ever cooked on my own without parental supervision, French toast holds a special place in my heart. It probably wasn't very good, but I did get the basics down: Give stale bread a quick soak in eggs beaten with milk, cinnamon, and vanilla; put the slices in a skillet to brown; flip them to brown more; and breakfast is served. It's still my favorite breakfast, but at a diner recently I encountered something new to me, and even better: crunchy French toast, which combined the soft, slightly sweet, custardy interior of classic French toast with a satisfyingly crunchy exterior. As soon as I took a bite, I knew I had to learn how to make it.

Back in the test kitchen, I did some research and turned up a few recipes. The egg-and-dairy mixtures ("custards," in kitchen speak) varied slightly in ingredients and proportions; crushed cornflakes was the usual coating; and some of the recipes called for sautéing the French toast, while others required shallow-frying it in a few inches of oil. I set out the ingredients and got down to work.

Unfortunately, many of these toasts had flaws that a gallon of maple syrup couldn't cover up. The questions they raised were many and perplexing: How do you get the coating to stick? (I quickly learned that it has a tendency to slough off in the frying pan.) How do you keep the coating from getting soggy when it meets the wet custard? How do you keep the coating from burning yet ensure that the inside cooks through? And I also wondered just what would make for a tasty coating—my tasters were lukewarm about the cornflakes.

This first round of testing did lead to a few helpful discoveries, though. First, fat 1-inch-thick slices produced the best ratio of soft inside to crunchy outside. Next, shallow-fried French toast produced hyper-crunchy slices that beat the pants off slices that were merely sautéed. But since I definitely didn't want the bother and mess of frying first thing in the morning (and in multiple batches), I'd have to figure out an easier way.

Cherry-picking these winning features from the sample recipes, I started again: To yield eight slices, I used a custard made from milk, eggs, and the standard flavorings, and I used cornflakes, for now, to coat. The immediate problem

The keys to big crunch? A carefully timed custard soak (to prevent sogginess) and a secret ingredient in the coating.

was that in order to saturate the thick slices, I needed extra custard. I doubled the amounts and found success. My next concern was getting the cornflakes to stick. I figured that if the custard were thicker, it would have better adhesive powers. I replaced the 2½ cups of milk with an equal amount of half-and-half. Problem solved. Along the way, as I adjusted here and tweaked there, I found that dipping the slices in the custard

mixture for just 15 seconds per side let the custard saturate the slices without producing wet, squishy toast.

Now it was time to deal with the cornflake coating, which we'd never liked much. One taster had compared it (kindly, I thought) to cardboard. So I rounded up some other candidates: Frosted Flakes, Cap'n Crunch, Honey Bunches of Oats, and panko, a Japanese-style bread crumb that the test kitchen

often uses for its extreme crunch. Cap'n Crunch won the day by a long shot. Ground down to a coarse crumb, it adhered well to the moistened bread without soaking up too much liquid, and tasters deemed it crunchy, satisfyingly sweet, and kid-friendly, too, as one mom in the group added.

Up until now I had been shallow-frying the toast in batches in a skillet. That meant that, in order to make eight pieces of this Texas-size toast, I had to do four separate batches, which was tedious to say the least. I got the idea to try making the toasts in the oven, assuming I could preserve the crunch. Leaning on a recipe that we'd developed a few years ago for oven-baked French toast, I baked almost 20 batches over six days, making a series of adjustments as I went along: I set each piece to rest on a wire cooling rack after I dredged it in the cereal so that the bottoms wouldn't get soggy before I'd even started cooking. I didn't merely grease the baking sheet; I simulated frying by pouring in a generous ½ cup of oil (butter tasted good, but unfortunately it burned). To guarantee great crunch, first I let the baking sheet get good and hot; then I let the oil heat up; and only at that point did I carefully slide in the custard-soaked, cereal-coated French toast pieces. The loud sizzling boded well.

Twenty minutes (and one flip) later, I took a batch out of the oven, poured on

Which syrup tastes [be]st? Read our taste [te]st of maple and [pa]ncake syrup at [Co]oksCountry.com/ [ma]plesyrup.

the maple syrup, and called my tasters. Their smiles, the empty plates, and the sound of crunching told me all I needed to know.

CRUNCHY FRENCH TOAST

Serves 6 to 8
Day-old challah works best. To crush the cereal, pour it into a 1-gallon zipper-lock bag, seal, and use a rolling pin to roll over it several times.

6	cups Cap'n Crunch cereal, crushed coarse
2½	cups half-and-half
3	large eggs
3	tablespoons sugar
1	tablespoon vanilla extract
1½	teaspoons ground cinnamon
½	teaspoon salt
1	(12 by 5-inch) loaf challah, cut into eight 1-inch-thick slices
½	cup vegetable oil

1. Adjust oven rack to middle position, place rimmed baking sheet on rack, and heat oven to 450 degrees. Set wire cooling rack inside second rimmed baking sheet. Place cereal in 13 by 9-inch baking dish. Whisk half-and-half, eggs, sugar, vanilla, cinnamon, and salt together in large bowl until combined.

2. Working with 2 slices of bread at a time, soak in half-and-half mixture until just saturated, about 15 seconds per side. Transfer soaked bread to cereal and press lightly to adhere; transfer to prepared wire rack. Repeat with remaining bread.

3. Add oil to preheated sheet, tilting to coat evenly. Return sheet to oven and heat until oil is just smoking, about 4 minutes. Carefully remove sheet from oven and arrange bread in even layer on sheet. Bake until exterior is golden brown and crunchy, about 20 minutes, flipping once and rotating sheet halfway through baking. Transfer toast to clean wire cooling rack and let cool for 5 minutes. Serve.

SECRET INGREDIENT
Cap'n Crunch
Most recipes call for coating French toast with cornflakes to make crunchy French toast. We found a cereal that stood up better to the custard without getting soggy. With Cap'n Crunch, we had our golden-brown, crunchy exterior locked up.

CRUNCHY COATING
Think outside the bowl.

TASTING FROZEN ORANGE JUICE CONCENTRATE

Frozen concentrated orange juice is easy to carry home, lasts up to two years in the freezer, is cheaper than refrigerated juice, and takes up little space until you reconstitute it. But we'd long written it off as a relic from the 1950s, when convenience often trumped freshness. To test our assumption, we bought three nationally available products, added water according to directions, and held a blind taste test. We were shocked to find that we actually liked two of the products.

It turns out that frozen and refrigerated juice are more similar than we knew: All commercial orange juice is extracted mechanically and strained of pulp to varying degrees. Refrigerated orange juice is then pasteurized. Juice destined to be frozen concentrate goes to an evaporation chamber, where heat removes the water; the concentrate is then frozen. Both types of orange juice may be enhanced with oils extracted from peels, and both are tested for Brix (sweetness) and acidity and then blended to suit brand specifications. So we tasted our favorite frozen concentrate again, this time alongside our winning refrigerated orange juice, Tropicana Pure Premium 100% Pure Orange Juice with Some Pulp. The refrigerated brand barely eked out a win, and we were shocked all over again.

So what of the lousy frozen orange juice that many of us remember from childhood? These days, the evaporation process goes much faster than in the past, minimizing off flavors, according to Kristen Gunter, executive director of the Florida Citrus Processors Association. She added that most frozen concentrate now includes pulp for a more natural texture. From now on, we'll stock our freezer with Minute Maid Original Frozen Concentrated Orange Juice—and never be caught without OJ again. –HANNAH CROWLEY

RECOMMENDED		TASTERS' NOTES
MINUTE MAID Original Frozen Concentrated Orange Juice **Price:** $1.50 for 12 oz (3 cents per reconstituted oz)		This "bright" juice was "slightly floral" and "orangey upfront." "Just the right amount of sugar and acid," said one taster; "easy to drink," said another. With "minimal" pulp yet an appealing "full-bodied" texture, it was the one in our lineup "most like fresh squeezed."
TROPICANA 100% Juice Frozen Concentrated Orange Juice **Price:** $1.79 for 12 oz (4 cents per reconstituted oz)		This juice had a "fuller" flavor that was "lively," "tart," and "not too sweet"; it was more "pucker-y" than the others, "like grapefruit juice" or "orange zest." The "small pulpy bits" made for "thicker juice" with "home-squeezed" texture.
NOT RECOMMENDED		
CASCADIAN FARM Organic Orange Juice Frozen Concentrate **Price:** $4.39 for 12 oz (9 cents per reconstituted oz)		Tasters missed the "acid pucker" in this organic brand, which had a "very sweet start." It was thin, with "zero pulp." (It's the only brand to list water as an ingredient.) It reminded one taster, unfavorably, of "Tang or SunnyD."

TEST KITCHEN TECHNIQUE **Making Crunchy French Toast**

1. Dipping the thick slices of bread in the custard mixture for just 15 seconds per side gives the finished toast a custardy (but not soggy) center.

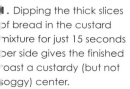

2. Dredging each custard-soaked slice in coarsely crushed Cap'n Crunch makes for the best crunchy coating. (The Cap'n is aptly named.)

3. Cooking our French toast on a preheated baking sheet in a generous amount of oil simulates shallow frying and guarantees a crunchy crust.

OVEN-COOKED BACON

Serves 4 to 6
The amount of bacon you can cook at one time will vary depending on the size of the bacon slices and the size of your baking sheet.

1 pound bacon

Adjust oven rack to middle position and heat oven to 400 degrees. Line rimmed baking sheet with aluminum foil. Arrange bacon on prepared sheet (slices can overlap slightly). Bake until brown and crisp, 10 to 15 minutes, rotating sheet halfway through baking. Transfer bacon to paper towel–lined plate to drain. Serve.

Getting to Know Shoots and Stalks

Come spring, shoots and stalks are everywhere. Here are a dozen that could end up in your kitchen and on your plate. BY REBECCAH MARSTERS

Swiss Chard Stalks
TWOFER

With edible stalks *and* leaves, Swiss chard is one vegetable in two. We often keep them together, chopping the tougher, more fibrous stalks smaller than the leaves or giving them a head start in the pan to soften them. But you can also roast, braise, or even pickle the stalks by themselves. Whether red, yellow, or white, the stalks will taste the same (and the colors will fade when the chard is cooked). To stem Swiss chard, fold each leaf in half along the stalk and cut out the stalk with a knife.

Asparagus
SPRING HERALD

Thanks to a global market, asparagus is now sold year-round, but its appearance at the store used to mean that spring had sprung. Store spears, cut end down, in a glass of water in the refrigerator. Steam the thinner spears and broil, roast, or grill thicker ones. Or try them with goat cheese and olives in our Asparagus–Goat Cheese Tart (page 13). Asparagus are members of the lily family.

White Asparagus
OLD-WORLD CRUSH

White asparagus is actually just green asparagus that was grown covered in hay or soil: Shielded from sunlight, there's no photosynthesis. Europeans love their white asparagus (the Germans even hold spring festivals in its honor). In America, any fresh spears you find probably come from Peru. Try them poached or steamed and dressed in herb vinaigrette. Canned or preserved white asparagus are mushy and taste tinny—walk on by.

Garlic Scapes
LESS OF A STINKING ROSE

Garlic scapes are the flower stalk of the garlic bulb. Each bright green shoot loops in a circle and ends in a mini clove called a bulbil. A darling of foodies, garlic scapes show up at farmers' markets in the late spring or early summer. Snipping them promotes growth underground, meaning plump garlic cloves—plus it gives farmers two products to sell. The scapes taste like very mild garlic. Sauté them in olive oil or puree into a white bean dip or pesto.

Celery
CARROT STICK'S BFF

Celery is indispensable—whether it's sent to school in a child's lunch box; served raw with dip as crudités; or sautéed with onions, carrots, and herbs to make a *mirepoix* (the classic building block for soups, sauces, stuffing, and much more). Next time you're chopping it up to add crunch to chicken or egg salad, throw in the leaves, too: They carry lots of flavor.

Chinese Celery
ASIAN ANCESTOR

The Chinese form of celery has skinny, hollow stalks, which are woodier than those of common North American celery. Other differences? Chinese celery is leafier (the leaves look and taste somewhat like parsley), and it has a pungent, peppery flavor. Chinese celery is a nearer relative of wild celery than the cultivated variety we eat in America. Asian cooks use it in soups and stir-fries as both an herb and a vegetable.

Rhubarb
PIE PLANT

Because it's usually paired with strawberries and made into pie, rhubarb is often mistaken for a fruit. Actually, it's a vegetable, and though very tart and astringent, sugar transforms it into dessert. Buy it red or green: The color doesn't indicate ripeness or affect the taste. Slice rhubarb thinly across the grain to reduce stringiness. Don't eat the leaves; they are poisonous.

Fennel
VEGETABLE CANDY

Once a specialty Italian ingredient, licorice-flavored fennel is now familiar to most Americans. To prep it, slice off the stalks, trim the bottom of the bulb, halve the bulb lengthwise, and remove and discard the hard core. Cut the remaining bulb into chunks and roast them, or slice it thinly (across the grain to prevent stringiness) to eat raw in salads and slaws. Treat the feathery fronds like an herb to add mild anise flavor to a dish.

Hearts of Palm
THE TURNAROUND KID

Once referred to as "swamp cabbage," hearts of palm took a turn for the gourmet in the 1950s. They come from the innermost portion of the cabbage palm tree, which grows in South and Central America. Many grocery stores carry canned or jarred versions. Fresh, they are smooth and white, crisp yet creamy, and slightly tart. Use them in salads with seafood, corn, papaya, and/ or avocados.

Bamboo Shoots
STIR-FRY STAPLE

Asian cooks simmer, braise, stir-fry, and even grill this off-white shoot of the bamboo plant, which is crisp and slightly bitter. To prepare fresh shoots, peel back the tough outer layers (carefully: They have bristles) and parboil the shoots for 20 minutes to let the bitter compounds dissipate. Unless you shop at Asian markets, though, you will probably be using canned, in which case you should drain, rinse, and dry the shoots before using.

Fiddleheads
FOREST FERN

The young, unfurled shoots of several types of ferns are a much-prized early spring vegetable. Their high price reflects the fact that they're wild, delicate, and highly perishable, plus the season is short. Fiddleheads have a "grassy, nutty" flavor similar to that of asparagus and green beans. Clean them carefully before blanching them in boiling water, shocking them in an ice bath, and briefly sautéing them in butter.

Lemongrass
MISS POPULARITY

Ubiquitous in curries, soups, and salads across Southeast Asia, lemongrass reached America more than a decade ago; many supermarkets now carry it in the produce section. Lemongrass has a delicate, citrusy, slightly "peppery" flavor. To prepare it, first peel and discard the tough, outer layers. Then mince or grate the pale lower stalk (freeze it first for easy grating) or bruise it by pounding it and leave it whole to infuse stocks and soups.

SPRING RISOTTO WITH PEAS,
FAVA BEANS, AND ARUGULA

SKILLET BROCCOLI MACARONI AND CHEESE

OVEN-FRIED FISH STICKS WITH
OLD BAY DIPPING SAUCE

SWEET AND SPICY PORK LETTUCE WRAPS

SKILLET BROCCOLI MACARONI AND CHEESE

Serves 4

WHY THIS RECIPE WORKS: We use evaporated milk in the sauce to ensure that it won't curdle.

- 3¾ cups water
- 1 (12-ounce) can evaporated milk
- Salt and pepper
- 12 ounces (3 cups) elbow macaroni
- 12 ounces broccoli florets, cut into 1-inch pieces
- 2 teaspoons hot sauce
- 1 teaspoon cornstarch
- 8 ounces sharp cheddar cheese, shredded (2 cups)
- 8 ounces Monterey Jack cheese, shredded (2 cups)

1. Bring water, 1¼ cups evaporated milk, and ½ teaspoon salt to simmer in 12-inch nonstick skillet over medium-high heat. Add macaroni and cook, stirring often, until almost tender, about 5 minutes. Add broccoli and cook, stirring frequently, until broccoli and macaroni are tender, 3 to 5 minutes.

2. Whisk remaining ¼ cup evaporated milk, hot sauce, and cornstarch together in bowl, then stir into macaroni. Bring to simmer and cook until slightly thickened, about 1 minute. Off heat, stir in cheddar and Monterey Jack. Season with salt and pepper to taste. Serve.

TEST KITCHEN NOTE: You can use cauliflower in place of the broccoli.

SPRING RISOTTO WITH PEAS, FAVA BEANS, AND ARUGULA

Serves 4

WHY THIS RECIPE WORKS: Giving the rice a head start in the microwave lets you make risotto with far less hands-on stirring than usual.

- 4 cups low-sodium chicken broth
- 1 cup Arborio rice
- 6 tablespoons unsalted butter
- 1 onion, chopped fine
- 2 garlic cloves, minced
- 1 cup frozen peas, thawed
- 1 cup frozen fava beans, thawed
- 2 ounces (2 cups) baby arugula, chopped rough
- 2 ounces Parmesan cheese, grated (1 cup)
- Salt and pepper

1. Microwave 3 cups broth, rice, and 2 tablespoons butter in large covered bowl until most of liquid is absorbed, 14 to 16 minutes.

2. Melt 2 tablespoons butter in 12-inch nonstick skillet over medium heat. Add onion and cook until softened, about 5 minutes. Stir in garlic and cook until fragrant, about 30 seconds. Add parcooked rice and remaining 1 cup broth. Bring to simmer and cook, stirring constantly, until rice is almost tender, 4 to 6 minutes. Stir in peas and fava beans and cook until heated through, about 1 minute. Off heat, stir in arugula, Parmesan, and remaining 2 tablespoons butter. Season with salt and pepper to taste. Serve.

TEST KITCHEN NOTE: You can use frozen lima beans or an additional cup of frozen peas in place of the fava beans.

SWEET AND SPICY PORK LETTUCE WRAPS Serves 4

WHY THIS RECIPE WORKS: By using a whole pork tenderloin instead of preground pork, our meat mixture is juicy, tender, and flavorful.

- ¼ cup hoisin sauce
- 3 tablespoons soy sauce
- 2 tablespoons water
- 1 tablespoon Asian chili-garlic sauce
- 1 (16-ounce) pork tenderloin, trimmed and cut into 1-inch chunks
- 2 tablespoons vegetable oil
- 1 red bell pepper, stemmed, seeded, and cut into ¼-inch pieces
- 1 (8-ounce) can water chestnuts, drained and chopped
- 1 tablespoon grated fresh ginger
- 1 head Bibb lettuce (8 ounces), leaves separated

1. Whisk hoisin sauce, soy sauce, water, and chili-garlic sauce together in large bowl; set aside. Pulse half of pork in food processor until coarsely chopped, about 5 pulses. Transfer to separate bowl and repeat with remaining pork.

2. Heat 1 tablespoon oil in 12-inch nonstick skillet over medium-high heat until just smoking. Cook pork until no longer pink, about 4 minutes. Transfer pork to bowl with hoisin mixture. Stir to combine.

3. Heat remaining 1 tablespoon oil in now-empty skillet over medium-high heat until shimmering. Cook bell pepper and water chestnuts until bell pepper softens, about 3 minutes. Add ginger and cook until fragrant, about 30 seconds. Add pork mixture to skillet, bring to simmer, and cook until thickened, about 1 minute. Transfer to serving dish. To serve, spoon pork mixture into lettuce leaves.

TEST KITCHEN NOTE: You can substitute one minced clove of garlic and ¼ teaspoon of cayenne pepper for the Asian chili-garlic sauce.

OVEN-FRIED FISH STICKS WITH OLD BAY DIPPING SAUCE

Serves 4

WHY THIS RECIPE WORKS: Firm, meaty haddock holds its shape during cooking.

- ½ cup plain Greek yogurt
- ½ cup mayonnaise
- 3 tablespoons Dijon mustard
- 2 tablespoons Old Bay seasoning
- Salt and pepper
- ¾ cup all-purpose flour
- 2 large eggs
- 2 cups panko bread crumbs
- 2 tablespoons vegetable oil
- 2 pounds skinless haddock fillet, 1 inch thick, sliced crosswise into 1-inch-wide strips

1. Adjust oven rack to middle position and heat oven to 450 degrees. Set wire rack in rimmed baking sheet and spray with vegetable oil spray. Whisk yogurt, ¼ cup mayonnaise, 1 tablespoon mustard, and 1 tablespoon Old Bay together in bowl. Season with salt and pepper to taste; set aside.

2. Combine ½ cup flour, remaining 1 tablespoon Old Bay, ¼ teaspoon salt, and ⅛ teaspoon pepper in shallow dish. Whisk remaining ¼ cup mayonnaise, remaining ¼ cup flour, eggs, and remaining 2 tablespoons mustard together in second shallow dish. Combine panko and oil in 12-inch skillet and toast over medium-high heat until lightly browned, about 5 minutes. Transfer toasted panko to third shallow dish. Pat haddock dry with paper towels and season with salt and pepper. Working with 1 strip at a time, coat haddock strips lightly with flour mixture; dip in egg mixture; and dredge in panko, pressing to adhere. Transfer to prepared wire rack and bake until crumbs are golden and haddock is cooked through, 10 to 12 minutes. Serve with reserved sauce.

INDOOR BURGERS WITH CRISPY ONIONS

CHICKEN WITH TARRAGON BREAD CRUMBS

BONELESS PORK CHOPS WITH MANGO-MINT SALSA

SKILLET CITRUS CHICKEN TENDERS

CHICKEN WITH TARRAGON BREAD CRUMBS
Serves 4

WHY THIS RECIPE WORKS: Tarragon and lemon add bright flavor to simple chicken cutlets.

- ½ cup all-purpose flour
- 3 large eggs
- 5 slices hearty white sandwich bread, torn into pieces
- ½ cup chopped fresh tarragon
- 1 tablespoon unsalted butter, chilled
- 2 teaspoons grated lemon zest
  Salt and pepper
- 8 (3- to 4-ounce) chicken cutlets, ½ inch thick, trimmed
- 6 tablespoons vegetable oil

1. Adjust oven rack to middle position and heat oven to 200 degrees. Set wire rack in rimmed baking sheet. Place flour in shallow dish. Beat eggs in second shallow dish. Pulse bread, tarragon, butter, lemon zest, ¼ teaspoon salt, and ¼ teaspoon pepper in food processor until coarsely ground, about 10 pulses; transfer to third shallow dish.

2. Pat cutlets dry with paper towels and season with salt and pepper. Working with 1 cutlet at a time, coat cutlets lightly with flour; dip in egg; and dredge in bread crumbs, pressing to adhere. Transfer to plate.

3. Heat 3 tablespoons oil in 12-inch nonstick skillet over medium-high heat until shimmering. Cook half of cutlets until golden brown and cooked through, about 3 minutes per side. Transfer to prepared wire rack and keep warm in oven. Wipe out skillet and repeat with remaining 3 table-spoons oil and remaining cutlets. Serve.

TEST KITCHEN NOTE: You can use parsley in place of the tarragon.

SKILLET CITRUS CHICKEN TENDERS
Serves 4

WHY THIS RECIPE WORKS: Sautéing the chicken in two batches ensures that it will brown, not steam.

- 2 pounds chicken tenderloins, trimmed
  Salt and pepper
- 2 tablespoons vegetable oil
- 3 tablespoons unsalted butter
- 3 garlic cloves, minced
- 1 tablespoon all-purpose flour
- 1 cup low-sodium chicken broth
- 1 tablespoon grated orange zest plus ¼ cup juice
- 2 teaspoons grated lemon zest plus 3 tablespoons juice
- 2 tablespoons minced fresh parsley

1. Pat chicken dry with paper towels and season with salt and pepper. Heat 1 tablespoon oil in 12-inch nonstick skillet over medium-high heat until just smoking. Cook half of chicken until golden brown and cooked through, about 2 minutes per side. Transfer to plate and tent with aluminum foil. Repeat with remaining 1 tablespoon oil and remaining chicken.

2. Melt 1 tablespoon butter in now-empty skillet. Add garlic and cook until fragrant, about 30 seconds. Stir in flour and cook for 1 minute. Stir in broth, orange juice, and lemon juice and bring to simmer, scraping up any browned bits. Cook until slightly thickened, about 3 minutes. Off heat, whisk in parsley, remaining 2 tablespoons butter, orange zest, and lemon zest. Stir in browned chicken. Season with salt and pepper to taste. Serve.

TEST KITCHEN NOTE: If you can't find chicken tenderloins, slice boneless, skinless chicken breasts lengthwise into ¾-inch-thick strips.

INDOOR BURGERS WITH CRISPY ONIONS Serves 4

WHY THIS RECIPE WORKS: The fried onion rings get extra crunch from the vinegar and cream of tartar.

- 1 onion, sliced into thin rings
- ½ cup white vinegar
- ½ cup all-purpose flour
  Salt and pepper
- ¼ teaspoon cream of tartar
- 2 pounds 85 percent lean ground beef
- 3 garlic cloves, minced
- 2 teaspoons plus 2 cups vegetable oil
- 4 slices deli American cheese (4 ounces)
- 4 hamburger buns, toasted and buttered

1. Adjust oven rack to middle position and heat oven to 300 degrees. Separate onion rings and combine with vinegar in bowl. Combine flour, ½ teaspoon salt, ¼ teaspoon pepper, and cream of tartar in large bowl.

2. Gently knead beef, garlic, ¾ teaspoon salt, and ½ teaspoon pepper together in bowl until well combined. Shape beef mixture into four ¾-inch-thick patties and press shallow divot in center of each. Heat 2 teaspoons oil in 12-inch nonstick skillet over high heat until just smoking. Transfer burgers to skillet and cook without moving them for 2 minutes. Flip burgers and cook for 2 minutes on second side. Transfer to rimmed baking sheet, place 1 slice of cheese on each burger, and bake until burgers register 125 degrees (for medium-rare), about 5 minutes.

3. Meanwhile, wipe skillet clean and heat remaining 2 cups oil over medium-high heat to 350 degrees. Drain onion rings and toss in flour mixture until evenly coated. Fry onion rings, stirring occasionally, until golden brown and crisp, about 5 minutes. Transfer to paper towel–lined plate. Place burgers on bun bottoms, add desired condiments, and top with onion rings. Serve.

BONELESS PORK CHOPS WITH MANGO-MINT SALSA
Serves 4

WHY THIS RECIPE WORKS: Frozen mango is always ripe and already peeled, making this salsa a quick and delicious side to the pan-seared pork.

- 10 ounces (1½ cups) frozen mango, thawed and chopped fine
- ¼ cup olive oil
- 3 tablespoons lime juice (2 limes)
- 1 jalapeño chile, stemmed, seeded, and minced
- 2 tablespoons chopped fresh mint
  Salt and pepper
- 4 (8-ounce) boneless pork chops, ¾ to 1 inch thick, trimmed

1. Combine mango, 3 tablespoons oil, lime juice, jalapeño, and mint in bowl. Season with salt and pepper to taste.

2. Pat chops dry with paper towels and season with salt and pepper. Heat remaining 1 tablespoon oil in 12-inch nonstick skillet over medium-high heat until just smoking. Cook chops until well browned and meat registers 145 degrees, about 5 minutes per side. Transfer to platter, tent loosely with aluminum foil, and let rest for 5 minutes. Serve chops with mango-mint salsa.

TEST KITCHEN NOTE: You can substitute one fresh mango for the frozen mango.

Chicken Noodle Casserole

This creamy, homey casserole is a surefire dinner-table pleaser—if you can keep the noodles and the chicken from overcooking. BY CAROLYNN PURPURA MACKAY

PLENTY HAVE GONE before us riffing on chicken noodle casserole, a recipe first conceived and developed by the Campbell's company in the 1940s as a way to boost sales of its canned condensed soup. The simplest (and in my opinion, scariest) version I found of this classic casserole called for canned condensed soup, canned vegetables, and canned chicken. Gloppy, bland, and gross, it didn't justify even the minimal effort involved. But creamy, satisfying casseroles are our stock-in-trade in the Country; I was confident we were the right folks for this job.

Since the test kitchen had already figured out a replacement for canned soup in its recipe for tuna noodle casserole, and since the two recipes are similar, I decided to start with it. Instead of canned chicken (it's precooked, like canned tuna), I used store-bought rotisserie chicken, which plenty of recipes call for, and then I loosely followed the instructions for tuna noodle casserole.

I sautéed some diced onion and built a flour-thickened sauce from a little chicken stock (1½ cups) and a lot of half-and-half (3½ cups). I stirred in 1 cup each of cheddar and Monterey Jack cheeses; the diced rotisserie chicken; and cooled, boiled egg noodles (cooked to barely al dente, since they'd continue to cook while the casserole baked). I poured the mixture into a dish, which I stuck in the oven for just 15 minutes. This casserole was a big improvement over the all-canned version. That said, it hadn't translated perfectly from tuna. While the plentiful half-and-half softened the fishy tuna, with milder chicken the sauce was bland. Meanwhile, the chicken itself was tough and rubbery.

To lighten the sauce, I went down on the half-and-half and up on the chicken broth. But this sauce separated—fat helps keep a sauce from breaking—so I'd have to compensate for its loss. I was able to stabilize the sauce by melting in cream cheese, which contains stabilizers that can help prevent curdling, in place of the Monterey Jack. But the tangy flavor was jarring. Casting about for a mellower cheese that also has stabilizers, I landed on American cheese. Ultimately, a combination of American and cheddar cheeses, plus 2½ cups each of half-and-half and chicken broth, yielded a tasty, lighter, but still cohesive sauce.

For crunch and extra richness, we top our creamy casserole with crushed Ritz Crackers.

Now how to fix the rubbery chicken? When I tried raw chicken in the casserole, it didn't cook through. But the rotisserie chicken overcooked during its round in the oven. It was a Catch-22. Hang on . . . what if we abandoned the rotisserie chicken and instead cooked raw chicken on the stovetop, slightly undercooking it, before stirring it into the casserole to gently finish in the oven? White meat was a given. All recipes for chicken noodle casserole use it, and it suits this old-fashioned dish. I settled on boneless, skinless chicken breasts and employed a method the test kitchen has used with success before, namely poaching the meat in the thickened cream sauce, stopping just before it is cooked through, and then cubing it.

It worked here (and, as a bonus, added nice chicken flavor to the sauce). A few tests later, I opted to shred (not cube) the chicken so that it would meld better with the other ingredients. My method—some 10 minutes of hands-off poaching—was barely more work than if I had bought a rotisserie chicken.

I had two more decisions to make: the vegetables and a crunchy topping. Recipes variously call for peas, carrots, peppers, celery, and mushrooms. All tasted fine, but our favorite was a combination of peas and red bell peppers. For the topping, after testing the usual (and some unusual) suspects, I landed on Ritz Crackers. Buttery, crunchy, and retro, they suited this creamy, cheesy comfort casserole perfectly.

CHICKEN NOODLE CASSEROLE
Serves 8 to 10

Cooking the egg noodles until just al dente and then shocking them in cold water prevents them from overcooking.

- 12 ounces (7¾ cups) wide egg noodles
  Salt and pepper
- 3 tablespoons unsalted butter
- 1 red bell pepper, stemmed, seeded, and chopped fine
- 1 onion, chopped fine
- 3 tablespoons all-purpose flour
- 2½ cups half-and-half
- 2½ cups low-sodium chicken broth
- 1 pound boneless, skinless chicken breasts, halved lengthwise and trimmed
- 4 ounces deli American cheese, chopped coarse
- 4 ounces sharp cheddar cheese, shredded (1 cup)
- 1½ cups frozen peas
- 25 Ritz Crackers, crushed coarse

1. Bring 4 quarts water to boil in Dutch oven. Add noodles and 1 tablespoon salt and cook, stirring often, until just al dente, about 3 minutes. Drain noodles and rinse with cold water until cool, about 2 minutes. Drain again and set aside.

2. Melt 1 tablespoon butter in now-empty pot over medium-high heat. Add bell pepper and onion and cook, stirring occasionally, until softened, about 5 minutes. Transfer to bowl; set aside. In now-empty pot, melt remaining 2 tablespoons butter over medium heat. Add flour and cook, whisking constantly, for 1 minute. Slowly whisk in half-and-half and broth and bring to boil. Reduce heat to medium-low and simmer until slightly thickened, about 5 minutes. Add chicken and cook until no longer pink, 8 to 10 minutes.

3. Adjust oven rack to upper-middle position and heat oven to 425 degrees. Remove pot from heat, transfer chicken to plate, and shred into bite-size pieces once cool enough to handle. Whisk American and cheddar cheeses into sauce until smooth. Stir shredded chicken, noodles, bell pepper mixture, peas, 1½ teaspoons salt, and 1¼ teaspoons pepper into cheese sauce.

4. Transfer mixture to 13 by 9-inch baking dish and top with crackers. Bake until golden brown and bubbling, about 15 minutes. Let casserole cool on wire rack for 10 minutes. Serve.

Milk-Can Supper

Cowboys used to set a big milk can loaded with meat and vegetables over a campfire to cook. Could we adapt this open-range meal for your kitchen range? BY NICK IVERSON

A MILK-CAN SUPPER IS the cowboy equivalent of all-in-one meals like the New England clambake or the Low-Country shrimp boil. In this case, everything—enough meat (usually sausage) and vegetables to feed a crowd—is cooked together in a 10-gallon milk can over a campfire. The ingredients for a milk-can supper are layered in the pot according to their cooking times: Items that need more cooking go in toward the bottom, where the pot will be hotter, while more delicate ingredients get piled in toward the top. If all goes according to plan, the flavors mingle, all the ingredients are done at the same time, and the meal is enjoyed with a minimum of fuss and ceremony. It's a quick, easy, and inexpensive crowd-pleaser.

Like many such folk dishes, milk-can supper derived from a combination of necessity and hospitality. Before the days of refrigerated train cars and 18-wheelers, cowboys drove large herds of cattle north from Texas by horseback to the railroad lines in the northern plains. Cattle became big business in the plains, and with the boom came the need for more open range. Ranchers set their gaze toward the relatively untouched grasslands of Nebraska, South Dakota, and Wyoming to establish new ranches. Some of the busiest times on these ranches were branding days. Ranchers showed their appreciation to all who lent a hand by offering supper—often cooked in the giant tin cans used for milk delivery to accommodate the huge amount of food. Local home cooks soon started cooking large meals in the cans, and a tradition was born.

I don't own a ranch, I have no cowhands to feed, and I don't live in the plains states. Still, a milk-can supper sounded like fun. I was excited to cook this dish for myself (on the stovetop, not an open fire). To do so, I'd need to get my hands on a milk can. Luckily that was a simple matter of searching online; I found a company out of Nebraska that sells stainless steel milk cans for cooking. I ordered the modest 1-gallon can (which feeds about six people; the company sells much bigger cans). When it arrived, I was happy to see that it came with a recipe for a traditional milk-can supper. After adding this recipe to the others that I had collected, I got busy

You need a big, deep serving vessel for our Milk-Can Supper; we didn't cook it in a roasting pan, but it makes sense to serve it in one.

prepping ingredients in the test kitchen.

In the old days, cooks would line the bottom of the can with rocks to keep the food from scorching; instead, the manufacturer of my shiny new can recommended using canning rings to elevate the food, so I loaded them in. Then came the long-cooking vegetables that were standard in all milk-can supper recipes: cabbage, corn, and potatoes. After that, recipes vary widely in terms of what other vegetables they call for.

I settled on the most common, piling in onion, carrots, celery, summer squash, bell peppers, sweet potatoes, and broccoli. Following the standard operating procedure of most recipes, I placed a few pounds of bratwurst on top, poured in a bottle of Bud, and brought it all to a boil on the stovetop. At this point I turned down the heat, put on the lid, and let the lot cook for 30 minutes. Then I poured the contents into a large roasting pan (I didn't have a serving

platter big enough to corral all that food) and called over my tasters.

To be honest, I was expecting mushy, watery vegetables and gray, spent bratwurst. To our surprise, many of the vegetables were perfectly tender, and the savory juice from the cooking bratwurst had dripped down and infused the vegetables with meaty flavor and deep seasoning. Still, there were a few issues to work through. Even with the sausage seasoning the other ingredients, my

A: A big metal can that, back in the day, farmers used to transport milk from the farm to the dairy, where the milk would be processed.

milk-can supper needed more baseline flavor. Beyond that, certain vegetables were problematic. The summer squash and peppers had turned to mush—they cooked faster than the other vegetables and fell apart. I'd omit the squash moving forward (it didn't add much flavor), but my tasters lobbied to keep the green bell peppers, so next time I'd add them partway through cooking. Also, all those vegetables created a mishmash of flavors. With input from my tasters, I nixed the celery, sweet potatoes, and broccoli.

After starting my next test in a Dutch oven, I immediately realized that the pot was going to have trouble accommodating all the ingredients. I wondered if I could save a little room by leaving out

the canning rings and placing sturdy red potatoes on the bottom of the pot. It worked well; the potatoes protected the other vegetables without burning. For more flavor, I added garlic, thyme, and a couple of bay leaves to the mix with good results. Next I tested the liquid that I was adding. I had been using American lager, which is traditional, but now I pitted it against four other liquids: dark ale, chicken stock, plain water, and white wine (which might not be very "cowboy," but hey, I went to culinary school). The cowboys were right: The lager was the clear winner, as it added a balanced, toasty depth that the other liquids didn't. (The cowboys probably didn't call it "toasty depth" either.)

So far so good. But I still needed to bump up the overall flavor. Could the sausages do a little more in this regard? Maybe, I thought, I could coax more flavor out of those bratwursts by browning them first. It turned out that I could, and this step also created tasty fond on the bottom of the pot that was released into the cooking liquid to nice effect. Plus, the browned sausages looked much more appealing than they had when they were simply steamed.

I made one more batch. I browned the brats, removed them from the pot, and cut them in half (so they'd release more juices to flavor the pot); I layered in the potatoes, cabbage, and corn and then the carrots, onion, garlic, thyme sprigs, and bay leaves. I poured in the beer; put the browned, sliced brats on top of everything; and turned on the burner. After 15 minutes, I added the quick-cooking bell peppers. After another 15 minutes, I emptied the Dutch oven into a roasting pan to serve, reserving some of the juices for passing

at the table. I called over my tasters for one (hopefully) final tasting. Though we hadn't worked up a big, cowboy-size appetite rounding up and branding cattle, we loved this milk-can supper: The vegetables were tender, the brats juicy, and the flavor delicious. Altogether, this dinner was unfussy and just plain fun to eat—no milk can or branding irons necessary.

MILK-CAN SUPPER
Serves 6 to 8
If your Dutch oven is slightly smaller than 8 quarts, the lid may not close all the way when you start cooking. But as the contents of the pot cook, they will decrease in volume, so you'll soon be able to clamp on the lid. Use small red potatoes, measuring 1 to 2 inches in diameter. Light-bodied American lagers, such as Budweiser, work best in this recipe.

- 1 tablespoon vegetable oil
- 2½ pounds bratwurst (10 sausages)
- 2 pounds small red potatoes, unpeeled
- 1 head green cabbage (2 pounds), cored and cut into 8 wedges
- 3 ears corn, husks and silk removed, ears cut into 3 pieces
- 6 carrots, peeled and cut into 2-inch pieces
- 1 onion, halved and cut through root end into 8 wedges
- 4 garlic cloves, peeled and smashed
- 10 sprigs fresh thyme
- 2 bay leaves
  Salt and pepper
- 1½ cups beer
- 2 green bell peppers, stemmed, seeded, and cut into 1-inch-wide strips

1. Heat oil in 8-quart Dutch oven over medium heat until shimmering. Add bratwurst and cook until browned all over, 6 to 8 minutes. Remove pot from heat. Transfer bratwurst to cutting board and halve crosswise.

2. Place potatoes in single layer in now-empty Dutch oven. Arrange cabbage wedges in single layer on top of potatoes. Layer corn, carrots, onion, garlic, thyme, bay leaves, 1 teaspoon salt, and ½ teaspoon pepper over cabbage. Pour beer over vegetables and arrange browned bratwursts on top.

3. Bring to boil over medium-high heat (wisps of steam will be visible). Cover, reduce heat to medium, and simmer for 15 minutes. Add bell peppers and continue to simmer, covered, until potatoes are tender, about 15 minutes. (Use long skewer to test potatoes for doneness.)

4. Transfer bratwurst and vegetables to large serving platter (or roasting pan, if your platter isn't large enough); discard thyme sprigs and bay leaves. Pour 1 cup cooking liquid over platter. Season with salt and pepper to taste. Serve, passing remaining cooking liquid separately.

TEST KITCHEN TECHNIQUE **Layers of Flavor**
Cooking all the vegetables and sausage in one pot has advantages: It's easy, the flavors mingle, and the beer and sausage drippings season the lot. But you have to plan ahead to make sure that everything is done at the same time. Knowing that the pot is hottest at the bottom (closest to the heat source), we put the longest-cooking items in first and layer everything else accordingly.

TAKE IT FROM THE BOTTOM
Potatoes, cabbage, corn, carrots, onions, bratwurst, and peppers (added halfway through).

Braciole

What cut of beef to use? What to stuff it with? How to develop the flavor yet minimize the work?
These were just a few of the questions we explored while perfecting this Italian American classic. BY DIANE UNGER

I
F YOU GREW up in an Italian American household (especially if your old-country ancestors came from southern Italy), you know braciole. You most likely ate it for supper as part of "Sunday gravy," a long-simmered tomato sauce that's also packed with meatballs and sausage. If you're not familiar with this dish, you're in for a real treat. The basic description—rolled, stuffed beef that is browned and simmered in tomato sauce—doesn't do justice to its savory deliciousness. (And by the way, it's pronounced "brah-ZHUL.")

There are as many versions as there are Italian grandmothers. To get a handle on them, I questioned Italian American colleagues and trolled the test kitchen's cookbook library. Of the dozens of recipes I found, I selected five that represented different braciole techniques and variations, and then I slipped on my chef's jacket and got busy. After a few days of rolling, stuffing, searing, and braising, I plated my five versions and convened my tasters. What did we learn?

Although all of the recipes used beef, there were cuts from the chuck, rump, flank, and brisket; there were delicately bundled mini-steaks and huge roasts pounded out to the size of pillowcases; fillings were based on bread, herbs, vegetables, and/or cheese; and the tomato sauces seemed to function merely as color accents—they didn't have much flavor. Furthermore, some of the meats were stringy and chewy and tasted washed-out. And last, some of these recipes were a lot of work. On the plus side, I had no trouble coming up with goals: tender, flavorful beef; a filling with some zip; and plenty of tasty tomato sauce—all with a minimum of fuss and effort.

First, I'd determine what cut of beef to use. Making little bundles of individually sized braciole was tedious; I'd make one large braciole and slice it into portions. In my initial tests, brisket took too long to tenderize, so that was out. Top round, bottom round, and chuck-eye steaks had shown promise as smaller rolls, so I tested those cuts in roast form (butchering and/or pounding about 2 pounds of each into big sheets) against flank steak, our favorite larger cut from our original five-recipe test. I rolled each

We brush the steak with garlic oil before stuffing it with a mixture of raisins, Parmesan, herbs, more garlic, and red pepper flakes.

one up (for now I was working without filling), tied them with kitchen twine, seared them in a skillet, poured crushed tomatoes over them, covered them, and braised them over a low flame until they were tender. The flank steak was beefy and the most tender of the steaks that I tested (although not perfectly so), and hence it was the winner.

On to the filling. My tasters voiced strong opinions about the stuffings they had tried. Stuffings based on bread or

bread crumbs were stodgy. Stuffings with vegetables tasted steamed and bland. At first it was a mystery to me why they deemed one nonvegetable stuffing bland, as I had put cups of cheese in there. But when I took a look, I saw that the cheese had melted out of the meat altogether. To keep the flank steak the focus, the sausage had to go, too. Over several tests, I fiddled with ingredients, eventually landing on a simple stir-together filling of raisins

(common in savory southern Italian dishes), Parmesan, fresh herbs, lots of garlic, oregano, and red pepper flakes. I chopped the raisins because the smaller pieces were less apt to fall out when I rolled up the meat. Also, brushing the meat with olive oil before spreading on the filling helped it adhere, both while I was rolling up the meat and later when it came time to slice the braciole.

With the filling figured out, I turned to fine-tuning my recipe steps. The techniques that I'd seen in braciole recipes were as varied as the ingredients; I'd run through them all to sort out the best. For starters, some recipes don't brown the braciole at all before braising, while others call for a deep, dark sear. I found that the middle ground—a nice light brown color all over—worked best to add flavor without toughening the meat. Likewise, cooking times and meat rest periods ran the gamut. I got the best results—tender, moist, and flavorful braciole—from cooking the dish covered for 1½ hours in a low oven and then resting the meat in the sauce for another 30 minutes. To get good garlic flavor without having to worry about bits of minced garlic burning, I came up with my own innovation: I made a quick garlic-infused oil in the microwave, which I used to sauté the onion for the tomato sauce (using the same pan in which I'd browned the meat) as well as to brush on the raw meat. I patted myself on the back for adding my own touch to this old and esteemed recipe.

After working through these details, I called over tasters to sample what I hoped was the finished product. From the bold, tangy, spicy sauce and the big, beefy slices of moist meat to the occasional sweet raisin nugget, the dish was a hit. To add to its appeal, I could make it ahead. And I discovered something else the day after my testing was done: The leftovers taste even better.

BRACIOLE
Serves 4 to 6
Look for flank steak of even thickness, without tapered ends. Braciole is usually served with pasta, sometimes together and sometimes separately, as when a pasta course with the sauce is followed by the meat. Our recipe makes enough sauce for at least 1 pound of pasta.

- 1 (2-pound) flank steak, trimmed
- 10 garlic cloves, sliced thin
- ¼ cup extra-virgin olive oil
- ½ cup golden raisins, chopped coarse
- 1 ounce Parmesan cheese, grated (½ cup), plus extra for serving
- ½ cup chopped fresh basil
- ¼ cup chopped fresh parsley
- 1 teaspoon dried oregano
- ½ teaspoon red pepper flakes
  Salt and pepper
- 1 onion, chopped
- 3 tablespoons tomato paste
- 2 (28-ounce) cans crushed tomatoes

1. Adjust oven rack to middle position and heat oven to 325 degrees. Position steak on cutting board so long edge is parallel to counter edge. Cover with plastic wrap and pound to even ½-inch thickness. Trim any ragged edges to create rough rectangle about 11 by 9 inches. Pat steak dry with paper towels.

2. Combine garlic and oil in bowl and microwave until fragrant, about 1 minute. Let cool slightly, then remove garlic from oil with fork. Separately reserve garlic and garlic oil. Combine raisins, Parmesan, ¼ cup basil, parsley, half of garlic, ½ teaspoon oregano, and ¼ teaspoon pepper flakes in bowl.

3. Brush exposed side of steak with 1 tablespoon garlic oil and season with ½ teaspoon salt and ¾ teaspoon pepper. Spread raisin mixture evenly over steak, pressing to adhere, leaving 1-inch border along top edge. Starting from bottom edge and rolling away from you, roll steak into tight log, finally resting seam side down. Tie kitchen twine around braciole at 1-inch intervals.

4. Heat 1 tablespoon garlic oil in 12-inch nonstick skillet over medium-high heat until just smoking. Add braciole, seam side down, and cook until lightly browned all over, about 5 minutes. Transfer to 13 by 9-inch baking dish.

5. Reduce heat to medium and add onion, remaining garlic oil, remaining ½ teaspoon oregano, and remaining ¼ teaspoon pepper flakes to now-empty skillet. Cook until onion just begins to soften, about 3 minutes. Stir in tomato paste and remaining half of garlic and cook until fragrant and tomato paste is lightly browned, about 1 minute. Stir in tomatoes, bring to simmer, and pour sauce over braciole. Cover dish tightly with aluminum foil and bake until fork slips easily in and out of braciole, 1½ to 1¾ hours. Transfer baking dish to wire rack, spoon sauce over braciole, re-cover, and let rest in sauce for 30 minutes.

6. Transfer braciole to carving board, seam side down; cut and discard twine; and cut into ¾-inch-thick slices. Stir remaining ¼ cup basil into sauce and season with salt and pepper to taste. Ladle 2 cups sauce onto serving platter. Transfer braciole slices to platter. Serve, passing remaining sauce and extra Parmesan separately.

TO MAKE AHEAD Follow recipe through step 5, letting braciole cool completely in sauce. Refrigerate braciole and sauce separately. To serve, adjust oven rack to middle position and heat oven to 350 degrees. Bring sauce to simmer over medium heat in large saucepan. Stir remaining ¼ cup basil into sauce and season with salt and pepper to taste. Transfer braciole to carving board, seam side down; discard twine; and cut into ¾-inch-thick slices. Pour 2 cups sauce into 13 by 9-inch baking dish. Arrange braciole slices on top of sauce, cover tightly with aluminum foil, and bake until meat is heated through, about 15 minutes. Serve, passing remaining sauce separately.

RATING TWINES AND TIES

Kitchen twine is indispensable for trussing whole chickens, tying roasts and rolled stuffed meats, and making bundles of herbs for flavoring stews. (Never cook with twines that aren't specifically labeled "kitchen" or "food-safe.") Does it matter which kind you use? And what about reusable food ties made of silicone? We tested cotton and linen kitchen twine as well as two brands of silicone food ties, using them on stuffed 11-inch-long flank steaks for braciole and to truss chickens. When all was said and done, nothing beat cotton twine. It never frayed, singed, split, or broke, and it stayed put when we tied knots. It's inexpensive and efficient. Linen twine worked equally well but was more expensive. We'll stick with Librett Cotton Butcher's Twine for our cooking needs. –AMY GRAVES

KEY **Good** ★★★ **Fair** ★★ **Poor** ★

HIGHLY RECOMMENDED	CRITERIA		TESTERS' NOTES
LIBRETT Cotton Butcher's Twine **Price:** $8.29 (2 cents per foot) **Material:** cotton **Source:** lifeandhome.com	Ease of Use Performance	★★★ ★★★	This ball of 100 percent cotton twine tied and held foods without burning, fraying, splitting, or breaking. It made neat, even ties around braciole and whole chicken and stayed in place without slipping. Although any cotton twine might perform as well, this brand releases string from the center of the ball, letting us pay it out with no danger of it rolling off the counter.

RECOMMENDED

FRENCH LINEN Butcher's Twine **Price:** $9.99 (3 cents per foot) **Material:** linen **Source:** cutleryandmore.com	Ease of Use Performance	★★★ ★★★	This compact ball of linen twine comes in a clear plastic container with an opening for the string and a small blade for portioning lengths, but we still needed our kitchen shears to snip off ends after tying. Thinner than cotton twine and slightly more expensive, linen proved just as strong and simple to use.

RECOMMENDED WITH RESERVATIONS

TRUDEAU Food Tie Wraps **Price:** $14.20; reusable **Material:** silicone; heat resistant to 480 degrees 	Ease of Use Performance	★★ ★★	These flexible, stretchy, 11-inch silicone ties come in a set of six—not enough to tie our braciole at 1-inch intervals. Using a tab and loop mechanism, they were easier to tie than another silicone product but proved slippery. The ties didn't melt in a hot skillet or a 450-degree oven, and we could pull and secure them to truss a chicken evenly for uniform roasting.

NOT RECOMMENDED

FUSIONBRANDS The FoodLoop Trussing Tool **Price:** $10; reusable **Material:** silicone; heat resistant to 675 degrees 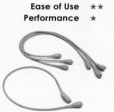	Ease of Use Performance	★★ ★	Although they held up to searing in a hot pan and roasting in a 450-degree oven, we needed more than one set of four textured 13½-inch silicone ties to tie our braciole at 1-inch intervals. Spaced 2 inches apart, they let the rolled meat bulge in between and left ugly indentations. As for trussing a chicken, these loops pulled the legs to one side as we tightened the cinch, making the bird lean, which resulted in lopsided roasting.

KEY STEPS **Building Your Braciole**
Here's how to get tender meat that holds the filling in place.

POUND IT OUT
Trim a 2-pound flank steak of excess fat and then pound it to an even ½-inch thickness.

STUFF AND ROLL
Brush the steak with garlic oil, season it, spread on the stuffing, and roll tightly.

TIE IT UP
After you've rolled the steak into a spiral, use kitchen twine to tie it into a tight cylinder.

Dakota Bread

This big, multigrain loaf from America's breadbasket presented the usual multigrain baking challenge: producing a hearty loaf, not a leaden one. BY CRISTIN WALSH

IN 1989, NORTH DAKOTA celebrated the 100th anniversary of its statehood in a manner that we here at *Cook's Country* heartily approve: with a recipe. Dakota bread—chock-full of whole-wheat and rye flours, barley, oats, sunflower seeds, and more—was created as a tribute to the state's bountiful harvest. It is also a rustic, hearty, and truly delicious loaf.

I rounded up some recipes. Even before I mixed, kneaded, shaped, and baked my way through them, I was taken aback by the lengthy lists of ingredients. Recipes called for so many types of flours, grains, and seeds that I'd need a granary instead of a pantry. But how could I streamline without losing its complex, nutty taste and moist and chewy texture? As I made the bread, other questions arose: Which flours were best? Recipes called for all sorts. How long to let the dough rise? Again, recipes ran the gamut. Naturally, these recipes produced quite different results, too. Some doughs yielded loaves that were closer to airy white sandwich bread than to multigrain bread. Other doughs made for heavy, dense loaves. My version would meet in the middle, with a hearty yet light crumb and a pared-down ingredient list that still captured the many flavors and textures that made this bread so appealing in the first place.

I put together a working recipe that picked up the features we liked best from my initial test. My first order of business was to trim back the ingredients. Fortunately, I already had an idea: seven-grain cereal, which I figured could provide a multigrain fix in a single, easy package. I made a loaf using all-purpose flour (for now) in combination with the cereal—tallying up the amount of individual grains and non-white flours and replacing the lot with the same volume of cereal. I found that I needed to soften the cereal first, so I soaked it in warm water for 10 minutes before making the dough; while I was at it, I added the other wet ingredients—oil and honey—too.

I did a few more tests to work out the best ratio of cereal to flour. With 1½ cups of cereal combined with 3½ cups of the all-purpose flour (plus seeds added at the end of kneading), this Dakota bread had a wholesome flavor and was pleasantly coarse. Alas, the loaf was somewhat flat and saggy; it got

little to no gluten (which is what gives dough elasticity and structure) from the grains in the seven-grain cereal. I didn't want to cut back on the grains—that was the whole point, after all—so I hoped that using a different type of flour would help. I was pretty sure that whole-wheat flour would only make the problem worse, as the bran in the flour inhibits gluten development. That's why 100 percent whole-wheat flour breads are so often heavy and dense. But (white) bread flour is designed to maximize gluten development. Sure enough, bread flour combined with the seven-grain cereal made a strong, flexible dough and bread with a tender, light crumb.

Even with the bread flour, I knew that this dough would still need all the

This hearty, easy bread is topped with seeds: pepitas, sunflower, sesame, and poppy.

help it could get in order to rise and form a tall, domed loaf rather than a short, squat one. My first step was to bake it at a toasty 425 degrees. The nice, hot oven would aid "oven spring," a term for the fast expansion of bread dough in the first few minutes of baking, thanks to an initial blast of hot air and steam that encourages the gasses inside dough to swell. I learned the hard way that it also encourages burning; the seeds on the top of the loaf were especially vulnerable. Things worked better when I preheated the oven to 425 and then dropped it to 375 as soon as I put in the dough to bake. But I still had a problem. The crust of the loaf set too quickly in the still-quite-hot oven, which meant that the dough couldn't take

advantage of oven spring. To address that, I put a loaf pan in the bottom of the oven and filled it with boiling water. The humidity from the water kept the dough moist, allowing it to rise impressively high before the crust set.

I baked a final loaf. The smell was awesome, and the loaf emerged from the oven tall, round, and even, with a beautiful brown sheen. When I cut into it, I was pleased to see that the grain-speckled crumb was even and tight. Best of all, it tasted fantastic. This Dakota bread was definitely something to celebrate.

DAKOTA BREAD
Makes one 10-inch loaf
In step 2, if the dough is still sticking to the sides of the mixing bowl after 2 minutes, add more flour 1 tablespoon at a time, up to 3 tablespoons. Be sure to use hot cereal mix, not boxed cold breakfast cereals, which may also be labeled "seven-grain."

- 2   cups warm water (110 degrees)
- 1½ cups (7½ ounces) seven-grain hot cereal mix
- 2   tablespoons honey
- 2   tablespoons vegetable oil
- 3½ cups (19¼ ounces) bread flour
- 1¾ teaspoons salt
- 1   teaspoon instant or rapid-rise yeast
- 3   tablespoons raw, unsalted pepitas
- 3   tablespoons raw, unsalted sunflower seeds
- 1   teaspoon sesame seeds
- 1   teaspoon poppy seeds
- 1   large egg, lightly beaten

1. Grease large bowl. Line rimmed baking sheet with parchment paper. In bowl of stand mixer, combine water, cereal, honey, and oil and let sit for 10 minutes.

2. Add flour, salt, and yeast to cereal mixture. Fit stand mixer with dough hook and knead on low speed until dough is smooth and elastic, 4 to 6 minutes. Add 2 tablespoons pepitas and 2 tablespoons sunflower seeds to dough and knead for 1 minute longer. Turn out dough onto lightly floured counter and knead until seeds are evenly distributed, about 2 minutes.

3. Transfer dough to greased bowl and cover with plastic wrap. Let dough rise at room temperature until almost doubled in size and fingertip depression in dough springs back slowly, 60 to 90 minutes.

4. Gently press down on center of dough to deflate. Transfer dough to lightly floured counter and shape into tight round ball. Place dough on prepared sheet. Cover dough loosely with plastic and let rise at room temperature until almost doubled in size, 60 to 90 minutes.

5. Adjust oven racks to upper-middle and lowest positions and heat oven to 425 degrees. Combine remaining 1 tablespoon pepitas, remaining 1 tablespoon sunflower seeds, sesame seeds, and poppy seeds in small bowl. Using sharp knife, make ¼-inch-deep cross, 5 inches long, on top of loaf. Brush loaf with egg and sprinkle seed mixture evenly over top.

6. Place 8½ by 4½-inch loaf pan on lowest oven rack and fill with 1 cup boiling water. Place baking sheet with dough on upper-middle rack and reduce oven to 375 degrees. Bake until crust is dark brown and bread registers 200 degrees, 40 to 50 minutes. Transfer loaf to wire rack and let cool completely, about 2 hours. Serve.

Chocolate Sugar Cookies

Turning a chewy sugar cookie into a chewy *chocolate* sugar cookie takes a little more than simply stirring in chocolate. BY CAROLYNN PURPURA MACKAY

I HAVE A THING for sugar cookies, especially the kind with crisp edges, chewy centers, and crunchy, crackled, sugary tops. The ones I'm talking about require no laborious rolling out—just shape the dough into balls, dip in sugar, flatten, and bake. I hoped to create a chocolate version.

I started with the test kitchen's recipe for chewy brown sugar cookies. It's an unusual recipe: It calls for melted, browned butter, whereas most recipes use ordinary chilled butter. The browning adds flavor, while the melting adds chew. This recipe also uses lots of dark brown sugar and vanilla for extra flavor.

So I mixed 1¾ cups of brown sugar, vanilla, and salt into 14 tablespoons of melted browned butter; then stirred in 1 ounce of cooled, melted chocolate and the eggs; and, lastly, added leavener and 2¼ cups of flour. I repeated this test several times, increasing the amount of chocolate, but by the time the cookies were chocolaty enough (which took 4 ounces), they were no longer chewy. How about cocoa powder? After several experiments, I found that I was able to use 2¼ ounces of cocoa to replace some of the flour (if I used too much cocoa, the cookies crumbled). Fortunately, since cocoa is more intense than bar chocolate, the flavor was just as good despite the reduction—plus, the cookies were chewy again.

Browning the butter was bothersome. I had to watch it like a dog on a squirrel or it would go from brown to burnt in an instant. With so much chocolate, was it even adding anything? I made two new batches of cookies, one with browned butter, the other with merely melted. As it turned out, few of us could tell the difference.

My chocolate sugar cookie recipe had come together quickly, but one problem remained. The results were inconsistent from batch to batch. Blame the butter. If it was too hot when I added it to the dough, the cookies spread too much. To foolproof my recipe, I melted most (but not all) of the butter and then stirred in the remaining cold butter to cool it down.

Using this technique, I was able to produce round, even cookies with deep chocolate flavor; nice chew; and fissured, sugary tops—every time. Now all I needed was a glass of milk.

These cookies get their intense flavor from cocoa and plenty of vanilla and dark brown sugar.

CHOCOLATE SUGAR COOKIES
Makes 24 cookies

- ⅓ cup (2⅓ ounces) granulated sugar
- 1½ cups plus 2 tablespoons (8⅛ ounces) all-purpose flour
- ¾ cup (2¼ ounces) unsweetened cocoa powder
- ½ teaspoon baking soda
- ¼ teaspoon baking powder
- 14 tablespoons unsalted butter
- 1¾ cups packed (12¼ ounces) dark brown sugar
- 1 tablespoon vanilla extract
- ½ teaspoon salt
- 1 large egg plus 1 large yolk

1. Adjust oven rack to middle position and heat oven to 350 degrees. Line 2 baking sheets with parchment paper. Place granulated sugar in shallow dish; set aside. Combine flour, cocoa, baking soda, and baking powder in bowl.

2. Microwave 10 tablespoons butter, covered, in large bowl until melted, about 1 minute. Remove from microwave and stir in remaining 4 tablespoons butter until melted. Allow butter to cool to 90 to 95 degrees, about 5 minutes.

3. Whisk brown sugar, vanilla, and salt into butter until no lumps remain, scraping down bowl as needed. Whisk in egg and yolk until smooth. Stir in flour mixture until just combined.

4. Working with 2 tablespoons dough at a time, roll into balls. Working in batches, roll balls in granulated sugar and divide between baking sheets. Using bottom of drinking glass, flatten cookies to 2 inches in diameter. Sprinkle each sheet of cookies with 1½ teaspoons remaining granulated sugar.

5. Bake 1 sheet at a time until cookies are slightly puffy and edges have begun to set, about 15 minutes, rotating sheet halfway through baking (cookies will look slightly underdone between cracks). Let cookies cool on sheets for 5 minutes, then transfer to wire rack. Let cookies cool completely before serving.

Cooking Class Sheet Pan Pizza

Also called Sicilian or cafeteria-style pizza, sheet pan pizza is delicious, feeds a crowd, and is much less fussy than thin-crust pizza. Lengthy fermenting times, pizza stones, and super-hot ovens not required. BY SCOTT KATHAN

SHEET PAN PIZZA

Serves 12

After it's mixed in step 1, the dough will be very sticky, so coat your hands with flour before you move it to the greased bowl. The test kitchen's favorite brand of tomato paste is Goya. The fresh basil is important here; if all you have is dried, skip the basil altogether.

DOUGH

- 1¾ cups warm water (110 degrees)
- ½ cup plus 1 tablespoon extra-virgin olive oil
- 1 tablespoon sugar
- 5 cups (25 ounces) all-purpose flour
- 4½ teaspoons instant or rapid-rise yeast
- 2 teaspoons salt

SAUCE AND TOPPINGS

- 1 tablespoon extra-virgin olive oil
- 3 garlic cloves, minced
- 1½ teaspoons dried oregano
- ¼ teaspoon red pepper flakes
- 2 tablespoons tomato paste
- 1 (28-ounce) can crushed tomatoes
  Salt
- 3 ounces Parmesan cheese, grated (1½ cups)
- 12 ounces mozzarella cheese, shredded (3 cups)
- 2 tablespoons chopped fresh basil

1. FOR THE DOUGH: Grease large bowl. Combine water, ¼ cup oil, and sugar in 2-cup liquid measuring cup. Using stand mixer fitted with dough hook, mix flour, yeast, and salt on low speed until combined, about 30 seconds. Increase speed to medium-low, add water mixture, and knead until dough is uniform in texture, about 3 minutes. Transfer dough to prepared bowl, cover with plastic wrap, and let rise at room temperature until doubled in size, 1 to 1½ hours.

2. Evenly coat rimmed baking sheet with ¼ cup oil. On lightly floured work surface, use rolling pin to roll dough into 16 by 12-inch rectangle. Transfer dough to prepared sheet and stretch dough to cover sheet, pressing dough into corners. Brush dough evenly with remaining 1 tablespoon oil and cover with plastic. Set in warm spot (not oven) until slightly risen, about 20 minutes.

3. FOR THE SAUCE AND TOPPINGS: While dough rises, heat oil in large saucepan over medium heat until

It takes just minutes to mix and knead the dough for this pizza in the mixer.

shimmering. Cook garlic, oregano, and pepper flakes until fragrant, about 30 seconds. Stir in tomato paste and cook until just beginning to brown, about 2 minutes. Add tomatoes and simmer until reduced to 3 cups, about 10 minutes. Off heat, season with salt to taste.

4. Adjust oven rack to lowest position and heat oven to 450 degrees. Remove plastic and, using your fingers, make indentations all over dough. Sprinkle dough with 1 cup Parmesan and bake until cheese begins to melt, 7 to 10 minutes. Remove sheet from oven and spoon sauce over pizza, leaving 1-inch border. Bake until sauce is deep red and steaming, 7 to 10 minutes.

5. Sprinkle mozzarella and remaining ½ cup Parmesan evenly over sauce and bake until cheese is golden brown, about 12 minutes. Remove pizza from oven and let rest for 5 minutes. Sprinkle with basil. Serve.

MEAT MANIA SHEET PAN PIZZA

While dough rises, cook 1 pound sweet Italian sausage, casings removed, in

12-inch nonstick skillet over medium heat, breaking up pieces with spoon, until no longer pink, about 8 minutes. Transfer to paper towel–lined plate and let cool completely, about 15 minutes. Arrange 3½ ounces thinly sliced deli pepperoni in single layer on separate paper towel–lined plate. Cover with 2 more paper towels and microwave for 1 minute. Let cool completely, about 15 minutes. Once meats have cooled, toss with mozzarella and use this mixture in step 5.

VEGETABLE DELIGHT SHEET PAN PIZZA

While dough rises, heat 1 tablespoon olive oil in 12-inch nonstick skillet over medium-high heat until shimmering. Add 10 ounces white mushrooms, trimmed and sliced thin; 1 stemmed, seeded, and chopped red bell pepper; 1 stemmed, seeded, and chopped green bell pepper; and 1 chopped onion and cook until browned, about 10 minutes. Season with salt and pepper to taste. Transfer to plate and let cool completely, about 15 minutes. Once vegetables have cooled, toss with mozzarella and use this mixture in step 5.

Core Techniques

TEST KITCHEN TIPS FOR ANY SHEET PAN PIZZA

Knead Briefly

Gluten is a protein that's formed in flour that, when activated by moisture, helps give baked goods their structure. Lots of kneading develops lots of gluten, which results in lots of chew, a quality you don't want in dense, tender sheet pan pizza crust. So how do you limit gluten formation in dough? Add oil and restrict kneading. The oil coats the flour granules and hinders the formation of gluten. Keeping the kneading to only about 3 minutes also helps limit the gluten formation to ensure a tender crust.

Make a Rich Dough

Thin-crust pizza doughs get complex flavor from long fermentation (up to four days) and baking on hot pizza stones. Well, not everyone has a pizza stone, and who wants to wait a day (or three) for their pizza? Sheet pan pizza

is ready to eat in just a few hours. To get flavorful crust quickly, we add sugar and olive oil to the dough.

"Oven-Fry" for Flavor

The sugar and olive oil add flavor, but that's not all. In conjunction with extra olive oil on the baking sheet, they help the bottom of the crust "fry" to delicious crispness without a pizza stone. Bake the pizza on the lowest oven rack, which is nearest to the heating element.

12 Steps to Sheet Pan Pizza

1. MAKE DOUGH Mix warm water, oil, sugar, flour, yeast, and salt in a mixer fitted with a dough hook; knead briefly in the machine.
WHY? Kneading builds gluten, which gives dough its structure. For a tender crust, knead for just 3 minutes or so.

2. LET RISE Move the dough to a greased bowl, cover it with plastic wrap, and let it rise at room temperature until it has doubled in size, 1 to 1½ hours.
WHY? All yeast doughs need time to create carbon dioxide, which causes the dough to rise.

3. OIL THE BAKING SHEET Coat the baking sheet with ¼ cup of olive oil.
WHY? This oil, in combination with the oil that's in the dough, helps the bottom of the pizza brown and crisp as it bakes.

4. ROLL AND PRESS Roll the dough into a rectangle, place it on the baking sheet, and stretch and press the dough into the corners.
WHY? This dough is stiff so it requires rolling out before stretching the corners to fully line the baking sheet.

5. LET RISE AGAIN Brush the dough with oil to keep it moist, cover it with plastic, and let it set for 20 minutes.
WHY? This waiting period allows the gluten in the dough to relax, which prevents the dough from shrinking and helps optimize a nice, fast rise in the oven.

6. START SAUCE Sauté garlic, oregano, and red pepper flakes in hot oil for 30 seconds.
WHY? By "blooming" the aromatics, we bring out their full flavor—and with a thick crust like this one, the sauce needs to be potent.

7. BROWN PASTE Stir in tomato paste and brown it lightly, about 2 minutes.
WHY? Browning deepens the flavor of the tomato paste.

8. SIMMER SAUCE Add the canned crushed tomatoes and simmer for 10 minutes.
WHY? Simmering evaporates moisture, in turn thickening the sauce and concentrating its flavor. A thicker sauce reduces the chances of a soggy crust.

9. BAKE WITH PARMESAN Dimple the dough, sprinkle it with Parmesan, and bake it at 450 for 7 to 10 minutes.
WHY? This thick crust needs parbaking. Baking the Parmesan onto the crust creates a ragged surface the sauce can stick to.

10. BAKE WITH SAUCE Remove the pizza from the oven and spoon on the sauce, leaving the edges bare. Bake for 7 to 10 minutes longer.
WHY? The crust needs more parbaking time; for this stretch, we top it with the sauce so it can concentrate even further.

11. FINAL BAKE Top with mozzarella and more Parmesan and bake until done, about 12 more minutes.
WHY? Now that parbaking has firmed up the crust and the sauce has further reduced, it's time to load on the cheese and cook the pizza through.

12. REST AND SLICE Wait 5 minutes before you slice and serve the pizza.
WHY? This oversize pizza needs time to set up and cool slightly so that you can serve tidy squares: If it's too hot when you slice it, the toppings will slide off.

KEY EQUIPMENT
Pizza Wheel
Are all pizza wheels created equal? Absolutely not. In our most recent testing, we found that some wheels made a mess of cutting pizzas: The wheels were dull, uncomfortable, and awkward to use. Our favorite pizza wheel is a 4-inch model from OXO (we also liked their wheel that's designed for nonstick pans). This pizza wheel is sharp and agile, with a comfortable handle and a protective thumb guard—all traits that make it easy to neatly cut any pizza into slices.

OUR FAVORITE WHEEL
OXO Good Grips 4" Pizza Wheel

SHOPPING
Which Parmesan Should You Buy?
In our taste tests, we have found that nothing beats the rich, nutty flavor of authentic Parmigiano-Reggiano cheese, and if price is no object, it is always our first choice (especially when we're eating it on its own or on a cheese plate). But it is expensive; we've discovered that much more affordable American-made Parmesan cheeses are acceptable substitutes in most recipes (including this pizza). Our favorite inexpensive Parmesans are BelGioioso and SarVecchio (formerly Stravecchio); visit **CooksCountry.com/parmesan** to read the full tasting of eight supermarket Parmesans.

DOMESTIC PARMESANS:
BELGIOIOSO AND SARVECCHIO
Fine in most recipes.

Our online cooking school offers personalized instruction in pizza and dozens of other topics. Our program helps home cooks master techniques, not just recipes. For details, including how to start a free 14-day trial membership, visit **OnlineCookingSchool.com**.

Recipe Makeover Eggplant Parmesan

Most eggplant Parmesans are made with so much cheese and crunchy coating that you could swap cardboard for the eggplant and hardly notice. We set out to make a lighter version. BY CAROLYNN PURPURA MACKAY

HOW DO YOU encourage fussy eaters to eat eggplant? One surefire way is to bread and fry it, pour on the tomato sauce, load it up with cheese, and bake it until it's deliciously soft and gooey. Small wonder eggplant Parmesan is so popular—and so in need of a nutritional makeover. A single serving can contain almost 700 calories and 50 grams of fat. I wanted a healthier version of the dish, and incidentally, wouldn't it be nice if you could actually taste the eggplant?

Turns out that recipes already abound for slimmed-down versions, many of which involve baking or grilling eggplant with no breading. Although some of those versions were tasty in their own way, they felt like cheating—what's eggplant Parm without the breading? Having said that, the oven "fry" method—in conjunction with crumbs—did show some promise. For these recipes, the eggplant slices were dipped in egg, coated in crumbs (the best version used a combination of toasted panko and a little oil and Parmesan), and baked in a hot oven until tender within and crunchy without.

I gave this method a shot, using beaten egg whites instead of whole eggs to reduce fat; the eggplant looked great as I pulled it out of the oven. Then, following standard protocol, I spread sauce (I used a test kitchen quick marinara recipe modified to incorporate only a tablespoon of olive oil) in the bottom of a baking dish, layered in the crisp eggplant, spooned in more sauce, sprinkled on cheese, and then repeated the layering. After the casserole finished baking, my tasters dug in. The once-crisp coating was soggy. Not good.

I was absentmindedly prodding this failed version with a fork and thinking about what had gone wrong when it occurred to me that I needed to be more strategic about how I layered in the sauce, since the breaded eggplant had obviously absorbed too much moisture from it. Not wanting to cut back on the 3 cups that I was using, however, I began by bottom-loading the dish with 1½ cups of sauce. Then I used just ¾ cup of sauce each for the upper two layers, dolloping the sauce in the center of each eggplant slice to avoid a sodden blanket over the vegetable. I topped the casserole with cheese and baked it for about 10 minutes. After the

casserole cooled slightly, I portioned some out and tasted a forkful, eager to see whether the new infrastructure had succeeded. The eggplant on top of the casserole was perfect—crisp at the edges where the breading was exposed and saucy and cheesy in the middle.

The bottom layer of eggplant, however, hadn't fared as well—the breading, once crispy, was still mushy and pasty. But my tasters were so happy with the top layer that several wondered if the bottom layer of eggplant needed breading at all. Less breading means less fat and fewer calories, so I was eager to give it a try. I made another version with the bottom layer of eggplant baked naked (with a little vegetable oil spray) and the top layer breaded and baked. I assembled the casserole as before and cooked it. It was delicious, and, happily, we didn't miss the breading on the bottom layer of eggplant. The top of the top layer of eggplant was so nice and crisp, though, that I couldn't help noticing that its underside suffered from soggy bottom syndrome. I tried breading just one side of the eggplant and baking it crumb side up. With just one surface—at the very top of the casserole—of the two layers of eggplant now breaded, this casserole was the best yet.

With less breading, you could actually tell you were eating a vegetable, but there was still enough crunch on top to make it register as a traditional eggplant Parmesan. I'd managed to cut 320 calories and 31 grams of fat. But I knew I had really succeeded when I did a final side-by-side test with my healthy version and the original fried full-fat version. We liked the healthy version better, praising its crunch, its real eggplant flavor, and the lack of greasiness. Who says low-fat has to taste like diet food?

The Numbers

Traditional Eggplant Parmesan
All nutritional information is for one serving.
CALORIES **680**
FAT **47 g**   SATURATED FAT **10 g**

Cook's Country **Reduced-Fat Eggplant Parmesan**
CALORIES **360**
FAT **16 g**   SATURATED FAT **7 g**

Full-fat versions can be greasy and sloppy. Our low-fat eggplant Parm is firm, bright, and tasty.

How It Stacks Up
We lose the deep fry and the egg yolks, minimize the cheese, and bread just the uppermost surface of the eggplant. Here's how it comes together.

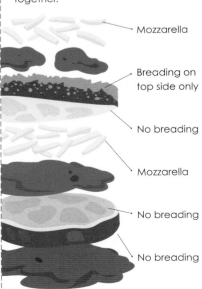

- Mozzarella
- Breading on top side only
- No breading
- Mozzarella
- No breading
- No breading

REDUCED-FAT EGGPLANT PARMESAN
Serves 6
Measure the eggplant slices when slicing. Breading just half of the eggplant slices, and on just one side, saves on calories. We recommend two brands of crushed tomatoes: Muir Glen Organic Crushed Tomatoes with Basil and Tuttorosso Crushed Tomatoes in Thick Puree with Basil.

    Vegetable oil spray
1 cup panko bread crumbs
2 tablespoons extra-virgin olive oil
2 ounces Parmesan cheese, grated (1 cup)
2 large egg whites
1 tablespoon water
3 pounds eggplant, sliced into ½-inch-thick rounds
    Salt and pepper
¼ cup finely chopped onion
2 garlic cloves, minced
1 (28-ounce) can crushed tomatoes
¼ teaspoon sugar
1 tablespoon chopped fresh basil
8 ounces part-skim mozzarella cheese, shredded (2 cups)

---

1. Adjust oven racks to upper-middle and lower-middle positions and heat oven to 475 degrees. Line rimmed baking sheets with aluminum foil and spray with vegetable oil spray. Combine panko and 1 tablespoon oil in medium saucepan and cook over medium heat, stirring often, until golden, 7 to 10 minutes. Transfer to shallow dish and let cool for 10 minutes. Combine ½ cup Parmesan with cooled panko. In second shallow dish, whisk egg whites and water together until combined.

2. Season eggplant all over with ½ teaspoon salt and ½ teaspoon pepper. Place half of eggplant slices in single layer on first prepared sheet and set aside. Dip 1 side of each remaining slice of eggplant into egg white mixture, then dredge same side in panko mixture (only 1 side of eggplant should be coated). Transfer, panko side up, to second prepared sheet in single layer. Spray all eggplant slices lightly with vegetable oil spray. Transfer breaded eggplant to upper-middle oven rack and unbreaded eggplant to lower-middle oven rack. Bake until eggplant is tender and breaded tops are crisp, about 25 minutes, rotating and switching sheets halfway through baking.

3. Meanwhile, heat remaining tablespoon oil in medium saucepan over medium-low heat until shimmering. Add onion and ½ teaspoon salt and cook, stirring occasionally, until golden brown, 3 to 5 minutes. Add garlic and cook until fragrant, about 30 seconds. Stir in tomatoes and sugar, increase heat to high, and bring to boil. Reduce heat to medium-low and simmer until thickened slightly, about 10 minutes. Off heat, stir in remaining ½ cup Parmesan and basil. Season with salt and pepper to taste.

4. Spread 1½ cups tomato sauce in bottom of 13 by 9-inch baking dish. Place unbreaded eggplant slices on top of sauce, overlapping as needed to fit all slices. Spread ¾ cup sauce over eggplant and sprinkle with 1 cup mozzarella. Layer breaded eggplant over top, panko side up, overlapping as needed to fit all slices. Dollop remaining ¾ cup tomato sauce over top, leaving majority of eggplant exposed so it remains crisp. Sprinkle with remaining 1 cup mozzarella. Bake on upper-middle oven rack until bubbling and mozzarella is beginning to brown, 10 to 15 minutes. Let cool for minutes. Serve.

This chicken is as smoky, sweet, and tender as recipes cooked outside in a smoker.

your grill. Could I make pulled chicken inside in the slow cooker instead?

Apparently yes, as I found lots of recipes for slow-cooker pulled chicken. I selected five representative ones and started cooking. All used either breasts or thighs—with bones and skin or without. Most recipes called for tossing the raw chicken in the cooker with barbecue sauce, letting it cook for several hours, taking out the chicken, discarding the skin and bones, and "pulling" the chicken into shreds before tossing it back into the sauce. The big problems were overcooked meat, a "chopped" (not pulled) texture, and lousy-tasting bottled sauce. I learned that breast meat pulled into nice long strands while dark meat didn't "pull" as well; I'd go with bone-in, skin-on breasts because the skin and bones help insulate the white meat from overcooking. I'd supplement them with some boneless thighs for their deeper flavor and moister texture.

Moving on to the sauce, I knew I'd make my own. But from-scratch sauces usually start with sautéed onion and require simmering to thicken and concentrate the flavors. I hoped to shortcut the sautéing and simmering. I whisked together a simple "dump-and-stir" sauce from ketchup, molasses, cider vinegar, hot sauce, and a dash of liquid smoke. While this sauce was simple, it was too thin and lacked big barbecue flavor.

Using tomato paste in place of some of the ketchup helped thicken and enrich the sauce. For more "barbecue" flavor, I added brown mustard, chili powder, and cayenne pepper and tripled the amount of liquid smoke to make up for the absent grill flavor.

There was one final missing piece: the oniony, aromatic sauce base. Since I wanted to avoid a stovetop sauté, I tried the microwave. After some fiddling,

I found microwaving a cup of finely chopped onion for 3 minutes provided a solid oniony foundation for the sauce. Microwaving the chili powder, cayenne, garlic, and tomato paste with the onion bloomed their flavors, giving my sauce even more depth.

I gathered tasters, spooned the saucy shredded chicken onto rolls, doled out the sandwiches, and waited. After a few moments, I broke the silence by asking if the chicken needed anything. "A cold beer on the side," said one. "And some coleslaw," said another. I took that as a sign of success.

SLOW-COOKER PULLED CHICKEN
Serves 10

Use a relatively mild hot sauce, like Frank's, or the sauce will be too hot.

- 5 (10- to 12-ounce) bone-in split chicken breasts, trimmed
- 7 (3-ounce) boneless, skinless chicken thighs, trimmed
  Salt and pepper
- 1 onion, chopped fine
- ½ cup tomato paste
- 2 tablespoons vegetable oil
- 5 teaspoons chili powder
- 3 garlic cloves, minced
- ¼ teaspoon cayenne pepper
- 1 cup ketchup
- ⅓ cup molasses
- 2 tablespoons brown mustard
- 4 teaspoons cider vinegar
- 4 teaspoons hot sauce
- ¾ teaspoon liquid smoke
- 10 sandwich rolls

1. Pat chicken dry with paper towels and season with salt and pepper. Combine onion, tomato paste, oil, chili powder, garlic, and cayenne in bowl and microwave until onion softens slightly, about 3 minutes, stirring halfway through microwaving. Transfer mixture to slow cooker and whisk in ketchup, molasses, mustard, and vinegar. Add chicken to slow cooker and toss to combine with sauce. Cover and cook on low until chicken shreds easily with fork, about 5 hours.

2. Transfer cooked chicken to carving board, tent loosely with aluminum foil, and let rest for 15 minutes. Using large spoon, remove any fat from surface of sauce. Whisk hot sauce and liquid smoke into sauce and cover to keep warm. Remove and discard chicken skin and bones. Roughly chop thigh meat into ½-inch pieces. Shred breast meat into thin strands using 2 forks. Return meat to slow cooker and toss to coat with sauce. Season with salt and pepper to taste. Serve on sandwich rolls.

Pretty good.
- Not too sweet.
- Needs a little more "barbecue" character
* - maybe chipotle?*

Cooking for Two Yankee Pot Roast

Does downsizing a pot roast mean sacrificing deep flavor? Not necessarily. We figured out how to replicate long-cooked flavor for two. BY ADAM RIED

A BIG PIECE of beef braised slowly with lots of onions, carrots, and potatoes—Yankee pot roast is a hearty one-pot dinner that feeds all the farmhands. For just two, though, that same pot roast becomes a week's worth of boring repeat meals. I assumed that downscaling for a pair would be as easy as cutting back on the beef and vegetables, but my first few attempts proved me wrong. The sauce turned out to be an unexpected challenge: It lacked the deep flavor and meaty richness begat by braising a large piece of meat for 3 to 4 hours. My goals were super-tender meat for two and a truly full-flavored sauce despite the quicker braising time of a smaller cut.

Pot roast typically relies on a largish piece—about 4 pounds—of cheap, tough beef from the sirloin, round, or chuck. Tasters agreed that chuck, a cut from the shoulder, was the right stuff: Its plentiful fat and connective tissue melt during cooking, resulting in juicy, silky meat. I went on to try four small cuts from the chuck, each about 1¼ pounds to serve two: chuck-eye roast (I tied it for a neat shape), boneless chuck-eye steaks, chuck under-blade steaks, and chuck top blade steaks. I browned and braised each, and though all four became tender and succulent after about 2¼ hours in the oven at 325 degrees, the top blade was the beefiest. For tender but not mushy vegetables, I added them in the last hour of braising.

The modest quantities of meat, vegetables, and liquid in my dish for two meant that the usual pot, a Dutch oven, was too big. A sturdy 12-inch ovensafe skillet, able to go from stovetop to oven, made an excellent substitute. The braising liquid reached about halfway up the sides of the meat—perfect.

Now I set my sights on improving the sauce. The braising liquid that eventually becomes the sauce is usually water or broth, either beef or chicken (the Yankees eschewed wine in their pot roast). Tasters favored chicken broth for its clean, savory flavor. To transform the braising liquid into a sauce, some recipes call for thickening it with flour, others for reducing it after the meat and vegetables have cooked. For me, the choice was a no-brainer: Reducing the liquid also concentrates its flavor, which was one of my primary goals.

That helped, but the sauce still

We enhance the meaty flavor of the sauce with 2 teaspoons of soy sauce.

needed a boost. Starting out by sautéing chopped onions, carrots, and celery—a mixture that the French call *mirepoix*—is a go-to strategy for building flavor. Since I was already two-thirds of the way there with the big chunks of onion and carrot in the dish, I decided to chop some of each, add the necessary celery, and sauté them right after browning the meat. Adding some garlic, thyme, and a bay leaf advanced the flavor even further.

But still not enough. To introduce yet more savory depth, I turned to several known *umami* builders. ("Umami" is the fifth taste and is used to describe savory flavor.) Tomato is an umami treasure trove, so I added 2 teaspoons of tomato paste, which enhanced the overall flavor without claiming the spotlight. A small amount of soy sauce, another umami powerhouse, balanced the sweetness of the onion and carrots.

By this point, the meat was fork-tender and silky, the vegetables were tender, and the sauce was deeply flavored. All the sauce lacked was a bit of spark—the telltale mark of an acidic ingredient. Here I asserted the Yankee

spirit of independence (even while breaking further with traditional Yankee pot roast) by finishing the sauce with a small hit of balsamic vinegar.

TEST KITCHEN TECHNIQUE
Cutting Pot Roast Down to Size
A big pot roast requires a big pot; our Yankee Pot Roast for Two does not.

BLADE STEAKS
Smaller cut cooks faster.

12-INCH SKILLET
Goes from stovetop to oven.

YANKEE POT ROAST FOR TWO

If your skillet doesn't have a lid, use potholders to cover it with foil.

- 2 (8- to 10-ounce) beef top blade steak
  Salt and pepper
- 4 teaspoons vegetable oil
- 3 carrots, peeled (½ carrot chopped fine
  2½ carrots cut into 1½-inch pieces)
- 1 onion (½ onion chopped fine, ½ onion
  cut into 4 wedges through root end)
- 1 celery rib, minced
- 2 garlic cloves, minced
- 2 teaspoons tomato paste
- 1¾ cups low-sodium chicken broth
- 2 teaspoons soy sauce
- 1 sprig fresh thyme
- 1 bay leaf
- 10 ounces red potatoes, unpeeled, cut
  into 1-inch pieces
- 2 tablespoons minced fresh parsley
- 1 teaspoon balsamic vinegar

1. Adjust oven rack to middle position and heat oven to 325 degrees. Pat steaks dry with paper towels and season with salt and pepper. Heat 2 teaspoons oil in 12-inch ovensafe skillet over medium-high heat until just smoking. Brown steaks on both sides, about 3 minutes per side; transfer to plate.

2. Reduce heat to medium, add remaining 2 teaspoons oil to now-empt skillet, and heat until shimmering. Add chopped carrot, chopped onion, celery, and ½ teaspoon salt and cook until golden, about 5 minutes. Stir in garlic and tomato paste and cook until fragrant, about 30 seconds. Stir in brot soy sauce, thyme, and bay leaf and brin to boil. Return steaks and any accumulated juices to skillet. Cover and bake fo 1¼ hours.

3. Flip steaks and add carrot pieces, onion wedges, and potatoes to skillet. Cover and bake until vegetables are tender and fork slips easily in and out o meat, 50 to 60 minutes. Transfer steaks and vegetables to platter with slotted spoon and tent loosely with aluminum foil.

4. Defat braising liquid with large spoon and discard thyme sprig and bay leaf. Bring liquid to boil over medium-high heat and cook until reduced to 1 cup, about 3 minutes. Off heat, stir in parsley and vinegar. Season with salt an pepper to taste. Pour sauce over steaks and vegetables. Serve.

No need to smother it in cheese sauce. Roasting brings out cauliflower's sweet side.

BY NICK IVERSON

UNTIL RECENTLY, CAULIFLOWER, at least for me, either lived on a crudités tray—the obligatory one that my mom makes for Thanksgiving—or in the freezer section, paired with broccoli and carrots and sold as a "vegetable medley." Both fates were equally bad, which probably explains why I never liked cauliflower. When I discovered the test kitchen's roasted cauliflower recipe, though, I began to see it in a whole new light.

Most recipes call for tossing the florets with oil and roasting them on a baking sheet in a very hot oven. But because of their shape, the florets don't brown evenly. Also, the high heat dehydrates the florets before very much browning can take place—and browning equals flavor. Our solution is twofold: First, instead of slicing florets, we cut a head of cauliflower into just eight wedges, which gives us more—and flatter—surface area for browning. A bonus? There are fewer pieces to flip partway through roasting.

Next, we devised a hybrid steaming/roasting technique. We arrange the wedges on a baking sheet, cover them tightly with foil, and set them in a 475-degree oven. The cauliflower begins to steam in its own moisture. When we remove the foil 10 minutes later, the cauliflower has enough time to caramelize but not to dry out. After 15 minutes on the first side, we flip the wedges, and 15 minutes after that, we've got

intensely sweet, tender cauliflower.

As a recent and avid convert to the virtues of roasted cauliflower, I borrowed this technique to develop four flavor variations. Paired with smoked paprika and chorizo in one, and bacon and scallions in another, the cauliflower tastes so substantial it could almost be a meal. Combined with curry, cilantro, and cashews, the hearty winter vegetable shows its exotic side. And finished with capers and lemon, it takes a detour to the Mediterranean.

ROASTED CAULIFLOWER Serves 4 to 6
Wedges are easy to flip and have a lot of surface area in contact with the pan, which leads to great browning.

    1   head cauliflower (2 pounds)
    ¼   cup extra-virgin olive oil
        Kosher salt and pepper

1. Adjust oven rack to lowest position and heat oven to 475 degrees. Trim outer leaves of cauliflower and cut stem flush with bottom of head. Cut head into 8 equal wedges, keeping core and florets intact. Place wedges cut side down on parchment paper–lined rimmed baking sheet. Drizzle with 2 tablespoons oil and season with salt and pepper to taste; rub gently to distribute oil and seasonings.

2. Cover sheet tightly with aluminum foil and cook for 10 minutes. Remove foil and continue to roast until bottoms of cauliflower wedges are golden, about 15 minutes. Remove sheet from oven and, using spatula, carefully flip wedges. Return sheet to oven and continue to roast until cauliflower is golden all over, about 15 minutes longer. Season with salt and pepper to taste, transfer to platter, drizzle with remaining 2 tablespoons oil, and serve.

ROASTED CAULIFLOWER WITH BACON AND SCALLIONS
In step 1, combine 2 tablespoons oil and 4 minced garlic cloves in small bowl before drizzling over cauliflower. Distribute 6 slices bacon, cut into ½-inch pieces, and ½ onion, cut into ½-inch-thick slices, on baking sheet around cauliflower before roasting. In step 2, whisk remaining 2 tablespoons oil with 2 teaspoons cider vinegar in large bowl. Toss roasted cauliflower mixture with

oil-vinegar mixture. Season with salt and pepper to taste, transfer to platter, and sprinkle with 2 thinly sliced scallions.

ROASTED CAULIFLOWER WITH CURRY AND LIME
In step 1, combine 2 tablespoons oil and 1½ teaspoons curry powder in small bowl before drizzling over cauliflower. Distribute ½ onion, cut into ½-inch-thick slices, on baking sheet around cauliflower before roasting. In step 2, whisk remaining 2 tablespoons oil with 2 teaspoons lime juice in large bowl. Toss roasted cauliflower with oil–lime juice mixture. Season with salt and pepper to taste; transfer to platter; and sprinkle with ¼ cup cashews, toasted and chopped, and 2 tablespoons chopped fresh cilantro.

ROASTED CAULIFLOWER WITH LEMON AND CAPERS
In step 1, combine 2 tablespoons oil and 1½ teaspoons chopped fresh thyme in small bowl before drizzling over cauliflower. Distribute 2 shallots, cut into ¼-inch-thick rings, on baking sheet around cauliflower before roasting. In

step 2, whisk remaining 2 tablespoons oil with ¼ teaspoon grated lemon zest and 2 teaspoons lemon juice in large bowl. Toss roasted cauliflower mixture with oil-lemon mixture. Season with salt and pepper to taste; transfer to platter; and sprinkle with 2 tablespoons rinsed, chopped capers.

ROASTED CAULIFLOWER WITH PAPRIKA AND CHORIZO
In step 1, combine 2 tablespoons oil and 1½ teaspoons smoked paprika in small bowl before drizzling over cauliflower. Distribute ½ red onion, cut into ½-inch-thick slices, on baking sheet around cauliflower before roasting. In step 2, when removing aluminum foil, distribute 6 ounces chorizo sausage, halved lengthwise and sliced ½ inch thick, on sheet. In step 2, whisk remaining 2 tablespoons oil with 2 teaspoons sherry vinegar in large bowl. Toss roasted cauliflower mixture with oil-vinegar mixture. Season with salt and pepper to taste, transfer to platter, and sprinkle with 2 tablespoons chopped fresh parsley.

Cauliflower is utterly transformed by a very hot oven, olive oil, salt, and pepper.

TEST KITCHEN DISCOVERY
Cut into Wedges

For the best browning, we cut the head of cauliflower into eight wedges. First, trim the outer leaves and cut the stem flush with the bottom of the head. Next cut the wedges, keeping the florets attached to the pieces of the core.

Equipment Review Salad Spinners

Obviously, a good spinner needs to get greens dry, but that's just for starters. We considered capacity, ease of use, design, and sturdiness, too. BY TAIZETH SIERRA

WE FIRST CHOSE the OXO salad spinner as our favorite in 1999, and although we've tested other brands over the years, we've never found a better one. It is newly redesigned. Could the maker improve on great? At the same time, new products have entered the market. We put eight through their paces, including the newest OXO model.

All salad spinners share a basic design: a perforated basket that balances on a point in the center of a larger bowl. The lid houses a mechanism that grabs the basket and makes it spin. Centrifugal force created by the spinning basket propels the contents of the spinner away from the center; greens are trapped while water passes through the perforations and collects in the outer bowl. But the spinning mechanisms, and other differences in design, affect how well salad spinners work.

Of the eight spinners we tested, two used a pump action, two had retractable cords, two had levers, one used a ratchet handle, and one had a crank. The crank was tricky to get started, and because the direction of the force being applied by the user was the same as the spinning of the basket, this model was prone to jump around on the counter. The ratcheting model was clearly designed for the right hand and proved awkward for lefties. Pull-string mechanisms work, but with time the retracting component can wear out so the string needs to be rewound manually. Plus, pulling the string away from the spinner can bring the lid with it. Lastly, when the string becomes wet or soiled, bacteria can grow. With lever mechanisms, because the force being applied is slightly off to one side, the spinner can become unstable. Our favorite method is the pump: The simple up-and-down motion takes little effort, and since it's set in the center, the spinner won't dance around on the counter.

As we were considering spinning mechanisms, we also noticed that spinners with conical shapes had smaller bases, which made them wobble at high speed. They were out of the running.

To test capacity, we made a Caesar salad recipe that calls for 2 pounds of romaine hearts cut into pieces. We recorded how many batches it took each spinner to dry the lettuce: two for the best performers, four for the smallest.

Turning to drying ability, we weighed the greens before and after washing and spinning. One salad spinner threw off about a tablespoon more water than any of the others. The worst performer, a collapsible model, trapped water; it left behind 76 grams of water on the greens. (To get greens completely dry, blot them with a clean dish towel after spinning.)

Concerned that violent spinning might bruise delicate herbs, we washed and dried a bunch of cilantro in each spinner and examined how well the spinners removed sandy soil. Every spinner cleaned the cilantro without bruising it, but long sprigs of cilantro did not fit comfortably in all models.

Once the greens are clean, it's time to clean the spinners. Green baskets obscured any trapped greens when we were washing up; we preferred clear or white baskets. Complicated lids were also harder to clean, which made us appreciate one new model that comes apart for thorough washing and drying. And we were grateful for lids that compress for easy storage and stacking.

After all was said and done, the OXO Good Grips Salad Spinner ($29.99) once again carried the day. Fourteen years and counting . . .

HIGHLY RECOMMENDED		CRITERIA		TESTERS' NOTES
OXO GOOD GRIPS Salad Spinner **Model:** 32480V2 **Price:** $29.99 **Source:** oxo.com **Spin Mechanism:** Pump **Capacity:** 4½ qt **Water Left Behind After Spinning:** 44 g		Ease of Use Cleanup Sturdiness	★★★ ★★★ ★★★	Our redesigned favorite is better than ever. Its pump mechanism was the easiest to use among the models we tested, and its performance remained superb, holding plenty of greens and getting them driest. The new, wider base provides more stability, the smaller pump increases the spinner's capacity, and the flat lid comes apart for easy cleaning and storage.
RECOMMENDED				
ZYLISS Smart Touch Salad Spinner **Model:** 15912 **Price:** $29.95 **Source:** surlatable.com **Spin Mechanism:** Lever **Capacity:** 5 qt **Water Left Behind After Spinning:** 59 g		Ease of Use Cleanup Sturdiness	★★½ ★★★ ★★½	We liked the large capacity, which let us wash and dry 2 pounds of greens in two batches. The lever was easy to use and worked similarly to the pump on the OXO model, and it locked down for easy storage. However, because the lever pushes slightly to one side, this spinner did hop about a bit. It comes in green or white; the white is easier to clean, as you can see any trapped herbs.
RECOMMENDED WITH RESERVATIONS				
CHEF'N Large Salad Spinner **Model:** 83845018216 **Price:** $19.95 **Spin Mechanism:** Lever **Capacity:** 3½ qt **Water Left Behind After Spinning:** 63 g		Ease of Use Cleanup Sturdiness	★★ ★★ ★★	This spinner got the job done, but its combined flaws lowered its rank. It took three batches to clean 2 pounds of greens, and while the spinner did an adequate job drying them, its lever made disconcerting clicking noises, making us worry that it might wear out quickly. Its lid does not collapse for storage, and its green basket made trapped particles difficult to see.
PROGRESSIVE Ratchet Salad Spinner **Model:** SAL-100 **Price:** $37.71 **Spin Mechanism:** Ratchet handle **Capacity:** 5 qt **Water Left Behind After Spinning:** 64 g		Ease of Use Cleanup Sturdiness	★★ ★★ ★★	We have few complaints about this model's performance. It has a large capacity, and the ratchet mechanism is effortless to use (though slightly uncomfortable if you are left-handed). Unfortunately, the basket's conical shape reduced its usable capacity, and it is harder to store because it's taller than other models, with a lid that makes stacking impossible.
ZYLISS Easy Spin Salad Spinner **Model:** 15103 **Price:** $24.99 **Spin Mechanism:** Self-retracting cord **Capacity:** 5 qt **Water Left Behind After Spinning:** 49 g		Ease of Use Cleanup Sturdiness	★½ ★½ ★½	This model placed just behind our winner when it came to drying ability, and it spun 2 pounds of greens in a respectable three batches. However, the spinning mechanism (a pull cord) makes you pull away from the spinner, so you have to apply significant pressure to hold down the lid, occasionally causing it to go askew and partially fall into the spinner.
NOT RECOMMENDED				
PROGRESSIVE Collapsible Salad Spinner **Model:** CSS-1 **Price:** $29.95 **Spin Mechanism:** Self-retracting cord **Capacity:** 4 qt **Water Left Behind After Spinning:** 76 g		Ease of Use Cleanup Sturdiness	★½ ★ ★½	The single reason to buy this collapsible model is if your kitchen is very cramped; it has no other advantages. The solid band of silicone that makes this spinner collapsible also traps water in the drainage basket. Both basket and bowl were stiff and required substantial force to expand.
NORPRO Salad Spinner **Model:** 813 **Price:** $22.49 **Spin Mechanism:** Crank **Capacity:** 3 qt **Water Left Behind After Spinning:** 71 g		Ease of Use Cleanup Sturdiness	★ ★½ ★	This spinner had the smallest capacity of the models we tested, requiring us to dry 2 pounds of greens in four batches. Both bowl and basket flexed and felt flimsy when full of water and greens. The crank was at times difficult to get going and, once spinning, tended to make the spinner jump around.
KITCHENAID Professional Salad Spinner **Model:** KG308ER **Price:** $34.99 **Spin Mechanism:** Pump **Capacity:** 5 qt **Water Left Behind After Spinning:** 63 g		Ease of Use Cleanup Sturdiness	½ ★½ ★	This model had a fatal flaw: Push the pump too far down and the spinning basket locks, requiring you to stop, remove the lid, turn the pump until it unlocks, and rethread the pump through the lid before you can (finally) continue spinning. Also, the pump runs down the center of the basket, taking up space, and the bowl's narrow base reduces stability.

What did we learn when we sampled America's own artisanal, cured pork? It's (almost) all good. BY HANNAH CROWLEY

EUROPE HAS ITS fabled cured hams—prosciutto in Italy, *jamón ibérico* in Spain—but did you know that we've got one, too? Country ham is a strong, salty, dry-cured product produced primarily in Virginia, North Carolina, Tennessee, Kentucky, and Missouri. Just seven million country hams are sold annually in the United States, but with increased interest in artisanal and local foods, the current love affair with anything pig, and the explosion of Internet mail ordering, these small-town Southern hams seem poised to hit the big time. Being ham lovers ourselves, we wanted in.

By definition, a ham is the cut of meat taken from the upper part of a pig's back leg; for many, it's a holiday table centerpiece, spiral-cut and lacquered with a sugary glaze. But that is a city ham, made by injecting or soaking a fresh ham in brine and sold cooked, to be simply heated and served.

While city hams can be ready for market in 24 hours, country hams cure for anywhere from three months to years. Traditionally, it was a way to preserve the meat in prerefrigeration days: Hogs were slaughtered in the fall; the hams were rubbed with salt, sugar, and spices and then left to cure during the winter, with the salt drawing out moisture. Come spring, they were cleaned and hung, and some were smoked. Finally, in the warm summer months, the hams were aged. The heat accelerated enzymatic activity, which imparted the robust, pungent flavors that one producer has described as the ham's "country twang." This centuries-old seasonal style of making country ham is known as an "ambient" cure. Today, virtually all commercial cured-ham makers use special aging rooms to mimic the seasons, with temperature, airflow, and humidity under carefully monitored control.

Country ham is sold whole or sliced, cooked or uncooked. We ordered ours online from individual company websites; you can also buy these hams in some Southern supermarkets and warehouse club stores. (The hams may have mold on them. It's harmless—just wipe it off.) We chose whole uncooked hams and slow-cooked them for 4 to 5 hours, according to a test kitchen recipe. We selected country hams that were aged from three to six months because these are the most widely sold. Much as barbecue fanatics fight over Memphis versus Carolina versus Texas, country ham pros have partisan loyalties. Tasting hams from different states, they warned us, was like comparing apples with oranges. We ignored their advice and investigated hams across the geographic range. Then we held a blind taste test. Because these hams are so salty, we kept our palates fresh by serving thin slices with biscuits, water, and unsalted crackers.

When we tallied the results, we learned that of the seven products, we had serious reservations about just one. The top five, all recommended, were in a virtual tie. They were porky and complex with the robust flavors that develop from aging temperatures that run 10 to 30 degrees hotter than those used for European cured hams. Next—and we say this with all due respect—it's not apples and oranges. McIntosh and Granny Smith might be more apt. All of the hams were made by the same methods, with the same ingredients, and from the same breed of pig, a crossbred packinghouse hog called American Landrace. (We did not taste fancy heritage breeds; these makers do not raise their own pigs.) Six products that we tasted are hickory smoked; the seventh is not (we liked that ham, too).

So if every producer starts with the same product, adds the same ingredients, and undertakes the same preservation method, what accounts for differences? Time, temperature, airflow, and humidity inside the curing and aging rooms, we learned. Producers can tailor each of these factors, ham by ham, to get the exact product they want to sell. Hams aged in rooms with more airflow will be drier; hams aged for longer will have more concentrated flavor; hams aged at higher temperatures will have stronger flavors. To achieve their goals, makers inspect and smell the hams daily.

In the end, only one brand didn't pass muster (a brand that happens to be made by the largest pork producer in the world). Yes, country ham is salty, but this brand was so salty that's all we could taste. Our second-to-last-place finisher, recommended with reservations, was strong and gamy, characteristics that split our tasters. You can't go wrong with any of the remaining five brands, but our top choice is Harper's Grand Champion Whole Country Ham, made in Kentucky. It had robust pork flavor and balanced salt levels and would have no trouble holding its own among the better-known European hams.

RECOMMENDED

	TASTERS' NOTES
HARPER'S Grand Champion Whole Country Ham **Price:** $61.21 for a 14- to 15-lb ham (shipping included) **Origin:** Kentucky **Sodium:** 1980 mg per 3-oz serving **Cure and Age Time:** 3-month minimum	Our top country ham pick was "delicious and savory"; "bacony"; "rich and deeply flavored"; "quietly smoky," with an "interesting mineral taste"; "well balanced"; and "not overwhelmed by salt." It was on the "tender" side of the spectrum with "moist," "juicy" meat.
BURGERS' SMOKEHOUSE Ready to Cook Country Ham **Price:** $69.95 for a 13- to 15-lb ham (shipping included) **Origin:** Missouri **Sodium:** 1490 mg per 3-oz serving **Cure and Age Time:** 4 to 6 months	This "balanced" ham had a "nuanced," "rich, fatty" ham flavor that was "very deep" and spoke of "awesome bacon" with "a nice amount of fat to balance flavor." Slices were "silky," tender, and "slightly dry."
EDWARDS VIRGINIA TRADITIONS Uncooked Virginia Ham **Price:** $97.53 for a 13- to 14-lb ham (shipping included) **Origin:** Virginia **Sodium:** 2272 mg per 3-oz serving **Cure and Age Time:** 4 to 6 months	The smoke flavor was stronger here, in this "very meaty"; "porky, nutty, and complex"; and "very deep, bacony" ham. It was drier than some other samples, with a "firm, good chew" that was "dense" and "compact" yet remained "tender" with "marbled fat." With all these winning characteristics, the relatively high salt level didn't bother us.
TRIPP COUNTRY HAMS Whole Country Ham **Price:** $66.20 for a 13- to 14-lb ham (shipping included) **Origin:** Tennessee **Sodium:** 1620 mg per 3-oz serving **Cure and Age Time:** 4 to 5 months	This "super-concentrated" ham was "meaty," with a "slightly gamy" aftertaste and "intense pig flavor" combined with "some sweetness." Salt levels were balanced by the porky complexity. Slices were "moist," "plump, and juicy."
GOODNIGHT BROTHERS Whole Country Ham **Price:** $61.78 for a 12- to 15-lb ham (shipping included) **Origin:** North Carolina **Sodium:** 1618 mg per 3-oz serving **Cure and Age Time:** 3 to 4 months	This ham was salt-forward with "wild, funky" flavors balanced by a "strong *umami* flavor." This was the only unsmoked ham in our lineup, and a few tasters missed the smoke. It was on the dry side, with a "fatty" and "dense" bite.

RECOMMENDED WITH RESERVATIONS

JOHNSTON COUNTY HAMS INC. Whole Uncooked Country Ham **Price:** $75.95 for a 13-lb ham (shipping included) **Origin:** North Carolina **Sodium:** 1620 mg per 3-oz serving **Cure and Age Time:** 4 months	This ham was "intense," with "hints of sweetness" and a "slightly funky, gamy" flavor. Tasters found its robust, complex taste "good in small amounts" but wished for more ham flavor beyond "funk." The texture was "lean" and "drier" than most.

NOT RECOMMENDED

SMITHFIELD HAMS Country Whole Ham (Uncooked) **Price:** $79.99 for a 14- to 17-lb ham (shipping included) **Origin:** Virginia **Sodium:** 2500 mg per 3-oz serving **Cure and Age Time:** 3 months	This ham was nearly "inedible" due to a "mouth-puckering" saltiness combined with a funky, smoky flavor that was "like licking a smokehouse." "Lots going on here covering up the pork flavor," said one taster. The texture was "tough" and "leathery."

Looking for a Recipe

Have you lost a recipe you treasure? Ask a reader. While you're at it, answer a reader. Post queries and finds at **CooksCountry.com/magazine**; click on **Looking for a Recipe** (or write to Looking for a Recipe, *Cook's Country*, P.O. Box 470739, Brookline, MA 02447). We'll share all of your submissions online and one recipe on this page; include your name and mailing address.

Jewish Honey Cake
Avi Mandell, White Plains, N.Y.

I've been trying for years to make a light, moist, tender honey cake, the kind that uses oil in place of butter. I've tinkered with many recipes but have never quite been able to produce one that I love. Do you have a tried-and-true recipe for honey cake that you're willing to share with me?

Bar Pizza
Cindy Schlager, Rockland, Mass.

Do you know the pizza tradition of bar pies? These are pizzas sold on the South Shore of Massachusetts, just south of Boston. The pizza is baked in an oiled metal pan. The crust is buttery and gets really crisp, especially at the edges. I'd love to figure out how to make it at home. Does anyone have a recipe?

Pittsburgh Barbecue Chipped Ham Sandwiches
Mary Birnie, Chantilly, Va.

Does anybody know how to make a proper barbecue chipped ham sandwich, like those I used to eat at school cafeterias in the Pittsburgh, Pennsylvania, area? I moved away several years ago, and not a soul I've met since has ever even heard of this sandwich.

Caramel Apple Blossoms
Deborah Johnson, Two Harbors, Minn.

Do any of you know apple blossoms? They are similar to apple dumplings, but there is caramel inside, too, not just fruit. I've heard that the recipe was developed in the 1930s and that home bakers won many a contest with them. Lately, I've noticed that a company named Chudleigh's is selling "blossoms" to supermarkets. I'd rather prepare them myself, but I don't know how to make a good version. Can you help?

Fig Bars
Joanna Cossette, Miami, Fla.

I grew up in New Jersey and my father used to bring these bars home from New York City for me and my sister. They were very simple: fig jam with pie dough on either side and a light glaze on top. I'd love to make these to surprise my sister.

CARROT-RAISIN SALAD
Serves 6 to 8
Becky Archibald, Memphis, Tenn.

"My mom used to make this salad every year for holiday dinners, as part of her relish tray. I wonder whatever happened to that tradition." You can grate the carrots on the large holes of a box grater or use a food processor with the grating disk. We don't recommend buying preshredded carrots, which can be dry and tasteless. This salad is delicious with baked ham.

- ½ cup extra-virgin olive oil
- 6 tablespoons cider vinegar
- 2 tablespoons honey
- 1 tablespoon Dijon mustard
  Salt and pepper
- 2 pounds carrots, peeled and shredded
- 1 cup raisins
- 1 (8-ounce) can crushed pineapple, drained

1. Whisk oil, vinegar, honey, mustard, ½ teaspoon salt, and ½ teaspoon pepper together in large bowl. Add carrots, raisins, and pineapple and toss thoroughly to combine.

2. Season with salt and pepper to taste. Cover and refrigerate for at least 1 hour or up to 24 hours. Serve.

RC = Recipe Card

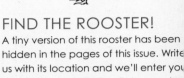

FIND THE ROOSTER!
A tiny version of this rooster has been hidden in the pages of this issue. Write us with its location and we'll enter you a random drawing. The first correct e drawn will win our top-rated salad spi (see page 30), and each of the next will receive a free one-year subscripti to *Cook's Country*. To enter, visit **CooksCountry.com/rooster** by May 3 2013, or write to Rooster, *Cook's Cour* P.O. Box 470739, Brookline, MA 02447. Include your name and address. Car Trosper of Silver Spring, Md., found the rooster in the December/January 201 issue on page 7 and won our favorite moderately priced 12-inch skillet.

WEB EXTRAS
Free for 4 months online at
CooksCountry.com

Fluffy Cream Cheese Frosting
Maple Syrup Tasting
Mayonnaise Tasting
One-Minute Salsa
Parmesan Tasting
Pink-Sugared Lemon Slices
Single-Crust Pie Dough
Strawberry Sauce

COOK'S COUNTRY IS NO ON iPAD!

Download the new *Cook's Country* app for iPad and start a free trial subscription or purchase a single issue of the magazine.
All issues are enhanced with full-colo Cooking Mode slide shows that provi step-by-step instructions for completi recipes, plus expanded reviews and ratings. Go to **CooksCountry.com/iPe** to download our app through iTunes

 Follow us on **Twitter**
twitter.com/TestKitchen

 Find us on **Facebook**
facebook.com/CooksCountry

Pink Lemonade Cake

When life gives you lemons, make our Pink Lemonade Cake, a tender chiffon cake with lemony cream cheese frosting and a pretty-in-pink hue.

To make this cake you will need:

- **5 large eggs, separated**
- **1 teaspoon cream of tartar**
- **1½ cups (10½ ounces) sugar**
- **1⅓ cups (5⅓ ounces) cake flour**
- **2 teaspoons baking powder**
- **½ teaspoon salt**
- **⅔ cup water**
- **½ cup vegetable oil**
- **4 teaspoons grated lemon zest plus 2 tablespoons juice (2 lemons)**
- **Red food coloring**
- **2 recipes Fluffy Cream Cheese Frosting***
- **1 recipe Pink-Sugared Lemon Slices***

FOR THE CAKE: Adjust oven rack to lower-middle position and heat oven to 325 degrees. Using stand mixer fitted with whisk, whip egg whites and cream of tartar on medium-low speed until foamy, about 1 minute. Increase speed to medium-high and whip whites to soft, billowy mounds, about 1 minute. Gradually add 2 tablespoons sugar and whip until glossy, stiff peaks form, 2 to 3 minutes. Combine flour, remaining sugar, baking powder, and salt in large bowl. Whisk egg yolks, water, oil, lemon zest and 2 tablespoons juice, and 5 to 7 drops food coloring together in medium bowl until smooth. Whisk yolk mixture into flour mixture until smooth. Whisk one-third of whipped egg whites into batter, then gently fold in remaining whites in 2 additions until well combined. Pour mixture into ungreased 16-cup tube pan. Bake until skewer inserted in center comes out clean and cracks in cake appear dry, 55 to 65 minutes. Invert pan onto wire rack and let cake cool completely in pan, about 3 hours.

TO ASSEMBLE: Stir 3 to 4 drops food coloring into frosting until well combined. Unmold cake onto plate and frost top and sides in even layer. Decorate along bottom edge with sugared lemon slices and serve.

▶ *Go to CooksCountry.com for our recipes for **Fluffy Cream Cheese Frosting** and **Pink-Sugared Lemon Slices.**

Cook's Country

JUNE/JULY 2013

Best Lemon Icebox Pie

Picnic Fried Chicken

The Ultimate Grilled Steak

Summer Squash Casserole
Bland and Watery? No More

Grilled Chicken Quarters
Crisp Skin, Flavorful Meat

Muffin Tin Doughnuts
No Frying Required

Memphis Wet Ribs
Enough to Feed a Crowd

All About Grilling Shrimp
Step-by-Step Instructions

Natchitoches Meat Pies
Fragrant Two-Meat Turnovers

Chicken Divan for Two
Quicker and Better

Summer Berry Pudding
Fresh, Bright Flavors

Testing Two-Slice Toasters
Are They All Losers?

CooksCountry.com
$5.95 U.S./$6.95 CANADA

Invented in the South, where no-bake pies and condensed milk ruled summer months, **Lemon Icebox Pie** *is a well-loved classic. But after making 30-some versions, we found an approach that made it even better.* PAGE 23

Cook's Country

Dear Country Cook,

My grandfather, Charles Stanley White, owned a small farm in Leesburg, Virginia, in the days before it became a suburban community. His love of chickens was passed along to my mother, Mary Alice. The result was a child-hood photo of yours truly in an old-fashioned baby carriage with a rooster standing proudly on the handlebars. My mother's lifetime obsession with chickens included doorstops, paintings, metal sculptures, and, of course, large flocks of laying hens on her farm in northwest Connecticut.

In later years, we celebrated Easter on the farm. The Berkshires were usually cool and clear on Easter morning, the sky egg blue with wisps of streaking clouds. Wildly colored eggs were scattered among the bushes, flower beds, and woodpiles, the search area bordered by the chicken coop and the small putty-colored farmhouse. Guinea hens, Rhode Island Reds, and wyandottes scattered as grandchildren, legs and arms awry, ran to fill woven baskets.

Mary Alice watched silently, a lone figure, a mother hen to her chicks. It's funny how human life imitates nature, how we finally become what we love.

Christopher Kimball
Founder and Editor, Cook's Country

July 1934: Dusting hens with talcum powder hides their scent—a time-tested way to keep them from pecking one another.

Cook's Country

Founder and Editor Christopher Kimball
Editorial Director Jack Bishop
Editorial Director, Magazines John Willoughby
Executive Editor Peggy Grodinsky
Managing Editor Scott Kathan
Senior Editors Lisa McManus, Bryan Roof, Diane Unger
Test Kitchen Director Erin McMurrer
Associate Editors Hannah Crowley, Amy Graves, Rebeccah Marsters
Test Cooks Sarah Gabriel, Nick Iverson, Carolynn Purpura MacKay, Cristin Walsh
Assistant Editors Shannon Friedmann Hatch, Taizeth Sierra
Copy Editors Nell Beram, Megan Ginsberg
Executive Assistant Christine Gordon
Test Kitchen Manager Leah Rovner
Senior Kitchen Assistants Michelle Blodget, Meryl MacCormack
Kitchen Assistants Maria Elena Delgado, Ena Gudiel, Andrew Straaberg Finfrock
Executive Producer Melissa Baldino
Co-Executive Producer Stephanie Stender
Production Assistant Kaitlin Hammond

Contributing Editors Erika Bruce, Eva Katz, Jeremy Sauer
Consulting Editors Anne Mendelson, Meg Ragland
Science Editor Guy Crosby, Ph.D.
Executive Food Editor, TV, Radio & Media Bridget Lancaster

Managing Editor, Web Christine Liu
Senior Editor, Cooking School Mari Levine
Associate Editors, Web Eric Grzymkowski, Roger Metcalf
Assistant Editors, Web Jill Fisher, Charlotte Wilder
Senior Video Editor Nick Dakoulas

Design Director Amy Klee
Art Director Julie Cote
Deputy Art Director Susan Levin
Associate Art Director Lindsey Timko
Deputy Art Director, Marketing/Web Jennifer Cox
Staff Photographer Daniel J. van Ackere
Color Food Photography Keller + Keller
Styling Catrine Kelty, Marie Piraino
Associate Art Director, Marketing/Web Mariah Tarvainen
Production Designer, Marketing/Web Judy Blomquist
Photo Editor Steve Klise

Vice President, Marketing David Mack
Circulation Director Doug Wicinski
Circulation & Fulfillment Manager Carrie Fethe
Partnership Marketing Manager Pamela Putprush
Marketing Assistant Joyce Liao
Customer Service Manager Jacqueline Valerio
Customer Service Representatives Megan Hamner, Jessica Haskin

Production Director Guy Rochford
Director of Project Management Alice Carpenter
Workflow & Digital Asset Manager Andrew Mannone
Production & Traffic Coordinator Brittany Allen
Senior Color & Imaging Specialist Lauren Pettapiece
Production & Imaging Specialists Heather Dube, Lauren Robbins
Systems Administrators Scott Norwood, Marcus Walser
Helpdesk Support Technician Brianna Brothers
Senior Business Analyst Wendy Tseng
Web Developer Chris Candelora
Human Resources Manager Adele Shapiro

VP New Media Product Development Barry Kelly
Development Manager Mike Serio
Developer Patrick Hereford
Chief Financial Officer Sharyn Chabot
Director of Sponsorship Sales Anne Traficante
Retail Sales & Marketing Manager Emily Logan
Client Services Associate Kate May
Sponsorship Sales Representative Morgan Ryan
Publicity Deborah Broide

ON THE COVER:
Lemon Icebox Pie
Keller + Keller, Catrine Kelty
ILLUSTRATION: Greg Stevenson

Cook's Country magazine (ISSN 1552-1990), number 51, published bimonthly by Boston Common Press Limited Partnership, 17 Station St., Brookline, MA 02445. Copyright 2013 Boston Common Press Limited Partnership. Periodicals postage paid at Boston, Mass., and additional mailing offices, USPS #023453. Publications Mail Agreement No. 40020778. Return undeliverable Canadian addresses to P.O. Box 875, Station A, Windsor, ON N9A 6P2. POSTMASTER: Send address changes to Cook's Country, P.O. Box 6018, Harlan, IA 51593-1518. For subscription and gift subscription orders, subscription inquiries, or change-of-address notices, visit americasTestKitchen.com/customerservice, call 800-526-8442 in the U.S. or 515-248-7684 from outside the U.S., or write to Cook's Country, P.O. Box 6018, Harlan, IA 51593-1518. PRINTED IN THE USA

Contents

GRILLED CAESAR SALAD, 13

SPICY TOMATO JAM, 7

GRILLED CHICKEN LEG QUARTERS, 6

Features

Departments

America's Test Kitchen is a very real 2,500-square-foot kitchen located just outside Boston. It is the home of *Cook's Country* and *Cook's Illustrated* magazines and is the workday destination of more than three dozen test cooks, editors, and cookware specialists. Our mission is to test recipes over and over again until we understand how and why they work and until we arrive at the best version. We also test kitchen equipment and supermarket ingredients in search of brands that offer the best value and performance. You can watch us work by tuning in to *Cook's Country from America's Test Kitchen* (CooksCountryTV.com) and *America's Test Kitchen* (AmericasTestKitchenTV.com) on public television.

RECIPES THAT WORK®

Ask Cook's Country

BY SARAH GABRIEL

I can't seem to grill chicken pieces without flare-ups as fat drips down into the grill. Do you have any tips to combat that?

Mark Steudel, Seattle, Wash.

Beyond being scary and dangerous, flare-ups also can make the difference between pleasant charred grill flavor and burnt food. Flare-ups are usually caused by fat or by excess oily marinade dripping off the meat and catching fire. To avoid them, trim meat carefully and pat dry any foods marinated with oil with paper towels before grilling (see our recipe for Grilled Chicken Leg Quarters with Lime Dressing on page 7).

Additionally, many gas grills have grease traps on their undersides; when your grill is completely cool, remove the shallow pan from under your grill and give it a good cleaning to prevent it from catching fire. Sometimes, despite our best preventive measures, we still get flare-ups. Keep long tongs and grill gloves handy so that you can quickly and safely move the food to an area of the grill not directly over the fire. The flare-up will die down fast, and you'll have the grill back under your control. Briefly covering the grill can also help quelch flare-ups.

THE BOTTOM LINE: Minimize flare-ups by removing excess fat and marinade from food before grilling. Keep long tongs and grill gloves handy so you can safely move food while managing a flare-up.

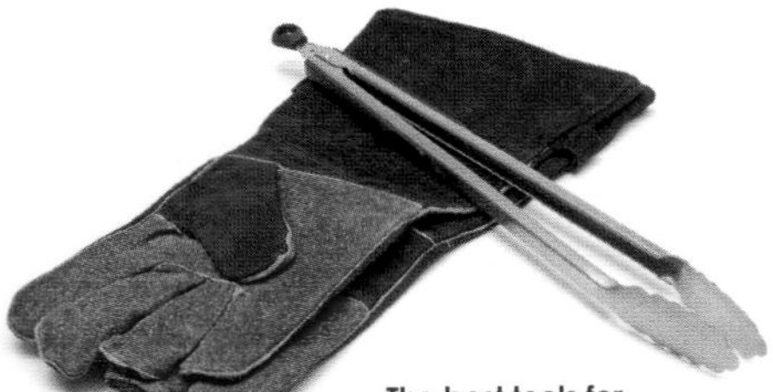

The best tools for combatting flare-ups on the grill.

My grocery store sells baby bananas and red bananas. How are they different from regular bananas?

Margaret Walsh, Nashville, Tenn.

The banana most Americans think of as a "regular" banana is a variety called Cavendish. But red and baby bananas are becoming more common in grocery stores. Tasting them plain, we found the red banana to be "more floral" and the baby "coconutty" and "denser" than the Cavendish. Both were delicious, but how would they fare in our favorite banana bread recipes? One recipe calls for three mashed (Cavendish) bananas, which measures 1½ cups. To get the same cup amount, we needed seven red bananas and 11 baby bananas. The bread made with baby bananas came out slightly darker (baby bananas have darker yellow flesh), and tasters concluded that the bread made with Cavendish bananas had the most intense banana flavor. That said, all three loaves were delicious. Another banana bread recipe we like calls for microwaving the bananas to extract their juice. When we tested this one, we found that both red and baby bananas released less liquid than an equal weight of Cavendish bananas, so the breads made with those varieties were slightly drier. The baby bananas once again produced a darker-colored loaf and the Cavendish bananas yielded the most intense banana flavor . . . but we happily polished off all three loaves.

THE BOTTOM LINE: Expand your horizons. Try different banana varieties. The flavors and textures of red and baby bananas are somewhat different from those of the more common Cavendish banana, but they're all delicious, and all work in recipes for banana bread.

11 baby bananas = 7 red bananas = 3 Cavendish bananas = 1½ cups of mashed banana

I don't drink white wine, so if I open a bottle for cooking, it often goes bad before I get through it. Is there a substitute that keeps better?

Danika Oliverio, Gainesville, Fla.

Since few of us want to open a bottle of white wine just to use ½ cup for a sauce, vermouth—which is much more shelf-stable—seemed as though it might be a good alternative. To find out, we replaced white wine with dry vermouth—an idea made famous by Julia Child—in sauces for chicken, fish, and vegetables. It worked fine in every instance. Our tasters found the sauces made with dry vermouth to be a little sweeter and "more herbal" than the same sauces made with white wine, but the difference was subtle.

Just what is vermouth, anyhow? It's made from wine fortified with additional alcohol, bringing the alcohol content to around 18 percent, versus about 12 percent for white wine. The additional alcohol in vermouth helps inhibit the growth of vinegar-producing microbes that can spoil wine. Vermouth and other fortified wines are also exposed to more air during production, which, our science editor explained, reduces the level of oxidizable compounds, making the wine more stable than white wine once the bottle is opened. Keeping vermouth in the refrigerator, where it's dark and cool, further reduces oxidation.

So how long does a bottle of vermouth last? There isn't a hard-and-fast rule, but most sources say that refrigerated vermouth will continue to taste good for three to nine months, whereas white wine goes south in just days. Even if you store the bottle in the refrigerator, though, expect the flavor of vermouth to slowly deteriorate (it will lose aroma and complexity) long before it actually goes bad. We have a couple of open bottles of vermouth in our fridge right now, and we will let you know for sure—in three to nine months.

THE BOTTOM LINE: Dry vermouth is a useful substitute for white wine in sauces. Open bottles will last several months in the refrigerator.

So many foods are labeled "low fat," "reduced fat," "fat free," etc. Do those terms mean anything?

Tim Huggins, Princeton, N.J.

If you think the labels are tough to decode, try reading the extensively foot-noted, jargon-heavy, microscopically printed U.S. Food and Drug Administration (FDA) regulations. Yes, those brightly colored starbursts on food products are, indeed, regulated. Basically, there are three categories of descriptors: those indicating the absence of fat or calories, those indicating small amounts, and those indicating comparatively less than the regular version of that food (what the FDA calls the "reference food"). Descriptors don't necessarily mean precisely what you'd think. Our chart summarizes these terms, but don't look for "light" (or "lite")—its definition can change, depending on the percentage of calories from fat in the original product, whether the food is considered a meal, and several other complicating factors.

CALORIES	FAT
Zero: Less than 5 calories per serving	**Free:** Less than 0.5 gram fat per serving
Low: 40 calories or fewer per serving	**Low:** 3 grams of fat or fewer per serving
Reduced: 25 percent fewer calories than reference food	**Reduced:** 25 percent less fat than reference food

THE BOTTOM LINE: To compare products accurately, use the nutrition information chart on the backs of packages and not the bold claims on the fronts. For a full explanation of nutrient content claims, visit the FDA website at www.fda.gov.

Why is cold-brewed iced coffee so much better than regular coffee poured over ice?

Dan Schomburg, Portland, Ore.

The flavor of coffee is made up of many different compounds. Some astringent and bitter compounds dissolve better in hot water than in cold, which means that coffee brewed in hot water will be more bitter and astringent than coffee brewed in cold water. As for the aromatic oils in coffee, they do not dissolve in water, hot or cold; rather, they leach out into it, and they do so much faster in hot water—that why it takes a long time (about 24 hours) to make cold-brewed coffee. For a step-by-step photographic guide to making cold-brewed iced coffee at home, visit **CooksCountry.com/coldbrewcoffee**.

THE BOTTOM LINE: Cold-brewed iced coffee tastes mellower because cold water dissolves fewer of coffee's bitter flavor components.

To ask us a cooking question, visit **CooksCountry.com/askcookscountry**. Or write to Ask Cook's Country, P.O. Box 470739, Brookline, MA 02447. Just try to stump us!

Kitchen Shortcuts

COMPILED BY NICK IVERSON

DOUBLE DUTY
No-Fuss Hash Browns
Denise Hines, Burlington, Mass.

My favorite part of a diner breakfast has always been the crispy hash brown potatoes. But making them at home is a hassle, and they never seemed to come out cooked correctly—never, that is, until I cracked the code using an unlikely piece of kitchen equipment: my waffle iron. Just grate potatoes, season with salt and pepper, add a little oil, plop them into the preheated iron, and close the lid. In about 15 minutes, you have perfect hash browns with no stirring, flipping, burning, or mess.

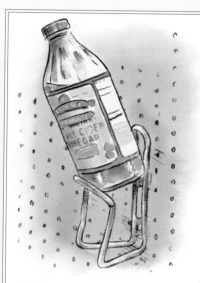

DOUBLE DUTY
Bottle Rack
Tim Collins, Madison, Wis.

Like Julia Child, I keep a large Peg-Board on a door in my kitchen: It's great for hanging pots, pans, and kitchen utensils. Recently, I was cleaning out my garage and found a half-dozen water bottle cages from our family's bicycles through the years. Not wanting to throw them out, I mounted them on the board, and now I store bottles of vinegar in them so that they're at arm's reach at all times. A friend of mine liked this idea so much that he mounted a few water bottle cages right on his kitchen wall.

CLEVER TIP Book Lock
Colm Peirce, Arlington, Mass.

I cook from cookbooks most nights. But two issues can make this difficult in my small kitchen: First, the book can get dirty, or worse, ruined, from oil, molasses, honey, ketchup, etc. And second, the pages in a stiff book often flip on their own. To solve these problems, I set the opened cookbook in a rimmed baking sheet and stretch two rubber bands across the pages on either side (this also works great with magazines). This way I can lean the book against the wall for easy, out-of-the-way, and protected reading, and the pages don't flip on me.

CLEVER TIP No-Waste Paste
Michael Lowenstein, Olympia, Wash.

I used to cringe whenever a recipe called for tomato paste: I would open the can, use a tablespoon or two, and stash the remainder in my fridge until I found it a few months later covered with green fuzz. But I came up with a solution. After using however much a particular recipe calls for, I now take the can and freeze it. Once the tomato paste is frozen, I open the other end of the can and push the frozen paste log into a zipper-lock bag. Now when I need some tomato paste, I just slice off what's required and put the rest back in the freezer.

EASY CLEANUP
Foiled Again
Margaret Rooney, Cary, N.C.

My husband cooks a big breakfast for our family every Sunday, but he's notoriously bad about disposing of the bacon grease—we've had a few clogged drains and several melted trash bags to show for his efforts. Now whenever I smell the bacon cooking, I take a small bowl and line it with foil for my husband to pour the hot grease into. Once the grease cools and solidifies, I simply wad up the foil and toss it.

EASY CLEANUP Paper or Plastic?
Leslie Lowe, Syracuse, N.Y.

Recently, while visiting friends in Florida, I saw a trick that I thought was particularly great. My friend had taken a large brown paper grocery bag, opened it, and placed the end of the cutting board just inside the bag. As she cut and chopped various vegetables, she just slid the scraps and peels into the bag as she went. No wasted motion or trips to the garbage can.

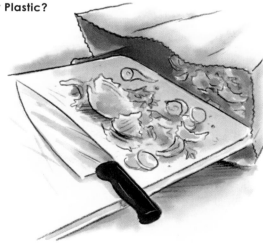

NEAT TRICK Blown Away
Tommy Folsom, Lexington, Ky.

I love grilling with charcoal, but gas grills are much faster (I use both at home). Recently, I was watching a barbecue show on TV and saw a guy stoking his fire with a leaf blower. While this seemed excessive, it got me thinking that I could use an old hair dryer (with an extension cord) to get a lit chimney starter fully ignited faster: You light the starter and point the hair dryer at the bottom for 3 minutes. The charcoal is ready to go in about 15 minutes, which shaves about 15 minutes off of the usual prep time.

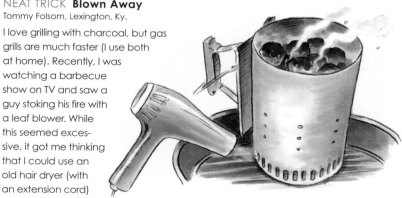

Submit a tip online at **CooksCountry.com/kitchenshortcuts** or send a letter to Kitchen Shortcuts, *Cook's Country*, P.O. Box 470739, Brookline, MA 02447. Include your name, address, and phone number. If we publish your tip, you will receive a free one-year subscription to *Cook's Country*. Letters may be edited for clarity and length.

The Ultimate Steak

If you like steak, you owe it to yourself to try the very best:
Introducing grilled cowboy-cut rib eyes. BY NICK IVERSON

WHEN IT COMES to steak, you generally get what you pay for. Sure, there are some affordable cuts that, with careful preparation to boost flavor and/or minimize chew, can make for some pretty nice eating. But high-quality premium cuts like rib eye, strip, and tenderloin will always cost you. And you know what? That's just fine with me because these steaks, and especially a rib eye—the steak with the best balance of huge flavor and tender texture—are worth it. And the absolute acme of steaks is the cowboy-cut rib eye. I'm talking 2-inch-thick, 1½-pound, bone-in behemoths that can cost upwards of $25 each at the supermarket. What's the advantage to buying huge steaks? Aside from impressing your guests, these big steaks stay on the grill longer than smaller steaks, which means (with careful cooking) they soak up more smoke and grill flavor. It was time to add these big beauties to my repertoire.

The challenge when grilling any piece of meat is cooking the inside to just the right temperature while getting a dark, flavorful sear on the outside. The larger the piece of meat the harder it is to get these things to happen at the same time. If you put a big steak over a hot fire, in the short time it takes to get a good sear, the inside won't have time to cook through. But if you put the steak over a cooler fire, when the inside is a perfect medium-rare, the outside still won't have enough char. To solve this difficulty, most grilling experts instruct the cook to create a fire with hotter and cooler zones: You sear the steaks on both sides over a hot fire, and then you move them to a cooler area of the grill to finish cooking. I gave this method a go and ended up with steaks that looked mouthwatering: The center registered a nice 125 degrees (exactly medium-rare) and the exterior had a nice, crusty char. But when I sliced into one, a serious problem emerged. Although pink in the center, the steak had a large gray band of overcooked meat around the exterior—a sure sign that it had been cooked too aggressively.

I wasn't discouraged; I had another idea. Instead of searing the steaks first and then finishing them gently, what if I reversed the order, cooking them gently most of the way (to about 100 degrees) and then moving them to a hot fire to

To carve, cut the meat off the bone and slice it. Each of these mammoth steaks serves two to three people.

finish cooking and achieve that flavorful sear? I hoped that the low heat would eliminate the gray band and that when the time came, the coals on the hotter side would still have enough juice to provide a nice char. In preparation, I set up the grill with a layer of lit coals on one side and no coals on the other. I put the steaks on the cooler side and waited patiently. And waited some more, periodically checking the steaks' internal temperature. After almost an hour, the meat finally hit 100 degrees—but by that time, the coals had burned down so much that a good sear was impossible. How could I speed up the slower "roasting" portion of cooking so that I'd have enough fire to quickly sear the steaks at the end?

I headed inside and took the temperature of the eight steaks that still remained in the refrigerator. They registered an appropriately chilly 35 to 40 degrees—no wonder it was taking the low heat so long to warm the center of the steaks. I needed to "acclimate" the steaks so that they weren't so cold when they hit the grill. To do so, I unwrapped the steaks and set them out on the counter. To increase air circulation for more even warming, I put them on a wire rack. I came back after an hour and checked their temperature again. The steaks registered roughly 55 degrees, a difference of about 20 degrees. As it turned out, those 20 degrees shaved a good 30 minutes off the initial cooking time. But after moving the steaks to the hotter part of the grill, I still wasn't getting the solid sear that these hefty steaks deserve.

It was time to bust out my trump card: the Minion method. This is a charcoal setup (named for the guy who popularized it on the barbecue circuit) in which you put a pile of unlit charcoal in the grill and then pour lit charcoal on top; as the fire burns, the unlit fuel ignites, providing a longer-burning fire. It's a technique often used for long-cooking items like ribs and pork shoulders so you don't have to add more charcoal in the middle of grilling.

I scaled down the amounts to fit the time my steaks needed on the grill and gave it a try. By the time the steaks were done roasting, there was plenty of heat left to create a crusty sear on the outside of the rib eyes. (This took about 4 minutes per side.) Two other tricks ensured success: When searing, I bucked tradition and kept the grill covered to minimize flare-ups and to make sure the steaks cooked all the way through. Also, side-by-side tests proved that rubbing the steaks with oil before grilling helped them pick up a little base color during the first part of cooking, leading to an improved sear at the end. I'd achieved sweet, tasty success.

With my cooking method worked out, I turned to flavoring the steaks. Most cooks, me included, don't mess too much with rib eyes—why cover up that wonderful beefy flavor with spice rubs or pastes? So it would be just salt and pepper. But I wanted the seasoning to be more than superficial. Since I was pulling the steaks out of the refrigerator an hour before cooking anyway, I tried salting a batch and then letting them sit while the chill came off. The prolonged salting worked wonders, seasoning these hefty slabs throughout. I finally had steaks that were flavorful and juicy, without a gray band or a burned exterior; frankly, this was the best steak I'd ever

Our recipe for classic **Wedge Salad** is perfect alongside these steaks. Find it at CooksCountry.com/wedgesalad.

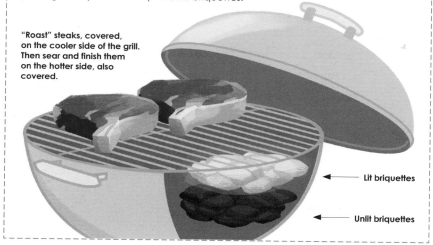
eaten. These steaks are expensive, sure, but when cooked right, they're worth every penny.

GRILLED COWBOY-CUT RIB EYES
Serves 4 to 6

Don't start grilling until the steaks' internal temperatures have reached 55 degrees. Otherwise, the times and temperatures in this recipe will be inaccurate. You will need a wire rack and a rimmed baking sheet for this recipe.

- 2 (1¼- to 1½-pound) double-cut bone-in rib-eye steaks, 1¾ to 2 inches thick, trimmed
- 4 teaspoons kosher salt
- 2 teaspoons vegetable oil
- 2 teaspoons pepper

1. Set wire rack inside rimmed baking sheet. Pat steaks dry with paper towels and sprinkle all over with salt. Place steaks on prepared rack and let stand at room temperature until meat registers 55 degrees, about 1 hour. Rub steaks with oil and sprinkle with pepper.

2A. FOR A CHARCOAL GRILL: Open bottom vent halfway. Arrange 4 quarts unlit charcoal briquettes in even layer over half of grill. Light large chimney starter one-third filled with charcoal briquettes (2 quarts). When

top coals are partially covered with ash, pour evenly over unlit coals. Set cooking grate in place, cover, and open lid vent halfway. Heat grill until hot, about 5 minutes.

2B. FOR A GAS GRILL: Turn all burners to high, cover, and heat grill until hot, about 15 minutes. Turn primary burner to medium-low and turn off other burner(s). Adjust primary burner as needed to maintain grill temperature of 300 degrees.

3. Clean and oil cooking grate. Place steaks on cooler side of grill with bones facing fire. Cover and cook until steaks register 75 degrees, 10 to 20 minutes. Flip steaks, keeping bones facing fire. Cover and continue to cook until steaks register 95 degrees, 10 to 20 minutes.

4. If using charcoal, slide steaks to hotter part of grill. If using gas, remove steaks from grill, turn primary burner to high, and heat until hot, about 5 minutes; place steaks over primary burner. Cover and cook until well browned and steaks register 120 degrees (for medium-rare), about 4 minutes per side. Transfer steaks to clean wire rack set in rimmed baking sheet, tent loosely with foil, and let rest for 15 minutes. Transfer steaks to carving board, cut meat from bone, and slice into ½-inch-thick slices. Serve.

SHOPPING In Praise of Cowboy Steaks

Rib-eye steaks are deeply marbled, tender, and beefy—they're from the same part of the steer that's used for prime rib. Bone-in steaks (like these) have more flavor than boneless, and the bone protects against overcooking. Of special interest is the exterior band of fat and meat on a rib eye called the deckle; connoisseurs say it is the most flavorful part of the cow.

BIGGER IS BETTER
Cowboy-cut rib eyes are double-thick bone-in steaks. They take longer to cook than single-serving rib eyes, so they have more time to soak up smoky grill flavor.

Grilled Chicken Leg Quarters

Leg quarters have a lot of promise: juicy dark meat and flavorful skin. But the thick joint makes it hard to cook them through without burning the outside. BY SARAH GABRIEL

WHEN IT COMES to grilled chicken, I always prefer juicy and flavorful dark meat. Bone-in, skin-on thighs are my go-to, but recently I spied whole chicken leg quarters at the meat counter for about half the price. Hmmm, I thought. Maybe this combination of leg and thigh—the perfect serving size, with rich dark meat and plenty of skin to crisp up—could become my new standard and save me some cash. I headed to the test kitchen's cookbook library to see what I could learn about cooking chicken leg quarters.

There are, as you might guess, already plenty of grilling recipes out there for this cut. The seasonings and grilling methods vary pretty widely, so I picked out a collection of recipes to try that used a broad range of ingredients and techniques. While there were several tasty seasoning combinations, my tasters and I were particularly enamored with a bold, Latin-inspired combination of lime zest, cilantro, garlic, oregano, cumin, salt, pepper, sugar, and cayenne mixed with just enough oil to create a paste—this combination really popped with flavor. The cooking method, however, proved more elusive.

As a professional cook and avid griller, I can't say I was surprised when the recipe that called for cooking over a hot fire the entire time produced chicken that burned on the outside before the inside was done. Or that a recipe that cooked over a low fire the entire time resulted in nicely cooked meat with sodden, rubbery skin. One seemingly promising recipe recommended using a two-level fire (with hotter and cooler cooking areas), searing the meat over the hotter side and then moving it to the cooler side to finish cooking, which sounded perfectly logical . . . but resulted in a smoky, charred mess when the fat rendering from the skin dripped onto the hot fire and flared up, causing scorching.

In the end, the two-level fire was the answer; I just had to start the quarters on the cooler side to render some of the fat where it wouldn't flare up. Once the leg quarters were mostly cooked through and most of the fat had melted out (this took about 20 minutes), I moved them to the hotter side to sear and finish cooking.

We use our Latin-inspired seasoning mixture as a marinade and then transform it into a bright finishing sauce.

With the basic cooking method resolved, my recipe was taking shape. That said, there remained a few important issues to figure out. The meat was good but not quite perfectly cooked (the edges and the skin were slightly overdone and dry by the time the thick joint was fully cooked through), and the seasoning, while potent, didn't penetrate as deeply and thoroughly into the meat as I wanted.

I decided to try borrowing a technique I'd previously used successfully with much larger cuts of meat. With large beef or pork roasts, we often deeply score the fat and meat to achieve the dual goals of exposing more of the roast to the seasonings and speeding up the rendering and cooking. This technique seemed odd with relatively small leg quarters, but I gave it a go, making several slashes through the meat down to the bone on each piece. I rubbed the seasoning paste into the slashes and let the legs sit for an hour before grilling. This time I had deeply seasoned meat (subsequent tests proved that the chicken gets even more flavorful with longer marination), and the slashes sped up and evened out the cooking. My tasters were impressed with the crisp ski[n] and evenly cooked meat but wondered [if] there was a way to add a bit more fresh flavor.

Experience has taught me that marinades are valuable flavor-building tools, but they can take a dish only so far. I needed something to add bold, fresh seasoning to the chicken after it was cooked. A squeeze of lime was an improvement, but it was one-dimensional. I made one more batch of chicken, this time leaving the herbs out of the marinade and setting aside 2 teaspoons of the garlic, lime zest, and spice mixture before rubbing the rest on the chicken. I let the meat sit as usual and then fired up the grill. After grilling, I mixed the fragrant reserved paste with lime juice, extra olive oil, and fresh oregano and cilantro to make an assertively bright and flavorful dressing for the cooked chicken.

Need a side dish? Try our recipe for **Creamy Buttermilk Coleslaw** at CooksCountry.com/buttermilkcoleslaw.

It's a good thing that leg quarters are a bargain because with this recipe's skin-crisping grilling method, deep seasoning, and tastebud-awakening finishing sauce, you may end up eating twice as much chicken as you normally would.

GRILLED CHICKEN LEG QUARTERS WITH LIME DRESSING Serves 4

A garlic press makes quick work of mincing the 6 cloves called for here. You can use 1 teaspoon of dried oregano in place of the fresh called for in the dressing. Do not (ever) use dried cilantro.

- 6 garlic cloves, minced
- 4 teaspoons kosher salt
- 1 tablespoon sugar
- 2 teaspoons grated lime zest plus 2 tablespoons juice
- 2 teaspoons plus ¼ cup extra-virgin olive oil
- 1½ teaspoons ground cumin
- 1 teaspoon pepper
- ½ teaspoon cayenne pepper
- 4 (10-ounce) chicken leg quarters, trimmed
- 2 tablespoons chopped fresh cilantro
- 2 teaspoons chopped fresh oregano

1. Combine garlic, salt, sugar, lime zest, 2 teaspoons oil, cumin, pepper, and cayenne in bowl and mix to form paste. Reserve 2 teaspoons garlic paste for dressing.

2. Position chicken skin side up on cutting board and pat dry with paper towels. Leaving drumsticks and thighs attached, make 4 parallel diagonal slashes in chicken: 1 across drumsticks, 1 across leg joints; and 2 across thighs (each slash should reach bone). Flip chicken over and make 1 more diagonal slash across back of drumsticks. Rub remaining garlic paste all over chicken and into slashes. Refrigerate chicken for at least 1 hour or up to 24 hours.

3A. FOR A CHARCOAL GRILL: Open bottom vent completely. Light large chimney starter filled with charcoal briquettes (6 quarts). When top coals are partially covered with ash, pour two-thirds evenly over half of grill, then pour remaining coals over other half of grill. Set cooking grate in place, cover, and open lid vent completely. Heat grill until hot, about 5 minutes.

3B. FOR A GAS GRILL: Turn all burners to high, cover, and heat grill until hot, about 15 minutes. Turn primary burner to medium and turn other burner(s) to low. (Adjust primary burner as needed to maintain grill temperature of 400 to 425 degrees.)

4. Clean and oil cooking grate. Place chicken on cooler side of grill, skin side up. Cover and cook until underside of chicken is lightly browned, 9 to 12 minutes. Flip chicken, cover, and cook until leg joint registers 165 degrees, 7 to 10 minutes.

5. Transfer chicken to hotter side of grill, skin side down, and cook (covered if using gas) until skin is well browned, 3 to 5 minutes. Flip chicken and continue to cook until leg joint registers 175 degrees, about 3 minutes longer. Transfer to platter, tent loosely with aluminum foil, and let rest for 5 to 10 minutes.

6. Meanwhile, whisk remaining ¼ cup oil, lime juice, cilantro, oregano, and reserved garlic paste together in bowl. Spoon half of dressing over chicken and serve, passing remaining dressing separately.

KEY STEPS To Flavorful, Well-Cooked Chicken Leg Quarters

Here's how we get the most out of this inexpensive cut.

SLASH Make bone-deep slashes in each quarter so the seasonings can penetrate and the meat cooks more readily.

RUB Massage the garlicky seasoning paste into the slashes and all over the chicken and refrigerate for up to 24 hours.

DRESS Transform the remaining seasoning paste into a bright dressing for the cooked chicken.

Spicy Tomato Jam

It may sound strange, but it doesn't taste that way. Tomatoes are a fruit, not a vegetable, after all. BY NICK IVERSON

EVERY SUMMER, FOR one brief, fleeting moment, sweet, juicy, vine-ripened tomatoes abound, and then, just like that, they're gone. So how do you take advantage? Make jam. OK, that might not have been your first answer, and truth be told it wasn't mine either. I had the mistaken idea that jam making was difficult and laborious. Tomato jam, an old-fashioned sweet-savory preserve that's enjoying a resurgence of late, taught me otherwise.

I collected recipes, old and new. In the kitchen, I peeled and chopped tomatoes and onions, tossed in herbs and spices, simmered batches in pots, and filled pint jars. If you're not sterilizing, canning, and sealing the jars, that's really all there is to it. But some jams tasted too sweet and others too complicated, snuffing out the tomatoes with competing flavors. On the plus side, I gleaned that brown sugar gave tomato jam depth, lemon juice gave it brightness, and onion a savory quality. Also, we liked chunky jams.

I combined these results into a decent working recipe and set to testing tomato types. All worked pretty well, but I settled on plum tomatoes for their consistently good quality. Throughout several subsequent tests, I tried various herbs and spices, eventually picking fresh ginger and cumin for warmth and pepper flakes for a touch of heat.

My jam was very tasty, but could I speed up the more than 1-hour-long process? Instead of mincing the ingredients, I gave them a rough chop and then pulsed them in the food processor. Next, I dispensed with the tomato peeling and seeding that other recipes called for. The test kitchen has found that the seeds and surrounding "jelly" contain the most tomato flavor anyway. Lastly, I traded my pot for a nonstick skillet—an old restaurant trick for reducing sauces quickly. The increased surface area of the skillet speeds up evaporation. In the skillet, I could produce jam in about 20 minutes.

I can't make time stop. But I have found a way to extend summer.

Since we don't process our jam, it's simple to make. It lasts in the fridge for two weeks.

TOMATO JAM

Makes about 2 cups

It's important to use plum tomatoes; globe tomatoes are juicier and need to cook longer. Use tomato jam in a turkey or egg salad sandwich, slather it on a burger, spread it on a buttered English muffin, or serve it with your favorite cheese. Store the jam in the refrigerator for up to two weeks.

- 2 pounds plum tomatoes, cored and chopped
- 1 cup packed light brown sugar
- ½ onion, chopped
- 3 tablespoons lemon juice
- 2 teaspoons grated fresh ginger
- 1 teaspoon ground cumin
- ¾ teaspoon salt
- ⅛ teaspoon red pepper flakes

1. Pulse all ingredients in food processor until coarsely ground, about 8 pulses. Transfer mixture to 12-inch nonstick skillet and bring to boil over medium heat.

2. Reduce heat to medium-low and simmer, stirring occasionally, until mixture is thick and syrupy (spatula should leave wide trail when dragged through jam), 20 to 25 minutes. Transfer tomato jam to bowl (or jar) and refrigerate until cool, about 2 hours.

Summer Squash Casserole

Summer squash is mostly composed of water. So how could we turn it into a casserole that wasn't wet and bland? BY DIANE UNGER

MORE OFTEN THAN not, summer squash gratins are watery and flavorless. Does it have to be that way? As an experienced professional cook, I refused to believe it. I was convinced that good technique applied to a difficult vegetable could create a delicious casserole. Since zucchini and yellow summer squash are 95 percent water, I'd need to remove extra water and keep the crumbs that topped the casserole crisp. Also, I'd season with a free hand.

The test kitchen has a technique of salting sliced squash to extract water before cooking it—if you have 45-plus minutes to spare. I hoped to develop a faster method, and I had a hunch that heat might be the answer. To test my hypothesis, I experimented with the microwave; I tossed 3 pounds of sliced squash with 2 teaspoons of salt and zapped the vegetable for various intervals. Ultimately, 8 minutes drew out excess water without annihilating the squash. (Our science editor explained why this works: Salt draws out moisture by osmosis, but the water needs time to cross many cell walls. Microwaving breaks down cell walls. Since the water runs into fewer barriers, he said, it comes out faster.) After removing the slices from the microwave, I drained them and pressed them dry.

The bread crumbs add an essential textural contrast that can make or break a gratin, so I spent several days figuring out which kind to use and how best to employ them. Eventually, I opted for ultracrispy Japanese-style panko. Traditionally, a gratin is vegetable layers *topped* with bread crumbs. With squash, though, employing them throughout was key since crumbs layered in the bottom and middle absorbed moisture released by the baking squash. After the casserole baked, covered, for 15 minutes, I added a final layer of crumbs, which browned—but didn't soak—while the gratin baked for a final 15 minutes.

To season the casserole, I incorporated a layer of nicely caramelized onions, which I perked up with garlic, thyme, and a little white wine. For even more flavor, I tossed in chopped kalamata olives, and since I'd drifted into the Mediterranean, I sprinkled on fresh basil, too. At this point, I circled back to the bread crumbs and tossed them with lots of grated Parmesan. Combined, these assertive seasonings proved perfect foils for relatively bland summer squash.

I baked a last casserole and then watched with pleasure as my coworkers attacked it. I hate to say I told you so, but . . .

SUMMER SQUASH GRATIN
Serves 6 to 8

- 2 tablespoons unsalted butter, softened, plus 4 tablespoons melted
- 2 onions, halved and sliced thin
  Salt and pepper
- 3 garlic cloves, minced
- 1 tablespoon minced fresh thyme
- ½ cup dry white wine
- ½ cup pitted kalamata olives, chopped fine
- ¼ cup chopped fresh basil
- 1½ pounds zucchini, sliced ¼ inch thick
- 1½ pounds yellow summer squash, sliced ¼ inch thick
- 1 cup panko bread crumbs
- 2 ounces Parmesan cheese, grated (1 cup)

1. Melt 1 tablespoon softened butter in 12-inch nonstick skillet over medium heat. Add onions, ½ teaspoon salt, and ¼ teaspoon pepper and cook, stirring occasionally, until onions are soft and golden brown, 15 to 20 minutes. Stir in garlic and thyme and cook until fragrant, about 30 seconds. Stir in wine and cook until evaporated, about 3 minutes. Off heat, stir in olives and 2 tablespoons basil; set aside.

2. Meanwhile, toss zucchini and yellow squash with 2 teaspoons salt in large bowl. Microwave, covered, stirring halfway through microwaving, until slightly softened and some liquid is released, about 8 minutes. Drain in colander and let cool slightly. Arrange zucchini and yellow squash on triple layer of paper towels, then cover with another triple layer of paper towels. Press slices firmly to remove as much liquid as possible.

3. Adjust oven rack to middle position and heat oven to 450 degrees. Grease bottom and sides of 13 by 9-inch baking dish with remaining 1 tablespoon softened butter. Combine panko, Parmesan, and 1 teaspoon pepper in bowl. Evenly coat baking dish with 6 tablespoons panko mixture. Stir melted butter into remaining panko mixture until well combined; set aside.

4. Arrange half of squash in prepared dish and season with pepper to taste. Sprinkle ¼ cup panko mixture evenly over squash. Spread onion mixture in even layer over crumbs. Arrange remaining half of squash over onion mixture and season with pepper to taste. Cover with aluminum foil and bake until just tender, about 15 minutes.

5. Remove dish from oven; discard foil. Sprinkle remaining panko mixture evenly over top. Bake, uncovered, until bubbling around edges and crumbs are golden brown, 10 to 15 minutes. Transfer to wire rack and let cool for 15 minutes. Sprinkle with remaining 2 tablespoons basil. Serve.

Kalamata olives and fresh basil give our casserole a Mediterranean slant.

Water: Gratin Killer

This recipe calls for a total of 3 pounds of sliced zucchini and summer squash. To rid the watery vegetables of the excess liquid that would sabotage the gratin, we slice, salt, microwave, and drain them before assembling the gratin.

LOSE THE LIQUID
This is the amount we throw out.

Grilled Eggplant with Yogurt Sauce

Smoke and fire—plus our flavored oil and easy stir-together sauce—transform mild eggplant.

BY NICK IVERSON

FEW VEGETABLES LOVE smoke and char as much as eggplant does. This often misunderstood vegetable becomes tender and smoky on the grill, where it soaks up flavor and seasonings. When it's done well, grilled eggplant is fantastic. Unfortunately, most of the grilled eggplant that I've had (including, sad to say, some that I've grilled myself) has ended up either leathery or spongy and bland.

As with many items that you put on the grill, the size of the pieces is key because you want each piece to simultaneously get good char—on both sides—and become tender. I got my testing underway with "butchering": I cut one eggplant into long planks and another into thick rounds; brushed them with olive oil to encourage browning and prevent them from sticking to the grill; seasoned them with salt and pepper; and grilled them over medium-high heat for about 10 minutes, flipping once, until they were tender. The planks cooked evenly but were unwieldy, both on the grate and the plate. Rounds were easier to cook and serve. After a series of tests, I found that ¼ inch was the optimal thickness for rounds that would be just tender by the time they were nicely marked by the grill.

Since eggplant is something of a blank canvas for other flavors, I'd settle on the seasonings next. I was already brushing the rounds with oil, so it was an obvious next move to flavor that oil. Garlic and chiles are natural partners for eggplant; I knew that I'd have to use heat to get them to give up their flavor to the oil. I didn't want to dirty a saucepan, so I turned to the ever handy microwave. I stirred five minced garlic cloves and a good pinch of red pepper flakes into about ⅓ cup of olive oil, and I microwaved the mixture until the garlic turned golden, which took about 2 minutes. Now the oil had roasted garlic flavor and a little spring in its step from the red pepper flakes. Strained and brushed on the raw eggplant rounds, the oil generously spread its flavor around.

Grilled eggplant is delicious on its own, but it's even better with a creamy sauce. With "easy" as my mantra, I looked to the Middle East for inspiration—they're masters of eggplant cookery in that region. I mixed yogurt with lemon juice and zest, cumin, mint, and some of my flavored oil. This no-cook, stir-together sauce proved the perfect foil for the smoky, garlicky, slightly spicy eggplant.

Have you been stumped by what to do with the piles of beautiful eggplants you see at farmers' markets each summer? This recipe is your answer.

GRILLED EGGPLANT WITH YOGURT SAUCE
Serves 6 to 8

For spicier eggplant, increase the amount of red pepper flakes to ¼ teaspoon.

- 6 tablespoons extra-virgin olive oil
- 5 garlic cloves, minced
- ⅛ teaspoon red pepper flakes
- ½ cup plain whole-milk yogurt
- 3 tablespoons chopped fresh mint
- 1 teaspoon grated lemon zest plus 2 teaspoons juice
- 1 teaspoon ground cumin
  Salt and pepper
- 2 pounds eggplant, sliced into ¼-inch-thick rounds

1. Combine oil, garlic, and pepper flakes in bowl. Microwave, uncovered, until garlic is golden brown and crispy, about 2 minutes. Strain garlic oil through fine-mesh strainer into small bowl. Reserve garlic oil and crispy garlic separately.

2. Combine yogurt, mint, 1 tablespoon garlic oil, lemon zest and juice, cumin, and ¼ teaspoon salt in separate bowl; set aside while preparing eggplant.

3A. FOR A CHARCOAL GRILL: Open bottom vent completely. Light large chimney starter filled with charcoal briquettes (6 quarts). When top coals are partially covered with ash, pour evenly over grill. Set cooking grate in place, cover, and open lid vent completely. Heat grill until hot, about 5 minutes.

3B. FOR A GAS GRILL: Turn all burners to high, cover, and heat grill until hot, about 15 minutes. Turn all burners to medium-high.

4. Clean and oil cooking grate. Brush eggplant all over with remaining garlic oil and season with salt and pepper. Arrange half of eggplant on grill and cook (covered if using gas) until browned and tender, about 4 minutes per side. Transfer to platter. Repeat with remaining eggplant. Serve eggplant with yogurt sauce and sprinkle with crispy garlic.

The smoky grilled eggplant is topped with a lemony yogurt sauce and crispy garlic bits.

TEST KITCHEN DISCOVERY Eggplant Even Goldilocks Could Love
If the eggplant slices are too thick, the exterior will nicely char, but the inside will be spongy and underdone. We found that ¼-inch-thick slices are the optimal size for eggplant rounds destined for the grill.

¼-INCH-THICK SLICES—JUST RIGHT

TOO THICK

Picnic Fried Chicken

Packing up cooled fried chicken to take on a picnic sounds like a grand idea. But in our experience, the sun shines, the kids play—and the chicken turns soggy. Unless . . . BY DIANE UNGER

FRIED CHICKEN IS a picnic staple, but I've often wondered why. In my experience, cold fried chicken is usually bland and soggy. Even if you don't fry much chicken yourself, you probably know that intuitively. As they sit around, French fries turn limp, fritters toughen, and fried chicken gets soggy. Was crispy cold fried chicken an oxymoron?

I looked around for specialized recipes. What I found was fried chicken made in the usual ways with a final injunction: "Serve cold." I tested these recipes anyway and was unimpressed. So on one marathon Fryday, I made six of the test kitchen's recipes for fried chicken and then refrigerated each batch for about 5 hours. This round didn't fare much better than the first.

I managed to pick up a few pointers, though. I used them to put together a working recipe that combined several features customized to facilitate fried chicken that could handle the cold. To begin, I'd brine in salty water, a step that seasons chicken deeply and keeps it moist. Next, I'd include both baking powder and cornstarch in the flour coating. In previously developed test kitchen recipes, these ingredients produced ultralight, crispy coatings—qualities that I'd need in spades for chicken I planned to eat cold.

Beyond these, all bets were off, so every day for the next eight weeks I tested all parts and procedures, trying to figure out how to fry several hours ahead yet retain the crunch. Test by test, the way grew clearer. I settled on my dredging procedure: I'd dredge the pieces in my flour mixture, then in beaten eggs, and then in a second flour dredge, this last one mixed with a little water to make it lumpy. Dipping twice would prevent a

> ▶ We fry this chicken in a Dutch oven. Read our testing of these versatile pots at CooksCountry.com/dutchovens.

"thin and wimpy" coating, as one taster put it, while adding water to the second dredge would help achieve a craggy coating, which gave us more to crunch on. I let the raw, dredged chicken chill for at least 30 minutes to evenly hydrate the coating; otherwise, dry spots became soggy when they hit the oil.

Finally, I settled on my frying procedure: I'd double-fry, a technique that involves parcooking the chicken pieces, removing them from the oil for a few minutes to let moisture evaporate from the skin, and returning them to the hot oil to finish cooking. It's extra work, but it makes a big difference.

I was making progress, but despite these adjustments, truly crunchy, cold fried chicken still seemed an impossible dream. Maybe that's why over the next week, my testing grew steadily wackier. (See "False Starts.") But one afternoon, my luck changed. Scientist Nathan Myhrvold—author of *Modernist Cuisine*, a definitive six-volume, 2,400-page tome on science-based cooking—dropped by the test kitchen. If anyone could help me, he could. He suggested an industrial crisping ingredient that manufacturers use. Um, can you buy that at the supermarket? I asked. OK then, he said, try combining Wondra with potato starch, which should give you a similar result.

When I got back to my desk, I phoned our science editor to get the whys and wherefores. He explained that Wondra has just enough protein content to give the coating strength without sacrificing the crispy, brittle structure of the potato starch. Also, Wondra is precooked (pregelatinized) and dried, he said, so it doesn't absorb moisture readily. But he advised me to stick with cornstarch, which has more amylose starch molecules than potato starch does. Amylose, he explained, does the lion's share of the work in achieving a crispy coating. Back in the kitchen, I grabbed

We fry twice: Moisture evaporates with the first fry, making crispy chicken skin easier to achieve.

a canister of Wondra and cornstarch (it's also more pantry-friendly than potato starch) and got to work. The resulting chicken was crispy when hot—and it was crispy when cold. Hallelujah.

I made a few last refinements. I replaced the egg dredge with plain water because the fat in the egg was softening the coating. And since sensitivity to taste is lower when food is cold, I bumped up the seasoning, adding plenty of pepper, garlic powder, sage, and thyme to the second dredge. The final key to crispiness was as simple as cooling the fried chicken uncovered in the refrigerator.

Fast and easy this recipe is not, but bear in mind that the chicken is made ahead. Come picnic time, simply apply the sunscreen, unfurl the blanket, and dig in.

PICNIC FRIED CHICKEN Serves 4

We like it best the day it's made, but you can refrigerate this fried chicken for up to 24 hours. Use a Dutch oven that holds 6 quarts or more.

- Salt and pepper
- 3 pounds bone-in chicken pieces (split breasts cut in half crosswise, drumsticks, and/or thighs), trimmed
- 1½ cups Wondra flour
- 1½ cups cornstarch
- 2 teaspoons white pepper
- 1½ teaspoons baking powder
- 1 teaspoon dried thyme
- 1 teaspoon dried sage leaves
- 1 teaspoon garlic powder
- ¼ teaspoon cayenne pepper
- 3 quarts peanut or vegetable oil

KITCHEN TESTING False Starts

We took a few wrong turns in our quest for chicken that would stay crispy when cold.

Lose the Skin?
Was flabby skin to blame for the soggy coating? But when skinless, it was . . . not really fried chicken.

Add Gelatin or Pectin?
Neither gave the coating more structure. And both turned doughy when cold.

Chinese Takeout Trick?
Pulverizing wonton wrappers for the coating was a cool idea. Too bad it tasted like cardboard.

1. Dissolve ¼ cup salt in 1 quart cold water in large container. Submerge chicken in brine, cover, and refrigerate for 1 hour.

2. Whisk flour and cornstarch together in large bowl. Transfer 1 cup flour mixture to shallow dish; set aside. Whisk 1 tablespoon pepper, white pepper, baking powder, thyme, sage, garlic powder, 1 teaspoon salt, and cayenne into remaining flour mixture. Add ¼ cup water to seasoned flour mixture. Rub flour and water together with your fingers until water is evenly incorporated and mixture contains craggy bits of dough. Pour 2 cups cold water into medium bowl.

3. Set wire rack in rimmed baking sheet. Working with 2 pieces of chicken at a time, remove chicken from brine and dip in unseasoned flour mixture, pressing to adhere; dunk quickly in water, letting excess drip off; and dredge in seasoned flour mixture, pressing to adhere. Place chicken on prepared wire rack and refrigerate for at least 30 minutes or up to 2 hours.

4. Add oil to large Dutch oven until it measures about 2 inches deep and heat over medium-high heat to 350 degrees. Fry half of chicken until lightly golden and just beginning to crisp, 5 to 7 minutes. Adjust burner, if necessary, to maintain oil temperature between 300 and 325 degrees. Chicken will not be cooked through at this point.) Return parcooked chicken to wire rack. Return oil to 350 degrees and repeat with remaining raw chicken. Let each batch of chicken rest for 5 to 7 minutes.

5. Return oil to 350 degrees. Return first batch of chicken to oil and fry until breasts register 160 degrees and thighs/drumsticks register 175 degrees, 5 to 7 minutes. Adjust burner, if necessary, to maintain oil temperature between 300 and 325 degrees. Transfer chicken to clean wire rack. Return oil to 350 degrees and repeat with remaining chicken. Let chicken cool to room temperature, transfer to paper towel–lined plate, and refrigerate uncovered until ready to eat, up to 24 hours in advance. (Serve cold or let chicken come to room temperature.)

Texas Potato Salad

A mustardy potato salad that packs heat? Sounds like something we should have thought of a long time ago. BY CRISTIN WALSH

CRANK UP THE flavor of potato salad with yellow mustard and chopped jalapeños, and you've got what's popularly called Texas potato salad. I liked the sound of it. Since we've already perfected classic potato salad in the test kitchen, I'd start there and Tex it up.

I boiled Yukon Gold potatoes to tenderness and tossed the hot spuds with dill pickle juice to season them. After waiting 30 minutes for the flavors to deepen (and the potatoes to cool), I mixed in the usual mayonnaise, onions, celery, pickles, and hard-cooked eggs. But instead of the modest 1 tablespoon of mustard our recipe calls for, I lavished the potato salad with 6 tablespoons, and then I stirred in chopped fresh jalapeños.

The punchy mustard flavor was great, but as for the jalapeños—ouch. They were raw and hot. For my next test, I replaced them with a jar of pickled jalapeños. But supermarket pickled jalapeños, it turns out, have little zip. To make my own quick pickle, I heated vinegar, sugar, and lots of mustard seeds—to reinforce the mustardy flavor—and then I stirred in jalapeño and onion slices and let the mixture cool for 20 minutes. As I was swapping out the dill pickles in the original recipe for my homemade pickled jalapeños, I realized that I could also replace the dill pickle juice with my homemade pickling solution. My next batch of potato salad reflected those changes—and was awfully good. For extra kick, I added ¼ teaspoon of cayenne.

My Texas Potato Salad is spicy, bold, and bright no matter where you eat it—Brownsville or Jacksonville, Austin or Boston.

What makes our potato salad so distinctive? Fast, easy, homemade pickled jalapeños.

TEXAS POTATO SALAD Serves 8

Annie's Naturals Organic Yellow Mustard is our favorite brand of yellow mustard.

- ½ cup red wine vinegar
- 1½ tablespoons sugar
  Salt and pepper
- 1 teaspoon yellow mustard seeds
- ½ small red onion, sliced thin
- 2 jalapeño chiles (1 sliced into thin rings; 1 stemmed, seeded, and minced)
- 3 pounds Yukon Gold potatoes, peeled and cut into ¾-inch pieces
- 6 tablespoons mayonnaise
- 6 tablespoons yellow mustard
- ¼ teaspoon cayenne pepper
- 2 large hard-cooked eggs, cut into ¼-inch pieces
- 1 celery rib, minced

1. Combine vinegar, sugar, 1½ teaspoons salt, and mustard seeds in bowl and microwave until steaming, about 2 minutes. Whisk until sugar and salt are dissolved. Add onion and jalapeños and set aside until cool, 15 to 20 minutes. Strain onion and jalapeños through fine-mesh strainer set over bowl. Reserve pickled vegetables and vinegar mixture separately.

2. Meanwhile, combine potatoes, 8 cups water, and 1 tablespoon salt in Dutch oven and bring to boil over high heat. Reduce heat to medium and simmer until potatoes are just tender, 10 to 15 minutes.

3. Drain potatoes thoroughly, then transfer to large bowl. Drizzle 2 tablespoons reserved vinegar mixture over hot potatoes and toss gently until evenly coated. (Reserve remaining vinegar mixture for another use.) Refrigerate until cool, about 30 minutes, stirring once halfway through chilling.

4. Whisk mayonnaise, mustard, ½ teaspoon pepper, and cayenne together in bowl until combined. Add mayonnaise mixture, reserved pickled vegetables, eggs, and celery to potatoes and stir gently to combine. Season with salt and pepper to taste. Cover and refrigerate to let flavors blend, about 30 minutes. Serve. (Salad can be refrigerated for up to 2 days.)

Pork Chops with Vinegar Peppers

Our objective? To avoid the common cooking pitfalls that often spoil this Italian American classic: dry chops and sour sauces. BY REBECCAH MARSTERS

THICK, MEATY CHOPS braised with tangy vinegar peppers has been an Italian American restaurant favorite for decades. Given how simple it looks—combine chops, jarred pickled peppers, and vinegar—the dish seems ideally suited for a weeknight dinner at home. The recipes I found promised deep yet bright flavor and the fall-off-the-bone tenderness that comes from long braising. I was dubious; pork chops risk drying out if cooked for very long. One recipe claimed that the acid in the vinegar had a tenderizing effect—really?

Keeping an open mind, I prepared a handful of recipes. Most used center-cut or rib chops, which were browned and then braised—some for up to 45 minutes. One recipe called for nearly a cup of vinegar; others used just a few tablespoons of pickling liquid, with chicken broth making up the bulk of the braising liquid. Recipes variously used sweet or spicy pickled peppers.

Sad to say, my skepticism was justified: These chops were uniformly dry and chalky and the sauces thin and sour; those made with the jarred brine tasted tinny. So much for tenderizing vinegar. Despite these flaws, I spied the potential for a satisfying, rustic dish. The best of this bad lot included rosemary sprigs and whole garlic cloves.

My first task was to figure out the peppers and the pork. I ran through my pickled pepper choices: Cherry peppers were too spicy, and heat turned *pepperoncini* mushy. Short of pickling my own peppers—not realistic for a weeknight meal—I was left with sweet vinegar peppers. Their mild tang complemented the savory pork, and they were sturdy enough to hold up to braising.

Improving the pork should be easy, I thought—I'd just avoid overcooking it. Lean center-cut chops are prone to dry out when braised, so I used thick, bone-in rib chops, which have more fat, connective tissue, and flavor. For extra insurance against dry meat and to season the chops deeply, I brined them for 30 minutes. I knew that a lengthy braise was out, but I hoped that if I nailed the timing, I could simmer the chops just long enough to cook them through and allow for some flavor transfer between the meat and the sauce. After the chops browned for a few minutes, I removed them from the pan and added the garlic and rosemary I'd liked, plus white wine

At this point in the recipe, we remove the chops, reduce the sauce, and then stir in butter.

vinegar and the sliced peppers. I nestled the meat back into the pan and let it finish cooking at a gentle simmer. It took less than 10 minutes to arrive at juicy, perfectly cooked pork.

Those 10 minutes were enough time for the flavors of the meat and sauce to mingle, but the sauce lacked the complexity of a long-cooked braising liquid. Also, without time to reduce, it was too thin. To bolster the sauce, I sautéed sliced onions along with the garlic before adding the peppers to the pan. Most recipes use white wine vinegar, but we preferred red wine vinegar combined with chicken broth.

I was making headway, but the sauce still lacked enough flavor and heft. Running through a mental list of potent ingredients in the Italian larder, I came up with an unexpected flavor booster: anchovies. A few fillets sautéed with the aromatics added depth and seasoning without being identifiable as fish. To thicken the sauce, I floured the chops before I seared them, which had the serendipitous side effect of boosting the flavorful browning.

To maintain the crust I'd created with this step, I seared the chops on just one side, flipped them, and was careful to keep the seared side above the braising liquid. Once the chops were cooked, I set them aside on a plate and reduced the sauce for a few minutes until it was thick and silky. Finally, I swirled in a pat of butter, bringing the whole now-delicious dish together.

PORK CHOPS WITH VINEGAR PEPPERS Serves 4

- 3 tablespoons sugar
- Salt and pepper
- 4 (8- to 10-ounce) bone-in pork rib chops, 1 inch thick, trimmed
- ⅓ cup all-purpose flour
- 2 tablespoons olive oil
- 1 onion, halved and sliced thin
- 8 garlic cloves, lightly crushed and peeled
- 2 anchovy fillets, rinsed, patted dry, and minced
- 2 cups thinly sliced sweet green vinegar peppers
- 1 sprig fresh rosemary
- 1 cup chicken broth
- ½ cup red wine vinegar
- 1 tablespoon unsalted butter

1. Dissolve sugar and 3 tablespoons salt in 1½ quarts cold water in large container. Add chops, cover, and refrigerate for 30 minutes or up to 1 hour.

2. Place flour in shallow dish. Remove chops from brine. Pat chops dry with paper towels and season with pepper. Working with 1 chop at a time, dredge both sides in flour, shaking off excess. Heat 1 tablespoon oil in 12-inch skillet over medium-high heat until just smoking. Add chops and cook until well browned on first side, 5 to 7 minutes. Flip chops and cook on second side for 1 minute; transfer to plate, browned side up.

3. Reduce heat to medium and add remaining 1 tablespoon oil, onion, garlic, and anchovies to now-empty skillet. Cook, stirring frequently, until onion is softened and golden brown, 6 to 8 minutes. Add peppers and rosemary and cook until peppers begin to caramelize, about 5 minutes. Add broth and vinegar and bring to boil.

4. Arrange chops, browned side up, in skillet and add any accumulated juices from plate. Reduce heat to low, cover, and simmer until chops register 145 degrees, 6 to 10 minutes. Transfer chops to serving platter and tent loosely with aluminum foil.

5. Increase heat to high and boil sauce until slightly thickened, about 3 minutes. Off heat, stir in butter and season with salt and pepper to taste. Stir any accumulated juices from platter into sauce. Discard rosemary and spoon sauce over chops. Serve.

Grilled Caesar Salad

A smoky char makes this classic American salad better than ever.
But must you give up crispness to get smokiness? BY CRISTIN WALSH

GRILL CAESAR SALAD? Introduce delicate lettuce to hot coals? It sounded like a terrible idea. But as I paged through recipes, the universally enthusiastic descriptions piqued my interest. The smoky char of the grill, I read, brings a whole new dimension to Caesar salad. Curious, I tried a few recipes—and my doubts returned. On the grill, the lettuce scorched and wilted. At any rate, the challenge was clear: maintain crispness yet develop smokiness.

I did pick up a few good ideas, though. I'd use romaine hearts, not heads. The sturdier, more compact hearts withstood the heat better. Before grilling, I'd halve them lengthwise, keeping the cores attached. This gave them plenty of surface area to develop char while preventing the leaves from falling into the fire. To improve the odds of getting softness and char, as opposed to limpness and flabbiness, I'd grill the hearts on just one side.

I started again, brushing the halved romaine hearts with oil to encourage char and minimize sticking and then grilling them over a hot fire. In 5 minutes, I had smokiness and char. Unfortunately, I also had wilted, slimy lettuce. To get char faster, so that the heat wouldn't have time to penetrate (read: wilt) the inner leaves, how about a hot fire? Within a minute or two, the romaine had both distinct char and a crunchy interior.

For the Caesar dressing, I used a test kitchen recipe that replaces the classic raw egg with mayonnaise. It's bold, well seasoned, and delicious—so good that I got the idea to brush it on the cut side of the uncooked lettuce in place of the olive oil I'd been using. In just 1 minute over the heat, the dressing picked up a mildly smoky flavor.

For the croutons, I'd need big slices that couldn't fall through the grill grates. I cut a baguette into slices on the bias, brushed them with olive oil, and toasted them over the coals. Borrowing an idea from bruschetta, I rubbed the slices with a cut raw garlic clove.

I combined the lettuce and the bread, drizzled on extra dressing, dusted everything with more Parmesan, and called tasters. The salad disappeared and so did my skepticism. With apologies to Shakespeare: It's not that I love Caesar less, but that I love grilled Caesar more.

GRILLED CAESAR SALAD Serves 6

DRESSING
- 1 tablespoon lemon juice
- 1 garlic clove, minced
- ½ cup mayonnaise
- ½ ounce Parmesan cheese, grated (¼ cup)
- 1 tablespoon white wine vinegar
- 1 tablespoon Worcestershire sauce
- 1 tablespoon Dijon mustard
- 2 anchovy fillets, rinsed
- ½ teaspoon salt
- ½ teaspoon pepper
- ¼ cup extra-virgin olive oil

SALAD
- 1 (12-inch) baguette, cut on bias into 5-inch-long, ½-inch-thick slices
- 3 tablespoons extra-virgin olive oil
- 1 garlic clove, peeled
- 3 romaine lettuce hearts (18 ounces), halved lengthwise through cores
- ½ ounce Parmesan cheese, grated (¼ cup)

1. FOR THE DRESSING: Combine lemon juice and garlic in bowl and let stand for 10 minutes. Process mayonnaise, Parmesan, lemon-garlic mixture, vinegar, Worcestershire, mustard, anchovies, salt, and pepper in blender for about 30 seconds. With blender running, slowly add oil. Reserve 6 tablespoons dressing for brushing romaine.

2A. FOR A CHARCOAL GRILL: Open bottom vent completely. Light large chimney starter filled with charcoal briquettes (6 quarts). When top coals are partially covered with ash, pour evenly over half of grill. Set cooking grate in place, cover, and open lid vent completely. Heat grill until hot, about 5 minutes.

2B. FOR A GAS GRILL: Turn all burners to high, cover, and heat grill until hot, about 15 minutes. Leave all burners on high.

3. FOR THE SALAD: Clean and oil cooking grate. Brush bread with oil and grill (over coals if using charcoal), uncovered, until browned, about 1 minute per side. Transfer to platter and rub with garlic clove. Brush cut sides of romaine with reserved dressing; place half of romaine, cut side down, on grill (over coals if using charcoal). Grill, uncovered, until lightly charred, 1 to 2 minutes. Move to platter with bread. Repeat. Drizzle romaine with remaining dressing. Sprinkle with Parmesan. Serve.

We leave the core of the romaine intact so the leaves won't fall apart on the grill.

STEP BY STEP **Salad Prep for Grilled Caesar**
We get twice the flavor by using the dressing before and after grilling.

1. Brush our easy homemade Caesar dressing onto the halved romaine hearts before grilling.

2. Grill the dressed romaine halves on just one side to keep the lettuce from wilting.

3. Once the charred lettuce comes off the grill, finish it with more Caesar dressing.

Inexpensive Roast Beef on the Grill

Slow-roasting beef on the grill is easy with pricey cuts. But could we make it work with bargain beef?

BY JEREMY SAUER

TO BE HONEST, it's pretty easy to grill-roast a beautifully marbled roast from the rib or top loin: Just rub the exterior with salt and herbs, sear it over high heat, and then move it to a cooler part of the grill to slowly cook to the desired temperature. The intensely charred crust and smoky flavor are phenomenal on these tender, beefy roasts. But what if you want a grill-roasted beef roast without the exorbitant price tag of those premium cuts?

"Inexpensive" beef roasts aren't new territory in the test kitchen. Through the years we've tested every possible cut and have picked top sirloin as our preferred inexpensive choice for most recipes. But at roughly $10 a pound, a 4-pound top sirloin roast isn't that inexpensive. I set out to develop a recipe for roast beef on the grill that used a truly cheap roast like top round, bottom round, rump, or eye round. After doing a bit of exploratory cooking—and tasting—of these cuts, I landed on the eye round in part for its almost perfectly cylindrical shape; the other roasts were blocky or tapered and thus more challenging to cook evenly. Eye round's $5-per-pound price tag didn't hurt either.

I began testing with an eye toward texture. In the past, the test kitchen has helped tenderize tough beef roasts by salting the meat for several hours, searing it quickly on the stovetop, and then roasting it at around 225 degrees. The low temperature lets enzymes in the meat work their tenderizing magic while minimizing shrinkage of muscle fibers (which would force out moisture and toughen the meat) and also lessens the likelihood of overcooking. Since these techniques were proven in the oven, they'd surely translate to the grill, right?

I started by searing the salted roast over a hot fire to develop a tasty browned crust and then sliding it to a cooler part of the grill to finish with indirect heat—grill roasting 101. Unfortunately, the cooler side of the grill was too hot for true low-and-slow cooking so the outside of the roast overcooked. I tried pulling it off the grill for a few minutes after searing while the grill cooled down, but the finished roast still had an overcooked exterior in the form of a gray band of meat surrounding the pink center. Shifting gears, I skipped the searing and just cooked the beef with

Deep, rich, and flavorful, this beef has evenly cooked meat that is pink throughout—no small achievement with an eye-round roast.

low, indirect heat. This was an improvement (though the roast was, for the time being, devoid of a crust), but the roast was cooking unevenly—often one side of the meat was cooked considerably more than the other.

The problem is that even with indirect grilling, the side of the roast that faces the heat cooks more quickly than the other. While not a deal breaker for dishes like ribs and pulled pork that are

not cooked to a specific temperature, we like our roast beef cooked to 125 degrees for medium-rare—the direct heat on one side of the meat was killing me here. I toyed with different heat levels and tried flipping halfway, but nothing helped. Thankfully, a colleague made a simple suggestion: Block the radiant heat. I laid a sheet of aluminum foil on the cooler side of the grill, set the raw seasoned roast on it, and wrapped

the foil over the meat in a loose cylinder. This foil "shield" deflected the heat and created a consistent ambient cooking temperature that resulted in beautifully cooked beef.

Now I could move on to building more flavor. The presalting was a start, but some dried herbs (rosemary, oregano, and thyme) and pepper really amped up the crust. My tasters clamored for smoke to amplify the "grilled" flavor so I obliged them by adding a cup of soaked wood chips to the fire. Although the roast was properly seasoned, it still lacked beefiness. The "beef" flavor of lean eye round just can't compare with that of better-marbled cuts—but I hoped that a little kitchen chicanery might bridge the gap.

It's no secret that *umami*-rich ingredients like mushrooms, soy sauce, and Parmesan cheese contribute "meaty," savory taste to recipes. I found a recipe that created a flavorful crust by calling for rubbing a beef roast with pulverized dried porcini mushrooms. We tried it and liked it, but porcini didn't exactly track with the "inexpensive" theme. I followed up with a Parmesan rub, a soy "brine," and even a miso glaze. Nothing gave me the results I sought. Then one of my editors had an idea: Try rubbing the roast with ketchup. Tomatoes *are* umami-rich, but could ketchup really work here? You bet—just 2 tablespoons rubbed into the exterior (with the salt and herbs) definitely made the roast taste beefier and in the process turned our preconceptions on their head.

One problem remained: the crust. I'd already dismissed searing upfront, so I hoped that searing after grill-roasting would work. For my next test, once the roast was a hair shy of medium-rare, I cranked the grill to high and seared the roast until it was charred all over. The crust looked great, but the final blast of heat sent the internal temperature soaring and overcooked the exterior of the roast. I tried turning up the heat earlier and earlier with no more success. Then it hit me: What if I let the roast rest before I seared it? This way, the internal temperature of the roast would stabilize—as the carryover cooking would have time to peter out—and the searing would affect only the exterior of the meat (plus, the resting would give me time to light and add more briquettes for the charcoal grill version). On my next test, I pulled the roast off the grill at 122 degrees; let it rest for 30 minutes, until it was 130 degrees; and then seared it over high heat. When I pulled it off the grill for the second time, it still registered 130 degrees but it looked—and tasted—awesome. Finally, I had a warm-weather roast beef at a weekly discount price.

SMOKED ROAST BEEF Serves 6 to 8

For those of you using charcoal, this recipe calls for lighting two fires: the first to slow-smoke the meat, and the second to sear it after a prolonged rest. For medium roast beef, cook it to an internal temperature of 130 to 135 degrees. You don't need to rest the meat again after searing it in step 5; the roast may be served immediately.

- 2 tablespoons ketchup
- 4 teaspoons salt
- 2 teaspoons pepper
- ½ teaspoon dried thyme
- ½ teaspoon dried oregano
- ½ teaspoon dried rosemary
- 1 (4-pound) boneless eye-round roast, trimmed
- 1 cup wood chips
- 2 teaspoons vegetable oil

1. Combine ketchup, salt, pepper, thyme, oregano, and rosemary in bowl. Rub ketchup mixture all over roast, then wrap roast with plastic wrap and refrigerate for at least 6 hours or up to 24 hours. Just before grilling, soak wood chips in water for 15 minutes, then drain. Using large piece of heavy-duty aluminum foil, wrap soaked chips in foil packet and cut several vent holes in top.

2A. FOR A CHARCOAL GRILL: Open bottom vent halfway. Light large chimney starter half filled with charcoal briquettes (3 quarts). When top coals are partially covered with ash, pour into steeply banked pile against side of grill. Place wood chip packet on coals. Set cooking grate in place, cover, and open lid vent halfway. Heat grill until hot and chips are smoking, about 5 minutes.

2B. FOR A GAS GRILL: Place wood chip packet over primary burner. Turn all burners to high, cover, and heat grill until hot and wood chips are smoking, about 15 minutes. Turn primary burner to medium-high and turn off other burner(s). (Adjust primary burner as needed to maintain grill temperature of 325 degrees.)

3. Set wire rack inside rimmed baking sheet. Unwrap roast. Arrange 18 by 12-inch sheet of foil on cooler side of grill and place roast on top of 1 end of foil. Loosely roll foil over roast, then tuck end of foil under roast to form loose cylinder around roast. Cook, covered, until meat registers 125 degrees (for medium-rare), 1½ to 1¾ hours. Remove roast from grill, transfer to prepared wire rack, and tent loosely with foil. Let roast rest for 30 minutes or up to 1 hour.

4A. FOR A CHARCOAL GRILL: Open bottom vent completely. Light large chimney starter filled with charcoal briquettes (6 quarts). When top coals are partially covered with ash, pour into pile over spent coals. Set cooking grate in place, cover, and open lid vent completely. Heat grill until hot, about 5 minutes.

4B. FOR A GAS GRILL: Turn all burners to high, cover, and heat grill until hot, about 5 minutes. Leave all burners on high.

5. Clean and oil cooking grate. Brush roast all over with oil. Grill (directly over coals for charcoal; covered if using gas), turning frequently, until charred on all sides, 8 to 12 minutes. Transfer meat to carving board, slice thin, and serve.

TASTING FROZEN FRENCH FRIES

Frozen French fries are not a promising food group, but get real: Making homemade fries is a project. So do any frozen fries deserve a passing grade? We sought the answer by tasting four straight-cut frozen French fry products with a side of ketchup. (We left crinkle cuts and steak fries for another day.)

Before you bake them at home, frozen fries that come in bags have already been cooked—twice. In the factory, the potatoes are blanched in hot water and then fried in vegetable oil. One product we tried uses only Yukon Gold potatoes; the rest rely on russets or a combination of russets and other yellow potatoes.

The standout fries had a "savory," "potato-y" flavor and a "creamy," "fluffy" interior. They were not peeled, which probably contributed to the "earthy" flavor. This product also had the fewest ingredients: just the potatoes, oil, sea salt, and citric acid (to preserve color). By contrast, two fry products that use sodium acid pyrophosphate, also a color preservative, tasted "packaged," and a product with no added salt tasted "bland" even after we added enough salt to level the playing field. This no-added-salt product uses apple juice concentrate to promote browning; the fries browned, yes, but they were "oddly sweet."

From now on, when we don't have time to peel, cut, blanch, and fry potatoes, we'll be reaching for Organic Yukon Select Fries from Alexia. –AMY GRAVES

RECOMMENDED

ALEXIA Organic Yukon Select Fries
Price: $2.99 for 15 oz (20 cents per oz)
Ingredients: Organic Yukon Gold potatoes, organic canola or sunflower or safflower oil, sea salt, citric acid
Sodium: 200 mg per 3-oz serving
Thickness: 7 mm

These "most potato-y" fries were "nice and crispy" with a "fluffy," "creamy interior." "This feels like a fry, not a mushy stick of starch," one taster said. This organic product also earned plaudits for the "earthy" taste of potato skin on the ends.

ORE-IDA Golden Fries
Price: $3.99 for 32 oz (12 cents per oz)
Ingredients: Potatoes, vegetable oil (sunflower, cottonseed, soybean, and/or canola oil), salt, dextrose, disodium dihydrogen pyrophosphate, annatto (vegetable color)
Sodium: 290 mg per 3-oz serving
Thickness: 10 mm

Our second-favorite fries were thicker-cut, "potato-y"-tasting sticks that were also "buttery," "crisp," and "very flavorful." They lost a few points for a "mealy interior" that some found "almost bready" and "starchy."

RECOMMENDED WITH RESERVATIONS

CASCADIAN FARM Shoe String French Fries
Price: $2.99 for 16 oz (19 cents per oz)
Ingredients: Organic potatoes, canola oil, apple juice concentrate (to promote browning), citric acid (to preserve color)
Sodium: 10 mg per 3-oz serving
Thickness: 6 mm

The thinnest fries in our lineup were nice and "crunchy" but had "almost no interior." Some praised their "potato flavor"; others found them "bland," with one taster complaining, "These don't taste like anything."

NOT RECOMMENDED

McCAIN Classic Cut French Fried Potatoes
Price: $3.99 for 32 oz (12 cents per oz)
Ingredients: Potatoes, canola and cottonseed oil, sea salt, annatto and caramel (color), sodium acid pyrophosphate (preserves natural color)
Sodium: 220 mg per 3-oz serving
Thickness: 10 mm

A few tasters liked the "almost cheesy/buttery flavor" of these thick fries, but many rated them "starchy" and "limp." A few of us picked up on a "fake" aftertaste, "like a processed baked potato." Caramel coloring accounted for the orangey hue and possibly affected the flavor, too.

TEST KITCHEN TECHNIQUE **Smoked Roast Beef on (and off) the Grill**
Follow these directions for flavorful beef that's rosy throughout.

1. COOK LOW with a foil shield.

2. REST to prevent overcooking.

3. SEAR over high heat.

Getting to Know Essential Pork Cuts

Here are the 12 cuts of pork we use most often in the test kitchen, along with notes on how to cook them. BY REBECCAH MARSTERS

Pork Loin
SUNDAY ROAST

The large, tender loin is from the pig's back, and it's best roasted (we like to sear it first to provide extra flavor). Lean pork loin can dry out if cooked beyond 140 degrees—use an instant-read thermometer to make sure you cook it correctly. You can buy the loin bone-in or boneless. One way we enjoy a boneless loin roast is seared then roasted with a honey glaze. Find the recipe at **CooksCountry.com/ honeyglazedporkloin**.

Pork Chops
SINGLE SERVE

Pork chops come thin or thick cut; bone-in or boneless; and from the sirloin or from the shoulder, rib, or center of the loin. In the test kitchen, we prefer bone-in rib and center-cut loin chops for sautéing or grilling; blade chops (cut from the shoulder) are fattier and better braised. To avoid overcooking, cook lean chops to an internal temperature of 145 degrees. For extra insurance against dried-out chops, brine them before cooking.

Pork Butt
SLOWPOKE

To coax the most from pork butt, a tough, fatty, relatively inexpensive cut from the upper part of the pig's shoulder, slowly smoke, roast, or braise it to tenderness. This cut—also called Boston butt— comes bone-in or boneless, weighs 6 to 8 pounds, and is often shredded after cooking. If we don't plan to shred it, we tie the roast before cooking. Find our recipe for Lexington-Style Pulled Pork at **CooksCountry.com/lexingtonpork**.

Ham Hocks
FLAVORING AGENT

Ham hocks give porky (and sometimes smoky) flavor to soups, stews, and pots of long-simmered greens. Cut from the lower portion of the pig's hind leg, the hock has lots of fat, bone, and connective tissue, plus a little meat, so it requires long cooking to release flavor and tenderize. Ham hocks are usually sold smoked or cured, although fresh ones are available, too.

Picnic Shoulder
CRACKLIN' CACHE

Just below the pork butt, where the pig's front leg meets its torso, is the picnic shoulder, also called the pork shoulder. Like the pork butt, the shoulder is fatty and needs long cooking, but unlike the butt, it's usually sold bone-in. The picnic shoulder has a considerable cap of fat and skin—perfect for making crackling. Don't confuse picnic shoulders with picnic hams: The latter are smoked.

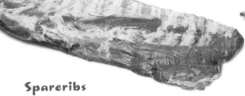

Spareribs
BBQ CHAMP

Cut from near the fatty belly of the pig, spareribs include the rib bones, the meat between them, and the brisket bone near the pig's chest. They can weigh more than 4 pounds per rack. We prefer the slightly smaller St. Louis–style ribs (seen here), which fit better on a backyard grill because the bones and meat from the brisket section have been removed. They cook more quickly and evenly, too.

Baby Back Ribs
PARTY FAVORITE

These ribs come from the back of the pig, along the vertebrae. They're smaller than spareribs, usually less than 2 pounds per rack. These ribs have more meat and less connective tissue than spareribs do, which is good, but there is a drawback: Baby backs are relatively lean, so they can easily dry out if overcooked. Find our recipe for roasted baby backs at **CooksCountry.com/honeyroastedribs**.

Country-Style Ribs
MIX AND MATCH

These ribs are made from halved or butterflied rib chops from the blade (shoulder) end of the tenderloin. They contain both dark meat from the shoulder and light meat from the loin; we like to brine them (to keep the white meat moist) and then pound them to an even thickness (so the dark meat cooks through faster), as we do in our recipe for Barbecued Country-Style Ribs: **CooksCountry. com/bbqcountrystyleribs**.

Pork Tenderloin
THE OTHER WHITE MEAT

Pork tenderloin, the muscle that runs down either side of the backbone, is lean, mild, and, yes, tender—in fact, it's the single most tender part of the pig. We like to sear tenderloins and then finish them either in the oven or on the cooler part of the grill. Before you start cooking, trim off the shiny membrane (it's called the silverskin, and it's unpleasantly chewy).

Fresh Ham
HEFTY HINDQUARTERS

Most of us think of ham as a pink haunch that's smoked, fully cooked, and ready to eat. Fresh ham is none of those things: It's simply the pig's upper hind leg. Whole fresh hams can weigh up to 25 pounds, so they're usually broken down into the sirloin (or "butt") end closer to the torso, and the tapered shank end (seen here; we prefer this cut for easy carving). Brine fresh ham before cooking it to keep it moist.

Cured Ham
HOLIDAY CLASSIC

Cured city hams are wet-cured in brine, while country hams are dry-cured in salt and then aged. If the label says anything more than "ham" or "ham with natural juices," don't buy it. Also avoid boneless hams, which can be spongy. Our favorite country ham is Harper's Grand Champion Whole Country Ham. Our winning spiral ham is Cook's Spiral Sliced Hickory Smoked Bone-In Honey Ham.

Pork Belly
PORCINE PRIZE

The fatty, succulent pork belly has become a hugely popular restaurant cut. Chefs braise and sear sections of the belly to create a dish that's crisp on the outside and unctuous within. Bacon is pork belly that's been salted, (usually) sugared, and smoked. Pancetta, sometimes called Italian bacon, is similar but not smoked.

Illustration: Jay Layman

SEARED SHRIMP WITH TOMATO, LIME, AND AVOCADO

GRILLED CHICKEN SAUSAGE WITH MUSTARD SAUCE AND ZUCCHINI SLAW

GRILLED MEATLOAF BURGERS

FARMERS' MARKET PASTA WITH LEEKS, SPINACH, AND SUMMER SQUASH

GRILLED CHICKEN SAUSAGE WITH MUSTARD SAUCE AND ZUCCHINI SLAW Serves 4

WHY THIS RECIPE WORKS: Salting the grated zucchini and squeezing the shreds dry ensures that they won't water down the slaw. You can use the same sauce and slaw with pork sausage.

- 3 zucchini (8 ounces each), shredded
  Salt and pepper
- ½ cup honey mustard
- 3 tablespoons cider vinegar
- 3 tablespoons olive oil
- 2 tablespoons plain yogurt
- 1 tablespoon lemon juice
- 1½ pounds chicken sausage
- 1 cup thinly sliced onion
- 1 red bell pepper, stemmed, seeded, and cut into ¼-inch pieces

1. Toss zucchini with 1 teaspoon salt in bowl, then transfer to colander in sink to drain. Whisk mustard and vinegar together in large bowl. Transfer ⅓ cup mustard-vinegar mixture to small bowl and reserve for dipping sauce. Add oil, yogurt, and lemon juice to mustard-vinegar mixture still in large bowl to make yogurt dressing.

2. Grill sausage over hot fire until browned and meat registers 165 degrees, 8 to 10 minutes, turning every 2 to 3 minutes.

3. Press zucchini with rubber spatula to force out as much liquid as possible. Add zucchini, onion, and bell pepper to yogurt dressing and toss to combine. Season with salt and pepper to taste. Serve sausage with dipping sauce and zucchini slaw.

TEST KITCHEN NOTE: You can use summer squash instead of zucchini.

FARMERS' MARKET PASTA WITH LEEKS, SPINACH, AND SUMMER SQUASH Serves 4

WHY THIS RECIPE WORKS: The leeks melt into the sauce and bind the pasta and vegetables.

- 1 pound penne
  Salt and pepper
- 2 tablespoons olive oil
- 1½ pounds leeks, white and light green parts only, halved lengthwise, sliced thin, and washed thoroughly
- 3 garlic cloves, minced
- 2 yellow summer squash (8 ounces each), halved lengthwise and sliced ¼ inch thick
- 6 ounces (6 cups) baby spinach, chopped coarse
- 2 ounces Pecorino Romano cheese, grated (1 cup), plus extra for serving
- ½ cup chopped fresh basil
- 2 tablespoons unsalted butter

1. Bring 4 quarts water to boil in Dutch oven. Add penne and 1 tablespoon salt and cook, stirring often, until al dente. Reserve ¾ cup cooking water, then drain penne.

2. Heat oil in now-empty pot over medium-high heat until shimmering. Add leeks and 1 teaspoon salt and cook until softened, about 3 minutes. Add garlic and cook until fragrant, about 30 seconds. Add squash and ¼ cup reserved cooking water and cook, covered, until squash is tender, about 4 minutes. Stir in penne, spinach, Pecorino, basil, remaining ½ cup reserved cooking water, and butter until combined. Remove from heat and season with salt and pepper to taste. Serve, passing extra Pecorino separately.

TEST KITCHEN NOTE: You can substitute watercress or baby arugula for the spinach.

SEARED SHRIMP WITH TOMATO, LIME, AND AVOCADO
Serves 4

WHY THIS RECIPE WORKS: Cooking the shrimp in two batches in a 12-inch skillet allows them to brown, not steam.

- 1 pound tomatoes, cored and cut into ½-inch pieces
- 6 scallions, white and green parts separated, sliced thin
- ¼ cup minced fresh cilantro
- 3 garlic cloves, minced
- 2 teaspoons minced canned chipotle chile in adobo sauce
  Salt and pepper
- 1½ pounds peeled and deveined extra-large shrimp (21 to 25 per pound)
- 2 tablespoons vegetable oil
- 1 tablespoon lime juice, plus lime wedges for serving
- 1 avocado, halved, pitted, and cut into ½-inch pieces

1. Combine tomatoes, scallion whites, cilantro, garlic, chipotle, and ¾ teaspoon salt in bowl; set aside.

2. Combine shrimp, ¼ teaspoon salt, and ¼ teaspoon pepper in separate bowl. Heat 1 tablespoon oil in 12-inch nonstick skillet over medium-high heat until just smoking. Add half of shrimp to pan in single layer and cook, without moving them, until spotty brown and edges turn pink on bottom side, about 1 minute. Flip each shrimp and continue to cook until all but very center is opaque, about 30 seconds. Transfer shrimp to large plate. Repeat with remaining 1 tablespoon oil and remaining shrimp.

3. Return skillet to medium-high heat. Add tomato mixture and lime juice and cook until tomatoes soften slightly, about 1 minute. Stir in shrimp and cook until shrimp are cooked through, about 1 minute. Transfer to platter and sprinkle with scallion greens and avocado. Serve with lime wedges.

GRILLED MEATLOAF BURGERS Serves 4

WHY THIS RECIPE WORKS: These burgers mimic the flavor of meatloaf but cook in far less time.

- 1½ pounds meatloaf mix
- 1 large egg
- 2 teaspoons Worcestershire sauce
- 1 teaspoon minced fresh thyme
  Salt and pepper
- ½ cup ketchup
- 2 tablespoons packed brown sugar
- 2 teaspoons cider vinegar
- 4 hamburger buns

1. Combine meatloaf mix, egg, Worcestershire, thyme, ½ teaspoon salt, and ½ teaspoon pepper in bowl. Shape mixture into four ¾-inch-thick patties. Whisk ketchup, sugar, and vinegar together in bowl until combined. Reserve 5 tablespoons glaze for serving.

2. Grill burgers over medium-hot fire until well browned on first side, 5 to 7 minutes. Flip burgers and brush with remaining glaze. Cook until meat registers 160 degrees, about 7 minutes. Transfer burgers to plate and tent loosely with aluminum foil; let rest for 5 minutes. Serve burgers on buns with reserved glaze.

TEST KITCHEN NOTE: You can substitute equal parts ground beef and ground pork for the meatloaf mix.

GRILLED CHICKEN PARMESAN

ROAST PORK TENDERLOIN WITH CARROT SALAD

ASIAN CHICKEN AND CELLOPHANE NOODLE SALAD

GRILLED STEAK TIPS WITH RED POTATO SKEWERS

ROAST PORK TENDERLOIN WITH CARROT SALAD Serves 4

✓ **WHY THIS RECIPE WORKS:** By finishing the tenderloin on a wire rack in the oven, we ensure that it cooks evenly all around.

        Salt and pepper
1½ teaspoons ground cumin
 2   (16-ounce) pork tenderloins, trimmed
 1   tablespoon plus ½ cup extra-virgin olive oil
 2   tablespoons lemon juice
¼   teaspoon cayenne pepper
 1   pound carrots, peeled and shredded
 1   (14-ounce) can chickpeas, rinsed
 2   ounces (2 cups) baby arugula, roughly chopped

1. Adjust oven rack to middle position and heat oven to 450 degrees. Set wire rack in aluminum foil–lined rimmed baking sheet. Combine 1 teaspoon salt, ½ teaspoon pepper, and ½ teaspoon cumin in bowl. Pat tenderloins dry with paper towels and season with spice mixture.

2. Heat 1 tablespoon oil in 12-inch nonstick skillet over medium-high heat until just smoking. Cook tenderloins until browned on all sides, 5 to 7 minutes. Transfer tenderloins to wire rack. Roast until meat registers 140 degrees, 15 to 18 minutes. Transfer to cutting board, tent with foil, and let rest for 5 minutes.

3. Meanwhile, whisk remaining ½ cup oil, lemon juice, remaining 1 teaspoon cumin, and cayenne together in large bowl. Add carrots, chickpeas, and arugula and toss to combine. Season with salt and pepper to taste. Slice tenderloins and serve with carrot salad.

TEST KITCHEN NOTE: You can use lime juice in place of the lemon juice.

GRILLED CHICKEN PARMESAN Serves 4

✓ **WHY THIS RECIPE WORKS:** Smoky flavor makes chicken Parm even better.

 1   tablespoon unsalted butter
 2   tablespoons finely chopped onion
     Salt and pepper
 1   garlic clove, minced
 1   (14.5-ounce) can diced tomatoes
 1   ounce Parmesan cheese, grated (½ cup)
 2   tablespoons chopped fresh basil
 1   tablespoon extra-virgin olive oil
 6   (3- to 4-ounce) chicken cutlets, ½ inch thick, trimmed
 4   ounces mozzarella cheese, shredded (1 cup)

1. Melt butter in medium saucepan over medium-low heat. Add onion and ½ teaspoon salt and cook until onion is golden brown, about 3 minutes. Add garlic and cook until fragrant, about 30 seconds. Stir in tomatoes and their juice and mash with potato masher until coarsely ground. Increase heat to high and bring to boil. Reduce heat to medium-low and simmer until thickened slightly, about 10 minutes. Off heat, stir in Parmesan, basil, and oil. Season with salt and pepper to taste.

2. Pat chicken dry with paper towels and season with salt and pepper. Grill chicken over hot fire until well browned on first side, about 3 minutes. Flip chicken over and top each cutlet with 2 tablespoons tomato sauce. Divide mozzarella among cutlets. Cover and cook until mozzarella starts to melt and chicken registers 160 degrees, about 3 minutes. Transfer chicken to plate, tent loosely with aluminum foil, and let rest for 5 minutes. Serve, passing remaining tomato sauce separately.

TEST KITCHEN NOTE: Hunt's are our favorite canned diced tomatoes.

GRILLED STEAK TIPS WITH RED POTATO SKEWERS Serves 4

✓ **WHY THIS RECIPE WORKS:** The potatoes and steak tips are seasoned with the same infused oil.

 2   pounds sirloin steak tips, trimmed and cut into 2½-inch pieces
     Salt and pepper
½   cup olive oil
 6   garlic cloves, minced
 1   tablespoon chopped fresh rosemary
1½ pounds small red potatoes, unpeeled, halved
 9   wooden skewers
 2   tablespoons minced fresh chives

1. Pat beef dry with paper towels and season with salt and pepper. Combine oil, garlic, and ½ teaspoon salt in small bowl. Microwave until garlic is golden brown, about 2 minutes. Stir in rosemary.

2. Thread potatoes onto skewers. Place in single layer on large plate, brush all over with ¼ cup oil mixture, and season liberally with salt. Microwave until potatoes offer slight resistance when pierced with tip of paring knife, flipping halfway through microwaving, about 8 minutes.

3. Grill beef over hotter side of 2-level fire, until well browned all over and temperature registers 125 degrees (for medium-rare), 8 to 10 minutes. Transfer to platter, brush with 2 tablespoons oil mixture, tent loosely with aluminum foil, and let rest while potatoes cook.

4. Meanwhile, grill potatoes, covered, over hotter part of grill until marked on both sides, about 2 minutes per side. Move potatoes to cooler part of grill and continue to cook, covered, until tender, 5 to 8 minutes longer. Transfer to platter with beef, brush with remaining oil mixture, and sprinkle with chives. Serve.

ASIAN CHICKEN AND CELLOPHANE NOODLE SALAD Serves 4

✓ **WHY THIS RECIPE WORKS:** We quick-pickle the vegetables while the noodles cook.

 8   ounces cellophane noodles or rice vermicelli
 3   carrots, peeled and cut into 2-inch-long matchsticks
 2   seedless English cucumbers, peeled and cut into 2-inch-long matchsticks
 6   tablespoons rice vinegar
⅓   cup soy sauce
 2   tablespoons vegetable oil
 1   tablespoon toasted sesame oil
 1   tablespoon grated fresh ginger
 1   garlic clove, minced
 2   cups shredded rotisserie chicken

1. Bring 4 quarts water to boil in large pot. Add noodles and cook until tender. Drain, rinse with cold water, and drain again to remove as much water as possible.

2. Meanwhile, toss carrots and cucumbers with 2 tablespoons vinegar in large bowl; set aside to marinate for 10 minutes. Whisk soy sauce, remaining ¼ cup vinegar, vegetable oil, sesame oil, ginger, and garlic together in bowl.

3. Drain and discard vinegar from marinating vegetables. Add noodles, chicken, and dressing to bowl with vegetables and toss to thoroughly combine. Serve.

TEST KITCHEN NOTE: We prefer English cucumbers in this recipe. If you use regular cucumbers, seed them or they will water down the dressing.

Muffin Tin Doughnuts

What tastes like a doughnut but doesn't require frying?

BY SARAH GABRIEL

BEING A DOUGHNUT devotee, I took notice when something called a doughnut muffin appeared at my local coffee shop. Could a baked item possibly achieve the sugary, fried deliciousness that has me hooked on doughnuts?

In the scheme of pastry family resemblance, the doughnut muffin was more cousin than fraternal twin to the doughnut; the crumb was unevenly bubbly, unlike the compact, tender, almost crumbly texture of a true doughnut. But the cinnamon sugar coating and the nutmeg inside were undeniably reminiscent of a classic cake doughnut. This particular fauxnut was imperfect, but judging from the preponderance of recipes (some called doughnut muffins, others muffin doughnuts), perfection should be achievable.

I baked off six batches of muffin tin doughnuts from popular recipes, and while none was bad, none captured both the essence of a doughnut and the ease of a muffin. I collated our tasting notes and jotted down all the characteristics that this muffin would need to persuade eaters that it was a cake doughnut in disguise: a very tender crumb, a crisp exterior, nutmeg and cinnamon flavors, and a buttery spiced coating. What I wanted was great doughnuts without rolling, cutting, or a pot of hot oil.

I picked the best of the lot: a recipe that had yielded doughnut muffins with good flavor and crumb structure. But they were a little tough and dry, the coating method was problematic, and they required that I cream butter and sugar in a stand mixer—I hoped for a simpler method. I started by nixing

These buttery muffins not only taste like doughnuts, they have a similar texture, too.

KEY STEP Brush with Butter

We brush the warm muffins liberally with melted butter before rolling them in the cinnamon sugar. The butter helps the coating stick and makes the muffins taste more fried.

the mixer; instead, I simply switched to melting the butter and then whisking the wet ingredients (butter, eggs, and buttermilk) into the dry (flour, sugar, baking powder, salt, and nutmeg).

To fix the texture, I first tried an extra egg yolk. That tenderized the crumb slightly and also made my doughnut muffins a little moister and richer. Next I tried replacing the all-purpose flour with cake flour, which is lower in stretchy gluten, the protein network that gives baked goods their structure. Now the doughnuts were too tender: They disintegrated into crumb-y messes all over our shirts. I considered using half cake flour and half all-purpose, but two flours seemed too fussy. We occasionally cut all-purpose flour with cornstarch as an emergency substitute for cake flour, so I tested varying proportions of each.

Ultimately, 2¾ cups of flour and ¼ cup of cornstarch gave me a tender but adequately resilient crumb.

To replicate the crispy exterior frying achieves, I tried scooping the batter into a hot, heavily buttered muffin tin and then rolling the finished doughnuts in cinnamon sugar. Fail. The edges of the doughnuts were cracked, and the sugar didn't adhere. The real solution came from simply increasing the oven temperature from 325 to 400 degrees, which crisped the crust nicely.

Time to figure out the mechanics of the coating, which had frustrated me from the start. Dipping the muffin tops in melted butter and then sprinkling on cinnamon sugar, as some recipes suggest, was easy, but it didn't produce a crisp, rich, sugary layer on the tops and it left the bottoms naked. Rolling

the baked muffins in melted butter and then cinnamon sugar, as other recipes required, yielded the rich exterior of a real fried doughnut, but as the butter level dropped, it was hard to coat the last few. Exasperated, I tried a pastry brush, applying the butter all over. Sweet relief: Tender and consistently coated, these treats "really do taste like doughnuts," one taster said, dusting the cinnamon sugar from her fingers.

MUFFIN TIN DOUGHNUTS

Makes 12 doughnuts

In step 3, brush the doughnuts generously, using up all the melted butter. Use your hand to press the cinnamon sugar onto the doughnuts to coat them completely.

DOUGHNUTS

- 2¾ cups (13¾ ounces) all-purpose flour
- 1 cup (7 ounces) sugar
- ¼ cup cornstarch
- 1 tablespoon baking powder
- 1 teaspoon salt
- ½ teaspoon ground nutmeg
- 1 cup buttermilk
- 8 tablespoons unsalted butter, melted
- 2 large eggs plus 1 large yolk

COATING

- 1 cup sugar
- 2 teaspoons ground cinnamon
- 8 tablespoons unsalted butter, melted

1. FOR THE DOUGHNUTS: Adjust oven rack to middle position and heat oven to 400 degrees. Spray 12-cup muffin tin with vegetable oil spray. Whisk flour, sugar, cornstarch, baking powder, salt, and nutmeg together in bowl. Whisk buttermilk, melted butter, and eggs and yolk together in separate bowl. Add wet ingredients to dry ingredients and stir with rubber spatula until just combined.

2. Scoop batter into prepared tin. Bake until doughnuts are lightly browned and toothpick inserted in center comes out clean, 19 to 22 minutes. Let doughnuts cool in tin for 5 minutes.

3. FOR THE COATING: Whisk sugar and cinnamon together in bowl. Remove doughnuts from tin. Working with 1 doughnut at a time, brush all over with melted butter, then roll in cinnamon sugar, pressing lightly to adhere. Transfer to wire rack and let cool for 15 minutes. Serve.

Natchitoches Meat Pies

First we had to learn to pronounce the name of Louisiana's fragrant, deep-fried meat turnovers. Then we had to learn how to make them. BY REBECCAH MARSTERS

NEW ORLEANS IS one of the best food towns in America, so why on a recent trip to the region did I find myself driving away from the city in search of a recipe? Three words: Natchitoches meat pies. Wrapped in dough (sturdier than pie crust, flakier than pizza dough), these half-moon-shaped, hand-held, simply seasoned turnovers are filled with ground beef, pork, or both and then deep-fried. They are deeply delicious.

In search of Natchitoches ("NACK-uh-dish") meat pies, I had flown from Boston to New Orleans and then zipped along Louisiana highways and bayous, on a 250-mile drive to the city of Natchitoches, which sits near the Texas border. It's the oldest permanent settlement in Louisiana and the star of the 1980s movie *Steel Magnolias*. Nice, but I wasn't interested in stars; I was there to eat and evaluate, in order to engineer my own meat pies back in the test kitchen.

Culinary historians argue about the origins of these fried turnovers (see "On the Road"), but no one disputes that in the late 1960s, James Lasyone revived their popularity at Lasyone's Meat Pie Restaurant. Today his daughter Angela runs the place, so that's where I headed when I got to Natchitoches. Soon I was sitting inside with a hot meat pie before me, Angela across the table, and James's original cast-iron frying pot on the sideboard. I paused to savor the moment and breathe in the pie's fragrant steam. Then I made quick work of it—but not without noting the meat pie's yellow-tinged, crackery crust; rich, stewlike filling; and whisper of heat. Angela told me enough to tantalize without giving away her secrets: The filling was 80 percent beef and 20 percent pork and included chopped onions and green peppers.

Natchitoches meat pies are also sold at gas stations all over town, I soon discovered. Don't bother. But if you run into the exceptionally generous Gay Melder, you're in luck. Every December, she makes hundreds of meat pies for the town's annual Christmas festival, and she was willing to show me how. In her kitchen, she eyeballed the measurements for both filling and dough and then organized her visiting friends and family (and me) into an assembly line to form the pies; in short order, we had a

These turnovers are filled with a mix of ground beef and pork, green peppers, and scallions.

growing pile. Gay slipped the meat pies into shimmering oil to fry, and some 15 minutes later they were ready to taste. The crust was delicate and flaky, the filling moist and well seasoned. But that doesn't begin to do them justice; these pies were much more than the sum of their parts. Could I ever do as well?

Back in the test kitchen the following week, I had to quantify and foolproof what Gay did by instinct. For starters, I'd need to pin down her instructions to add "just enough" flour and to salt generously until I thought I'd "ruined it." Plus, I was willing to bet that no other home outside Louisiana had the customized meat-pie-crimping appliance that Gay owned, so instructions for forming the pies were in order. I'd bring to bear all my test kitchen expertise so that even meat pie novices (like me) could pull off the recipe.

Like Gay, I started with equal amounts of ground pork and beef—not too lean, she had warned. Still following her instructions, I sautéed the meat with the onion, green pepper, garlic, and scallion whites (adding the greens at the end for a fresh, mild, oniony hit). I drained off and discarded most of the meat juices, as I'd seen her do. And finally I thickened the filling with flour. (Unlike her, I measured. I measured the salt, pepper, and cayenne, too.) To simplify the dough, I used the food processor, mixing flour, salt, and

baking powder; cutting in the shortening; and finally adding eggs and milk. It was an unusual dough, like a cross between pastry and pasta dough. Gay's had been sturdy, smooth, and slightly glossy, so I aimed for the same. I rolled out balls of dough, filled and crimped meat pies by hand, and dropped them into hot oil. In 10 minutes they were golden brown.

But this first attempt missed the mark. The filling was crumbly, the meat pebbly and overcooked, and the flavor flat. To buttress the flavor, I relied on the test kitchen's full repertoire of time-tested techniques. I sautéed the cayenne in fat at the start to unlock its flavor. I added chicken broth to reinforce the filling's savory flavor. And I retained the meat juices and succulent fat to take advantage of their flavor, too. Finally, I discovered that the pies were better if I sautéed the meat and vegetables sequentially. This way, the vegetables browned in the meat drippings rather than steaming with the browning meat.

At this point, I ran into a piece of luck: The dry, pebbly meat situation resolved itself. Since I'd removed the browned meat from the pan, it couldn't overcook while waiting for the onion and green pepper to soften.

My kitchen work had an unfortunate side effect, though. The added broth and meat juices made the filling less cohesive than ever. To fix it, I simply added more flour. Bad move—unless you like the taste of raw flour. I needed more flour but less flour taste. I know—instead of adding it at the end, I sautéed it with the meat to cook out its raw taste. The pies were much better for it.

I was proud of my filling, so I got to work on the dough. To be honest, there wasn't much room for improvement (though not for lack of testing). To cite just one example, normally we *Cook's Country* natives can't live without butter, but when I substituted butter for shortening in this dough, the meat pies' superlative tenderness

vanished. In the end, I made just one small change, and it happened like this: One afternoon, I had some chicken broth left over from making the filling. On a hunch, I used it in place of the milk in the dough. It made the most tender and flavorful crust yet.

I consolidated everything I'd learned into one last batch and then set out a platter of beautiful Natchitoches meat pies for my coworkers. The filling was thick, rich, and cohesive, they said, the dough tender and savory. Against all odds, these deep-fried, meat-stuffed pies tasted subtle, even delicate. A good cook's intuition, which Gay had in spades, is hard to capture on paper, and when I'd tasted her meat pies in Natchitoches, I'd feared I never would. Now I realized that I hadn't messed much with perfection. I'd just spread the news.

NATCHITOCHES MEAT PIES
Makes 16 pies
You can make the dough and the filling up to 24 hours ahead and refrigerate them separately. You can also shape and fill the pies, refrigerating them for up to 24 hours before frying. Use a Dutch oven that holds 6 quarts or more.

FILLING
- 5 teaspoons vegetable oil
- ¾ pound 85 percent lean ground beef
- ¾ pound ground pork
  Salt and pepper
- 1 onion, chopped fine
- 1 green bell pepper, stemmed, seeded, and minced
- 6 scallions, white parts minced, green parts sliced thin
- 3 garlic cloves, minced
- ¼ teaspoon cayenne pepper
- 2 tablespoons all-purpose flour
- 1 cup chicken broth

DOUGH
- 4 cups (20 ounces) all-purpose flour
- 2 teaspoons salt
- 1 teaspoon baking powder
- 8 tablespoons vegetable shortening, cut into ½-inch pieces
- 1 cup chicken broth
- 2 large eggs, lightly beaten

- 1 quart vegetable oil for frying

1. FOR THE FILLING: Heat 2 teaspoons oil in 12-inch skillet over medium-high heat until just smoking. Add beef, pork, 1 teaspoon salt, and ½ teaspoon pepper and cook, breaking up pieces with spoon, until no longer pink, 8 to 10 minutes. Transfer meat to bowl.

2. Add remaining 1 tablespoon oil to now-empty skillet and heat over medium-high heat until shimmering. Add onion, bell pepper, scallion whites, ½ teaspoon salt, and ½ teaspoon pepper and cook until vegetables are just starting to brown, 3 to 5 minutes.

Stir in garlic and cayenne and cook until fragrant, about 30 seconds.

3. Return meat and any accumulated juices to skillet with vegetables. Sprinkle flour over meat and cook, stirring constantly, until evenly coated, about 1 minute. Add broth, bring to boil, and cook until slightly thickened, about 3 minutes. Transfer filling to bowl and stir in scallion greens. Refrigerate until completely cool, about 1 hour. (Filling can be refrigerated for up to 24 hours.)

4. FOR THE DOUGH: Process flour, salt, and baking powder in food processor until combined, about 3 seconds. Add shortening and pulse until mixture resembles coarse cornmeal, 6 to 8 pulses. Add broth and eggs and pulse until dough just comes together, about 5 pulses. Transfer dough to lightly floured counter and knead until dough forms smooth ball, about 20 seconds. Divide dough into 16 equal pieces. (Dough can be covered and refrigerated for up to 24 hours.)

5. Line rimmed baking sheet with parchment paper. Working with 1 piece of dough at a time, roll into 6-inch circle on lightly floured counter. Place ¼ cup filling in center of dough round. Brush edges of dough with water and fold dough over filling. Press to seal, trim any ragged edges, and crimp edges with tines of fork. Transfer to prepared sheet. (Filled pies can be covered and refrigerated for up to 24 hours.)

6. Adjust oven rack to middle position and heat oven to 200 degrees. Set wire rack in second rimmed baking sheet. Add 1 quart oil to large Dutch oven until it measures about ¾ inch deep and heat over medium-high heat to 350 degrees. Place 4 pies in oil and fry until golden brown, 3 to 5 minutes per side, using slotted spatula or spider to flip. Adjust burner, if necessary, to maintain oil temperature between 325 and 350 degrees. Transfer pies to prepared wire rack and place in oven to keep warm. Return oil to 350 degrees and repeat with remaining pies. Serve.

TEST KITCHEN TECHNIQUE **Sealing Meat Pies**

1. Brush the edges of each round with water and fold one side over the filling to form a half-moon. For tidy pies, trim the edges with a pastry wheel.

2. Use the tines of a fork to make a decorative crimp that tightly seals the pies.

Memphis Wet Ribs for a Crowd

After much trial and error, we perfected our backyard version of these ribs. But could we make enough to serve a crowd? BY DIANE UNGER

WET OR DRY? You'd better be prepared to answer that question when ordering ribs in Memphis, a city that has the highest density of barbecue establishments in the country. Memphis dry ribs are just what they sound like—spice-rubbed slow-smoked ribs served dry, meaning without sauce—while wet ribs are sauced, usually both during and after cooking. The sauce in Memphis is a tangy, tomato-based concoction that falls somewhere between the sharp, vinegary bite of North Carolina–style sauces and the heavy sweetness of Kansas City sauces.

While I appreciate the clean, minimalist approach of dry ribs, for me it's just not barbecue without sauce. My mission was to create a backyard recipe for wet ribs that a Memphis pit master would be proud to serve.

The test kitchen has more than 20 years of experience cooking pork ribs, so I wasn't starting from scratch. I knew, for instance, that I'd use St. Louis–cut ribs, which are spareribs with the bulky brisket bone and meat cut off; St. Louis–cut ribs are easier to eat, cook faster, and fit better on a backyard kettle grill than full spareribs. With that in mind, I sorted through dozens of recipes and whittled them down to six that claimed to create the best, most "authentic" Memphis wet ribs. On the day of reckoning, I prepped the recipes and stepped into the alley behind the test kitchen to do some serious smoking (and I don't mean cigarettes).

About 6 hours later I hauled the ribs inside, sliced them up, and called my colleagues to come taste. Their bright-eyed enthusiasm quickly faded. While none was downright awful, we were disappointed by ribs that were dry or tough and by rubs and sauces that were acrid and harsh or almost unnoticeable.

While this initial test was discouraging, at least it gave me the freedom to begin my testing with a clean slate. My first task was the rub. A good spice rub provides balanced flavor without dominating the pork; I threw together a basic barbecue mixture of paprika, brown sugar, salt, pepper, onion powder, and granulated garlic (a few of the recipes I'd tested had used garlic powder and cayenne, both of which tasted harsh). As for the sauce, I mail-ordered several

We keep these ribs moist by mopping them with a thin sauce several times during cooking. We slather on the barbecue sauce at the end.

sauces from Memphis restaurants known for their wet ribs and put together a recipe based on our favorite, from Charlie Vergo's Rendezvous. I used some of the spice rub in the sauce, along with ketchup, yellow mustard, apple juice, cider vinegar, Worcestershire, and molasses. A 20-minute simmer thickened it and brought all the flavors together.

Ribs take at least 4 hours of low-and-slow cooking to become tender. Three-quarters of a chimney's worth of charcoal (our preferred amount for ribs) burns for about 2 hours. This means that on a charcoal kettle grill—the kind most of us have at home—you must refuel the grill at least once or the heat will go out before the ribs tenderize. Thankfully, the test kitchen has a better way: We smoke the ribs with indirect heat on the grill for 2 hours before

bringing them inside to finish in the controlled heat of a 250-degree oven. It may not be traditional, but it creates reliably smoky, tender ribs. I basted the ribs with the sauce several times during the last 45 minutes in the oven and painted them with sauce again when they were done. Now my tasters were really smiling.

But I wasn't. The ribs were tender, saucy, and plenty tasty, yes. But this recipe (like all of our barbecued rib recipes) made two racks, which is all you can fit on a backyard grill when cooking with indirect heat, since the meat can never sit directly over the fire. Two racks feed just four people: too few eaters for the hefty 4-hour time investment. I was determined to double the recipe to four racks without using a second grill.

My editors and I talked about this and came up with several ideas. I tried smoking four racks in several configurations—in V-racks, stacked up in a tower with large onion rounds in between, and even in a wire file folder—but nothing worked. After days of trial and error, though, my perseverance finally paid off: I tied two racks together (bone sides facing each other) with kitchen twine and then positioned them as before on the cooler side. This arrangement didn't change the footprint of the meat on the grill, but it did require me to tweak the method.

First, with twice the amount of meat, I needed more heat on the grill. The solution here was something called the Minion method, a barbecue trick for which you put unlit briquettes in the grill and then cover them with lit ones to create a longer-burning fire. With more heat in play, I had to take extra measures to avoid drying out the meat. A disposable roasting pan with some water in it below the ribs on the grill created steam that helped the ribs render and stay moist. A simple barbecue mop (or thin basting sauce) of apple juice, cider vinegar, and yellow mustard—ingredients that were already in my sauce—cooled the surface of the ribs (and prevented overcooking) while adding subtle flavor. I mopped the ribs twice during their time on the grill and once more before moving them to the oven. Speaking of the oven, I found that I had to turn it up a little, to 300 degrees, to make sure that all the ribs fully tenderized.

It takes a bit of engineering, but if you want Memphis wet ribs—and a lot of them—that taste like they were born in Tennessee, what are you waiting for?

MEMPHIS-STYLE WET RIBS FOR A CROWD
Serves 8 to 12
This recipe requires heavy-duty aluminum foil; a 13 by 9-inch disposable aluminum pan (or an 8½ by 4½-inch loaf pan for a gas grill); kitchen twine; and two rimmed baking sheets. You'll get the best results from a charcoal grill. If you're cooking with gas, you'll need a large grill with at least three burners. If you'd like to use wood chunks instead of wood chips when using a charcoal grill, substitute two medium wood chunks, soaked in water for 1 hour, for the wood chip packet.

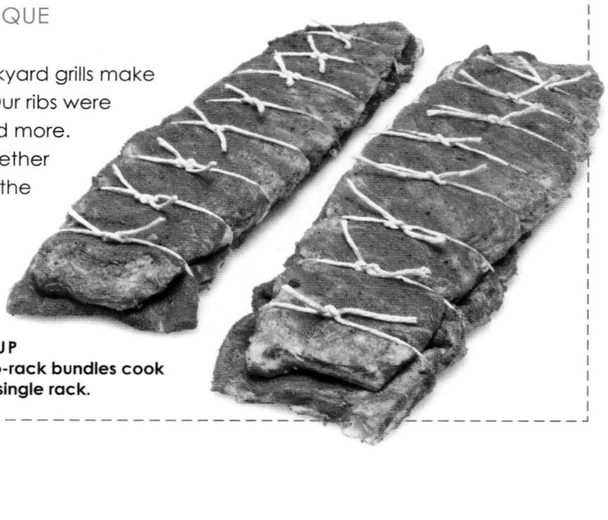

SPICE RUB
- ¼ cup paprika
- 2 tablespoons packed brown sugar
- 2 tablespoons salt
- 2 teaspoons pepper
- 2 teaspoons onion powder
- 2 teaspoons granulated garlic

BARBECUE SAUCE
- 1½ cups ketchup
- ¾ cup apple juice
- ¼ cup molasses
- ¼ cup cider vinegar
- ¼ cup Worcestershire sauce
- 2 tablespoons yellow mustard
- 2 teaspoons pepper

MOP
- ½ cup apple juice
- ¼ cup cider vinegar
- 1 tablespoon yellow mustard

RIBS
- 4 (2½- to 3-pound) racks St. Louis–style spareribs, trimmed, membrane removed
- 2 cups wood chips, soaked in water for 15 minutes and drained
- 1 (13 by 9-inch) disposable aluminum roasting pan (if using charcoal) or 1 (8½ by 6-inch) disposable aluminum pan (if using gas)

1. FOR THE SPICE RUB: Combine all ingredients in bowl.

2. FOR THE BARBECUE SAUCE: Combine ketchup, apple juice, molasses, vinegar, Worcestershire, mustard, and 2 tablespoons spice rub in medium saucepan and bring to boil over medium heat. Reduce heat to medium-low and simmer until thickened and reduced to 2 cups, about 20 minutes. Off heat, stir in pepper; set aside.

3. FOR THE MOP: Whisk apple juice, vinegar, mustard, and ¼ cup barbecue sauce together in bowl.

4. FOR THE RIBS: Pat ribs dry with paper towels and season all over with remaining spice rub. Place 1 rack of ribs, meaty side down, on cutting board. Place second rack of ribs, meaty side up, directly on top of first rack, arranging thick end over tapered end. Tie racks together at 2-inch intervals with kitchen twine. Repeat with remaining 2 racks of ribs. (You should have 2 bundles of ribs.) Using large piece of heavy-duty aluminum foil, wrap soaked chips in foil packet and cut several vent holes in top.

5A. FOR A CHARCOAL GRILL: Open bottom vent halfway and place disposable roasting pan on 1 side of grill. Fill pan with 2 quarts water. Arrange 3 quarts unlit charcoal briquettes on other side of grill. Light large chimney starter half filled with charcoal briquettes (3 quarts). When top coals are partially covered with ash, pour evenly over unlit coals. Place wood chip packet on coals. Set cooking grate in place, cover, and open lid vent halfway. Heat grill until hot and wood chips are smoking, about 5 minutes.

5B. FOR A GAS GRILL: Place wood chip packet and disposable pan over primary burner and fill pan with 2 cups water. Turn primary burner to high (leave other burners off), cover, and heat grill until hot and wood chips are smoking, about 15 minutes. (Adjust primary burner as needed to maintain grill temperature of 275 to 300 degrees.)

6. Clean and oil cooking grate. Place ribs on cooler side of grill and baste with one-third of mop. Cover (positioning lid vent over ribs for charcoal) and cook for 2 hours, flipping and switching positions of ribs and basting again with half of remaining mop halfway through cooking.

7. Adjust oven racks to upper-middle and lower-middle positions and heat oven to 300 degrees. Line 2 rimmed baking sheets with foil. Cut kitchen twine from racks. Transfer 2 racks, meaty side up, to each sheet. Baste with remaining mop and bake for 2 hours, switching and rotating sheets halfway through baking.

8. Remove ribs from oven and brush evenly with ½ cup barbecue sauce. Return to oven and continue to bake until tender, basting with ½ cup barbecue sauce and rotating and switching sheets twice during baking, about 45 minutes. (Ribs do not need to be flipped and should remain meaty side up during baking.)

9. Transfer ribs to carving board. Brush evenly with remaining ½ cup barbecue sauce, tent loosely with foil, and let rest for 20 minutes. Cut ribs in between bones to separate. Serve.

TANGY CORN RELISH
Makes about 5 cups
You can substitute 4½ cups of frozen corn kernels for the ears of corn. The relish can be stored, covered, in the refrigerator for up to one week. Enjoy it on its own or as a topping for grilled meat or fish.

- ½ cup sugar
- ¼ cup all-purpose flour
- 1 tablespoon salt
- 2 teaspoons pepper
- 1¾ cups distilled white vinegar
- ¼ cup water
- 6 ears corn, kernels cut from cobs
- 1 onion, chopped fine
- 1 red bell pepper, stemmed, seeded, and chopped fine
- 1 teaspoon yellow mustard seeds
- ½ teaspoon celery seeds

Combine, simmer, stir. In 40 minutes, you've got relish.

1. Whisk sugar, flour, salt, and pepper together in Dutch oven until combined. Slowly whisk vinegar and water into sugar mixture until incorporated.

2. Add corn, onion, bell pepper, mustard seeds, and celery seeds to pot. Bring to boil over medium-high heat. Reduce heat to medium-low and simmer, stirring occasionally, until vegetables are tender and mixture has thickened slightly, about 40 minutes. Transfer to bowl and refrigerate until cool, at least 2 hours.

Summer Berry Pudding

Most recipes for this traditional British dessert—sweetened berries encased in bread—barely qualify as cooking. So why is it so hard to get it right? BY CRISTIN WALSH

SUMMER BERRY PUDDING is more common in the United Kingdom than in the United States, but given the success of sticky toffee pudding, I say that we're due for another British invasion. To make it, a pudding mold—or often simply a bowl—is lined snugly with crustless bread, filled with lightly sweetened and cooked berries, and topped with a bread "lid." The pudding is compressed for some 8 hours with weights before it's inverted and unmolded. During the wait (and the weight), the berry juices permeate the bread, making for a sliceable magenta sweet that's a homey paean to summer.

But it's in such breezily, seemingly simple recipes that the most can go wrong, as I quickly found out. Things appeared to be under control when I refrigerated my first test puddings for the night, but when I unmolded them the next day, berries collapsed into runny piles and bread cases disintegrated. Structural problems aside, the berries tasted long-stewed, and the bread was either slimy and wet or patchy and unevenly saturated. Still, I kept the faith. I knew that fresh berries and good bread should, could, and would add up to a delicious dessert—eventually.

Surveying the berry-bread wreckage, I made two decisions. Many traditional British recipes call for red currants, but their season is fleeting, if you can find them at all. Instead I'd use a mix of blueberries, blackberries, strawberries, and raspberries. Second, to develop a recipe that would work consistently, I'd replace the bowl. Bowls don't come in standard sizes, and they had produced wobbly puddings. I'd try a loaf pan, as I'd seen one recipe call for.

I lined a loaf pan with plastic wrap, lined the sides and bottom with white bread, filled it, and covered it with more bread. As I'd hoped, the rectangular shape proved much more stable (the filling was still too wet—I'd get to that). I proceeded to make three more puddings, testing wheat bread, challah, and sliced pound cake. The wheat bread was soggy and the flavor was wrong. The cake veered too close to trifle. But the challah was tasty and reasonably sturdy.

"Reasonably sturdy" was no guarantee. I'd read that summer pudding originated as a way to use up stale bread. So why don't most recipes call for it? I'd try toasting the challah in the oven as added

With blueberries, blackberries, raspberries, and strawberries, our pudding lives up to its name.

insurance against a mushy, unstable bread casing. I lined the loaf pan with my staled bread, poured in the berries, and weighted and waited. It worked nicely.

Over several weeks of testing, I'd been frustrated that truly ripe, juicy berries soaked the bread case through, often too much so, while lower-quality berries made for patchy, dry cases. As I perfected the filling, I'd need to correct for the variability of fresh berries. A coworker suggested that I strain out the juice after cooking the berries and sugar and add a measured amount back to the pudding. I went one better: I strained the berries and then dipped my oven-staled challah slices in the juices. Now I controlled how wet they'd get. I lined the pan with soaked-just-enough bread and filled it with the strained berries.

This new method worked so well that I was ready to wrap up. But then one of my coworkers suddenly raised the bar: Summer berry pudding should emphasize the berries, she said; yours has too much bread. I had to admit that she was right. Maybe I could eliminate the bread that lined the sides of the loaf pan—but only if I could make the filling firmer. I tested possible thickeners: Flour, cornstarch, and tapioca required longer cooking to activate the starches, which degraded the fresh berry flavor. But a mixture of tangy apricot preserves and gelatin tasted right and ensured that the structure would hold.

To make the filling even more fresh and bright, I cooked just half of the berries and folded in the rest off heat. My pudding was ready to cross the Atlantic.

SUMMER BERRY PUDDING Serves 6

Fill in any gaps in pudding crusts with toast trimmings.

- 8 (¼-inch-thick) slices challah, crusts removed
- 12 ounces strawberries, hulled and chopped (2 cups)
- 8 ounces blackberries, halved (1½ cups)
- 8 ounces (1½ cups) blueberries
- 5 ounces (1 cup) raspberries
- ½ cup (3½ ounces) granulated sugar
- 1 teaspoon unflavored gelatin
- 2 tablespoons cold water
- ½ cup (5½ ounces) apricot preserves
- 1 cup heavy cream, chilled
- 1 tablespoon confectioners' sugar

1. Adjust oven rack to middle position and heat oven to 350 degrees. Line 8½ by 4½-inch loaf pan with plastic wrap, pushing plastic into corners and up sides of pan and allowing excess to overhang long sides. Make cardboard cutout just large enough to fit inside pan.

2. Place challah on wire rack set in rimmed baking sheet. Bake until dry, about 10 minutes, flipping challah and rotating sheet halfway through baking. Let challah cool completely.

3. Combine strawberries, blackberries, blueberries, and raspberries in bowl. Transfer half of mixture to medium saucepan, add granulated sugar, and bring to simmer over medium-low heat, stirring occasionally. Reduce heat to low and continue to cook until berries release their juices and raspberries begin to break down, about 5 minutes. Off heat, stir in remaining berries. After 2 minutes, strain berries through fine-mesh strainer set over medium bowl for 10 minutes, stirring berries once halfway through straining (do not press on berries). Reserve berry juice. (You should have ¾ to 1 cup.)

4. Sprinkle gelatin over water in bowl and let sit until gelatin softens, about 5 minutes. Microwave until mixture is bubbling around edges and gelatin dissolves, about 30 seconds. Whisk preserves and gelatin mixture together in large bowl. Fold in strained berries.

5. Trim 4 slices of challah to fit snugly side by side in bottom of loaf pan (you may have extra challah). Dip slices in reserved berry juice until saturated, about 30 seconds per side, then place in bottom of pan. Spoon berry mixture over challah.

Trim remaining 4 slices of challah to fit snugly side by side on top of berries (you may have extra challah). Dip slices in reserved berry juice until saturated, about 30 seconds per side, then place on top of berries. Cover pan loosely with plastic and place in 13 by 9-inch baking dish. Place cardboard cutout on top of pudding. Top with 3 soup cans to weigh down pudding. Refrigerate pudding for at least 8 hours or up to 24 hours.

6. Using stand mixer fitted with whisk, whip cream and confectioners' sugar on medium-low speed until foamy, about 1 minute. Increase speed to high and whip until soft peaks form, 1 to 3 minutes. Transfer to serving bowl. Remove cans, cardboard, and plastic from top of pudding. Loosen pudding by pulling up on edges of plastic. Place inverted platter over top of loaf pan and flip platter and pan upside down to unmold pudding. Discard plastic. Slice pudding with serrated knife and serve with whipped cream.

Summer Pudding Blueprint
Follow our plan for a juicy but firm pudding. Place the filled loaf pan in a baking dish to catch drips while the pudding sets in the refrigerator.

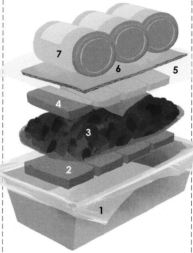

1. Plastic wrap lines the loaf pan for easier unmolding.

2. Challah saturated with juices.

3. Sweetened four-berry mix.

4. Challah saturated with juices.

5. Plastic wrap on top seals the pudding while it chills.

6. Cardboard cutout distributes the weight.

7. Soup cans compress the pudding.

Lemon Icebox Pie

With so many variations on this recipe, someone needed to figure out which was best—clearly, a job for the test kitchen. BY CAROLYNN PURPURA MACKAY

LEMON ICEBOX PIE, a close relative of Key lime pie, is a favorite in the South. Like Key lime pie, it has a graham cracker crust that holds a citrusy filling based on one can of sweetened condensed milk and egg yolks and is typically topped with whipped cream. It started as a no-bake pie—a bonus in the relentlessly hot and humid South—that's stored in the refrigerator and served chilled. Eaters love it for its cool, oh-so-creamy, sweet yet tart deliciousness. Home bakers love it because it's so easy to make.

Because many Americans are nervous about eating raw eggs, many modern recipes call for baking the pie, for anywhere from 10 to 25 minutes. And that's not the only discrepancy. Some recipes use cream cheese, others gelatin, and a few two cans of milk, and one that I found uses no canned milk whatsoever—which seemed particularly weird because canned milk is the very definition of this pie. The amounts of lemon juice were all over the map, too. The craziest recipe of the bunch mixed crushed lemon drops into both crust and whipped cream. Not wanting to be hidebound by tradition, I made a slew of these variations alongside the classic pie and invited my coworkers to a *Cook's Country* pie social.

Based on their comments, the cream cheese was out; I wasn't making cheesecake, after all. The gelatin added unnecessary fussiness, and the crushed lemon drops were good in theory but bad in practice. I opted to use three egg yolks, for richness, and two cans of sweetened condensed milk, which made for tall, generous slices. So far we were on the side of tradition. But one new innovation made it through: The baked pies set up and sliced much better, so after a few tests, I settled on 15 minutes' oven time.

Now I just needed to figure out the right amount of lemon. Other recipes call for as little as 2 tablespoons of juice (bland) and as much as 2 cups (inedibly sour). Many pies later, I established perfect pucker at 1 cup.

I was about to sweeten the whipped cream topping with sugar, as we usually do, when I realized that I could get the same effect by borrowing canned milk from the filling. Three tablespoons did the job nicely, but it threw off the balance of the pie. I tinkered and eventually found that by decreasing the lemon juice slightly, I could reestablish harmony.

This pie needs just 15 minutes in the oven.

LEMON ICEBOX PIE Serves 8
We like Keebler Graham Crackers Original.

- 9 whole graham crackers, broken into 1-inch pieces
- 3 tablespoons sugar
- 5 tablespoons unsalted butter, melted
- 2 (14-ounce) cans sweetened condensed milk
- 3 large egg yolks
- ¾ cup plus 2 tablespoons lemon juice (5 lemons)
- 1 cup heavy cream
- ½ teaspoon vanilla extract

1. Adjust oven rack to middle position and heat oven to 325 degrees. Process graham crackers and sugar in food processor until finely ground, about 30 seconds. Add melted butter and pulse until combined, about 8 pulses. Transfer crumbs to 9-inch pie plate. Using bottom of measuring cup, press crumbs into bottom and up sides of plate. Bake until crust is fragrant and beginning to brown, about 15 minutes. Let crust cool completely on wire rack, about 35 minutes. Increase oven temperature to 375 degrees.

2. Reserve 3 tablespoons condensed milk. Whisk remaining condensed milk and egg yolks together in bowl until smooth. Slowly whisk in lemon juice. Pour filling into cooled pie crust. Bake pie until edges are beginning to set but center still jiggles when shaken, about 15 minutes. Let cool for 1 hour on wire rack. Refrigerate until chilled and set, at least 3 hours or up to 24 hours.

3. Using stand mixer fitted with whisk, whip cream, reserved condensed milk, and vanilla on medium-low speed until foamy, about 1 minute. Increase speed to high and whip until stiff peaks form, 1 to 3 minutes. Spread whipped cream evenly over top of pie. Serve.

Cooking Class How to Grill Shrimp

Protect the crustacean. Follow our easy techniques to ensure tender, plump, flavorful shrimp.

BY SCOTT KATHAN

A smoky char brings out shrimp's natural sweetness.

GRILLED JALAPEÑO AND LIME SHRIMP SKEWERS

Serves 4

You will need four 14-inch metal skewers for this recipe. We prefer flat skewers.

MARINADE

- 1 jalapeño chile, stemmed, seeded, and minced
- 3 tablespoons olive oil
- 6 garlic cloves, minced
- 1 teaspoon grated lime zest plus 5 tablespoons juice (3 limes)
- ½ teaspoon salt
- ½ teaspoon ground cumin
- ¼ teaspoon cayenne pepper

SHRIMP

- 1½ pounds extra-large shrimp (21 to 25 per pound), peeled and deveined
- ½ teaspoon sugar
- 1 tablespoon minced fresh cilantro

1. FOR THE MARINADE: Process all ingredients in food processor until finely ground, about 20 seconds. Reserve 2 tablespoons marinade for finishing cooked shrimp. Transfer remaining marinade to medium bowl.

2. FOR THE SHRIMP: Pat shrimp dry with paper towels, add to bowl with remaining marinade, and toss to coat. Cover and refrigerate for at least 30 minutes or up to 1 hour. Thread marinated shrimp tightly onto 4 skewers (8 to 9 shrimp per skewer), alternating direction of each shrimp. Sprinkle 1 side of shrimp skewers with sugar.

3A. FOR A CHARCOAL GRILL: Open bottom vent completely. Light large chimney starter filled with charcoal briquettes (6 quarts). When top coals are partially covered with ash, pour evenly over half of grill. Set cooking grate in place, cover, and open lid vent completely. Heat grill until hot, about 5 minutes.

3B. FOR A GAS GRILL: Turn all burners to high, cover, and heat grill until hot, about 15 minutes. Leave primary burner on high and turn other burner(s) to low.

4. Clean and oil cooking grate. Grill shrimp sugared side down over hotter part of grill, uncovered, until lightly charred, 3 to 4 minutes. Flip skewers and move to cooler part of grill. Cover and continue to cook until shrimp are uniformly pink, 1 to 2 minutes.

5. Holding skewers with potholder, use tongs to slide shrimp off skewers into medium bowl. Add reserved marinade and toss to coat. Transfer shrimp to platter and sprinkle with cilantro. Serve.

Core Techniques

The primary problem with cooking shrimp on the grill is they cook so quickly that, if you're not careful, you'll end up with dry, overcooked crustaceans. You have a very short window in which to achieve nice grill char before they overcook. Here are a few ways to handle that challenge.

Pack Tightly on Skewer

Cooking shrimp on skewers makes it easier to flip them—you don't have to turn each one individually. But packing shrimp into a tight mass on a skewer has another benefit: It protects against overcooking and allows the skewers to stay over a hot fire long enough to pick up some tasty char.

Add Sugar

Sugar browns faster than shrimp (or any other animal protein), so sprinkling the skewers—on one side only—with a light dusting of granulated sugar lets them pick up color and char more quickly than they otherwise would. This technique helps build flavor while guarding against overcooking.

Start Hot

A good, hot fire will ensure that the shrimp sear quickly. If your fire isn't hot enough, it will take too long for the shrimp to pick up flavorful browning. By the time they've done so, they'll be overcooked.

Finish Gently

Our testing shows that good browning and char on just one side still gives the shrimp plenty of flavor. So after charring the first side, we finish the shrimp over low heat without any sugar to gently cook them through.

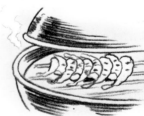

Q&A

What kind of skewers are best?

If you do a lot of grilling, it's worth investing in a good set of metal skewers; wood skewers can burn with prolonged grilling time—yes, even if you soak them. But not all metal skewers are created equal. Skewered food may spin on round skewers, making even cooking a challenge. We prefer flat metal skewers because the food stays put.

BEST CHOICE
Flat metal skewers

Will the shrimp be more flavorful if I marinate them overnight?

No. Don't marinate the shrimp (or most fish, for that matter) for longer than an hour. The acid in the marinade will start to "cook" the shrimp, making them mushy.

Why pat the shrimp dry only to toss them with (wet) marinade?

Because most shrimp are sold frozen (and we recommend buying them that way), they shed liquid when you defrost them. By patting the shrimp dry before marinating, you minimize that moisture, which otherwise would water down the marinade.

Twelve Steps to Perfect Grilled Shrimp

1. MAKE MARINADE
Buzz jalapeño, olive oil, garlic, lime zest and juice, salt, cumin, and cayenne in a food processor.
WHY? Turning these potent ingredients into a paste ensures even distribution of flavors.

2. RESERVE 2 TABLESPOONS
Put the marinade in a bowl, setting aside 2 tablespoons to sauce the cooked shrimp later.
WHY? Using the same mixture as a marinade and finishing sauce saves time and effort.

3. PREP SHRIMP
If the shrimp are unpeeled, peel them. Then make a shallow cut (about ⅛ inch) down the outside curve of the flesh.
WHY? Peeled shrimp are easier to eat. The incision exposes the "vein" and opens up more surface area.

4. DEVEIN
Remove and discard the vein.
WHY? What's commonly called the vein is actually the digestive tract. Removing it creates more surface area to soak up flavor.

5. MARINATE
Add the shrimp to the bowl with the marinade, toss to coat, cover, and refrigerate for 30 to 60 minutes.
WHY? For flavor. Fish and shellfish marinate for less time than meat because their muscle fibers are shorter and more delicate.

6. SKEWER
Thread the shrimp tightly onto skewers, alternating the direction of each shrimp. You should be able to fit 8 or 9 shrimp on each skewer.
WHY? A tightly packed skewer helps prevent the shrimp from overcooking.

7. SUGAR
Sprinkle one side of each skewer with a small amount of granulated sugar.
WHY? The sugar leads to much faster browning.

8. GRILL HOT
Cook the skewers, sugared side down, over the hotter part of the grill until charred, 3 to 4 minutes.
WHY? You're grilling. The char flavor is the point.

9. GRILL COOL
Flip the skewers and grill, covered, over the cooler part of the grill until the shrimp are uniformly pink, 1 to 2 minutes.
WHY? Finishing the shrimp gently keeps them from overcooking.

10. DE-SKEWER
Slide the shrimp off the skewers into a clean bowl.
WHY? Take the shrimp off the skewers so they're easier to eat and the sauce will coat them evenly.

11. TOSS WITH SAUCE
Add the reserved marinade, toss to coat the shrimp, and then transfer to platter.
WHY? The reserved marinade paste adds a blast of flavor to the cooked shrimp.

12. FINISH WITH CILANTRO
Sprinkle the cooked, sauced shrimp with fresh cilantro.
WHY? Like many fresh herbs, cilantro loses some of its flavor when it's cooked. We sprinkle it on at the end to take full advantage of its potency.

Shopping for Shrimp

Black Tiger versus White
Most of the shrimp sold in U.S. supermarkets are farmed black tiger shrimp from Asia, and they are usually acceptable. If you can find them, though, we prefer white shrimp from either the Mexican Pacific or the Gulf of Mexico.

Wild versus Farmed
We've found that wild shrimp are slightly sweeter and firmer than farmed shrimp. But they are more expensive and your market may not carry them. Our recipes all work with good-quality farmed shrimp.

Fresh versus Frozen
Buyer beware: The vast majority of "fresh" shrimp sold in markets has actually been previously frozen and then defrosted. Unfortunately, you never know how they were defrosted or how long they've been sitting in the case—shrimp spoil quickly and can taste noticeably less fresh just a day after defrosting. Bagged frozen shrimp is a safer bet because bagged shrimp has been individually quick frozen (IQF), which locks in quality and freshness; freezing masses of shrimp in blocks compromises quality. With bagged shrimp, you—the cook—control the thawing and storage. Also, you can thaw exactly the amount you need and keep the rest frozen. Check the ingredient list on the bag of frozen shrimp before you buy: It should list nothing but "shrimp."

Sizing 'em Up
Naming conventions for shrimp sizes are confusing: One fishmonger's "extra-large" may be another's "jumbo." To eliminate ambiguity, go by the numbers. The count per pound is usually listed on the package. Our recipe for **Grilled Jalapeño and Lime Shrimp Skewers** calls for extra-large shrimp, which come 21 to 25 to a pound (so are sometimes referred to as "21/25s"). These shrimp may be labeled U25s; the *U* stands for "under," meaning that there are fewer than 25 shrimp per pound.

WHO ARE YOU CALLING A SHRIMP?
Extra-large (21/25 per pound) shrimp, shown actual size.

Slow Cooker Baked Ziti

Mushy or bloated? Were those the only, er, pastabilities from the slow cooker?

BY SARAH GABRIEL

"BAKED" ZITI IN the slow cooker? It's a strange idea, but maybe it's a smart one. The appliance keeps the kitchen cooler than the oven and eliminates the threat of smoky sauce spillovers. I'd give it a try.

Most oven-baked ziti recipes work like this: Brown meat, onions, and garlic; add tomatoes; simmer; season; stir in partially cooked ziti; alternate layers of sauced ziti and cheese in a baking dish; and bake. Slow-cooker recipe methods diverged in two key ways: how to handle the ziti before putting it in the appliance (parcook, fully cook, or use it raw) and when to add the cheese (at the start or the finish).

I tested recipes with all these variables, as well as numerous add-ins and tomato products. If I put (even just slightly) cooked pasta in, mushy pasta came out. But raw pasta didn't work either: Cooked for 4 hours, it soaked up all the liquid, becoming bloated and leaving the dish dry and burnt onto the sides of the cooker. Cheese added before cooking was greasy by the end, and cheese added just before serving failed to melt completely. Technical difficulties aside, a batch with sausage, onion, garlic, oregano, diced tomatoes, and tomato sauce plus a topping of ricotta and mozzarella tasted pretty good. If I could get the pasta to cook properly and the cheese to melt well, I'd be in business.

Cooked pasta was a lost cause, so I'd start with raw. I browned sausage and onion in a skillet, added the spices and tomatoes, and then combined the mixture with raw ziti in the slow cooker. Four hours had proven too long, so I

Our "baked" ziti is finished with dollops of creamy ricotta cheese and fresh basil.

set the cooker for 3 hours on high. With just 10 minutes to go on the timer, I dotted the top with the cheeses. The pasta was slimy, bloated, and burnt, as before; the ricotta was cool in the center and the mozzarella greasy.

Luckily, the test kitchen has a method for preventing the edges of slow-cooker casseroles from scorching: a foil collar. I folded foil into strips, lined the slow-cooker insert, and greased the strips before adding everything. Scorching solved. To melt the cheese more evenly, I dolloped it in after the cooker had shut off and then replaced the lid. After 20 minutes, the ricotta was hot throughout and the mozzarella melted but not greasy. On to the pasta.

I tried switching the cooker setting to low, but the outside of the ziti was still slimy and now the interior was tough and starchy. Thinking that more liquid might help, I added another can of tomato sauce, but that made things worse. I was bemoaning my unevenly cooked ziti one day when a colleague chimed in: "Could you waterproof it by coating it in oil?" Cooking rice in oil before adding the liquid to make pilaf and risotto helps it hold its shape. Could the technique work for pasta, too? I stirred the raw ziti into the browned sausage and onion on the stove. After a couple of minutes, it began to look translucent at the edges, just as rice would. I stirred in the tomatoes, poured everything into the foil-lined slow

cooker, and crossed my fingers. To my relief, this pasta cooked evenly all the way through after 3 hours on low.

The main structural elements of pasta are starch and protein, our science editor explained. When we cook pasta in boiling water, the moisture causes the starch to swell up; simultaneously, the heat causes the protein to set, constraining the expansion of the starch. In the slow cooker, the liquid heats up slowly, so the starch has more time to swell before being checked by the protein. Precooking the pasta in oil presets the protein, stopping bloated pasta before it starts— and giving me another delicious dinner from the slow cooker.

SLOW-COOKER BAKED ZITI Serves 6

- 2 tablespoons olive oil
- 1 pound hot or sweet Italian sausage, casings removed
- 1 onion, chopped
- 3 garlic cloves, minced
- ½ teaspoon dried oregano
- ½ teaspoon salt
- ½ teaspoon pepper
- 8 ounces (2½ cups) ziti
- 1 (28-ounce) can crushed tomatoes
- 1 (15-ounce) can tomato sauce
- 8 ounces (1 cup) whole-milk ricotta cheese
- 4 ounces mozzarella cheese, shredded (1 cup)
- 2 tablespoons thinly sliced fresh basil

1. Make aluminum foil collar for slow cooker by folding 2 (18-inch-long) pieces of foil to make 2 (18 by 4-inch) strips. Line perimeter of slow cooker with foil strips and spray with vegetable oil spray.

2. Heat oil in Dutch oven over medium-high heat until just smoking. Cook sausage, breaking up pieces with spoon, until well browned, 6 to 8 minutes. Add onion and cook until lightly browned, about 5 minutes. Stir in garlic, oregano, salt, and pepper and cook until fragrant, about 1 minute.

3. Reduce heat to medium-low. Add ziti and cook, stirring constantly, until edges of pasta become translucent, about 4 minutes. Off heat, stir in crushed tomatoes and tomato sauce, scraping up any browned bits. Transfer mixture to prepared slow cooker. Cover and cook on low until pasta is tender, about 3 hours.

4. Using tongs, remove foil collar from slow cooker. Dollop ricotta over ziti and sprinkle with mozzarella. Cover and let sit for 20 minutes to let cheeses melt. Garnish with basil and serve.

KEY STEPS To Great Slow-Cooker "Baked" Ziti

1. To prevent burning, fold aluminum foil into two strips and use them to line the perimeter of the slow cooker.

2. After hours in the slow cooker, pasta turns slimy and bloated. To avoid that, we first sauté it with the sausage and onion.

Cooking for Two Chicken Divan

Quick and easy shouldn't have to mean bland and boring, even when it comes to everyday ingredients like chicken and broccoli. BY REBECCAH MARSTERS

CHICKEN DIVAN BEGAN its life in a fancy New York restaurant, where chefs combined poached chicken and broccoli with both béchamel and hollandaise sauces, fortified with Parmesan cheese and whipped cream. Modern versions are considerably more down-market—typically giant casseroles made from canned soup, frozen broccoli, sour cream, and mayonnaise. I wanted neither. I hoped to bring this 20th century classic into the 21st century, with neither heavy, fancy sauces on the one hand nor convenience products on the other. Also, I wanted a version to serve two people, so the casserole would have to go.

After I made a few of the modern versions, I also ruled out newer additions to the dish (rice, sliced almonds, and even curry powder have crept into recipes). So what would be in it? First off, I'd use boneless, skinless chicken breasts for ease. Also, fresh broccoli florets, not frozen, plus the Parm would stay. Beyond these, I didn't want to spend time making the fussy hollandaise of the original, but if I held on to the cream, maybe I could build a simple sauce based on a flour-and-butter roux.

I started by steaming broccoli florets and setting them aside. Next, I dredged chicken breasts lightly in flour to help them develop a golden crust, and I browned them in oil in a skillet. I set aside the chicken, too; I'd used the fond left behind in the skillet to enrich the sauce. I put a pat of butter into that pan, sautéed minced shallot, whisked in a little flour to make the roux, and poured in cream. I returned the chicken to the skillet to finish cooking in the simmering sauce, removed it again, added Parmesan to the sauce, and let it reduce and concentrate. When I poured the sauce over the chicken and broccoli and called tasters over, we agreed that the results were OK, if plain. Apparently you can't just add cream sauce to chicken and broccoli and call it divan. The dish wasn't cohesive and the sauce was boring.

To breathe more life into it, I'd have to maximize flavor. Cream provides richness and silkiness, but it's hardly an electrifying flavor. A combination of cream and chicken broth worked much better. To bump it up further, I added Worcestershire sauce, and for brightness, I finished it with a squeeze

For easy cooking and cleanup, we cook our Chicken Divan for Two in a skillet, start to finish.

of lemon juice. My newly flavorful sauce got me to wondering if I could coax more from the broccoli, too. I did more testing and eventually modified my method—browning the broccoli lightly in the skillet and then steaming it in savory chicken broth instead of plain water. This chicken divan was much better; the sauce had gained complexity and was rich but not over the top, while the broccoli was a big step up from simply steamed. I'd seen some recipes for chicken divan with sherry—was that worth adding? Yes. A good glug gave my version depth and sophistication.

I missed the crusty browned top that forms on the casserole version of divan as it bakes. Sure I liked the ease of preparing the dish in one skillet on the stove, but did that have to preclude the crusty top? For my next test, I sliced the chicken before returning it, with the broccoli, to the simmering sauce in the skillet. I sprinkled on more Parmesan and ran the skillet under the broiler until the sauce bubbled and the surface crisped and browned, about 5 minutes. This divan was truly divine.

Divan's Unfortunate History
Blame the airlines and their uninspiring culinary programs. Or maybe the producers of TV dinners. During the 20th century, the once elegant, restrained chicken divan devolved into a gloppy casserole or frozen entrée. Today, many "convenience" divan recipes are made with a grab bag of inappropriate ingredients, such as canned condensed soups, frozen broccoli, canned mushrooms, mayonnaise, cooking sherry, and curry powder.

NOT FOR HUMAN CONSUMPTION
Gloppy and gross.

CHICKEN DIVAN FOR TWO
Be sure to use an ovensafe skillet. You can substitute dry white wine for the sherry.

    5 teaspoons vegetable oil
   12 ounces broccoli florets, cut into
       1½-inch pieces
  1¼   cups chicken broth
    2 tablespoons plus 2 teaspoons
       all-purpose flour
    2 (6- to 8-ounce) boneless, skinless
       chicken breasts, trimmed
       Salt and pepper
    1 tablespoon unsalted butter
    1 shallot, minced
   ½   cup heavy cream
   ¼   cup dry sherry
    1 teaspoon Worcestershire sauce
  1½   ounces Parmesan cheese, grated
       (¾ cup)
    2 teaspoons lemon juice

1. Heat 2 teaspoons oil in 10-inch ovensafe skillet over medium-high heat until just smoking. Add broccoli and cook until spotty brown, about 2 minutes. Add ¼ cup broth, cover, and cook until just tender, about 2 minutes. Transfer broccoli to plate and wipe out skillet with paper towels.

2. Place 2 tablespoons flour in shallow dish. Pat chicken dry with paper towels and season with salt and pepper. Dredge chicken in flour, shaking to remove excess. Heat remaining 1 tablespoon oil in now-empty skillet over medium-high heat until just smoking. Cook chicken until golden brown, about 3 minutes per side. Transfer chicken to plate.

3. Reduce heat to medium, add butter and shallot to now-empty skillet, and cook until fragrant, about 30 seconds. Stir in remaining 2 teaspoons flour and cook for 1 minute. Whisk in remaining 1 cup broth, cream, sherry, and Worcestershire and bring to simmer, scraping up any browned bits. Return chicken to skillet and simmer until it registers 160 degrees, 8 to 10 minutes, flipping halfway through cooking.

4. Adjust oven rack 9 inches from broiler element and heat broiler. Transfer chicken to cutting board and continue to simmer sauce until reduced to ½ cup, 5 to 7 minutes. Off heat, whisk in ¼ cup Parmesan and lemon juice. Season sauce with salt and pepper to taste. Cut chicken into ½-inch-thick slices and stir chicken and broccoli into sauce in skillet. Sprinkle with remaining ½ cup Parmesan and broil until spotty brown, about 5 minutes. Serve.

Recipe Makeover Corn Chowder

The secret to our reduced-fat corn chowder is butter—but not the type you think.

BY CAROLYNN PURPURA MACKAY

I ADORE CORN chowder. Unfortunately, at 600 calories and 36 grams of fat, even the occasional bowl feels like overindulgence. Surely there's a way to lighten it up without messing it up. Or maybe not: I test-drove several recipes from healthy cookbooks, but . . . well, see for yourself: "Lean," "vegetal," "like bad diet food," "funky," "grainy," and "punishing," tasters said. Since these recipes were so far off the mark, I decided to skip them and their wrong-headed ingredients—turkey bacon, skim milk, and low-fat buttermilk (a fine ingredient but wrong for chowder). Instead, I'd start with my favorite full-fat recipe and whittle it down.

As is standard, this recipe suspends lots of corn, potatoes, and bacon in a thick and delicious creamy base. The corn and potatoes could stay, but lots of bacon, whole milk, and heavy cream? Doubtful. I'd have to think of something else. I began by exchanging the cream and milk for 1 percent milk and using two slices of bacon instead of the four originally called for. I fried the bacon and then extended its salty, porky flavor by sautéing chopped onion and garlic in its fat. I followed the rest of the recipe exactly as written. Even before tasting it, I was concerned. The soup looked like thin gruel, plus, since I know that fat carries flavor and I definitely know that bacon packs flavor, I didn't expect it to generate much enthusiasm. I was right. As one jokester said, "No question it's low calorie if none of us eats it."

To boost the flavor, I tried something a bit odd. Instead of removing the cooked bacon and stirring it back in at the end, I left the diced bacon in the simmering soup. The pieces melted away, sort of, infusing the soup with a nice background smokiness. Looking for other ways to boost flavor, I tried the time-tested test kitchen technique of replacing milk with more savory chicken broth. Over several batches, I tinkered with ratios, eventually landing on 3¾ cups of broth combined with 1¾ cups of 1 percent milk. The soup wasn't bland anymore, but instead of chowder, it tasted like milky chicken soup.

"Corn chowder should taste like corn," a taster declared. I was briefly annoyed, and then I got to thinking:

We're not kidding: This reduced-fat chowder tastes better than most full-fat versions.

How come corn chowder rarely does taste like corn? What it tastes like is bacon and cream. But I had an idea for infusing the entire soup with corn flavor—something I'd recently read about online called corn butter. There's actually no butter in it, which was good, since I couldn't afford butter's fat or calories. Instead, corn butter is made by juicing pureed corn kernels and cooking the extracted liquid to the texture of soft butter. It's said to be a powerhouse of corn flavor—just what my soup needed.

I removed the kernels from five ears of corn, pureed them in the food processor, transferred them to a double layer of cheesecloth, and squeezed the liquid into a measuring cup. I then discarded the solids and added the corn liquid to the sautéed onion and garlic. After a few minutes on the stove, it thickened to the consistency of butter, as promised. I added the milk and chicken broth, followed by diced potatoes, herbs, and kernels from five more ears of corn. About 20 minutes later, we dipped in our spoons. The flavor was

astonishing—corn to the nth degree.

On top of that, the corn butter also helpfully contributed body to the chowder. Our science editor explained what was going on: Sweet corn contains lots of starch and sugars. As the corn juice cooks, the starch granules swell and thicken; that, along with the sugars in the corn and the onion solids, leads to the chowder's creamy texture. To thicken the soup a little more, I tried cornstarch (not creamy enough), pureed potatoes (muddled flavors), and flour (yes, good). The next time I made a batch of soup, I whisked the flour and corn liquid together before adding them to the chowder.

At this point, my recipe was so slender that I was able to sneak some fat and calories back in, specifically ⅓ cup of half-and-half. My made-over corn chowder had lost more than 200 calories and upwards of 20 grams of fat per serving, yet it remained deeply creamy and imbued with corn flavor. There was no question that making the recipe required an extra step or two. And there was no question that it was worth it.

The Numbers
Traditional Corn Chowder
All nutritional information is for one serving.
CALORIES **600**
FAT **36 g** SATURATED FAT **17 g**

***Cook's Country* Reduced-Fat Corn Chowder**
CALORIES **390**
FAT **14 g** SATURATED FAT **3.5 g**

TEST KITCHEN TECHNIQUE
Cooking with Corn, Two Ways
We use lots of fresh corn in our reduced-fat chowder. Half of the kernels go directly into the soup, and the remainder form the base of a naturally sweet, starchy liquid.

HALF OF KERNELS
These get processed until smooth.

We then strain the pureed kernels and discard the solids.

The resulting 1¼ cups of liquid is the base for our flavorful corn butter.

+

REMAINING KERNELS
These get added, whole, to the simmering soup.

With hardly any work, you can do much better than the bland and monotonously smooth store-bought versions. BY NICK IVERSON

REDUCED-FAT CORN CHOWDER

Serves 6

Don't substitute frozen corn for fresh. Because it's parcooked, frozen corn won't release the starchy liquid that flavors and thickens our soup.

- 10 ears corn, kernels cut from cobs (7½ cups)
- ¼ cup all-purpose flour
- 2 slices bacon, chopped fine
- 1 onion, chopped fine
  Salt and pepper
- 2 garlic cloves, minced
- 3¾ cups chicken broth
- 1¾ cups 1 percent low-fat milk
- 10 ounces red potatoes, unpeeled, cut into ½-inch pieces
- 1 teaspoon minced fresh thyme
- 1 bay leaf
- ⅓ cup half-and-half
- 2 tablespoons minced fresh chives

1. Process 3¾ cups corn kernels in food processor until smooth, about 2 minutes. Set fine-mesh strainer over 2-cup liquid measuring cup and line strainer with double layer of cheesecloth. Transfer pureed corn to strainer, gather corners of cheesecloth together, and squeeze 1¼ cups liquid from corn into measuring cup. Discard corn solids. Whisk flour into corn liquid until no lumps remain.

2. Cook bacon in Dutch oven over medium heat until beginning to crisp, about 5 minutes. Reduce heat to low; add onion, 1 teaspoon salt, and ½ teaspoon pepper; and cook, covered, until softened, about 10 minutes. Add garlic and cook until fragrant, about 30 seconds. Add corn liquid mixture and cook, stirring constantly, until thickened to paste-like consistency, about 3 minutes. Slowly whisk in broth until incorporated. Cook until thickened slightly, about 5 minutes.

3. Add milk, potatoes, thyme, and bay leaf and bring to boil over medium-high heat. Reduce heat to medium-low and simmer for 7 minutes. Add remaining 3¾ cups corn and half-and-half and return to simmer. Simmer until kernels are tender yet firm, 10 to 12 minutes. Discard bay leaf. Stir in chives. Season with salt and pepper to taste. Serve.

WHY WOULD ANYONE ever buy the guacamole that comes in those hermetically-sealed bags at the grocery store? Guacamole takes only a few minutes to make (with no cooking) and the store-bought stuff lacks what makes home-made guacamole so good: freshness and an appealing chunky texture.

But recipes for this easy dip have their flaws, too. Many call for cooks to pulverize the ingredients by hand or, worse, puree them in a food processor. The uniform, ultrasmooth guacamole that results also harks back to baby food. In the test kitchen we prefer guacamole with some lumps and chunks, so we've created a recipe to produce those: We mash one avocado with the seasonings and then gently stir in dice from two more avocados. We use the traditional seasonings to flavor it: onion, garlic, cumin, cilantro, jalapeño, and a squeeze of lime juice to brighten everything up.

I'm not ashamed to admit that I'm obsessed with the stuff. I decided to take the test kitchen's core guacamole recipe and create four spin-offs that switch up the flavors. Two variations stay with a Mexican theme: I add chipotle peppers and toasted pepitas (pumpkin seeds) to one and mango and habanero chiles to the other. For a more American take, bacon and tomato make a guacamole fit for any party or barbecue. A final variation features feta and arugula, which give this dip a decidedly Mediterranean feel—try it with toasted pita wedges.

TEST KITCHEN TECHNIQUE
Dicing Avocados

After cutting a crosshatch pattern through the flesh to the peel of the avocado halves, use a spoon to scoop out the cubes.

Our guacamole is brightened by lime and cilantro—and just enough (but not too much) garlic.

GUACAMOLE

Makes 2½ to 3 cups; serves 4 to 6

Store guacamole for up to 24 hours by pressing plastic wrap directly against its surface.

- 3 ripe avocados
- ¼ cup chopped fresh cilantro
- 1 jalapeño chile, stemmed, seeded, and minced
- 2 tablespoons finely chopped onion
- 2 tablespoons lime juice
- 2 garlic cloves, minced
  Salt
- ½ teaspoon ground cumin

1. Halve 1 avocado, remove pit, and scoop flesh into medium bowl. Add cilantro, jalapeño, onion, lime juice, garlic, ¾ teaspoon salt, and cumin and mash with potato masher (or fork) until mostly smooth.

2. Halve and pit remaining 2 avocados. Carefully make ½-inch crosshatch incisions in flesh with butter knife, cutting down to but not through skin. Insert spoon between skin and flesh, gently scoop out avocado cubes, and add to mashed mixture. Gently mash until mixture is well combined but still coarse. Season with salt to taste. Serve.

BACON AND TOMATO GUACAMOLE

Add 6 slices chopped and cooked bacon and 1 tomato, cored and cut into ¼-inch pieces, with avocados in step 2.

CHIPOTLE AND PEPITA GUACAMOLE

Substitute 1 tablespoon minced canned chipotle chile in adobo sauce for jalapeño in step 1. Add ¼ cup toasted pepitas with avocados in step 2.

FETA AND ARUGULA GUACAMOLE

Substitute ½ cup chopped baby arugula for cilantro in step 1. Add 1 cup crumbled feta cheese with avocados in step 2.

HABANERO AND MANGO GUACAMOLE

Substitute 1 stemmed, seeded, and minced habanero chile for jalapeño in step 1. Add ½ mango, peeled and cut into ¼-inch pieces, with avocados in step 2.

Equipment Review Two-Slice Toasters

If we can send a robot to Mars, why can't anybody make a decent toaster?

BY TAIZETH SIERRA

KEY Good ★★★   Fair ★★   Poor ★

IS GOOD TOAST really too much to ask? Every few years, we find ourselves hunting for a dependable toaster. Apparently, manufacturers are on the same quest, given how fast they develop and (as in the case of our most recent favorite) discontinue new toasters. So, like Sisyphus, we are starting over.

We set a reasonable limit—$100 or less—and then lined up seven qualifying toasters from major brands. We toasted more than 1,000 slices of sandwich bread. Then we tackled bagels, toaster pastries, English muffins, and frozen waffles.

At the very least, toasters should pop out nicely browned bread in the shade that you select. But that's just where most fail. Set to "light," every toaster in our lineup produced dried-out, pale, slightly warm slices. A few couldn't make medium toast either, unless they were set on "dark." So what happened on "dark" settings? For some models, the toast burned. Others rendered all three shades across a single slice or toasted only one side properly. Just one toaster out of seven earned perfect marks.

Could these toasters handle a crowd? We made three batches of toast in rapid succession. The good news is that most of our lineup performed consistently, batch after batch. The bad news is that the quality was not very high.

Next, we tested the toasters' durability, making 50 slices of toast in each machine using alternating slots. Our lone front-runner fumbled, producing patchy, uneven toast, sometimes barely warming the bread, though we never changed the setting; the problem worsened the longer we used the toaster. Exactly the opposite happened with a different model. Its lackluster performance improved with use . . . kind of: It still struggled to toast a single slice evenly and would occasionally fail to toast the bread at all.

So where were we? In three years, we'd tested 14 two-slot toasters, and we didn't love a single one. The only one we'd ever found acceptable had been discontinued. So far, our current testing yielded just one toaster that we liked enough to recommend, and with reservations at that. All the rest were so unreliable that we rated them "not recommended." For $90 we expected to be able to recommend a toaster without reservations. Maybe the price cap was the problem. If money were no object,

could we finally get perfect toast? We bought three models at the opposite end of the price spectrum—between $240 and $300—and repeated our tests.

All three performed better than our favorite reasonably priced toaster. The first had impressive features: It sensed when bread was in the slot and automatically lowered it into the toaster. A pleasing tone announced when toast was ready, a clever "little longer" button let us top off the shade without fear of burning the bread, and the "keep warm" function automatically engaged if the toast was not removed within 45

seconds. Unfortunately, all those luxury features were beside the point: On "medium," the bread emerged too light overall and much darker on one side than on the other. After we flipped the slice and hit the "little longer" button, it was perfect, but wouldn't our patience for fiddling run out after paying $300?

On the other end of the spectrum was a minimalist model. Two dials let you control the heating elements, depending on whether you are toasting one or two slices of bread or one side of a bagel. A manual toast ejector lets you remove toast mid-cycle or preheat

the toaster before adding the bread (which improved toasting performance significantly). You must remember what position on the dial makes your favorite toast, resetting the dial every time—no presets here. This model produced nice-looking toast, but again, only with active fiddling.

The third toaster was the best of the three. Its controls are simple, and it produced flawless single slices of toast time after time, which we could view through a clear window, and we could hit a central "stop" button if we wanted to arrest the browning. However, when we tried

---

RECOMMENDED

	CRITERIA		TESTERS' NOTES
MAGIMIX BY ROBOT-COUPE Vision Toaster **Model:** 11526US **Price:** $249.95 **Source:** williams-sonoma.com **Extras:** Defrost, bagel, reheat, cancel, clear window 	Consistency Evenness of Color Design	★★½ ★★★ ★★★	The most reliable and efficient toaster in the lineup has quartz elements for even heating and one long slot that can fit two pieces of sandwich bread or a long slice of artisanal bread. We loved its clear windows, which let us keep track of browning, and its "stop" button. Our only quibble: The heat seems to concentrate in the middle of the slot, so single slices of bread placed in the middle brown perfectly but two slices side by side come out lighter at the outer edges.

RECOMMENDED WITH RESERVATIONS

	CRITERIA		TESTERS' NOTES
DUALIT 2-Slice NewGen Classic Toaster **Model:** 27150 **Price:** $239.99 **Source:** bedbathandbeyond.com **Extras:** Defrost, bagel, manual ejector, replaceable elements	Consistency Evenness of Color Design	★★ ★★ ★★½	If you're hands-on, this is the toaster for you. You decide how long to set the timer and when to lower the bread and remove it. (This becomes easy after a few uses.) The manual even instructs you on how to replace elements if they burn out. Too bad the toasting consistency was not that great.
KITCHENAID Pro Line Toaster **Model:** KMT2203 **Price:** $299.95 **Source:** williams-sonoma.com **Extras:** Defrost, bagel, keep warm, "little longer" button, cancel	Consistency Evenness of Color Design	★½ ★½ ★★★	This handsome machine was a joy to use and has just about every feature you could want—if only it would toast bread evenly. Every time we used it, the results were (literally) spotty. When we flipped the bread over and hit the "little longer" button, we did get lovely toast, but having to do so is a deal breaker.
KITCHENAID 2 Slice Manual High-Lift Lever Toaster with LCD Display **Model:** KMT222OB **Price:** $89.99 **Source:** kitchenaid.com **Extras:** Digital display, cancel, bagel, defrost, reheat *BEST BUY*	Consistency Evenness of Color Design	★★ ★★ ★½	Spotty heating and unevenness side to side was an issue when we started using this toaster. To our surprise, the toaster improved with time. Still, on occasion it failed to toast or else burned the odd piece of bread.

NOT RECOMMENDED

	CRITERIA		TESTERS' NOTES
CUISINART Touch to Toast Leverless 2-Slice Toaster **Model:** CPT-420 **Price:** $79.95 **Extras:** Digital display, button instead of lever, bagel, defrost, reheat, cancel 	Consistency Evenness of Color Design	★ ★½ ★★	This toaster has nice features and is easy to use and clean. It produced perfect toast at first, making ideal light, medium, and dark shades. Unfortunately, the longer we used the toaster the more the toast quality suffered.
BREVILLE Ikon 2-Slice Toaster **Model:** CT70XL **Price:** $69.99 **Extras:** "Lift and look," defrost, reheat, bagel, cancel	Consistency Evenness of Color Design	★ ★ ★★	This toaster was consistently inconsistent, making spotty, uneven toast and struggling to get both sides of the toast the same shade. The "lift and look" lever allows users to check the progress of the toast mid-cycle so that they can adjust the slice or cancel the cycle, but we still didn't get reliable results.
BODUM Bistro Toaster **Model:** 10709 **Price:** $50 **Extras:** Defrost, cancel, warming rack	Consistency Evenness of Color Design	½ ½ ★	The slots on this model were too shallow to fit our favorite sandwich bread, and it repeatedly browned the bottom of the toast more than the top. Not surprisingly, we found that the heating elements were concentrated toward the bottom of the machine.

to toast two slices of our favorite (slightly oversize) sandwich bread, the edges were lighter than the rest of the slice. Toward the end of our "50 slices" test, this toaster sometimes produced unevenly browned toast. Still, for simplicity and the most consistent overall performance, this one was our winner. In the end, all three higher-end toasters delivered better results than their less expensive counterparts.

Why were some toasters better than others? The heating elements—their material, number, design, and placement—all affect performance. Most toasters have heating elements made of Nichrome wires (the trade name for an alloy of nickel and chromium), which are wrapped across a flameproof mica sheet. As electricity flows through the wires, they radiate heat. Toasters with abundant, evenly spaced Nichrome wires heated most evenly. One of the worst performers had eight wires on one side of the slot and four on the other; another had 10 wires on one side, seven of which were concentrated on the bottom half of the mica sheet.

Our favorite high-end toaster was the only model with quartz heating elements. Large quartz rods are placed along the top and bottom of each side of a single long slot. Quartz is highly responsive, cooling and heating rapidly, and it emits intense heat to toast the exterior of the slice while leaving the inside moist. Better-performing toasters also featured baskets inside the slots that centered the bread, keeping each slice equidistant from heating elements; otherwise, bread tended to lean closer to one set of elements and become darker on that side of the slice.

In the end, we liked the Magimix by Robot-Coupe Vision Toaster best. If you think $250 is just too much to pay for excellent toast, we recommend (with reservations) the KitchenAid 2 Slice Manual High-Lift Lever Toaster, which costs $89.99.

EDITORS' NOTE: We tested three toasters that don't appear in our chart. They were made by Proctor Silex, Dualit, and Hamilton Beach and we can't recommend them. For more details, go to **CooksCountry.com/toasters**.

Taste Test Pepper Jack Cheese

We sought heat, smooth meltability, and cheese with character.

BY HANNAH CROWLEY

ADD HOT PICKLED peppers to Monterey Jack, a mild California cow's-milk cheese, and you've got pepper Jack. As American enthusiasm for spicy food continues to rise, pepper Jack has become one of the country's fastest-growing sellers, according to Datassential, a restaurant market research firm.

Here in the test kitchen, we like pepper Jack for its creamy melting properties, and we've used it in enchiladas, biscuits, nachos, seven-layer dip, Tex-Mex meatloaf, and much more. To select a favorite product, we tasted seven nationally available cheeses: six in block form and one preshredded from a prominent brand that doesn't sell blocks. We tried the cheeses on their own and melted in quesadillas.

Although every product uses jalapeños (with one adding habanero), the heat levels ranged. None was tear-inducingly hot, but some were tear-inducingly tame: "Where is the heat?!" demanded one exasperated taster of an especially bland sample. When we tallied the results, a pattern emerged: We preferred the spicier cheeses.

Peppers aside, the cheeses themselves ranged from "bland" and "kid-friendly" to pleasingly "sharp," "grassy," "buttery," and "tangy." Tasters compared the products we liked with sharper cheeses, such as cheddar and Swiss, and those with more "bite and sharpness" could take on the hot peppers. Fat played a role in our rankings, too, providing buttery, creamy, rounded background to the tang, saltiness, and heat of pepper Jack, as well as helping the cheese melt smoothly. Unsurprisingly, our bottom two products had 1 less gram of fat than the other samples.

As for the lone preshredded product? It got off to a bad start when we tasted it plain, and it didn't fare much better in quesadillas: The potato starch and powdered cellulose coating that is added to preshredded cheese to keep the shreds from clumping made it "chalky" and "oddly dry."

With 9 grams of fat per ounce, our winning product, Boar's Head Monterey Jack Cheese with Jalapeño, was "creamy" and "buttery." It melted nicely, and its cheddarlike tang easily accommodated the "assertive kick" of peppers. Made with the Boar's Head cheese, even a plain cheese quesadilla was lively and flavorful.

Hot 🌶🌶🌶 **Medium** 🌶🌶 **Mild** 🌶

RECOMMENDED

	TASTERS' NOTES
BOAR'S HEAD Monterey Jack Cheese with Jalapeño **Price:** $6.99 for 8 oz (87 cents per oz) **Style:** Block **Peppers:** Jalapeño **Fat:** 9 g per oz **Heat:** 🌶🌶🌶	This "buttery" cheese had a "tangy," "cheddarlike" flavor that was "clean" and "nicely balanced," and the jalapeños gave it a "bright," "assertive" kick. The texture was "even and firm" yet "creamy."
TILLAMOOK Pepper Jack Cheese **Price:** $16 for 2 lb (50 cents per oz) **Style:** Block **Peppers:** Jalapeño **Fat:** 9 g per oz **Heat:** 🌶🌶	This cheese's "very strong, sharp flavor" was "more tangy than milky," "fairly acidic," and "complex." The heat was "moderate" and the texture "soft."

RECOMMENDED WITH RESERVATIONS

VELLA Jalapeño Jack **Price:** $24 for 2.5 lb (60 cents per oz) **Style:** Block **Peppers:** Jalapeño **Fat:** 9 g per oz **Heat:** 🌶 ½ 	Vella's "full milky flavor" was "creamy" and "rich," while the spice level was "mild but consistent"; some tasters preferred hotter products. The cheese was "soft," "smooth," and "nearly gooey."
CABOT Pepper Jack **Price:** $3.59 for 8 oz (45 cents per oz) **Style:** Block **Peppers:** Jalapeño **Fat:** 9 g per oz **Heat:** 🌶🌶 	This pepper Jack reminded us of "mild cheddar." The large chunks of jalapeño gave it a "vegetal," "fruity" pepper flavor. Good, but alas, the texture was "waxy" and "rubbery."
LAND O'LAKES Hot Pepper Jack **Price:** $6.99 per lb (44 cents per oz) **Style:** Block **Peppers:** Jalapeño **Fat:** 9 g per oz **Heat:** 🌶🌶	Tasters wished for "more sharpness" in this "bland" cheese, although at least the pepper flavor was "pronounced" and "lingering." The texture was "weirdly soft, like bad American cheese," said one taster; another compared it to Cheez Whiz.

NOT RECOMMENDED

ORGANIC VALLEY Pepper Jack Cheese **Price:** $7.99 for 8 oz ($1 per oz) **Style:** Block **Peppers:** Jalapeño **Fat:** 8 g per oz **Heat:** 🌶	The flavor was "subtle" in this "very mild," "kid-friendly" cheese, which had "almost no heat," with "sweet," "not at all spicy" peppers. We found the texture "mushy" and "sticky."
SARGENTO OFF THE BLOCK Pepper Jack Traditional Cut **Price:** $3.59 for 8 oz (45 cents per oz) **Style:** Shredded **Peppers:** Jalapeño and habanero **Fat:** 8 g per oz **Heat:** 🌶🌶🌶	We liked the definite pepper heat in this preshredded cheese (it includes habanero as well as jalapeño). But the ingredients added to prevent caking (potato starch and powdered cellulose) made the cheese chalky and powdery when eaten plain and "stiff" and "grainy" when melted.

Looking for a Recipe

Have you lost a recipe you treasure? Ask a reader. While you're at it, answer a reader. Post queries and finds at **CooksCountry.com/magazine**; click on **Looking for a Recipe** (or write to Looking for a Recipe, *Cook's Country*, P.O. Box 470739, Brookline, MA 02447). We'll share all of your submissions online and one recipe on this page; please include your name and mailing address.

Mississippi Comeback Sauce
Sarah French, Birmingham, Ala.

I'm trying to find a recipe for Mississippi comeback sauce, which is delicious on just about anything from fried green tomatoes to burgers and fries. Most recipes that I've seen make it by combining mayonnaise, ketchup, and pepper, but these versions taste nothing like the sauces I've enjoyed in Jackson, Mississippi.

Frikadeller
Peter Grinager, St. Paul, Minn.

I'm looking for a good recipe for Danish meatballs—well, actually, they're more like patties. They're made with beef and pork and are usually pan-fried. I think they're called *frikadeller* in Danish, and they usually go with buttered potatoes. Have you got an authentic recipe, one that makes meatballs that don't fall apart in the skillet? If so, I'd love to try it.

No-Knead Yeast Rolls
Bill Carter, Astatula, Fla.

Hello there! I used to have a Spry shortening cookbook that had a wonderful recipe for yeast rolls that required no kneading. Because of that, they were super-easy to make, and they tasted great, too. Can you help me track down this recipe?

Almond Meringue Cookies
Julie Jahn, Decatur, Ind.

When I was young, my mom used to make the most wonderful cookies; I've never been able to duplicate them. She beat four or five egg whites with sugar as though she were making meringue. To half of the beaten whites she added pulverized almonds. That's it—there was nothing else in these cookies. She'd spread the almond–egg white mixture on a cookie sheet to a depth of ¼ inch and cover that base with the plain whipped, sugared egg whites. She cut this dough into rectangles and baked them until the cookies were golden. The tops were basically a meringue cookie and the bottoms wonderful almond cookies. I have tried to make these too many times with no luck—I am so frustrated. Can anyone help?

CREAM OF CELERY SOUP
Serves 6 to 8
From Molly Mioduszewski, Fitchburg, Mass.

4	tablespoons unsalted butter
12	celery ribs, chopped
1	pound russet potatoes, peeled, quartered, and sliced thin
2	onions, chopped
2	tablespoons sugar
2	teaspoons dried sage
	Salt and pepper
2	tablespoons all-purpose flour
6	cups chicken broth
1	bay leaf
½	cup heavy cream

1. Melt butter in Dutch oven over medium-low heat. Add celery, potatoes, onions, sugar, sage, ½ teaspoon salt, and ½ teaspoon pepper and cook, covered, until celery and onions soften, about 15 minutes.

2. Stir in flour and cook for 1 minute. Stir in broth and bay leaf and bring to boil over high heat. Reduce heat to medium-low and simmer, uncovered, until potatoes are tender, about 20 minutes. Discard bay leaf.

3. Working in batches, process soup in blender until smooth, 1 to 2 minutes. Return soup to clean pot, stir in cream, and bring to simmer over medium heat. Season with salt and pepper to taste. Serve.

FIND THE ROOSTER!
A tiny version of this rooster has been hidden in the pages of this issue. Write to us with its location and we'll enter you in a random drawing. The first correct entry drawn will win our Best Buy two-slot toaster (see page 30), an each of the next five will receive a free one-year subscription to *Cook's Country*. To enter, visit **CooksCountry. com/rooster** by July 31, 2013, or write Rooster JJ13, *Cook's Country*, P.O. Bo 470739, Brookline, MA 02447. Include your name and address. **Audrey Woo Manhattan, Kansas**, found the rooster the February/March 2013 issue on pa 4 and won our favorite cookie sheet.

WEB EXTRAS
Free for 4 months online at **CooksCountry.com**

Barbecued Country-Style Ribs
Creamy Buttermilk Coleslaw
Dutch Oven Testing
Honey-Glazed Pork Loin
Honey-Roasted Ribs
Lexington-Style Pulled Pork
Two-Slice Toasters (full chart)
Wedge Salad
Yellow Layer Cake

COOK'S COUNTRY IS NC ON iPAD!

Download the new *Cook's Country* app for iPad and start a free trial subscription or purchase a single issue of the magazine. All issues are enhanced with full-color Cooking Mode slide shows that provide step-b step instructions for completing recipe plus expanded reviews and ratings. G **CooksCountry.com/iPad** to downloa app through iTunes.

Follow us on **Twitter**
twitter.com/TestKitchen

Find us on **Facebook**
facebook.com/CooksCountry

Piña Colada Cake

We turn a classic tropical cocktail into an irresistible cake.

To make this cake you will need:

- 1 tablespoon instant tapioca
- 1 pineapple, peeled, cored, and quartered lengthwise
- ⅓ cup (2⅓ ounces) granulated sugar
- ¼ cup spiced rum
  Salt
- 20 tablespoons (2½ sticks) unsalted butter, softened
- 3 tablespoons canned coconut milk
- 1 teaspoon vanilla extract
- ½ teaspoon coconut extract
- 2¼ cups (9 ounces) confectioners' sugar
- 2 (9-inch) yellow cake rounds*
- 1 cup (3 ounces) sweetened shredded coconut, toasted

FOR THE FILLING: Grind tapioca to fine powder in spice grinder, about 30 seconds. Coarsely chop 2 pineapple quarters, then pulse in food processor until coarsely ground, 8 to 10 pulses (you should have about 1½ cups). Slice one of remaining pineapple quarters into ⅛-inch-thick slices and reserve to decorate cake. (Eat remaining pineapple quarter—cook's treat!) Transfer ground pineapple to medium saucepan and add granulated sugar, rum, ground tapioca, and ⅛ teaspoon salt. Bring to boil over medium heat and cook until thickened, about 4 minutes. Off heat, stir in 2 tablespoons butter until incorporated. Transfer to bowl and refrigerate until set, at least 4 hours or up to 24 hours.

FOR THE FROSTING: Using stand mixer fitted with whisk, whip remaining 18 tablespoons butter, coconut milk, vanilla, coconut extract, and ⅛ teaspoon salt on medium-low speed until combined. Slowly add confectioners' sugar and continue to whip until smooth, about 2 minutes. Increase speed to medium-high and whip until light and fluffy, about 5 minutes.

TO ASSEMBLE: Place 1 cake round on plate or pedestal. Spread filling evenly over top. Top with second cake round, press lightly to adhere, then spread frosting evenly over top and sides of cake. Gently press coconut onto sides of cake. Fan pineapple slices in circle around top edge of cake. Serve.

▶ *Go to **CooksCountry.com/yellowlayercake** for our **Yellow Layer Cake** recipe or use your own.

Inside This Issue

Grilled Chicken Leg Quarters 6

Smoked Roast Beef 14

Natchitoches Meat Pies 18

Summer Berry Pudding 22

Pork Chops with Peppers 12

Farmers' Market Pasta RC

Reduced-Fat Corn Chowder 28

Grilled Chicken Sausage RC

Tangy Corn Relish 21

Guacamole 29

Muffin Tin Doughnuts 17

Grilled Caesar Salad 13

Slow-Cooker Baked Ziti 26

Grilled Cowboy-Cut Rib Eyes 4

Grilled Shrimp Skewers 24

Texas Potato Salad 11

Memphis Wet Ribs 20

Roast Pork Tenderloin RC

Grilled Eggplant 9

Picnic Fried Chicken 10

Tomato Jam 7

Chicken Divan for Two 27

Grilled Chicken Parmesan RC

Asian Chicken Noodle Salad RC

Summer Squash Gratin 8

Cook's Country

AUGUST/SEPTEMBER 2013

Tar Heel Pie

Puerto Rican Roast Pork

Chicken Diavolo

California Fish Tacos
Light, Crunchy Coating

Chopped Caprese Salad
Italian Flavors, American Style

Frittata Breakfast Muffins
A Meal in a Muffin

Grilled Chuck Steaks
Technique for Tenderness

Tasting Jarred Salsas
Are Any Worth Buying?

Backyard BBQ Brisket
Step-by-Step Instructions

Pesto Potatoes
New Summer Classic

Testing Small Slow Cookers
Is Smaller Just as Good?

Peach Cobbler for Two
Juicy, Not Soggy

Strawberry Pretzel Salad
Midwest Favorite Updated

CooksCountry.com
$5.95 U.S./$6.95 CANADA

*Billed as "sensational" in a 1953 magazine, **Tar Heel Pie** ideally combines the best of a pie with the best of a gooey, fudgy brownie. After a couple of weeks in our test kitchen, we had perfected a pie that does just that.* PAGE 22

7 25274 05251 6

09>

Dear Country Cook,

Harvest in our small Vermont town was never like what you see in the photo below—I didn't show up in knee-highs, shorts, and a cardigan cradling a watermelon. But the fall harvest was still a special time. The last bale of hay was in the barn, the wild apples were in large sacks ready for pressing, the honey was spun and bottled, the beets and carrots were stored in baskets of sand, the potatoes were stored in the root cellar, and the eating apples were kept separately in the cold cellar.

These days, it seems as if we are constantly celebrating, whether it's victory on the baseball field, our 10-year-old's soccer game, or at a restaurant on a Saturday night. Our grandparents, however, were more frugal in celebration; it was the rare occasion that provided a break from the daily routine.

That reminds me of the story of the Vermonter who was visiting his brother in Texas. He was having lunch at a small diner, and as he was leaving, he remarked to the owner and his young son that it looked as though it might rain. "Hope so," said the owner, peering up at the sky. "Not so much for my own sake as for the boy's. I've seen it rain."

Well, I guess even the simplest things can be worth celebrating. Just don't overdo it!

All the best,

Christopher Kimball
Founder and Editor

Heading to the harvest festival, 1941.

Cook's Country

AUGUST/SEPTEMBER 2013

Contents

Founder and Editor Christopher Kimball
Editorial Director Jack Bishop
Editorial Director, Magazines John Willoughby
Executive Editor Peggy Grodinsky
Managing Editor Scott Kathan
Senior Editors Lisa McManus, Bryan Roof, Diane Unger
Test Kitchen Director Erin McMurrer
Associate Editors Hannah Crowley, Amy Graves, Rebeccah Marsters
Test Cooks Sarah Gabriel, Nick Iverson, Christie Morrison, Carolynn Purpura MacKay, Cristin Walsh
Assistant Editors Shannon Friedmann Hatch, Taizeth Sierra
Copy Editors Nell Beram, Megan Ginsberg
Executive Assistant Christine Gordon
Test Kitchen Manager Leah Rovner
Senior Kitchen Assistants Michelle Blodget, Meryl MacCormack
Kitchen Assistants Maria Elena Delgado, Ena Gudiel
Executive Producer Melissa Baldino
Co-Executive Producer Stephanie Stender
Production Assistant Kaitlin Hammond

Contributing Editors Erika Bruce, Eva Katz, Jeremy Sauer
Consulting Editors Anne Mendelson, Meg Ragland
Science Editor Guy Crosby, Ph.D.
Executive Food Editor, TV, Radio & Media Bridget Lancaster

Managing Editor, Web Christine Liu
Senior Editor, Cooking School Mari Levine
Associate Editors, Web Eric Grzymkowski, Roger Metcalf
Assistant Editors, Web Jill Fisher, Charlotte Wilder
Senior Video Editor Nick Dakoulas

Design Director Amy Klee
Art Director Julie Cote
Deputy Art Director Susan Levin
Associate Art Director Lindsey Timko
Deputy Art Director, Marketing/Web Jennifer Cox
Staff Photographer Daniel J. van Ackere
Color Food Photography Keller + Keller
Styling Catrine Kelty, Marie Piraino
Associate Art Director, Marketing/Web Mariah Tarvainen
Production Designer, Marketing/Web Judy Blomquist
Photo Editor Steve Klise

Vice President, Marketing David Mack
Circulation Director Doug Wicinski
Circulation & Fulfillment Manager Carrie Fethe
Partnership Marketing Manager Pamela Putprush
Marketing Assistant Joyce Liao

VP, Technology, Product Development Barry Kelly
Director, Project Management Alice Carpenter
Production & Traffic Coordinator Brittany Allen
Development Manager Mike Serio

Chief Operating Officer Rob Ristagno
Production Director Guy Rochford
Workflow & Digital Asset Manager Andrew Mannone
Senior Color & Imaging Specialist Lauren Pettapiece
Production & Imaging Specialists Heather Dube, Lauren Robbins
Director of Sponsorship Sales Anne Traficante
Client Services Associate Kate May
Sponsorship Sales Representative Morgan Ryan
Customer Service Manager Jacqueline Valerio
Customer Service Representatives Megan Hamner, Jessica Haskin, Andrew Straaberg Frinfrock

Chief Financial Officer Sharyn Chabot
Retail Sales & Marketing Manager Emily Logan
Human Resources Manager Adele Shapiro
Publicity Deborah Broide

ON THE COVER:
Tar Heel Pie
Keller + Keller, Catrine Kelty
ILLUSTRATION: Greg Stevenson

Cook's Country magazine (ISSN 1552-1990), number 52, is published bimonthly by Boston Common Press Limited Partnership, 17 Station St., Brookline, MA 02445. Copyright 2013 Boston Common Press Limited Partnership. Periodicals postage paid at Boston, Mass., and additional mailing offices. USPS #023453. Publications Mail Agreement No. 40020778. Return undeliverable Canadian addresses to P.O. Box 875, Station A, Windsor, ON N9A 6P2. POSTMASTER: Send address changes to Cook's Country, P.O. Box 6018, Harlan, IA 51593-1518. For subscription and gift subscription orders, subscription inquiries, or change-of-address notices, visit americasTestKitchen.com/customerservice, call 800-526-8442 in the U.S. or 515-248-7684 from outside the U.S., or write to Cook's Country, P.O. Box 6018, Harlan, IA 51593-1518. PRINTED IN THE USA

GRILLED CHUCK STEAKS, 4

REDUCED-FAT BLONDIES, 28

CHOPPED CAPRESE SALAD, 5

Features

Departments

RECIPES THAT WORK®

America's Test Kitchen is a very real 2,500-square-foot kitchen located just outside Boston. It is the home of Cook's Country and Cook's Illustrated magazines and is the workday destination of more than three dozen test cooks, editors, and cookware specialists. Our mission is to test recipes over and over again until we understand how and why they work and until we arrive at the best version. We also test kitchen equipment and supermarket ingredients in search of brands that offer the best value and performance. You can watch us work by tuning in to Cook's Country from America's Test Kitchen (CooksCountryTV.com) and America's Test Kitchen (AmericasTestKitchenTV.com) on public television.

Ask Cook's Country

BY SARAH GABRIEL

I grill whole chickens a lot in the summer. Can I use the carcasses to make stock?

Eileen Carque, New Ashford, Mass.

To answer your question, we grilled a whole chicken (this technique is called "grill roasting"), took the meat off the breasts and legs, and then broke up the carcass. We simmered it with onions, carrots, and celery for about 3 hours to make stock. The steam from the pot had a faint smoky odor, and the stock came out tasting smoky but not unpleasant; this stock couldn't pass for regular stock, but we loved it in soups with strong flavors, like our Chicken Tortilla Soup. In a follow-up test, we took the extra step of removing every bit of skin from the wings. The resulting stock had barely perceptible smoke flavor. We repeated these tests with a smoked chicken. As long as we carefully removed all the skin, the stock was pleasantly smoky—we'd be happy to use it in any number of boldly seasoned recipes. But if we left on any skin whatsoever, the stock was acrid and unusable.

THE BOTTOM LINE: Stock made from grilled whole chickens has a smoky flavor that can be an asset in recipes with strong flavors. That's also true of stock made from smoked chickens, as long as you diligently remove and discard the skin first.

I see TV chefs sprinkle salt on garlic when they chop it. Why?

Mary Anne Maher, Avon, Conn.

We usually use a garlic press in the test kitchen, but to answer your question, we minced garlic cloves with knives after sprinkling half of the cloves with salt. We found that the salt made little difference in the ease of mincing (the salt does help prevent the garlic from sticking to the knife blade), but the salted minced garlic was wetter. When it came to mashing the minced garlic into a paste with the broad side of a knife (as you might do to help raw garlic incorporate better into a vinaigrette), the salted cloves turned into a creamy paste in about half of the time. Our science editor explained that the salt draws moisture out of the garlic cells, accounting for the moister mince. As the cells lose moisture, they collapse and soften, which explains why it was so much easier to mash the salted garlic. Furthermore, the grains of salt act as an abrasive, helping grind the garlic particles as you mash.

THE BOTTOM LINE: Sprinkling minced garlic with salt can speed the process of mashing it. Be sure to use less salt when seasoning the dish you use it in.

I read in a magazine that you can substitute mashed avocado for butter in cookies. That sounds insane. Could it possibly be true?

Rachel Hackett, Northampton, Mass.

That does sound insane. But sure enough, an Internet search of "substitute avocado for butter" returned more than 50,000 results—some for cookies, others for cakes. We did some calculations and found that one mashed avocado weighs about the same as a stick of butter but has about one-quarter of the calories and fat—about 95 percent less saturated fat and no cholesterol versus 234 milligrams of cholesterol for a stick of butter. So if the substitution worked, the payoff would be huge.

We made chocolate chip and oatmeal cookies, replacing all the butter with ripe avocado. When creaming the avocado and sugar, the mixture never became fluffy, as it would have with butter, and the avocado color intensified. In the oven, the cookies made with butter spread as the butter melted, but those made with avocado never did. Beneath their dry, pale green surface, these cookies were dense and damp. We tried again using half butter and half avocado, but the results weren't any more appetizing. So the answer to the cookie question is an emphatic no.

But what about cakes? Yellow cake was a nonstarter—we didn't like the green color or the vegetal flavor. But could chocolate cover up those things? We made three chocolate cakes, one with butter, one with half butter and half avocado, and the third with all avocado. They looked slightly different, but we all liked the half-avocado version, and two-thirds of us liked the all-avocado cake, too; the rest of us found it "wetter" or "gummier" than the original.

THE BOTTOM LINE: Don't use avocado in place of butter in cookies—it demeans both the avocado and the cookie. But it's fine to use it to replace at least half of the butter in chocolate cake.

OATMEAL COOKIE
Tastes as bad as it looks.

"YELLOW" CAKE
Not even for St. Patty's.

CHOCOLATE CAKE
Surprisingly OK.

My grocery store carries dozens of different mustards. How many do I need?

David Mitchell, Madison, Maine

Four main characteristics account for the differences among mustards: type of mustard seeds (white, brown, or black), grind size (from whole seeds to powder), liquid ingredients (vinegar, wine, beer, fruit juice), and seasonings (horseradish, paprika, and other spices).

Usually, Dijon mustard is made from moderately hot brown mustard seeds. The liquid—white wine or the sour juice of unripe grapes, called verjuice—adds tang. Although some Dijon mustards are coarsely ground, the most widely available products are smooth. While any mustard will help emulsify vinaigrette, the balanced heat, smooth consistency, and muted color of Dijon mustard make it perfect for this task. It's also good as a condiment.

Spicy brown mustard uses brown mustard seeds, too, but it's more coarsely ground, so it has a speckled appearance. Spicy brown mustard usually contains vinegar. Its heat is often bolstered by horseradish (some brands call spicy brown mustard with horseradish "deli-style"). Spicy brown and deli-style mustards pair well with salty foods like ham, hot dogs, and pretzels and can add spicy punch to barbecue sauces.

Whole-grain mustards come in a variety of flavors and are made with various liquids and spices. What they all have in common is that the mustard seeds are whole rather than ground or crushed. This rustic-style mustard is often served with cured sausages or used on meat or fish when showcasing the mustard is the goal.

The primary difference between yellow mustard (sometimes called "American-style") and other styles is that the yellow mustard is made from milder white mustard seeds. The texture is smooth, the liquid is usually vinegar, and the spices—generally turmeric and paprika—are tame. Yellow mustard is a classic hot dog condiment or may be used in dressing for potato salad; it adds zip but won't overwhelm sensitive palates.

THE BOTTOM LINE: You don't need to keep five different mustard products on hand, but since mustard has a shelf life of a year or more, you can stock several without worrying about spoilage.

Is the coconut milk next to the soy milk at the store the same as the canned stuff I cook with?

Lauren Myrick, Wichita, Kan.

We went to the nondairy "milk" section of the grocery store and found the coconut milk beverage that you mention. We bought a few different kinds, tasted them, and compared labels. Here's what we learned: Canned coconut milk—the stuff you cook with—is made by steeping shredded coconut in water or milk and then pressing it to yield a creamy, coconut-flavored liquid. (Coconut water, which is usually sold with the sports drinks, is simply the watery liquid from the hollow insides of young coconuts.) The carton-packed coconut milk beverage you saw is made by blending coconut milk with water and additional ingredients such as sugar, flavors, vitamins, preservatives, and thickeners. These make it creamy, despite the water that it contains. The carton-packed coconut milk beverage has about an eighth of the fat content of canned coconut milk. We tasted it: Even the coconut milk beverages that weren't flavored with chocolate or vanilla didn't taste like coconut, and the unsweetened version tasted surprisingly bland.

THE BOTTOM LINE: The two products are not the same. Don't cook with the coconut milk beverage.

PERFECT FOR COOKING

FOR DRINKING ONLY

To ask us a cooking question, visit **CooksCountry.com/askcookscountry.** Or write to Ask *Cook's Country*, P.O. Box 470739, Brookline, MA 02447. Just try to stump us!

Kitchen Shortcuts

COMPILED BY NICK IVERSON

SMART PREP
Anchors Aweigh
Jeremy Gelfand, Rochester, N.Y.

I brine chicken all the time and have a special brining bucket just for this task. I came up with an easy technique that keeps the chicken submerged instead of floating with the top sticking out of the brine. I fill a gallon-size zipper-lock bag with pie weights and drape the bag over the chicken in the bucket. The weighted bag conforms to the chicken's shape and keeps it below the surface of the liquid, for more efficient brining.

DOUBLE DUTY
Cake Stand Stand-In
Mark Hinemann, Albert Lea, Minn.

Every year I like to bake a cake for my wife's birthday. I've considered getting a rotating cake stand to make frosting cakes easier, but they're heavy and take up a lot of space (our kitchen is quite small). I found a "hack" that actually works pretty well: I take the insert out of a tube pan and invert it (cone side down) in a Mason jar. I put the cake on the flat part and can rotate it to facilitate frosting. It's surprisingly stable and works great.

TIDY TIP Teed Off
Jon Register, Birmingham, Ala.

For those of us who don't own cake carriers, the usual way to transport frosted cakes is to stick the cake with toothpicks and loosely drape plastic wrap over them. But the sharp toothpicks can puncture the wrap and make a mess. Instead of using toothpicks, I stick about a dozen clean, unused golf tees in the cake. Their blunt ends hold—but don't puncture—the plastic. And when the cake reaches its destination, I can smooth over the holes in the icing after I remove the tees.

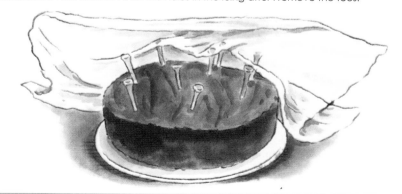

Submit a tip online at **CooksCountry.com/kitchenshortcuts** or send a letter to Kitchen Shortcuts, *Cook's Country*, P.O. Box 470739, Brookline, MA 02447. Include your name, address, and phone number. If we publish your tip, you will receive a free one-year subscription to *Cook's Country*. Letters may be edited for clarity and length.

TWICE AS NICE Waste Not . . .
Nicky Mendoza, Oak Park. Ill.

I have three young boys at home, and you wouldn't believe the number of paper towels our household goes through each week—no matter how much I admonish them to go easy, the kids always seem to wad two or three sheets around their fists, even for small jobs. Recently, it occurred to me that I could take control of this waste by downsizing the roll—I use my bread knife to saw through the roll of paper towels, leaving me with two mini rolls that I put on the dispenser one at a time. Cutting the rolls in half has cut our paper towel consumption in half.

NEAT TRICK
Big Footprint
Tammy Berg, Rapid City, S.D.

Following the test kitchen's advice, I keep an oven thermometer in my oven. But there is a problem with the one I have: If I hang it from an oven rack, I invariably knock it off while cooking. It isn't big enough to rest on the rack without falling through the bars. I was frustrated until I came up with this solution: I folded a sheet of aluminum foil around the base of the thermometer a few times to create a bigger "foot" so the device can sit on the oven rack without falling off.

CLEVER TIP
Egg Shell Game
Colin Maguire, Oklahoma City, Okla.

I like having hard-cooked eggs on hand—they're great as a to-go breakfast, in a green salad, as a quick snack, or chopped up for egg salad. But there are few things more frustrating than trying to peel an egg with a shell that doesn't easily come free. Instead of wrestling with (and sometimes crunching on) shell fragments, now I cut the eggs in half and run a spoon between the shell and the egg to scoop it out. Less frustration, quicker results.

DOUBLE DUTY
Sliced Thin
Jaine Nistico, Oak Ridge, Tenn.

I love raw onion on my sandwiches, but too much can ruin your lunch—and make your breath peel paint. I found a trick to simulate the paper-thin slices you get on deli sandwiches (for which they slice the onions on a meat slicer). I cut an onion in half and use a vegetable peeler to shave thin slices off the cut side. The peeler makes thin and tidy slices that have just enough flavor.

Grilled Chuck Steaks

Chuck is a supremely flavorful cut of beef, but it requires long cooking to make it tender. Could we get this inexpensive cut to work as a steak? BY NICK IVERSON

DOES A GOOD steak dinner have to cost an arm and a leg? Hoping that the answer was no, I hit the meat counter looking for an inexpensive alternative to pricey strip, tenderloin, and rib-eye steaks. I talked to a butcher who recommended chuck steaks; he pointed to some in the case that were nicely marbled and looked pretty good. Chuck is cut from the hardworking shoulder of the steer, which means it's laden with both flavorful fat and tough connective tissue. Until now I'd always passed on buying chuck steaks, figuring that they could never become tender without long, slow cooking. But recently I've been hearing from my chef buddies that chuck steaks can be great grilled, so I figured it was time to give chuck a chance.

I started my testing as we always do in the test kitchen: by gathering recipes. Most were frustratingly vague in that they called for "chuck steaks," which could mean any slab of meat from the chuck. (I knew from experience that the many different muscles of the chuck all cook—and eat—quite differently.) A few recipes offered more direction, specifying blade, flat-iron, chuck-eye, and seven-bone steaks, all of which are cut from the chuck. Most of the recipes require seasoning the meat before cooking, via a marinade or a heavily spiced rub. All cooked for a short time over high heat—standard steak protocol.

I cooked off the steaks and called my tasters. I'll give it to you straight: The steaks were not very good. But these failures were instructive and helped me start to shape my recipe. Steaks that were marinated never achieved a good, hard, flavor-building sear (even when I patted them dry before grilling). We preferred the spice-rubbed steaks for their flavorful, well-browned crusts. More importantly, I figured out which cut of beef to use. The seven-bone and blade steaks were out because they were as tough as a dog's chew toy. Flat-iron steaks are hard to come by (I had to get them from a restaurant supplier), so those, too, were off the list. But my tasters did think that the chuck-eye steaks had some promise: While not melt-in-your-mouth tender, they were by far the least chewy of the bunch, and they had great beefy flavor.

A simple-yet-bold spice rub adds complex flavor to these beefy steaks.

Now that I'd decided on chuck-eye steaks, I needed to learn about them in more detail. With a little research, I discovered that the chuck eye comes from the intersection of the fifth and sixth ribs of the cow; this intersection is also the border between the chuck and the rib primal cuts. In other words, chuck-eye steaks come from the part of the cow closest to where rib eyes are cut from, which helps explain why they are more tender than other chuck cuts. I ordered more steaks to continue testing, but the steaks that came in from the market were inconsistent in size and shape, so they cooked at different rates. But there was a bigger problem: Even though everything I was getting was labeled "chuck-eye steaks," the steaks were so wildly different that I had to believe they were incorrectly marked.

To make sure that I was really getting chuck-eye steaks and that they would be consistent, I'd have to buy chuck-eye roasts and cut my own steaks. I ordered a few large chuck-eye roasts, which are basically two lobes of meat connected by a seam of fat that runs their length. I removed the seam, making two smaller roasts, and then cut each smaller roast into two hefty steaks, creating four steaks that were a good 1 to 1½ inches thick (depending on the roast). Just as

I had hoped, fabricating my own consistently sized steaks meant that they now cooked at the same rate.

As for the grilling, my first order of business was a good sear for flavor. First I tried the most straightforward approach—I grilled the steaks over a hot fire until they were charred on both sides, which took about 10 minutes total. But the steaks weren't yet cooked through. I had better luck creating hotter and cooler cooking areas: I could sear the steaks over the hotter part of the grill and then move them to the cooler area to cook through without burning the exterior. Brushing the steaks with a little vegetable oil right before cooking helped create even better char. Slicing the cooked meat thin against the grain, after a rest, of course (to let the juices redistribute), minimized the chewiness. Now all I had to do was perfect the spice rub.

I pieced together a working rub from the ones that we had liked best in the initial recipes, and then I tested and tweaked various iterations over the course of several days. Chipotle chile powder gave the rub a suitably assertive, complex base, and plenty of salt was an obvious addition. Granulated garlic and coriander added complementary flavors, and an unexpected ingredient—cocoa powder—lent great depth, with brown sugar helping smooth out the bitter edges. The rub tasted good on the steaks, but the seasoning was superficial. There was an easy fix for this: time. I found that if I rubbed the steaks and refrigerated them for at least 6 (or up to 24) hours, the salt and spice flavor was much more pervasive.

I was curious but a little skeptical when I began testing. But as I chowed down on this relatively tender, definitely affordable steak, I realized I was ready to proselytize: Give chuck a chance!

Ever wonder which type charcoal burns hotter, briquettes or hardwood? Visit CooksCountry.com/charcoal for the answer.

GRILLED CHUCK STEAKS Serves 4

Choose a roast without too much fat at the natural seam.

- 1 tablespoon kosher salt
- 1 tablespoon chipotle chile powder
- 1 teaspoon unsweetened cocoa powder
- 1 teaspoon packed brown sugar
- ½ teaspoon ground coriander
- ½ teaspoon granulated garlic
- 1 (2½- to 3-pound) boneless beef chuck-eye roast
- 2 tablespoons vegetable oil

1. Combine salt, chile powder, cocoa, sugar, coriander, and granulated garlic in bowl. Separate roast into 2 pieces along natural seam. Turn each piece on its side and cut in half lengthwise against grain. Remove silverskin and trim fat to ¼-inch thickness. Pat steaks dry with paper towels and rub with spice mixture. Transfer steaks to zipper-lock bag and refrigerate for at least 6 hours or up to 24 hours.

2A. FOR A CHARCOAL GRILL: Open bottom vent halfway. Light large chimney starter filled with charcoal briquettes (6 quarts). When top coals are partially covered with ash, pour evenly over half of grill. Set cooking grate in place, cover, and open lid vent halfway. Heat grill until hot, about 5 minutes.

2B. FOR A GAS GRILL: Turn all burners to high, cover, and heat grill until hot, about 15 minutes. Turn primary burner to medium-high and secondary burner(s) to medium-low.

3. Clean and oil cooking grate. Brush steaks all over with oil. Place steaks over hotter side of grill and cook (covered if using gas) until well charred on both sides, about 5 minutes per side. Move steaks to cooler side of grill and continue to cook (covered if using gas) until steaks register 125 degrees (for medium-rare), 5 to 8 minutes.

4. Transfer steaks to carving board, tent loosely with foil, and let rest for 10 minutes. Slice steaks thin. Serve.

TEST KITCHEN TECHNIQUE

Creating Chuck Steaks at Home

We weren't satisfied with what we found labeled "chuck steaks" in stores, so we made our own. Start with a 2½- to 3-pound boneless beef chuck-eye roast and follow these simple steps to yield four steaks.

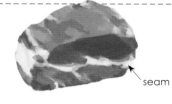

seam

CHUCK-EYE ROAST

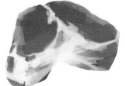

DIVIDE ROAST IN TWO
Use your hands to separate the roast at the natural seam.

CUT EACH HALF IN TWO
Turn each piece on its side and cut it in half lengthwise, against the grain.

TRIM EACH STEAK
Remove and discard the chewy silverskin and any excess fat.

Chopped Caprese Salad

We had to keep a few things from getting lost in translation when we turned this Italian classic into a hearty chopped salad. BY NICK IVERSON

We punch up the traditional mozzarella-tomato-basil trio with kalamata olives.

TO ME, NO DINNER is complete without a giant green salad on the table. Since I'm always looking for new salad combinations, it occurred to me to take inspiration from the tomato, fresh mozzarella, basil, and olive oil combination of Caprese salad. I wanted the bulk and bounty of a green salad with the flavors and simplicity of spirit of classic Caprese.

I decided to make this a chopped salad so the ingredients would be well integrated and easy to eat. To figure out a starting point, I tossed two chopped romaine hearts with diced globe tomatoes, cubes of fresh mozzarella, and basil and dressed the mix with a simple vinaigrette of red wine vinegar and extra-virgin olive oil. This salad had some problems. First, the juicy tomatoes broke down and their liquid washed out the dressing. Second, the mozzarella didn't taste well seasoned. And third, the basil got lost in the shuffle.

I immediately ditched the juicy, round tomatoes. I tested Roma, cherry, and grape tomatoes, eventually selecting grape tomatoes for their compact size and year-round consistency. To keep them from diluting the vinaigrette, I halved the tomatoes, tossed them with salt to draw out some of their moisture, and left them to drain in a colander for 15 minutes before adding them to the salad.

To give the mozzarella more pop, I bathed it in extra-virgin olive oil that I flavored generously with chopped basil, garlic, and shallot. After I'd removed the mozzarella, I realized that all I had to do was add vinegar to the marinade and I'd have a flavorful vinaigrette. Perfect. To reinforce the fragrant basil, I tossed torn leaves in with the romaine, and to add extra dimension to the salad, I mixed in chopped kalamata olives.

I prepared the salad for (fingers crossed) one final test. The comments from tasters were music to my ears: "Well-balanced." "Perfectly dressed." "Straightforward." Looks like my salad menu just expanded.

CHOPPED CAPRESE SALAD

Serves 4 to 6

You can use cherry tomatoes in place of the grape tomatoes.

- 8 ounces fresh mozzarella, cut into ½-inch pieces (1 cup)
- 3 tablespoons extra-virgin olive oil
- 2 tablespoons minced shallot
- 1 garlic clove, minced
  Salt and pepper
- ½ cup fresh basil leaves
- 1½ pounds grape tomatoes, cut in half lengthwise
- 2 romaine hearts (12 ounces), quartered lengthwise and cut into ½-inch pieces
- ¼ cup pitted kalamata olives, chopped
- 3 tablespoons red wine vinegar

1. Combine mozzarella, oil, shallot, garlic, ¼ teaspoon salt, and ¼ teaspoon pepper in bowl. Coarsely chop half of basil leaves and add to mozzarella mixture; set aside while preparing tomatoes. Combine tomatoes and 1 teaspoon salt in separate bowl; transfer to colander set in sink; and let drain for 15 minutes, stirring occasionally. (Tomatoes can be prepared up to 1 hour in advance.)

2. Tear remaining basil leaves into ½-inch pieces. Gently toss tomatoes, romaine, olives, vinegar, mozzarella mixture, and basil together in large bowl. Season with salt and pepper to taste, and serve.

Puerto Rican Pork Roast

Introducing *pernil*, a Latin dish of tender, super-flavorful slow-roasted pork with the ultimate crispy skin. BY SARAH GABRIEL

PERNIL IS A much-loved Puerto Rican preparation of long-cooked, heavily seasoned pork roast that is chopped or shredded; it's often served at the holidays or at parties both on the island and in Puerto Rican communities in the States. As with American barbecue, aficionados love to debate the proper cut (fresh ham or picnic shoulder?), the proper seasonings (dry spices, a wet marinade, or a paste of aromatics and herbs called a *sofrito*?), and the best cooking method. I was easily sold on pernil—even before I heard about the crispy skin. For devotees, munching away on bits of crunchy, burnished skin glossed with salty, buttery fat is the kind of ecstatic experience that seems too good to be legal. I jumped at the chance to develop my own recipe for this classic dish.

Picnic shoulder is much more widely available than fresh ham, so I'd use a bone-in, skin-on picnic shoulder. I collected and prepared six pernil recipes that represented different takes on the other variables. The good news? Every recipe that got the meat to 200 degrees yielded tender, flavorful meat. The bad? No matter the cooking time, oven temperature, or covering-uncovering regimen, crackling, crispy brown skin eluded me; the skin was either pale and rubbery or else dark and hard as ebony.

My plan was to fine-tune the seasonings and then tackle the issue of the skin. Bottled spice blends like Goya Sazón, which is common in modern pernil recipes, were too heavy on dehydrated onion and dusty spices. My tasters much preferred pork seasoned with a sofrito. After a bit of tinkering, I landed on a knockout sofrito by grinding onion, garlic, cilantro, cumin, dried oregano, kosher salt, and pepper in the food processor. By making the sofrito salty and rubbing it into the meat 12 to 24 hours before roasting, the salt had a chance to penetrate the pork and help keep it moist (as with a brine) when cooked. I turned to the skin.

I quickly learned that pork skin is finicky: It gets hard and dark if you cook it in a dry environment and pale and rubbery when cooked in a covered, moist environment. I hoped to split the difference with a hybrid method, cooking it covered for half of the time and uncovered for the remainder. I rubbed a 7-pound shoulder with the sofrito; let

We like our Pork Pernil coarsely chopped and served with rice.

it sit overnight; and roasted it, skin side up, at 375 degrees, covered tightly with foil, for 3 hours. Then I uncovered it and continued to cook it until the meat reached 200 degrees, which took about 3 hours more. The juices started to burn off and smoke, so I added some water to the pan midway through cooking. This didn't work: In the end, the skin was too dark and too leathery to chew. The added water had created steam that

prevented the skin from crisping. But without the water, the pernil smoked out the kitchen.

I continued to test different roasting variables over the course of several weeks; some tests were abject failures, while others offered glimpses of techniques that I thought might help me. As I tested and tested, the ideal method slowly took shape, and here is where I landed: First, for perfectly cooked pork,

I roasted it, covered, skin side down for 90 minutes at 450 degrees. I made sure there was plenty of water in the pan to create lots of steam that would jump-start the transformation of the roast's tough collagen into tender gelatin. Next I removed the foil and turned down the oven to 375 degrees for a good 2½ hours of roasting (if the roast was covered during this period, the meat would taste steamed). The prolonged braising of the skin—a technique that I borrowed from recipes for *chicharrón* (deep-fried pork skin)—helped break down the skin's rubbery connective tissue so that it would hopefully crisp up later (with dry heat) without hardening.

At this point I elevated the roast, skin side up, on a V-rack and roasted it for another hour so that the now-softened skin could dry out while the meat cooked to 195 degrees, just shy of done. Finally, I moved the pork—still on the V-rack—to a clean, foil-lined baking sheet, turned up the oven to 500, and high-roasted for 15 to 30 minutes, until the skin was well-browned and perfectly crispy—finally. Letting the roast rest for 30 minutes before serving allowed the juices to redistribute and resulted in moist meat throughout. Normally we'd tent the meat with foil to keep it warm, but I found that the foil trapped steam that turned the crispy skin soggy.

I caught more than one taster crunching away at a big, crispy slab of mahogany pork skin, transfixed by the combination of potent seasoning, rich fat, and addictive crunch. But I had one last order of business: a quick sauce to dress the meat after I chopped it. Combining the pan drippings with lime juice, lime zest, and chopped cilantro couldn't be simpler, and the bright citrusy punch was an ideal foil for the rich and salty meat. After weeks of work—and more than 40 roasts—I finally had the enormously flavorful, crisp-skinned pernil I had set out to find.

PORK PERNIL Serves 8 to 10

Depending on their size, you may need two bunches of cilantro. Crimp the foil tightly over the edges of the roasting pan in step 2 to minimize evaporation. Make sure to spray the V-rack in step 3.

- 1½ cups chopped fresh cilantro leaves and stems
- 1 onion, chopped coarse
- ¼ cup kosher salt
- ¼ cup olive oil
- 10 garlic cloves, peeled
- 2 tablespoons pepper
- 1 tablespoon dried oregano
- 1 tablespoon ground cumin
- 1 (7-pound) bone-in pork picnic shoulder
- 1 tablespoon grated lime zest plus ⅓ cup juice (3 limes)

1. Pulse 1 cup cilantro, onion, salt, oil, garlic, pepper, oregano, and cumin in food processor until finely ground, about 15 pulses, scraping down sides of bowl as needed. Pat pork dry with paper towels and rub sofrito all over. Wrap pork in plastic wrap and refrigerate for at least 2 hours or up to 24 hours.

2. Adjust oven rack to lower-middle position and heat oven to 450 degrees. Pour 8 cups water in large roasting

How to Cook *Pernil*
We started cooking the marinated pork roast skin side down in a roasting pan, covered and with some water, to render the fat and soften the skin. Then we flipped the roast skin side up and elevated it on a V-rack to finish cooking and crisp the flavorful skin.

pan. Unwrap pork and place skin side down in pan. Cover pan tightly with aluminum foil and roast for 90 minutes. Remove foil, reduce oven temperature to 375 degrees, and continue to roast for 2½ hours.

3. Remove pan from oven. Spray V-rack with vegetable oil spray. Gently slide metal spatula under pork to release skin from pan. Using folded dish towels, grasp ends of pork and transfer to V-rack, skin side up. Wipe skin dry with paper towels. Place V-rack with pork in roasting pan. If pan looks dry, add 1 cup water. Return to oven and roast until pork registers 195 degrees, about 1 hour. (Add water as needed to keep bottom of pan from drying out.)

4. Line rimmed baking sheet with foil. Remove pan from oven. Transfer V-rack and pork to prepared sheet and return to oven. Immediately increase oven temperature to 500 degrees. Cook until pork skin is well browned and crispy (when tapped lightly with tongs, skin will sound hollow), 15 to 30 minutes, rotating sheet halfway through cooking. Transfer pork to carving board and let rest for 30 minutes.

5. Meanwhile, pour juices from pan into fat separator. Let liquid settle for 5 minutes, then pour off 1 cup defatted juices into large bowl. (If juices measure less than 1 cup, make up difference with water.) Whisk remaining ½ cup cilantro and lime zest and juice into bowl.

6. Remove crispy skin from pork in 1 large piece. Coarsely chop skin into bite-size pieces and set aside. Trim and discard excess fat from pork. Remove pork from bone and chop coarse. Transfer pork to bowl with cilantro-lime sauce and toss to combine. Serve pork, with crispy skin on side.

WHAT TO DO WITH LEFTOVERS
Philadelphia Pork Sandwiches

With a little know-how, *pernil* leftovers become the perfect base for Philly's other famous sandwich.

BY SARAH GABRIEL

IF YOU THINK a cheesesteak is the only sandwich worth standing in line for in Philadelphia, think again: The Italian roast pork sandwich might be even more popular with locals. While no two purveyors make the sandwich exactly the same way, the classic version is a hoagie roll piled with moist, tender pork and topped with garlicky sautéed broccoli rabe and melted provolone. As I stared at a platter of our leftover Pork Pernil in a test kitchen refrigerator, my mind wandered to Philly: Could our Pork Pernil leftovers have a new life in Italian American roast pork sandwiches?

Picking up a test kitchen method for the broccoli rabe, I trimmed the vegetable, chopped it into 2-inch pieces, and cooked it (covered) in a 12-inch skillet with a little water, olive oil, and salt until it was just tender, about 4 minutes. Then I removed the lid to let the water evaporate; after about 3 minutes, the liquid was gone and the rabe began to sizzle in the oil. I added garlic and red pepper flakes and cooked the rabe for another minute. It was tender and very flavorful.

When the rabe was done, I pulled it from the skillet and added the shredded pork with ½ cup of chicken broth, covered it, and cooked it over medium heat until the meat was hot throughout. Then I warmed six sub rolls in the oven; loaded them up with the juicy pork, broccoli rabe, and ¼ cup each of shredded aged provolone; and returned the sandwiches to the oven just to melt the cheese.

Judging from the speed with which the tray was emptied, I think it's safe to say that my tasters forgot all about that other Philly sandwich.

PHILADELPHIA ROAST PORK SANDWICHES
Makes 6 sandwiches
If you can't find aged provolone, use sliced deli provolone.

- 6 (6-inch) Italian sub rolls, split lengthwise
- 12 ounces broccoli rabe, trimmed and cut into 2-inch pieces
- 1 tablespoon olive oil

Broccoli rabe adds pleasant bitterness to this satisfying sandwich.

- ¼ teaspoon salt
- 3 garlic cloves, minced
- ¼ teaspoon red pepper flakes
- 3 cups Pork Pernil
- ½ cup chicken broth
- 6 ounces aged provolone cheese, shredded (1½ cups)

1. Adjust oven rack to middle position and heat oven to 350 degrees. Arrange rolls on rimmed baking sheet. Bring ½ cup water to boil over medium-high heat in 12-inch nonstick skillet. Add broccoli rabe, oil, and salt. Cover and cook until just tender, 3 to 5 minutes. Uncover and cook until water evaporates and broccoli rabe begins to sizzle, about 3 minutes. Add garlic and pepper flakes and cook until fragrant, about 1 minute. Transfer to plate and set aside.

2. Add pork and broth to now-empty skillet. Cover and cook over medium heat, stirring occasionally, until hot, about 5 minutes.

3. Meanwhile, warm rolls in oven for 5 minutes. Divide pork, broccoli rabe, and provolone among rolls. Bake sandwiches until cheese is melted, 6 to 9 minutes. Serve.

Grilled Chicken Diavolo

To transform this chicken from dull to diabolical, you need your marinade to do double duty. BY SARAH GABRIEL

CHICKEN DIAVOLO IS one of those dishes that have no universally accepted definition. The one constant (other than the chicken, of course) is heat provided by plenty of black and/or dried red pepper. We tested a handful of recipes that used a range of different flavors and cooking techniques and came away most impressed by those that were grilled. That's what mine would be: spicy, smoky, devilishly good chicken diavolo.

I assembled recipes calling for chicken in various forms (whole or parts), with spices from various sources (black pepper, red pepper flakes, or cayenne) added to the chicken either dry or mixed into a marinade. As we tasted the results, it became clear that I had a ways to go. But the optimist in me was pleased that I at least had a place to start: Pieces were easiest to handle and picked up the most grill flavor, so I'd forgo whole birds. Lemon juice seemed like a perfect contrast to the chicken's heat, but a lemony marinade didn't provide much flavor. An oil-based marinade yielded potent, well-distributed spiciness, but my tasters' sweaty brows were a signal that I needed to turn down the heat. Also, the oily marinade caused hellacious flare-ups over high heat, leaving the chicken skin blackened in some places and pale and flabby in others.

The test kitchen has a few marinade building blocks: Salt helps with seasoning (obviously) and juiciness. Oil dissolves flavor compounds in herbs, spices, garlic, and citrus peels and distributes them evenly over the surface of the meat. And sugar ensures speedier browning. Hoping for a potent yet balanced marinade, I added red pepper flakes, black pepper, rosemary, and a modest amount of paprika to a foundation of salt, oil, and sugar. Looking at past test kitchen recipes, I remembered that acids make the surface of meat mushy or tough, so I tried replacing the lemon juice in my recipe with lemon zest, which is packed with flavor compounds that dissolve well in oil. I poured this mixture into a zipper-lock bag with the chicken and stashed it in the fridge for an hour.

While the chicken was marinating, I headed out to set up the grill. I wanted the chicken well seared but not burnt, so I built a two-level fire with two-thirds of the coals on one side of the grill and

Some of the infused oil that we use for the marinade serves as the base for a supercharged vinaigrette that we spoon over the grilled chicken.

one-third on the other side; now I had a hot spot on one-half and gentler heat over the rest of the grill. In the spirit of an Italian recipe that called for cooking over a wood fire, I tossed a foil packet of soaked wood chips onto the charcoal to add some smoky flavor.

When I was ready to grill, I blotted the excess marinade to prevent it from dripping off and flaring up and then seared the chicken pieces on the

hotter side of the grill. But despite my precautions, fat rendering from the skin fueled out-of-control flames. Scorched outside and raw inside, this batch of chicken went straight into the trash. I tried again, this time grilling the chicken on the cooler side first to render some of the fat and cook the meat through before moving it to the hotter side to sear. Now it was properly cooked and perfectly browned, so I

called the tasters. We deemed the grilling method a success, but the marinade? Not so much. While potent on its own, the marinade had barely penetrated the meat, so the chicken tasted ho-hum.

I whisked up a new batch of marinade, doubling the red pepper flakes. Unfortunately, turning up the heat knocked the flavor off-balance. I went back to the kitchen and doubled all the spices, but that was a nonstarter. There was so much debris in the oil that the chicken emerged covered in bits of garlic and a paste of spices that charred badly on the grill. Since by itself the marinade had plenty of oomph, it occurred to me to hold back a few tablespoons to drizzle on the chicken after it was cooked. I tried it. This double dose of marinade did intensify the flavor, but the raw garlic tasted harsh, plus the chicken was dull and salty.

The brand of black pepper you use does make a difference. Read our taste test of black pepper at **CooksCountry. com/blackpeppercorns.**

I gave this concept another try. This time I divided the marinade into two portions at the start, before I added the salt. The portion that went in the bag with the raw chicken got a hefty dose of salt. I heated the rest of the marinade for several minutes in a saucepan on the stovetop until the garlic was golden and mellow. I gave this half a modest sprinkling of salt and a shot of fresh lemon juice; after grilling the chicken, I drizzled on this doctored dose of marinade. Happily, it added just enough extra kick, bright lemon, and toasty garlic to complement the fiery flavor. My Chicken Diavolo was redeemed.

GRILLED CHICKEN DIAVOLO

Serves 4

If you are buying a whole chicken and cutting it into pieces yourself, use the backbone and wings to make stock. To use wood chunks on a charcoal grill, substitute one medium wood chunk, soaked in water for 1 hour, for the wood chip packet.

- 3 **pounds bone-in chicken pieces (split breasts cut in half, drumsticks, and/or thighs), trimmed**
- ½ **cup extra-virgin olive oil**
- 4 **garlic cloves, minced**
- 1 **tablespoon chopped fresh rosemary**
- 2 **teaspoons grated lemon zest plus 4 teaspoons juice**
- 2 **teaspoons red pepper flakes**
- 1 **teaspoon sugar**
  Salt and pepper
- ½ **teaspoon paprika**
- 1 **cup wood chips**

1. Pat chicken dry with paper towels. Whisk oil, garlic, rosemary, lemon zest, pepper flakes, sugar, 1 teaspoon pepper, and paprika together in bowl until combined. Reserve ¼ cup oil mixture for sauce. (Oil mixture can be covered and refrigerated for up to 24 hours.) Whisk 2¼ teaspoons salt into oil mixture remaining in bowl and transfer to 1-gallon zipper-lock bag. Add chicken, turn to coat, and refrigerate for at least 1 hour or up to 24 hours. Just before grilling, soak wood chips in water for 15 minutes, then drain. Using large piece of heavy-duty aluminum foil, wrap soaked chips in foil

packet and cut several vent holes in top.

2A. FOR A CHARCOAL GRILL: Open bottom vent halfway. Light large chimney starter filled with charcoal briquettes (6 quarts). When top coals are partially covered with ash, pour two-thirds evenly over half of grill, then pour remaining coals over other half of grill. Place wood chip packet on larger pile of coals. Set cooking grate in place, cover, and open lid vent halfway. Heat grill until hot and wood chips are smoking, about 5 minutes.

2B. FOR A GAS GRILL: Place wood chip packet over primary burner. Turn all burners to high, cover, and heat grill until hot and wood chips are smoking, about 15 minutes. Turn primary burner to medium and turn other burner(s) to low. (Adjust primary burner as needed to maintain grill temperature of 400 to 425 degrees.)

3. Remove chicken from marinade and pat dry with paper towels. Discard used marinade. Clean and oil cooking grate. Place chicken on cooler side of grill, skin side up. Cover and cook until underside of chicken is lightly browned, 8 to 12 minutes. Flip chicken, cover, and cook until white meat registers 155 degrees and dark meat registers 170 degrees, 7 to 10 minutes.

4. Transfer chicken to hotter side of grill, skin side down, and cook (covered if using gas) until skin is well browned, about 3 minutes. Flip and continue to cook (covered if using gas) until white meat registers 160 degrees and dark meat registers 175 degrees, 1 to 3 minutes. Transfer chicken to platter, tent loosely with foil, and let rest for 5 to 10 minutes.

5. Meanwhile, heat reserved oil mixture in small saucepan over low heat until fragrant and garlic begins to brown, 3 to 5 minutes. Off heat, whisk in lemon juice and ¼ teaspoon salt. Spoon sauce over chicken. Serve.

TEST KITCHEN TECHNIQUE
The Right Fire
A two-level fire lets us gently cook the chicken on the cooler side and then sear it on the hotter side for flavorful char. To get good smoky flavor, we place an aluminum foil–wrapped packet of soaked wood chips on the larger pile of charcoal.

Grilled Cabbage

Putting cabbage over fire can transform it into a soft, sweet, deliciously smoky dish.

BY CAROLYNN PURPURA MACKAY

EXCEPT FOR COLESLAW, few people give cabbage much thought. That's a pity because if you really want to see cabbage come into its own, you ought to try grilling it. The cabbage sweetens and softens, picking up gentle smoke and char.

I did, slicing some heads and cutting others into wedges. But without toothpicks or skewers to hold the leaves together, the slices fell apart on the grill when I flipped them. I opted for wedges; since the core was left intact, the leaves held together naturally.

Some recipes call for grilling the cabbage with nothing but salt and pepper. Better to brush the cabbage with oil first, I found. It produced more browning, which meant that the cabbage tasted sweeter. High heat helped develop good color, too, but the timing was tricky. The cabbage was nicely brown, yes, but the interior was raw. In the test kitchen we prevent soggy coleslaw by salting chopped cabbage. The salt draws out moisture, which we drain off before we dress the coleslaw. I salted the cabbage wedges, hoping the moisture drawn out between the leaves would turn to steam on the grill, and that the steam would cook the wedges through. And it did.

Even better, the flavor of the cabbage improved. And I had an idea to press home my advantage: I whisked together a simple lemon-herb vinaigrette, which I brushed on the cabbage in place of the oil, before grilling and—in a moment of inspiration—about 20 minutes later, after grilling, too. We tasted the wedges again. Could this really be cabbage—the vegetable many people love to loathe? It was transformed.

GRILLED CABBAGE Serves 4
Leave the core intact so the cabbage wedges don't fall apart on the grill.

- **Salt and pepper**
- 1 **head green cabbage (2 pounds), cut into 8 wedges through core**
- 1 **tablespoon minced fresh thyme**
- 2 **teaspoons minced shallot**
- 2 **teaspoons honey**
- 1 **teaspoon Dijon mustard**
- ½ **teaspoon grated lemon zest plus 2 tablespoons juice**
- 6 **tablespoons extra-virgin olive oil**

We season the wedges with vinaigrette both before and after grilling.

1. Sprinkle 1 teaspoon salt all over cabbage wedges and let sit for 45 minutes. Combine thyme, shallot, honey, mustard, lemon zest and juice, and ¼ teaspoon pepper in bowl. Slowly whisk in oil until incorporated. Reserve ¼ cup vinaigrette for serving.

2A. FOR A CHARCOAL GRILL: Open bottom vent completely. Light large chimney starter filled with charcoal briquettes (6 quarts). When top coals are partially covered with ash, pour evenly over grill. Set cooking grate in place, cover, and open lid vent completely. Heat grill until hot, about 5 minutes.

2B. FOR A GAS GRILL: Turn all burners to high, cover, and heat grill until hot, about 15 minutes. Turn all burners to medium.

3. Clean and oil cooking grate. Brush 1 cut side of cabbage wedges with half of vinaigrette. Place cabbage on grill, vinaigrette side down, and grill, covered for gas grill, until well browned, 7 to 10 minutes. Brush tops of wedges with remaining vinaigrette; flip and grill, covered for gas, until second side is well browned and fork-tender, 7 to 10 minutes. Transfer cabbage to platter and drizzle with reserved vinaigrette. Season with salt and pepper to taste. Serve.

California-Style Fish Tacos

You can't just wrap a fish in a tortilla and call it a California-style taco. You need light, crisp fried fish, the perfect toppings, and high-contrast flavors and textures. BY REBECCAH MARSTERS

NAMED AFTER THE region in Mexico where they originated, Baja fish tacos have been making their way across the United States, gaining popularity as they go, since the first Rubio's opened in San Diego in 1983. It's easy to see the appeal of these tacos: The crispy fried whitefish, crunchy cabbage, and creamy white sauce, all piled onto a corn tortilla (or two), come together to deliver an irresistible combination of flavors and textures.

Determined to make a tasty version that was easy enough for a weeknight dinner, I weeded through a bevy of recipes for Baja tacos—rejecting those that required grilling or sautéing or that called for "creative" ingredients like blackened salmon or pineapple salsa—until I'd found several traditional versions to test.

After battering and frying what seemed like several schools' worth of fish, I called in my tasters to eat through a buffet of tacos. One obvious takeaway was that less was more when it came to the batter coating. We liked the yeasty, slightly bitter flavor that beer imparted to the batter, but the texture was another story. Most coatings—including the beer batters—were thick and heavy, obscuring the delicate fish. Toppings ran the gamut from avocado *crema* to fried jalapeños, and while they were all good, there were just too many of them, which meant that (once again) the fish got lost. I'd start simple—just the essential crunchy cabbage and creamy white sauce.

Focusing on the fish, I started with cod—the whitefish that's most available here in the Northeast. I stirred together a simple batter of flour, beer, and salt, and after cutting the fish into 4 by 1-inch strips (the perfect size to fit inside a corn tortilla) and seasoning them, I dipped and fried the strips. As with my initial attempts, the coating was thick and cumbersome. Taking a cue from Japanese tempura batter—a super-thin batter that creates a crispy, light coating—I increased the ratio of beer to flour, thinning out the batter until it was just thick enough to coat the fish. As it turned out, equal parts flour and liquid was just right. I had good flavor and a thin coating . . . but still not enough crunch. To lighten the batter so it would fry up crispier, I used the test kitchen technique of replacing about a quarter of the flour

Our simple garnishes include pickled onions, crispy cabbage, fresh cilantro, and sour cream–lime and green sauces.

with cornstarch. I was definitely making progress, and I had another trick up my sleeve: baking powder. Many batters use baking powder because when the powder is activated, it produces carbon dioxide, which makes for a light coating. It worked: With a combination of cornstarch and baking powder, my coating was ethereally thin, light, and crispy. Some recipes call for frying in deep vats of oil, but I found that I needed

to fill my Dutch oven only 3/4 inch deep. A few extra tests showed that this recipe works equally well with haddock and halibut.

With the batter and frying perfected, I moved on to the toppings. The cabbage was easy enough—I simply sliced it thin. The white sauce served with these tacos is usually a mixture of mayonnaise and yogurt or sour cream thinned to drizzling consistency. We found that

equal parts mayonnaise and sour cream supplied the right balance of tang and richness, that lime juice introduced brightness, and that a splash of milk thinned the sauce without damaging its creamy appeal.

Some of the initial test recipes went overboard on the toppings. But I had overcorrected. My fried fish and creamy sauce definitely needed something spicy and tart for contrast. A test recipe had called for topping the tacos with pickled onions; I took that idea and ran with it. To make a quick pickle, I heated vinegar, lime juice, sugar, and salt and poured the mixture over a sliced red onion. I added a couple of sliced jalapeños for heat, and after just 30 minutes for the flavors to meld, I had a third topping. Unfortunately, next to these flavorful homemade pickles, the naked shredded cabbage tasted lackluster. But I had an idea. Before assembling the tacos, I took ¼ cup of the pickling liquid from the onions and tossed it with the cabbage. This seasoned the cabbage and softened it slightly without taking away its crunch.

I laid out the toppings and fried a last batch of fish. Before calling tasters over, I warmed a stack of corn tortillas, set out a jar of green salsa, and completed the spread with a bowl of cilantro leaves. We filled, topped, and tasted. The tacos were a happy tangle of crunchy, creamy, rich, bright, and fresh.

CALIFORNIA FISH TACOS
Serves 6

Although this recipe looks involved, all the components are easy to execute and most can be made in advance. Light-bodied American lagers, such as Budweiser, work best here. Cut the fish on a slight bias if your fillets aren't quite 4 inches wide. You should end up with about 24 pieces of fish. Serve with green salsa, if desired.

PICKLED ONIONS
- 1   small red onion, halved and sliced thin
- 2   jalapeño chiles, stemmed and sliced into thin rings
- 1   cup white wine vinegar
- 2   tablespoons lime juice
- 1   tablespoon sugar
- 1   teaspoon salt

CABBAGE
- 3   cups shredded green cabbage
- ¼   cup pickling liquid from pickled onions
- ½   teaspoon salt
- ½   teaspoon pepper

WHITE SAUCE
- ½   cup mayonnaise
- ½   cup sour cream
- 2   tablespoons lime juice
- 2   tablespoons milk

FISH
- 2   pounds skinless whitefish fillets, such as cod, haddock, or halibut, cut crosswise into 4 by 1-inch strips
    Salt and pepper
- ¾   cup all-purpose flour
- ¼   cup cornstarch
- 1   teaspoon baking powder
- 1   cup beer
- 1   quart peanut or vegetable oil
- 24 (6-inch) corn tortillas, warmed
- 1   cup fresh cilantro leaves

Easier than It Looks
This recipe has several parts, but they come together faster than you might think.

Quick Pickled Onions
Just slice the onion and jalapeños, pour the vinegar mixture over, and let sit for at least 30 minutes. This can be done up to two days ahead.

No-Cook Cabbage
Simply shred the cabbage (by hand or in a food processor) and toss with the onion pickling liquid.

Simple White Sauce
Measure ingredients and whisk together. This can be done up to two days ahead.

1. FOR THE PICKLED ONIONS: Combine onion and jalapeños in medium bowl. Bring vinegar, lime juice, sugar, and salt to boil in small saucepan. Pour vinegar mixture over onion mixture and let sit for at least 30 minutes. (Pickled onions can be made and refrigerated up to 2 days in advance.)

2. FOR THE CABBAGE: Toss all ingredients together in bowl.

3. FOR THE WHITE SAUCE: Whisk all ingredients together in bowl. (Sauce can be made and refrigerated up to 2 days in advance.)

4. FOR THE FISH: Adjust oven rack to middle position and heat oven to 200 degrees. Set wire rack inside rimmed baking sheet. Pat fish dry with paper towels and season with salt and pepper. Whisk flour, cornstarch, baking powder, and 1 teaspoon salt together in large bowl. Add beer and whisk until smooth. Transfer fish to batter and toss until evenly coated.

5. Add oil to large Dutch oven until it measures about ¾ inch deep and heat over medium-high heat to 350 degrees. Working with 5 to 6 pieces at a time, remove fish from batter, allowing excess to drip back into bowl, and add to hot oil, briefly dragging fish along surface of oil to prevent sticking. Adjust burner, if necessary, to maintain oil temperature between 325 and 350 degrees. Fry fish, stirring gently to prevent pieces from sticking together, until golden brown and crispy, about 2 minutes per side. Transfer fish to prepared wire rack and place in oven to keep warm. Return oil to 350 degrees and repeat with remaining fish.

6. Divide fish evenly among tortillas. Top with pickled onions, cabbage, white sauce, and cilantro. Serve.

TASTING JARRED GREEN SALSA

Mexican-style *salsa verde*—made from tomatillos, green chiles, onion, and cilantro—adds tangy zest to tacos, enchiladas, eggs, and much more. You can also use it as a dip. To figure out which one to buy, we rounded up five nationally available, shelf-stable products and tasted them plain and with tortilla chips. We learned that flavor mattered more to us than either heat level or texture; bright, fresh-tasting salsas came out on top, but we also liked the complexity of roasted tomatillos. The products all contained very similar ingredients, so why did they taste different? The nutrition labels showed us that we liked salsas with higher levels of vitamins A and C (measured as percentage of daily value based on a 2,000-calorie diet). The vitamins reveal which salsas have more and fresher fruits and vegetables processed at a lower temperature; these vitamins degrade in older produce and at higher temperatures. Moreover, our favorite salsa had neither preservatives nor stabilizers. –TAIZETH SIERRA

RECOMMENDED

FRONTERA Tomatillo Salsa
Price: $4.49 for 16 oz (28 cents per oz)
Vitamin A: 2% (per 2-tablespoon serving) **Vitamin C:** 6%
Ingredients: Tomatillos, tomatoes, filtered water, onions, serrano chiles, cilantro, garlic, salt, evaporated cane juice, spices

TASTERS' NOTES
This roasted tomatillo salsa was a "powerhouse of flavor"; "sweet and nuanced"; and "roasted, smoky, and a little sour," with "a good amount of heat." Not everyone recognized the black flecks as bits of charred tomatillo skin, but many tasters praised the complex, roasted taste.

RECOMMENDED WITH RESERVATIONS

ORTEGA Salsa Verde, Medium
Price: $3.99 for 16 oz (25 cents per oz)
Vitamin A: 2% **Vitamin C:** 6%
Ingredients: Fresh tomatillos, fresh jalapeño peppers, water, fresh onions, salt, garlic, cilantro, xanthan gum, spices, natural flavor

This "chunky" product was "bright, fresh, sour, tangy, and sweet"; it had a "nice balance" of flavors. But most tasters agreed that this salsa lacked heat, despite the "medium" in its name.

NOT RECOMMENDED

PACE Garlic & Lime Verde Restaurant Style Salsa
Price: $3.29 for 16 oz (21 cents per oz)
Vitamin A: 0% **Vitamin C:** 2%
Ingredients: Yellow tomato puree (water, yellow tomato paste), tomatillos, water, fresh jalapeño peppers, fresh onions, red peppers, cilantro, dehydrated onions, lime juice concentrate, salt, sugar, garlic, distilled vinegar, natural flavoring

This product used more tomato puree than tomatillos. Many found it "sour, flat, watery, and too pickle-ish, without heat to balance." Tasters also objected to its "soupy" texture, comparing the salsa, unfavorably, to "pickle relish."

EMBASA Salsa Verde
Price: $1.79 for 7 oz (26 cents per oz)
Vitamin A: 2% **Vitamin C:** 0%
Ingredients: Tomatillo, chiles, onions, cilantro, salt, xanthan gum, sodium benzoate (as a preservative), garlic powder, and citric acid

The only salsa to come in a can, this "bland" product tasted "cooked," "like canned peas," one taster said. It also lost points for a range of "stale" off-flavors, suggesting everything from "lawn clippings" and "green tea" to "cleaning products" and "old cheese."

HERDEZ Salsa Verde
Price: $3.67 for 16 oz (23 cents per oz)
Vitamin A: 0% **Vitamin C:** 0%
Ingredients: Green tomato, chile peppers, onions, iodized salt, cilantro, and xanthan gum

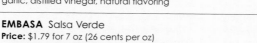

Tasting of "hay," this "salty" salsa offered "weird candy sweetness" and "weak pepper flavor." We confirmed with the manufacturer that the "green tomato" on the ingredient list is indeed tomatillo.

Porcupine Meatballs

This homey, old-fashioned recipe was due for a comeback—if only we could get the rice and the ground meat on the same schedule. BY DIANE UNGER

RECIPES FOR PORCUPINE meatballs abound in old community cookbooks and advertisements for tomato sauce, tomato soup, and electric skillets. A reader recently sent me a Xerox from a spiral-bound 1950s cookbook with four recipes: "a whole page of porcupines," as she put it. The meatballs, a homey early 20th-century classic, are made from ground beef mixed with raw rice. They simmer on the stove in a tomato-based sauce for up to 2 hours. During that time, the rice swells and softens (its starch helping to thicken the sauce) and pokes out from the meatballs like quills on a porcupine. Once a way to stretch meat for folks on a limited budget, today porcupine meatballs make a warming, satisfying supper.

Or should. In the recipes I tried, if the rice was plump and soft, the meatballs were tough, and if the meatballs were tender, the rice was inedibly hard. Diced raw onion added an unpleasant secondary crunch. The sauce made matters worse: Recipes variously called for watered-down condensed soups, canned sauces, or canned juices flavored with a hodgepodge of unnecessary ingredients like ketchup, cloves, celery salt, green pepper, poultry seasoning, and chili powder. Still, despite the plates of barely touched meatballs before me, I was sure the core concept was solid. I didn't want to turn this old-fashioned dish into something fussy, but I did want to bring the recipe into the 21st century.

To keep things easy, I started by doctoring canned tomato sauce. We'd liked the sweet-and-sour quality of one of the test recipes, so I'd use it as my model. After several tests, I settled on sautéing onion, garlic, paprika, and red pepper flakes; pouring in tomato sauce; flavoring with thyme and bay leaf; and using vinegar and brown sugar for a balanced tang. Normally, the sauce is thinned with water; I tried chicken broth instead. Taken together, these measures produced a delicious yet simple sauce.

I expected the meatballs to be a tougher challenge (literally and figuratively). Since I'd added browned onion to the sauce, I no longer needed raw onion in the meat mix. But how could I keep the meatballs moist and tender during an extended simmer? I'd employ a panade, a mix of milk and bread that the test kitchen relies on for moist,

The rice grains stick out of the meatballs like porcupines' quills, hence the fanciful name.

tender meatloaf. That worked better, but with relatively lean beef, these meatballs were still tough. I swapped out half of the beef for fattier meats. Ground pork and Italian sausage each had fans, but bratwurst carried the day. It not only tenderized the meatballs but goosed their flavor, too.

The nubby bits of hard rice definitely had to go. To speed up their cooking, I tested instant and ready rice; both turned to mush. As for converted rice, we didn't like its aggressive flavor. If I couldn't fix the problem through ingredients, I'd need to examine my technique. Some recipes use a different procedure, rolling the raw meatballs in the raw rice—but it was too much work. Soaking the raw rice before mixing it

into the beef-bratwurst mixture didn't produce tender rice. Fortunately, parboiling the rice (like you'd cook pasta), did. After testing a range of boiling times, I landed on 8 minutes. Given this head start, the grains softened before the meatballs overcooked—especially once I switched the meatballs from stovetop to oven so they'd cook most evenly.

I ran through the recipe once more, parcooking the rice, draining it at the 8-minute mark, and rinsing it to cool it down before adding it to the meat mixture and shaping 16 meatballs. I arranged these in a single layer in a 13 by 9-inch pan. I poured my souped-up tomato sauce over them, sealed the casserole tightly with foil, and baked it for 1 hour. Porcupine perfection.

PORCUPINE MEATBALLS
Serves 4 to 6
Use canned tomato sauce, not jarred.

Salt and pepper
¾ cup long-grain white rice
2 tablespoons olive oil
1 onion, chopped fine
4 garlic cloves, minced
1 teaspoon paprika
¼ teaspoon red pepper flakes
2 cups chicken broth
1 (15-ounce) can tomato sauce
2 tablespoons cider vinegar
1 tablespoon packed brown sugar
1 teaspoon minced fresh thyme
1 bay leaf
2 slices hearty white sandwich bread, torn into 1-inch pieces
½ cup milk
12 ounces bratwurst, casings removed
12 ounces 90 percent lean ground beef

1. Bring 4 cups water and 1 teaspoon salt to boil in medium saucepan over medium-high heat. Add rice, return to boil, and cook for 8 minutes, stirring occasionally. Drain rice through fine-mesh strainer, rinse with cold water, and drain again; set aside.

2. Heat oil in now-empty saucepan over medium heat until shimmering. Add onion and cook until lightly browned, about 5 minutes. Stir in garlic, paprika, and pepper flakes and cook until fragrant, about 30 seconds. Stir in broth, tomato sauce, vinegar, sugar, thyme, and bay leaf and bring to simmer. Season with salt and pepper to taste. Remove from heat, cover, and keep warm.

3. Adjust oven rack to middle position and heat oven to 350 degrees. Mash bread and milk together with fork in large bowl to form paste. Add bratwurst, beef, parcooked rice, 1 teaspoon pepper, and ½ teaspoon salt and mix with hands until thoroughly combined.

4. Divide meat mixture into 16 portions (about ¼ cup each) and, with wet hands, roll each portion into meatball; transfer to 13 by 9-inch baking dish. Pour sauce over meatballs. Cover dish tightly with aluminum foil and bake until cooked through and rice is tender, about 1 hour. Let meatballs rest in sauce, covered, for 15 minutes. Transfer meatballs to rimmed serving platter. Skim any fat from surface of sauce with spoon, discard bay leaf, and pour defatted sauce over meatballs. Serve.

Pesto Potatoes

Simply stirring pesto into boiled potatoes doesn't work.
To get it right, the pesto required some customizing. BY REBECCAH MARSTERS

THERE ARE PLENTY of potato recipes in the *Cook's Country* arsenal but never enough. So when I ran across a recipe for pesto potatoes, I jumped on it.

Here's what the instructions said: Combine diced, boiled potatoes with pesto and serve. When I looked up other recipes, they said about the same. All of them produced oily, bland results. Did pesto, so fresh and fragrant on pasta, need reengineering to work with potatoes?

Since the test kitchen already has an excellent recipe for pesto, I decided to use it as my starting point. It deviates from typical recipes in two ways: First, we toast the pine nuts to bring out their flavor. Next, we toast the garlic cloves, unpeeled, to temper their raw bite. The nuts and peeled garlic are then processed, as usual, with fresh basil, olive oil, and Parmesan cheese. I tossed our pesto with peeled, cubed, boiled, and still warm Yukon Gold potatoes—a test kitchen favorite. But here they were mealy and they fell apart. Also, the warm potatoes absorbed the pesto's moisture to the point of making the dish dry.

I tested other potato varieties and settled on red potatoes. Their sturdy, waxy texture suited this dish better, plus their thin, tender skins didn't require peeling. Because they were sturdier, I decided to try slicing them into thin rounds instead of the usual chunks to create more surface area, and thus (hopefully) more flavor absorption. Also, sliced potatoes cook faster. I tested these theories in the kitchen and was pleased with how well they worked out.

To make up for all the moisture that the potatoes were stealing from the pesto, I'd need to make a wetter pesto. I started by adding lemon juice, which turned out to have additional advantages: It helped the pesto retain a nice green color and gave the flavor another boost. I poured in more olive oil, too; as long as I was careful to gradually emulsify it into the pesto, it didn't produce oily potatoes. And I decided to steal the pine nuts from the pesto and instead sprinkle them on the potatoes at the end. This modified thinner, slicker pesto coated the potatoes thoroughly and evenly, plus we liked the crunch.

But despite the Parmesan and garlic, the potatoes were still bland. To flavor the slices more deeply, I borrowed a technique that we use when we make

To make pesto minus the raw-garlic burn, we toast the garlic cloves before pureeing them.

potato salad: dressing the warm potatoes with an acidic ingredient, in this case the lemon. However, the slices broke apart when I stirred in the lemon. Eventually, I figured out that if I let them cool for 20 minutes before dressing them with the pesto, the slices remained intact yet still warm enough to absorb flavor. Then

I added three ingredients that gave my dish more pizzazz: shallot, capers, and lemon zest. My last move was to double the Parmesan, sprinkling half of it on at the end. Mashed, baked, and roasted—I still love 'em, but now when I want a fresher, brighter potato dish, I know just what to make.

PESTO POTATOES Serves 8

Use small red potatoes measuring 1 to 2 inches in diameter. High-quality Parmesan makes a difference here.

- 3 pounds small red potatoes, unpeeled, sliced ¼ inch thick
  Salt and pepper
- 3 garlic cloves, unpeeled
- ⅓ cup pine nuts
- 3 cups fresh basil leaves
- 1 ounce Parmesan cheese, grated (½ cup)
- 1 teaspoon grated lemon zest plus 2 tablespoons juice
- ½ cup extra-virgin olive oil
- ¼ cup capers, rinsed and minced
- 1 large shallot, minced

1. Combine 2 quarts water, potatoes, and 1 tablespoon salt in Dutch oven and bring to boil over high heat. Reduce heat to medium and simmer until potatoes are easily pierced with tip of paring knife but do not break apart, 5 to 8 minutes. Drain potatoes thoroughly and transfer to large bowl. Let potatoes cool slightly, about 20 minutes.

2. Meanwhile, toast garlic in 10-inch skillet over medium heat, stirring occasionally, until skins are just beginning to brown, about 5 minutes. Add pine nuts and continue to toast until garlic is spotty brown and pine nuts are golden, 2 to 3 minutes. Transfer to plate and let cool slightly.

3. When cool enough to handle, peel garlic. Process garlic, basil, ¼ cup Parmesan, lemon zest and juice, and 1 teaspoon salt in food processor until coarsely ground, about 30 seconds, scraping down sides of bowl as needed. With processor running, slowly add oil and process until smooth, about 1 minute.

4. Add pesto, capers, shallot, pine nuts, and remaining ¼ cup Parmesan to potatoes and stir gently to combine. Season with salt and pepper to taste. Serve slightly warm or at room temperature.

TEST KITCHEN DISCOVERY **Custom Pesto**
To keep the pesto from weighing down the potatoes, we made it lighter and brighter. How? By withholding half of the cheese and all the pine nuts from the initial puree and by adding several flavorful power players. Before serving the dish, we sprinkled whole toasted pine nuts over it.

A BRIGHTER START
We add lemon juice and zest to the traditional basil, garlic, Parmesan, and oil.

A FLAVORFUL FINISH
We stir in capers and shallots for extra flavor and add pine nuts, whole, for crunch.

Monterey Chicken

Grilled chicken. Smoky bacon. Melted cheese. Honey mustard. Sounds delicious, but how do you combine them in a grill recipe that doesn't go up in smoke? BY CRISTIN WALSH

THE LATE DAN BLOCKER was famous for playing the friendly, lighthearted Hoss Cartwright on the TV show *Bonanza*, but I think his real star turn was his role in creating the popular restaurant dish Monterey chicken. Blocker founded the Bonanza Steakhouse chain in 1963, and in 1982 Chicken Monterey found its place on the menu. It was a boneless chicken breast that was marinated in the restaurant's "exclusive Monterey marinade," flame-broiled, and then topped with bacon strips and melted Monterey Jack cheese (hence the name). The dish is incredibly popular in many chain restaurants and diners today—although no two places seem to make it the same way. My challenge was to convert it into a recipe for home grillers.

I found plenty of restaurant recipes claiming to be versions of Monterey chicken, so I selected six of the most promising and got to work. My tasters were optimistic as I laid platters of nicely charred, cheese-draped chicken in front of them. But they were not happy with the bland, dry, overcooked meat that these recipes produced. The marinades were mostly variations of Italian dressing and gave the chicken little or no flavor. The store-bought barbecue sauces or honey mustards used to baste and sauce the chicken also failed to impress. And the bacon and cheese were treated like afterthoughts, with the cheese only partially (if at all) melted and the bacon usually sliding off somewhere between grill and mouth. Something had obviously gone awry between the restaurant version and these "copycat" recipes. This script was going to need a total rewrite if my tasters were ever going to give it the green light.

Grilling a boneless chicken breast can be a challenge because, with a thin end and a thick end, it's hard to cook it evenly. In the test kitchen, we get around this problem by either pounding or butterflying the breasts to an even thickness or else brining them to guard against the thinner part drying out. I tried all three methods. Pounding was OK some of the time, but the delicate breast meat had a tendency to shred or tear. Brining worked fine, but I wanted to marinate for more flavor, so I decided to go with the butterflying. The process is easy: Just slice (parallel to the cutting

We top the marinated, grilled chicken breasts with bacon-fat-basted onions, bacon, cheese, and pico de gallo.

board) through the thickest part of the breast, keeping the "hinge" intact on the other side, and fold the top half open like a book. These heart-shaped breasts were thin enough to cook quickly and had extra surface area to soak up marinade and grill flavor.

Chicken breast is best cooked to 160 degrees, but when grilled over a medium fire, as most recipes instruct, the chicken reached that temperature without flavorful grill marks. I tried again, slathering test batches with homemade versions of both barbecue and honey-mustard sauce at the beginning of grilling, hoping that the sugar in the sauces would get the char going. While I did learn that my tasters greatly preferred the version sauced with the honey mustard, the chicken still had inferior char. Bumping up the fire from medium to medium-hot solved the problem.

Using some of the honey-mustard sauce as a marinade and reserving some for basting intensified the flavor even further.

This spicy, sweet, and smoky chicken was ready for its supporting players. I had already learned that bacon and cheese added after cooking didn't adhere because the cheese didn't melt. But I had an idea. I got grilling again, but this time, as the temperature of the chicken was nearing 160 degrees, I pulled the charred breasts onto the cooler side, topped them with the crisp bacon slices and sliced Monterey Jack, and put the lid on. Covering the grill created an oven effect that melted the cheese during the last few minutes of cooking. I also found that the bacon and cheese adhered better if I cut the bacon into pieces before crisping and then shredded the cheese and mixed it with the bacon pieces to create a unified topping.

Many Monterey chicken recipes feature an extra component, such as sautéed mushrooms, but that meant more work in the kitchen—and I was already reluctant to be cooking the bacon inside when I preferred to be standing at my grill. Thinking of an item that I could prepare on the grill, it occurred to me to try red onion. I quickly figured out that if grilled onion is good, then grilled onion basted with bacon fat (which I had at the ready) is even better. I grilled bacon fat–painted slices of onion on the cooler side of the grill until they were softened, slightly charred, and very smoky. Then I separated the rings, divided them among the breasts, and added the bacon-cheese mixture. A final dress change for the cheese—replacing the mild Monterey Jack with the more lively pepper Jack—and our Monterey Chicken was ready for the spotlight at last. Thanks, Hoss.

MONTEREY CHICKEN Serves 4

We skewer the onion slices with a toothpick to keep them from falling apart on the grill. You won't need an entire red onion for this recipe; you can use the remainder to make Pico de Gallo (recipe follows).

- ½ cup Dijon mustard
- ¼ cup honey
  Salt and pepper
- 4 (6- to 8-ounce) boneless, skinless chicken breasts, trimmed
- 4 slices bacon, cut into ½-inch pieces
- 6 ounces pepper Jack cheese, shredded (1½ cups)
- 4 ½-inch-thick slices red onion
  Lime wedges

1. Whisk mustard, honey, 1 teaspoon salt, and ½ teaspoon pepper together in bowl. Reserve ¼ cup honey-mustard mixture for basting chicken. Transfer remaining honey-mustard mixture to 1-gallon zipper-lock bag.

2. Working with 1 breast at a time, starting on thick side, cut chicken in half horizontally, stopping ½ inch from edge so halves remain attached. Open up breast like book, creating single flat piece. Place chicken in bag with honey-mustard mixture, toss to coat, and refrigerate for at least 30 minutes or up to 1 hour.

3. Meanwhile, cook bacon in 10-inch

skillet over medium heat until crisp, 5 to 7 minutes. Using slotted spoon, transfer bacon to paper towel–lined plate. Reserve bacon fat. Once cool, toss bacon with pepper Jack.

4A. FOR A CHARCOAL GRILL: Open bottom vent completely. Light large chimney starter filled with charcoal briquettes (6 quarts). When top coals are partially covered with ash, pour two-thirds evenly over half of grill, then pour remaining coals over other half of grill. Set cooking grate in place, cover, and open lid vent completely. Heat grill until hot, about 5 minutes.

4B. FOR A GAS GRILL: Turn all burners to high, cover, and heat grill until hot, about 15 minutes. Leave primary burner on high and turn other burner(s) to medium. (Adjust primary burner as needed to maintain grill temperature of 350 to 400 degrees.)

5. Clean and oil cooking grate. Push toothpick horizontally through each onion slice to keep rings intact while grilling. Brush onion slices lightly with reserved bacon fat and place on cooler side of grill. Place chicken on hotter side of grill, cover, and cook until lightly charred, about 5 minutes. Flip onion slices and chicken. Brush chicken with reserved honey-mustard mixture, cover, and cook until lightly charred on second side, about 5 minutes.

6. Remove onion slices from grill and move chicken to cooler side of grill. Quickly remove toothpicks and separate onion rings. Divide onion rings evenly among chicken breasts. Divide bacon–pepper Jack mixture evenly over onion rings. Cover and cook until pepper Jack is melted and chicken registers 160 degrees, about 2 minutes. Transfer chicken to platter, tent loosely with aluminum foil, and let rest for 5 to 10 minutes. Serve with lime wedges.

PICO DE GALLO
Serves 4

While pico de gallo is not part of the original Bonanza steakhouse recipe, we did find it in a few copycat recipes. It's delicious spooned over our Monterey Chicken. To make it spicier, include the jalapeño seeds.

- 3 tomatoes, cored and chopped
  Salt and pepper
- ¼ cup finely chopped red onion
- ¼ cup chopped fresh cilantro
- 1 jalapeño chile, stemmed, seeded, and minced
- 1 tablespoon lime juice
- 1 garlic clove, minced

Toss tomatoes with ¼ teaspoon salt in bowl. Transfer to colander and let drain for 30 minutes. Combine drained tomatoes, onion, cilantro, jalapeño, lime juice, and garlic in bowl. Season with salt and pepper to taste. Serve.

TEST KITCHEN TECHNIQUE A Trip to Monterey
The bacon fat–basted onion slices cook on the cooler side of the grill as the butterflied chicken breasts cook on the hotter side. When the chicken is almost done, we move it to the cooler side and top it with the softened onions, crisp bacon, and shredded cheese.

Getting to Know Vinegar Pickles

Pickling in vinegar-based brine originated eons ago as a practical means of preserving foods. These days, everyone from star chefs to home cooks is doing it mainly for the distinctive flavor. BY CHRISTIE MORRISON

Sweet Pickles
SUGAR AND SPICE

Their porous flesh makes cucumbers perfect for pickling. Add a lot of sugar to the brine—plus mustard seeds, celery seeds, cider vinegar, and turmeric—and you have sweet pickles. The category includes sweet gherkins, made from immature cucumbers, and waffle-cut bread-and-butter chips. Find a recipe at **CooksCountry.com/ breadandbutterpickles**.

Dill Pickles
BURGER BUDDY

Dill pickles come in several varieties, all flavored with dill, salt, and vinegar. Add garlic for kosher dills or slice them thin for hamburger dills. In the test kitchen, we use the brine, too, as in our All-American Potato Salad (get the recipe at **CooksCountry. com/allamericanpotatosalad**). Garlicky, crisp Boar's Head Kosher Dill Pickles are our taste-test winner.

Pickled Peppers
PETER'S PICK

Pickled peppers, both hot and sweet, come in all shapes and colors. Some of the types we like to use in the test kitchen are pickled jalapeños (pictured), *pepperoncini*, and sweet cherry peppers. Introduce pickled peppers to pizza or sandwiches, or mix them into sauces or relish; the brine makes a spicy addition to vinaigrettes. You can cook with them, too.

Giardiniera
GARDEN RELISH

In this country *giardiniera* refers to a combination of pickled cauliflower, carrots, celery, and sweet and hot peppers; in Italy, the term is more generic. Its "sharp, vinegary tang" cuts the richness of fatty meats and cheeses on an antipasto platter. Our favorite supermarket brand of giardiniera is Pastene.

Capers
BOLD BUDS

Capers—the sun-dried pickled flower buds of the caper bush—are used in Mediterranean recipes to provide briny punch. Their flavor develops as they are cured, most commonly in a salt and vinegar brine or more unusually (and expensively) in salt. Rinse and drain capers before using them. Capers are essential for tartar sauce and chicken piccata; find our recipe at **CooksCountry. com/chickenpiccata**. Reese Non Pareil Capers are our favorite.

Pickled Beet Eggs
AMISH TREAT

To produce this snack and salad staple, the Pennsylvania Dutch combine sliced pickled beets and shelled hard-cooked eggs. The two go in brine with spices like caraway, mustard seeds, cloves, cinnamon, and star anise. The acidic vinegar balances the earthy, sweet beets. As for the eggs, the longer they stay in the brine the deeper the beet color penetrates, until even the yolks are tinged with purple. Try our recipe and see for yourself: **CooksCountry.com/ pickledbeeteggs**.

Dilly Beans
SWIZZLE STICK

Aromatic and super-crunchy, dilly beans are green or yellow wax beans in a pungent dill, garlic, mustard seed, and peppercorn brine. Some versions include dried or fresh red chile for a spicy kick. Snack on dilly beans, add them to salad, or dunk them in a Bloody Mary. They're so easy and inexpensive to make that we hope you'll pickle your own: **CooksCountry.com/dillybeans**.

Cocktail Onions
GIBSON GARNISH

Pearl onions add the final touch to classic *boeuf bourguignon*, the famous French beef stew, or they simmer in cream for a classic steakhouse side dish. When immersed in pickling brine and jarred, these mild, naturally sweet alliums become the signature garnish of the Gibson, the gin and vermouth cocktail. When you put down your drink, try pickled cocktail onions on an antipasto platter or in a green salad.

Pickled Ginger
SUSHI CHASER

Unlike wasabi, its partner on a plate of sushi, pickled ginger isn't there as a condiment. Traditionally, pickled ginger is eaten after sushi, since ginger is a natural palate cleanser. To make pickled ginger, slice the root very thin and marinate it in a vinegar and sugar solution; the resulting pickle ranges in color from pink to light yellow, although most commercial ginger is tinted pink with vegetable-based dye.

Pickled Okra
SLIME STOPPER

Southerners fry, smother, and bake okra, but the rest of the country knows it best for its role as a thickener in gumbo, thanks to the viscous liquid (some call it slime) inside the pods. When you pickle okra, the salt pulls out moisture, giving the pods a nice crunch without any gooey texture. Add pickled okra to shrimp or potato salads, or roll it in cream cheese–slathered ham slices for okra pinwheels, a beloved Southern appetizer.

Pickled Watermelon Rind
SWEET SCRAPS

Most people throw out the rind of the watermelon. But did you know that it makes a terrific pickle? (And no wonder: The melons are cousins of the cucumber.) The rinds are peeled, cooked, and pickled—a process that produces sticky-sweet pickles in a sugary, syrupy brine. This classic Southern pickle is a treat straight from the jar, added to a cocktail, or wrapped in bacon for an appetizer.

Pickled Pigs' Feet
GLOBE TROTTER

To the uninitiated, they're alarming. But pickled pigs' feet are beloved in the American South (also in Korea, the Caribbean, and parts of Europe). They are made by salting and smoking, then pickling in a vinegar solution. Alternatively, they are brined in a saltwater solution, boiled, and pickled. Commercial versions often add dye. Find the trotters in giant jars on the counters of bars and mom-and-pop grocery stores. Snack on them straight from the jar, with a cold beer.

GRILLED STEAK FAJITA PIZZA

PAN-SEARED SALMON WITH CHIMICHURRI

GRILLED CHICKEN TERIYAKI WITH PINEAPPLE

SPAGHETTI WITH SHIITAKES AND LEMON

PAN-SEARED SALMON WITH CHIMICHURRI Serves 4

✓ **WHY THIS RECIPE WORKS:** Thanks to the food processor, this recipe comes together quickly. The bright flavors of parsley and cilantro cut the richness of the salmon.

- 1 cup fresh parsley leaves
- 1 cup fresh cilantro leaves
- 2 garlic cloves, minced
  Salt and pepper
- ¼ teaspoon red pepper flakes
- ½ cup plus 1 tablespoon extra-virgin olive oil
- ¼ cup red wine vinegar
- 4 (6-ounce) skin-on salmon fillets, 1¼ inches thick

1. Combine parsley, cilantro, garlic, 1 teaspoon salt, and pepper flakes in food processor; pulse until coarsely chopped, about 5 pulses. Add ½ cup oil and vinegar; pulse, scraping down bowl as needed, until mixture is combined but still chunky, about 5 pulses. Transfer to bowl; set aside.

2. Pat salmon dry with paper towels and season with salt and pepper. Heat remaining 1 tablespoon oil in 12-inch nonstick skillet over medium-high heat until just smoking. Cook salmon, skin side up, until well browned, 4 to 6 minutes. Flip and continue to cook until well browned on skin side, 4 to 6 minutes. Transfer to platter. Spoon chimichurri over top. Serve.

TEST KITCHEN NOTE: You can make the chimichurri up to 24 hours in advance and store it in the refrigerator.

GRILLED STEAK FAJITA PIZZA Serves 4

✓ **WHY THIS RECIPE WORKS:** We use smoky chipotle chile powder both in our easy no-cook pizza sauce and as a rub for the steak.

- 2 teaspoons dried oregano
- 1 teaspoon chipotle chile powder
  Salt and pepper
- 1 (14.5-ounce) can diced tomatoes
- 8 ounces skirt steak, trimmed
- 1 poblano chile, stemmed and seeded
- 1 red onion, cut into ½-inch-thick slices
- 1 pound pizza dough
- 8 ounces shredded Mexican cheese blend (2 cups)
- ½ cup chopped fresh cilantro

1. Combine oregano, chile powder, 1 teaspoon salt, and ½ teaspoon pepper in bowl. Pulse tomatoes and their juice with half of spice mixture in food processor until coarsely chopped, about 5 pulses; transfer to bowl. Pat steak dry with paper towels and rub with remaining spice mixture. Grill steak, poblano, and onion, uncovered, over hot fire until well charred and meat registers 125 degrees, about 3 minutes per side for steak and 4 minutes per side for vegetables. Transfer steak and vegetables to carving board, tent with aluminum foil, and let rest for 5 minutes. Thinly slice steak against grain; slice poblano into thin strips; separate onion rings.

2. Roll dough into 12-inch circle on lightly floured counter. Grill dough, uncovered, over hot fire until underside is spotty brown and top is bubbly, about 3 minutes. Flip dough and top with tomato sauce, steak, poblano, onion, and cheese. Continue to grill, covered, until cheese is melted and dough is cooked through, about 3 minutes. Transfer to carving board and sprinkle with cilantro. Serve.

SPAGHETTI WITH SHIITAKES AND LEMON Serves 4 to 6

✓ **WHY THIS RECIPE WORKS:** Letting the dish sit briefly before serving allows the flavors to meld and the sauce to thicken.

- 1 pound spaghetti
  Salt and pepper
- 5 tablespoons extra-virgin olive oil, plus extra for drizzling
- 12 ounces shiitake mushrooms, stemmed and sliced thin
- 1 shallot, minced
- ¼ cup heavy cream
- 1 ounce Parmesan cheese, grated (½ cup), plus extra for sprinkling
- 2 teaspoons grated lemon zest plus ¼ cup juice (2 lemons)
- 2 tablespoons thinly sliced fresh basil

1. Bring 4 quarts water to boil in Dutch oven. Add spaghetti and 1 tablespoon salt and cook, stirring often, until al dente. Reserve 1¾ cups cooking water, then drain spaghetti and set aside.

2. Heat 2 tablespoons oil in now-empty Dutch oven over medium heat until shimmering. Add mushrooms, shallot, and ½ teaspoon salt and cook until lightly browned, about 7 minutes. Add 1½ cups reserved cooking water and cream and bring to boil. Reduce heat to medium-low and simmer for 2 minutes. Remove from heat and stir in spaghetti, Parmesan, lemon zest and juice, ½ teaspoon pepper, and remaining 3 tablespoons oil. Cover and let stand for 2 minutes, tossing halfway through.

3. Add remaining ¼ cup cooking water as needed to adjust consistency. Stir in basil and season with salt and pepper to taste. Serve, drizzling individual portions with extra oil and sprinkling with extra Parmesan.

TEST KITCHEN NOTE: You can use cremini mushrooms in place of the shiitakes.

GRILLED CHICKEN TERIYAKI WITH PINEAPPLE Serves 4

✓ **WHY THIS RECIPE WORKS:** Pineapple and teriyaki are a natural pairing. The soy sauce in the glaze seasons the meat sufficiently so that no salt is required.

- ⅓ cup soy sauce
- ¼ cup sugar
- 2 tablespoons mirin
- 1 tablespoon grated fresh ginger
- 1 teaspoon cornstarch
- 3 pounds bone-in chicken thighs, trimmed
- 1 pineapple, peeled, cored, and cut into ½-inch-thick rings

1. Whisk soy sauce, sugar, mirin, ginger, and cornstarch together in small saucepan. Bring to boil over medium-high heat and cook until thickened, about 2 minutes.

2. Grill chicken skin side up over medium-hot fire, covered, until underside is browned, 8 to 10 minutes. Flip and grill, covered, until skin is well browned and meat registers 175 degrees, 6 to 8 minutes. Brush chicken all over with half of sauce and continue to grill, uncovered and flipping often, until sauce begins to caramelize, about 2 minutes. Transfer chicken to serving platter and tent loosely with aluminum foil.

3. Brush pineapple rings with half of remaining sauce and grill, uncovered, until lightly charred on both sides, 1 to 2 minutes per side. Transfer to platter with chicken. Pour remaining sauce over chicken and pineapple. Serve.

TEST KITCHEN NOTE: Many supermarkets carry fresh peeled and cored pineapple. Canned pineapple rings will work in a pinch.

CHICKEN IN CREAMY PARMESAN SAUCE WITH
ARTICHOKES AND TOMATOES

GRILLED BEEF WITH PEANUT SAUCE

GRILLED PORK CUTLETS AND ZUCCHINI WITH FETA
AND MINT COMPOUND BUTTER

CARIBBEAN CHICKEN SALAD

GRILLED BEEF WITH PEANUT SAUCE Serves 4

☑ **WHY THIS RECIPE WORKS:** Red curry paste does double duty by serving as an ingredient in both our steak rub and our peanut sauce.

- 3 tablespoons Thai red curry paste
- 2 tablespoons vegetable oil
- 1 tablespoon plus 1 teaspoon soy sauce
- 1 (2-pound) flank steak, trimmed
- 3 tablespoons packed dark brown sugar
- 2 garlic cloves, minced
- 1 cup canned coconut milk
- ⅓ cup chunky peanut butter
- 1 tablespoon fish sauce
- 1 tablespoon lime juice

1. Combine 2 tablespoons curry paste, 1 tablespoon oil, and 1 tablespoon soy sauce in bowl and rub all over steak. Let sit for 10 minutes.

2. Meanwhile, heat remaining 1 tablespoon oil in small saucepan over medium heat until shimmering. Add sugar, garlic, and remaining 1 tablespoon curry paste and cook until fragrant, about 30 seconds. Add coconut milk and bring to boil. Whisk in peanut butter, fish sauce, lime juice, and remaining 1 teaspoon soy sauce until combined. Remove from heat; set aside.

3. Grill steak over hot fire until medium-rare (125 degrees), about 6 minutes per side. Transfer to carving board, tent loosely with aluminum foil, and let rest for 5 minutes. Slice thin against grain. Serve with peanut sauce.

TEST KITCHEN NOTE: Light or regular coconut milk may be used.

CHICKEN IN CREAMY PARMESAN SAUCE WITH ARTICHOKES AND TOMATOES Serves 4

☑ **WHY THIS RECIPE WORKS:** Sweet-tart cherry tomatoes and fresh parsley bring a burst of color and flavor to this hearty dish.

- 4 (6- to 8-ounce) boneless, skinless chicken breasts, trimmed
  Salt and pepper
- 2 tablespoons olive oil
- 1 shallot, minced
- 9 ounces frozen artichoke hearts, thawed and patted dry
- ½ cup heavy cream
- ½ cup chicken broth
- 6 ounces cherry tomatoes, halved
- 2 ounces Parmesan cheese, grated (1 cup)
- 2 tablespoons minced fresh parsley

1. Pat chicken dry with paper towels and season with salt and pepper. Heat 1 tablespoon oil in 12-inch skillet over medium-high heat until just smoking. Cook chicken until golden brown, about 5 minutes per side; transfer to plate.

2. Add remaining 1 tablespoon oil and shallot to now-empty skillet and cook over medium heat until shallot is softened, about 1 minute. Add artichokes and cook until beginning to brown, 6 to 8 minutes. Add cream and broth and bring to simmer. Return chicken to skillet and cook until meat registers 160 degrees, about 10 minutes, flipping chicken halfway through cooking. Remove skillet from heat and transfer chicken to clean plate.

3. Stir tomatoes, Parmesan, and parsley into sauce. Season with salt and pepper to taste. Pour sauce over chicken and serve.

TEST KITCHEN NOTE: Serve with bread or egg noodles.

CARIBBEAN CHICKEN SALAD Serves 4

☑ **WHY THIS RECIPE WORKS:** Lime and Jamaican jerk paste enliven mayonnaise, which we use to bind mango, jicama, red bell pepper, and red onion into a vibrant chicken salad.

- 2 (8-inch) pita breads
- ½ cup mayonnaise
- ¼ cup lime juice (2 limes)
- 1 tablespoon Jamaican jerk paste
- 1 (2½-pound) rotisserie chicken, skin and bones discarded, meat shredded into bite-size pieces (3 cups)
- 2 romaine lettuce hearts (12 ounces), chopped
- 1 mango, peeled, pitted, and cut into ½-inch pieces
- 1 small jicama, peeled and cut into ½-inch pieces
- 1 red bell pepper, stemmed, seeded, and cut into ½-inch pieces
- ¼ red onion, sliced thin

1. Adjust oven rack to middle position and heat oven to 425 degrees. Place pita breads on rimmed baking sheet and bake until crisp and lightly toasted, 12 to 15 minutes.

2. Meanwhile, whisk mayonnaise, lime juice, and jerk paste together in large bowl. Add chicken, romaine, mango, jicama, bell pepper, and onion and toss to combine. Cut each pita into quarters and serve with salad.

TEST KITCHEN NOTE: Jamaican jerk paste is a mix of oil and jerk spices that is sold with the spice mixes in supermarkets. If you can't find it, use 1 tablespoon jerk seasoning and add an extra tablespoon of mayonnaise to the dressing.

GRILLED PORK CUTLETS AND ZUCCHINI WITH FETA AND MINT COMPOUND BUTTER Serves 4

☑ **WHY THIS RECIPE WORKS:** Packaged pork loin cutlets are inconsistent. Instead of using them, we make our own cutlets with pork tenderloin.

- 2 (12- to 16-ounce) pork tenderloins, trimmed, each cut into 4 equal pieces and pounded to ¼-inch thickness
  Salt and pepper
- 4 tablespoons unsalted butter, softened
- 1 ounce feta cheese, crumbled (¼ cup)
- 1 tablespoon chopped fresh mint
- ½ teaspoon grated orange zest
- 4 small zucchini (6 ounces each), halved lengthwise
- 1 tablespoon vegetable oil

1. Pat pork dry with paper towels and season with salt and pepper. Let sit for 10 minutes.

2. Meanwhile, combine butter, feta, mint, orange zest, ¼ teaspoon salt, and ¼ teaspoon pepper in bowl; set aside. Brush zucchini with oil and season with salt and pepper.

3. Grill pork over hot fire, uncovered, until lightly charred and cooked through, about 2 minutes per side. Transfer to serving platter, tent loosely with aluminum foil, and let rest while cooking zucchini. Grill zucchini, uncovered, until tender, about 3 minutes per side. Top pork and zucchini with compound butter. Serve.

TEST KITCHEN NOTE: You can use lemon zest in place of the orange zest.

Pasta with Spinach and Fresh Tomato Sauce

Who would have thought a little chopped spinach would be so temperamental?

BY CRISTIN WALSH

ON A HOT August evening, faced with a bag of spinach and some juicy summer tomatoes that needed using up fast, I set out to develop a recipe for fettuccine with a bright, light, spinach-flecked tomato sauce. Although the combination sounds basic, when I tried existing recipes, I encountered slimy, flavorless, or negligible spinach with tomato sauces that ran the gamut from watery to dull.

Given their poor performance, I ditched the sauces in favor of a proven test kitchen recipe. I heated olive oil, garlic, tomato paste, and red pepper flakes in a skillet, letting the paste darken and intensify to give the sauce depth and a little density. Next, I stirred in 3 pounds of tomatoes (we tested several varieties and all worked fine; peeling wasn't necessary). In 15 minutes, the mixture simmered, thickened, and transformed into just the bright, chunky sauce I sought. I gave the sauce a test run over fettuccine and got the thumbs-up.

The spinach proved more of a slog. After a couple of tests, I exchanged the curly-leaf spinach that other recipes use for baby spinach, which comes conveniently prewashed and bagged, and with tender stems that don't need trimming. I made the dish with ever-increasing amounts of spinach until I settled on

16 cups for 1 pound of pasta. It was too much to fit in my skillet, but I knew that with a little heat, the spinach would wilt into a manageable mound. I loaded up a bowl, microwaved the 16 cups with a little water, and watched it wilt to half its volume.

That wilted spinach went into the skillet with the tomatoes. But as the tomatoes cooked, the spinach clumped and slimed, and the taste was as anemic as ever. Several tests taught me how to fix the texture: Chop and squeeze the microwaved spinach dry and then let the tomatoes cook down before stirring the spinach into the skillet. You'd think that since the spinach was no longer watery, its flavor would pop. Not so. Puzzled, I called our science editor. He explained that when spinach is cooked in a moist, acidic environment, such as tomato sauce, the flavor compounds don't develop fully. Sauté it by itself in oil, he suggested, where it can get hotter, bringing out sulfur compounds that eaters perceive as more flavorful.

Following his instructions, I sautéed the wilted spinach in oil (plus more garlic), and I cooked the tomatoes separately. I combined them and added the fettuccine, along with a bit of the starchy cooking water to help the sauce adhere. What a difference: The spinach registered, making the sauce fresher and brighter than ever. A sprinkle of Pecorino was all the enhancement this dish needed.

COOK THE SPINACH IN HOT OIL
To bring out its flavor, sauté the spinach without acid.

Skip the hearty, meaty sauce. Our lighter, brighter pasta is tailor-made for summer.

PASTA WITH SPINACH AND TOMATOES
Serves 6

You can use linguine or pappardelle in place of the fettuccine.

- 1 pound (16 cups) baby spinach
- 6 tablespoons extra-virgin olive oil
- 4 garlic cloves, minced
- 2 tablespoons tomato paste
- ¼ teaspoon red pepper flakes
- 3 pounds tomatoes, cored and chopped
  Salt and pepper
- 1 pound fettuccine
  Grated Pecorino Romano cheese

1. Place spinach and ¼ cup water in large bowl. Cover bowl with large dinner plate and microwave until spinach is wilted and decreased in volume by half, about 5 minutes. Using potholders, remove bowl from microwave and keep covered, 1 minute. Carefully remove plate and transfer spinach to colander set in sink. Using rubber spatula, gently press spinach against colander to release excess liquid. Transfer spinach to cutting board and roughly chop, then place in clean dish towel and squeeze to remove excess water.

2. Heat 2 tablespoons oil in 12-inch skillet over medium-high heat until shimmering. Add half of garlic and cook until fragrant, about 30 seconds. Add spinach and cook until glossy green, about 2 minutes. Transfer spinach to bowl and set aside.

3. Reduce heat to medium and add remaining 4 tablespoons oil, remaining garlic, tomato paste, and pepper flakes to now-empty skillet and cook until fragrant and tomato paste has darkened slightly, about 1 minute. Add tomatoes and 1 teaspoon salt and bring to strong simmer. Cook, stirring occasionally, until tomato sauce has thickened slightly and few tomato chunks remain, 15 to 18 minutes. Season with salt and pepper to taste. Add spinach to sauce, cover, and keep warm.

4. Meanwhile, bring 4 quarts water to boil in large pot. Add fettuccine and 1 tablespoon salt and cook, stirring often, until al dente. Reserve ½ cup cooking water, then drain fettuccine and return it to pot. Add sauce and toss to combine. Adjust consistency with reserved cooking water as needed. Serve with Pecorino.

Muffin Tin Frittatas

What looks like a muffin but tastes like an omelet? And where has this delicious and handy recipe been all our lives? BY DIANE UNGER

IF YOU'RE MAKINGS eggs for a brunch crowd, frittata is an excellent choice. It's like a thick, open-faced omelet, but it's easier to make because the additions are mixed right into the raw eggs, and there's no delicate flipping or timing. You can add just about anything to a frittata; plus, it's as tasty at room temperature as it is when warm.

I was interested in a particular variation on this theme. Instead of cooking a frittata in a skillet, as usual, I wanted to bake individual frittatas in a muffin tin, something that I'd enjoyed at a party recently. This method would let me customize batches, even within a single tin. So I took a frittata recipe that we'd developed in the test kitchen and made it several times, divvying up the seasoned egg-milk mixture among the greased cups of a muffin tin and baking it. But in some batches the eggs were too pale, and in others they were overcooked and rubbery. Sticking was a problem, too. I'd need to adjust the recipe and figure out the best cooking times and temperatures.

My first task was to prevent sticking.

> ▶ Get two more recipes for fillings at CooksCountry.com/ sept13: Asparagus, Dill, and Goat Cheese and Mushroom, Chive, and Gruyère.

I did the sensible things: I double-checked that I was using an unscratched nonstick muffin tin and took special care to spray it very thoroughly. But even after these precautions, the frittatas didn't release easily. I was at a loss until a coworker suggested that I increase the fat quotient in the frittatas. A little half-and-half and a lot of cheese later, the frittatas came out of the muffin tins without any trouble. It didn't hurt that they were richer and cheesier than before.

I did a series of tests to get just the right amount of browning on my individual frittatas. While I wanted some color, I didn't want overcooked eggs, which is a greater danger in a muffin tin than on the stovetop because the delicate custard mix is closely surrounded by hot metal. Ultimately, I learned that 425 degrees was perfect. Any higher and the frittatas overcooked, plus they souffléd and then sank; any lower and they failed to adequately brown.

You can flavor a frittata with just about anything—and believe me, I did. For one batch, I combined potato, red bell pepper, and cheddar cheese. For others, I switched it up with add-ins ranging from asparagus to chorizo to mushrooms. I found that I could indeed easily make half batches of the fillings, so I baked two different types of frittatas in one muffin tin. Now if I could just perfect my Bloody Mary . . .

MUFFIN TIN FRITTATAS
Makes 12 muffins

Use a nonstick muffin tin or the eggs will stick. You can prepare the egg and filling mixtures up to a day in advance; refrigerate them separately. Make two different types of frittatas in a single muffin tin by making half batches of two different filling recipes. You'll need to reduce the sauté time to 8 to 10 minutes and use a 10-inch skillet.

- 8 large eggs
- ¼ cup half-and-half
- ½ teaspoon pepper
- ¼ teaspoon salt
- 1 recipe frittata filling (recipes follow)

1. Adjust oven rack to lower-middle position and heat oven to 425 degrees. Generously spray 12-cup nonstick muffin tin with vegetable oil spray. Whisk eggs, half-and-half, pepper, and salt together in large bowl.

2. Divide frittata filling evenly among muffin cups. Using ladle, evenly distribute egg mixture over filling in muffin cups. Bake until frittatas are lightly puffed and just set in center, 9 to 11 minutes. Transfer muffin tin to wire rack and let cool for 10 minutes. Run plastic knife around edges of frittatas, if necessary, to loosen from muffin tin, then gently remove and serve.

CHORIZO, PARSLEY, AND PEPPER JACK FILLING
Makes enough for 12 muffin tin frittatas

- 1 tablespoon olive oil
- 8 ounces Spanish-style chorizo sausage, quartered lengthwise and sliced thin
- 8 ounces Yukon Gold potatoes, unpeeled, quartered lengthwise and sliced thin
- 1 large onion, chopped fine
- ½ teaspoon salt
- 2 garlic cloves, minced
- 6 ounces pepper Jack cheese, shredded (1½ cups)
- 3 tablespoons minced fresh parsley

Serve these frittata muffins for brunch or eat them as a grab-and-go breakfast.

Heat oil in 12-inch nonstick skillet over medium heat until shimmering. Add chorizo, potatoes, onion, and salt and cook, stirring occasionally, until potatoes are tender, 10 to 15 minutes. Stir in garlic and cook until fragrant, about 30 seconds. Transfer to bowl and let cool for 15 minutes. Stir in pepper Jack and parsley.

POTATO, BELL PEPPER, AND CHEDDAR FILLING
Makes enough for 12 muffin tin frittatas

High quality cheddar makes a difference here. Do not use dried basil in this (or any other) recipe.

- 2 tablespoons olive oil
- 8 ounces Yukon Gold potatoes, unpeeled, quartered lengthwise and sliced thin
- 1 large onion, chopped fine
- 1 large red bell pepper, stemmed, seeded, and chopped
- ½ teaspoon salt
- 2 garlic cloves, minced
- 6 ounces sharp cheddar cheese, shredded (1½ cups)
- 3 tablespoons minced fresh basil

Heat oil in 12-inch nonstick skillet over medium heat until shimmering. Add potatoes, onion, bell pepper, and salt and cook, stirring occasionally, until potatoes are tender, 10 to 15 minutes. Stir in garlic and cook until fragrant, about 30 seconds. Transfer to bowl and let cool for 15 minutes. Stir in cheddar and basil.

Ham Steak with Red-Eye Gravy

Cooking a slab of salty ham in strong coffee may sound odd. Prepare to become a fan. BY DIANE UNGER

HAM WITH RED-EYE gravy, a time-honored tradition in the South, is made by using a splash of strong coffee to deglaze a skillet in which meaty, deliciously salty ham steaks are fried. There is an origin story starring President Andrew Jackson that is probably hokum, but what's not under dispute is how good this dish can be.

I picked out a handful of recipes, from simple (ham simmered in coffee) to gussied-up (including butter, beef stock, and heavy cream). The bare bones recipes yielded thin, bitter gravy—salty coffee with a side of ham. The more complex recipes tasted better but seemed overwrought for what should be a simple dish.

To develop my recipe, I first needed to choose the right cut. Southern cooks make this dish with country ham. Ordinary bone-in ham steak is easier for most cooks to find, so I used that instead. But I soon discovered that bone-in supermarket ham steaks are trimmed so well that they don't render enough fat to cook in. I decided to add fat—and smoky flavor—by starting with bacon, rendering two slices in a large skillet. I dried the ham steak well with paper towels so that the steak would brown not steam. Then I fried it in the bacon fat to a beautiful golden brown, just 5 minutes or so. I moved the ham to a platter and made the gravy.

Instead of heading straight for the coffee maker, I added chopped onion to the now-empty skillet to brown, thinking that it would lend complexity. To give the sauce body, I threw in a teaspoon of flour. I was now at the point when most recipes call for pouring in the brewed coffee and boiling it down to concentrate its flavor. Say what? Anyone who has ever tried to reheat a cup of coffee knows that boiling, or even simmering, coffee makes it bitter and undrinkable. I figured, therefore, that the best gravy would use the coffee as a flavor rather than a base. I'd use a more traditional gravy ingredient, chicken broth, and concentrate it before adding the coffee component. But what was the right coffee component?

Brewed coffee was a nonstarter. By the time I'd used enough to actually taste the coffee, the gravy was bitter. I steeped whole coffee beans in the gravy base. They barely registered. I tried crushed coffee beans (still scant flavor) and then freshly ground ones (plenty of flavor, but I couldn't strain out all of the grounds). I turned to instant coffee, stirred into the gravy at the last minute. Instant coffee doesn't make good coffee, and it makes even worse ham steak. But instant espresso powder, added off the heat, worked wonders.

To balance the coffee flavor, I tested sweeteners from sugar to honey to molasses before hitting the mark with a single tablespoon of (admittedly Northern) maple syrup. To make the gravy smoother and richer, I whisked in 3 tablespoons of butter, and I seasoned it with just pepper—delicious. It was time to put the two elements together.

I poured the gravy over the resting ham steak and carved a hunk. It was so salty that I couldn't eat it. After a few minutes' thought, I realized why: As the ham steak sat on the platter, it released salty meat juices, which then mixed into the gravy. For my next batch, I discarded the accumulated juices before saucing the ham. Finally, the bracing, eye-opening gravy and the well-browned, slightly crispy ham made perfect sense.

It may look like dinner, but ham steak with red-eye gravy is usually served for breakfast.

Visit **CooksCountry.com/hashedpotatoes** for our recipe for **Potatoes Hashed in Cream**, which are a great accompaniment to these ham steaks.

HAM STEAK WITH RED-EYE GRAVY
Serves 4

Pat the ham steak dry before cooking so it will brown well. Before pouring the gravy over the ham in step 3, discard any accumulated juices on the platter, as they will make the sauce too salty.

- 1 (1¼-pound) bone-in ham steak
  Pepper
- 2 slices bacon
- 2 tablespoons finely chopped onion
- 1 teaspoon all-purpose flour
- 1½ cups chicken broth
- 1 tablespoon maple syrup
- 3 tablespoons unsalted butter, cut into 3 pieces and chilled
- 2 teaspoons instant espresso powder

1. Pat ham dry with paper towels and season with pepper. Cook bacon in 12-inch skillet over medium heat until crisp, about 5 minutes. Remove bacon from skillet (leaving bacon fat behind) and reserve for another use. Add ham to skillet with bacon fat and cook until well browned on first side, about 5 minutes. Flip ham and cook on second side until lightly browned, about 2 minutes. Transfer ham to platter and tent loosely with aluminum foil.

2. Add onion to now-empty skillet and cook until just beginning to brown, about 1 minute. Stir in flour and cook for 15 seconds. Whisk in broth and maple syrup, scraping up any browned bits. Bring to simmer and cook until mixture is reduced to ¾ cup and slightly thickened, 5 to 7 minutes.

3. Off heat, whisk in butter and espresso powder. Season with pepper to taste. Discard any juices on ham platter. Carve ham steak into 4 equal portions. Pour red-eye gravy over ham. Serve.

TEST KITCHEN DISCOVERY
Powder Power

We tried freshly brewed coffee, coffee beans, instant coffee, and more. In the end, instant espresso powder made the perfect red-eye gravy.

WAKE UP AND SMELL THE ESPRESSO

Strawberry Pretzel Salad

Even in its "convenience food" version, this beloved Midwest favorite has a fantastic combination of salty and sweet, crunchy and creamy. How great would it be without the fake ingredients? BY NICK IVERSON

I N MY FAMILY, it's just not a holiday unless Mom's pretzel salad is on the table. She lines a 13 by 9-inch baking pan with a mix of crushed pretzels, sugar, and melted butter and bakes it into a crust; she spreads it with a combination of sweetened cream cheese and whipped topping; and then she covers it all with a layer of strawberry Jell-O mixed with syrupy berries. The ingredients would make you think it's for dessert, but it's actually eaten with dinner. Confused? So were my colleagues. But this unlikely yet beloved dish holds a place of honor at backyard barbecues, potlucks, and holiday dinners all over the Midwest. And with good reason—the stuff is deliciously salty and sweet and creamy and crunchy.

All recipes for the salad are very similar; I made several with small variations, layering components and letting the salads chill. After a few hours, I called over my colleagues. They were pleasantly surprised. "That's actually pretty good," one conceded. But I'd still need to repair some flaws: crumbly crusts; bouncy, fake-tasting Jell-O tops; and enough sugar to open a candy store. Also, the store-bought whipped topping would have to go. Yes, these changes might mean extra kitchen work, but a fresher, fruitier pretzel salad sounded appealing. (Sorry, Mom.)

The crust was easy to fix—it was a simple matter of using pretzel sticks instead of classically shaped pretzels. The sticks crushed evenly, making for a sturdier crust. That done, I moved up a layer, replacing the Cool Whip with homemade whipped cream. I folded it into cream cheese that I'd beaten with sugar in a stand mixer. While this substitution worked nicely, the mixture was still too sweet and the process bothersome. Over several tests, I decreased the sugar from 1 cup to just ½ cup, and in an attempt to simplify the procedure, I tried slowly pouring the cream into the mixer with the cream cheese and sugar instead of whipping it separately. To my surprise, the mixture whipped up fine. I spread it over the cooled pretzel crust, chilled it, and tried a bite. Honest-to-goodness cream versus artificial whipped dairy topping? No contest.

For the gelatin layer, I hoped to ditch the artificially flavored boxed Jell-O and overly sweet frozen berries in syrup and pack in as much real

This is a salad in name only. That said, pretzel salad is served as a side dish—not a dessert—in much of the Midwest.

strawberry flavor as I could. To do so, I'd make homemade Jell-O. After some experimentation, I had my game plan: Puree berries, strain to extract strawberry juice, heat liquid with sugar, and thicken with gelatin. By the time I was done, I was whizzing 2 entire pounds of frozen (for year-round consistency), thawed berries in the food processor and setting things to a relaxed wiggle

with just 4½ teaspoons of gelatin. Instead of the strawberries in syrup, I folded in another full pound of sliced berries. Now I controlled the sweetness level—1½ cups of sugar proved to be enough. I chilled the strawberry topping for 30 minutes before layering it on the salad. Otherwise, as I learned from hard-won experience, it melted the cream and soaked the crust.

I checked all my modifications in a final pretzel salad and then called over tasters to judge it, though truthfully, the opinion I most cared about was my own. I chewed attentively and gave myself a pat on the back. The sweet-salty, creamy-crunchy contrasts mirrored my mom's version. The intense strawberry flavor and soft homemade cream were my own.

STRAWBERRY PRETZEL SALAD

Serves 10 to 12

For a sturdier crust, use (thinner) pretzel sticks not (fatter) rods. Thaw the strawberries in the refrigerator the night before you begin the recipe. You'll puree 2 pounds of the strawberries and slice the remaining 1 pound.

6½	ounces pretzel sticks
2¼	cups (15¾ ounces) sugar
12	tablespoons unsalted butter, melted and cooled
8	ounces cream cheese
1	cup heavy cream
3	pounds (10½ cups) frozen strawberries, thawed
¼	teaspoon salt
4½	teaspoons unflavored gelatin
½	cup cold water

1. Adjust oven rack to middle position and heat oven to 400 degrees. Spray 13 by 9-inch baking pan with vegetable oil spray. Pulse pretzels and ¼ cup sugar in food processor until coarsely ground, about 15 pulses. Add melted butter and pulse until combined, about 10 pulses. Transfer pretzel mixture to prepared pan. Using bottom of measuring cup, press crumbs into bottom of pan. Bake until crust is fragrant and beginning to brown, about 10 minutes, rotating pan halfway through baking. Set aside crust, letting it cool slightly, about 20 minutes.

2. Using stand mixer fitted with whisk, whip cream cheese and ½ cup sugar on medium speed until light and fluffy, about 2 minutes. Increase speed to medium-high and, with mixer still running, slowly add cream in steady stream. Continue to whip until soft peaks form, scraping down bowl as needed, about 1 minute longer. Spread whipped cream cheese mixture evenly over cooled crust. Refrigerate until set, about 30 minutes.

3. Meanwhile, process 2 pounds strawberries in now-empty food processor until pureed, about 30 seconds. Strain mixture through fine-mesh strainer set over medium saucepan, using underside of small ladle to push puree through strainer. Add remaining 1½ cups sugar and salt to strawberry puree in saucepan and cook over medium-high heat, whisking occasionally, until bubbles begin to appear around sides of pan and sugar is dissolved, about 5 minutes; remove from heat.

4. Sprinkle gelatin over water in large bowl and let sit until gelatin softens, about 5 minutes. Whisk strawberry puree into gelatin. Slice remaining strawberries and stir into strawberry-gelatin mixture. Refrigerate until gelatin thickens slightly and starts to cling to sides of bowl, about 30 minutes. Carefully pour gelatin mixture evenly over whipped cream cheese layer. Refrigerate salad until gelatin is fully set, at least 4 hours or up to 24 hours. Serve.

The American Table
Salad Days

Baked beans, marshmallows, fruit cocktail, flavored gelatin, grated American cheese, ginger ale, sauerkraut . . . Do the words "salad fixings" spring to mind?

Probably not, but then you aren't a well-bred, middle-class lady living at the turn of the 20th century, or in 1920, or even in 1954. Had you been reared on the tenets of the domestic science movement that dominated American cooking in the first half of the 20th century, such a list would indeed have suggested salad. As a "progressive housekeeper," you would have cringed at the very idea of what we call salad today—raw vegetables tossed together. Perish the thought.

To the early 20th-century housewife, such a haphazard arrangement smacked of crudity. As culinary historian Laura Shapiro has detailed in *Perfection Salad: Women and Cooking at the Turn of the Century*, vegetables had to be tamed—boiled to death, smothered in thick white sauce, or, in the case of "salads," confined in dainty asparagus stalk "wheels" and pineapple ring borders. The very best way to render untidy raw vegetables harmless was to encase them in gelatin.

Fortunately, home cooks no longer needed to simmer, strain, and skim calves' feet to make it, nor even purify sheet gelatin. The early 20th-century salad maker need only have reached for commercial powdered gelatin. Then, after molding and chilling her salad, she could gild the lily with a few stuffed prunes, rolled cottage cheese balls, rococo swirls of thinned mayonnaise, and a carved tomato tulip.

Pretzel salad is a direct descendent of such "Festive for Special Occasions Salads," as *Betty Crocker's New Picture Cookbook* grouped similar concoctions as late as 1961. And even today, despite the Cool Whip and the strawberry Jell-O, pretzel salad is not dessert—it's a salad.

Maque Choux

The secret to this humble Cajun dish was getting the texture of the corn right. BY DIANE UNGER

Maque choux is traditionally served over rice.

JUST ABOUT EVERY Cajun family has its own version of *maque choux*, a stewed corn dish that dates back more than 300 years and includes bell pepper, celery, onion, garlic, cayenne, and whatever else you've got around—shrimp, crawfish, tomato, tasso (Louisiana spicy smoked pork). As maque choux (pronounced "mock SHOE") slowly cooks on the stovetop, the starches in the sweet corn come out, making for a creamy, slightly soupy dish.

Following instructions from Louisiana cookbooks, I sautéed vegetables, browned meat, stirred in corn kernels and water, and stewed. An hour later, I understood the challenges: Where was the much-vaunted creaminess? And why were the kernels of corn blowing out? Before addressing those questions, though, I nixed the tasso (delicious but hard to come by) and replaced it with andouille, a more widely sold Cajun sausage. To reinforce its smoky, meaty flavor, I added bacon, using its fat to brown the vegetables.

Instead of merely stripping the corn, I grated two of the eight cobs I was using to encourage faster release of the starches. As I'd hoped, this made for thicker, creamier maque choux. But after 30 minutes, the corn was still blown out. I had been stirring in canned tomatoes at the end. Our science editor suggested I do so at the start instead. The acid in the tomatoes should strengthen the pectin in the corn kernels, preventing blowouts. It worked. I'd perfected my own version.

MAQUE CHOUX Serves 4 to 6

Fresh corn is best. For frozen corn, use 6 cups of thawed kernels; process 1½ cups of kernels with ½ cup of water in a blender until coarsely ground to replace the grated corn in step 1.

8	ears corn, husks and silk removed
4	slices bacon, chopped fine
2	tablespoons vegetable oil
5	ounces andouille sausage, halved lengthwise and sliced thin
1	green bell pepper, stemmed, seeded, and chopped
1	onion, chopped
1	celery rib, minced
	Salt and pepper
4	garlic cloves, minced
1	tablespoon tomato paste
¼	teaspoon cayenne pepper
2	cups water
1	(14.5-ounce) can diced tomatoes, drained with juice reserved
6	scallions, sliced thin

1. Cut kernels from 6 ears of corn. Break remaining 2 ears in half and grate over plate on large holes of box grater. Combine cut kernels, grated corn, and any accumulated corn milk in bowl; set aside. Cook bacon in Dutch oven over medium heat until crisp, 6 to 8 minutes. Using slotted spoon, transfer bacon to bowl with corn.

2. Add oil to rendered bacon fat in pot and return to medium heat. Add andouille and cook until lightly browned, about 2 minutes. Add bell pepper, onion, celery, and ½ teaspoon salt and cook, stirring occasionally, until vegetables begin to soften and brown, 8 to 10 minutes. Stir in garlic, tomato paste, and cayenne and cook until fragrant, about 30 seconds.

3. Stir in corn-bacon mixture, water, and tomatoes and bring to boil, scraping up any browned bits. Reduce heat to low and simmer, stirring often, until liquid has reduced by three-fourths, 25 to 30 minutes. Stir in reserved tomato juice and cook until liquid is reduced by two-thirds and mixture is slightly thickened and creamy, about 10 minutes longer. Off heat, stir in scallions and season with salt and pepper to taste. Serve.

MAQUE CHOUX WITH SHRIMP

Stir in 1½ pounds extra-large shrimp (21 to 25 per pound), peeled and deveined, after tomato juices have reduced in step 3. Cook until shrimp are cooked through, about 5 minutes. Add scallions, and serve.

Tar Heel Pie

This brownie pie should be sweet, not saccharine, and deeply fudgy.
But whenever we got the texture right, the flavor went south—and vice versa. BY SARAH GABRIEL

I FIRST ENCOUNTERED Tar Heel pie in a pie cookbook, and I wondered if it was widely known. When I dug deeper into old food magazines and Southern community cookbooks, I found my answer: There are hundreds—if not thousands—of (very similar) recipes for this pie.

Melt a stick of butter with 1 cup of semisweet chocolate chips; whisk in ½ cup each of brown and granulated sugars, ½ cup of flour, a pinch of salt, and a cup of chopped pecans; pour the batter into an uncooked pie shell; and bake it until the edges brown and the filling sets. One version included shredded coconut and a few called for adding chocolate chunks, but by and large the recipes were identical.

Along the way, I learned that the pie dates back to at least the 1950s, although this particular name came into being only a few decades ago. The story goes that a secretary at a postcard company in North Carolina dubbed "brownie pie" Tar Heel pie. A postcard with a picture of the pie was distributed, and the new name stuck.

I made a few pies—whatever they're called—with and without added coconut and chocolate chunks, and after the team tasted each one, I tallied up the pros and cons. Combine pie and brownie and you should get doubly delicious results, right? Apparently not. The filling was far too sweet, as well as gloppy rather than fudgy, plus the chocolate flavor was wimpy; the underdone crust was more pasty than pastry; and the nuts were mealy.

Some of our problems with the pie (pasty, raw crust and mealy nuts), while significant, were hardly mysterious. None of the recipes that I had found called for a parbaked pie shell or toasted pecans. Buried in wet batter, neither had a chance of crisping up. I'd try starting with a parbaked shell and toasted nuts. Using the filling recipe from the first round with a parbaked shell and toasted pecans, I baked a new pie at 325 degrees until it was set but still moist, about 35 minutes. The filling was still too sweet and lackluster in the chocolate flavor department, but the crust was flaky and the pecans were crunchy.

Encouraged by these early successes, I pressed on. Could curbing the cloying sweetness be as simple as using less sugar? Well, yes and no.

"Sensational New Kind of Pie!" gushed a 1953 magazine ad we unearthed in our research. Tar Heel pie is back and better than ever.

When I eliminated 2 tablespoons each of granulated sugar and brown sugar, the sweetness level was correct, but the pie was bland and no longer fudgy. Sugar behaves like a wet ingredient in baked goods, dissolving in the oven and making the finished product moister. I returned to the original amounts and tried replacing the semisweet chocolate with unsweetened. This pie was dry and brittle, like unsweetened chocolate itself.

I circled back to semisweet chocolate. Brown sugar is moister than granulated, so maybe I could rein in the sweetness without harming the texture by switching to all brown sugar and using less of it. At last, real progress: ¾ cup of brown sugar did just that, plus its molasses undertones bolstered the chocolate flavor.

Adding cocoa powder gave the chocolate flavor an extra push, and doubling the salt and the vanilla extract filled out the background tastes. Since the flavor and the texture were so entangled, I wondered if I could take them both one step further by exchanging the light brown sugar for dark. Flavor, check: The pie now tasted delicious. While conducting these tests, I discovered something interesting: If I mixed the eggs separately with the sugar, the pie developed a crackly, shiny, attractive top.

Nice, but otherwise, the texture still needed work. Going for gooey, I decided to try backing down from the ½ cup of flour. Reducing it by half definitely upped the fudgy factor, but any less and this would be a custard pie. I'd leave the flour at ¼ cup and try to find another way to further tenderize the filling.

Fat can tenderize baked goods, but I was already using a stick of butter; would more be overkill? As I was putting the second stick of butter back in the fridge, I got an idea. Maybe it wasn't more fat I needed but a softer fat—a liquid fat, to be exact. Chewy boxed brownies call for vegetable oil rather than butter, and a few years back a colleague cracked the code to chewy homemade brownies by using a combo of butter and vegetable oil. I made my pie again, this time using 4 tablespoons each of butter and oil. Now the crust wasn't just an extra. For people who like brownies so fudgy and barely cooked that they are too messy to eat out of hand, this pie was a must.

▶ Which store-bought pie dough is best? Read our tasting at CooksCountry.com/piecrusttasting.

FUDGY TAR HEEL PIE Serves 8
Serve with ice cream.

1   (9-inch) single-crust pie dough
1   cup (6 ounces) semisweet chocolate chips
4   tablespoons unsalted butter
¼   cup vegetable oil
2   tablespoons unsweetened cocoa powder
¾   cup packed (5¼ ounces) dark brown sugar
2   large eggs
1   tablespoon vanilla extract
¾   teaspoon salt
¼   cup (1¼ ounces) all-purpose flour
1¼   cups pecans, toasted and chopped coarse

1. Adjust oven rack to lower-middle position and heat oven to 375 degrees. Roll dough into 12-inch circle on lightly floured counter. Loosely roll dough around rolling pin and gently unroll it onto 9-inch pie plate, letting excess dough hang over edge. Ease dough into plate by gently lifting edge of dough with 1 hand while pressing into plate bottom with your other hand. Leave any dough that overhangs plate in place. Trim overhang to ½ inch beyond lip of pie plate. Tuck overhang under itself; folded edge should be flush with edge of pie plate. Crimp dough evenly around edge of pie using your fingers. Wrap dough-lined pie plate loosely in plastic wrap and place in freezer until dough is fully chilled and firm, about 15 minutes.

2. Line chilled pie shell with two 12-inch squares of parchment paper, letting parchment lie over edges of dough, and fill with pie weights. Bake until lightly golden around edges, 18 to 25 minutes. Carefully remove parchment and weights, rotate pie shell, and continue to bake until center begins to look opaque and slightly drier, 3 to 6 minutes. Let cool completely.

3. Reduce oven to 325 degrees. Microwave ⅔ cup chocolate chips and butter in bowl, stirring often, until melted, 60 to 90 seconds. Whisk in oil and cocoa until smooth.

4. In separate bowl, whisk sugar, eggs, vanilla, and salt together until smooth. Whisk chocolate mixture into sugar mixture until incorporated. Stir in flour and remaining ⅓ cup chocolate chips until just combined.

5. Spread pecans in bottom of pie shell, then pour batter over top, using spatula to level. Bake pie until toothpick inserted in center comes out with thin coating of batter attached, 30 to 35 minutes. Let pie cool on wire rack until barely warm, about 1½ hours. Serve. (Pie can be reheated, uncovered, in a 300 degree oven until warm throughout, 10 to 15 minutes.)

TEST KITCHEN DISCOVERY Nut Regimen

1. For better flavor and to ensure that the pecans don't get soggy, toast them in a 350-degree oven for about 5 minutes.

2. Sprinkle the nuts in the bottom of the prebaked pie shell; don't mix them into the filling. This way, the pie shell won't get soggy and the pie will be easy to slice.

TESTING APRONS

We waded through a lot of ruffles, pleats, and chintz—and fronts reading "Kiss the Cook"—to round up seven no-nonsense, utilitarian cooks' aprons in different materials and lengths, priced from $6 to $69. Since grease and other kinds of splatters often land above the waist, we stuck with bib-style aprons. Styles ranged from the most basic, no-pockets, nonadjustable shapes to feature-laden designs such as one that included a towel in its own carrying loop and a built-in corduroy potholder.

We enlisted seven test cooks, including men and women of different heights and girths, to try them all on and assess their comfort and fit. Then we assigned each cook one apron to wear for a week in the kitchen. We got the aprons back, along with an earful about what worked and what didn't. While making our Tar Heel Pie, we saw the advantage of the widest apron of the lot, a 39-inch-wide cotton/linen combination that wrapped completely around all testers and offered handy coverage for chocolate splatters.

Last came our stain-making test: a dousing of yellow mustard, soy sauce, chocolate, and coffee that we let soak into each apron overnight. Not everything came out in the wash. The only apron to get completely clean in one wash was the white Travail Apron from Bragard. This was a nice addition to its other advantages of comfort and coverage. With an adjustable neck strap, long strings that wrap around the back to tie in front, and a chest area reinforced with an extra layer of fabric, it was soft but rugged. Its look is pure practicality—which suits us just fine. –AMY GRAVES

KEY Good ★★★ Fair ★★ Poor ★

HIGHLY RECOMMENDED

	CRITERIA		TESTERS' NOTES
BRAGARD Travail Apron **Model:** 9804-0256 **Price:** $26.95 **Source:** bragardusa.com **Material:** 55% linen/45% cotton **Size:** 39 by 39 in	Protection ★★★ Comfort and Fit ★★★ After Washing ★★★		This wide apron gave cooks total coverage. Its adjustable neck strap ties at the front, as do the long waist strings. Washing instructions call for bleach, which obliterated tough stains, and it's dryer-friendly.

RECOMMENDED WITH RESERVATIONS

	CRITERIA		TESTERS' NOTES
MU KITCHEN MU In Cotton Apron **Model:** 6002-0906 **Price:** $14.99 **Material:** Cotton **Size:** 34.5 by 28 in	Protection ★★★ Comfort and Fit ★★ After Washing ★½		This comfortable cotton apron was long and thick—stains never soaked through and they came out in the wash. But it shrank 3 inches in length and width from five runs through the dryer.
LE CREUSET Chef's Apron **Model:** TH4900-67 **Price:** $39.95 **Material:** Cotton canvas **Size:** 31.5 by 33.5 in	Protection ★★★ Comfort and Fit ★★ After Washing ★½		This thick apron softened after washing, which failed to remove an olive oil stain in five tries. It shrank an inch in the dryer. Two of its four pockets stuck out. But no stains soaked through.
DISH WISH Smart Apron **Model:** 25 **Price:** $34.99 **Material:** Cotton **Size:** 33 by 28 in	Protection ★★ Comfort and Fit ★★ After Washing ★★		The corduroy patch worked for wiping hands or holding pots, and the flat pockets worked well. But the towel stuck out, and the apron shrank and remained stained after five washes.

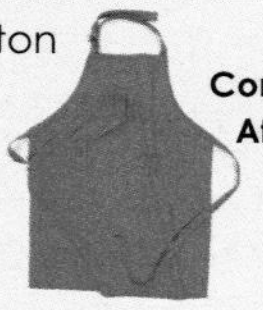

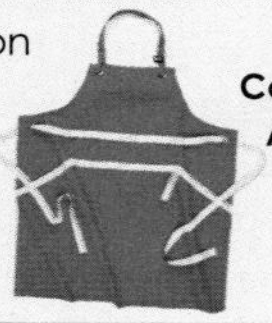

NOT RECOMMENDED

	CRITERIA		TESTERS' NOTES
CHEF WORKS Bib Chef Apron **Model:** APKDC **Price:** $6.15 **Material:** 65% polyester/35% cotton **Size:** 33 by 27.5 in	Protection ★ Comfort and Fit ★★½ After Washing ★		This simple apron felt lightweight and comfortable. But it gaped in the back on larger cooks, and a mustard stain soaked through to clothing. Tougher stains never came out.
LIBECO Amherst Apron **Model:** 82586 **Price:** $69 **Material:** Linen **Size:** 38 by 28 in	Protection ★ Comfort and Fit ★★ After Washing ★		This rough linen apron held on to towels tucked into the waist-level strings, but its tie scratched at our testers' necks. Machine drying is prohibited—an inconvenience. Mustard soaked through and stayed on.
CHEF WORKS Three-Pocket Bib Apron **Model:** F10 **Price:** $14.44 **Material:** 65% polyester/35% cotton **Size:** 24 by 28 in	Protection ★ Comfort and Fit ★ After Washing ½		This apron was not long enough even for our shortest tester. Mustard soaked through the thin fabric and remained after five laundry cycles.

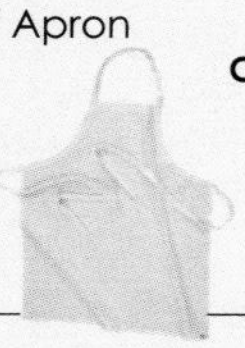

Cooking Class How to Make Barbecued Brisket

Good news: Even without a barbecue pit in your backyard, you can make smoky, succulent barbecued brisket at home. BY REBECCAH MARSTERS

KANSAS CITY BARBECUED BRISKET Serves 8 to 10

To use wood chunks when using a charcoal grill, substitute two medium chunks, soaked in water for 1 hour, for the wood chip packet.

- 1½ tablespoons paprika
- 1½ tablespoons packed brown sugar
- 1 tablespoon chili powder
- 1 tablespoon pepper
- 2 teaspoons salt
- 1 teaspoon granulated garlic
- 1 teaspoon onion powder
- 1 (5- to 6-pound) beef brisket, flat cut, fat trimmed to ¼ inch
- 2 cups wood chips
- 1 (13 by 9-inch) disposable aluminum roasting pan
- 1 cup ketchup
- 1 cup water
- 3 tablespoons molasses
- 1 tablespoon hot sauce

1. Combine paprika, sugar, chili powder, pepper, salt, granulated garlic, and onion powder in small bowl. Cut ½-inch crosshatch pattern through brisket fat cap, ¼ inch deep. Rub brisket with spice mixture. Wrap brisket in plastic wrap and refrigerate for at least 6 or up to 24 hours. Just before grilling, soak wood chips in water for 15 minutes, then drain. Using large piece of heavy-duty aluminum foil, wrap soaked chips in foil packet

and cut several vent holes in top.

2A. FOR A CHARCOAL GRILL: Open bottom vent halfway. Light large chimney starter filled with charcoal briquettes (6 quarts). When top coals are partially covered with ash, pour evenly over half of grill. Place wood chip packet on coals. Set cooking grate in place, cover, and open lid vent halfway. Heat grill until hot and wood chips are smoking, about 5 minutes.

2B. FOR A GAS GRILL: Place wood chip packet over primary burner. Turn all burners to high, cover, and heat grill until hot and wood chips are smoking, about 15 minutes. Leave primary burner on high and turn off other burners.

3. Pat brisket dry with paper towels and transfer to disposable pan. Set pan with brisket on cooler side of grill and cook, covered, with lid vent positioned above brisket, for 2 hours.

4. Adjust oven rack to lower-middle position and heat oven to 300 degrees. Whisk ketchup, water, molasses, and hot sauce together in bowl and pour over brisket. Cover pan tightly with foil and transfer to oven. Cook until brisket registers 195 degrees, 2½ to 3 hours. Turn off heat and let brisket rest in oven for 1 hour.

5. Transfer brisket to carving board. Skim fat from sauce. Slice brisket against grain into ¼-inch-thick slices. Serve with sauce.

Core Techniques

Whether you're in Kansas City, Texas, or your own backyard, the key to good barbecued brisket is the right balance of smoke, fat, moisture, and tenderness. A low temperature for a long period of time is a given for this tough cut of meat. We've developed a few other strategies as well.

TEST KITCHEN TIPS FOR ANY BARBECUED BRISKET

Keep the Fat (and Score It)

Most steaks and roasts are marbled with fat throughout. Not flat-cut brisket. It has a large cap of fat, but the meat itself is fairly lean and prone to dry out. For moist meat, buy a brisket with a considerable fat cap. Trim any hard or particularly thick fat off, but leave at least ¼ inch attached. Then score the fat in a crosshatch pattern to encourage it to render and baste the brisket as it cooks.

Go from Grill to Oven

A Texas pit master might scoff, but for home cooks, using the oven is the key to moist, tender barbecued brisket. You need the grill for smoke—that's nonnegotiable. But to cook a brisket all the way to tenderness on a charcoal grill (our preferred grill for this recipe), you would need to keep the fire lit and at a constant temperature for more than 5 hours, carefully monitoring it and refueling with fresh charcoal at least once. It's much easier to regulate the heat in the oven, so after grilling it for a few hours, we finish our brisket in the oven, low and slow. Don't reverse the process. If you go from oven to grill, the smoke flavor will never permeate the meat.

Position the Vents

To keep charcoal lit, you need air flow in the grill—fire needs oxygen to burn. The bottom and lid vents provide the ventilation. The lid vent has another important function, too: It directs the path of the smoke coming off the wood chips, drawing it out of the grill. By placing the vent above the brisket, you direct the smoke right where you want it: over the meat. (This is moot on gas grills, as most don't have lid vents.)

Give It Time

There is no hurrying a brisket. To season it deeply, we coat it with a spice rub and let it rest for at least 6 hours. The salt in the rub penetrates and seasons the meat. For large cuts like brisket, season for 24 hours if you can. Give brisket plenty of time to cook, too. The tough connective tissue, collagen, will slowly break down into gelatin; gelatin dissolves in the moisture within the meat. Remain patient, even after the brisket is cooked. As meat cooks, the muscle fibers contract, squeezing out moisture. Let it rest in its own juices—at least an hour and as long as overnight. During the rest, the brisket reabsorbs some moisture and becomes more flavorful.

Twelve Steps to Kansas City Barbecued Brisket

1. TRIM THE FAT
Use a knife to trim the brisket's fat cap to ¼ inch.
WHY? You want a glossy sauce not a greasy one.

2. SCORE THE MEAT
Cut a crosshatch pattern in the remaining fat cap.
WHY? To help the fat render and let the flavors of the rub permeate the brisket.

3. RUB AND WAIT
Massage the rub into the brisket. Then wrap the brisket in plastic, refrigerate, and wait.
WHY? Salting the meat draws moisture to its surface. The moisture dissolves the salt, and then the meat reabsorbs it, which seasons the meat.

4. SET IN PAN
Blot the brisket dry and place it in a disposable pan.
WHY? A dry brisket forms a better crust. The pan keeps the brisket from burning while letting it develop char and absorb smoke. And it catches the juices for the sauce.

5. MAKE FOIL PACKET
Briefly soak the wood chips (hickory is traditional) in water, drain, and wrap in foil. Cut vent holes.
WHY? For subtle smokiness. Wrapped, the chips won't burn too fast, while the vents let the smoke escape gradually and flavor the brisket.

6. BUILD TWO-LEVEL FIRE
Pour a full chimney of charcoal briquettes in an even layer over half of the grill. Place the wood chip packet on top of the coals and let the grill heat up.
WHY? This setup creates a cooler side, where the brisket can cook relatively gently.

7. SMOKE BRISKET
Once the wood chips start to smoke, place the brisket in its pan on the grill, opposite the coals. Cook, covered, for 2 hours.
WHY? Smoke needs plenty of time to penetrate such a large hunk of meat. It wouldn't be barbecue without smoke.

8. BUILD SAUCE
After removing the brisket from the grill, whisk ketchup, water, molasses, and hot sauce together and pour over brisket.
WHY? For deep, spicy-sweet flavor. Adding the sauce before the brisket moves to the oven allows it to flavor the meat and vice versa.

9. MOVE TO OVEN
Seal the disposable pan with foil and move it to a 300-degree oven.
WHY? It takes hours for brisket to tenderize. Instead of refueling the grill, we finish the meat in the oven, roasting it for 2½ to 3 hours.

10. LET COOL IN OVEN
When the meat reaches 195 degrees, turn off the oven. Let the brisket rest in the cooling oven for an hour.
WHY? As the meat gently cools, it can reabsorb some of the flavorful juices it expelled.

11. DEFAT SAUCE
Move the meat to a cutting board. Skim the fat from the surface of the sauce, or pour the juices into a fat separator.
WHY? You don't want to ruin your brisket with greasy sauce.

12. SLICE AND ENJOY
Slice the brisket across the grain and serve it with the sauce.
WHY? The brisket is a hard-working muscle with a heavy grain. Slicing across the grain ensures that it's tender.

Anatomy of a Brisket
Cut from the breast of the cow, a whole brisket weighs about 12 pounds. It's a well-exercised muscle, which makes for coarse-grained, tough meat. Butchers usually break down whole briskets into two cuts: The flat (or first) cut is separated from the point (or second) cut by a thick layer of fat that runs diagonally through the fat end of the brisket. The knobby, irregularly shaped point cut is more marbled and has more overall fat. Few grocery stores carry it. Here in the test kitchen, we prefer the thinner, rectangular flat cut anyhow; it's leaner and once cooked is easier to slice. The flat cut usually weighs about 5 pounds, although butchers occasionally break it down further into two (2- to 3-pound) roasts.

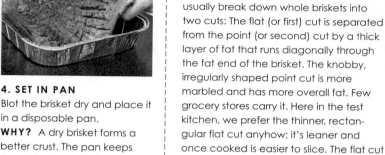

POINT CUT
Irregularly shaped.

FLAT CUT
Cooks—and slices—evenly.

ESSENTIAL GEAR
Slicing Knife
A good slicing knife should be about 12 inches long, have a thin blade with heft and balance, and be slightly flexible yet have enough sturdiness to ensure a straight cutting path. In our tests, knives with small, oval scallops cut out of either side along the blade, a style known as a granton edge, cut the thinnest slices with the least effort. The hollows allow for a razor-thin cutting edge while maintaining heft at the top of the blade. A rounded tip is also essential. It prevents the blade from getting caught as it slices the meat. But the most important characteristic is sharpness. Most knives are sharp when they're new, but the best knives hold an edge for longer.

OUR FAVORITE SLICER
Victorinox 12-Inch Granton Edge Slicing Knife.

Slow Cooker Ratatouille

Normally, ratatouille cooks uncovered to let moisture evaporate. So how do you get this summery vegetable stew to work in the slow cooker, where the lid stays on the whole time? BY CAROLYNN PURPURA MACKAY

THE KEY TO great ratatouille is cooking down the tomatoes, eggplant, zucchini, onions, and peppers so that their moisture is driven off and their flavors concentrate and meld into a thick, intensely satisfying mélange. Most of this cooking is done with the pan(s) uncovered so the moisture that comes out of these juicy vegetables can evaporate. While ratatouille could be considered a stew—and slow cookers are literally built for cooking stews—it is a stew that requires evaporation. And evaporation is the appliance's Achilles' heel.

Recipes abound for slow-cooker ratatouille, and they are more or less all the same: Chop your vegetables and toss them into the insert with tomatoes (often canned), salt, pepper, and herbs; throw on the lid; turn on the slow cooker; and wait. Seems awfully simple, right? I collected five such recipes, hoping the recipe writers knew something that I didn't about making this dish in the slow cooker. When I went back to the slow cookers 4 hours later, I found a collection of messes—bloated, soggy vegetables bobbing in puddles of bland liquid. Just as I suspected, I needed to find a way to get rid of that excess liquid.

I started with the tomatoes, the most watery vegetable in the mix. The recipes I'd made called for either chopped fresh tomatoes, canned diced tomatoes, or tomato sauce. But since moisture was the enemy here, I hoped to find a drier tomato product. My mind immediately went to tomato paste—thicker and far less watery and the very essence of concentrated tomato. I was sure this would solve my problems—but it didn't. The ratatouille made with tomato paste had unevenly cooked vegetables—some were tender; others still seemed raw.

To finish, we stir in Parmesan cheese. Yes, it's Italian, but who's quibbling? It suits ratatouille.

It turns out that the liquid was holding the temperature in the cooker constant; without it (and without stirring), the vegetables nearest the heating element were cooking through while those farther away were not. I lost the tomato paste and tested fresh tomatoes, sauce, and canned diced tomatoes again, eventually settling on the last for its appealing chunks and inherent moisture (I drained them so I had more control over the texture). The moral of the story: You need some, but not too much, liquid in the slow cooker to ensure that the vegetables cook properly.

Time to move on to the eggplant, another notoriously watery vegetable. I knew I'd need to get rid of some of its moisture before it went into the slow cooker, so I tried sautéing cubed eggplant. This produced good ratatouille but took more hands-on work than I wanted. Turning to the oven, I considered roasting but wondered if broiling would be faster and also give me better (read: more flavorful) browning. I cut the eggplant into chunks, tossed the chunks with a little olive oil, and broiled them for about 10 minutes until they had nicely shrunken and browned.

The batch of ratatouille made with the broiled eggplant was so much better that I wondered if there would be additional improvement if I broiled the zucchini, peppers, and onions, too. For the next batch I mixed all the vegetables except the canned diced tomatoes in a bowl with olive oil, sugar, garlic, and herbes de Provence and broiled them for 10 minutes (I had to do this in two batches). I then put the browned, softened vegetables in the slow cooker and stirred in the tomatoes and flour. The vegetables were cooked through after 4 hours on low; I finished the ratatouille with Parmesan cheese and fresh basil. My tasters and I agreed that my work was done here. With a little help from the broiler, I had rich, complex, tender slow-cooker ratatouille that tasted just as good as the stovetop version.

SLOW-COOKER RATATOUILLE
Serves 8 to 10
Herbes de Provence is a French blend that usually includes rosemary, marjoram, thyme, lavender, and fennel. If you can't find it, you can use 1 teaspoon each of dried rosemary and dried thyme.

- 2 pounds eggplant, cut into ½-inch pieces
- 3 zucchini (8 ounces each), quartered lengthwise and cut into 1-inch pieces
- 2 red bell peppers, stemmed, seeded, and cut into ½-inch pieces
- 2 onions, chopped
- ½ cup extra-virgin olive oil
- 1 tablespoon sugar
- 2 garlic cloves, minced
- 2 teaspoons herbes de Provence
- 1 (28-ounce) can diced tomatoes, drained
- ¼ cup all-purpose flour
  Salt and pepper
- ¼ cup grated Parmesan cheese
- ¼ cup chopped fresh basil

1. Adjust oven rack 4 inches from broiler element and heat broiler. Line 2 rimmed baking sheets with aluminum foil and spray with vegetable oil spray. Combine eggplant, zucchini, bell peppers, onions, 6 tablespoons oil, sugar, garlic, and herbes de Provence in large bowl. Divide vegetables evenly between prepared sheets and spread in single layer. Broil, 1 sheet at a time, until vegetables begin to brown, 10 to 12 minutes, rotating sheet halfway through broiling. Transfer broiled vegetables and tomatoes to slow cooker.

2. Stir flour, 2½ teaspoons salt, and 1 teaspoon pepper into vegetables in slow cooker. Cover and cook until vegetables are tender, about 4 hours on low. Stir in Parmesan, basil, and remaining 2 tablespoons oil. Season with salt and pepper to taste. Serve.

Get Rid of Excess Moisture
Many of the vegetables in ratatouille—eggplant and zucchini to name two—contain a lot of water. Since it can't evaporate in the slow cooker, it waters down the ratatouille.
To get the vegetables to release moisture before we slow-cook them, we brown them under the broiler first. Its high heat evaporates the moisture, and the browning boosts flavor, too.

BROIL FIRST
Broiling the vegetables adds flavor and prevents soupy ratatouille.

Sure, packaged couscous is convenient, but it comes out mushy, and the packaged spices are second-rate. With a clever technique and a few mix-ins, our couscous is consistently fluffy and flavorful. BY CRISTIN WALSH

COUSCOUS, WHICH LOOKS like a small grain but is actually pasta made from semolina flour and water, dates back centuries as a staple of Mediterranean diets. These days, it can be found in every American supermarket, boxed and usually accompanied by a spice packet for convenience. Thankfully, the test kitchen has found a way to draw big flavor out of this tiny pasta—and it starts with throwing away the dusty-tasting spice packet.

Back-of-the-box instructions tell cooks to boil water (or broth) and butter or oil, stir in the couscous, let the mixture sit off heat for 5 minutes while the pasta absorbs the water, and then fluff with a fork before serving. But the result is often soggy, mushy grains that clump together. And bad as the spice packet is, without it, the couscous needs a flavor boost.

The test kitchen's method borrows a technique used for rice pilaf to keep the pearls of couscous fluffy and separate and add flavor at the same time: We toast the grains in butter. We melt butter in a pot and add the couscous, stirring the tiny pasta granules until they are lightly browned and have a nutty aroma. The toasting sets the proteins in the pasta, which helps set the shape of the starch granules and prevents them from absorbing too much water (thus turning to mush).

These salads are not only tasty but fast, too: The couscous cooks in just 12 minutes.

The toasting also deepens the flavor of the couscous. At this point, we add the liquid, a combination of water and chicken broth for its savory but not overwhelming flavor.

This method for basic couscous is a great jumping-off point for flavorful salads: Couscous takes well to dressing up. To get the couscous primped for the company of other ingredients, I added minced garlic to the butter before toasting it. Then I settled on a formula of dressing the cooked pasta with an olive oil, citrus, and herb vinaigrette as the main flavor-delivery system.

I flavored my most basic version of couscous salad with Mediterranean ingredients that have long been paired with this tiny pasta: fresh parsley, scallions, lemon juice, and toasted almonds, the last for crunch. I crafted one elegant variation with arugula, pecans, dried cherries, and crumbled goat cheese.

While playing with different ingredients, I discovered that couscous takes very well to Latin flavors, which led to two more salads: one with chorizo, orange, cilantro, and cashews (not strictly a Latin ingredient, but we liked them here), and another with cumin, lime, more cilantro, and roasted pepitas (pumpkin seeds). Finally, for a Greek-inspired salad, I used red onion, cucumber, feta cheese, and kalamata olives.

LEMON AND PARSLEY COUSCOUS SALAD
Serves 4 to 6
You can eat the salad immediately, but it will improve if you let the flavors meld for 30 minutes or so.

- 2 tablespoons unsalted butter
- 2 garlic cloves, minced
- 2 cups couscous
- 1 cup water
- 1 cup chicken broth
  Salt and pepper
- 1 cup sliced almonds, toasted
- 6 tablespoons extra-virgin olive oil
- ¼ cup chopped fresh parsley
- 4 scallions, sliced thin
- 3 tablespoons lemon juice

1. Melt butter in medium saucepan over medium-high heat. Stir in garlic and cook until fragrant, about 30 seconds. Add couscous and cook, stirring frequently, until grains begin to brown, about 5 minutes. Add water, broth, and 1 teaspoon salt; stir briefly to combine, cover, and remove pan from heat. Let stand until liquid is absorbed and couscous is tender, about 7 minutes. Uncover and fluff couscous with fork.

2. Combine almonds, oil, parsley, scallions, and lemon juice in large bowl. Stir in couscous until well combined. Season with salt and pepper to taste. Serve.

CHERRY AND GOAT CHEESE COUSCOUS SALAD
In step 2, substitute 1 cup pecans, toasted and chopped, for almonds and 1 cup chopped arugula for parsley. Add 1 cup dried cherries, chopped, and 1 cup crumbled goat cheese.

CHORIZO AND ORANGE COUSCOUS SALAD
In step 1, add 6 ounces chopped Spanish-style chorizo sausage to melted butter in saucepan (before adding garlic) and cook until lightly browned, about 2 minutes. Proceed with step 1, adding ½ teaspoon cayenne pepper to couscous with broth. In step 2, substitute 1 cup roasted cashews, chopped, for almonds; ½ cup chopped fresh cilantro for parsley; and 1 teaspoon grated orange zest plus ¼ cup orange juice for lemon juice.

CILANTRO AND PEPITA COUSCOUS SALAD
In step 1, add 2½ teaspoons ground cumin and ½ teaspoon cayenne pepper to couscous with broth. In step 2, substitute roasted, salted pepitas for almonds; ½ cup chopped fresh cilantro for parsley; and 3 tablespoons lime juice (2 limes) for lemon juice.

FETA AND OLIVE COUSCOUS SALAD
In step 2, substitute 1 finely chopped small red onion for scallions. Add 1½ cups crumbled feta cheese; 1 cucumber, peeled, seeded, and chopped fine; and 1 cup pitted kalamata olives, chopped coarse.

TEST KITCHEN TECHNIQUE
Toast to Maximize Flavor

Most recipes call for pouring the liquid over the couscous, covering it, and waiting. We add a lot of flavor, and improve the texture, by first toasting the couscous on the stovetop in garlicky butter. Stir the grains frequently while they are toasting to keep them from burning.

Recipe Makeover Blondies

To lighten up blondies, we'd need to get rid of more than half of the butter. But when we did so, our problems cascaded. BY CAROLYNN PURPURA MACKAY

SURE WE WANT to cut fat and calories from our diets, but give up blondies? Not on your life. The chewy, golden, butterscotch-flavored cousin to brownies has been a favorite of mine since grade school. I'd just have to find a way to slim them down.

There is no shortage of low-fat blondie recipes, but they are indisputably weird. Ordinary blondies are made from butter, brown sugar, flour, eggs, vanilla extract, leavener, chocolate chips, and nuts. The recipes that I found tried every trick in the book to replace the fat and sugar, from mashed chickpeas, apple juice, fake sugars, and carob chips to pureed pumpkin and egg substitutes. Trying to rein in my skepticism, I pulled out mixing bowls and tested them.

After I tasted the results, my initial fears were confirmed; they were uniformly horrible. Switching course, I pulled out our own terrific recipe for full-fat blondies, intending to trim where I could. The primary trouble was easy to pinpoint: 12 tablespoons of butter for 16 bars. To get even close to making my fat allowance, I'd need to cut that back by more than half. I tried just straight-out slashing it to the requisite 5 tablespoons but immediately ran into three big problems. First, because butter adds moisture as well as fat, the batter was so dry that I could barely mix it. Second, because butter both carries flavor and has so much flavor itself, the blondies were practically tasteless. And third, because fat is essential to chewiness, these blondies had lost their distinctive chew. I'd need to find ingredients to mimic each of these qualities.

To moisten the batter, I stirred in, by turns, buttermilk, nonfat yogurt, skim milk, and even water. These turned what should be chewy blondies ever more cakey. Changing course, I tried supplementing the butter with almond butter, thinking it could replace both butter and nuts. Unfortunately, it covered up the butterscotch that is the hallmark of a good blondie. At this point, I got a kooky idea: I'd go up on the moist brown sugar. Sure, it was counterintuitive for a recipe makeover, but I'd cut so many (butter) calories already that I had some leeway, and it wouldn't add any fat. As I'd hoped, an extra ¼ cup of brown sugar moistened the batter further, and it helpfully underlined the butterscotch flavor.

But while the brown sugar was an improvement, the batter was still dry and the blondies themselves cakey. Our science editor suggested that I add vinegar. Beyond the obvious fact that it would add moisture, he said that if I combined the vinegar with the eggs, the acid would begin to coagulate the proteins, providing the bars with more chewy structure. I tried it, combining 1½ teaspoons of cider vinegar with the eggs. Amazingly, this batter baked into properly chewy blondies.

But my fat count still wasn't low enough. Getting rid of egg yolks is a basic makeover strategy, so I decided to try replacing the two whole eggs in our full-fat recipe with an equal volume of egg whites (I'd need four). But as one taster commented, with so little tenderizing fat this was "one tough blonde." I restored one whole egg, using it in combination with two whites. Better.

Now that I'd solved the triple problems created by drastically cutting the butter, it was time to think about the nuts and chocolate, which also add considerable fat and calories. To mimic their crunch, I tested a range of substitutes, including Grape-Nuts cereal, chopped-up Heath bars (actually less fat, believe it or not), and steel-cut and regular oats. A few of these things (like the Heath bars) changed blondies into something they weren't (like toffee squares). Another (the Grape-Nuts) just wasn't good, adding grit, not crunch. In the end, I stuck with both the nuts and the chocolate but in smaller quantities than in the original recipe. To get the same mileage out of less, I toasted the nuts and replaced the chocolate chips with gooier chopped bar chocolate.

My grade school favorite was still delicious, but now I could eat it with a clear conscience.

The Numbers
Nutritional information is for one blondie.
Traditional Blondies
CALORIES **310**
FAT **18 g**   SATURATED FAT **8 g**

***Cook's Country* Reduced-Fat Blondies**
CALORIES **220**
FAT **7 g**   SATURATED FAT **3.5 g**

The secret to our tasty Reduced-Fat Blondies? Moderation (and a little vinegar).

REDUCED-FAT BLONDIES
Makes 16 blondies
Use room-temperature ingredients, which will make the batter easier to spread.

- 2 cups (10 ounces) all-purpose flour
- ¾ teaspoon salt
- ¼ teaspoon baking soda
- 1¾ cups packed (12¼ ounces) brown sugar
- 5 tablespoons unsalted butter, melted
- 1 large egg plus 2 large whites, room temperature
- 4 teaspoons vanilla extract
- 1½ teaspoons cider vinegar
- 2 ounces bittersweet chocolate, chopped fine
- ¼ cup pecans, toasted and chopped

1. Adjust oven rack to middle position and heat oven to 350 degrees. Make foil sling for 13 by 9-inch baking pan by folding 2 long sheets of aluminum foil; first sheet should be 13 inches wide and second sheet should be 9 inches wide. Lay sheets of foil in pan perpendicular to each other, with extra foil hanging over edges of pan. Push foil into corners and up sides of pan, smoothing foil flush to pan. Lightly spray with vegetable oil spray.

2. Whisk flour, salt, and baking soda together in bowl. Whisk sugar, melted butter, egg and whites, vanilla, and vinegar together in large bowl until smooth. Stir in flour mixture, chocolate and pecans with rubber spatula until just combined.

3. Transfer batter to prepared pan and smooth top. Bake until toothpick inserted in center comes out with few moist crumbs attached, 17 to 20 minutes, rotating pan halfway through baking. Let blondies cool completely in pan on wire rack, about 2 hours. Using foil overhang, lift blondies out of pan. Cut into 16 pieces and serve.

Don't Do It!
We found "diet" blondie recipes that called for ingredients like canned pumpkin, apple juice, carob chips, and, yes, even canned chickpeas.

Biscuits are delicious. Peaches are delicious. So why, when you combine them, is the sum of the parts less than the whole? BY REBECCAH MARSTERS

I LOVE EATING peach cobbler, but making it is another story. Rustic and homey, it looks like it's casually tossed together. In fact, it's a troublemaker. The juiciness that makes a raw ripe peach so luscious out of hand is precisely what waters down and washes out cobbler filling and drenches biscuit crust. To prepare peach cobbler for two—or four or eight or any number—I'd need, in effect, to wring out the juice.

Most cobblers are made by stirring sliced raw peaches with sugar and a little flour (or cornstarch) to thicken. The peach mixture is topped with biscuit dough and baked. The result? To repeat: soggy biscuits and bland filling. That's why I immediately turned to a test kitchen technique designed to handle juicy fruit. I tossed the peach slices with the sugar and let them sit for half an hour. This maceration draws out the juice, which I then drained and discarded. Now I stirred in the flour, put the mixture into ramekins, and topped each with drop biscuits (made using a test kitchen recipe that I quartered to serve two). When I took the ramekins out of the oven about 20 minutes later, it appeared that I'd overcorrected. The cobblers were dry, and by throwing out the flavorful peach juice, I'd thrown out much of the flavor.

The next time I made the cobblers, I saved the strained juice, cooked it on the stovetop to concentrate it, and returned the thicker, more flavorful liquid to the peaches. The technique worked, but it felt awfully fussy for what I thought of as an easy dessert.

Should I reconsider using flour? It occurred to me that perhaps the timing was to blame. Only after the peaches released all their juice during baking would the flour get to work thickening that juice. But in the meantime, the damage had been done: The biscuits were soggy.

What if I thickened the peach juice before introducing the topping? This time, I melted butter in a skillet, added the peaches, and cooked them—covered to speed up their cooking—until the juice just began to flow and bubble. Then I stirred in the sugar and the flour mixed with a little water to make a "slurry," which prevents flour lumps). I divided this cooked filling between the ramekins, dropped on the biscuits,

Sauté the peaches in a skillet for syrupy juices, dollop on the topping, and then put the whole skillet in the oven.

and baked the cobblers. Bingo—thick, syrupy peaches and crisp biscuits.

Throughout my testing, tasters had been fighting over the especially tasty bits of cobbler where the peaches caramelized at the edges of the ramekins. To spread that delicious flavor around, I switched from the white sugar I'd been using to brown sugar, and I stirred it in the skillet with the butter so it could begin to caramelize before I added the fruit. I also introduced lemon juice for brightness and vanilla extract and cinnamon to round out the flavors.

As for the topping, I made just one small adjustment: sprinkling sugar over the raw biscuits to give the cobbler a slight crackly crunch. One afternoon, I was divvying up peaches and biscuit dough between ramekins when I got to wondering why I was bothering. Since I was sautéing the peaches in a skillet, why not just dollop the topping on and place the entire skillet in the oven? I tried it in an 8-inch skillet. When I pulled the skillet from the oven, the biscuits were golden and the peach juice gurgling. I had two generous portions, plus the

additional surface area had given the topping extra room to crisp. Admiring my handiwork, I had a happy thought: Now that I know how to make a perfect peach cobbler for two, I can have it whenever I like.

DON'T MAKE THIS MISTAKE

Soggy Biscuit, Flavorless Filling
Peaches are very juicy. That's part of their appeal and—when it comes to cobbler—their challenge. We precook the fruit, concentrating its juice and flavors, and ensuring that wet peaches don't produce soggy biscuits that spread rather than rise.

CRUMMY COBBLER

PEACH COBBLER FOR TWO

If you use frozen peaches, don't thaw them, but do increase their cooking time in step 1 to about 7 minutes. A serrated peeler makes quick work of peeling fresh peaches. If you don't have buttermilk, combine ¼ cup of milk with 1 teaspoon of lemon juice and let the mixture sit for 10 minutes before proceeding with step 2 of the recipe.

FILLING
- 3 tablespoons packed brown sugar
- 1 tablespoon unsalted butter
- ⅛ teaspoon salt
- ⅛ teaspoon ground cinnamon
- 1¼ pounds fresh peaches, peeled, halved, pitted, and cut into ½-inch wedges, or 1 pound frozen sliced peaches
- 1 tablespoon water
- 1½ teaspoons lemon juice
- 1 teaspoon all-purpose flour
- ½ teaspoon vanilla extract

TOPPING
- ½ cup (2½ ounces) all-purpose flour
- 2 tablespoons plus 1 teaspoon granulated sugar
- ½ teaspoon baking powder
- ⅛ teaspoon baking soda
- ⅛ teaspoon salt
- ¼ cup buttermilk
- 2 tablespoons unsalted butter, melted

1. FOR THE FILLING: Adjust oven rack to middle position and heat oven to 400 degrees. Combine sugar, butter, salt, and cinnamon in 8-inch ovensafe skillet over medium-high heat. Cook until sugar is dissolved, about 2 minutes. Add peaches and cook, covered, until peaches release their juice, about 5 minutes. Whisk water, lemon juice, and flour together in bowl and stir into peaches. Off heat, stir in vanilla. Cover and set aside.

2. FOR THE TOPPING: Whisk flour, 2 tablespoons sugar, baking powder, baking soda, and salt together in bowl. Add buttermilk and butter and stir until dough forms.

3. Using spoon, drop 1-inch pieces of dough evenly over hot peach mixture in skillet. Sprinkle with remaining 1 teaspoon sugar and bake until topping is golden brown, 20 to 25 minutes. Let cool on wire rack for 20 minutes. Serve.

Equipment Review Small Slow Cookers

We looked for a model that was consistent and easy to use—and could guarantee perfectly cooked dinners.

BY TAIZETH SIERRA

KEY **Good** ★★★   **Fair** ★★   **Poor** ★

RECOMMENDED		CRITERIA		TESTERS' NOTES

CUISINART 4-Quart Programmable Slow Cooker
Model: PSC-400
Price: $79.95
Source: cuisinart.com
Controls: Digital programmable
Maximum Temperature: 186 degrees on low, 212 degrees on high

Cooking ★★★
Design ★★½

This model produced perfect chicken, steaks, and ribs. Its programmable timer can be set to cook for up to 24 hours and then automatically switches over to "keep warm" for another 8 hours. We also like its dishwasher-safe insert, large handles, and retractable cord for easy storage. Our only gripe: Its big, square casing is bulky, taking up almost as much counter space as our 6-quart slow cooker does.

HAMILTON BEACH Stay or Go 4-Quart Slow Cooker
Model: 33246T
Price: $26.99
Source: hamiltonbeach.com
Controls: Manual
Maximum Temperature: 191 degrees on low, 206 degrees on high

Cooking ★★★
Design ★★

BEST BUY

This cooker performed well, producing perfect ribs, steak, and chicken. A gasket and clips on the lid let you take your cooker to a potluck without risking spills. It's comparatively low-tech: The "off," "low," "high," and "warm" settings are on a manual dial—which is its drawback. You can't set it to turn off or switch to "keep warm" on its own.

RECOMMENDED WITH RESERVATIONS

WEST BEND 4 Qt. Oval Crockery Cooker
Model: 84384
Price: $29.99
Controls: Manual
Maximum Temperature: 209 degrees on low, 212 degrees on high

Cooking ★★
Design ★★

This model performed fine with chicken Provençal, bringing the thighs north of 140 degrees in about an hour. It cooked steak to tenderness (although the sauce scorched slightly). But ribs developed a tough leathery crust wherever they touched the hot bottom of the insert. The model is manually controlled, which means you must switch off the cooker to stop cooking.

BREVILLE the Risotto Plus
Model: BRC600XL
Price: $129.99
Controls: Digital programmable
Maximum Temperature: 212 degrees on low, 212 degrees on high

Cooking ★★
Design ★½

This 4-quart model is a slow cooker, rice cooker, and risotto maker, and it works OK, as long as you don't cook low-moisture recipes, like our ribs, which turned into jerky. The instruction manual calls for a greater minimum amount of liquid than we call for in some of our recipes. The insert lacks handles and is the only insert that isn't dishwasher-safe. On the plus side, the sauté function worked perfectly—no need to brown foods in a separate pan before placing them in the slow cooker.

PROCTOR SILEX 4 Quart Slow Cooker
Model: 33043
Price: $19.99
Controls: Manual
Maximum Temperature: 192 degrees on low, 209 degrees on high

Cooking ★★
Design ★½

The least expensive model we tested, this cooker produced good chicken and steaks. But without liquid to buffer the ribs, the very hot surface of the insert burned their edges and overcooked them; plus, when we removed the ribs, they fell apart. Because the cooker is manually controlled, you can't set it to turn off or switch to "keep warm." The insert's handles were small.

NOT RECOMMENDED

CROCK-POT 4-Qt. Programmable Slow Cooker
Model: PVP400-S
Price: $39.99
Controls: Digital programmable
Maximum Temperature: 195 degrees on low, 203 degrees on high

Cooking ★
Design ★

While this model is programmable, it has silly limits: You can set it for only 4 to 6 hours on high or 8 to 10 hours on low, and the warm setting runs for only 1 hour—as opposed to 8 hours with our winner. If you're making a recipe that has to cook for 3 hours, say, you're out of luck. While ribs cooked fine, the steaks were tough, and the chicken thighs never passed 169 degrees—short of our desired 175 degrees (although safe to eat).

CALPHALON 4 Qt. Digital Slow Cooker
Model: 1793835
Price: $79.95
Controls: Digital programmable
Maximum Temperature: 206 degrees on low, 210 degrees on high

Cooking ★
Design ★

With its easy-to-set timer and digital controls, this model seemed promising. The elongated rectangular shape fit foods nicely, and we liked the large handles on the dishwasher-safe insert. Chicken cooked well and its abundant sauce thickened perfectly. However, sauces in other tests burned in the oversized insert. Steaks were overcooked and onions burned. Ribs tasted bitter and scorched.

CROCK-POT Manual Slow Cooker
Model: SCV401-TR
Price: $24.99
Controls: Manual
Maximum Temperature: 189 degrees on low, 204 degrees on high

Cooking ½
Design ★½

Chicken thighs never reached a safe temperature. The water-temperature performance was inconsistent, and cooking results reflected that. We retested the model by ordering other copies, but we had the same problems. While manual controls were our only design gripe, this model's cooking was fatally flawed.

WE USED TO turn to our slow cooker only when we were cooking for company or making a big batch of stew meant to last for several meals (our favorite model holds 6 quarts). But these days, many manufacturers are selling smaller models, too, offering the same set-it-and-forget-it convenience to small families—or for small kitchens. (For comparison, a 6-quart slow cooker can fit eight chicken thighs or more; smaller cookers fit about four thighs.)

To assess these smaller versions, we bought eight 4-quart models priced from about $20 to $130. Half featured digital programmable timers; the rest had manual controls that can't be programmed. One model lets you brown food right in the pot rather than in a separate pan and doubles as a rice and risotto cooker. Another has a latching lid so that it can travel without spills.

Slow cookers are designed to cook food gently over a long period of time. Such low-and-slow cooking turns tough meats tender and succulent and produces flavorful sauces and stews. We looked for a model that would heat up quickly to get food into the safe zone and then maintain a simmer; according to the U.S. Food and Drug Administration, the meat's internal temperature must reach at least 140 degrees within 2 hours.

A good slow cooker should also produce perfect results on both low and high settings, and in recipes with lots of sauce or very little. For our first test, we made chicken thighs in a hearty tomato sauce, a recipe that has plenty of liquid and cooks on high for 3 to 4 hours. All but one of the cookers easily reached a safe 140 degrees in less than 2 hours. And even after 5 hours that same problem cooker—plus one other model—failed to bring the chicken to doneness (175 degrees). The other models produced juicy chicken in nice thick, chunky sauces.

Next we made smothered steaks for two, which braise for 4 to 5 hours on the high setting with a moderate amount of liquid. Here one of the models that had struggled in the previous test produced tough, chewy steaks; two other models ran hot and scorched the sauce. But the rest performed well. Pushing our slow cookers to the max, we ran an extreme test: sweet-and-sour sticky ribs for two. This dish cooks on low with very little moisture for 7 to 8 hours. Only two of the cookers yielded juicy, tender ribs. The two models that

Taste Test Jarred Medium Salsa

Sure, it sells well, but is salsa from the supermarket actually any good?

BY HANNAH CROWLEY

succeeded had also aced the chicken and steak tests.

To help us understand these recipe test results, we recorded the temperature of each cooker while heating 2½ quarts of water for 6 hours, first on high and then on low. Some cookers shot up to the boiling point of 212 degrees and maintained a roaring boil throughout the tests—these were the very models that overcooked ribs and scorched steaks. One model's temperature climbed painfully slowly, as it had when cooking chicken. Each subsequent time that we tested this particular model, it behaved differently. We ordered additional copies of the same model and repeated our tests. The copies performed no better. The best slow cookers reached 140 degrees quickly and then slowly climbed over a period of hours. With these models, foods reached safe temperatures and then simmered gently to tenderness.

Which models were easy to use? Cookers with manual controls required that the user return several hours later to switch the pot to "off" or a "keep warm" setting—so much for set it and forget it. We much preferred cookers with digital programmable controls that automatically switched over to "warm."

As for design, we liked dishwasher-safe inserts with large, easy-to-grip handles. The shape of the inserts mattered less. Although food fit slightly more easily in oval inserts, round and oval cookers performed about the same. In fact, we had one of each for our two top performers. That said, a cooker with an especially spacious oblong insert burned the sauce for the ribs and the steaks. When you're making smaller amounts of food, too much space is a disadvantage.

In the end, we can recommend two small slow cookers. The Cuisinart 4-Quart Programmable Slow Cooker was simple to set, and its digital timer meant that we could just walk away. It cooked food well if a little more slowly than other models. One drawback: If your kitchen is cramped, be aware that it is nearly as big as a full-size slow cooker. Our Best Buy is the Hamilton Beach Stay or Go 4-Quart Slow Cooker. With manual controls and no timer, it was far less convenient, but it performed perfectly.

IN AN IDEAL WORLD, we'd always make homemade salsa. In the real world, when we're pressed for time, we rely on the open-the-jar convenience of store-bought. But the sheer number of products and variations is daunting. Which tastes best?

We focused on the red Tex-Mex style, which dominates U.S. sales, and on a medium level of heat. Medium salsa outsells both mild and hot versions two to one, according to commercial salsa makers and among our own readers. Sales figures compiled by Chicago market research firm IRi gave us the seven top-selling national jarred products.

We tasted them plain and with tortilla chips. And when all was said and done, just one salsa was left standing. Tasters had reservations, or worse, about the other six. How did that one product get it right?

To begin, while many of the other salsas were marred by "mushy," "slimy" vegetables, "with no textural contrast," our top pick included firm, crunchy, evenly diced vegetables. Moreover, where other salsas were out of whack—overdoing the tomatoes or hot peppers or onions—our favorite got the ratios right.

No question, the heat level mattered, too. Salsas that used bell pepper were too mild. At the other end of the spectrum, we knocked points off one product that was too hot. Is it too much to ask that medium salsa be medium? We preferred medium heat from chile peppers, specifically the jalapeño chiles that our top three products used.

When we scrutinized labels, we discovered that our top three contained more sugar per serving than the bottom four. Not granulated sugar, mind you. Two products used granulated sugar to sweeten the salsa, an addition our tasters considered misguided. The better salsas derived complexity from naturally sweet tomatoes. Products with less natural sugar seemed unbalanced—too hot or too sour (the acid, incidentally, came from vinegar, not lime juice, which is used in many homemade salsas). A few salsas tasted too salty. But beyond that observation, salt levels didn't illuminate much about our likes and dislikes.

While it pains us to find fault in six of the seven products in our lineup, we prefer to focus on the positive: Chi-Chi's Medium Thick and Chunky Salsa is balanced, fresh-tasting, and has a nice level of heat. It's still not homemade, but it's the next best thing.

RECOMMENDED

CHI-CHI'S Medium Thick and Chunky Salsa
Price: $2.50 for 16 oz (16 cents per oz)
Sugar: 2 g per 2-tablespoon serving
Peppers: Jalapeño

TASTERS' NOTES

This salsa was balanced, vibrant, and "bright with acidity." Tasters found it "spicy, fresh, and tomatoey," with "plenty of heat" that was "pleasant, not overpowering." It also had a "good texture" that was "not too thin or thick," placing it squarely "in between [the] stewed and the crunchiest" salsas. In sum: It offered a "good dipping consistency."

RECOMMENDED WITH RESERVATIONS

TOSTITOS Chunky Salsa, Medium
Price: $3 for 15.5 oz (19 cents per oz)
Sugar: 2 g per 2-tablespoon serving
Peppers: Jalapeño

Familiar, mild, and sweet, this salsa had big chunks of peppers and onions and a kid-friendly flavor. Tasters described it as "classic jarred salsa": "pleasant" but "not very spicy or complex," with a rich red sauce and a vinegary kick. Some found it too salty when eaten with chips, plus it tasted cooked, not fresh.

PACE Chunky Salsa, Medium
Price: $2.49 for 16 oz (16 cents per oz)
Sugar: 2 g per 2-tablespoon serving
Peppers: Jalapeño

Tasters liked the "nice lingering heat" of this salsa, as well as its "smoky, heavy on the chiles" flavor. But it was somewhat "vinegar-heavy." While we appreciated "very firm" vegetable chunks, the surrounding liquid was "too runny" and "doesn't stay on the chip."

ORTEGA Original Salsa, Medium
Price: $2.50 for 16 oz (16 cents per oz)
Sugar: 1 g per 2-tablespoon serving
Peppers: Red bell, green bell, chili pepper puree, jalapeño

Though this salsa had a "nice, thick texture," with big chunks of sweet peppers in thick sauce, tasters found it off balance: The "heat took over all other flavor." With two kinds of hot peppers and not enough sugar to balance it, this salsa also registered as salty, "bitter," and "tinny."

NOT RECOMMENDED

NEWMAN'S OWN Medium Salsa
Price: $2.50 for 16 oz (16 cents per oz)
Sugar: 1 g per 2-tablespoon serving
Peppers: Green chili, green bell, red jalapeño, red bell

This salsa was nice and chunky with crunchy contrast. Unfortunately, the appealing texture couldn't make up for the nasty flavor. With too much black pepper and a slew of dusty dried herbs, it didn't taste fresh. Plus the seasonings were strange: "Too sweet," tasters said, and oddly "Italian American," with oregano and basil.

LA VICTORIA Thick'n Chunky Salsa, Medium
Price: $3.60 for 16 oz (23 cents per oz)
Sugar: 1 g per 2-tablespoon serving
Peppers: Jalapeño, green chiles

This underseasoned salsa tasted like cooked tomatoes and not much else. Tasters compared it to "mild tomato puree," "tomato soup," and "marinara sauce." The vegetables were "mushy." Diced too fine, they disappeared into the puree, leaving the salsa "soupy," "like ketchup."

HERDEZ Salsa Casera, Medium
Price: $2.69 for 16 oz (17 cents per oz)
Sugar: 1 g per 2-tablespoon serving
Peppers: Serrano

Serranos are usually hotter than jalapeños—not here. "Where's the HEAT?" tasters demanded. These particular chiles were either too few or on the mild end of the heat spectrum. This sample tasted like "bad gazpacho," with "mushy" vegetables in "thin tomato water." It had the second highest level of sodium among the salsas we tasted, with no balancing vinegar or heat.

Looking for a Recipe

Have you lost a recipe you treasure? Ask a reader. While you're at it, answer a reader. Post queries and finds at **CooksCountry.com/magazine**; click on **Looking for a Recipe** (or write to Looking for a Recipe, *Cook's Country*, P.O. Box 470739, Brookline, MA 02447). We'll share all of your submissions online and one recipe on this page; please include your name and mailing address.

Cowboy Caviar
Dianne Geissal, Monticello, Ill.

Costco makes a terrific salad that it calls cowboy caviar. It includes black beans, black-eyed peas, red peppers, tomatoes, and roasted corn, all tossed in a spicy dressing. I'd love to make it at home. Do you have a recipe that comes close?

George Washington Cake
Bob Kelly, Las Vegas, Nev.

When I was growing up in Philadelphia, we used to buy a cake from a local bakery called George Washington cake. It was a hearty spice cake, with chocolate frosting, that was baked in sheets, frosted, and sold in squares. I would love to find a recipe for it.

Hot Chicken Salad in Cheese Crust
E. Brown, Buffalo, Wyo.

I have searched for years for a recipe that I once clipped from a magazine for a hot chicken salad inside a yeasted cheese crust. I've mislaid the recipe but I remember that the slightly sweet cheese crust was made with cheddar cheese. The dish was unique, and everybody I ever served it to loved it. I am so hoping that someone has this recipe for me.

Golden Raisin Cookies
Barb Weismann, Sacramento, Calif.

I can no longer find the golden raisin cookies produced by Nabisco. Maybe they don't make them anymore? They are (were?) bar cookies filled with a thin layer of raisin puree. Has anybody developed a recipe for something similar? If so, please share it with me. I've tried to create my own version but can't seem to get the texture of either the filling or the crust right.

Woodford Pudding with Butterscotch Sauce
Sarah Dudley, via email

My grandmother used to make a delicious dessert that she called Woodford pudding. It had blackberry jam, cinnamon, and a batter that formed a cakelike pudding. She served it warm with a sauce that was good enough to drink. I never got the recipe from her, but I'd love to be able to re-create it.

PASTITA
Serves 10 to 12
Julia Purpura, via email

Pastita is a very rich Italian pasta casserole. We like it drizzled with extra-virgin olive oil.

- 1 pound spaghetti
  Salt and pepper
- 5 tablespoons unsalted butter, softened
- 3 ounces Parmesan cheese, grated (1½ cups)
- 2 pounds (4 cups) whole-milk ricotta cheese
- 2 ounces Pecorino Romano cheese, grated (1 cup)
- 4 large eggs, lightly beaten
- ¼ cup minced fresh parsley
- 3 cups whole milk

1. Bring 4 quarts water to boil in large pot. Add spaghetti and 1 tablespoon salt and cook, stirring often, until al dente. Drain spaghetti, return it to pot, and toss with 3 tablespoons butter. Let spaghetti cool for 5 minutes.

2. Meanwhile, adjust oven rack to middle position and heat oven to 350 degrees. Grease 13 by 9-inch baking dish with remaining 2 tablespoons butter, then coat evenly with ½ cup Parmesan. Combine ricotta, Pecorino, eggs, parsley, 2 teaspoons pepper, 1 teaspoon salt, and remaining 1 cup Parmesan in large bowl. Slowly whisk in milk until combined.

3. Stir spaghetti into ricotta mixture until thoroughly combined. Transfer to prepared dish and press into even layer. Bake until casserole is firm and slightly puffed, 50 to 60 minutes. Transfer to wire rack and let cool for 30 minutes. Serve.

Follow us on **Twitter**
twitter.com/TestKitchen

Find us on **Facebook**
facebook.com/CooksCountry

FIND THE ROOSTER!

A tiny version of this rooster has been hidden in the pages of this issue. Write us with its location and we'll enter you in a random drawing. The first correct entry drawn will win our winning small slow cooker (see page 30), and each the next five will receive a free one-ye subscription to *Cook's Country*. To ent visit **CooksCountry.com/rooster** by September 30, 2013, or write to Rooste AS/13, *Cook's Country*, P.O. Box 4707 Brookline, MA 02447. Include your nam and address. **Marge Thomssen** of Linc Neb., found the rooster in the April/M 2013 issue on page 13 and won our to rated salad spinner.

WEB EXTRAS
Free for 4 months online at
CooksCountry.com

All-American Potato Salad
Black Peppercorn Tasting
Bread and Butter Pickles
Candied Orange Peel
Charcoal Test
Chicken Piccata
Dilly Beans
Frittata Fillings
    Asparagus, Dill, and Goat Cheese
    Mushroom, Chive, and Gruyère
Pickled Beet Eggs
Pie Crust Tasting
Potatoes Hashed in Cream
White Cake Round

FIND US ON iPAD

Download the new *Cook's Country* a for iPad and start a free trial subscripti or purchase a single issue of the magazine. All issues are enhanced wi full-color Cooking Mode slide shows th provide step-by-step instructions for completing recipes, plus expanded reviews and ratings. Go to **CooksCountry. com/iPad** to download our app through iTunes.

Orange Creamsicle Ice Cream Cake

We transform an ice cream truck treat into a special occasion ice cream cake.

To make this cake you will need:

- 1 cup orange marmalade
- ¼ cup water
- 3 tablespoons orange-flavored gelatin
- 24 cake-style ladyfingers
- 1 (8-inch) white cake round*
- 1½ pints orange sherbet
- 1½ pints vanilla ice cream
- 2 tablespoons candied orange peel*

FOR THE LADYFINGERS: Grease 9-inch springform pan and line bottom with parchment paper. Line sides of pan with 3-inch-wide strip of parchment, then grease parchment. Process marmalade and water in food processor until no large pieces of rind remain, about 30 seconds. Transfer to small saucepan and bring to boil over medium heat. Off heat, whisk in gelatin until dissolved. Let cool slightly, about 15 minutes. Dip each ladyfinger quickly into marmalade mixture, flipping once to coat both sides, then place on wire rack set in rimmed baking sheet.

TO ASSEMBLE: Center cake round in bottom of prepared pan. Line sides of pan with coated ladyfingers, flat sides facing in, gently wedging ladyfingers between cake and pan. Brush 3 tablespoons remaining marmalade mixture (some may be left over) evenly over top of cake. Scoop sherbet into bowl and mash with wooden spoon until softened. Spread in even layer over cake. Cover with plastic wrap; freeze until very firm, at least 2 hours. Scoop ice cream into bowl and mash with wooden spoon until softened. Spread in even layer over sherbet. Cover with plastic; freeze until very firm, at least 2 hours. To serve, remove sides of pan. Using large metal spatula, transfer cake from pan bottom to plate or pedestal, then gently peel off parchment from sides. Arrange candied peel in center of cake. Serve.

▶ *Go to **CooksCountry.com/sept13** for our recipes for **White Cake Round** and **Candied Orange Peel**, or use your own.

Inside This Issue

Cook's Country

OCTOBER/NOVEMBER 2013

Quicker, Better Cinnamon Buns

Spice-Rubbed Grilled Turkey

Slow-Cooker BBQ Pork

Best Baked Chicken Wings
Crispy Skin Without Frying

10 Steps to Perfect Meatloaf
Never Dry or Bland

Oven-Roasted Mushrooms
Sweet-Tart Glaze

Chuck Roast and Po' Boys
Cook Once, Eat Twice

Chocolate Cake in a Mug
Instant Microwave Dessert

Featherbed Eggs
Breakfast Casserole Reinvented

Testing Cake Pans
Wrong Choice Ruins Cakes

Lighter Sausage and Biscuits
Full Flavor, One-Third the Fat

Sweet Potato Pie
Silkier than Pumpkin

CooksCountry.com
$5.95 U.S./$6.95 CANADA

We wanted the speed of a biscuit but the pull-apart texture of a slow-rising yeast bread. After a few weeks in the test kitchen, we had perfected a novel approach that gave us the best of both in our **Quicker Cinnamon Buns.** PAGE 18

Cook's Country

Dear Country Cook,

One of my all-time favorite movies is Jason and the Argonauts, since it was filmed using stop-motion animation, a technique, incidentally, pioneered by Ray Harryhausen, who died earlier this year. That is also why I love the Macy's Thanksgiving Day Parade; the charm of old-fashioned floats is so much more appealing than Hollywood special effects. When anything is possible, everything is taken for granted.

That is, I suppose, why I love to cook. Almost any dish can be created in the world of expensive, celebrity-chef restaurants, yet the smallest success in the kitchen is worthy of an Oscar nomination since it is made at home and, most important, by hand. A nicely grilled steak, a perfect sugar cookie, or a slice of creamy, just-set pumpkin pie is a personal triumph.

That is the charm, I suppose, of imperfection. When the cookies are slightly burnt on the bottom, or the meatloaf is a tad overbaked, or the Macy's Thanksgiving Day balloons are hard to handle in the high November winds, we are reminded that perfection is rare. That way, we can better appreciate what we have today rather than what might be just around the corner.

Cordially,

Christopher Kimball
Founder, Cook's Country

Macy's Thanksgiving Day Parade, Times Square, New York City, 1960.

Cook's Country

Founder and Editor Christopher Kimball
Editorial Director Jack Bishop
Editorial Director, Magazines John Willoughby
Executive Editor Peggy Grodinsky
Managing Editor Scott Kathan
Senior Editors Lisa McManus, Bryan Roof, Diane Unger
Test Kitchen Director Erin McMurrer
Associate Editors Hannah Crowley,
Amy Graves, Rebeccah Marsters, Christie Morrison
Test Cooks Sarah Gabriel, Nick Iverson,
Carolynn Purpura MacKay, Cristin Walsh
Assistant Editors
Shannon Friedmann Hatch, Taizeth Sierra
Copy Editors Nell Beram, Megan Ginsberg
Executive Assistant Christine Gordon
Test Kitchen Manager Leah Rovner
Senior Kitchen Assistants
Michelle Blodget, Meryl MacCormack
Kitchen Assistants
Maria Elena Delgado, Shane Drips, Ena Gudiel
Executive Producer Melissa Baldino
Co-Executive Producer Stephanie Stender
Production Assistant Kaitlin Hammond

Contributing Editors Erika Bruce,
Eva Katz, Jeremy Sauer
Consulting Editors Anne Mendelson, Meg Ragland
Science Editor Guy Crosby, Ph.D.
Executive Food Editor, TV, Radio & Media
Bridget Lancaster

Managing Editor, Web Christine Liu
Senior Editor, Cooking School Mari Levine
Associate Editors, Web Eric Grzymkowski, Roger Metcalf
Assistant Editors, Web Jill Fisher, Charlotte Wilder
Senior Video Editor Nick Dakoulas

Design Director Amy Klee
Art Director Julie Cote
Deputy Art Director Susan Levin
Associate Art Director Lindsey Timko
Deputy Art Director, Marketing/Web Jennifer Cox
Staff Photographer Daniel J. van Ackere
Color Food Photography Keller + Keller, Carl Tremblay
Styling Catrine Kelty, Marie Piraino
Associate Art Director, Marketing/Web
Mariah Tarvainen
Designer, Marketing/Web Judy Blomquist
Photo Editor Steve Klise

Vice President, Marketing David Mack
Circulation Director Doug Wicinski
Circulation & Fulfillment Manager Carrie Fethe
Partnership Marketing Manager Pamela Putprush
Marketing Assistant Joyce Liao

VP, Technology, Product Development Barry Kelly
Director, Project Management Alice Carpenter
Production & Traffic Coordinator Brittany Allen
Development Manager Mike Serio

Chief Operating Officer Rob Ristagno
Production Director Guy Rochford
Workflow & Digital Asset Manager Andrew Mannone
Senior Color & Imaging Specialist Lauren Pettapiece
Production & Imaging Specialists
Heather Dube, Lauren Robbins
Director of Sponsorship Sales Anne Traficante
Client Services Associate Kate May
Sponsorship Sales Representative Morgan Ryan
Customer Service Manager Jacqueline Valerio
Customer Service Representatives
Megan Hamner, Jessica Haskin,
Andrew Straaberg Finfrock

Chief Financial Officer Sharyn Chabot
Retail Sales & Marketing Manager Emily Logan
Human Resources Manager Adele Shapiro
Publicity Deborah Broide

ON THE COVER: *Quicker Cinnamon Buns,* Keller + Keller,
Catrine Kelty
ILLUSTRATION: Greg Stevenson

Follow us on **Twitter**
twitter.com/TestKitchen

Find us on **Facebook**
facebook.com/CooksCountry

Cook's Country magazine (ISSN 1552-1990), number 53, published bimonthly by Boston Common Press Limited Partnership, 17 Station St., Brookline, MA 02445. Copyright 2013 Boston Common Press Limited Partnership. Periodicals postage paid at Boston, Mass., and additional mailing offices, USPS #023453. Publications Mail Agreement No. 40020778. Return undeliverable Canadian addresses to P.O. Box 875, Station A, Windsor, ON N9A 6P2. POSTMASTER: Send address changes to Cook's Country, P.O. Box 6018, Harlan, IA 51593-1518. For subscription and gift subscription orders, subscription inquiries, or change-of-address notices, visit AmericasTestKitchen.com/customerservice, call 800-526-8442 in the U.S. or 515-248-7684 from outside the U.S., or write Cook's Country, P.O. Box 6018, Harlan, IA 51593-1518. PRINTED IN THE USA

OCTOBER/NOVEMBER 2013

Contents

CRISPY SKILLET STUFFING, 6

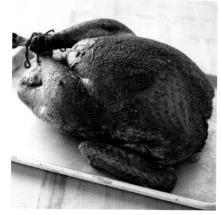
SPICE-RUBBED GRILL-ROASTED TURKEY, 4

SMOKY TURKEY COBB SALAD, 13

Features

Departments

America's TEST KITCHEN
RECIPES THAT WORK®

America's Test Kitchen is a very real 2,500-square-foot kitchen located just outside Boston. It is the home of *Cook's Country* and *Cook's Illustrated* magazines and is the workday destination of more than three dozen test cooks, editors, and cookware specialists. Our mission is to test recipes over and over again until we understand how and why they work and until we arrive at the best version. We also test kitchen equipment and supermarket ingredients in search of brands that offer the best value and performance. You can watch us work by tuning in to *Cook's Country from America's Test Kitchen* (CooksCountryTV.com) and *America's Test Kitchen* (AmericasTestKitchenTV.com) on public television.

Ask Cook's Country

BY SARAH GABRIEL

When a recipe calls for finishing a sauce with butter, why must you add it off the heat?
Greg Johnson, Frederic, Wis.

Finishing a pan sauce with butter adds three things: flavor, richness, and body. To achieve the last of these, you need to remove the pan from the heat before stirring in the butter. Why? Because butter is an emulsion, a mixture of two things that ordinarily do not mix well. This particular emulsion is of water in fat; standard American butter is about 16 percent water and 80 percent fat. What binds these two ordinarily unfriendly molecules is a third type of molecule, called a phospholipid, which has a tail that attracts water and a head that weakly attracts fats. As long as there is enough phospholipid to coat the water droplets, the emulsion will be stable. But when you introduce butter into a liquid, as you do when finishing a sauce, suddenly there are many more water molecules than fat molecules, and there is too little phospholipid to go around. If you leave the sauce on the heat, the heat causes the molecules to move faster and jostle one another more, which makes it just that much harder for the phospholipid to hold on to the fat and water molecules. The result? At about 160 degrees, the fat separates out from the water, and instead of a nicely thickened sauce, what you have is a liquid with a pool of floating fat.
THE BOTTOM LINE: Add butter to pan sauces off heat to prevent the butter from separating and leaving an oil slick on top.

DON'T DO IT
This sauce broke because the butter was added on the heat.

I usually oven-dry the bread for stuffing, but once I left it out to stale instead. The stuffing was slimy. Why?
Mayda Torres, Fresno, Calif.

To answer your question, we reenacted your Turkey Day tragedy. We made two batches of our Back-to-Basics Bread Stuffing (October/November 2011), one according to the instructions (dry diced bread for almost 1 hour at 325 degrees) and the other with bread that we had diced and left out to stale. Both batches of bread felt dry and hard, but when we mixed in the liquid, the counter-staled bread disintegrated into a paste, while

the oven-dried bread stayed more or less intact. We baked both batches and then called over some tasters. The stuffing made with dried bread came out moist and tender; not surprisingly, the one with staled bread was gluey and wet. To figure out why, we did some research, and here's what we learned: The dried bread felt dry and hard because it had lost moisture in the oven and actually *was* dry. The stale bread, on the other hand, only *felt* dry. When bread goes stale, the starch crystallizes, locking the bread's moisture inside the starch crystals, which makes the bread feel hard and dry even though it still contains most of its original moisture. So when we added the liquid to the staled bread, we were adding liquid to already-moist bread, which is why the result was wet and pasty.
THE BOTTOM LINE: If your stuffing recipe calls for oven-dried bread, stale bread is not a good substitute: The stuffing will be too wet.

If a recipe calls for canned diced tomatoes and all I have is canned whole tomatoes, I can dice up the whole tomatoes, can't I?
Richard Taigue, Lynbrook, N.Y.

To find out, we made batches of soup and macaroni and cheese following recipes that call for tomatoes. We found that the canned diced tomatoes were firmer than whole peeled tomatoes cut to resemble diced. But while the differences were detectable, we decided that in cooked preparations in which intact pieces of tomato aren't the focus, cut-up whole peeled tomatoes work perfectly well in place of canned diced. When used raw, however, hand-chopped canned whole peeled tomatoes did not perform as well. In salsa, tasters found the diced tomatoes pleasantly resilient, while the

chopped whole tomatoes were "squishy" and "limp." Likewise, in our Maque Choux (August/September 2013), a stewed corn-and-tomato dish, diced tomatoes kept their shape, while chopped whole tomatoes stewed into a pulpy puree.

Why are diced tomatoes firmer and more durable? The juice in which diced tomatoes are packed is treated with calcium chloride, which fortifies the cell walls and helps the tomatoes hold their shape. Many whole tomato products are also packed in calcium chloride–laced juice, but the solution acts only near the surface of the whole tomatoes, leaving the interior fragile.
THE BOTTOM LINE: Hand-cut canned whole peeled tomatoes will stand in for diced when you don't need the diced to hold their shape. When distinct chunks are important, stick with canned diced.

My pie crust recipe uses butter and shortening. Can I replace the shortening with coconut oil?
Toby Pendergast, Winters, Calif.

Despite being high in saturated fat, coconut oil is said to lower cholesterol; it is also high in antioxidants and is said to boost immunity. The oil comes in two basic varieties: refined and virgin (or unrefined), both of which—like shortening—are solid at room temperature. Virgin oil tastes like coconut, which works nicely in some recipes, but obviously not for pie crust, so for our test, we used neutral-tasting refined oil.

Pie dough recipes call for shortening, a pure fat, because it's easy to work with and produces flaky crusts. Butter, with fat plus water, is fussier, but it tastes better—and also contributes to flakiness. Many pie crust recipes, including most of ours, call for both butter and shortening for the best combination of flavor and flakiness.

We made a pie dough using butter

When you make beer can chicken, does it matter what kind of beer you use?
Rafael Goncalves, Grand Rapids, Mich.

We tried making beer can chicken with several varieties of beer and found that, whether light or dark, hoppy or malty, cheap or spendy, all produced great-all-around crispy-skinned birds. That got us thinking: Did it even matter if we used beer at all? We roasted three chickens on vertical roasters (which function just like beer cans), each with a different liquid in the reservoir under the chicken cavity. One roaster contained water, the second beer, and the third wine. We tasted the three chickens side by side, and not one of our tasters could identify the difference.

If the liquid in a vertical roaster doesn't flavor the meat, did we need any liquid at all? We made two more chickens, filling the reservoir of one vertical roaster with water and leaving the other dry. Both chickens came out equally moist and flavorful. If you use a beer can rather than a store-bought vertical roaster, you may still want to keep liquid in the can because the added weight will make the rig steadier. (Drink the beer and refill the can with water if you like.)
THE BOTTOM LINE: The liquid in a vertical roaster or beer can has no impact on the flavor of beer can chicken. Our advice: Drink the beer.

VERTICAL ROASTING
The beer flavor isn't the point. The all-the-way-around crispy skin that comes from roasting a bird vertically is.

plus coconut oil, another pure fat, in place of the shortening. It was just as eas to roll out, and we all liked it; some tasters even preferred it to the original recipe. Impressed, we tried coconut oil in anothe baked good that commonly calls for a combination of butter and shortening: biscuits. Again, the coconut oil performe as well as or better than the shortening.
THE BOTTOM LINE: Yes, you can. Refined coconut oil can replace the shortening in pie dough and biscuit recipes that also contain butter.

I made angel food cake, inverting the pan to cool, as the recipe instructed. The cake fell out. Why?
Alyssa Smith, Akron, Ohio

Angel food cake is cooled upside down i its pan so it won't collapse under its own weight and come out rubbery and dense Some tube pans, like our favorite, the Chi cago Metallic Professional Nonstick Ange Food Cake Pan with Feet, are designed to stand upside down (hence the feet), while others need to be set on the neck of a bottle to let the tall baked cake coo upside down. In both cases, obviously it's necessary that the cake hang on to the pan. Our recipes call for ungreased tube pans, but when we looked at a sampling of other recipes, they didn't all specify; the lack of grease lets the batter climb th cake pan. We sprayed our favorite tube pan and then baked an angel food cake in it. Sure enough, the cake slid right out when inverted, which is what you want fo other types of cakes, but not this one.
THE BOTTOM LINE: Never grease a tube pan when making angel food cake.

To ask us a cooking question, visit **CooksCountry.com/askcookscountry**. Or write to Ask *Cook's Country*, P.O. Box 470739, Brookline, MA 02447. Just try to stump us!

Kitchen Shortcuts

COMPILED BY NICK IVERSON

RECYCLE IT
The Inside Scoop
Tyler Taylor, Little Silver, N.J.

I keep my flour in a canister on the counter. I didn't have a scoop, so I made one out of the top of a clean quart milk jug. All it took was a pair of scissors and a little imagination.

CLEVER TIP Cookie Protection
Maggie Swanick, Birmingham, Ala.

My mom taught me how to bake, and I like to send her a batch of her favorite cookies a few times a year. I never have a cookie tin around when I need one, but I found that an empty hot chocolate container works great for shipping a stack of big cookies across the country. The container even perfumes the cookies with chocolate, a definite plus!

CLEVER TIP Deep Freeze
Peter Dudley, Middletown, Conn.

When I make large batches of my famous spaghetti sauce for freezing, I need to cool down the finished sauce as quickly as possible. I've seen tips that call for filling an old soda bottle with water, freezing it, and submerging it in the sauce, but I never have enough forethought to do that. Instead, I put a few ice packs in a zipper-lock bag and stir the bag around in the sauce to cool it.

RECYCLE IT
Utensil Holder
Debbie Robbins, Shaker Heights, Ohio

Like many home cooks, I keep a big ceramic crock of spatulas, wooden and slotted spoons, and tongs at the ready near the stove. The problem is that I also need smaller items like measuring spoons, my instant-read thermometer, and my garlic press nearby, and they get lost at the bottom of the big crock or in a drawer. Now I use an empty (and clean) 28-ounce tomato can as a smaller "crock" to hold my smaller cooking essentials. I know where everything is, and I can find my small utensils easily.

BETTER BAKING
Pinching Pie Dough
India Lydon, Los Gatos, Calif.

Most cakes have frosting to hide their imperfections, but with pies, all is exposed. A friend who is an expert pie maker recently showed me a tip to prevent what was a common problem for me: having the edges of the dough crack when I rolled it out (which makes it hard to crimp and edge). My friend showed me how to pinch the edge of the dough disk before rolling; this puts less pin pressure on the edges as you start to roll it out, which leads to fewer cracks. It sounds simple and silly, but it really works.

CLEVER TIP
Air Cushion
Tamara Joseph, Kittery, Maine

After crushing some expensive lobster mushrooms on my way to a friend's house last summer, I came up with a nifty trick for transporting delicate produce. I put the mushrooms (or herbs, tomatoes, etc.) in a zipper-lock bag that I seal up around a straw. I fill the bag with air through the straw, remove the straw, and fully seal the bag. It becomes a balloon that protects the produce from getting squished and ruined.

TIDY TIP Got It Covered
Ella McWilliams, Austin, Texas

I finally had it with getting caught in a "flour tornado" when adding dry ingredients to my running mixer. I tried covering the bowl with a dish towel, but I was worried that the towel would fall and catch on the paddle. I improvised a pretty good cover by cutting an opening in a clean gallon-size ice cream container lid. The opening is big enough to accommodate the attachment and also allows me to add ingredients. No more floury face.

Submit a tip online at CooksCountry.com/kitchenshortcuts or send a letter to Kitchen Shortcuts, Cook's Country, P.O. Box 470739, Brookline, MA 02447. Include your name, address, and phone number. If we publish your tip, you will receive a free one-year subscription to Cook's Country. Letters may be edited for clarity and length.

Spice-Rubbed Grilled Turkey

Mild turkey is a perfect candidate for amping up with smoke and spice, but how could we keep the charcoal going long enough to cook the big bird? BY REBECCAH MARSTERS

COOKING THE TURKEY on the grill is great because it frees up the oven on the busiest cooking day of the year—but it should do more than that. Since grill-roasted turkey isn't the same old Thanksgiving dinner to start with, why not take things to a whole new level by adding lots of spice to the smoky flavor? Bold flavors are my Thanksgiving theme this year, and it all starts with the turkey.

We've grill-roasted our fair share of turkeys in the test kitchen, so I had some knowledge to help me get started. First of all, I knew that gentle, indirect heat would be key; a 12-pound bird takes a long time to cook, and high heat would burn the skin and dry out the meat before it could cook through. To create indirect heat on a charcoal grill, you put the charcoal in a pile on one side of the lower grate and place the food—in this case, the turkey—on the other side of the upper (cooking) grate, away from the heat. I also decided to place a disposable baking pan filled with water next to the coals; the water pan not only creates steam to help keep the turkey moist but also absorbs heat to moderate the temperature inside the grill. I use a water pan in the gas-grill version of this recipe, too.

Next, I knew that because of the lengthy cooking time, I'd need to either refuel the charcoal grill during cooking (not ideal) or use the Minion method. With the Minion method, you place lit charcoal on top of unlit charcoal to create a longer-burning fire. This is the technique I'd use. And finally, to address the white-meat breast and dark-meat legs cooking to different temperatures, I'd position the bird with the legs closest to the fire and the breast farthest away. (Since a turkey won't fit this way on most gas grills, for gas I position the bird with one side facing the heat and rotate it halfway through cooking.)

A trial run confirmed that my basic method resulted in a nicely cooked bird, so I turned to seasoning the turkey. To add smoky flavor, I followed test kitchen protocol and wrapped soaked wood chips in foil, pierced the foil packet with a few vent holes, and placed it on the hot coals. Except this time I used double the amount of wood chips that we normally do (from 1 to 2 cups) in order to give the turkey deeply smoky flavor.

With good smoke flavor on the bird, I moved on to the spice. I started by

With spiced butter rubbed under the skin, this turkey has a slightly exotic flavor.

creating a spice rub to flavor the skin of the bird. After a bit of trial and error, I landed on an extremely flavorful mix of five-spice powder, cumin, granulated garlic, cayenne, and cardamom (plus salt and pepper) that I rubbed on the exterior of the turkey before grilling. But the spice rub, while flavorful, ended up dry and dusty on the cooked turkey. Mixing the spice rub with a couple of tablespoons of vegetable oil before rub-

bing it on the bird solved the problem.

As good as this spice rub was, however, it was seasoning just the skin and not the meat. To flavor the turkey under the skin, I turned to the classic technique of carefully loosening the turkey skin from the meat (I like to use my fingers, but the handle of a wooden spoon works, too, if you're gentle and take care not to tear the skin) and rubbing softened butter—with some of my spice

rub mixed in—all over the meat under the skin. Adding a little brown sugar to the seasoned butter rounded it out and helped emphasize the "warm spice" flavors in the spice mix.

The turkey finally had smoke and spice, but the skin was a little dry. I was already applying seasoned oil before the turkey went on the grill, so I tried brushing on more of the oil during cooking. This worked, but on a quest for more flavor, I decided to switch to butter; I bloomed more of my spice mixture in melted butter to draw out more depth and then brushed it on the turkey during the last half-hour of grilling.

This not only added another layer of spicy, buttery flavor but also helped crisp and burnish the skin (butter enhances browning). As I carted my last turkey into the kitchen from outside, I knew I had my holiday centerpiece figured out; the bird was deeply browned with juicy, smoky meat and buttery, spicy skin. My Thanksgiving just got a lot more flavorful.

SPICE-RUBBED GRILL-ROASTED TURKEY
Serves 10 to 12

We prefer a Butterball turkey for this recipe. If you prefer natural, unenhanced turkey, we recommend brining: Dissolve 1 cup of salt in 2 gallons of cold water; submerge the turkey in the brine, cover, and refrigerate for 6 to 12 hours. Make sure you have plenty of fuel if you're using a gas grill.

- 2 teaspoons five-spice powder
  Salt and pepper
- 1½ teaspoons ground cumin
- 1 teaspoon granulated garlic
- ¼ teaspoon cayenne pepper
- ¼ teaspoon ground cardamom
- 2 tablespoons unsalted butter, softened, plus 4 tablespoons unsalted butter
- 1 tablespoon packed brown sugar
- 2 tablespoons vegetable oil
- 1 (12- to 14-pound) turkey, neck and giblets discarded
- 2 cups wood chips, soaked in water for 15 minutes and drained
- 1 (13 by 9-inch) disposable aluminum pan (if using charcoal) or 2 (9-inch) disposable aluminum pie plates (if using gas)

1. Combine five-spice powder, 2 teaspoons salt, cumin, 1 teaspoon pepper, granulated garlic, cayenne, and cardamom in bowl. Combine 1 tablespoon spice mixture with softened butter and sugar in second bowl. Combine 1 tablespoon spice mixture with oil in third bowl.

2. Dry turkey thoroughly inside and out with paper towels. With turkey breast side up on work surface, use your fingers or handle of wooden spoon to carefully separate skin from breast. Rub spiced butter evenly under skin of breast. Tuck wings underneath turkey and tie legs together with kitchen twine. Rub spiced oil evenly over entire surface of turkey. Using large piece of heavy-duty aluminum foil, wrap soaked chips in foil packet and cut several vent holes in top.

3A. FOR A CHARCOAL GRILL: Open bottom vent completely and place disposable pan filled with 3 cups water on 1 side of grill, with long side of pan facing center of grill. Arrange 3 quarts unlit charcoal briquettes in even layer on opposite side of grill. Light large chimney starter three-quarters filled with charcoal briquettes (4½ quarts). When top coals are partially covered with ash, pour evenly over unlit coals. Place wood chip packet on coals. Set cooking grate in place, cover, and open lid vent completely. Heat grill until hot and wood chips are smoking, about 5 minutes.

3B. FOR A GAS GRILL: Place wood chip packet directly on primary burner. Place disposable pie plates with 2 cups water in each directly on secondary burner(s). Turn all burners to high, cover, and heat grill until hot and wood chips are smoking, about 15 minutes. Leave primary burner on high and turn off other burner(s). (Adjust primary burner as needed to maintain grill temperature of 325 degrees.)

4. Clean and oil cooking grate. Place turkey, breast side up, over pan(s), with legs pointing toward fire for charcoal grill or with 1 side of turkey facing primary burner for gas. Cover (placing lid vent over turkey on charcoal grill) and cook for 1 hour.

5. Meanwhile, melt remaining 4 tablespoons butter in small saucepan over medium heat. Add remaining 2 teaspoons spice mixture and cook until fragrant, about 1 minute. Remove from heat. After turkey has been on grill for 1 hour, brush all over with spiced butter, rotating turkey if using gas grill (if turkey looks too dark, cover breast lightly with foil). Cover and continue to cook until breast registers 160 degrees and thighs/drumsticks register 175 degrees, 1 to 2 hours longer.

6. Transfer turkey to carving board and let rest, uncovered, for 45 minutes. Carve turkey and serve.

KEY TECHNIQUE Moderating the Heat

One of the keys to roasting a turkey on the grill for 2 to 3 hours is moderating the heat—the fire needs to be hot enough to cook the turkey, but not so hot that it cooks unevenly or burns. For both gas and charcoal, we place disposable aluminum pans filled with water on the bottom of the grill (next to the briquettes for charcoal, directly on the secondary burners for gas). The water absorbs heat and helps keep the temperature consistently low.

FOR CHARCOAL
Use a 13 by 9-inch disposable lasagna pan.

FOR GAS
Use 9-inch disposable pie plates.

Mashed Butternut Squash

Winter squash is often wet and stringy. Was this dish a hopeless cause?

BY NICK IVERSON

Cumin, coriander, cinnamon, cayenne, and maple syrup bring out the earthy sweetness of butternut squash.

SQUASH IS GOOD for you, sure, but based on the handful of recipes I tested as Thanksgiving neared, it just isn't good. I'd picked the recipes to represent a range of approaches, cutting up the butternut squash variously and either baking, roasting, steaming, or boiling before mashing it to a rustic puree. Alas, after we tasted the different preparations, the same words kept coming up: soupy, fibrous, washed out.

On the positive side, these tests did reveal that how I cut the squash was critical. Squash that I cooked whole or halved saved work on the front end but exacerbated the stringiness. Once the squash was cooked, no matter how vigorously I mashed, it proved impossible to cut through the tough fibers. By cubing the raw squash, though, I could cut through the fibers, making them vanish into the finished dish. As for cooking method, roasting at high heat evaporated extra moisture; plus, it concentrated the squash's flavor and sweetness.

Most recipes I found were quite sweet, but in my initial test, our favorite recipe called for onions and garlic. I sweated chopped onion in butter on the stove and then tossed in a range of spices, eventually settling on cumin, cinnamon, and coriander for their warm notes and cayenne for background heat. After the spices and garlic "bloomed" briefly, I added the roasted squash and mashed the mix. Despite the spices, the dish tasted oddly flat. I brainstormed harvest ingredients and flavors, eventually landing on shredded Granny Smith apples. They perked up the squash and added a fruity sweetness, which I underlined with maple syrup.

Now the mash was neither stringy nor soupy, and its flavor was almost mysterious. Eating it, you might not be able to identify the add-ins, but you could name their effect: delicious.

MASHED BUTTERNUT SQUASH
Serves 8

Cutting the squash into uniform chunks ensures even cooking.

- 4 pounds butternut squash, peeled, seeded, and cut into 1-inch pieces (10 cups)
- 3 tablespoons vegetable oil
  Salt and pepper
- 4 tablespoons unsalted butter
- 2 Granny Smith apples, peeled and shredded (2 cups)
- 1 onion, chopped fine
- 1 garlic clove, minced
- ½ teaspoon ground cumin
- ½ teaspoon ground coriander
- ¼ teaspoon ground cinnamon
- ⅛ teaspoon cayenne pepper
- 3 tablespoons maple syrup

1. Adjust oven rack to upper-middle position and heat oven to 425 degrees. Line rimmed baking sheet with parchment paper. Combine squash, oil, 1 teaspoon salt, and ½ teaspoon pepper in bowl. Spread squash in even layer on prepared sheet. Roast until tender and starting to brown, 40 to 50 minutes, rotating sheet halfway through roasting.

2. Meanwhile, melt butter in Dutch oven over medium-low heat. Add apples, onion, and ¼ teaspoon salt and cook, covered, until apples are soft, about 5 minutes. Uncover and continue to cook, stirring occasionally, until apples and onion are golden brown, 5 to 7 minutes longer. Add garlic, cumin, coriander, cinnamon, and cayenne and cook until fragrant, about 30 seconds. Remove from heat, cover, and set aside while squash finishes roasting.

3. Add squash and maple syrup to pot. Mash with potato masher until mostly smooth. Season with salt and pepper to taste. Serve.

Crispy Skillet Stuffing

For stuffing with a high crunch quotient, we grabbed a skillet.
But that was just the starting point. BY CRISTIN WALSH

TO MAKE CLASSIC Thanksgiving stuffing, you sauté onions and celery in a skillet with herbs, moisten dried bread cubes with broth and possibly eggs, combine everything, and bake the mixture in a casserole dish (unless you're stuffing the turkey). My family always fights over the crispy top crust, so this year I wondered if I could double the effect by baking the stuffing right in the skillet. My theory was that the heat from below (from contact with the hot skillet) coupled with the heat from above (from the hot oven) would produce twice the delicious crust.

> ▶ You can find a variation of this recipe with sausage and apple at **CooksCountry. com/nov13.**

I found some recipes that tried this. But by and large they failed to deliver the serious crunch and moist, but not soggy, interior that I envisioned. Still, I put together a recipe drawing on their more successful parts and our collective test kitchen expertise. After I dried white bread cubes in a 300-degree oven for nearly an hour, I mixed them in a bowl with the chicken broth, eggs, and sautéed vegetables and then let the mixture sit to saturate the bread. I melted a generous lump of butter in a 12-inch nonstick skillet (the same one I'd used for sautéing the veg) and piled in the stuffing, patting it down to an even layer. I brushed the top with extra butter to encourage more browning, and therefore crunch, and I baked it in a 350-degree oven.

When I pulled the skillet out some 50 minutes later, the stuffing had an impressive golden top. But disappointment lurked below. The bottom crust wasn't particularly crispy, and the middle was wet mush. I tried using less broth, but I'd merely traded one evil (slimy bread in the center) for another (dry, chewy bread). Was the bread itself the problem? I tested my recipe using challah, whole wheat, supermarket Italian, and a baguette. The baguette held up well, plus

its high ratio of crust to crumb helped with the crunch. And it gave me an idea. Instead of drying the bread in a low oven—standard test kitchen procedure—what if I toasted the bread? Might the whole loaf be more like the hard crust of the baguette and thus better withstand moisture? I toasted the cubes in a

450-degree oven until they were golden, which took less than 15 minutes. Then I made the stuffing in the skillet as before.

Better, but the bottom crust still wasn't crunchy enough. To get it going, once I'd packed the stuffing into the skillet, I kept the burner on low, basically frying the stuffing. I checked the

This stuffing has the time-tested flavors of onion, celery, sage, and thyme. It's the crispy, crunchy texture that sets it apart.

bottom crust every so often by lifting it up with a spatula. When it was brown, after not quite 10 minutes, I stuck the skillet in the still very hot oven to encourage yet more browning on top of the stuffing. It came out perfectly. If, like me, you prefer the crusty portion of stuffing, then this is the recipe for you.

EXTRA-CRISPY SKILLET STUFFING
Serves 8

If your nonstick skillet doesn't have a metal handle, wrap the handle in a double layer of foil before placing it in the oven.

1½	pounds baguette, cut into ½-inch cubes (18 cups)
3¾	cups chicken broth
4	large eggs, lightly beaten
8	tablespoons unsalted butter
2	onions, chopped fine
3	celery ribs, minced
1½	teaspoons salt
1½	tablespoons minced fresh thyme
1½	tablespoons minced fresh sage
3	garlic cloves, minced
¾	teaspoon pepper

1. Adjust oven rack to upper-middle position and heat oven to 450 degrees. Arrange bread evenly on rimmed baking sheet and bake until light golden brown, 12 to 15 minutes, stirring halfway through. Let bread cool completely.

2. Whisk broth and eggs together in large bowl. Stir bread into broth mixture until evenly coated. Set aside, stirring occasionally, to saturate bread.

3. Melt 2 tablespoons butter in skillet over medium heat. Add onions, celery, and salt and cook until browned, 10 to 12 minutes. Stir in thyme, sage, garlic, and pepper and cook until fragrant, about 30 seconds. Stir onion mixture into bread mixture.

4. Melt 3 tablespoons butter in now-empty skillet over low heat. Add stuffing to skillet, pressing down firmly into even layer with spatula (skillet will be very full). Cook until bottom of stuffing is browned around edges when lifted with spatula, 7 to 10 minutes.

5. Melt remaining 3 tablespoons butter in microwave and brush evenly over top of stuffing. Transfer skillet to oven and bake until center of stuffing is hot and top is golden brown, about 20 minutes, rotating skillet halfway through baking. Let cool for 10 minutes. Serve.

Browning = Flavor and Crunch

For the ultimate crunch, we don't merely dry the bread; we toast it at high heat. To further develop its crust, we fry the stuffing in butter on the stovetop, without stirring. Then we brush the top with melted butter and put the skillet in a hot oven so the top can develop a similarly brown, crunchy crust.

GOOD COLOR
These toasted bread cubes are unusually dark for stuffing.

GREAT CRUNCH
Our method makes stuffing that is crispy on the top *and* on the bottom.

Brussels Sprout Salad

This appealing new salad was just a few tweaks away from a permanent place on our table.

BY CAROLYNN PURPURA MACKAY

IT WASN'T THAT long ago that Brussels sprouts ranked high on the list of America's most hated vegetables. The picture began to change when roasting came into vogue; this technique produced Brussels sprouts so caramelized, so tender, and so downright delicious that it turned loathers into lovers. Recently, another recipe has been making the rounds that I think has a good shot at converting any remaining skeptics: Brussels sprout salad.

Instead of calling for roasting the sprouts at high heat to make them taste great, this recipe requires no heat whatsoever: The Brussels sprouts are raw. This isn't as weird as it sounds. Brussels sprouts are very much like miniature cabbages, and we think nothing of eating cabbage raw; coleslaw, anyone? To make Brussels sprout salad, you thinly slice the sprouts and then, depending on which recipe you are following, toss them with variously flavored vinaigrettes. Recipes I looked at called for apple cider vinegar, balsamic vinegar, and Dijon mustard, to name a few. The salads are dressed up with equally variable add-ins, such as bacon, pomegranate seeds, sunflower seeds, dried cranberries, walnuts, feta cheese, Parmesan . . . the list goes on. Brussels sprouts, it was clear, can accommodate many flavors and textures.

In the kitchen, I lined up packages of Brussels sprouts and got to work slicing, whisking, tasting, and judging. The consensus? We liked them all pretty well. I could see that some of my work would be simply picking and choosing among options. That said, every recipe I made shared one not insignificant flaw: The Brussels sprouts themselves tasted underseasoned, and they were raw in a bad way; I felt rabbity munching on them. Before I fixed that, however, I'd settle on a dressing. When push came to shove, a bright, lemony vinaigrette—with a touch of Dijon— seemed to give the most balance to the earthy Brussels sprouts.

To both soften and season the Brussels sprouts, I sliced them, tossed them with salt, and put them in a colander so that the water drawn out by the salt could drain away. I stole this idea from our test kitchen coleslaw method. But as I was waiting, it occurred to me that I could simplify. I made the salad again, this time without salting; I simply let the salad marinate in its lemony vinaigrette. The marinating proved just as effective, and it let me skip a step. A test of intervals of time revealed that the sprouts needed 30 minutes to become properly seasoned and softened.

With the method down and the dressing decided, I tested different flavor combinations. Many test salads later, my tasters and I agreed on a combination of minced shallot, minced garlic, toasted pine nuts, and shredded Pecorino Romano—the last two added just before serving. With this salad, I think that unfairly maligned Brussels sprouts may have shed their reputation for good.

BRUSSELS SPROUT SALAD Serves 8

Slice the sprouts as thin as possible. Shred the Pecorino Romano on the large holes of a box grater.

- 3 tablespoons lemon juice
- 2 tablespoons Dijon mustard
- 1 small shallot, minced
- 1 garlic clove, minced
  Salt and pepper
- 6 tablespoons extra-virgin olive oil
- 2 pounds Brussels sprouts, trimmed, halved, and sliced very thin
- 3 ounces Pecorino Romano cheese, shredded (1 cup)
- ½ cup pine nuts, toasted

1. Whisk lemon juice, mustard, shallot, garlic, and ½ teaspoon salt together in large bowl. Slowly whisk in oil until incorporated. Toss Brussels sprouts with vinaigrette and let sit for at least 30 minutes or up to 2 hours.

2. Fold in Pecorino and pine nuts. Season with salt and pepper to taste. Serve.

BRUSSELS SPROUT SALAD WITH CHEDDAR, HAZELNUTS, AND APPLE

Substitute 1 cup shredded sharp cheddar for Pecorino and ½ cup hazelnuts, toasted, skinned, and chopped, for pine nuts. Add 1 Granny Smith apple, cored and cut into ½-inch pieces.

BRUSSELS SPROUT SALAD WITH SMOKED GOUDA, PECANS, AND DRIED CHERRIES

Substitute 1 cup shredded smoked gouda for Pecorino and ½ cup pecans, toasted and chopped, for pine nuts. Add ½ cup chopped dried cherries.

This variation dresses up the sprouts with smoked gouda, toasted pecans, and dried cherries.

STEP BY STEP How to Slice Brussels Sprouts

You can use the slicing disk of your food processor or slice the sprouts with a chef's knife. Follow these steps to do the latter safely and quickly.

1. TRIM Trim the stem end of each sprout and then cut each sprout in half through the cut end.

2. SLICE With the flat surface on the cutting board, thinly slice each half.

Sweet Potato Pie

Pies with heavy, grainy, cloying fillings were not our idea of holiday dessert. To do this pie justice, we needed time . . . and lots of tubers. BY CAROLYNN PURPURA MACKAY AND CHRISTIE MORRISON

IN 1936, FAMED scientist George Washington Carver published a bulletin in which he offered 32 recipes that make use of the sweet potato, which grew (and grows) abundantly in the South. Traditional sweet potato pie was No. 6 on his list. Carver's recipe didn't use precise measurements—he called for sugar in quantities of teacups. But other than that, his method and basic set of ingredients were consistent with most modern recipes that we found and tested.

These recipes instruct home bakers to cook the sweet potatoes; mash or beat the flesh; make a custard of eggs, milk or cream, sugar, and spices; and whisk the custard into the mash. The filling is then poured into a pie shell and baked until it puffs and the center is set. We baked our way through a number of these simple-sounding recipes but were underwhelmed by the pies they produced, which were variously overspiced, far too sweet, or heavy instead of rich. Mashed fillings (as opposed to pureed) were grainy, plus the pies failed to slice neatly. This classic needed an upgrade.

Since pie making is, by definition, a bit of a production, we hoped to streamline where we could. The obvious place? Cooking the sweet potatoes as quickly and easily as possible. Recipes took an assortment of approaches, from baking the potatoes for an hour to laboriously peeling, dicing, and boiling them. We also tried the microwave, which was a simple matter of poking holes in the sweet potatoes to release steam (bursting potatoes were definitely not part of our game plan) and stopping a few times to turn them for even cooking. Given the minimal prep, the 20-minute timetable, and the fluffy, sweet results, the microwave bested both stovetop and oven. Once the sweet potatoes were tender, the food processor gave us a super-smooth, creamy puree.

Since most of the recipes we had tested called for three eggs to about 2 cups of puree, we'd follow suit—for now. As similar as these recipes were, the choice of dairy product was the one area where they diverged. We lined up eight parbaked pie crusts and tested, in turn, custards with milk, half-and-half, heavy cream, evaporated milk, sweetened condensed milk, buttermilk, sour cream, and cream cheese. Then we called over tasters for a sweet potato pie extravaganza.

Look closely: We added a layer of brown sugar between the crust and the filling. The sugar melts into a gooey faux caramel in the oven.

We polished off all the pies without much trouble, but when push came to shove, we voted for the sour cream filling for its lovely tang and silky texture.

The pie didn't yet slice cleanly, but we knew what to do. We added a few extra yolks to the 3 whole eggs—one was good, two even better. The yolks both firmed the filling and added richness, which suited a pie that we planned as the capstone for Thanksgiving dinner.

Come to think of it . . . we stirred 4 tablespoons of melted butter into the custard, too. It made the pie more satisfyingly rich but not heavy, and it solidified when the pie cooled, which made for cleaner slices.

As for sweetener, we baked a few more pies and carried out a few more tests before settling on 1 cup of light brown sugar. Its molasses edge echoed the earthiness of the sweet potatoes. To

season the filling further, we ran through all the spices that signal fall/warmth/fireside/harvest, namely cinnamon, cloves, ginger, pumpkin pie spice, nutmeg, and allspice. As with our initial test pies, less—just cinnamon and nutmeg—was more. We "bloomed" the pair in the hot melted butter to deepen their flavor and then combined the spiced butter with the custard. A shot of smoky bourbon and some vanilla extract rounded everything out.

At this point, there were no complaints—far from it—but was our pie truly as good as it could be? To take it to the next level, we toyed with sprinkling something on the parbaked crust before pouring in the filling. We tried chopped chocolate—"off point," the tasters ruled. Ditto for toasted coconut. With toasted pecans, at least we were in the right neck of the woods (the South), but they were soggy. What worked was a layer of just ¼ cup of brown sugar, which melted to a gooey faux caramel as the pie baked. It added an unexpected molten sugar layer to each bite and kicked this already satisfying pie into holiday table territory.

▶ Have extra sweet potatoes on hand? Visit CooksCountry. com/sweetpotatofries for our recipe for Crispy Sweet Potato Fries.

SWEET POTATO PIE Serves 8

The best pies use homemade crust. Find our recipe at CooksCountry.com/ piedough. If you're pressed for time, try our favorite store-bought crust, Wholly Wholesome 9" Certified Organic Traditional Bake at Home Rolled Pie Dough. Choose sweet potatoes that are about the same size so that they'll cook evenly.

1   (9-inch) single-crust pie dough
1¼ cups packed (8¾ ounces) light brown sugar
1¾ pounds sweet potatoes, unpeeled
½   teaspoon salt
4   tablespoons unsalted butter
½   teaspoon ground cinnamon
¼   teaspoon ground nutmeg
1   cup sour cream
3   large eggs plus 2 large yolks
2   tablespoons bourbon (optional)
1   teaspoon vanilla extract

1. Adjust oven rack to middle position and heat oven to 375 degrees. Roll dough into 12-inch circle on lightly floured counter. Loosely roll dough around rolling pin and gently unroll it onto 9-inch pie plate, letting excess dough hang over edge. Ease dough into plate by gently lifting edge of dough with your hand while pressing into plate bottom with your other hand.

2. Trim overhang to ½ inch beyond lip of pie plate. Tuck overhang under itself; folded edge should be flush with edge of pie plate. Crimp dough evenly around edge of pie using your fingers. Wrap dough-lined pie plate loosely in plastic and freeze until dough is firm, about 15 minutes.

3. Line chilled pie shell with 2 (12-inch) squares of parchment paper, letting parchment lie over edges of dough, and fill with pie weights. Bake until lightly golden around edges, 18 to 25 minutes. Carefully remove parchment and weights, rotate crust, and continue to bake until center begins to look opaque and slightly drier, 3 to 6 minutes. Remove from oven. Let crust cool completely. Sprinkle ¼ cup sugar over bottom of crust; set aside. Reduce oven temperature to 350 degrees.

4. Meanwhile, prick potatoes all over with fork. Microwave on large plate until potatoes are very soft and surface is slightly wet, 15 to 20 minutes, flipping every 5 minutes. Immediately slice potatoes in half to release steam. When cool enough to handle, scoop flesh into bowl of food processor. Add salt and remaining 1 cup sugar and process until smooth, about 60 seconds, scraping down sides of bowl as needed. Melt butter with cinnamon and nutmeg in microwave, 15 to 30 seconds; stir to combine. Add spiced butter; sour cream; eggs and yolks; bourbon, if using; and vanilla to potatoes and process until incorporated, about 10 seconds, scraping down sides of bowl as needed.

5. Pour potato mixture into prepared pie shell. Bake until filling is set around edges but center registers 165 degrees and jiggles slightly when pie is shaken, 35 to 40 minutes. Let pie cool completely on wire rack, about 2 hours. Serve.

KEYS TO Rich and Silky Sweet Potato Pie

Too often, sweet potato pie is grainy or bland. Here's how we made our filling smooth, rich, and flavorful.

USE EXTRA YOLKS
Three eggs plus two extra yolks add richness and make the pie velvety smooth.

BLOOM SPICES
Heating the cinnamon and nutmeg in melting butter brings out their full flavor.

ADD SOUR CREAM
Sour cream makes for an especially creamy pie, plus its tang balances the sweetness.

BOURBON WHIPPED CREAM

Makes 3 cups

Keep the heavy cream cold until you start whipping. Confectioners' sugar produces a more stable whipped cream than granulated sugar.

1½ cups heavy cream, chilled
2   tablespoons bourbon
1½ tablespoons confectioners' sugar
¾   teaspoon vanilla extract

Using stand mixer fitted with whisk, mix all ingredients together on medium-low speed until foamy, about 1 minute. Increase speed to high and whip until stiff peaks form, 1 to 3 minutes.

TEST KITCHEN TECHNIQUE

Temp the Filling

Custard pies, such as sweet potato pie, require careful baking. Over-baked pies may crack and will lose their voluptuous creaminess. Under-baked pies won't set up and will be difficult to slice cleanly. Properly baked sweet potato pie is done when just the center jiggles slightly if you gently shake the pie. A fail-safe way to know: Take its temperature. When the custard is 165 degrees, the pie is done.

PROBLEM 1:
Overbaking.

PROBLEM 2:
Underbaking.

SOLUTION:
Use a thermometer. Our favorite inexpensive model is the ThermoWorks Super-Fast Waterproof Pocket Thermometer.

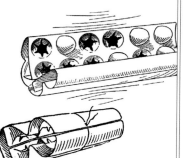

Sunday Roast, Weekday Po' Boys

We wanted to turn a tough braising cut into a tender roast—and plan a second supper
that was totally different but equally satisfying. BY REBECCAH MARSTERS

FOR BETTER OR for worse, speed and convenience rule in modern home cooking. Big batch cooking (eating the same roast, stew, casserole, etc., all week) is one way to go, but it's just not for me. I'm all for convenience, but I need variety in my diet. However, if I could cook once and get two different meals for two different nights, I'd be in business.

This time of year, my mind starts turning to beef roasts, and a roast beef has the advantage of being large enough to be reinvented for a second meal. But roasts can be very pricey, and I'm not interested in shelling out big bucks. We've developed lots of recipes for inexpensive beef roasts in the test kitchen, and we usually reach for lean top sirloin or eye-round roasts. I had an even more economical cut in mind: chuck-eye roast, which comes from the shoulder of the cow and has big, beefy flavor. The only problem is that there's a seam of intramuscular fat running through the middle—the reason it's usually cut up for beef stew or ground up for burgers. Undeterred, I ordered in a half-dozen hefty chuck-eye roasts—each one tipped the scale at nearly 6 pounds—and got to work.

I tried roasting one whole, fat and all, and was rewarded with juicy, beefy meat—in about every third bite. The slices of meat were so riddled with pockets of gristle and fat that it was a project just to eat. I needed to remove the large seam of fat in the middle of the roast, and it didn't take long to figure out how. The fat creates a natural separation between the two halves of the chuck roast; by simply pulling the pieces apart with my hands, I was left with two smaller roasts—one for each of my two meals. And with the majority of the fat on the outside, I could easily trim most of the fat away.

I took the larger of the two pieces for the roast beef, tied it up with kitchen twine (so it would cook more evenly), and seasoned it with salt, pepper, onion powder, and granulated garlic—flavors that work with almost any beef dish. I seared the tied roast in a skillet until it had a deeply browned crust and then transferred it—pan and all—to a low oven. Years of experience have taught us that low and slow is best for large cuts of beef; when the oven is

To make a tough cut tender, refrigerate it with a salt-based seasoning rub for at least 6 hours, cook it gently, and slice it thin.

too hot, the meat cooks unevenly and has an overcooked gray band around the edge by the time the center is medium-rare. We've gone as low as 225 degrees, but for the sake of faster cooking, I settled on a still-moderate 300. Less than an hour later, when the roast had reached 125 degrees (we usually prefer roast beef cooked to medium-rare), I pulled it out and let it rest before slicing it. The verdict? Great

beefy flavor; tough, chewy texture.

Chuck is a naturally tough cut of meat, which is why we usually braise or stew it for hours until all that tough connective tissue has melted out. I wanted this to be a sliceable roast, not a shredded pot roast, but maybe I could cook it longer than usual. I cooked three separate roasts to 130, 140, and 150 degrees and found, surprisingly, that the most "overcooked" meat was

the best. At 150 degrees, the beef was still juicy and a bit rosy in the center but didn't require a jaw workout. And the flavor was still fantastic. I whipped up a simple dump-and-stir horseradish sauce to serve with the beef, and I had one meal in the bag.

Eyeing the other half of the chuck-eye roast left on my cutting board, the first thing that came to mind was a po' boy sandwich. I sampled my first roast beef po' boy on a recent trip to New Orleans, and it was a game changer.

Po' boys, New Orleans' version of subs or hoagies, are served on long sections of squishy white bread. You can get them plain or "dressed" with lettuce, tomato, mayonnaise, and pickles. One style of roast beef po' boy left a particularly lasting impression. Most roast beef po' boys have sliced meat and gravy, but some bolster the gravy with the "debris," the bits of meat left over after cooking and slicing. The savory, messy roast beef po' boy with debris gravy that I had at a place called R & O's got high marks. I hoped to duplicate it in the test kitchen using the other half of my chuck roast.

For tender, shredded meat, I'd have to cook the chuck a lot longer than the hour my roast beef was in the oven. That meant the shredded meat needed a head start. To ensure that it cooked as fast as possible, I cut the small roast into chunks as if for stew. After browning the larger tied roast in the pan on the stovetop, I seasoned the cubed meat with the same mixture (salt, pepper, onion powder, and granulated garlic) and added it to the pan to brown. Then, following our basic method for beef stew, I sprinkled flour over the cubed meat and cooked it for a minute before deglazing the pan with red wine. Finally, I whisked in equal parts beef and chicken broths, brought the mixture to a boil, covered the pan, moved it to a 300-degree oven, and let the meat braise. Meanwhile, the seared roast rested on a plate.

After an hour, I uncovered the skillet and nestled the browned (but not cooked) roast on top of the stewing cubes. After another hour, when the roast reached 150 degrees, the braised cubes were fall-apart tender. I used a potato masher to coax them into shreds (they were so tender that a stern talking-to might have done the job), and since it was for my second meal, I cooled and refrigerated the shredded meat. The next day I heated it up and spooned it onto toasted mayo-smeared sub rolls, topping each with tomato, lettuce, and sliced pickles. My po' boys were beefy, savory, and satisfying—I had done this sandwich justice.

SLOW-ROASTED CHUCK ROAST
Serves 4 to 6
Refrigerate the meat with the seasoning rub for at least 6 hours before cooking.

BEEF
- 1 (5- to 6-pound) center-cut boneless beef chuck-eye roast
- 5 teaspoons kosher salt
- 2 teaspoons pepper
- 2 teaspoons onion powder
- 2 teaspoons granulated garlic
- 2 tablespoons vegetable oil
- ¼ cup all-purpose flour
- ½ cup red wine
- 1½ cups beef broth
- 1½ cups chicken broth

HORSERADISH SAUCE
- ½ cup heavy cream
- ½ cup sour cream
- ⅓ cup prepared horseradish, drained
- 1 tablespoon Dijon mustard
- 1 garlic clove, minced
- ½ teaspoon pepper

1. FOR THE BEEF: Pat roast dry with paper towels. Separate roast into 2 pieces along natural seam and trim fat to ¼-inch thickness. Tie kitchen twine around larger roast at 1-inch intervals. Cut smaller roast into 1-inch cubes. Combine salt, pepper, onion powder, and granulated garlic in bowl. Rub surface of tied roast evenly with half of spice mixture and wrap in plastic wrap. Transfer beef cubes to 1-gallon zipper-lock bag; add remaining spice mixture to bag, seal, and toss to coat beef cubes. Refrigerate tied roast and beef cubes for at least 6 hours or up to 24 hours.

2. Adjust oven rack to lower-middle position and heat oven to 300 degrees. Heat 1 tablespoon oil in 12-inch non-stick skillet over medium-high heat until just smoking. Brown tied roast on all sides, 10 to 12 minutes; transfer to plate.

3. Return now-empty skillet to medium-high heat, add remaining 1 tablespoon oil, and heat until just smoking. Add cubed beef and brown on all sides, 10 to 12 minutes. Sprinkle flour over meat and cook, stirring constantly, until beef is evenly coated, about 1 minute. Add wine and cook until pan is nearly dry, about 1 minute. Add beef

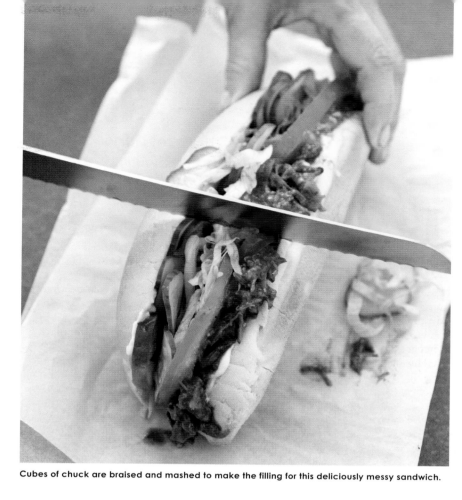

Cubes of chuck are braised and mashed to make the filling for this deliciously messy sandwich.

and chicken broths and bring to boil, scraping up any browned bits. Cover, transfer to oven, and cook for 1 hour.

4. FOR THE HORSERADISH SAUCE: Whisk all ingredients together in bowl until smooth. (Sauce can be refrigerated for up to 2 days.)

5. Uncover skillet and place browned roast on top of cubed meat. Return skillet to oven and continue to cook, uncovered, until cubed meat is fork-tender and roast registers 150 degrees, about 1 hour longer. Transfer roast to carving board, tent loosely with aluminum foil, and let rest for 20 minutes. Using potato masher, mash cubed meat until shredded into rough ½-inch pieces. Transfer shredded meat and gravy to bowl and let cool completely. Cover and refrigerate until ready to make Roast Beef Po' Boys, up to 2 days. Remove twine from roast and slice thin. Serve roast with horseradish sauce.

ROAST BEEF PO' BOYS
Serves 6
Toast rolls on a baking sheet in a 400-degree oven for 5 to 10 minutes.

- Reserved meat and gravy from Slow-Roasted Chuck Roast
- Salt and pepper
- 6 (8-inch) Italian sub rolls, split lengthwise and toasted
- ½ cup mayonnaise
- 2 large tomatoes, cored and sliced thin
- 2 cups shredded iceberg lettuce
- 3 whole dill pickles, sliced thin

1. In large saucepan, bring meat and gravy to boil over medium heat. Remove from heat and season with salt and pepper to taste.

2. Spread insides of rolls evenly with mayonnaise. Divide meat and gravy evenly among rolls, then top with tomatoes, lettuce, and pickles. Serve.

TEST KITCHEN TECHNIQUE **Cook Two Meals at Once**

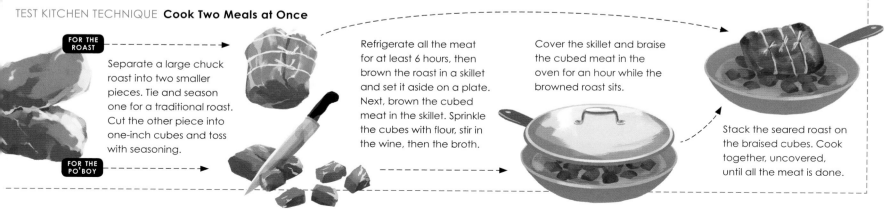

FOR THE ROAST Separate a large chuck roast into two smaller pieces. Tie and season one for a traditional roast. Cut the other piece into one-inch cubes and toss with seasoning.

Refrigerate all the meat for at least 6 hours, then brown the roast in a skillet and set it aside on a plate. Next, brown the cubed meat in the skillet. Sprinkle the cubes with flour, stir in the wine, then the broth.

Cover the skillet and braise the cubed meat in the oven for an hour while the browned roast sits.

FOR THE PO' BOY

Stack the seared roast on the braised cubes. Cook together, uncovered, until all the meat is done.

Featherbed Eggs

With a make-ahead element built into the recipe, strata is perfect for a big breakfast crowd. But the traditional sandwich bread doesn't bring much to the party. BY SARAH GABRIEL

LEAFING THROUGH AN old breakfast cookbook, I came across a recipe for featherbed eggs. The name was so enchanting that I did some more research. After a search in our cookbook library, I found that featherbed eggs is simply a name sometimes given to strata, a favorite brunch standby. Strata is a casserole of eggs, milk or cream, bread, and cheese that is assembled and then weighted and stored in the refrigerator overnight to let the custard permeate the bread. Recipes for classic strata usually call for white sandwich bread or French bread, which don't add much in either flavor or texture. But the recipes that really piqued my interest used cornbread.

▶ Serve the strata with fruit on the side. Read our guide to tropical fruit at CooksCountry.com/tropicalfruit.

Changing up the add-ins can spruce up an old strata recipe, but swapping the bread would give me a completely new base flavor; I selected half a dozen recipes that used cornbread. A few called for store-bought cornbread, while the rest called for making cornbread and letting it cool before continuing with the standard strata procedure of slicing or dicing the bread; oven-drying or staling it; and then mixing it with cheese, add-ins, and the custard. We found the store-bought cornbread too sweet and otherwise inconsistent, but homemade cornbread, while delicious, required significantly more work. I needed to whittle this down.

Rather than reinvent the wheel, I started with a simple dump-and-stir test kitchen cornbread recipe. To see if I could just skip the drying and staling routine, I baked and cooled a batch of cornbread, cut it up, and mixed it with shredded cheddar and sliced scallions in a baking dish. Then I poured in a working custard of six eggs and 4½ cups of milk and sprinkled more cheese over the top. After covering the dish with plastic wrap, I weighed it down and set it in the fridge overnight. In the morning, I baked it until it puffed up ever so slightly and the custard set. The pepper and cayenne had clumped in the custard and ended up in one spot, but that was the least of my problems. The cornbread had disintegrated and become slimy. I tried again with less custard; now the dish was denser, but the slimy bread persisted. Skipping the drying step was not an option.

So I needed dry bread—but I also needed an easy way to get it. I tried turning down the oven and baking the bread low and slow, essentially overcooking it on purpose to dry it out in just one trip through the oven. With this process the cornbread took an hour to bake and 45 minutes to cool. Only then could I cut it up to assemble the casserole. In other words, it took fewer steps but much more time. Maybe, I thought, I could decrease the cooking time by increasing the surface area. I spread the same amount of batter that I had been baking in an 8-inch square pan over an entire rimmed baking sheet. The batter, now only about ¼ inch deep in the pan, browned and pulled away from the edges of the pan in less than 20 minutes, and in just 10 more minutes it was almost completely cool. As an added advantage, this flat sheet of cornbread was easy to tear into pieces—no more

Our fast homemade cornbread gives the strata better flavor and texture.

slicing or dicing. I mixed the bread with the cheese and scallions, poured on the custard, covered the casserole, and weighed it down. The next morning, I baked it for about an hour. Ah, success.

Well, mostly. My baking sheet cornbread was dry enough to soak up the custard and remain intact so the texture of the strata was custardy, not slimy, but the spices still weren't evenly distributed. As I was mixing up the dry ingredients for the cornbread, I got an idea that I thought might solve my clumping-spice problem: Put the cayenne and pepper in the cornbread instead of in the custard. The bread came out nicely speckled and made an evenly seasoned batch of featherbed eggs. At last, I had a new brunch dish worth getting out of bed for.

FASTER, DRIER, EASIER
We bake the cornbread in a thin sheet.

TEST KITCHEN TECHNIQUE
Cornbread Quicker
Before we could even think about starting our strata, we needed to bake and stale cornbread for its base. But would the extra work torpedo the whole concept? Not if we could simplify. So we cooked cornbread in sheet form rather than baking it in the usual deeper pan. Spread thin, the batter baked very quickly. We let it overbake slightly so we could skip the step of staling or toasting it. No need to neatly cube it either; we tore up the sheet with our hands.

FEATHERBED EGGS
Serves 10 to 12
To weigh down the assembled strata so the custard permeates the bread, fill two 1-quart zipper-lock bags with rice or sugar and lay them side by side over the plastic-covered surface. Serve the strata with hot sauce.

CORNBREAD
- 1 cup (5 ounces) cornmeal
- 1 cup (5 ounces) all-purpose flour
- 2 teaspoons baking powder
- ½ teaspoon baking soda
- 1½ teaspoons pepper
- ½ teaspoon salt
- ¼ teaspoon cayenne pepper
- 1⅓ cups whole milk
- 2 large eggs, lightly beaten

CUSTARD
- 10 ounces sharp cheddar cheese, shredded (2½ cups)
- 6 scallions, sliced thin
- 4½ cups whole milk
- 6 large eggs, lightly beaten
- 2 teaspoons salt

1. FOR THE CORNBREAD: Adjust oven rack to middle position and heat oven to 400 degrees. Line rimmed baking sheet with parchment paper and spray with vegetable oil spray.

2. Whisk cornmeal, flour, baking powder, baking soda, pepper, salt, and cayenne together in bowl. Whisk milk and eggs together in separate bowl. Whisk milk-egg mixture into cornmeal mixture until just combined. Pour batter into prepared sheet and spread to cover entire sheet. Bake until lightly browned and edges of cornbread pull away from sides of sheet, 17 to 19 minutes. Let cornbread cool in sheet on wire rack for 10 minutes.

3. FOR THE CUSTARD: Spray 13 by 9-inch baking dish with oil spray. Tear cornbread into 1-inch pieces and place in prepared dish. Add 1½ cups cheddar and scallions to cornbread and toss to combine. Whisk milk, eggs, and salt in bowl; pour custard over cornbread mixture. Top casserole with remaining 1 cup cheddar. Cover with plastic wrap, weigh down, and refrigerate for 6 to 24 hours.

4. Adjust oven rack to middle position and heat oven to 325 degrees. Remove weights from casserole and discard plastic. Bake until lightly browned and center registers 170 degrees, 50 to 60 minutes. Let rest for 15 minutes. Serve.

MAPLE-SAUSAGE FEATHERBED EGGS

Bake 1 pound breakfast sausage links on middle rack of 400-degree oven until 165 degrees, about 10 minutes. Slice sausages into ½-inch pieces. Add sausage to cornbread pieces with cheddar and scallions. For custard, substitute ½ cup maple syrup for ½ cup milk and reduce salt to 1 teaspoon. Drizzle 1 tablespoon maple syrup over casserole just before baking.

PIMENTO-CHEESE FEATHERBED EGGS

Substitute extra-sharp cheddar cheese for sharp cheddar cheese and 2 minced shallots for scallions. Add ½ cup plus 2 tablespoons jarred chopped pimentos to cornbread pieces with cheddar and shallots. Add 1 tablespoon Dijon mustard and 1 tablespoon Worcestershire sauce to custard.

Smoky Turkey Cobb Salad

A subtly sweet maple vinaigrette, two kinds of smoky meat, and pan-seared cherry tomatoes lift this Cobb salad out of the ordinary.

BY REBECCAH MARSTERS

LEFTOVER TURKEY IS a given at Thanksgiving, but how many sandwiches can one person eat? I hoped to repurpose my bird into something a little more interesting: a main-course salad. Cobb salad came to mind. I made a salad from the classic ingredients: bacon, avocado, hard-cooked eggs, turkey, good blue cheese (we like Stilton), tomatoes, romaine lettuce, and a red wine vinaigrette. I tossed the dressed lettuce with the other ingredients, chopped and diced. The salad was salty, smoky, pungent, and creamy—not bad (quite good, actually) but missing some brightness and sweetness.

So I increased the ratio of vinegar in the dressing and stirred in minced shallot and Dijon mustard. To sweeten my tweaked vinaigrette, I landed on maple syrup, and in further testing, cider vinegar proved a good match for it. I dressed the lettuce with the bright, tangy-sweet vinaigrette, topped it, and tasted again. Every component was doing its part but one: the mushy, tasteless tomatoes. Out-of-season tomatoes are the worst, but how can you have Cobb salad without tomatoes?

I traded the chopped beefsteak tomatoes I had been using for cherry tomatoes, which are reliably sweet year-round. The salad improved, but it still wasn't stellar. What about cooking the tomatoes to concentrate their sugars? I already had the skillet out for the bacon, so I added a pint of cherry tomatoes to the hot bacon fat, shaking the pan until they were just charred and beginning to burst. The sweet, warm tomatoes invigorated the salad—it didn't hurt that they had picked up smoky bacon flavor. Unlike so much holiday food, this salad was fresh and bright, and definitely something to be thankful for.

▶ Visit CooksCountry.com/hardcookedeggs to learn how to make perfect hard-cooked eggs every time.

We soften cherry tomatoes in bacon fat to give the out-of-season tomatoes a helping hand.

SMOKY TURKEY COBB SALAD
Serves 4

You can use leftover smoked turkey from our Spice-Rubbed Grill-Roasted Turkey on page 5 or thick-sliced smoked turkey from the deli. Good quality blue cheese makes a difference here.

- 6 slices bacon
- 12 ounces cherry tomatoes
- 2 tablespoons cider vinegar
- 2 tablespoons maple syrup
- 1 teaspoon minced shallot
- 1 teaspoon Dijon mustard
  Salt and pepper
- 3 tablespoons extra-virgin olive oil
- 2 cups chopped smoked turkey
- 3 romaine lettuce hearts (18 ounces), cut into 1-inch pieces
- 4 large hard-cooked eggs, chopped
- 4 ounces blue cheese, crumbled (1 cup)
- 1 avocado, halved, pitted, and cut into ½-inch pieces

1. Cook bacon in 12-inch nonstick skillet over medium heat until crispy, 7 to 9 minutes; transfer to paper towel–lined plate. When bacon is cool enough to handle, crumble into bite-size pieces and set aside. Pour off all but 1 tablespoon fat from skillet and return to medium heat. Add tomatoes and cook, shaking pan often, until softened and spotty brown, 3 to 5 minutes. Remove from heat and let cool slightly.

2. Whisk vinegar, maple syrup, shallot, mustard, ¾ teaspoon salt, and ½ teaspoon pepper together in large bowl until combined. Slowly whisk in oil until incorporated. Transfer 1 tablespoon dressing to separate bowl, add turkey, and toss to combine. Toss romaine with remaining dressing. Season turkey and romaine with salt and pepper to taste.

3. Transfer romaine to serving platter or individual plates and top with bacon, tomatoes, turkey, eggs, cheese, and avocado. Serve.

Hearty Vegetable Chowder

We set out to make a satisfying, creamy soup that focused on the vegetables but was still hearty and flavorful. BY NICK IVERSON

CHOWDERS EXEMPLIFY THE straightforward, hearty, satisfying nature of New England's best dishes. Lobster, corn, and clam are the three best-known chowders, but I've also been intrigued by recipes for vegetable chowder.

Most read pretty much the same: Sweat onions, carrots, and celery in butter or pork fat (from bacon or salt pork); add flour to thicken; stir in broth; add your root vegetables of choice; simmer until tender; and finish with heavy cream. I followed a handful of recipes, and after many hours of peeling, dicing, stirring, and simmering, I asked my coworkers to evaluate the results. The different vegetable and flavor combinations helped us get a handle on what we wanted: We opted for a classic onion, carrot, celery, and thyme flavor base. Yukon Gold potatoes gave the chowder satisfying bulk and heft and held their shape in the chowder without breaking down too much. Bacon bested salt pork for its smoky depth. Chicken broth underpinned the chowder nicely with good savory taste. With simplicity and clarity of flavor in mind, we decided to leave it at that.

Now I was ready to address the issue of floury and stodgy chowder. I knew that the fault lay with the roux, the combination of flour and butter that thickens most chowders. I tried replacing the roux with a slurry of cornstarch and broth, but the chowder still lacked the light, clean flavor I was after. Then I remembered a soup trick I'd learned in

Pureed leeks and potatoes help give this soup its velvety smoothness.

Eliminate the Guesswork
The best chowders have a smooth, creamy base punctuated by chunks of vegetables. We achieved this by pureeing precisely measured amounts—1 cup of the softened vegetables and 2 cups of liquid—and using the puree to thicken the chowder.

CONTROL THE TEXTURE
Measure the solids and liquid before pureeing.

culinary school: adding cubed potatoes to the sweating aromatics and stirring vigorously. The constant stirring helps release the potatoes' sticky starch, which results in satiny smooth pureed soup. I'd borrow the technique, stirring the potatoes and then pureeing some of the vegetables in my chowder to thicken it.

Before trying the method, I switched to russet potatoes so I could take advantage of their higher starch content, and I substituted leeks for the onions for their silky quality when pureed. Now I began a new pot of chowder. After the leeks, carrots, and celery started to soften, I added the cubed russets and stirred constantly. Within 2 minutes, the potatoes were leaching a sticky starch that made all the vegetables tacky. I poured in the

broth and simmered the whole lot for about 20 minutes. Once the vegetables were tender, I removed a few cups of the soup to puree and then stirred the puree back into the chowder. (Subsequent tests showed that 1 cup of the veggies and 2 cups of the broth were ideal amounts.)

We liked the soup's consistency, but my tasters refused to believe that the stirring had anything to do with it. To prove it, I made two more batches, constantly stirring the potatoes in one and not at all in the other. The no-stir batch was watery and gritty, the other smooth and velvety. Our science editor explained that starch was released from the damaged potato cells because the potatoes had been cut into small cubes, which my stirring broke down further.

Most chowders are finished with heavy cream, but the cream muted the vegetable flavor. We preferred half-and-half. I was wrapping up, enjoying a last bowl, when it struck me that my chowder could use a finishing boost. I stirred in minced chives for a little freshness and added an enlivening squeeze of lemon. The vegetables were tender, the chowder creamy, substantial, bright—refined, even. How very New England.

HEARTY VEGETABLE CHOWDER
Serves 4 to 6

If your blender lid has a vent, open it (and cover with a towel) when blending so the steam can escape.

- 6 slices bacon, chopped
- 1 pound leeks, white and light green parts only, halved lengthwise, sliced thin, and washed thoroughly
- 4 carrots, peeled, halved lengthwise, and cut into 1-inch pieces
- 2 celery ribs, halved lengthwise and cut into ½-inch pieces
- 1 teaspoon minced fresh thyme
  Salt and pepper
- 1½ pounds russet potatoes, peeled and cut into 1-inch pieces
- 2 garlic cloves, minced
- 4 cups chicken broth
- 1 bay leaf
- ½ cup half-and-half
- 1 tablespoon minced fresh chives
- 1 teaspoon lemon juice

1. Cook bacon in Dutch oven over medium heat until fat has rendered and bacon is nearly crispy, 7 to 9 minutes. Add leeks, carrots, celery, thyme, and 1 teaspoon salt and cook until leeks are translucent, about 8 minutes. Add potatoes and cook, stirring constantly, until starch begins to release and coat vegetables, about 2 minutes. Add garlic and cook until fragrant, about 30 seconds. Add broth and bay leaf and bring to boil.

2. Reduce heat to low, cover, and simmer, stirring occasionally, until vegetables are tender, about 20 minutes. Discard bay leaf. Transfer 1 cup of vegetables (using slotted spoon) and 2 cups of soup broth to blender; process until smooth, about 1 minute. Stir processed soup back into pot. Stir in half-and-half, chives, and lemon juice and gently rewarm soup. Season with salt and pepper to taste. Serve.

Broccoli Dip in a Bread Bowl

Let's be honest: Most versions are gloppy and bland. Rescuing this party favorite meant opting for fresh broccoli and reconsidering the creamy base. BY SARAH GABRIEL

DIP IN A BREAD BOWL is, admittedly, a retro party snack, but the novelty never seems to wear off. Creamy broccoli dip is appealing on its own, but put it in an edible bowl and it's hard to resist. My goal was to rescue it from its usual fate—gloppy blandness.

Like other cold, creamy dips, broccoli dip starts with a base of sour cream, mayonnaise, or a combination. The cook stirs in chopped broccoli (fresh or frozen); oniony elements (minced onion, onion powder, minced garlic, garlic salt, or onion powder–heavy salad dressing mix); and add-ins like herbs, red pepper, or even canned water chestnuts. None of the recipes I tried was rave-worthy, but I got what these dips were driving at—creamy and green like spinach dip but with a livelier flavor and texture.

I'd start with the dip and then move on to the bowl. Frozen broccoli was spongy and bland; raw fresh broccoli was tough. Hoping that lightly cooked fresh broccoli would strike the right balance, I boiled the florets and the sliced stems for 2 minutes and then chopped them in the food processor. The florets were perfectly done, but the stalks were still woody. I tried pureeing the stalks into a base of equal parts mayonnaise and sour cream, but the stalks turned to stringy bits. I'd need to cook the stalks longer. I did, at the same time switching to the microwave for ease and steaming the broccoli (3 minutes for the florets, 5 for the stalks). With the fresher-tasting broccoli, the sour cream and mayonnaise combo seemed stifling; trading the sour

The vertical cuts on the "bowl" make it easy to tear off chunks of bread.

cream for lighter, tangier Greek yogurt was better.

I had some work to do on seasonings. Two tablespoons of minced shallot provided a savory kick. Exchanging garlic powder for a clove of the fresh stuff was another stride toward brighter flavor, but something was missing. I reluctantly admitted that recipes that used powdered salad dressing mix had a full, savory flavor that my fresher version lacked. They contained *umami* boosters, like monosodium glutamate and hydrolyzed yeast extract. Searching for similar flavor-boosting ingredients, I came across a block of Parmesan cheese. A quarter cup of finely grated Parmesan, plus salt, pepper, and cayenne, filled out the flavor. This dip was creamy and

vibrant; all it lacked was a bread bowl.

The prevailing bowl-making method called for slicing across the domed top of a round loaf and then pinching out bread to form the bowl. But the pinched-out pieces were too manhandled and flimsy for dipping. I tried cutting down into the loaf with the knife angled toward the center and working my way around the loaf, a couple of inches in from the edge, making a cone-shaped bread plug that I could remove in one piece and neatly dice. The depression held the dip comfortably. It was going great until the last bread chunk was gone. We tore into the dip-soaked bowl—delicious, sure, but a bit too messy.

Trying to engineer a tidier-to-eat bread bowl, I sliced vertically through its

rim in several spots and then spooned in dip, nervous about leaks. The bowl held, and we devoured both dip and bowl without embarrassing ourselves. Judging by the empty plate and clean-shirted tasters, I'd call it a success.

BROCCOLI DIP IN A BREAD BOWL Serves 12

Make the dip up to 24 hours ahead, but prepare and fill the bread bowl just before serving. Opt for a taller, domed loaf of sourdough over a flat, wide loaf. Serve with crudités, if desired.

- 12 ounces broccoli, florets cut into 1-inch pieces, stalks peeled and cut into ½-inch pieces
- ⅔ cup mayonnaise
- ¼ cup grated Parmesan cheese
- 2 tablespoons minced shallot
- 1 garlic clove, minced
- ½ teaspoon salt
- ¼ teaspoon pepper
- ⅛ teaspoon cayenne pepper
- ⅔ cup whole Greek yogurt
- 1 (8-inch) round sourdough bread

1. Combine broccoli stalks and 1 tablespoon water in bowl. Cover and microwave until tender, about 5 minutes. Transfer to colander, rinse under cold water, and drain thoroughly. Transfer to dish towel and pat dry. Combine broccoli florets and 1 tablespoon water in now-empty bowl. Cover and microwave until just tender, about 3 minutes. Transfer to colander, rinse under cold water, and drain thoroughly. Transfer to dish towel and pat dry. (Keep stalks and florets separate.)

2. Combine stalks, mayonnaise, Parmesan, shallot, garlic, salt, pepper, and cayenne in food processor and process until finely ground, about 30 seconds, scraping down sides of bowl as needed. Add florets and pulse until finely chopped, about 4 pulses. Transfer to bowl, stir in yogurt, and refrigerate for at least 30 minutes or up to 24 hours.

3. Using paring knife, cut into top of bread at 45-degree angle, about 1½ inches from edge. Continue to slice around bread at 45-degree angle in approximate 5-inch circle. Remove bread top and cut into bite-size pieces. Make vertical slices through perimeter of bread bowl at 1½-inch intervals, stopping just shy of bottom crust. Transfer dip to bread bowl. Serve, using bread pieces to dip.

Getting to Know Salts and Peppers

What one line do you find in nearly every savory recipe? "Season with salt and pepper." But not all salts and peppers are created equal. Here are 12 we like to cook with. BY CHRISTIE MORRISON

Table Salt
PEPPER'S PAL

Its small crystals and quickness at dissolving make table salt our go-to in most recipes. Calcium silicate, an anticaking agent, makes it fast-flowing. Iodine was added to this salt beginning in 1924 to prevent thyroid-related diseases; most table salt today is iodized. We use table salt to season, to make brines, and to preserve bright color when we're blanching green vegetables.

Black Peppercorns
SALT'S BETTER HALF

Whatever the variety, all peppercorns are defined by the heat-bearing compound piperine. Freshly ground pepper adds distinctive flavor and heat to many dishes and plays a starring role in our Steak Tips au Poivre (**CooksCountry.com/ steaktipsaupoivre**). For cracked pepper, gently crush peppercorns with the bottom of a heavy pan while using a rocking motion.

Kosher Salt
SIZE MATTERS

This coarse salt's large crystal size makes it easy to pick up with your fingers and distribute evenly on food; we often use it to season large cuts of meat. To convert table salt into kosher salt in recipes, you need a greater volume of the big crystals. The amounts are inconsistent from brand to brand: Increase the salt by 50 percent for Morton Coarse Kosher Salt (say from 1 to 1½ teaspoons) and by 100 percent for Diamond Crystal (from 1 to 2 teaspoons).

Pink Peppercorns
THE PRETENDER

This rose-hued pepper isn't a peppercorn at all: It's actually a berry from a tropical evergreen. In the 1980s, nouvelle cuisine made the pink peppercorn a star. Like true peppercorns, it has a savory heat but its "light, fruity flavor," as well as its pretty color make it an excellent addition to soft cheeses, salads, and popcorn. It's often sold as part of a mixed peppercorn medley.

Green Peppercorns
YOUNG 'UNS

Green peppercorns, which resemble capers, are simply unripe black pepper-corns and are usually soft (so put down that pepper mill). They are sold packed in brine or vinegar, so rinse them before using. Use them crushed or whole in light sauces or salads in which their "piney," "citrus-like," "juniper" flavors can shine.

Sea Salt
BAKED AND RAKED

Most sea salt comes from seawater held in large, shallow ponds or large pans. As the water evaporates—naturally or by heating—coarse salt crystals fall to the bottom. The crystals are then collected by raking. We sprinkle sea salt on salad, meat, and cooked vegetables just before serving so that it maintains its satisfying crunch. Our favorite, Maldon Sea Salt, has especially delicate, crunchy flakes.

Pink Curing Salt
PRETTY IN PORK

Commonly labeled pink salt, curing salt also answers to DQ Curing Salt and Insta Cure #1. This rose-colored salt contains sodium nitrite, which is a compound that inhibits bacterial growth, boosts meaty flavor, and preserves the color of fully cured bacon. Find curing salt in specialty food stores or order it online.

White Peppercorns
BEIGE ON BEIGE

White peppercorns are fully ripe black peppercorns; the black outer husk is removed and the berries are dried. They lose much of their heat in this process but have a sharpness and a pronounced citrus flavor ("floral," "potpourri," and "licorice," tasters noted). Many chefs like the way that these peppercorns blend into white sauces, while Asian cooks use them in stir-fries and to flavor hot-and-sour soup.

Pickling Salt
WELL PRESERVED

Made without anticaking agents, iodine, or other additives, pickling salt (also called canning salt) is prized for its purity as a brine maker—in fact, it's basically finely milled kosher salt. When mixed into a pickling brine, the crystals contribute to the flavor of the pickles without turning the brine cloudy or dark, as iodized salt will. You can find pickling salt at the grocery store or any hardware store that sells canning supplies.

Flavored Salts
SEASON-ALL

These spice cabinet staples range from stalwarts like Lawry's Seasoned Salt (a blend of salt, sugar, spices, and other ingredients) to celery salt, onion salt, and garlic salt. While many seasoned salts merely combine granulated spice powders with salt and an anticaking agent, some flavored salt blends add monosodium glutamate for deeper flavor. You can make your own flavored salt with table salt and just a few pantry ingredients: **CooksCountry.com/flavoredsalts**.

Rock Salt
ODD-JOBMAN

These large, chunky crystals are too big to dissolve easily in cooked dishes, but they're used around the kitchen for a number of odd jobs. Salt lowers the freezing point of water, so a rock salt and water solution will quickly chill a bottle of wine. Or mix rock salt with ice and you're on your way to chilling homemade ice cream. The crystals also make a suitable bed for shellfish dishes like clams casino. Buy food-grade rock salt, not the sort used to melt ice on roadways.

Sichuan Peppercorns
TONGUE TINGLER

Until recently, Sichuan peppercorns were banned from the United States; the shrub that bears them was thought to carry a disease that could harm citrus crops. These peppercorns are a staple in Sichuan recipes, such as ma pao tofu. They have an intense flavor that "hits you in the nose," but they are even better known for their numbing effect. Said one taster: "Musky and woodsy, and then my tongue went numb." Find them in Asian markets and large grocery stores.

PORK CHOPS WITH CHERRY SAUCE

QUICK ASIAN-STYLE DUMPLING SOUP

SKILLET CHEESEBURGER MACARONI

MEDITERRANEAN CHICKEN WRAPS

QUICK ASIAN-STYLE DUMPLING SOUP Serves 4

✓ **WHY THIS RECIPE WORKS:** For a fast weeknight soup, we rely on frozen dumplings, and we use bacon as a shortcut to a smoky meat base.

- 4 slices bacon, cut into ½-inch pieces
- 3 scallions, white and green parts separated, sliced thin on bias
- 2 teaspoons grated fresh ginger
- ¼ teaspoon red pepper flakes
- 4 ounces shiitake mushrooms, stemmed and sliced thin
- 6 cups chicken broth
- 2 (8-ounce) bags frozen Asian-style dumplings or potstickers
- 2 tablespoons fish sauce
- 2 tablespoons lime juice

1. Cook bacon in large saucepan over medium heat until crisp, 6 to 8 minutes. Using slotted spoon, transfer bacon to paper towel–lined plate. Pour off all but 2 tablespoons fat from pan and return pan to medium heat. Add scallion whites, ginger, and pepper flakes and cook until scallion whites have softened, about 2 minutes. Add mushrooms and cook until beginning to brown, about 5 minutes.

2. Add broth and bring to boil. Add dumplings and simmer over medium-low heat until dumplings are cooked through, 10 to 15 minutes. Remove from heat and stir in fish sauce and lime juice. Serve, sprinkled with scallion greens and bacon.

TEST KITCHEN NOTE: If you don't have enough fat in the pan after cooking the bacon, add enough vegetable oil to measure 2 tablespoons.

PORK CHOPS WITH CHERRY SAUCE Serves 4

✓ **WHY THIS RECIPE WORKS:** Thin-cut pork chops cook quickly, and the fruity sauce made with pantry ingredients tastes like the result of far more work than it is.

- 4 (8- to 10-ounce) bone-in pork rib chops, ½ inch thick, trimmed
   Salt and pepper
- 2 tablespoons olive oil
- 2 tablespoons minced shallot
- 3 garlic cloves, minced
- ½ teaspoon fennel seeds
- ¾ cup port
- ¼ cup balsamic vinegar
- ¼ cup dried cherries
- 1 tablespoon chopped fresh sage

1. Pat pork dry with paper towels and season with salt and pepper. Heat oil in 12-inch skillet over medium-high heat until just smoking. Add pork and cook until well browned and cooked through, about 4 minutes per side; transfer to plate and tent loosely with aluminum foil.

2. Add shallot, garlic, and fennel seeds to now-empty skillet and cook until shallot is softened, about 1 minute. Add port, vinegar, cherries, and sage and bring to boil. Reduce heat to medium-low and simmer until reduced to ½ cup and cherries are plump, about 10 minutes. Add accumulated pork juices to sauce. Pour sauce over pork. Serve.

TEST KITCHEN NOTE: Inexpensive ruby port is fine here. You can use dried cranberries in place of the dried cherries. Serve with mashed potatoes.

MEDITERRANEAN CHICKEN WRAPS Serves 4

✓ **WHY THIS RECIPE WORKS:** Starting with a rotisserie chicken means that most of the work is already done.

- 1 (2½-pound) rotisserie chicken, skin and bones discarded, meat shredded into bite-size pieces (3 cups)
- 4 ounces feta cheese, crumbled (1 cup)
- ½ cup plain Greek yogurt
- ½ cup jarred roasted red peppers, patted dry and chopped coarse
- ½ cup pitted kalamata olives, chopped coarse
- 2 tablespoons minced shallot
- 1 teaspoon grated lemon zest plus 2 teaspoons juice
- ½ teaspoon salt
- ¼ teaspoon pepper
- 4 (12-inch) flour tortillas
- 4 ounces (4 cups) baby arugula

1. Combine chicken, feta, yogurt, red peppers, olives, shallot, lemon zest and juice, salt, and pepper in bowl.

2. Lay tortillas on counter and divide arugula among tortillas. Top arugula with chicken mixture and roll up tightly. Serve.

TEST KITCHEN NOTE: You can use capers instead of olives.

SKILLET CHEESEBURGER MACARONI Serves 4 to 6

✓ **WHY THIS RECIPE WORKS:** We combine the flavors of our favorite burger—ground beef, dry mustard, American cheese, and dill pickles—with the convenience and heft of a one-skillet meal.

- 1 pound 85 percent lean ground beef
- 1 cup finely chopped onion
- 12 ounces (3 cups) elbow macaroni
- 2½ cups chicken broth
- 1 (15-ounce) can tomato sauce
- 1 tablespoon Worcestershire sauce
- 1 tablespoon dry mustard
   Salt and pepper
- 6 ounces chopped deli American cheese
- ½ cup chopped dill pickles

1. Cook beef and ½ cup onion in 12-inch nonstick skillet over medium-high heat until beef is no longer pink, about 7 minutes.

2. Add macaroni, broth, tomato sauce, Worcestershire, mustard, ½ teaspoon salt, and ¼ teaspoon pepper and bring to boil. Cover, reduce heat to low, and simmer, stirring occasionally, until macaroni is tender, 8 to 10 minutes. Stir in cheese, pickles, and remaining ½ cup onion. Season with salt and pepper to taste. Serve.

TEST KITCHEN NOTE: We like Boar's Head Kosher Dill Pickles.

GARLICKY SHRIMP PASTA WITH TARRAGON

SKILLET CHICKEN FAJITAS

SICHUAN-STYLE ORANGE BEEF
WITH SUGAR SNAP PEAS

SMOTHERED BONELESS PORK RIBS

SKILLET CHICKEN FAJITAS Serves 4

✔ **WHY THIS RECIPE WORKS:** Slicing the chicken breasts thin creates bite-size pieces that cook in minutes.

- 1 teaspoon chili powder
- ½ teaspoon ground cumin
- Salt and pepper
- 2 (6- to 8-ounce) boneless, skinless chicken breasts, trimmed and sliced thin crosswise
- ¼ cup vegetable oil
- 1 red bell pepper, stemmed, seeded, and sliced thin
- 1 onion, halved and sliced thin
- 2 tablespoons chopped fresh cilantro
- 4 teaspoons lime juice
- 8 (8-inch) flour tortillas, warmed

1. Combine chili powder, cumin, ½ teaspoon salt, and ¼ teaspoon pepper in bowl. Pat chicken dry with paper towels and season with spice mixture. Heat 2 tablespoons oil in 12-inch nonstick skillet over medium-high heat until just smoking. Add chicken and cook until well browned all over and cooked through, 6 to 8 minutes. Transfer to platter and tent loosely with aluminum foil.

2. Return now-empty skillet to medium-high heat and add remaining 2 tablespoons oil, bell pepper, onion, and ¼ teaspoon salt. Cover and cook, stirring occasionally, until vegetables are soft and beginning to brown, 6 to 8 minutes. Remove from heat and stir in cilantro and lime juice. Transfer to platter with chicken. Serve with tortillas.

TEST KITCHEN NOTE: Serve with salsa, shredded Monterey Jack cheese, lime wedges, and sour cream.

GARLICKY SHRIMP PASTA WITH TARRAGON Serves 4

✔ **WHY THIS RECIPE WORKS:** Tarragon and lemon juice brighten this creamy pasta dish, and quick-cooking shrimp make it weeknight-friendly.

- 1 pound spaghetti
- Salt and pepper
- 1½ pounds extra-large shrimp (21 to 25 per pound), peeled and deveined
- 3 tablespoons olive oil
- 1 shallot, minced
- 3 garlic cloves, minced
- ¼ cup dry white wine
- ½ cup heavy cream
- 2 tablespoons chopped fresh tarragon
- 2 teaspoons lemon juice

1. Bring 4 quarts water to boil in large pot. Add spaghetti and 1 tablespoon salt and cook, stirring often, until al dente. Reserve ¼ cup cooking water, then drain spaghetti and return it to pot.

2. Meanwhile, pat shrimp dry with paper towels and season with salt and pepper. Heat 1 tablespoon oil in 12-inch nonstick skillet over medium-high heat until just smoking. Add half of shrimp to pan in single layer and cook until spotty brown and cooked through, about 2 minutes per side. Transfer shrimp to plate and tent loosely with aluminum foil. Repeat with 1 tablespoon oil and remaining shrimp.

3. Return now-empty skillet to medium-high heat, add remaining 1 tablespoon oil and shallot, and cook until shallot is softened, about 2 minutes. Add garlic and cook until fragrant, about 30 seconds. Add wine, bring to boil, and cook until reduced by half, about 2 minutes. Stir in cream and reserved cooking water and bring to boil again. Off heat, stir in tarragon, lemon juice, ¼ teaspoon salt, ¼ teaspoon pepper, and shrimp. Add sauce to spaghetti and toss to coat. Serve.

SMOTHERED BONELESS PORK RIBS Serves 4 to 6

✔ **WHY THIS RECIPE WORKS:** Country-style ribs are meaty but tender; quick browning and 15 minutes of braising are all the cooking they need. We use the fond from browning them to flavor the sauce.

- 1 teaspoon onion powder
- ½ teaspoon paprika
- ½ teaspoon salt
- ½ teaspoon pepper
- 2 pounds boneless country-style pork ribs, trimmed
- ¼ cup vegetable oil
- 1 onion, halved and sliced thin
- 2 garlic cloves, minced
- ½ teaspoon minced fresh thyme
- 1 cup beef broth
- 1 teaspoon cider vinegar

1. Combine onion powder, paprika, salt, and pepper in bowl. Pat pork dry with paper towels and season with spice mixture. Heat 2 tablespoons oil in 12-inch skillet over medium-high heat until just smoking. Add pork and cook until well browned, about 4 minutes per side; set aside on plate.

2. Add remaining 2 tablespoons oil and onion to now-empty skillet. Cover and cook, stirring occasionally, until onion is soft and golden brown, about 6 minutes. Add garlic and thyme and cook until fragrant, about 30 seconds. Add broth and bring to boil. Return pork to pan, cover, and reduce heat to low. Cook until tender, about 15 minutes. Transfer pork to platter. Stir vinegar into sauce and spoon over pork. Serve.

TEST KITCHEN NOTE: Serve with egg noodles or mashed potatoes.

SICHUAN-STYLE ORANGE BEEF WITH SUGAR SNAP PEAS Serves 4

✔ **WHY THIS RECIPE WORKS:** Cooking the beef with the sauce flavors the meat, while the honey in the sauce aids in caramelization.

- 2 teaspoons grated orange zest plus ½ cup juice
- ¼ cup soy sauce
- 2 tablespoons toasted sesame oil
- 1 tablespoon honey
- 2 garlic cloves, minced
- ¼ teaspoon red pepper flakes
- 1½ pounds flank steak, trimmed, cut into thirds lengthwise, and sliced crosswise into ¼-inch-thick pieces
- 8 ounces sugar snap peas, strings removed
- 2 scallions, sliced thin

1. Combine orange zest and juice, soy sauce, oil, honey, garlic, and pepper flakes in bowl. Combine beef and ⅓ cup orange juice mixture in 12-inch nonstick skillet. Cook over medium-high heat, stirring occasionally, until liquid has evaporated and beef is caramelized, about 15 minutes. Transfer beef to plate and tent loosely with aluminum foil.

2. Add remaining orange juice mixture and snap peas to now-empty skillet and cook, covered, over medium heat, until snap peas are bright green, about 2 minutes. Uncover and continue to cook, stirring occasionally, until sauce thickens and snap peas are tender, about 1 minute. Return beef to skillet and toss with snap peas to combine. Transfer to platter and sprinkle with scallions. Serve.

TEST KITCHEN NOTE: Serve with white rice.

Glazed Mushrooms for a Crowd

It's easy to glaze a skillet of sautéed mushrooms with sweet-tart balsamic vinegar.
But what if you want to make a bigger batch? BY SARAH GABRIEL

WHAT CAN'T YOU glaze with balsamic vinegar? Steak, fish, chicken, squash, root vegetables, and even fruit often get this sweet-tart shellacking. Balsamic-glazed mushrooms are a popular steakhouse side; I wanted to create a recipe for home cooks that would yield meaty mushrooms with a glossy, balanced balsamic glaze. Oh, and one more thing: With the holidays approaching, I'd need enough for eight people.

Since quantity was part of my goal and I didn't want to break the bank, I'd develop this recipe using inexpensive white button mushrooms. I also knew that I'd use the oven to avoid tedious batch cooking of the 4 pounds of mushrooms I'd need to feed eight. The oven recipes I found called for either tossing white mushrooms with a vinegar mixture and then roasting them on a baking sheet or roasting the mushrooms "naked" and subsequently tossing them with vinegar that had been reduced on the stovetop.

Both approaches had problems. Mushrooms are watery on their own so adding vinegar at the start meant that it took nearly 2 hours to reduce the liquids to a glaze, leaving the mushrooms tasting boiled. Roasting the mushrooms in the oven while reducing the vinegar in a saucepan seemed like a better idea, but it required an extra pan, and the glaze didn't adhere well and tasted like an afterthought. Cooking already-reduced glaze on the mushrooms improved adhesion, but the concentrated vinegar scorched easily. I'd stick with the one-pan oven approach and try to strike a balance between boiling the mushrooms and scorching the vinegar; I'd roast the mushrooms partway and then add the vinegar.

I tried roasting 4 pounds of halved mushrooms in a 500-degree oven for a half-hour before pouring on the

Delicious right off the baking sheet, these mushrooms are even better when they're tossed with butter and thyme.

balsamic so it could reduce while the mushrooms finished cooking. No go—the mushroom liquid flooded the pan, making the mushrooms spongy from the steam before I even had the chance to add the vinegar. I had to get rid of the moisture before roasting.

The test kitchen often uses salt to draw moisture out of vegetables before cooking, so I tossed the mushrooms in salt. But after 30 minutes, only a few drops of liquid had beaded on the surface. I tried cooking them covered with foil for 15 minutes; they released their liquid quickly, but it took forever to evaporate. What about the microwave? Thankfully, it did the trick; after about 15 minutes in the microwave, covered, salted, and halved, my mushrooms

released about 2 cups of liquid.

I drained them in a colander, coated them with oil, and roasted them. The mushrooms had browned after 30 minutes, so I poured on the balsamic vinegar and returned the pan to the oven. After about 10 minutes, the vinegar had reduced to a glaze that coated the well-browned mushrooms. But beneath the glaze, the mushrooms had a tough, leathery surface. As they browned, they had dried out.

The fix here was simple: Preheat the baking sheet while I preheated the oven. The hot baking sheet jump-started browning, reducing the cooking time, so the mushrooms had less time to dry out. I added the vinegar and cooked the mushrooms for about 10 minutes

longer, stirring halfway through to prevent scorching. Unfortunately, the vinegar tasted one-dimensional and slightly harsh. Ultimately, the combined force of butter, brown sugar, garlic, vinegar, and thyme added dimension, balanced the acidity, and heightened the glaze's shine. These mushrooms—finally—are as good as any you'd get in a steakhouse. Even better, my version makes enough to feed a small crowd.

ROASTED BALSAMIC-GLAZED MUSHROOMS Serves 8

Buy mushrooms with caps about 1½ inches in diameter; use any smaller mushrooms whole. Once you add the vinegar, watch carefully so the mushrooms don't burn. If your microwave can't fit the mushrooms in one batch, microwave them in two batches, decreasing the microwave time to 10 minutes per batch.

- 4 pounds white mushrooms, trimmed and halved
- 1 tablespoon salt
- 3 tablespoons olive oil
- ¾ cup balsamic vinegar
- 3 garlic cloves, minced
- 1 teaspoon packed brown sugar
- ¾ teaspoon pepper
- 2 tablespoons unsalted butter, cut into 4 pieces
- 1 teaspoon minced fresh thyme

1. Adjust oven rack to lowest position, place rimmed baking sheet on rack, and heat oven to 500 degrees. Combine mushrooms and salt in large bowl. Cover with large plate and microwave until mushrooms release 1¾ to 2 cups liquid, 14 to 16 minutes, stirring halfway through microwaving. Strain mushrooms in colander and let sit for 5 minutes to drain completely. Return mushrooms to now-empty bowl, add oil, and stir to coat.

2. Transfer mushrooms to preheated sheet and roast until browned and liquid has evaporated, 22 to 25 minutes, stirring halfway through cooking. Whisk vinegar, garlic, sugar, and pepper together in 2-cup liquid measuring cup. Remove mushrooms from oven, pour vinegar mixture over mushrooms, and stir to coat. Return mushrooms to oven and roast until vinegar is reduced to glaze, 9 to 12 minutes, stirring halfway through cooking. Place mushrooms in serving bowl and stir in butter and thyme. Serve.

Mushroom Pretreatment

To rid the halved mushrooms of excess moisture so they'll brown properly, we salt and microwave them, covered, before roasting.

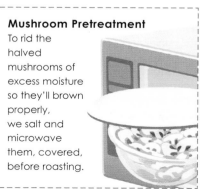

Quicker Cinnamon Buns

Making cinnamon buns is a project. Most shortcut recipes use quick biscuit dough, but the results just aren't the same. We wanted to find a way to make yeast hurry. BY DIANE UNGER

CINNAMON BUNS SHOULD be big and gooey, tender, and over-the-top sweet. And did I mention the requisite sweet, shiny glaze? Naturally, we have a recipe at America's Test Kitchen that produces just such a cinnamon bun. It's irresistible. So what's the problem? We rarely have time to make it. Between mixing, kneading, rising, shaping, rising again, and baking, these buns take more than 3 hours out of our overscheduled lives. I wanted to make cinnamon buns in half of the time.

I found plenty of recipes that claimed to deliver quick cinnamon buns. I made a half-dozen or so. They were delicious—but they weren't cinnamon buns. Instead, they were more like frosted cinnamon biscuits. No surprise, since these recipes called for taking ordinary biscuit dough (leavened with baking powder and/or soda), rolling it out in a rectangle, brushing it with butter, sprinkling it with cinnamon sugar, rolling it up, and slicing it into individual biscuits, which were then baked and glazed. Good as they were, they lacked the unmistakable yeasty flavor and sweet bread texture of a real cinnamon bun. I decided to take a "cinnamon biscuit" recipe, retain as much of its efficiency as possible, and try to restore the yeasted cinnamon bun taste and texture.

Taking the best of the biscuit recipes from my initial test (a basic buttermilk biscuit with a cream-cheese-and-butter glaze), I began its transformation. Almost all baked items are leavened, either by yeast (think bread or Danish) or by the chemical leaveners baking soda and baking powder (think cookies and cakes). But I had an idea based on an unusual Southern recipe known as angel biscuits. To get their famously light and fluffy texture, these biscuits pull out all the stops, incorporating baking powder, baking soda, and yeast. Similarly, I'd take my cinnamon "biscuit" dough and try adding back the yeast of a cinnamon bun.

My working recipe, which used 1¼ teaspoons of baking powder and ½ teaspoon of baking soda for 2¾ cups of flour, made eight buns. I tried the recipe with gradually increasing amounts of yeast, from 2¼ teaspoons (the amount in a single envelope of yeast) up to 2 tablespoons. I hit the sweet spot at 4 teaspoons; we liked the flavor that it gave these cinnamon buns,

We use cream cheese in our glaze to bring tang to this very sweet breakfast treat.

plus the amount—quite a bit relative to the amount of flour—produced lots of carbon dioxide gas fast. That meant that the buns, helped along by the two other leaveners, would rise quickly in the oven. To further speed along the yeast, I first dissolved it in warm milk with a little sugar. Once upon a time, this step, which is known as proofing the yeast, was part of every recipe calling for yeast. With instant yeast, which I was using,

it isn't necessary. But I did it anyway, since proofing accelerates rise and flavor development, and speed was my mantra.

Now that I was making a yeast dough, albeit an unusual one, two things came into play that don't with biscuit dough: kneading and rising. Our classic recipe for cinnamon buns calls for about 10 minutes of kneading in the mixer, followed by two rises, totaling 3 long hours, both before and

after shaping the dough into buns. Where was the line between cinnamon bun qualities (tender, yeasty, breadlike) and my desired cinnamon bun timetable? It took many tests to figure that out—not that I heard much complaining from coworkers, who cheerfully lined up to "evaluate" bun after bun. Eventually, I found the perfect compromise between time, taste, and texture: a mere 2 minutes of kneading by hand

and—after the dough was rolled out, filled, and cut into buns—a single 30-minute rise.

But I still had a problem. Despite the leaveners, the kneading, and the rise time, the buns remained somewhat squat; they didn't spring up in the oven, as they should. All along, I'd been baking them at 425 degrees—a standard oven temperature for biscuits. But with my hybrid biscuit bun, this high temperature worked against me: The golden-brown tops set before the combined leaveners had time to lift. In several tests, I turned down the oven in 25-degree increments. At 350 degrees, these quicker cinnamon buns reached their full height potential. Our science editor mentioned a second benefit to the cooler oven: Because the yeast was killed more slowly (yeast dies at 140 degrees), it had more time to multiply, ergo there was more flavor development.

The hard work was done. Now I tweaked the filling and the glaze, adding more brown sugar and butter to the former and a little vanilla to the latter. I retained the cream cheese in the glaze from the original biscuit recipe; its tang brought balance to these sugary buns. I was writing up the recipe when I spotted a chance to simplify. Could I switch from buttermilk to more convenient milk? Yep. And without acidic buttermilk, it turned out that I didn't need baking soda either. I wrote it out of the recipe, increasing the baking powder accordingly and making my cinnamon bun recipe shorter and simpler.

It would be an exaggeration to call these cinnamon buns "quick." If you count prepping, shaping, rising, and baking, they still take about 1½ hours. But that's less than half of the time needed to make ordinary cinnamon buns—for the same tender, oozy, and deliciously indulgent reward.

QUICKER CINNAMON BUNS
Makes 8 buns

Since the filling, dough, and glaze all require melted butter, it's easier to melt all 10 tablespoons in a liquid measuring cup and divvy it up as needed. Stir the melted butter before each use to redistribute the milk solids. We developed this recipe using a dark cake pan, which produces deeply caramelized buns. If your cake pan is light-colored, adjust the oven rack to the lowest position, heat the oven to 375 degrees, and increase the baking time to 29 to 32 minutes.

FILLING
- ¾ cup packed (5¼ ounces) light brown sugar
- ¼ cup (1¾ ounces) granulated sugar
- 1 tablespoon ground cinnamon
- ⅛ teaspoon salt
- 2 tablespoons unsalted butter, melted
- 1 teaspoon vanilla extract

DOUGH
- 1¼ cups whole milk, room temperature
- 4 teaspoons instant or rapid-rise yeast
- 2 tablespoons granulated sugar
- 2¾ cups (13¾ ounces) all-purpose flour
- 2½ teaspoons baking powder
- ¾ teaspoon salt
- 6 tablespoons unsalted butter, melted

GLAZE
- 3 ounces cream cheese, softened
- 2 tablespoons unsalted butter, melted
- 2 tablespoons whole milk
- ½ teaspoon vanilla extract
- ⅛ teaspoon salt
- 1 cup (4 ounces) confectioners' sugar, sifted

1. FOR THE FILLING: Combine brown sugar, granulated sugar, cinnamon, and salt in bowl. Stir in melted butter and vanilla until mixture resembles wet sand; set aside.

2. FOR THE DOUGH: Grease dark 9-inch round cake pan, line with parchment paper, and grease parchment. Pour ¼ cup milk in small bowl and

microwave until 110 degrees, 15 to 20 seconds. Stir in yeast and 1 teaspoon sugar and let sit until mixture is bubbly, about 5 minutes.

3. Whisk flour, baking powder, salt, and remaining 5 teaspoons sugar together in large bowl. Stir in 2 tablespoons butter, yeast mixture, and remaining 1 cup milk until dough forms (dough will be sticky). Transfer dough to well-floured counter and knead until smooth ball forms, about 2 minutes.

4. Roll dough into 12 by 9-inch rectangle, with long side parallel to counter edge. Brush dough all over with 2 tablespoons butter, leaving ½-inch border on far edge. Sprinkle dough evenly with filling, then press filling firmly into dough. Using bench scraper or metal spatula, loosen dough from counter. Roll dough away from you into tight log and pinch seam to seal.

5. Roll log seam side down and cut into 8 equal pieces. Stand buns on end and gently re-form ends that were pinched during cutting. Place 1 bun in center of prepared pan and others around perimeter of pan, seam sides facing in. Brush tops of buns with remaining 2 tablespoons butter. Cover buns loosely with plastic wrap and let rise for 30 minutes. Adjust oven rack to middle position and heat oven to 350 degrees.

6. Discard plastic and bake buns until edges are well browned, 23 to 25 minutes. Loosen buns from sides of pan with paring knife and let cool for 5 minutes. Invert large plate over cake pan. Using potholders, flip plate and pan upside down; remove pan and parchment. Reinvert buns onto wire rack, set wire rack inside parchment-lined rimmed baking sheet, and let cool for 5 minutes.

7. FOR THE GLAZE: Place cream cheese in large bowl and whisk in butter, milk, vanilla, and salt until smooth. Whisk in sugar until smooth. Pour glaze evenly over tops of buns, spreading with spatula to cover. Serve.

The Best Baked Chicken Wings

If you don't deep-fry, can you have chicken wings that are crispy on the outside and moist and tender within? We cooked more than 200 pounds of wings to find out. BY NICK IVERSON

VIRTUALLY EVERY COOK I've ever known—me included—is crazy about chicken wings. The reasons are clear: Wings have a high skin-to-meat ratio, and their dark meat is naturally flavorful and moist. So when you fry them until they're crispy and toss them in your sauce of choice, you've got everything that's good about chicken.

Most of us enjoy baskets of wings only in bars and restaurants because frying them at home can be a lot of work and too much mess. But what if I could figure out a way to make truly crispy wings in the oven?

Obviously, baked wings aren't a new idea; I've eaten my fair share of them, but I have never been very impressed. Baked wings, with their flabby, chewy skin and desiccated meat, always pale in comparison with their fried counterparts. I read up on how other cooks make their oven wings, and I discovered that recipes fall into one of two categories: those that are simply baked (the norm was at about 425 degrees for 1 hour on a rimmed baking sheet fitted with a rack for better air circulation) versus more "chef-y" recipes that pretreat the wings by either air-drying, steaming, boiling, or rubbing them with baking powder and salt and letting the wings sit for 24 hours before baking. Out of the seven recipes that I prepared for my tasters, none was great and the only two that showed any promise were the one with the baking powder rub and one of the boiled-and-then-baked recipes.

The challenge with wings, no matter how you're cooking them, is rendering the fat so that they aren't rubbery. The idea behind boiling is that the hot water should help melt out some of that fat so that the wings can crisp in the oven. But this method was a pain because I wanted to cook a good amount (about 4 pounds) of wings, which required boiling in two batches. More important, I was robbing Peter to pay Paul. Sure, the boiling rendered some fat, but the wings absorbed some of the water, so the skin couldn't crisp in the oven until the water evaporated, and by that time the meat was overcooked and dry.

The wings rubbed with baking powder were crispy and tender, but the recipe required that the wings sit for a day before baking. This was not exactly

Crispy skin, tender meat, and no deep-frying mess. Toss the wings in one of our easy sauces, like the Buffalo sauce here.

convenient, but since the baking powder wings were the most promising (see "Baking Powder"), I decided to pursue this approach anyway.

I knew that the baking powder and salt rub worked, but could I speed it up? I made three batches: one that was rubbed with the baking powder and salt mixture and left to sit (refrigerated on a wire rack) overnight, another that was chilled with the rub for an hour, and one that was rubbed and baked immediately. Even before the wings went into the oven, I could see that those that had been chilled overnight appeared drier on the surface. The other two batches had pasty beads of moisture—definitely a bad sign. When baked, the dry wings were far crispier than the others. Clearly, I had to find a way to dry the rubbed wings before they went into the oven.

Blotting the wings dry with paper towels would lift away the rub, so that wouldn't work. What about a low-temperature oven? I gave it a try, hoping that the mellow heat would evaporate the surface moisture without really cooking or drying out the meat. Then I could crank up the temperature to cook the wings and crisp the skin. As I was prepping the wings for this test, I discovered that I could shake the rub with the wings in a zipper-lock bag to distribute

LIKE MAGIC
A liberal dusting makes for the crispiest baked chicken wings.

the rub more easily and efficiently.

I layered the coated wings on a wire rack set in a rimmed baking sheet and placed them in a low oven for a half-hour. The results were promising, and with a few more tests I worked through the details. I dried the wings at 250 degrees on the lower-middle oven rack for 30 minutes. Then I turned up the oven to 425 degrees and moved the tray of wings to the upper-middle rack to capitalize on the reflected heat from the top of the oven for maximum browning. With a total cooking time of about 1½ hours, I'd saved about 22 hours from my overnight starting point. And the results were even better than I had hoped: tender meat and skin that was crisp enough to pass for fried.

One element of my recipe remained: the sauce. Traditional Buffalo sauce is usually just hot sauce and butter, but I decided to add a little molasses to my version for deeper flavor. And I didn't stop there. I made two other sauces: an easy dump-and-stir barbecue sauce and a Thai-inspired sauce. I made three more batches of the wings, tossed them with the sauces, and called my tasters. The wings were juicy and tender, and the crispy skin held the sauce without becoming soggy. My coworkers gave my recipe the best kind of affirmation: piles of stripped bones, sauce-smeared tasting sheets, lots of dirty napkins, and a satisfied, smiling silence.

OVEN-FRIED CHICKEN WINGS
Serves 4 to 6

If you buy chicken wings that are already split, with the tips removed, you will need only 3½ pounds.

- 4 pounds chicken wings, halved at joints, wingtips discarded
- 2 tablespoons baking powder
- ¾ teaspoon salt
- 1 recipe wing sauce (recipes follow)

1. Adjust oven racks to upper-middle and lower-middle positions and heat oven to 250 degrees. Set wire rack in aluminum foil–lined rimmed baking sheet. Pat wings dry with paper towels and transfer to 1-gallon zipper-lock bag. Combine baking powder and salt, add to wings,

seal bag, and toss to evenly coat.

2. Arrange wings, skin side up, in single layer on prepared wire rack. Bake wings on lower-middle oven rack for 30 minutes. Move wings to upper-middle rack, increase oven temperature to 425 degrees, and roast until wings are golden brown and crispy, 40 to 50 minutes longer, rotating sheet halfway through baking. Remove sheet from oven and let stand for 5 minutes. Transfer wings to bowl with wing sauce of your choice, toss to coat, and serve.

BUFFALO WING SAUCE
Makes about ¾ cup

Classic Buffalo sauce is made with Frank's RedHot Original Cayenne Pepper Sauce.

- ½ cup hot sauce
- 4 tablespoons unsalted butter, melted
- 1 tablespoon molasses

Combine all ingredients in large bowl.

SMOKY BARBECUE WING SAUCE
Makes about ¾ cup

- ¼ cup chicken broth
- ¼ cup ketchup
- 1 tablespoon molasses
- 1 tablespoon cider vinegar
- 1 tablespoon minced canned chipotle chile in adobo sauce
- ¼ teaspoon liquid smoke

Combine all ingredients in large bowl.

SWEET AND SPICY THAI WING SAUCE
Makes about ¾ cup

- ½ cup packed brown sugar
- ¼ cup lime juice (2 limes)
- 1 tablespoon toasted sesame oil
- 1 teaspoon red pepper flakes
- 1 garlic clove, minced
- 2 tablespoons fish sauce

Combine sugar, lime juice, oil, pepper flakes, and garlic in small saucepan; bring to simmer over medium heat. Cook until slightly thickened, about 5 minutes. Off heat, stir in fish sauce. Transfer to large bowl.

TASTING BLUE CHEESE DRESSING

Nothing dresses up a wedge of iceberg or offsets the spicy heat of Buffalo wings quite like blue cheese dressing. From dozens of supermarket options, we narrowed the field to seven top-selling national products, both shelf-stable and refrigerated, using a list compiled by Chicago-based market research firm IRi. (When a company made more than one version, we chose its best seller.) We sampled the dressings with celery sticks and with our Oven-Fried Chicken Wings tossed with our Buffalo Wing Sauce. Our findings were mostly common sense: Naturally, tasters demanded the unmistakable pungent flavor of blue cheese in their blue cheese dressing. Also, the thicker the dressing the better; runny and thin isn't for dipping. Finally, we preferred dressings with sizable, creamy chunks of cheese to those with negligible flecks. What we didn't expect was that we would be able to recommend five of the dressings that we tasted (one with reservations) and that a shelf-stable bottle would beat out refrigerated products. Its distinct blue cheese flavor and creamy texture made Wish-Bone Chunky Blue Cheese Dressing our top pick. For more tasting details, go to CooksCountry.com/nov13. –LISA McMANUS

RECOMMENDED		TASTERS' NOTES
WISH-BONE Chunky Blue Cheese Dressing **Price:** $3.29 for 16 oz (21 cents per oz) **Style:** Shelf-stable		"Actually tastes like blue cheese," many tasters noted, describing this dressing as "quite pungent but in an authentic way," with "nice chunks of very potent cheese." It had "distinctive blue flavor without being too sweet," was "creamy without being too thick or fatty," and was "ripe and rich."
MARZETTI Chunky Blue Cheese Dressing **Price:** $3.69 for 15 oz (25 cents per oz) **Style:** Refrigerated		This dressing was "very salty" and "pungent" with big chunks of cheese. It had a "tangy, rich" taste and a "great thick and chunky texture," with hints of Parmesan. A few tasters thought that the vinegar came on too strong.
KEN'S STEAK HOUSE Chunky Blue Cheese Dressing **Price:** $4.19 for 16 oz (26 cents per oz) **Style:** Shelf-stable		This dressing "tastes mightily of blue cheese," with "a good balance of acidity, saltiness, [and] creaminess" and a "nice tang" that's "not too overpowering." But several tasters found it "thin."
KRAFT Roka Blue Cheese Anything Dressing **Price:** $3.99 for 16 oz (25 cents per oz) **Style:** Shelf-stable		What's with the name? According to a company spokesperson, "For Kraft, 'Roka' is indicative of the Roquefort region in France known for their characteristic blue-veined cheese." That's nice, but our tasters found this product "not particularly flavored like blue cheese." We did, however, like its "really creamy and thick" texture and "salty, tangy" flavor.
RECOMMENDED WITH RESERVATIONS		
MARIE'S Chunky Blue Cheese Dressing **Price:** $5.49 for 25 oz (22 cents per oz) **Style:** Refrigerated		This dressing had "nice, real-tasting blue cheese chunks" and a "thick and creamy" texture that reminded some tasters of sour cream. Others found it a little "bland," like "ranch dressing or peppercorn Parm"—your "generic creamy, rich dressing." Since it had more buttermilk than blue cheese and the least sodium in the lineup, we weren't surprised.
NOT RECOMMENDED		
LITEHOUSE Chunky Bleu Cheese Dressing & Dip **Price:** $4.29 for 13 oz (33 cents per oz) **Style:** Refrigerated		"There's blue cheese in here?" asked one taster, who described this sample as "innocuous—not the way you want blue cheese dressing." Others agreed, comparing it to "watered-down mayo" and finding it overly "mellow" and "not very blue cheesy." "Can taste an 'herb' flavoring," said one taster. "Is this ranch?"
BRIANNAS Home Style True Blue Cheese Salad Dressing **Price:** $4.39 for 12 oz (37 cents per oz) **Style:** Shelf-stable		The most expensive dressing had four or more times the amount of sugar as every other blue cheese dressing we tested. But too sweet was the least of it. We also found it "sticky," "oily," "greasy," "runny and fake-tasting," and with a "sickly" taste, "like sugar mixed with mustard." Asked one taster, "How could you ruin Buffalo wings with this?"

Colorado Green Chili

More than 2 pounds of chiles go into this mildly spicy stew, making it as much about the green chile peppers as the pork. BY CHRISTIE MORRISON

MOST AMERICANS HAVE at least a glancing familiarity with Texas and New Mexico chilis, but not nearly so many realize that Denver, Colorado, also has a delicious chili tradition. Moderately spiced, this pork-based version is a relatively simple stew, but it has a complex and wonderful taste, thanks in part to the roasted green chiles from Hatch, New Mexico, that it contains. Denverites eat it as a main dish with flour tortillas or as a sauce of sorts, smothering everything from burgers to eggs to burritos.

Most recipes follow the same basic format: Roast green chiles until blistered and then peel, seed, and chop. Add the chiles to sautéed onions, garlic, and browned pork. Include cumin for spice. Pour in broth or water, stir in tomatoes, and thicken with *masa harina* (corn flour) or all-purpose flour. The Colorado chili simmers for an hour or three, and it's done when the meat is tender and the flavors have melded.

But because the ingredient amounts range, so do the resulting chilis, as I discovered when we tasted several versions that I'd made or mail-ordered from Denver. The ingredients produced chilis from thick to thin, hot to mild, muddy green to bright orange. The assortment did help us pin down what we liked: cohesive flavors, medium heat, and a noticeable vegetal taste. As the

cook, I also wanted a comparatively easy recipe. Since none of these recipes met my full list of requirements, I combined their best features, putting together a recipe from canned, diced tomatoes, lots of garlic and cumin, and more than 2 pounds of chiles to 3 pounds of meat. Hatch green chiles are readily available in the Southwest. Don't live there? Then you have to mail-order them. To avoid that, for now I'd use Anaheims; I'd test more rigorously later.

My first order of business, though, was to decide on the best cut of pork. I compared loin, tenderloin, boneless country-style ribs, and boneless butt and settled on the last because its rich marbling suits this long-braised dish. I cut the meat into 1-inch cubes, which I browned to develop crust and add depth to the chili. I had to do this in three batches to avoid overcrowding the pot, tediously turning the cubes to brown all sides. To streamline, I borrowed a method that the test kitchen developed for stews. We cram a skillet with cubed beef, add water, and cover the pan. After several minutes, we uncover it, let the water evaporate, stir the beef, and let it brown in its own fat. A test with the pork pieces yielded similar results: even browning and flavorful fond. This method wasn't fast, but it was more hands-off than the traditional approach.

Turning to the chiles, although the Anaheims tasted bright and vegetal, just like the Hatch chiles, they lacked heat. I tested canned hot green chiles, poblanos, and jalapeños (all are easy to find throughout the United States) in combination with the Anaheims. The jalapeños fared best, so I tried them every which way with the Anaheims. Eventually, I had a game plan: Roast both types of chiles whole under the broiler, set aside the jalapeños, puree half of the Anaheims, dice the remainder, and add both to the chili pot with the broth to braise alongside the other ingredients, introducing complexity and background heat. Meanwhile, I chopped and seeded the jalapeños (reserving the seeds to add later for more heat, if needed), and just before serving the dish, I stirred them into the pot. The jalapeños gave the stew a fresh, hot vigor.

Unfortunately, prepping the chiles was a hassle. I had to flip them all partway through cooking, plus once they were cool, they were slippery and

It's called Colorado Green Chili for the many green chile peppers it contains.

sticky, making them difficult to peel and even harder to seed. In culinary school I'd learned a great trick for roasting bell peppers. We sliced off the top and the bottom, made a cut down the side, removed the seeds and membranes, and then flattened the bell pepper; the flat surface broiled evenly, skin side up, and the skin subsequently came off easily. I successfully modified the technique for the Anaheims, and now I had to flip only the three jalapeños (which I continued to roast whole, to soften just slightly).

Colorado green chili should be thick enough to top a burger yet thin enough to eat on its own. I tested many possible thickeners: the usual masa harina and flour but also, in an effort to mimic masa

harina's flavor, crushed tortilla chips and pulverized corn tortillas. Flour was easy and convenient and worked perfectly—well, almost. Without frequent stirring, the thickened stew burned and stuck to the pot. I moved the pot to a low (325-degree) oven, where it could cook more evenly. This hands-off method produced very tender pork in just an hour or so, sans scorching. Additionally, I ran the diced tomatoes through the food processor so that they'd blend into the chili better.

I put a final batch of chili through its paces—as a topping, under a fried egg, and as a stew sopped up with tortillas—and it lived up to its Rocky Mountain hype. My only disappointment? How quickly it disappeared.

TEST KITCHEN TECHNIQUE
Easier Roasted Chiles
Roasting chiles whole and then seeding them—the usual procedure—makes a mess: The wet seeds stick to everything. We halve and seed the raw Anaheims. It's neater and lets us skip the usual flipping step. We leave the jalapeños whole; they soften but don't deeply roast.

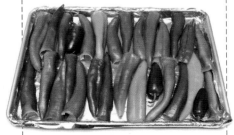

READY FOR ROASTING
Arrange the chiles head to foot for the best fit.

COLORADO GREEN CHILI Serves 6

The chiles can be roasted and refrigerated up to 24 hours in advance.

- 3 pounds boneless pork butt roast, trimmed and cut into 1-inch pieces
  Salt
- 2 pounds (10 to 12) Anaheim chiles, stemmed, halved lengthwise, and seeded
- 3 jalapeño chiles
- 1 (14.5-ounce) can diced tomatoes
- 1 tablespoon vegetable oil
- 2 onions, chopped fine
- 8 garlic cloves, minced
- 1 tablespoon ground cumin
- ¼ cup all-purpose flour
- 4 cups chicken broth
  Cayenne pepper
  Lime wedges

1. Combine pork, ½ cup water, and ½ teaspoon salt in Dutch oven over medium heat. Cover and cook for 20 minutes, stirring occasionally. Uncover, increase heat to medium-high, and continue to cook, stirring frequently, until liquid evaporates and pork browns in its own fat, 15 to 20 minutes. Transfer pork to bowl and set aside.

2. Meanwhile, adjust 1 oven rack to lowest position and second rack 6 inches from broiler element. Heat broiler. Line rimmed baking sheet with aluminum foil and spray with vegetable oil spray. Arrange Anaheims, skin side up, and jalapeños in single layer on prepared sheet. Place sheet on upper rack and broil until chiles are mostly blackened and soft, 15 to 20 minutes, rotating sheet and flipping only jalapeños halfway through broiling. Place Anaheims in large bowl and cover with plastic wrap; let cool for 5 minutes. Set aside jalapeños. Heat oven to 325 degrees.

3. Remove skins from Anaheims. Chop half of Anaheims into ½-inch pieces and transfer to bowl. Process remaining Anaheims in food processor until smooth, about 10 seconds; transfer to bowl with chopped Anaheims. Pulse tomatoes and their juice in now-empty food processor until coarsely ground, about 4 pulses.

4. Heat oil in now-empty Dutch oven over medium heat until shimmering. Add onions and cook until lightly browned, 5 to 7 minutes. Stir in garlic and cumin and cook until fragrant, about 30 seconds. Stir in flour and cook for 1 minute. Stir in broth, Anaheims, tomatoes, and pork with any accumulated juices and bring to simmer, scraping up any browned bits. Cover pot, transfer to lower oven rack, and cook until pork is tender, 1 to 1¼ hours.

5. Without peeling, stem and seed jalapeños and reserve seeds. Finely chop jalapeños and stir into chili. Season chili with salt, cayenne, and reserved jalapeño seeds to taste. Serve with lime wedges.

Sausage, Kale, and Bean Pasta

This classic combination should be a great one-pot dinner—if we could fix the anemic flavor, thin sauce, and unevenly cooked pasta. BY DIANE UNGER

AS THE DAYS grew cold, I found myself dreaming about the hearty combination of pasta with kale, sausage, and white beans. But I hoped to retool the dish for a single pot. I'd use a test kitchen method that cooks the pasta in broth with the other ingredients. It means fewer dishes, more flavorful pasta (it soaks up the broth), and instant sauce, as the pasta starches thicken the broth.

I realized on my first try that I'd need a Dutch oven to accommodate the amount of kale I wanted. Then, following test kitchen protocol, I browned crumbled sausage (we liked hot Italian) and set it aside. I sautéed chopped onion in the drippings; added spices; and stirred in raw pasta, kale, and broth (diluted, so it wouldn't make the dish too salty). I covered the pot for less than 10 minutes, uncovered it, and stirred in the beans and the browned sausage. I gave it a taste.

Uh-oh. The pasta was unevenly cooked, the sauce thin, and the dish as a whole anemic. To bump up the flavor, I'd try leaving in the sausage the entire time. Since the dish cooked pretty quickly, I hoped the texture of the meat wouldn't suffer. When I tried it, I found that the flavor had improved and the texture of the meat was just fine. Would anything be gained by doing the same with the beans? For my next test, I stirred them in with the onion. Some broke down into the sauce, turning it creamy; those that stayed intact absorbed meaty, savory flavor. A success on both counts.

But evenly cooked pasta remained elusive. I had a suspicion that the kale formed a barrier of sorts, keeping the pasta from being consistently surrounded by the broth. Eventually, I figured out a solution: I put just half of the kale in at the start to cook with the pasta. The remainder went in after 4 minutes, steaming in a layer on top of the pasta in the (still covered) Dutch oven. After another 4 minutes, I stirred this kale into the pot, removed the lid, and let the dish finish cooking.

The longer-cooked kale blended into the sauce, the shorter-cooked had more chew and distinction, the pasta was evenly al dente, the sauce was creamy, and the whole dish had plenty of flavor—a perfect weeknight dinner.

The orecchiette traps the sauce without getting entwined in the kale.

ONE-POT SAUSAGE, KALE, AND WHITE BEAN PASTA Serves 4

- 2 tablespoons extra-virgin olive oil
- 1 pound hot Italian sausage, casings removed, sausage broken into ½-inch pieces
- 1 onion, chopped fine
- 1 (15-ounce) can cannellini beans, rinsed
- 6 garlic cloves, minced
- ½ teaspoon fennel seeds
- ½ teaspoon dried oregano
- ⅛–¼ teaspoon red pepper flakes
- 3 cups chicken broth
- 1 cup water
- 8 ounces (2¼ cups) orecchiette
- 12 ounces kale, stemmed and chopped
- 1 ounce Pecorino Romano cheese, grated (½ cup), plus extra for serving
  Salt and pepper

1. Heat 1 tablespoon oil in Dutch oven over medium-high heat until just smoking. Add sausage and cook until lightly browned all over, 5 to 7 minutes. Add onion and beans and cook, stirring occasionally, until onion is lightly browned, about 5 minutes. Stir in garlic, fennel seeds, oregano, and pepper flakes and cook until fragrant, about 30 seconds.

2. Stir in broth and water and bring to boil. Stir in orecchiette and half of kale. Cover, reduce heat to medium, and simmer for 4 minutes. Without stirring, place remaining kale on top of orecchiette. Cover and continue to cook until kale is just tender, about 4 minutes longer.

3. Stir to incorporate kale into orecchiette. Simmer, uncovered and stirring occasionally, until most liquid is absorbed and orecchiette is al dente, 3 to 6 minutes. Off heat, stir in Pecorino and remaining 1 tablespoon oil. Season with salt and pepper to taste. Serve with extra Pecorino.

Cooking Class How to Make Meatloaf with Gravy

Meatloaf is an American favorite, but it's often no more than adequate. Learn how to make moist, tender meatloaf that never disappoints, plus a hearty mushroom gravy. BY REBECCAH MARSTERS

Core Techniques

TEST KITCHEN TIPS FOR ANY MEATLOAF

Whether basic or dressed up, glazed or plain, cooked in the oven or in the slow cooker, there are many kinds of meatloaf. These four universal principles can improve any meatloaf.

Skip the Meatloaf Mix

Not every store carries meatloaf mix, a combination of ground chuck, pork, and veal. Plus, the mix is inconsistent from store to store, and different ratios of meat and different fat percentages can affect how a recipe works. We prefer to buy ground beef and pork separately, and omit the harder-to-find veal altogether.

Use a Panade

Panade, a mixture of bread or cracker crumbs and liquid, helps keep meatloaves (and meatballs) moist. As meat cooks, the proteins shrink, wringing out moisture. The panade interrupts the meat's protein network, discouraging it from linking into a tough matrix and squeezing out liquid. Also, the starches in the panade form a gel, which traps moisture and fat inside the meat. The pieces of chopped mushrooms also work this way.

Precook Aromatics and Vegetables

No matter how long meatloaf bakes, aromatics and vegetables that are added raw will always taste raw. Sautéing the onion, garlic, and any other vegetables before incorporating them into the raw meat mixture improves their taste and texture.

Lose the Loaf Pan

Meatloaves made in loaf pans stew in their own juices, making their bottoms greasy and mushy. Avoid that by baking meatloaf on a baking sheet or, as we do here, in a skillet. Our method allows the excess moisture to evaporate, keeping the meatloaf from stewing or steaming. Also, when baked in a skillet or on a baking sheet, the meatloaf can form flavorful, browned crust on the sides.

Must-Haves

KEY INGREDIENTS **Flavor Boosters**

Meatloaf is mostly meat, but it can taste surprisingly mild. To beef up its flavor, we add ingredients that are high in the naturally occurring amino acids called glutamates. These ingredients contribute to a taste sensation known as *umami*, making food taste meatier and more robust. Our recipe contains Worcestershire sauce and two kinds of mushrooms—all of which are high in glutamates.

UMAMI BUILDERS
Glutamate-rich button and dried porcini mushrooms and Worcestershire sauce provide meaty flavor.

ESSENTIAL GEAR **Nonstick Skillet**
To prevent our meatloaf from sticking to the skillet and breaking when we try to remove it, it's important to use a nonstick skillet. Which is best? Nonstick coatings gradually wear off with use, but in our tests, one pan was more durable than others. We also liked it because it's ovensafe, which is key for this meatloaf and for other uses. This skillet is sturdy and has a broad cooking surface; low, flaring sides; and a comfortable handle. Finally, its thick bottom retains heat for even cooking but is not so hefty as to be unwieldy.

OUR FAVORITE
T-fal Professional Non-Stick Fry Pan, 12.5 inches.

STEP BY STEP **Making the Best Meatloaf with Gravy**

1. PREP PORCINI
Soften dried porcini in hot water for 5 minutes. Drain, setting aside the liquid and chopping the plumped mushrooms.
WHY? Dried porcini must be rehydrated before you can use them. The flavorful liquid will be used in both meatloaf and gravy.

2. GRIND SALTINES
Process the saltines in a food processor for about 30 seconds until they're finely ground.
WHY? A panade, in this case made with saltines, helps keep meatloaf moist. Using a food processor is more effective than crushing the crackers by hand.

3. GRIND MUSHROOMS
Set aside the saltines. In the now-empty processor, finely grind half of the white mushrooms.
WHY? Mushrooms flavor the meatloaf and keep it moist. The smaller pieces blend together into the raw meat, and pulsing them is faster than chopping by hand.

4. SAUTÉ VEGETABLES
Brown a chopped onion. Add the ground mushrooms and the garlic.
WHY? Vegetables added to the meatloaf raw will never soften. Browning the mushrooms and aromatics before mixing them with the raw meat softens them and develops their flavor.

5. MIX IN PORK
Add the vegetables to the panade. When they're cool, mix in the pork, the eggs, and some porcini liquid.
WHY? Because ground pork usually has more water than ground beef does, it combines better with the other ingredients.

esh and dried mushrooms add deep savor and help keep this meatloaf moist.

MEATLOAF WITH MUSHROOM GRAVY Serves 6 to 8

If you're short the 2 tablespoons of meatloaf drippings needed to make the gravy, supplement with melted butter or vegetable oil.

- 1 cup water
- ¼ ounce dried porcini mushrooms, rinsed
- 16 square or 18 round saltines
- 10 ounces white mushrooms, trimmed
- 1 tablespoon vegetable oil
- 1 onion, chopped fine
  Salt and pepper
- 4 garlic cloves, minced
- 1 pound ground pork
- 2 large eggs
- 1 tablespoon plus ¾ teaspoon Worcestershire sauce
- 1 pound 85 percent lean ground beef
- ¾ teaspoon minced fresh thyme
- ¼ cup all-purpose flour
- 2½ cups chicken broth

1. Adjust oven rack to middle position and heat oven to 375 degrees. Microwave water and porcini mushrooms in covered bowl until steaming, about 1 minute. Let sit until softened, about 5 minutes. Remove porcini from bowl with fork and mince. Strain porcini liquid through fine-mesh strainer lined with coffee filter; reserve ¾ cup.

2. Process saltines in food processor until finely ground, about 30 seconds; transfer to large bowl. Pulse half of white mushrooms in processor until finely ground, 8 to 10 pulses.

3. Heat oil in 12-inch nonstick oven-safe skillet over medium-high heat until shimmering. Add onion and cook until browned, 6 to 8 minutes. Add processed white mushrooms and ¼ teaspoon salt and cook until liquid evaporates and mushrooms begin to brown, about 5 minutes. Add garlic and cook until fragrant, about 30 seconds. Transfer to bowl with saltines and let cool completely, about 15 minutes.

4. Add pork, eggs, 1 tablespoon Worcestershire, 1 teaspoon salt, ¾ teaspoon pepper, and ¼ cup reserved porcini liquid to cooled white mushroom–saltine mixture and knead gently until mostly combined. Add beef and knead until well combined. Transfer meat mixture to now-empty skillet and shape into 10 by 6-inch loaf. Bake until meatloaf registers 160 degrees, 45 to 55 minutes. Transfer meatloaf to carving board using spatula and tent loosely with aluminum foil.

5. Thinly slice remaining white mushrooms. Discard any solids in skillet and pour off all but 2 tablespoons fat. Heat fat over medium-high heat until shimmering. Add sliced white mushrooms and minced porcini mushrooms and cook, stirring occasionally, until deep golden brown, 6 to 8 minutes. Stir in thyme and ¼ teaspoon salt and cook until fragrant, about 30 seconds. Add flour and cook, stirring frequently, until golden, about 2 minutes. Slowly whisk in broth, remaining ½ cup reserved porcini liquid, and remaining ¾ teaspoon Worcestershire, scraping up any browned bits, and bring to boil. Reduce heat to medium and simmer, whisking occasionally, until thickened, 10 to 15 minutes. Season with salt and pepper to taste. Slice meatloaf and serve with mushroom gravy.

SHAPE MEATLOAF
dd the beef and knead until ombined. Pat the mixture into a af right in the skillet.
HY? Now that the other ingreents are mixed, the ground beef easier to incorporate. Cooking e loaf free-form creates more rface area for a craggy crust.

7. BAKE IN SKILLET
Put the skillet in the oven and bake the meatloaf until it registers 160 degrees.
WHY? Using the same skillet to sauté the vegetables and bake the meatloaf keeps the loaf from steaming and means fewer dishes to clean up.

8. START GRAVY
Remove the meatloaf from the skillet. Slice the remaining white mushrooms and sauté them with the chopped porcini in the fat left in the skillet. Stir in flour to thicken.
WHY? The rendered fat adds rich base flavor.

9. DEGLAZE PAN
Add chicken broth, more porcini liquid, and Worcestershire sauce, whisking to incorporate the flour and scrape up the browned bits.
WHY? These additions, plus the fond, combine to make deeply flavorful gravy.

10. SIMMER AND SERVE
Simmer the gravy for 10 to 15 minutes to thicken. Slice the meatloaf and ladle on the gravy.
WHY? Flour-thickened liquids must boil in order to fully thicken. Simmering concentrates the gravy for the best flavor and texture.

Slow Cooker Chinese Barbecued Pork

The slow cooker does many things well. Who knew that making Chinese barbecued pork is among the things it does superbly? BY DIANE UNGER

IF YOU'VE VISITED a Chinatown, you've seen glossy, red-tinged *char siu*—Chinese barbecued pork—hanging in the windows of takeout shops. This rich, lacquered, sweet and savory pork can be simply sliced and served with white rice and greens or used to fortify wonton soup, fried rice, or stir-fries. Unlike what we typically think of as barbecue, this dish is cooked neither on a grill nor in a smoker: It's cooked and then glazed in an oven. The test kitchen has an oven-to-broiler recipe for Chinese barbecued pork that is out of this world, so I decided to see if I could adapt it for the slow cooker.

Our recipe calls for cutting a boneless pork butt roast—the cut typically used for pulled pork—into strips, trimming some (but not all) of the fat, and marinating the meat in a mixture of sugar, soy sauce, garlic, ginger, and hoisin sauce. The marinated pork then goes through a three-step cooking process: First it's covered with foil and steamed; then it's uncovered and roasted; finally, it's glazed under the broiler on both sides with a sauce of some reserved marinade mixture cooked with ketchup and honey. The finished product is tender and flavorful, with a shiny, slightly charred exterior

▶ Visit **CooksCountry. com/whiterice** for our recipe, which produces perfectly fluffy white rice every time.

that tastes even better than it looks. My colleagues refer to it fondly as "meat candy."

Since much of the point of the slow cooker is to make life easier, I was hoping that I could eliminate the marinating step. I'd simply cook the trimmed pork strips with the sauce in the slow cooker. But when I tried it, I was reminded that pork butt has a lot of flavor in part because it has a lot of fat and connective tissue that melt out of the meat as it cooks. By the time the meat was tender, after about 5 hours on low, the sauce had been diluted by the rendered fat and pork juices. Sure, I could run this cooking liquid through a fat separator and then reduce it on the stovetop to use as a glaze when broiling, but I didn't want to work that hard for a slow-cooker recipe.

What about using only dry seasonings in the cooker? I made a Chinese-style rub using powdered garlic, ginger, coriander, star anise, fennel seeds, cinnamon, salt, and pepper; rubbed it on the strips of pork shoulder; arranged them in the slow cooker; and set the

switch to "low." The meat rendered the same amount of fat and juices, but they combined with the spices to create a flavorful, more concentrated braising liquid for the meat, which now had deeper, richer flavor (I discarded the liquid when the slow cooking was done). I performed a few more tests and discovered that I could pare down my rub to just three ingredients—salt, pepper, and five-spice powder (the last handily collects five spices in one jar)—without sacrificing complexity.

To put the "char" in char siu and to properly lacquer the pork, I knew I'd have to finish it with sauce under the broiler, as we did in our original recipe. To streamline, though, I hoped that I wouldn't have to cook the sauce before brushing it on for the broiling step. After fiddling with various ratios of ingredients and testing the broiling mechanics, I found that I could use pretty much the same sauce as in our original recipe—without cooking it first—if I moved the oven rack up from the middle to about 4 inches from the broiler.

The stir-together sauce reduced into a sticky, clingy glaze right under the hot broiler. A little water in the pan prevented any sauce that dripped down from burning and smoking up the kitchen. With a slow cooker and this recipe, you're just a few hours away from incredibly tasty Chinese barbecued pork

SLOW-COOKER CHINESE BARBECUED PORK Serves 8

Pork butt roast is often labeled Boston butt in the supermarket. Look for five-spice powder and hoisin sauce in the international aisle at your supermarket.

- 1½ teaspoons salt
- 1½ teaspoons five-spice powder
- ½ teaspoon pepper
- 1 (5- to 6-pound) boneless pork butt roast, trimmed and sliced crosswise into 1-inch-thick steaks
- ⅓ cup hoisin sauce
- ⅓ cup honey
- ¼ cup sugar
- ¼ cup soy sauce
- ¼ cup ketchup
- 2 tablespoons dry sherry
- 1 tablespoon toasted sesame oil
- 1 tablespoon grated fresh ginger
- 2 garlic cloves, minced

1. Combine salt, ¾ teaspoon five-spice powder, and pepper in bowl. Rub spice mixture all over pork and transfer to slow cooker. Cover and cook on low until pork is just tender, 5 to 6 hours.

2. When pork is nearly done, combine hoisin, honey, sugar, soy sauce, ketchup, sherry, oil, ginger, garlic, and remaining ¾ teaspoon five-spice powder in bowl. Set wire rack inside aluminum foil–lined rimmed baking sheet. Pour 1 cup water into sheet. Adjust oven rack 4 inches from broiler element and heat broiler.

3. Using tongs, transfer pork from slow cooker to prepared wire rack in single layer. Brush pork with one-third of hoisin mixture and broil until lightly caramelized, 5 to 7 minutes. Flip pork, brush with half of remaining hoisin mixture, and broil until lightly caramelized on second side, 5 to 7 minutes. Brush pork with remaining hoisin mixture and broil until deep mahogany and crispy around edges, about 3 minutes. Transfer to carving board and let rest for 10 minutes. Slice crosswise into thin strips. Serve.

Once the meat is tender, we brush on glaze and broil to create the classic lacquered exterior.

TEST KITCHEN TECHNIQUE
Cutting Pork Steaks

Trim a 5- to 6-pound boneless pork butt roast of excess hard, waxy fat and then slice it into 1-inch-thick steaks. Most of the fat in the steaks will render during the slow cooking.

Recipe Makeover Biscuits with Sausage and Gravy

A great breakfast starts the day out right—but not if you have to take a nap right afterward. We set out to lighten this breakfast classic. BY CRISTIN WALSH

IF YOU WAKE before dawn to milk the cows and feed the pigs, biscuits with sausage and gravy might be just the thing to get your day rolling. In this largely sedentary era, though, few of us can afford those 600 calories and 35 grams of fat per serving. But does living a 21st-century life really mean that we have to relinquish this deeply satisfying breakfast? Not if I can help it.

Luckily, the test kitchen already has a low-fat biscuit recipe; it uses nonfat buttermilk plus low-fat cream cheese to replace much of the butter. That freed me up to focus on the gravy. To make ordinary sausage gravy, you brown bulk pork sausage in a saucepan, stir in flour as a thickener, and then add milk. After 10 minutes of simmering, it's ready to meet a biscuit. My challenge was to trim calories and fat but keep the full-bodied milkiness and flavor. Existing recipes for low-fat sausage gravy rely on such ingredients as canola oil (in place of the sausage fat), low-fat yogurt, skim milk, and meatless, fat-free "sausage." I tested an assortment of recipes, but they were "really repulsive," as one taster summed it up. I opted to start with the test kitchen's regular sausage gravy and trim the recipe myself, borrowing ideas as necessary from these other recipes.

Right away, I switched from fatty bulk pork sausage to leaner chicken sausage. But these meats diverged too much—in flavor, texture, and fat content—that I didn't want to pin my recipe on them. OK, I'd make my own chicken breakfast sausage. Ground turkey offers more fat-content options, I discovered, so I modified my plan, substituting 93 percent lean ground turkey for pork in what I hoped would be an easy, flavorful test kitchen recipe for breakfast sausage. Low in both fat and calories, the turkey looked perfect—on paper. In the pan, it turned rubbery and pebbly. Luckily, I remembered how we had solved this problem once before: We'd used baking soda, of all things, which works by raising the pH of the meat. That, in turn, loosens the structure of the muscle fibers, which dramatically increases how much of its own water and fat the meat can hang on to after it's cooked. I added baking soda to my mix and produced tender turkey sausage. One goal accomplished.

Turning to the actual gravy, I started

We make our own reduced-fat sausage with ground turkey and lots of spice.

by replacing the whole milk with skim milk. The gravy was wan, watery, and curdled. Low-fat milk had slightly more body but also curdled. Happily, my next idea, canned evaporated skim milk, had less fat, more body, and more stability (it contains stabilizers that prevent curdling).

To fix the gravy's meek flavor, I tried chicken broth in combination with the canned milk. As I had hoped, the broth added an underlying savory quality. Unfortunately, it also thinned out the gravy. To add back deep body and creaminess, I tried no-fat sour cream (too tangy), no-fat Greek yogurt (ditto), and low-fat cream cheese, aka neufchatel, which I was already using to make the biscuits. I found that if I first diluted the broth a little further with water, I could afford a small amount of neufchatel, stay within my target numbers, and give the gravy a real plush quality.

For a final test, I put together the two components: biscuits and gravy. With one-third fewer calories and two-thirds less fat, here was a breakfast tailor-made for a 21st-century office worker.

½   teaspoon dried thyme
¼   teaspoon baking soda
⅛   teaspoon cayenne pepper

GRAVY
1   teaspoon vegetable oil
¼   cup all-purpose flour
2   cups chicken broth
1½   cups evaporated skim milk
½   cup water
2   tablespoons ⅓ less fat cream cheese (neufchatel), softened

1. FOR THE BISCUITS: Adjust oven rack to middle position and heat oven to 450 degrees. Line rimmed baking sheet with parchment paper. Pulse flour, sugar, baking powder, baking soda, and salt in food processor until combined, about 3 pulses. Add butter and cream cheese and pulse until mixture resembles coarse meal, about 15 pulses. Transfer to bowl and stir in buttermilk until combined.

2. Knead dough on lightly floured counter until smooth, 8 to 10 turns. Pat dough into 7½ by 5-inch rectangle, about ¾ inch thick. Cut dough into 6 equal squares and space evenly on prepared sheet.

3. Bake biscuits for 5 minutes, then rotate sheet and reduce oven to 400 degrees. Continue to bake until golden brown, 12 to 15 minutes; transfer biscuits to wire rack.

4. FOR THE SAUSAGE: Mix all ingredients in bowl until thoroughly combined.

5. FOR THE GRAVY: Heat oil in Dutch oven over medium heat until shimmering. Add sausage and cook, breaking up pieces with spoon, until no longer pink, about 8 minutes. Sprinkle flour over sausage and cook for 1 minute. Slowly stir in broth, evaporated milk, and water and bring to simmer. Cook until sauce has thickened, 10 to 12 minutes. Remove from heat and whisk in cream cheese until combined. Serve over split biscuits.

REDUCED-FAT BISCUITS AND SAUSAGE GRAVY Serves 6
Remember to put the butter and neufchatel in the freezer at least 1 hour before you start making the biscuits.

BISCUITS
1½   cups (7½ ounces) all-purpose flour
1½   teaspoons sugar
1½   teaspoons baking powder
¼   teaspoon baking soda
½   teaspoon salt
2   tablespoons unsalted butter, cut into ½-inch pieces and frozen for 1 hour
1½   tablespoons ⅓ less fat cream cheese (neufchatel), cut into ½-inch pieces and frozen for 1 hour
½   cup plus 2 tablespoons nonfat buttermilk

SAUSAGE
1¼   pounds 93 percent lean ground turkey
2   teaspoons ground sage
1½   teaspoons pepper
1   teaspoon salt
1   garlic clove, minced
1   teaspoon ground fennel seeds

Cooking for Two Coffee Mug Chocolate Cake

Homemade molten chocolate cake in 5 minutes, start to finish? Amazing!
If only it actually worked. BY CRISTIN WALSH

IN THE 1970S, the microwave oven was the newest must-have toy for the kitchen, and for a time there was a steady stream of cookbooks devoted to it. But eventually the trend passed, and today, while just about every kitchen is equipped with a microwave, most of us relegate it to popping popcorn, reheating leftovers, and warming frozen meals.

But recently a recipe for an ingenious single-serving molten chocolate cake made in a coffee mug and "baked" in the microwave has been racing around the Internet. Moist and decadent, according to hundreds of user reviews, the cake is a "chocoholic's dream." Plus, it can be made from scratch in minutes: 2 to 4 minutes, to be exact. If its reviews were anywhere near true, it would be a perfect near-instant dessert for two.

I selected a few recipes to try, mixed ingredients, and tapped numbers into the microwave panel. Most recipes call for mixing cocoa powder, flour, sugar, eggs, oil, and milk, often right in the mug (or sometimes two mugs), and then hitting "Start." A few minutes later, my coworkers and I discovered that the hype was just that: hype. These cakes were bland, chalky, rubbery, heavy, and unevenly cooked. Several exploded over mug brims, looking like eighth-grade science experiments gone wrong. Yes, the recipe was ridiculously fast and easy, but the cakes weren't worth even this minimal effort.

Undeterred, I started over, this time working off a decadent (and reliable) test kitchen recipe for individual molten chocolate cakes, hoping to adapt it for the mug and the microwave. I cut back the recipe to fit into two mugs; then I streamlined the method, melting ¼ cup of butter and 4 ounces of chocolate together (in the microwave, of course) and stirring in two eggs, ¼ cup of sugar, a touch of salt, vanilla extract, and just a single tablespoon of flour (ordinarily, the recipe calls for whipping the eggs and sugar together). Based on reading I'd done, I instituted two techniques to get the cakes to cook more evenly: I set the mugs on opposite sides of the tray so they would be more evenly exposed to the microwaves. And I stirred the batter partway through.

I'd fixed the pockets of raw batter, and thanks to the butter and the chocolate, the flavor of the cakes was greatly improved. But I was still a long way from a cake I'd actually want to eat. This batter, too, had erupted and subsequently sunk, producing cakes as heavy as those in round one.

I'm a trained pastry chef, but baking in the microwave was virgin territory for me, so I enlisted the help of our science editor. He explained that microwaves heat food to very high temperatures, in particular raising the temperature of fat and water (contained in the eggs and butter) in the batter. The water then produces steam—in this case too much steam, causing excessive rise in the cakes. To moderate the eruptions, he suggested that I use less fat; it was the fat, he said, that was acting as a heat reservoir, providing so much heat to the water that it, in turn, produced that excessive steam. The easiest place to trim back fat was the chocolate, so I whittled it down, ounce by ounce. At 1 ounce, the cakes rose more or less normally and collapsed less dramatically, so they were lighter, if not yet light. Unfortunately, the flavor was back where it had started—in a word, weak. Some recipes boost the flavor with Nutella or peanut butter or hot cocoa mix. I tried all three, but in the end, the simplest solution proved best: 2 tablespoons of cocoa powder (cocoa has less fat than bar chocolate).

Now I redoubled my efforts to improve the texture. To strengthen the cake's structure, I gradually added more flour until I had quadrupled the original

We push a small piece of chocolate into the center of each cake toward the end of cooking; the chocolate softens into a "molten" center.

amount; flour forms gluten, which sets when hot. But while the mug cakes no longer fell, the rubbery texture had returned (plus they still weren't light, but I'd get to that later). Our science editor blamed the intense heat of the microwave. The gluten was setting too quickly, he said. Since water absorbs the energy of the microwaves, I thought cooking the cakes in a water bath would moderate the heat, but this was a total dud. The batter at the bottom, where the mug sat in the bath, never cooked; apparently, the water worked only too well. I conducted many more tests, fiddling endlessly with power settings and cooking times. My frustration was about to erupt, too, when I realized that the answer had been right under my nose: 50 percent power. It slowed the cooking just enough to let the flour gently develop structure. Just like that, the tough, rubbery quality vanished.

To make the mug cakes lighter, I could beat the sugar and eggs until light (standard molten cake procedure). Or, I could separate the eggs and fold stiffly beaten whites into the batter. No and

no—the point of this cake was ease and speed. Instead, I tried stirring baking powder into the batter. Amazingly, 3 minutes was enough time for the powder to produce plenty of gas so the cakes would have a nice light texture.

After more than 100 tests, my microwave molten chocolate mug cake was tender, moist, light, and flavorful. There was just one problem: It wasn't molten. In a conventional oven, cakes cook from the outside in, so you produce a molten cake by underbaking it slightly. Since a microwave doesn't cook that way, I'd have to improvise. Some recipes simplify molten cake for a conventional oven by inserting a piece of chocolate into the cake's center before baking; there it melts to perfect gushiness. I was stirring the batter partway through to ensure even cooking, so I'd need to modify that technique. I cooked the mug cakes for 45 seconds and stirred, cooked them for another 45 seconds, pushed chunks of bittersweet chocolate into their centers, and zapped them for a final 35 seconds. This produced the soft center I was looking for, with the ɔonus that it powerfully reinforced he chocolate flavor.

From start to finish, this cake akes about 5 minutes to make. It's niraculously fast; just as important, t's extremely delicious. I believe hey call that eating your cake and naving it, too.

ƆOFFEE MUG MOLTEN ƆHOCOLATE CAKE FOR TWO

Ve developed this recipe in a full-ize, 1200-watt microwave. If you're ısing a compact microwave with 800 vatts or fewer, increase the cooking ime to 90 seconds for each interval. or either size microwave, reset to 0 percent power at each stage of ooking. Use a mug that holds at least 1 ounces, or the batter will overflow. he bittersweet chocolate is added at wo points.

- 4 **tablespoons unsalted butter**
- 1 **ounce bittersweet chocolate, chopped, plus 1 ounce broken into 4 equal pieces**
- ¼ **cup (1¾ ounces) sugar**
- 2 **large eggs**
- 2 **tablespoons unsweetened cocoa powder**
- 1 **teaspoon vanilla extract**
- ¼ **teaspoon salt**
- ¼ **cup (1¼ ounces) all-purpose flour**
- ½ **teaspoon baking powder**

1. Microwave butter and chopped hocolate in large bowl, stirring ften, until melted, about 1 minute. Vhisk sugar, eggs, cocoa, vanilla, nd salt into chocolate mixture until mooth. In separate bowl, combine our and baking powder. Whisk our mixture into chocolate mixture ntil combined. Divide batter evenly etween 2 (11-ounce) coffee mugs.

2. Place mugs on opposite sides of ıicrowave turntable. Microwave at 0 percent power for 45 seconds. Stir atter and microwave at 50 percent ower for 45 seconds (batter will se to just below rim of mug). Press chocolate pieces into center of each ıke until chocolate is flush with top f cake. Microwave at 50 percent ower for 35 seconds (cake should be ightly wet around edges of mug and ɔmewhat drier toward center). Let ıkes rest for 2 minutes. Serve.

Five Easy Recipes Flavored Popcorn

We left no kernel unpopped in our search for crispy, light stovetop popcorn.

BY NICK IVERSON

SURE IT'S EASY to make, but microwave popcorn can be greasy, salty, and full of unpopped kernels at the bottom of the bag. If you try to compensate by popping it longer, it's easy to burn. Then there's the "artificial butter flavor," which can't hold a candle to real butter. If microwave popcorn is what you've become accustomed to, you owe it to yourself to revisit the genuine article: stovetop popcorn.

The test kitchen has developed an easy, foolproof stovetop method for popcorn. It starts with heating three kernels in vegetable oil in a medium saucepan. When the test kernels pop, you know the oil is hot enough—but don't dump in the rest of the kernels yet. Pull the pan off the heat first; then pour in the kernels and let them sit, covered and undisturbed, for 30 seconds before putting the pan back on the burner. This resting period preheats the raw popcorn so that it pops quickly and evenly, with a minimum of unpopped kernels, when returned to the heat.

There's no need to shake the pan; just keep the lid slightly ajar and wait for the popping to slow to about 2 seconds between pops. That's it: Now you have light, crispy popcorn in the same few minutes that it takes to make the much-inferior microwave variety.

Melted butter is just for starters . . .

You can, of course, simply toss the popcorn with melted butter and salt and settle into your couch to watch a movie. But if you're like me, you might want some flavor variations to keep it interesting. A ranch version flavored with buttermilk, onion, and garlic powders and fresh herbs is perfect for a western. Cinnamon, malt powder, and brown sugar provide a sweet twist for that romantic comedy. A combination of Parmesan cheese and black pepper is a great match for your favorite mafia flick. And Sriracha (Asian chili-garlic sauce) and lime zest give the popcorn a spicy kick fit for an action-packed martial arts movie.

BUTTERED POPCORN Makes 14 cups

You don't need to shake the pan as the corn pops.

- 3 **tablespoons vegetable oil**
- ½ **cup popcorn kernels**
- 2 **tablespoons unsalted butter, melted**
- ¼ **teaspoon salt**

1. Heat oil and 3 kernels in large saucepan over medium-high heat until kernels pop. Remove pan from heat, add remaining kernels, cover, and let sit for 30 seconds.

2. Return pan to medium-high heat. Continue to cook with lid slightly ajar until popping slows to about 2 seconds between pops. Transfer popcorn to large bowl. Add melted butter and toss to coat popcorn. Add salt and toss to combine. Serve.

BUTTERMILK RANCH POPCORN

Add 1 tablespoon buttermilk powder, 1 tablespoon chopped fresh cilantro, 2 teaspoons dried dill, ¼ teaspoon garlic powder, and ¼ teaspoon onion powder to salt.

CINNAMON-MALT POPCORN

Add 2 tablespoons malted milk powder, 2 tablespoons packed brown sugar, and 1 teaspoon ground cinnamon to salt.

PARMESAN-PEPPER POPCORN

Add ½ cup grated Parmesan and 2 teaspoons pepper to salt.

SRIRACHA-LIME POPCORN

Add 1½ teaspoons Sriracha sauce to melted butter. Add 1 teaspoon grated lime zest to salt.

TEST KITCHEN TECHNIQUE **Leave Lid Ajar**

With our method, you don't have to shake the pan steadily—or at all—while the corn pops. But do keep the lid slightly ajar so the steam, but not the popping kernels, can escape, guaranteeing crispy, light popcorn.

CRACK THE LID
A key to perfect popcorn.

Does the color of the pan you use affect the color of your cake? Yes, and it affects more than mere looks.

BY DAVID PAZMIÑO

WHY DON'T YOUR homemade layer cakes ever look as good as those from a bakery? Your cake pans could be at fault. A bad cake pan—flimsy, warped, worn out—makes lumpy, irregularly browned layers that stick, cling, and crack, no matter how much you grease it. A good cake pan is a baker's best friend.

Since the manufacturer discontinued what used to be our favorite 9-inch round cake pan, we were starting from scratch, but not without a few ideas. To produce tall layers and to accommodate voluminous fruit upside-down cakes, the replacement needed to be at least 2 inches deep. We vetoed angled sides because straight sides make better layer cakes. Handles on our former Best Buy cake pan (also discontinued) helped us move the pan from counter to oven without mishaps, but we couldn't find any suitable new pans with handles. Our old winner had a dark nonstick finish. Surveying the current field, we saw plenty of pans with light-colored nonstick finishes and a few without nonstick coating. To investigate all these alternatives, we bought seven different pans priced from $9.85 to $16.99 apiece (remember, you need two pans to make a layer cake).

Then we baked yellow cakes in pairs of each pan in the same oven, so we could observe how well each pan browned the cake and how it affected the shape of the layers. With layer cake, we want little to no doming. Domed cakes look unprofessional; moreover, domed layers indicate uneven heat transfer. As cake pans heat up, they often bake (and set) the batter that's in contact with the sides first, giving the batter in the center of the pan time to rise higher.

As the layers cooled, one result was clear: The darker the pan the darker the cake. A dark-colored pan absorbs heat more efficiently than a light-colored pan. While browning does improve flavor, darker pans also produced cakes that

were distinctly domed. Light-finish pans baked more evenly, producing taller, more level layers.

Two pans produced tall, airy layers with flat, even tops. Neither pan was dark; in fact, one wasn't even nonstick. Clearly, the lack of coating didn't matter with cake: We had prepared one set of pans with our usual regimen (grease, parchment, grease the parchment, and flour) and the other set with baking spray; every pan released the buttery cakes easily, nonstick-coated or not. So far, light-colored pans were in the lead.

But cake pans aren't just for cakes. Our Pepperoni Pan Pizza, for instance, also bakes in a cake pan. This time, nonstick coating made all the difference. Despite thorough greasing, pizza fused to the pans without nonstick coating. And once again the darkest pan made the brownest pizza crust, a decided plus.

At this point, we had two styles of pans in the lead, one light and the other dark, depending on what we were baking. To try to break the tie, we went back into the kitchen to make pineapple upside-down cake and cinnamon buns. Predictably, the light pan browned less, though acceptably, on upside-down cake. But it failed to adequately color the cinnamon buns; ultimately, we had to alter the recipe to make the light pan work here. (See page 19 for details.)

We were torn: Light pans made lovelier cake layers, but on anything other than cake we preferred the browning we got from dark pans. Reasoning that we use these pans primarily for cakes, we ultimately gave our light-colored winner the nod. The sturdy Nordic Ware Naturals Nonstick 9-Inch Round Cake Pan made tall layers with its 2½-inch straight sides (the others topped out at 2 inches). For deeper browning, to make recipes such as rolls, buns, and pizza, we also recommend our highest-ranking dark-finish choice, by Chicago Metallic.

HIGHLY RECOMMENDED		CRITERIA	TESTERS' NOTES
NORDIC WARE NATURALS Nonstick 9-Inch Round Cake Pan **Model:** 46950 **Price:** $14.32 **Source:** amazon.com **Nonstick/Color:** Yes, light **Material:** Aluminum, with galvanized steel–reinforced rim	Cake ★★★ Pizza ★★½		Solidly built, with light gold nonstick coating, this pan produced tall, fluffy, level cakes. Layers shaped up perfectly, no matter how the pan was greased. Upside-down cake and pizza released and browned well, but cinnamon buns were too pale.

RECOMMENDED			
USA PAN 9" Round Cake Pan **Model:** 1070LC **Price:** $14.99 **Source:** amazon.com **Nonstick/Color:** Yes, light silver **Material:** Aluminized steel	Cake ★★½ Pizza ★★½		This sturdy light-toned pan with a corrugated bottom browned consistently and produced level, tall cake layers, though they weren't quite as tall as those baked in our winner (and were slightly less attractive when we used baking spray). Pan pizza browned well but not as deeply as it did in darker pans.
CHICAGO METALLIC Non-Stick 9" Round Cake Pan **Model:** 16629 **Price:** $10.97 **Source:** amazon.com **Nonstick/Color:** Yes, dark **Material:** Aluminized steel	Cake ★½ Pizza ★★★ (BROWNS BEST)		This pan released perfectly but its dark finish radiated a lot of heat, setting the edges of the cake too quickly, which let the center rise to a dome. Layers were slightly less attractive when we used baking spray. But the dark finish browned pizza and cinnamon buns nicely.

RECOMMENDED WITH RESERVATIONS			
PARRISH MAGIC LINE 9" x 2" Round Cake Pan **Model:** PRD-92 **Price:** $10.42 **Nonstick/Color:** No, light **Material:** Aluminum	Cake ★★★ Pizza ★		Early on we admired this uncoated shiny aluminum pan for its tall, level cake layers with straight sides, which emerged evenly light brown, not overly dark. Cake released well, but pizza stuck firmly despite greasing; we had to chisel it out.
FAT DADDIO'S Professional Series Round Cake Pan Solid Bottom, 9" x 2" **Model:** PRD-92 **Price:** $9.99 **Nonstick/Color:** No, light **Material:** Anodized aluminum	Cake ★★½ Pizza ★		This thick, sturdy pan with a light, uncoated, matte finish produced mostly uniform cake layers with only slightly sloping edges. Cakes released fine, but with pizza, the lack of a nonstick coating was a big problem: Testers could hardly hack the pizza out of the pan.

NOT RECOMMENDED			
CUISINART Chef's Classic Non-Stick Bakeware 9" Round Cake Pan **Model:** AMB-9RCK **Price:** $9.85 **Nonstick/Color:** Yes, dark **Material:** Aluminized steel	Cake ★ Pizza ★★		The dark finish on this sturdy, heavy-weight pan overbrowned cake. Layers were sloped and visibly squat; one tester described the cake as "homely." The bottom of the pizza was a nice golden brown; unfortunately, a few pieces stuck and burned on the sides.
CALPHALON Nonstick Bakeware 9-Inch Round Cake Pan **Model:** 1826052 **Price:** $16.99 **Nonstick/Color:** Yes, dark **Material:** Steel	Cake ★ Pizza ★★		The cakes baked in this dark pan were some of the darkest and least risen among all the pans we tested and their edges shrank from the sides, making them slope. The manufacturer does not recommend baking spray, so we used shortening, which overcrisped the edges. Grease and flour are imperatives.

TEST KITCHEN DISCOVERY **Light Pan Makes Taller, More Level Cake**

Light-colored pans make tall, level layers, which make beautiful cakes with fluffy crumbs. Dark pans brown better (and browning equals flavor), but the cake layers come out sloped and short.

BAKED IN A DARK PAN

BAKED IN A LIGHT PAN

Taste Test Egg Noodles

What makes the best egg noodles? The right shape, right amount of fat, and right type of flour.

BY HANNAH CROWLEY

EGG NOODLES ARE the starchy soul of many of our favorite comfort foods. For beef stroganoff, goulash, tuna noodle casserole, and chicken noodle soup, we use them to anchor gravy, transport sauce, and add bulk to soup. The noodles should taste lightly wheaty, like traditional pasta, but with a richer flavor that comes from eggs in the pasta dough.

The last time we evaluated egg noodles, we found so many "bland" and "gummy" examples that we could recommend just two products. To see if our options have improved, we surveyed supermarket shelves and selected seven products to taste. We chose those that were widely available, and if the company offered multiple shapes, we focused on noodles labeled "wide" or "broad," as these are the most common type and what we typically call for in our recipes.

Twenty-one tasters evaluated each product twice, first cooked plain in lightly salted water and then tossed with a neutral-flavored oil to prevent sticking, and next in chicken noodle soup. We tabulated the results and were happily surprised: The egg noodle market has significantly improved, and we can recommend five of seven products. Of the other two, one was so-so; it contained only egg whites, no yolks, so it lacked flavor. The second was a frozen egg noodle that was very different from the others—short, straight, thick, and dumplinglike; tasters found it gummy.

Among the five products that we enjoyed, one stood out for being "buttery," "al dente" noodles in just the right shape. Since tasters liked their rich flavor, we compared the fat content among products. It ranged from 1 gram to 3 grams per 2-ounce

serving, and sure enough, our winning product had the most. Egg noodles have two primary ingredients: flour and eggs. So most of the fat is derived from the eggs, specifically the yolks. We inferred that with 3 grams of fat per serving, our winning noodles had the highest ratio of egg yolks, which imparted the winning rich flavor.

Rich, eggy flavor was a huge plus, but our winning noodles also stood out for their firm, chewy bite. The primary ingredient in every product was wheat flour, but three different kinds were used: standard wheat flour, durum flour, and semolina. The product with standard wheat flour was soft and gummy. The other two flours are both made from ground durum wheat, a high-protein variety that's often used in pasta because it develops more gluten, which helps noodles maintain their springy texture during cooking. The durum flour is finely ground, while semolina is coarser, and this difference was the key to our winner's resilient texture: The finer grains of durum flour break down more easily when cooked, so noodles turn mushy faster. Products at the top of our lineup use semolina.

One final factor explained our preferences: noodle shape, which ranged from broad pappardelle-like planks to short, narrow corkscrews; manufacturers interpreted the word "wide" in a variety of ways, as the industry does not have size standards. The optimal shape was somewhere in between. Tasters didn't like chasing thin noodles around their plates, and long flat noodles were unwieldy in soup, where they wiggled off our spoons, flicking broth in our faces. The most versatile shape was a wide corkscrew that was easy to spear with a fork yet short enough to be scooped up with a spoon. Four products offered this shape, including our winner.

We're glad to see that the egg noodle market has improved and are even happier that one brand was so good. We found these noodles rich and eggy, with the perfect tender chew and a versatile shape that works equally well as pasta and in soup. Pennsylvania Dutch Wide Egg Noodles beat a strong lineup to take the top spot. We'll be sure to choose them when available, but if they aren't sold at our supermarket, we're confident that we can find an alternative that's almost as good.

RECOMMENDED

	TASTERS' NOTES
PENNSYLVANIA DUTCH Wide Egg Noodles **Price:** $1.99 for 12 oz (17 cents per oz) **Fat:** 3 g **Flour:** Semolina, durum flour 	Our winning egg noodles had the most flavor, thanks to a higher ratio of yolks, which gave the pasta a "gentle egg flavor" that was "just rich enough." This product's high semolina content gave noodles a firm yet tender bite with a "nice, subtle chew." The wide, corkscrew shape worked in both soup and pasta.
DE CECCO Egg Pappardelle **Price:** $4.46 for 8.8 oz (51 cents per oz) **Fat:** 2 g **Flour:** Semolina 	These imported, expensive Italian noodles were "mildly eggy," with long, broad pappardelle-like planks that were "thin" and "delicate" but "not too soft." Their semolina content helped them remain "al dente," so they "held up" in soup. Their shape was great as pasta, but some tasters found them too long for soup, slithering off spoons.
LIGHT 'N FLUFFY Egg Noodles, Wide **Price:** $1.99 for 12 oz (17 cents per oz) **Fat:** 2.5 g **Flour:** Durum flour 	This product won our previous taste test, and we liked it again for its "classic," "light," "neutral" flavor, which was more wheaty than eggy. The "soft" noodles lacked the al dente bite of our winner but were perfectly passable and came in our preferred short, fat corkscrew shape.
BIONATURAE Traditional Egg Pasta Pappardelle **Price:** $3.53 for 8.8 oz (40 cents per oz) **Fat:** 2 g **Flour:** Organic semolina 	These wide planks were mild, "gentle," "neutral," and "clean," with "no off-flavors." They had "pleasant chew," with "thick" noodles that stayed "firm" but were best as pasta; in soup the shape was hard to eat, prompting one taster to dub them "the Chuck Norris of noodles. These are so big they kicked my chicken off the spoon!"
MANISCHEWITZ Wide Premium Enriched Egg Noodles **Price:** $2.79 for 12 oz (23 cents per oz) **Fat:** 2.5 g **Flour:** Durum flour 	These noodles were "a bit on the starchy side," with a "subtle" flavor that was "suitable" but "nothing to write home about." They were "softer" yet "didn't sog out" and had a versatile, short, fat corkscrew shape that was "spoon-friendly."

RECOMMENDED WITH RESERVATIONS

NO YOLKS Cholesterol Free Egg White Pasta, Broad **Price:** $2.39 for 12 oz (20 cents per oz) **Fat:** 1 g **Flour:** Durum flour, corn flour 	These noodles used egg whites but no yolks; tasters found them "very plain," and it was "hard to discern any flavor," but they were still "acceptable" and "neutral." (And to be fair, these noodles are marketed to people who are watching their fat and cholesterol intake.) It was the only noodle in our lineup to include corn flour, which according to the company is employed for its yellow color, firming texture, and smooth taste. The noodles' thin corkscrew shape was harder to scoop up: They were "a bit slippery."

NOT RECOMMENDED

REAMES Homestyle Egg Noodles **Price:** $4.25 for 24 oz (18 cents per oz) **Fat:** 1.9 g **Flour:** Bleached enriched wheat flour 	While they're sold as egg noodles, these frozen noodles were a very different sort from the rest in our lineup; they were short, thick planks that resembled dumplings. Also, they are made from all-purpose flour, not the more usual durum or semolina. No wonder tasters found them "bland," "floury," and "dense."

Looking for a Recipe

Have you lost a recipe you treasure? Ask a reader. While you're at it, answer a reader. Post queries and finds at **CooksCountry.com/magazine**; click on **Looking for a Recipe** (or write to Looking for a Recipe, *Cook's Country*, P.O. Box 470739, Brookline, MA 02447). We'll share all your submissions online and one recipe on this page; please include your name and mailing address.

Cranberry Jell-O Mold
Sarah Gendon, Bath, Maine

Every year at holiday time, my grandmother used to make the most wonderful Jell-O salad. Studded with cranberries and walnuts and filled with raspberries and strawberries, it was a head turner. She served it with a mayonnaise-based sauce. I never thought to get the recipe from her. Can anyone help me out?

Pickled Turnips
Mildred Katz, Newton, Mass.

I belong to a CSA (community-supported agriculture group), so every week I'm blessed with a bumper crop of organic vegetables (some of which I can't identify). Last month I got Macomber turnips and was told that they're great for pickling. Does anyone have a recipe? If so, please share.

Soupy Potatoes
Mara Grey, Langley, Wash.

I'm looking for a very simple recipe called soupy potatoes. It's one of my favorite comfort foods and was a standard in my mother's repertoire; she got it from an old Sierra Club cookbook from the 1930s. Potatoes, bacon, and onions are all cooked together and then roughly mashed. I'd really love to find the recipe

BREAKFAST COOKIES

Makes 16 cookies

Jill Marie Nevins, Davis, Calif.
"Cookies for breakfast?—no wonder I loved these as a kid. Odd as they sound, the salty-sweet thing really works, and lately I see a lot of bacon in sweets. My mom was ahead of her time!"

- 8 slices bacon
- 1¼ cups (6¼ ounces) all-purpose flour
- ½ cup (2 ounces) Grape-Nuts cereal
- ½ teaspoon salt
- ½ teaspoon baking powder
- ¼ teaspoon baking soda
- 8 tablespoons unsalted butter, softened
- 1 cup (7 ounces) granulated sugar
- ⅓ cup packed (2⅓ ounces) light brown sugar
- 1 large egg
- 2 tablespoons frozen orange juice concentrate, thawed
- ½ teaspoon grated orange zest

1. Cook bacon in 12-inch skillet over medium heat until crispy, 8 to 10 minutes. Transfer to paper towel–lined plate. Once cool, crumble coarsely; set aside. Adjust oven rack to middle position and heat oven to 325 degrees. Line 2 rimmed baking sheets with parchment paper.

2. Combine flour, Grape-Nuts, salt, baking powder, and baking soda in bowl. Using stand mixer fitted with paddle, beat butter, ⅔ cup granulated sugar, and brown sugar on medium-high speed until pale and fluffy, about 1 minute. Add egg, orange juice concentrate, and orange zest and beat until combined, about 30 seconds. Reduce speed to low, add flour mixture in 3 additions, and mix until just incorporated. Add bacon and mix until just combined, about 30 seconds.

3. Place remaining ⅓ cup granulated sugar in shallow dish. Working with 2 tablespoons dough at a time, roll into 16 balls, then roll balls in granulated sugar. Space balls on prepared sheets in staggered pattern. Using bottom of drinking glass, flatten balls to 2½ inches in diameter. Sprinkle each sheet with 1½ teaspoons granulated sugar from dish.

4. Bake cookies, 1 sheet at a time, until slightly puffy and light golden brown, 15 to 18 minutes, rotating sheets halfway through baking. Let cookies cool on sheet for 5 minutes, then transfer to wire rack. Let cookies cool completely before serving.

RECIPE INDEX

FIND THE ROOSTER!

A tiny version of this rooster has been hidden in the pages of this issue. Write us with its location and we'll enter you in a random drawing. The first correct entry drawn will win a set of our favorit[e] 9-inch cake pans (see page 30), and each of the next five will receive a fre[e] one-year subscription to *Cook's Coun[try]*. To enter, visit **CooksCountry.com/roos**[ter] by November 30, 2013, or write to Roo[ster] ON13, *Cook's Country*, P.O. Box 47073[9], Brookline, MA 02447. Include your nam[e] and address. **Nanette Campbell** of Po[rt] **Charlotte, Fla.**, found the rooster in the June/July 2013 issue on page 9 and w[on] our Best Buy two-slice toaster.

WEB EXTRAS

Free for 4 months online at
CooksCountry.com

Blue Cheese Dressing Tasting (full articl[e]
Classic Yellow Bundt Cake
Crispy Sweet Potato Fries
Flavored Salts
Getting to Know Tropical Fruit
Hard-Cooked Eggs
Sausage and Apple Skillet Stuffing
Steak Tips au Poivre
White Rice

COOK'S COUNTRY IS NO[W] ON iPAD!

Download the *Cook's Country* app for iPad and start a free trial subscription or purchase a single issue of the magazine. All issues are enhanced with full-color Cooking Mode slide shows that provide step-b[y] step instructions for completing recipe[s] plus expanded reviews and ratings. G[o to] **CooksCountry.com/iPad** to downloa[d] app through iTunes.

 Follow us on **Twitter**
twitter.com/TestKitchen

 Find us on **Facebook**
facebook.com/CooksCountry

Cranberry-Pecan Spice Cake

Some of our favorite elements of fall—toasty pecans, fragrant spices, and tart cranberries—are neatly packaged in a single cake.

To make this cake you will need:

- 8 ounces (2 cups) fresh or frozen cranberries
- ½ cup (3½ ounces) granulated sugar
- ½ cup orange juice
- 1½ cups pecans, toasted, cooled, and ground fine
- 1 tablespoon pumpkin pie spice
- 1 recipe Classic Yellow Bundt Cake* batter
- 2 tablespoons cream cheese, softened
- 2 tablespoons whole milk
- 1 cup (4 ounces) confectioners' sugar

FOR THE FILLING: Bring cranberries, granulated sugar, and orange juice to boil in medium saucepan over medium-high heat. Cook, stirring occasionally, until cranberries have broken down and juices have thickened slightly, 8 to 10 minutes. Transfer mixture to food processor and process until smooth, 10 to 15 seconds. Let cool completely.

FOR THE CAKE: Adjust oven rack to lower-middle position and heat oven to 325 degrees. Grease and flour 12-cup nonstick Bundt pan. Combine pecans and pie spice in small bowl, then stir into cake batter until incorporated. Spoon half of batter into prepared pan and smooth top. Using back of spoon, create ½-inch-deep channel in center of batter. Spoon half of filling into channel. Using butter knife, thoroughly swirl filling into batter. Repeat with remaining batter and filling. Bake until skewer inserted in center comes out clean, 70 to 75 minutes, rotating pan halfway through baking. Let cake cool in pan on wire rack for 10 minutes. Remove cake from pan and let cool completely on rack, about 2 hours.

FOR THE GLAZE: Whisk cream cheese and milk together in medium bowl until combined and no lumps remain. Whisk in confectioners' sugar until smooth. Drizzle evenly over top of cooled cake and let sit until glaze is firm, about 1 hour. Serve.

*Go to CooksCountry.com/yellowbundtcake for our **Classic Yellow Bundt Cake** recipe.

Inside This Issue

Cook's Country

DECEMBER/JANUARY 2014

Blitz Torte Revival

Chicken Baked in Foil

Bistro Steaks

Breakfast Sandwiches
Takeout Transformed

Prime Rib with Vegetables
Holiday Dinner in One Pan

Testing Roasting Pans
$200 Model Places Fourth

Shrimp Perloo
Low-Country Favorite

Chicken and Dumplings for Two
Downsizing the Effort

Slow-Cooker Beef Stew
Mediterranean Flavors

Pork Chop Casserole
Which Is the Right Chop?

Holiday Cookie Contest
Your Best Recipes

All About Dried Beans
Do You Have to Soak?

Spinach Gratin for a Crowd
Fresh Spinach Flavor

CooksCountry.com
$5.95 U.S./$6.95 CANADA

*A community cookbook staple, **Blitz Torte** was created by German immigrants as an easy version of elaborate European tortes. Perfected in the test kitchen, this cake-meringue-custard combo is ready for its revival.* PAGE 8

Cook's Country

Dear Country Cook,

In the 1980s, we had just built our farmhouse on the old Tikander farm. One neighbor brought over a freshly baked loaf of white bread and a shaker of salt as a form of Vermont welcome wagon. Another dropped off half of a cord of split oak. Another invited me rabbit hunting, which, over time, became a serious endeavor.

The next year, to repay a few outstanding debts, I made apple pies. One neighbor, Lucille, used to make her own crusts and now was buying store-bought. One taste of a real homemade crust, however, and she was converted back to the real thing. As she said at the time, "I had forgotten how an apple pie was supposed to taste."

Julia Child always said that knowing how things are supposed to taste is the better half of cooking. The old photo below of a pie factory, where they made upwards of 20,000 pies per day, is a reminder of how homemade became store-bought and America lost its culinary memory. Pie and cake recipes were no longer closely held secrets, using a variety of baking apples for a single pie became a lost art, and flaky lard crusts are now as rare as a loaf of anadama bread.

The good news is that we are all just one step away from the kitchen. We just have to know what to do when we get there!

Cordially,

Christopher Kimball
Founder and Editor, Cook's Country

At Chicago's Sunkist Pie Company in 1949, two bakers funnel fruit juices back into pies.

Cook's Country

Founder and Editor Christopher Kimball
Editorial Director Jack Bishop
Editorial Director, Magazines John Willoughby
Executive Editor Peggy Grodinsky
Managing Editor Scott Kathan
Senior Editors Lisa McManus, Bryan Roof, Diane Unger
Test Kitchen Director Erin McMurrer
Associate Editors Hannah Crowley,
Amy Graves, Rebeccah Marsters, Christie Morrison
Test Cooks Sarah Gabriel, Nick Iverson, Cristin Walsh
Assistant Editor Shannon Friedmann Hatch
Copy Editors Nell Beram, Megan Ginsberg
Executive Assistant Christine Gordon
Test Kitchen Manager Leah Rovner
Senior Kitchen Assistants
Michelle Blodget, Meryl MacCormack
Kitchen Assistants
Maria Elena Delgado, Shane Drips, Ena Gudiel
Executive Producer Melissa Baldino
Co-Executive Producer Stephanie Stender
Production Assistant Kaitlin Hammond

Contributing Editors Erika Bruce,
Eva Katz, Jeremy Sauer
Consulting Editors Anne Mendelson, Meg Ragland
Science Editor Guy Crosby, Ph.D.
Executive Food Editor, TV, Radio & Media
Bridget Lancaster

Managing Editor, Web Christine Liu
Senior Editor, Cooking School Mari Levine
Associate Editors, Web Eric Grzymkowski, Roger Metcalf
Assistant Editors, Web Jill Fisher, Charlotte Wilder
Senior Video Editor Nick Dakoulas

Design Director Amy Klee
Art Director Julie Cote
Deputy Art Director Susan Levin
Associate Art Director Lindsey Timko
Deputy Art Director, Marketing Jennifer Cox
Staff Photographer Daniel J. van Ackere
Color Food Photography Keller + Kelle
Styling Catrine Kelty, Marie Piraino
Associate Art Directors, Marketing Melanie Gryboski,
Mariah Tarvainen
Designer, Marketing Judy Blomquist
Photo Editor Steve Klise

Vice President, Marketing David Mack
Circulation Director Doug Wicinski
Circulation & Fulfillment Manager Carrie Fethe
Partnership Marketing Manager Pamela Putprush
Marketing Assistant Marina Tomao

VP, Technology, Product Development Barry Kelly
Director, Project Management Alice Carpenter
Development Manager Mike Serio

Chief Operating Officer Rob Ristagno
Production Director Guy Rochford
Workflow & Digital Asset Manager Andrew Mannone
Senior Color & Imaging Specialist Lauren Pettapiece
Production & Imaging Specialists
Heather Dube, Lauren Robbins
Director of Sponsorship Sales Anne Traficante
Client Services Associate Kate May
Sponsorship Sales Representative Morgan Ryan
Customer Service Manager Jacqueline Valerio
Customer Service Representatives
Megan Hamner, Jessica Haskin,
Andrew Straaberg Finfrock

Retail Sales & Marketing Manager Emily Logan
Human Resources Manager Adele Shapiro
Publicity Deborah Broide

ON THE COVER: *Blitz Torte*, Keller + Keller, Catrine Kelty
ILLUSTRATION: Greg Stevenson

Follow us on **Twitter**
twitter.com/TestKitchen

Find us on **Facebook**
facebook.com/CooksCountry

ok's Country magazine (ISSN 1552-1990), number 54,
ublished bimonthly by Boston Common Press Limited
tnership, 17 Station St., Brookline, MA 02445. Copyright
3 Boston Common Press Limited Partnership. Periodicals
tage paid at Boston, Mass., and additional mailing
ces, USPS #023453. Publications Mail Agreement No.
20778. Return undeliverable Canadian addresses to P.O.
875, Station A, Windsor, ON N9A 6P2. POSTMASTER: Send
dress changes to Cook's Country, P.O. Box 6018, Harlan,
1593-1518. For subscription and gift subscription orders,
scription inquiries, or change of address notices, visit
ericasTestKitchen.com/customerservice, call 800-526-
7 in the U.S. or 515-248-7684 from outside the U.S., or write
t Cook's Country, P.O. Box 6018, Harlan, IA 51593-1518.
TED IN THE USA

Contents

HOLIDAY PRIME RIB AND VEGETABLES, 4

GRAND-PRIZE-WINNING COOKIES, 20

CHICKEN BAKED IN FOIL, 10

Features

Departments

America's Test Kitchen is a very real 2,500-square-foot kitchen located just outside Boston. It is the home of *Cook's Country* and *Cook's Illustrated* magazines and is
the workday destination of more than three dozen test cooks, editors, and cookware specialists. Our mission is to test recipes over and over again until we understand
how and why they work and until we arrive at the best version. We also test kitchen equipment and supermarket ingredients in search of brands that offer the
best value and performance. You can watch us work by tuning in to *Cook's Country from America's Test Kitchen* (CooksCountry.com) and *America's Test Kitchen*
(AmericasTestKitchen.com) on public television.

RECIPES THAT WORK®

Ask Cook's Country

BY SARAH GABRIEL

I keep seeing recipes that call for "new potatoes," but what exactly does that mean? Are they just talking about small potatoes?
Joseph Olah, Kulpmont, Pa.

We did some digging on new potatoes and here's what we came up with: New potatoes are potatoes harvested before the skin sets so that they have delicate skins. But even after reading the definition, we were shaky on the details. What does it mean to "set" the skin? Are all new potatoes small? Are all small potatoes new? Can we use new potatoes in the same ways that we use regular potatoes?

For help, we called the United States Potato Board, a marketing organization for the potato industry. A spokeswoman explained that setting the skin is the process of cutting down the vines of the potato plants but leaving the tubers in the ground for two weeks to a month. During that time, their skin becomes thicker and better able to protect the spuds during storage and transit. New potatoes don't get that time to toughen up; they go straight to market with delicate skins that the spokeswoman described as "flaky." If you rub the skin of a new potato with your thumb, she said, it will rub right off. The potatoes that are harvested this way are almost always small. In most of the country, new potatoes are available in late summer and early fall. Because they are moist and sweet, they aren't well suited for frying: They'll brown too quickly and won't get as crispy as ordinary potatoes.

Are all small potatoes you find at the market new potatoes? No. If it's not the harvest season, chances are they are just smooth-skinned varieties that have been harvested while still small. Some varieties, such as rough-skinned russets, are never sold as new potatoes; you're not looking for moist and creamy in russets anyhow. If you're making a recipe that calls for new potatoes but they aren't in season, substitute a small, thin-skinned variety like fingerlings.

THE BOTTOM LINE: New potatoes are sweeter, moister, and thinner-skinned than ordinary small potatoes. You can substitute fingerlings and other small, naturally thin-skinned varieties.

THIN IS IN
New potatoes have thinner skins than regular small potatoes.

Whole chickens cost less per pound than parts but there's waste. Is it cheaper to buy whole chickens and break them down myself?
Tom Markunas, Red Hook, N.Y.

We broke down a half-dozen chickens and found that, on average, the trim (backs and wingtips) accounted for 20 percent of the weight of whole chickens. So to compare the price per pound of a whole chicken versus parts, multiply the per pound price of the whole bird by 1.25; if it's still lower than the price of the parts, then it's cheaper to cut up the whole bird. At our local supermarket, a whole chicken goes for $3.59 per pound, making a 3½-pound bird $12.57. If we were using that chicken for parts, accounting for the waste would make the price $15.71 ($12.57 times 1.25). If we were to buy all the parts separately, the total price would be $13.75 ($12.47 if we purchased the leg quarters instead of separated thighs and drumsticks).

Considering the prices at our local grocery store, unless we're going to use the backs and wingtips for stock, it's slightly more economical to buy the parts. So if breaking down a whole chicken for the parts may not save you money, why do the work? It does offer a few advantages in addition to trim for stock. If you buy the whole bird, you'll know that the size of the parts will be consistent, and you won't have any unpleasant surprises that make the real price of the parts hard to determine, like leg quarters with pieces of the backbone attached and split breasts with part of the rib cage left on.

THE BOTTOM LINE: Although buying a whole chicken and cutting it into parts may not save money, there are other advantages.

I read that adding 2 tablespoons of vinegar per quart of water before hard-cooking eggs will make peeling easier. Is that true?
Debbie Triplett, Saratoga Springs, N.Y.

We cooked six eggs with vinegar in the water alongside another six eggs in plain water, using our standard method, in which we put the eggs in a sauce pot with water, bring the water to a boil, turn off the heat, cover the pot, and let the eggs sit for 10 minutes before putting them in a bowl of ice water for 5 minutes. The vinegar didn't ease peeling. We tried it again using a popular hard-cooked egg method that calls for simmering the eggs for 10 minutes. That didn't ease peeling either. We asked our science editor if there was any basis to the vinegar theory. He explained that egg shells are made of calcium carbonate, which is soluble in acids like vinegar. But just 2 tablespoons in an entire quart of water can't dissolve nearly enough shell to ease peeling in the time that it takes to hard-cook an egg.

THE BOTTOM LINE: Adding vinegar to the cooking water won't make peeling easier. What will? Putting the eggs in ice water for 5 minutes after cooking and rolling them around under your palm to crack the shell all over before peeling.

I often freeze boneless chicken breasts. Can I add marinade to the bag before freezing so the meat is ready to cook when it thaws?
Ashley Parsons, Taylor, Texas

It would be awfully convenient to have a freezer full of ready-to-cook meat, so we mixed up an oil-and-herb based marinade and put it in bags along with six boneless, skinless chicken breasts and then froze the bags. We put six more chicken breasts in bags in the freezer without any marinade. After a few days, we thawed the chicken and marinated the batch that was frozen plain. Even before cooking, it was clear that the batch frozen in the marinade had

I saw something called "almond flour" at the grocery store. Is that just ground-up almonds? Can I use it in place of flour in cakes?
John Navarro, Somerville, Mass.

Almond flour is indeed ground-up almonds. If the almonds are blanched to remove their brown skins before grinding, the resulting coarse powder may be called almond flour. Almond meal is the same but may be made from nuts with or without their skins. You can't substitute almond flour or meal for wheat flour willy-nilly because almond flour contains less starch and more fat than flour, and it lacks the proteins glutenin and gliadin, which produce gluten, the stretchy network of proteins responsible for the structure that helps batters and doughs made with wheat flour hold air and stay together. Substitutions would lead to super-dense cakes that fall apart. However, almond meal is often used in addition to regular flour to add flavor and tenderize cookies and cakes. The delicacy of madeleines and the short and crumbly texture of Linzertorte can be attributed to the combination of almond and ordinary flour. We often use ground almonds in cookies and cakes in the test kitchen, but we usually start with whole nuts that we grind ourselves in the food processor. When overprocessed, nuts may turn to a paste (think peanut butter), so sometimes recipes call for grinding the nuts along with some or all of the sugar or wheat flour.

THE BOTTOM LINE: Don't use almond flour or almond meal in place of wheat flour, but ground almonds used *with* regular flour will tenderize baked goods.

DENSE DISASTER
This is what happens when you try to make a yellow cake using all almond flour. Used in conjunction with wheat flour, however, almond flour can lend tenderness and flavor.

changed: The meat was limp. Cooked, the marinated frozen chicken was mealy.

Our science editor explained why: When we put the chicken and marinade in the freezer, the water in the meat froze from the outside in. As the water slowly freezes, the substances like salt and sugar that are dissolved in it don't freeze; rather they become concentrated in the still-liquid water. The high concentration of dissolved substances in an ever-shrinking amount of unfrozen water draws water out of the muscle fibers, and when that water finally freezes, it crystallizes, tearing more holes in the fibers, in turn allowing even more water to leak out. We never recommend acidic marinades (like bottled Italian dressing) because the acid denatures the outside of the meat, but we tested a vinegar-based marinade here and it made the problems worse—the chicken was mushy as well as mealy.

THE BOTTOM LINE: Don't marinate meat before freezing; it will come out mushy and dry.

To ask us a cooking question, visit **CooksCountry.com/askcookscountry**. Or write to Ask *Cook's Country*, P.O. Box 470739, Brookline, MA 02447. Just try to stump us!

Kitchen Shortcuts

COMPILED BY NICK IVERSON

DOUBLE DUTY
Homemade Sugar Shaker
Rick Murphy, Kenosha, Wis.

I buy sugar—and most other staples—in bulk from warehouse stores. To create a container for pouring sugar for coffee or for baking, I took an empty cylindrical salt container, cut off the top (the cardboard round with the metal pouring spout) with a paring knife, and fit it to a quart-size Mason jar that I'd filled with sugar. Now I have the same convenience when it comes to measuring and pouring sugar as I do with salt.

EASY CLEANING **Wrap It**
Tobey Desebrais, Little Rock, Ark.

I used to dread cleaning my fridge. Sticky spills, mystery goo, and stuck-on gunk all required lots of hot water, elbow grease, and time. Thankfully, a friend clued me in to an easy solution. After one final deep clean, I carefully lined the refrigerator shelves with plastic wrap and put everything back in the fridge. Now when it comes time to clean, all I have to do is peel back the gunked-on plastic, toss it in the trash, and put down a fresh new piece. It saves me time and a lot of energy.

CLEVER TIP **A Smashing Success**
Sandy Wilson, Bloomington, Ind.

If you bake as much as I do, you know that chopping large quantities of nuts can be a bother—they can roll around on the counter and end up on the floor. I tried using the food processor, but it chops them unevenly, producing a combination of dust and nut butter. Instead of using a knife, I lay the nuts on my cutting board in an even layer, cover them with a sheet of plastic wrap, and give them a few controlled whacks with the bottom of a skillet. The skillet's heft and large surface area make quick, consistent work of chopping nuts. I've found that this method works best with rounder nuts, like peanuts or hazelnuts, but it will work with any nut.

DOUBLE DUTY **Knuckle Saver**
Virginia French, Sacramento, Calif.

Grating cheese on my box grater was always a semidangerous task. As the block of cheese diminished, I could count on inadvertently cutting my knuckle on the sharp holes—ouch. Recently, I hit on a neat idea: I use gardening gloves to protect my hands. In the garden, they're thin enough that I still have dexterity, but they prevent blisters and scratches. If I put a clean pair on when I am grating cheese, I no longer have to worry about cuts in the kitchen either.

DOUBLE DUTY **Good Gravy**
Chris Boyce, Portsmouth, N.H.

When my family starts passing around food at the Christmas dinner table, the first thing to get cold is the gravy. By the time it reaches the last person, it's tepid at best. Now I put the gravy in a clean coffee thermos. It looks funny on the table, but the gravy stays piping hot and pours easily.

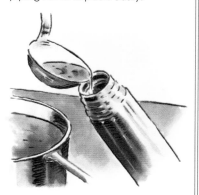

COOL TRICK **Cake Extender**
Sally Severson, Lancaster, Pa.

Every time I bake a cake for my family, about a quarter of it ends up with stale outside edges before we manage to eat it. To prevent this, I employ a trick my grandmother taught me: I use toothpicks to fasten a slice of white bread to each of the cut sides of the cake. The bread shields the exposed cuts, keeping the cake nice and moist.

CLEVER TIP **Smart Stacking**
Floyd Dutton, Corvallis, Ore.

My wife and I have a small microwave that can fit only one bowl at a time, annoying when we'd heat leftovers for the two of us. To increase the microwave's capacity, I put one bowl in and then put an inverted liquid measuring cup next to it. The second bowl goes on the "top shelf" on top of the measuring cup. Both bowls heat at the same time—so my wife and I can eat together.

Prime Rib and Vegetables

What's the most important ingredient for amazing prime rib?
Patience (even before you turn on the oven). BY CHRISTIE MORRISON

A BIG BEEF RIB ROAST is impressive-looking, impossibly tender, and delightfully meaty. It's also expensive. So the stakes were high for me as I set out to develop a simple, foolproof recipe for holiday prime rib with a side of roasted vegetables. In keeping with the "simple" theme, I wanted the oven to do the heavy lifting, leaving my hands free to focus on other parts of the meal (like holding my wineglass). But would the meat and vegetables cooperate?

I began by studying the test kitchen's archive of prime rib recipes. Most start with scoring the fat on top (to encourage it to render); salting the roast and refrigerating it, uncovered, for at least 24 hours; and then searing the meat in a skillet on the stovetop (for a flavorful crust) before roasting it in a low oven to ensure even cooking. The salting is important: It not only seasons the meat and enhances its beefy flavor but also breaks down proteins in the meat to make an already-tender cut even more buttery-tender. Additionally, this process encourages surface moisture to evaporate so that the meat will brown better. All this sounded good to me, with one caveat: Since I wanted to streamline and limit mess, I was hoping to avoid stovetop searing and brown the roast in the oven instead.

Choosing the right cut was easy: A first-cut roast is the best rib roast money can buy, and a 7-pound, three-bone first-cut rib roast would be enough to feed eight to 10 people at my holiday table. I started with three nearly identical such roasts. I scored and salted them and then refrigerated them for 24 hours. Then I put each roast on a V-rack in a large roasting pan. (Elevating the meat increases air circulation and ensures more even cooking.) Next I cut a few root vegetables—carrots and parsnips for now—into 1-inch pieces, tossed them in oil, and scattered them around the V-racks so that they could cook in the flavorful beef drippings. I started one roast in a 500-degree oven to sear and then turned the oven down to 300 degrees so that the meat could cook through gently and evenly. I reversed the process for the second roast: I cooked the beef in a low oven until it was almost done and then cranked the heat at the end to sear. I cooked the last roast at 300 degrees the entire time as

We slow-roast the beef and then roast the vegetables while the meat rests. Finally, we quickly broil the roast with the vegetables underneath.

a baseline and let all the roasts rest for 30 minutes before I sliced and sampled.

The high-to-low method yielded a pink interior with a wide gray band of overcooked meat around the perimeter of the roast, while the vegetables had leathery exteriors and undercooked interiors. The low-to-high method was kinder to the roast, producing a less prominent gray band, but the vegetables were undercooked—plus I had to wait

almost 20 minutes with the roast out of the oven for the oven to come up to the higher temperature for searing. Surprisingly, slow and steady produced the most promising prime rib—it was evenly cooked, with just a slight gray band around the edge and a good browned exterior—but the vegetables were undercooked and lacked flavorful browning. I decided to tackle the roast first and circle back to the vegetables later.

Encouraged by the low-and-slow method but determined to vanquish the gray band, I set the oven temperature 50 degrees lower. At 250 degrees, the roast took about 3 hours to cook to 120 degrees (the temperature continued to rise while the meat rested, bringing it to perfect medium-rare) and the meat was evenly red and juicy from edge to edge, with no gray band. And although it was cooked in a low oven, the roast had a nicely browned exterior. How could that be? Well, thanks to my 24-hour advance salting, most of the meat's surface moisture had evaporated before the roast went into the oven, and the Maillard reaction, which causes browning, can occur at relatively low temperatures if the surface of the meat is dry and the meat is cooked long enough.

Unfortunately, even though I had trimmed the fat cap on the roast until it was just ¼ inch thick and I'd scored it to promote rendering, it was greasy and pallid. Apparently, the low oven was unable to crisp it. But a 5-minute stint under a hot broiler solved the problem, turning the fat cap nicely crispy and golden.

Now I could focus on the vegetables. How could I get them to soften and brown—without drying out and turning leathery—in 3 hours in a low oven? My earlier test at 300 degrees yielded vegetables that had barely softened. While low-and-slow was the answer for tender prime rib, it seemed anathema to tender vegetables. To give the vegetables a head start before adding them to the pan, I microwaved them with a few tablespoons of water until they were almost tender, which took about 15 minutes. Then I repeated the test. No luck. While the vegetables were slightly more tender than before, they were still firm in the center, with no flavorful browning.

Frustrated, I took a step back and considered the dish as a whole. I had a perfectly roasted showstopper of a prime rib that needed 3 hours to cook and 30 to 60 minutes to rest after cooking. Plus, I had a roasting pan slick with flavorful beef fat. Why couldn't I use the time while the roast was resting to turn up the oven and roast the vegetables in the beef fat? Instead of forcing the

vegetables to work in concert with the beef, maybe I could let them fly solo for a while, as long as the whole dish could come together for the finish (and I could use the same pan). I started with a fresh roast, this time without vegetables in the pan. When the meat reached 120 degrees, I removed the entire rack from the roasting pan, set it on a carving board to rest, and tented the meat with aluminum foil to keep it warm. Then I increased the oven to 425 degrees, tossed the carrots and parsnips in the flavorful beef fat, and added salt and pepper. After about 40 minutes (with one break to stir), the vegetables were browned and tender at last. To finish the dish, I returned the V-rack and roast (sans foil) to the pan and broiled the lot for 5 minutes to crisp the fat cap.

Now that I had a working method in place, I took another look at the vegetables. After testing everything from potatoes to turnips to winter squash to fennel, I decided to add Brussels sprouts and a red onion to the mix. For even cooking, I cut the carrots into ½-inch-thick planks, the parsnips into ½-inch-thick slices, the onion into wedges, and the sprouts in half through the stem.

The roast and vegetables were fantastic on their own, but I thought that an easy sauce would take this meal over the top. After experimenting with several options, I settled on *chimichurri*, a bright mixture of parsley, red wine vinegar, red pepper flakes, onion, garlic, and salt emulsified with extra-virgin olive oil; Chimichurri hails from Argentina, where it's served with all manner of grilled meats. For a colorful twist on this classic, I added a tablespoon of earthy paprika. This fresh, bold sauce came together in minutes and gave my holiday meal the final flourish that it needed: an acidic complement to the richness of the meat and the caramelized sweetness of the vegetables. It was definitely a feast fit for a holiday—and I only had one pan to wash.

Looking for a fast, easy, and elegant soup to start your holiday meal? Find our recipe for **Simpler Shrimp Bisque** at cooksCountry.com/simplerbisque.

RED CHIMICHURRI SAUCE
Makes about 1½ cups
You can use sherry vinegar in place of the red wine vinegar. The sauce can be made and refrigerated up to three days in advance; let it come to room temperature before serving.

- 1 onion, chopped fine
- ½ cup minced fresh parsley
- ½ cup red wine vinegar
- ½ cup extra-virgin olive oil
- 3 garlic cloves, minced
- 1 tablespoon paprika
- ½ teaspoon kosher salt
- ¼ teaspoon red pepper flakes

Whisk all ingredients together in bowl. Cover with plastic wrap and let stand at room temperature, at least 30 minutes. Whisk again before serving.

Leftover sauce is great in sandwiches or spooned over scrambled eggs.

ONE-PAN PRIME RIB AND ROASTED VEGETABLES
Serves 8 to 10
The roast must be salted and then refrigerated for at least 24 hours before cooking; salting and refrigerating for the full 96 hours results in the most tender, flavorful meat. Serve with Red Chimichurri Sauce (recipe above), if desired.

- 1 (7-pound) first-cut beef standing rib roast (3 bones), fat trimmed to ¼ inch
  Kosher salt and pepper
  Vegetable oil
- 2 pounds carrots, peeled, cut into 2-inch lengths, halved or quartered lengthwise to create ½-inch-diameter pieces
- 1 pound parsnips, peeled and sliced ½ inch thick on bias
- 1 pound Brussels sprouts, trimmed and halved
- 1 red onion, halved and sliced through root end into ½-inch wedges
- 2 teaspoons minced fresh thyme

1. Using sharp knife, cut through roast's fat cap in 1-inch crosshatch pattern, being careful not to cut into meat. Rub 2 tablespoons salt over entire roast and into crosshatch. Transfer to large plate and refrigerate, uncovered, for at least 24 hours or up to 96 hours.

2. Adjust oven rack to lower-middle position and heat oven to 250 degrees. Season roast with pepper and arrange, fat side up, on V-rack set in large roasting pan. Roast until meat registers 115 degrees for rare, 120 degrees for medium-rare, or 125 degrees for medium, 3 to 3½ hours. Transfer V-rack with roast to carving board, tent loosely with aluminum foil, and let rest for about 1 hour.

3. Meanwhile, increase oven temperature to 425 degrees. Pour off all but 2 tablespoons fat from pan. (If there isn't enough fat in pan, add vegetable oil to equal 2 tablespoons.) Toss carrots, parsnips, Brussels sprouts, onion, thyme, 1 teaspoon salt, and ½ teaspoon pepper with fat in pan. Roast vegetables, stirring halfway through roasting, until tender and browned, 45 to 50 minutes.

4. Remove pan from oven and heat broiler. Carefully nestle V-rack with roast among vegetables in pan. Broil roast until fat cap is evenly browned, rotating pan as necessary, about 5 minutes. Transfer roast to carving board, carve meat from bones, and cut into ¾-inch-thick slices. Season vegetables with salt and pepper to taste. Serve roast with vegetables.

TEST KITCHEN TIP
Carving a Standing Rib Roast

Carving a bone-in rib roast may seem intimidating to the uninitiated, but it's really quite easy. Simply hold the roast in place with a carving fork and cut parallel to the rib bones to remove the meat in one big piece. Then slice and serve the meat.

SHOPPING **Buy the Right Roast**
This recipe calls for a first-cut, bone-in standing rib roast, which contains ribs 9, 10, and 11 (the ribs that are closest to the tail of the steer; butchers often label this cut "loin-end"). First-cut roasts contain the largest eye of meat. While second-cut roasts are pretty good, too, they are slightly fattier and more irregular, making them more difficult to cook evenly. Since these cuts are often priced the same, it's worth your while to ask for the superior first-cut roast.

FIRST CUT
More meat, larger eye.

SECOND CUT
More fat, smaller eye (but still good).

Spinach Gratin for a Crowd

We wanted the taste of fresh spinach but the convenience of frozen.

BY DIANE UNGER

AMONG THE MEAT and rich starches on my holiday table, a green vegetable dish is always welcome. My favorite is spinach gratin. For a large crowd, though, I'm caught between a rock and a hard place. I can either use frozen spinach, which makes for a stringy and listless casserole, or gird myself to face washing, stemming, chopping, wilting, and squeezing dry an enormous pile of fresh spinach; like all greens, spinach wilts to a fraction of its original volume when it's cooked. That prep is tedious, to say the least, plus even my biggest pot can't fit the amount of fresh spinach needed to serve eight. This year, I hoped to develop a recipe for a spinach gratin with a rich and creamy base; a crispy, buttery top; and great cheesy flavor—without the bother.

It occurred to me that creamed spinach, a similar recipe minus the cheese and topping, would make a good starting point, and the test kitchen already has an excellent recipe for it. We briefly wilt two 10-ounce bags of spinach, enough to feed four, and then squeeze the spinach dry; the recipe uses curly-leaf spinach because baby spinach can quickly cook into spinach slime. It calls for building a standard white sauce by sautéing chopped onion in butter, adding spices and flour (for thickening), whisking in milk, and then stirring in the wilted spinach.

To transform creamed spinach into spinach gratin for a holiday crowd, I'd need to add cheese and glamorize and double the recipe, plus develop a topping. But as soon as I upped the quantities, I had, predictably, too much spinach to comfortably handle. And when I tried the recipe with frozen chopped spinach, the results were, as I'd guessed, stringy and anemic. (Even though frozen chopped spinach is mechanically cut, in our experience it is inconsistent; many of the pieces are actually too small, and the box includes the stringy stems.) Eventually, after several tests, I managed to eliminate the stringiness in a counterintuitive way: I used frozen whole-leaf spinach, which I chopped myself. The large pieces were easier to squeeze dry, and the hand chopping fixed the texture. Admittedly, this added a few steps, but it was still easier than prepping a mountain of fresh spinach.

Unfortunately, my gratin still didn't taste remotely fresh. Hoping for fresh taste and frozen convenience, I tried combining fresh and frozen spinach. After several more tests, I found that I was able to quickly wilt 8 ounces of fresh curly-leaf spinach right in the white sauce. Off heat, I added four 10-ounce boxes of frozen whole-leaf spinach, which I'd thawed, squeezed dry, and chopped fine. I scraped the mixture into a 13 by 9-inch dish and

We brighten our gratin with a finishing sprinkle of lemon zest and parsley.

baked it. Happily, the modest amount of fresh spinach had an outsize impact.

For an elegant, holiday-appropriate sauce, I used Gruyère cheese and replaced the milk of the original with half-and-half—lots of it. I boosted the flavor with mustard, cayenne, nutmeg, and loads of garlic. For the gratin topping, I combined fresh bread crumbs with melted butter and more cheese. A mere 15 minutes in the oven browned the crumbs nicely without cooking the spinach down to sludge.

But while the half-and-half added luxuriant richness, now the gratin lacked zip. After a little thought, I mixed together chopped parsley and lemon zest and sprinkled my gratin gremolata over the casserole. Just the thing.

TEST KITCHEN DISCOVERY **Use a Combination of Fresh and Frozen**
Like all greens, spinach cooks down dramatically. To prepare the amount of fresh spinach you'd need to serve spinach gratin to a crowd, you'd be washing, stemming, steaming, and squeezing the amount shown here. Instead, our recipe uses just 8 ounces of fresh spinach plus 2½ pounds of frozen.

TOO MUCH OF A GOOD THING
To make the gratin from all fresh spinach, you'd need this much.

SPINACH GRATIN Serves 8 to 10
Thaw the frozen spinach in the refrigerator overnight. Before you use it, squeeze it as dry as you can using a dish towel.

- 2 slices hearty white sandwich bread, torn into 1-inch pieces
- 8 tablespoons unsalted butter
- 8 ounces Gruyère cheese, shredded (2 cups)
  Salt and pepper
- 1 onion, chopped fine
- 4 garlic cloves, minced
- ⅛ teaspoon cayenne pepper
- 2 tablespoons all-purpose flour
- 4 cups half-and-half
- 8 ounces curly-leaf spinach, stemmed and chopped coarse
- 1 tablespoon Dijon mustard

Melting Potatoes

It's easy to make a few potatoes with crispy outsides and creamy interiors in a skillet on the stovetop. But what about making a larger batch? BY CHRISTIE MORRISON

⅛ teaspoon ground nutmeg
2½ pounds frozen whole-leaf spinach, thawed, squeezed dry, and chopped fine
½ cup minced fresh parsley
1 teaspoon grated lemon zest, plus lemon wedges for serving

1. Adjust oven rack to upper-middle position and heat oven to 425 degrees. Pulse bread in food processor to fine crumbs, about 10 pulses; transfer to bowl. Melt 3 tablespoons butter in microwave, about 30 seconds. Stir melted butter, ½ cup Gruyère, ½ teaspoon salt, and ½ teaspoon pepper into crumbs; set aside.

2. Melt remaining 5 tablespoons butter in Dutch oven over medium heat. Add onion and cook until lightly browned, 7 to 9 minutes. Stir in garlic and cayenne and cook until fragrant, about 30 seconds. Stir in flour and cook for 1 minute. Slowly whisk in half-and-half and bring to simmer. Cook, whisking occasionally, until slightly thickened and reduced to about 3½ cups, about 10 minutes.

3. Stir in curly-leaf spinach and cook until just wilted, about 30 seconds. Off heat, stir in mustard, nutmeg, 1½ teaspoons salt, 1 teaspoon pepper, and remaining 1½ cups Gruyère until cheese is melted. Stir in thawed frozen spinach until thoroughly combined. Season with salt and pepper to taste. Transfer mixture to 13 by 9-inch baking dish.

4. Sprinkle crumb mixture evenly over spinach mixture. Bake until bubbling around edges and crumbs are golden brown, 15 to 17 minutes. Transfer to wire rack. Combine parsley and lemon zest in bowl; sprinkle over gratin. Let cool for 10 minutes. Serve with lemon wedges.

TO MAKE AHEAD
Crumb mixture can be covered and refrigerated for up to 24 hours. Spinach mixture can be cooled and refrigerated for up to 24 hours. When ready to serve, bake gratin until hot throughout, 15 to 20 minutes, then proceed with step 4.

▶ What's our top-rated broiler-safe baking dish? Visit CooksCountry.com/bakingdishes to find out.

IN THE TEST KITCHEN, it's rare to come across a potato recipe that we don't know backward and forward. Enter melting potatoes. I had heard them described as potatoes with crispy edges and creamy centers in a supremely buttery sauce. When I went looking for recipes, I discovered that this dish is popular in the United Kingdom, where it's known as fondant potatoes. I followed the six recipes that I'd gathered, and while none quite hit the mark, it was obvious that melting potatoes were indeed too good to languish in obscurity in the United States.

Most melting potato recipes instruct you to square off the ends of the spuds and cut them crosswise into disks, though a few call for wedges. The potatoes are then pan-fried in either oil or melted butter and braised to tenderness in broth. I followed this procedure in my initial test and then, based on the results, made a few decisions: I'd cut the potatoes into disks—the wedge cut called to mind steak fries and wasn't elegant enough for the holidays. I'd use Yukon Golds since russets were mealy and red potatoes were too small. I also opted for butter over oil for, well, buttery flavor.

Next I confronted my big problem. I wanted to make enough potatoes to serve six to eight people at the holiday table, but there was no way that a single skillet could brown the necessary 3 pounds. Since messing with multiple batches meant holding warm potatoes, pan frying was out. Roasting was the obvious choice, but could I achieve that deeply browned crust without the direct heat of the stovetop?

I cut the potatoes into 1-inch-thick disks, tossed them with melted butter, and laid them in a single layer in a 13 by 9-inch baking pan. I roasted them at 425 degrees until the bottoms began to color, about 20 minutes, and then flipped the potatoes. After they had spent 20 more minutes in the oven, I added about 2 cups of broth to the pan, to come about halfway up the sides of the potatoes, and then returned them to the oven to cook through. While these potatoes got some color, they were far from crispy. In pursuit of the crispiness of the pan-fried potatoes, I tried roasting them longer. A wrong turn—these potatoes were dried out and leathery. So what about roasting them at higher

Our method produces buttery potatoes with crispy tops and creamy interiors.

heat? I cranked the heat to 500 degrees. One side was beautifully browned, but the side that was face down to start was still a wimpy pale gold. I tried flipping the slices a second time, just before adding the broth. This method produced two beautifully bronzed sides.

As for the broth, I found that the potatoes needed just 1½ cups to braise. During cooking, the broth reduced and thickened from the potato starches, leaving just enough to drizzle over the gorgeously browned, buttery disks.

MELTING POTATOES Serves 6 to 8
Use potatoes at least 1½ inches in diameter. Do not use a glass baking dish, which could shatter.

3 pounds Yukon Gold potatoes, peeled
6 tablespoons unsalted butter, melted
1 tablespoon minced fresh thyme
1 teaspoon salt
½ teaspoon pepper
1½ cups chicken broth
2 garlic cloves, lightly crushed and peeled

1. Adjust oven rack to upper-middle position and heat oven to 500 degrees. Square off ends of potatoes and cut crosswise into 1-inch-thick disks. Toss potatoes with butter, thyme, salt, and pepper. Arrange potatoes in single layer in 13 by 9-inch baking pan.

2. Roast potatoes until bottoms are beginning to brown around edges, about 15 minutes. Remove pan from oven. Using flat metal spatula and tongs, loosen potatoes from bottom of pan and flip. Continue to roast until browned on second side, about 15 minutes longer.

3. Remove pan from oven, flip potatoes once more, and add broth and garlic. Roast until potatoes are tender and sauce has reduced slightly, about 15 minutes. Baste potatoes with sauce before serving.

Blitz Torte

Could this crazy way to make a cake—baking a meringue layer directly on top of yellow cake batter—ever work? BY REBECCAH MARSTERS

BLITZ TORTE—A BIG, gorgeous, many-layered dessert composed of cake, meringue, whipped cream (or custard), and fruit—sounds as though it comes straight from Germany. In fact, it's thought to be the invention of German immigrants to America: They wanted to duplicate the sort of elaborate cakes that they knew from their homeland, but with less time and effort. They named their creation *blitz*, or "lightning" in German, to imply that it could be made at lightning speed (admitted, some hyperbole here). I can't understand why the torte is so seldom seen today, but if you know where to look, you can find recipes in Junior League cookbooks, community cookbooks, and even a James Beard cookbook.

The beauty of blitz torte is that you get five impressive layers—cake, meringue, fruit-and-cream filling, more cake, and more meringue—plus a sprinkle of nuts for about the same amount of work required by an ordinary two-layer cake. That's because the recipe is so clever: Each meringue layer is baked directly atop the yellow cake batter instead of as a separate component. Also, the recipe is pleasingly symmetrical: The egg yolks go into the cake, while the whites go into the meringue. I chose five blitz torte recipes and headed to the kitchen.

I measured, greased, creamed, combined, whipped, and baked, after which my tasters and I tasted and evaluated. Lined up on the counter, these cakes looked fabulous, and everybody oohed and ahhed. But while their promise was obvious, the execution was problematic. The tortes shared some common faults—timing, for one. Typically, meringues bake in a low oven, about 250 degrees, for almost 2 hours (plus more time to cool in the turned-off oven), whereas yellow layer cakes bake at 350 degrees for 20 to 25 minutes. Getting both to come out right when baked together was a challenge, and judging by these samples, either the cake overbaked or the meringue underbaked. Next problem: The cakes were neither as tender nor as flavorful as a favorite test kitchen yellow cake recipe, which, as far as I'm concerned, is the gold standard. Also, a few of the yellow cakes domed, which caused the meringue layers to bulge and crimp and ultimately made the cakes harder to stack. Lastly, the fill-

Under construction: After we spread the lemony berry filling, we top it with a final yellow cake–meringue layer.

ings oozed out when I cut slices, turning showstoppers into sloppy heaps.

Rather than waste time repairing the yellow cake part of the torte, I'd use the test kitchen's recipe. We employ a technique that's known as reverse creaming: The dry ingredients (cake flour, sugar, baking powder, and salt) are mixed with butter before the wet ingredients (milk and eggs) are added. Coating the flour with fat before the liquid is introduced

minimizes gluten development, which makes for an amazingly velvety, tender crumb. Reverse creaming also limits the amount of air that gets incorporated into the batter, producing flatter cakes that are perfect for layering. How? Less air means less expansion of gases in the cake, making it less likely that the center will be pushed up before the cake's structure sets.

Unfortunately, our yellow cake

recipe uses whole eggs, which means that I'd need to crack extra eggs for the meringue layers in blitz torte, and I'd be stuck with leftover yolks. After several tests, I figured out a solution: I removed the egg whites from the batter (to use for the meringue) and made up the difference with extra milk. The milk kept the batter loose enough to spread and the cake itself nice and moist. Our recipe for yellow cake produces tall, beautiful layers. That's normally a good thing, but as I got to thinking about the meringue, I realized that I'd need to scale back the cake batter to make room for it. Reducing the cake batter by a third gave me layers of just the right height.

For the meringue, I whipped the egg whites that I'd set aside with cream of tartar (for stability), sugar, and vanilla. Once they were glossy and voluminous, I spread them over the cake batter that I'd already divided between the pans, sprinkled on sliced almonds (whole nuts deflated the delicate meringue, as I learned the hard way), and baked the cakes at 350 degrees for about 20 minutes, as our yellow cake recipe instructs. No good: When the cake was ready, the meringue was still wet in the center. I made the cake again and again, playing with time and temperature before the two components met in the middle—325 degrees and nearly an hour in the oven.

Much as we'd liked the custard fillings during my initials tests, in the end I couldn't justify the extra work for this easy (or at least easier-than-it-looks) torte. I'd use whipped cream. But to mimic custard's rich egginess and to perk up the filling, I got the idea to fold store-bought lemon curd into the whipped cream. This tasted beyond fantastic, but as before, slicing the cake caused a major collapse. To stabilize my curd-cream filling, I added unflavored gelatin. Though it sounds complicated, it took less than 5 minutes to make the creamy, lemony filling and, once it set up, it made neat slices of cake.

Most blitz torte recipes call for adding berries to the whipped cream. I settled on raspberries, which I macerated briefly with sugar and orange liqueur. After draining their juices, I tried simply folding the berries into the cream, but it turned a frightening shade of pink. Instead, I sandwiched the berries between two layers of whipped cream. As I assembled one last blitz torte, my tasters assembled, too (never a shortage of those for this torte). "Blitz torte?" said one taster as she set down her empty plate. "*Bliss* torte is more like it."

BLITZ TORTE
Serves 8 to 10

We developed this recipe using light-colored cake pans, which we prefer for baking cakes. If your pans are dark, reduce the baking time in step 6 to 30 to 35 minutes. In step 1, be sure to whip the heavy cream–gelatin mixture to firm, stiff peaks, and let the filling set up in the refrigerator for at least 1½ hours before assembling the cake.

FILLING
- 1 teaspoon unflavored gelatin
- 2 tablespoons water
- 1 cup heavy cream, chilled
- 1 teaspoon vanilla extract
- ½ cup lemon curd
- 10 ounces (2 cups) raspberries
- 2 tablespoons orange liqueur
- 1 tablespoon sugar

CAKE
- ½ cup whole milk
- 4 large egg yolks
- 1½ teaspoons vanilla extract
- 1¼ cups (5 ounces) cake flour
- 1 cup (7 ounces) sugar
- 1½ teaspoons baking powder
- ½ teaspoon salt
- 12 tablespoons unsalted butter, cut into 12 pieces and softened

MERINGUE
- 4 large egg whites
- ¼ teaspoon cream of tartar
- ¾ cup (5¼ ounces) sugar
- ½ teaspoon vanilla extract
- ½ cup sliced almonds

1. FOR THE FILLING: Sprinkle gelatin over water in small bowl and let sit until gelatin softens, about 5 minutes. Microwave until mixture is bubbling around edges and gelatin dissolves, 15 to 30 seconds. Using stand mixer fitted with whisk, whip cream and vanilla on medium-low speed until foamy, about 1 minute. Increase speed to medium-high and whip until soft peaks form, about 2 minutes. Add gelatin mixture and whip until stiff peaks form, about 1 minute.

2. Whisk lemon curd in large metal bowl to loosen. Gently fold whipped cream mixture into lemon curd. Refrigerate whipped cream filling for at least 1½ hours or up to 3 hours. (Filling may look slightly curdled before assembling cake.)

3. FOR THE CAKE: Meanwhile, adjust oven rack to middle position and heat oven to 325 degrees. Grease 2 light-colored 9-inch round cake pans, line with parchment paper, grease parchment, and flour pans.

4. Beat milk, yolks, and vanilla together with fork in 2-cup liquid measuring cup. Using stand mixer fitted with paddle, mix flour, sugar, baking powder, and salt on low speed until combined, about 5 seconds. Add butter, 1 piece at a time, and mix until only pea-size pieces remain, about 1 minute. Add half of milk mixture, increase speed to medium-high, and beat until light and fluffy, about 1 minute. Reduce speed to medium-low, add remaining milk mixture, and beat until incorporated, about 30 seconds (mixture may look curdled). Give batter final stir by hand. Divide batter evenly between prepared pans and spread into even layer using small offset spatula.

5. FOR THE MERINGUE: Using clean, dry mixer bowl and whisk, whip egg whites and cream of tartar on medium-low speed until foamy, about 1 minute. Increase speed to medium-high and whip whites to soft, billowy mounds, 1 to 3 minutes. Gradually add sugar and whip until glossy, stiff peaks form, 3 to 5 minutes. Add vanilla and whip until incorporated.

6. Divide meringue evenly between cake pans and spread evenly over cake batter to edges of pan. Use back of spoon to create peaks in meringue. Sprinkle meringue with almonds. Bake cakes until meringue is golden and has pulled away from sides of pan, 50 to 55 minutes, switching and rotating pans halfway through baking. Let cakes cool completely in pans on wire rack. (Cakes can be baked up to 24 hours in advance and stored, uncovered, in pans at room temperature.)

7. To finish filling, 10 minutes before assembling cake, combine raspberries, liqueur, and sugar in bowl and let sit, stirring occasionally.

8. Gently remove cakes from pans, discarding parchment. Place 1 cake layer on platter, meringue side up. Spread half of whipped cream filling evenly over top of meringue. Using slotted spoon, spoon raspberries evenly over filling, leaving juice in bowl. Gently spread remaining whipped cream filling over raspberries, covering raspberries completely. Top with second cake layer, meringue side up. Serve cake within 2 hours of assembly.

How the Layers Come Together

This multilayered, European-style cake is easier to make than it looks, in part because several of the components are combined.

TWO LAYERS BAKE AS ONE The meringue gets spread over the raw cake batter, and the two bake together.

A RICH FILLING We fortify the standard whipped cream filling with lemon curd and gelatin, and we layer it with raspberries.

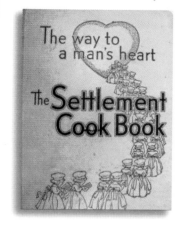

Chicken Baked in Foil

A quick-cooked meal of chicken and vegetables sounded great. Unfortunately, our first attempts were not much better than an old-style TV dinner. BY DIANE UNGER

RECENTLY I'VE BEEN hearing a lot about chicken baked in foil, the latest wrinkle in the time-honored tradition of cooking food sealed in packets. The boneless chicken breasts and chopped vegetables are sealed in foil pouches so that as they bake, the pouches trap steam and everything cooks in its own tasty juices. Each diner gets his or her own pouch, and when the pouches are opened—whoosh—plumes of fragrant, appetite-stoking steam invite everyone to dig in.

This sounded like a great weeknight dinner to me, so I found a half-dozen recipes and prepared them. As the first batch went into the oven, I started to feel uneasy: As a trained cook, I'm used to gauging when meat is properly cooked by monitoring how it looks, sounds, feels, and smells throughout the process. All those cues went out the window here.

Nevertheless, I followed the recipes and called over my tasters when it was showtime. The mushy vegetables, overcooked chicken, and prevailing blandness did not impress them. In fact, these packets were not that much better than old-fashioned TV dinners, which is what many of us think of when the idea of "cooking in foil" is mentioned. But I knew that this idea held promise, so I began redesigning the recipe.

My first task was improving the bland, almost nonexistent flavor. I knew right off that part of this fix would be adequate salting. I tried brining the chicken before wrapping it, and while this did season the chicken, nobody wants to brine for a weeknight dinner. I landed on sprinkling ⅛ teaspoon of salt over each side of each breast to guarantee thorough, even seasoning. As I repeatedly made the recipe, I found that the chicken took on deeper seasoning the longer it sat with the salt on it; although refrigerating the assembled packets for an hour improved them markedly, overnight proved ideal.

Now I turned my attention to the vegetables. I learned that soft varieties, like spinach and tomatoes, cooked into mushy messes; my foil-pouch method required heartier sorts. After working my way through most of the usual suspects, I ultimately decided on potatoes, carrots, and onion, which were just sturdy enough, when properly sliced, to cook at the same rate as the chicken.

For the most even, foolproof cooking, I found it best to layer the potato slices

Cooking in pouches results in great flavor. A bonus: no pots and pans to wash, plus this dish can be assembled up to a day ahead.

under the chicken in the pouches and to bake the pouches on a rimmed baking sheet on the lower rack of a 475-degree oven for about 20 minutes. This way, the potatoes absorb the direct heat and help insulate the chicken.

I also discovered that it was important to construct the pouches with plenty of headroom; this empty space at the top gave the steam room to circulate so that everything cooked at the same rate.

As for knowing when the chicken was properly cooked, at first I devised a method of placing one packet on an extra sheet of foil so I could open that packet, look at the chicken, and easily seal it again if need be. I then realized that this worked just as effectively as a way of plugging up the hole caused by sticking a thermometer through the foil to check the chicken's temperature, a much more reliable approach.

Now that I had the technique and cooking times down, I wanted to take the flavor even further, to make these packets seem like a special event rather than an ordinary dinner. So before putting them in the packets, I seasoned the vegetables with olive oil that I infused with lots of garlic, red pepper flakes, and fresh thyme.

As I watched my tasters gobble up what was my final recipe test, I knew

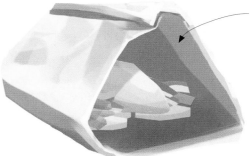

Leave headroom
(empty space) at the top to facilitate steam circulation.

Arrange carrots and onions
next to the chicken.

Place potato slices
on the bottom to insulate the chicken.

EXTRA CREDIT Place one packet on extra foil. After you've poked a thermometer through the packet to check the temperature of the chicken, you can reseal the packet with the extra sheet.

that chicken baked in foil was going to become a new weeknight staple in my house.

CHICKEN BAKED IN FOIL WITH POTATOES AND CARROTS Serves 4

To ensure even cooking, buy chicken breasts of the same size. If using table salt, use only ⅛ teaspoon for each entire breast. Refrigerate the pouches for at least 1 hour before cooking.

- 5 tablespoons extra-virgin olive oil
- 6 garlic cloves, sliced thin
- 1 teaspoon minced fresh thyme
- ¼ teaspoon red pepper flakes
- 12 ounces Yukon Gold potatoes, unpeeled, sliced ¼ inch thick
- 2 carrots, peeled, quartered lengthwise, and cut into 2-inch lengths
- ½ large red onion, sliced ½ inch thick, layers separated
  Kosher salt and pepper
- 4 (6-ounce) boneless, skinless chicken breasts, trimmed
- 2 tablespoons lemon juice
- 2 tablespoons minced fresh chives

1. Spray centers of four 20 by 12-inch sheets of heavy-duty aluminum foil with vegetable oil spray. Microwave oil, garlic, thyme, and pepper flakes in small bowl until garlic begins to brown, 1 to 1½ minutes. Combine potato slices, carrots, onion, 1 teaspoon salt, and garlic oil in large bowl.

2. Pat chicken dry with paper towels. Sprinkle ⅛ teaspoon salt evenly over each side of each chicken breast, then season with pepper. Position 1 piece of prepared foil with long side parallel to counter edge. In center of foil, arrange one-quarter of potato slices in 2 rows perpendicular to counter edge. Lay 1 chicken breast on top of potato slices. Place one-quarter of vegetables around chicken. Repeat with remaining foil, potato slices, chicken, and vegetables.

Drizzle any remaining oil mixture from bowl over chicken.

3. Bring short sides of foil together and crimp to seal tightly. Crimp remaining open ends of packets, leaving as much headroom as possible inside packets. Place packets on large plate and refrigerate for at least 1 hour or up to 24 hours.

4. Adjust oven rack to lowest position and heat oven to 475 degrees. Arrange packets on rimmed baking sheet. Bake until chicken registers 160 degrees, 18 to 23 minutes. (To check temperature, poke thermometer through foil of 1 packet and into chicken.) Let chicken rest in packets for 3 minutes.

5. Transfer chicken packets to individual dinner plates, open carefully (steam will escape), and slide contents onto plates. Drizzle lemon juice over chicken and vegetables and sprinkle with chives. Serve.

CHICKEN BAKED IN FOIL WITH FENNEL AND SUN-DRIED TOMATOES

Substitute 1 fennel bulb, stalks discarded, bulb halved, cored, and cut into ½-inch-thick wedges, layers separated, for carrots; balsamic vinegar for lemon juice; and minced fresh basil for chives. Add ¼ cup oil-packed sun-dried tomatoes, rinsed, patted dry, and chopped fine, and ¼ cup pitted kalamata olives, chopped fine, to vegetables in step 1.

CHICKEN BAKED IN FOIL WITH SWEET POTATO AND RADISH

Substitute 1 tablespoon grated fresh ginger for thyme; 12 ounces peeled sweet potato, sliced ¼ inch thick, for Yukon gold potatoes; 2 celery ribs, quartered lengthwise and cut into 2-inch lengths, for carrots; rice vinegar for lemon juice; and minced fresh cilantro for chives. Add 4 radishes, trimmed and quartered, to vegetables in step 1.

TESTING FOOD STORAGE GADGETS

Over the years, we've used up a lot of plastic bags, plastic wrap, and aluminum foil for the sake of saving a few morsels of food—only to end up tossing browned avocados and other moldering leftovers. So when we noticed a number of gadgets on the market promising to extend life, reduce refrigerator odors, and let us easily spot a range of food and drink in our overstuffed refrigerators—from avocados, to beer, to butter—we crossed our fingers and headed into the test kitchen. We monitored leftovers in these specialty reusable containers for several days. We like to do our bit for the environment, but some were so hard to open that we didn't want to use them again. In the end, we concluded that three of the six items we tested weren't worth buying, and a fourth we could recommend only with reservations. But the remaining two items—both from the same company—offered small solutions to small problems and are worth the small investment. –AMY GRAVES

HIGHLY RECOMMENDED	TESTERS' NOTES
SAVEBRANDS Beer Savers **Model:** 0006BS **Price:** $6.99 for six-pack **Source:** savebrands.com 	These silicone bottle caps fit the tops of 12-ounce glass beer and soda bottles. Tough but slightly stretchy, they come in packs of six, 12, or 54. (If you lose the top of a plastic bottle of seltzer or soda, they'll fit that, too.) Testing was fun: We downed half of a beer, capped the rest, and set it in the refrigerator. The beer was still effervescent the next evening. But don't wait too long: After 48 hours, the cap blew off one bottle and another beer was left a bit flat.
SAVEBRANDS Butter Saver **Model:** 0001BUTS **Price:** $4.99 **Source:** savebrands.com 	This square silicone cap fits the end of a butter stick. Its thickness exactly matches 1 tablespoon of butter in a standard-size stick, aiding both storage and usage. It alleviated the mess and guesswork of wrapping the end of a stick of butter and kept the butter from picking up refrigerator flavors for more than a week. Plus, it was tidier than folding the paper or foil liner over the exposed end of the stick.

RECOMMENDED WITH RESERVATIONS

PROGRESSIVE INTERNATIONAL Avocado Keeper **Model:** LKS-13DP **Price:** $5.59 	This small plastic container with a green lid in the shape of half of an avocado kept half of a lime-doused fruit almost completely green for a few hours longer than our usual method (we press plastic wrap on the surface of the citrus-spritzed avocado). It had the advantage of keeping the fruit from getting squashed in a packed refrigerator. The lid was devilishly hard to open.

NOT RECOMMENDED

PROGRESSIVE INTERNATIONAL Onion Keeper **Model:** OKS-07 **Price:** $9.35 	This small food storage container uses a stainless-steel disk set within its lid, which "reduces onion odors," according to the box. But the container worked no better than a plastic zipper-lock bag.
EVRIHOLDER Avo Saver **Model:** 11703 **Price:** $5.27	This avocado-shaped piece of hard plastic has a flexible silicone strap that presses down the avocado, but air and oxidation found their way in anyway, turning the edges of the exposed fruit brown within minutes (though the flesh nearest the pit was still green). We got better results pressing a plastic zipper-lock bag against a halved avocado.
HUTZLER Grapefruit Saver, Pepper Saver **Model:** 353-2 (grapefruit) 354-2 (pepper) **Price:** $7.99 for two 	These hard plastic cases, in the shape and color of half of a Ruby Red grapefruit, or a whole bell pepper, are designed to call attention to the item being stored (so you don't forget that it's in the fridge). But neither preserved the goods any better than plastic bags or wrap did, and they were hard to pry open.

Charleston Shrimp Perloo

Combine rice, shrimp, stock, green bell pepper, and celery in one big pot, and what do you get?
A deeply flavorful one-pot meal—or blown-out mush. Guess which we were aiming for. BY NICK IVERSON

I F YOU'RE NOT from Charleston, South Carolina, there's a good chance you've never heard of a *perloo* (pronounced "PUHR-low"). But it's a staple in South Carolina's Low Country, dating back to the 17th century. It's made by simmering long-grain white rice in broth with onions, celery, bell pepper, sometimes tomatoes, and meat—either chicken, game, or seafood. The rice soaks up the flavor of all the other ingredients as it cooks, making for an incredibly satisfying one-pot meal. It sounds straightforward enough, but I know that with these simple-seeming recipes, the devil is often lurking in the details. So I booked a plane ticket to Charleston to get some firsthand knowledge.

Down there, two amazing teachers walked me through the recipe. Chef Robert Stehling, of the famed Hominy Grill, made okra perloo in the oven, layering the ingredients in a roasting pan and then baking them for half an hour. My other guide was Mitchell Crosby, whom I'd found by nosing around Charleston's food community; if anyone can cook an authentic perloo, several people told me, it's Crosby. He cooked a shrimp perloo on the stovetop and made a point of resting the finished dish for 10 minutes, off heat. While the techniques were different, what both versions shared was tender, moist, just slightly sticky rice and fantastic flavor.

Back home in the test kitchen, I decided I'd tackle the recipe in three parts: broth, rice, and shrimp, in that order. And since I didn't need to make a roasting pan's worth, I'd stick with the stovetop.

Crosby's perloo, like many other modern ones, had used chicken broth. But after a couple of tests, I decided to go the classic route and make shrimp stock. I had the shells handy, and I knew from experience that shrimp stock is actually surprisingly easy to make. After peeling the shrimp, I sautéed the shells in butter with onions and celery until browned. Then I added water, bay leaves, peppercorns, and parsley and simmered for about 30 minutes. I strained out the solids and dipped in a spoon—excellent. I was off to a good start.

For the rice, I'd stick to the traditional flavors—the base of onions, celery, and bell pepper sautéed with garlic, thyme, and cayenne. I added a can of diced tomatoes (fresh tomatoes aren't reliable year-round), rice, and my shrimp stock. After everything had simmered, covered, for 20 minutes, I lifted the lid—and saw a pot of blown-out rice. I reviewed my notes and realized that I'd neglected a crucial step—Stehling had sautéed the rice before adding the stock to harden the grains' exterior starches and prevent mush.

Hoping that I'd identified the problem, I made another batch, adding the sautéing step. This batch was better but not perfect. Another test cook wondered if I'd failed to account for the liquid in the canned tomatoes. Rice is finicky to cook, and if you screw up the liquid-to-rice ratio, you're asking for trouble. I was using 2 cups of rice and 4 cups of shrimp stock. I tried again, this time using 3 cups of stock—bingo. The rice was tender, with separate grains.

And finally: the shrimp. These crustaceans are as finicky to cook as rice; one moment too long over the heat and they go from nicely firm to disastrously rubbery. Crosby had stressed the importance of the off-heat resting period, during which the residual heat inside the pot gently finishes the rice. I wondered if I could prevent rubbery shrimp by cooking them in that same gentle residual heat. I tried stirring in the shrimp as soon as I took the rice off the heat. They came out slightly underdone, so next I gently folded in the shrimp 5 minutes before turning off the rice and then let them rest, covered, as before. Perfect. This pot took me straight back to Charleston.

Never tasted *perloo*? Think drier, more tomatoey jambalaya without the smoked sausage.

CHARLESTON SHRIMP PERLOO
Serves 4 to 6
After adding the shrimp to the pot, fold it in gently; stirring the rice too vigorously will make it become mushy. Any extra stock can be refrigerated for three days or frozen for up to one month. Serve with hot sauce.

- 5 tablespoons unsalted butter
- 1½ pounds extra-large shrimp (21 to 25 per pound), peeled and deveined, shells reserved
- 2 onions, chopped
- 4 celery ribs, chopped
  Salt and pepper
- 4 cups water
- 1 tablespoon peppercorns
- 5 sprigs fresh parsley
- 2 bay leaves
- 1 green bell pepper, stemmed, seeded, and chopped
- 2 cups long-grain white rice
- 2 garlic cloves, minced
- 1 teaspoon minced fresh thyme
- ¼ teaspoon cayenne pepper
- 1 (14.5-ounce) can diced tomatoes

1. Melt 1 tablespoon butter in large saucepan over medium heat. Add shrimp shells, 1 cup onion, ½ cup celery, and 1 teaspoon salt and cook, stirring occasionally, until shells are spotty brown, about 10 minutes. Add water, peppercorns, parsley, and bay leaves. Increase heat to high and bring to boil. Reduce heat to low, cover, and simmer for 30 minutes. Strain shrimp stock through fine-mesh strainer set over large bowl, pressing on solids to extract as much liquid as possible; discard solids.

2. Melt remaining 4 tablespoons butter in Dutch oven over medium heat. Add bell pepper, remaining onion and celery, and ½ teaspoon salt and cook until vegetables are beginning to soften, 5 to 7 minutes. Add rice, garlic, thyme, and cayenne and cook until fragrant and rice is translucent, about 2 minutes. Stir in tomatoes and their juice and 3 cups shrimp stock (reserve remainder for another use) and bring to boil. Reduce heat to low, cover, and cook for 20 minutes.

3. Gently fold shrimp into rice until evenly distributed, cover, and continue to cook 5 minutes longer. Remove pot from heat and let sit, covered, until shrimp are cooked through and all liquid is absorbed, about 10 minutes. Serve.

Bistro Steaks

This rustic French restaurant dish is typically made with hanger steak, which can be hard to find in the United States. Could we make it work with a common American cut? BY REBECCAH MARSTERS

WHEN IT COMES to steak dinners, there are times when you want to splurge and times when you want to save. Splurge night is easy: Buy a rib, strip, or tenderloin steak; season it well; sear it; and don't overcook it. With a cheaper steak, technique becomes more important. My goal was to find a cut of meat and a cooking method for those days when both my stomach and my wallet feel light and I'm craving a great steak. As I searched for recipes for inexpensive steaks, I kept coming across some for bistro steak, which is a cheap but flavorful cut (hanger steaks are the most common, with skirt, flat-iron, and flap close behind) that's cooked in butter and served with a simple pan sauce.

Bistro steak sounded great except for one thing: Hanger, skirt, flat-iron, and flap steaks can be hard to find in supermarkets. Was there another inexpensive and flavorful but more common cut that I could dress up into a meal to impress? After touring several supermarkets and talking to butchers, I found three inexpensive cuts of beef that were readily available and had potential here: round, chuck, and flank steaks. I bought several of each and returned to the test kitchen to put the steaks through their paces.

Most bistro steak recipes call for cooking thin-cut steaks in butter; removing the meat from the pan; and then making a simple pan sauce based on the fond (the flavorful browned bits of caramelized meat and juices left in the pan after searing), white wine, and chopped shallot. Prepared in this manner, the round steaks were tough and tasted liver-y. While the chuck steaks were good, their loose, open grain didn't seem right here. Flank was the winner by far for its big flavor and relative tenderness (as long as it was sliced against the grain).

But there was a problem. I had cut

We cut a large flank steak into quarters before cooking it and serving it with a simple pan sauce.

four single-serving steaks from one 2-pound flank steak, but they were thicker and denser than hanger or skirt steaks, which meant that they didn't cook through with just a sear on both sides—when I had a beautiful crust on the meat and a deep brown fond on the

bottom of the pan, the steaks were still underdone in the middle. By the time the steaks were medium-rare, the fond had burned, ruining the resulting sauce. Luckily, the test kitchen has a fix for that: We simply put the steaks, still in the skillet, right in a hot oven to finish cooking in the ambient heat.

Before I started my next batch of steaks, I heated the oven to 400 degrees. Once the meat had browned, I put the whole skillet in the oven. It took only about 5 minutes for the steaks to finish cooking, and there wasn't any burning this time. I moved the steaks to a plate and put the skillet back on the stove to finish the sauce. I added butter and shallot as before and then the wine. I simmered the mixture until it was slightly

thickened and swirled in one last pat of butter off heat at the end for an extra-silky texture. I sliced the steaks, drizzled on some sauce, and took a bite. Big beefy flavor, juicy meat, well-balanced sauce, and only a half-dozen ingredients? Bistros are definitely onto something, and now you're in on the secret.

BISTRO-STYLE FLANK STEAKS
Serves 4

After cutting the meat into pieces, you should have four steaks with the grain (the long striations) running parallel to the long side. The amount of time that the steaks need in the oven will depend on the thickness of the meat—use an instant-read thermometer to check. Be careful when making the pan sauce, as the skillet handle will be hot.

- 1 (2-pound) flank steak, trimmed
  Salt and pepper
- 2 teaspoons vegetable oil
- 3 tablespoons unsalted butter
- 1 large shallot, minced
- ¾ cup dry white wine

1. Adjust oven rack to middle position and heat oven to 400 degrees. Cut steak in half lengthwise with grain, then cut each piece in half crosswise against grain to make 4 equal-size steaks. Pat steaks dry with paper towels and season with salt and pepper.

2. Heat oil in 12-inch skillet over medium-high heat until just smoking. Add 1 tablespoon butter and swirl to melt. Lay steaks in pan and cook until well browned, 3 to 5 minutes per side. Move skillet to oven and cook until steaks register 125 degrees (for medium-rare), 3 to 5 minutes. Transfer steaks to plate and tent loosely with aluminum foil.

3. Return skillet with drippings to medium-high heat (skillet handle will be hot). Add 1 tablespoon butter and shallot and cook until shallot is browned, about 2 minutes. Add wine and any accumulated beef juices from plate and bring to boil, scraping up any browned bits. Continue to boil until slightly thickened and reduced to about ½ cup, about 5 minutes.

4. Remove sauce from heat and swirl in remaining 1 tablespoon butter until melted. Season with salt and pepper to taste. Slice steaks thin against grain on bias and serve with sauce.

Shorter fibers mean more-tender steak.

KEY TECHNIQUE
Slicing Flank Against the Grain
Most of us are familiar with slicing a large flank steak against the grain: This shortens the muscle fibers and results in more-tender meat. The same principle holds true with individual steaks cut from flank, which is why we call for slicing them before serving.

Pork Chop Casserole

Odd as a casserole based on pork chops might sound, this rustic recipe had our tasters clamoring for more. BY NICK IVERSON

BEING FROM THE Midwest, I was raised on casseroles. My mom—and all my friends' moms who had me over for supper—would take whatever meat was on sale; add vegetables, maybe a starch, and a can of creamy soup; and bake it with crispy bread crumbs for a plentiful but economical stick-to-your-ribs meal. I thought I'd had just about every casserole in the book until I stumbled across some recipes for pork chop casserole. Pork chop casserole? This I had to try.

All the recipes I collected called for different types of chops: bone-in and boneless loin chops, rib chops, cutlets, and blade-cut chops. The accompanying vegetables were just as varied, with some recipes calling for onion and carrots, others sauerkraut and tomatoes, and still others cabbage and potatoes. As for the liquid component, most recipes used cans of condensed soup, while a few called for a roux-based sauce made with chicken broth or wine. I prepared these recipes and called my tasters to assess them.

While we didn't love any one recipe, I was able to assemble a jumping-off point by including what we liked and eliminating what we didn't. Loin and rib chops were so lean that they dried out: We preferred blade-cut chops, which have more fat—which means they have great flavor and are less apt to dry out. Potatoes, tomatoes, and sauerkraut lost out to onion, carrots, and cabbage. As for the liquid, we preferred the roux-based sauce to the canned soup.

Putting this working recipe to the test, I seared six bone-in blade-cut chops and arranged them in a 13 by 9-inch baking dish. I topped the chops with a heap of shredded cabbage, chopped carrots, and sliced onion, and then I built a quick sauce in the same pot in which I'd seared the chops by sautéing garlic with thyme and sage, stirring in flour, and adding equal parts chicken broth, wine, and cream. I poured this sauce over everything, covered the dish (I'd figure out the crumbs later), and baked it for an hour. The resulting casserole looked like a culinary junkyard. It was a mishmash of bones, wilted cabbage, sour onions, and watery sauce, all barely contained by an overloaded dish. I needed to reevaluate and pare this thing down.

To scale it down, I used four chops instead of six, and I removed their

Pork, carrots, cabbage, and onion are bound by a wine and cream reduction and topped with crispy crumbs in this hearty, savory casserole.

bones. The blade-cut chops were still juicy and flavorful, but now they took up less space and were easier to eat—especially when I cut them in half after searing. To remedy the watery sauce, I sautéed the cabbage, carrots, and onion to drive off some of their natural moisture before adding them to the casserole, and I simply eliminated the chicken broth. The sauce looked a little pasty when I put the dish in the oven, but that actually worked out perfectly, as the chops and vegetables gave off more liquid as they baked, which thinned the sauce to the proper consistency. The flavor and texture were spot-on, so I moved on to the last piece of the puzzle: the bread-crumb topping.

I wanted the topping to be easy, so

I went with a base of bread crumbs and butter, with Parmesan cheese and sage to boost the flavor. A quick buzz in the food processor and it was ready. After a few tests that featured soggy toppings, though, I realized that it was best to bake the casserole, covered but not yet topped, for an hour and then remove the cover and turn up the heat for another 15 minutes. This method let the top dry out before I sprinkled on the crumbs. At that point, I baked the dish for a final 15 minutes, letting the crumbs turn golden brown.

My tasters all agreed that this recipe was transformed. The chops were moist and flavorful, the vegetables tender, and the sauce had body and tied everything together. Mom would be proud.

PORK CHOP CASSEROLE Serves 6

The chops can fit in the pot in one batch.

- 4 slices hearty white sandwich bread, torn into 1-inch pieces
- 1 ounce Parmesan cheese, grated (½ cup)
- 4 tablespoons unsalted butter
- 2 tablespoons chopped fresh sage
  Salt and pepper
- 4 (8- to 10-ounce) bone-in blade-cut pork chops, about 1 inch thick, bones removed, trimmed
- 1 head green cabbage (2 pounds), cored and sliced ½ inch thick
- 4 carrots, peeled and cut into ½-inch pieces
- 1 onion, halved and sliced thin
- 4 garlic cloves, minced
- 1 tablespoon minced fresh thyme
- 2 tablespoons all-purpose flour
- ½ cup dry white wine
- ½ cup heavy cream

1. Adjust oven rack to middle position and heat oven to 300 degrees. Process bread, Parmesan, 2 tablespoons butter, 1 tablespoon sage, ½ teaspoon salt, and ½ teaspoon pepper in food processor until coarsely ground, about 8 pulses; set aside. Pat chops dry with paper towels and season with salt and pepper. Melt remaining 2 tablespoons butter in Dutch oven over medium-high heat. Add chops and cook until well browned, about 4 minutes per side. Transfer chops to cutting board, halve crosswise, and place in 13 by 9-inch baking dish.

2. Add cabbage, carrots, onion, ½ teaspoon salt, and ½ teaspoon pepper to now-empty pot and cook, covered, until cabbage is wilted, 7 to 10 minutes. Remove lid and continue to cook until onion is browned and moisture has evaporated, about 5 minutes.

3. Add garlic, thyme, and remaining 1 tablespoon sage and cook until fragrant, about 30 seconds. Add flour and cook for 1 minute. Add wine and cream, bring to boil, and cook until thickened, about 1 minute. Pour cabbage mixture over chops and cover dish with aluminum foil. Bake until chops are tender, about 1 hour.

4. Remove foil, increase oven to 425 degrees, and continue to cook until top of casserole is browned, about 15 minutes. Top casserole with bread-crumb mixture and continue to bake until golden brown, about 15 minutes. Let casserole cool for 15 minutes. Serve.

Chicken with Vinegar Sauce

This simple but flavorful dish from France has made its way into American restaurants.
But in the recipes that we tried, something was lost in translation. BY CRISTIN WALSH

TRUST THE FRENCH to come up with a stylish yet seemingly effortless approach to a fast weeknight chicken dinner: chicken with vinegar (*poulet au vinaigre*). To make this classic recipe, you brown bone-in chicken pieces in a skillet and then set them aside while you build a sauce from their fond, along with shallot, garlic, chicken broth, and a surprising amount of vinegar (it mellows as it cooks—or at least that's what they say). You set the chicken in the sauce to finish cooking, remove it again, boil down the sauce, and finish it with a lot of butter and herbs, usually tarragon. Bon appétit.

But judging from the recipes I tried, it was more like *mal* appétit. We encountered soggy chicken skin; sour, thin, or greasy sauces; and bullying garlic flavor. Determined to develop a reliable recipe that could provide a foolproof Tuesday night dinner for American cooks, I got down to work.

I knew what I would *not* do: cook the chicken with the lid on, as some recipes instruct. The steam made soggy skin inevitable. Nor would I keep turning the pieces in the sauce—another surefire recipe for soggy skin. Instead, I'd try a favorite test kitchen technique: starting the chicken on the stovetop and switching to a very hot oven. We brown the skin side of the chicken parts (I'd use 3 pounds to serve four people), and after we build our sauce, we return the

It may sound—and look—fancy, but this tasty braise is plenty fast enough for a weeknight.

chicken to the skillet and move it into the oven. The tops of the chicken parts sit above the sauce, so the skin gets seriously crispy while the bottoms, whether light or dark meat, cook gently and evenly in the simmering liquid. I tried the method here and was pleased to get the usual moist meat and crispy skin.

I turned to the sauce. Based on my initial tests, I was using 1 cup of chicken broth with ½ cup of white wine vinegar. But further tests revealed cider vinegar to be softer and sweeter, and perfect balance came when I added a touch of honey. To tame the garlic, I ran several tests on amounts and cuts: In the end, four lightly crushed cloves, added with the shallot, sweetened as the sauce gurgled. The garlic required almost no

work on my part and added another dimension to the dish.

Most recipes for chicken with vinegar finish the sauce with butter—as much as 4 tablespoons. It gives body, richness, and gloss. Alas, it also makes the recipe trickier: If the butter fails to emulsify into the sauce, it will pool greasily, on top. To create a more reliable dish, I determined that a mere teaspoon of cornstarch, stirred in early on in the sauce-building stage, contributed enough body, allowing me to whisk in just 1 tablespoon of butter, off heat, with the tarragon at the end.

The chicken looked a picture. The meat was moist, the skin crispy, and the sauce light and bright, with tart-sweet balance, mellow garlic, and a subtle taste

of tarragon. As for my recipe, it was straightforward, dependable, and fast—just 30 minutes of cooking, half of that hands-free. This recipe was a keeper in any language.

PAN-ROASTED CHICKEN WITH VINEGAR-TARRAGON SAUCE
Serves 4

- 1 teaspoon cornstarch
- 1 cup chicken broth
- ½ cup cider vinegar
- 2 teaspoons honey
- 3 pounds bone-in chicken pieces (split breasts cut in half crosswise, drumsticks, and/or thighs), trimmed
  Salt and pepper
- 2 teaspoons vegetable oil
- 1 shallot, minced
- 4 garlic cloves, lightly crushed and peeled
- 1 tablespoon unsalted butter
- 1 tablespoon chopped fresh tarragon

1. Adjust oven rack to upper-middle position and heat oven to 450 degrees. Dissolve cornstarch in 2 tablespoons broth in 2-cup liquid measuring cup. Whisk in vinegar, honey, and remaining broth; set aside.

2. Pat chicken dry with paper towels and season with salt and pepper. Heat oil in 12-inch ovensafe skillet over medium-high heat until just smoking. Cook chicken, skin side down, until well browned, 6 to 8 minutes. Transfer to plate, skin side up.

3. Pour off all but 1 tablespoon fat from skillet and return to medium-high heat. Add shallot and garlic and cook until fragrant, about 30 seconds. Whisk broth mixture to redistribute cornstarch and add to skillet, scraping up any browned bits. Bring to boil and return chicken to skillet, skin side up, along with any accumulated juices. Move skillet to oven and cook until breasts register 160 degrees and drumsticks/thighs register 175 degrees, 10 to 15 minutes.

4. Transfer chicken to serving platter, tent loosely with aluminum foil, and let rest while preparing sauce. Return skillet to medium-high heat (skillet handle will be hot), bring to boil, and cook until sauce is slightly thickened, 5 to 7 minutes. Off heat, whisk butter, tarragon, and any accumulated juices from platter into sauce. Season with salt and pepper to taste. Spoon sauce over chicken and serve.

TEST KITCHEN TECHNIQUE
Two-Heat Method

Most recipes call for making this dish on the stovetop from start to finish. By moving it into the oven after we brown the chicken, we ensure that the meat braises evenly and gently. The chicken skin stays above the liquid, where it continues to crisp. To finish, we return the skillet to the stovetop to reduce the sauce.

Getting to Know Umami Powerhouses

Umami, a quality of meaty savoriness that brings depth to many dishes, is widely considered the fifth taste. These 12 umami-enhancing ingredients boost the flavor of whatever we're cooking. BY CHRISTIE MORRISON

Soy Sauce
ASIAN UNIVERSAL

Soy sauce is practically synonymous with Asian cooking. Traditionally, manufacturers age this fermented liquid, made from soybeans and wheat, barley, or rice, for up to four years. Today, it can be chemically produced in just days, which explains the widely divergent flavors and qualities among brands. Lee Kum Kee Tabletop Soy Sauce is our favorite for cooking; we often use it to deepen the flavor of such American classics as beef stew, meatloaf, and chicken pot pie.

Fish Sauce
STRONG STUFF

Fish sauce—made from water, salt, sugar, and salted, fermented fish—has a pungent, funky aroma, but when used judiciously, it tastes neither strong nor fishy. Instead, the highly concentrated liquid adds salty complexity to many Southeast Asian dishes, including pad thai and stir-fries. Tiparos makes our favorite fish sauce.

Anchovies
HAIL CAESAR

Preserved anchovies are packed with umami-producing glutamates. They also contain other chemical compounds that can magnify the meaty taste of glutamates by up to 15 times. Traditionally, anchovies add dimension to Caesar dressing and puttanesca sauce, but we've also used them to intensify the savoriness of beef stew: Sauté two minced anchovies with the onions for stews using 3 to 4 pounds of meat. Our favorite are Ortiz Oil-Packed Anchovies.

Worcestershire Sauce
STEAK COHORT

English pharmacists Lea and Perrins concocted the fermented sauce in the early 1800s, combining malt vinegar, molasses, anchovies, and tamarind, among other ingredients, as a condiment for beef and fish. Glutamate-rich and salty, Worcestershire sauce has a pungent, fruity flavor. It typically introduces salty complexity to Caesar salad and Bloody Marys, and we've used it to add depth to cheddar cheese balls, too: **CooksCountry.com/cheddarcheeseball.**

Tomato Paste
CUT AND PASTE

Tomatoes in all their varied forms add savory qualities to foods, but ultraconcentrated tomato paste is the form that we turn to again and again to build umami. We add it to tomato soups and sauces to fortify tomato flavor, but we also use it in nontomato dishes like beef Burgundy and chicken paprikash. To develop its flavor, we sauté tomato paste with onions for 1 to 2 minutes until it darkens and smells fragrant. We like Goya Tomato Paste best.

Mushrooms
BEEF PROXY

Mushrooms are so high in umami that they routinely act as a stand-in for meat. We use them in our Reduced-Fat Meatballs and Marinara (page 29) to replace some of the meat, eliminating calories and fat in the process. But while all mushrooms contribute meaty flavor, dried mushrooms deliver the most umami because they are concentrated. We often use dried porcini or shiitake to build flavor in longer-cooking dishes.

Olives
BITTER FRUIT

Most olives are fermented or cured in salt or brine to remove oleuropein, the bitter compound that makes them unpalatable straight from the tree. Brine-cured olives are soaked in a salt solution, while salt-cured olives are first packed in salt to extract moisture and oleuropein and then submerged in oil for replumping. Olives have a decidedly meaty texture, but they also have a salty, meaty flavor that makes them a go-to umami enhancer in many meatless dishes.

Miso
SOUP FIX

Miso is having its moment in the United States, showing up in many a Western recipe. Japanese for "bean paste," miso is made by fermenting soybeans with rice, barley, or rye. In Japan, there are many hundreds of different types of miso. Here you're most likely to find mild, sweet white *shiro* (despite the name, it's light yellow) or fruity, intense red *aka*. We use miso to deepen the flavor and enrich the texture of salad dressings, marinades, sauces, and—of course—miso soup.

Parmesan Cheese
OLD FAITHFUL

While all cheeses contain umami, in this department aged Parmesan is unparalleled. Try to imagine a Caesar salad without it and you'll get the picture. But we also turn to it when depth—rather than cheese flavor—is what we're after: We use a Parmesan rind to deepen the savory flavor of soups like minestrone. Buying at the supermarket? Get Boar's Head Parmigiano-Reggiano.

Marmite
STRANGE BREW

Popular in Britain as a pungent spread for toast, Marmite has nearly twice the umami-producing glutamates of any other item on this page. Its sour, beefy flavor makes it an acquired taste, but we've found that it contributes meaty, long-simmered flavor to quick-cooked soups. Use a light hand—¼ teaspoon per serving. Find it in the international aisle of the grocery store or online.

Kombu
KELP HELP

Kombu, a type of kelp, is a mainstay in Japanese cooking. It's used in dashi, the Japanese stock, which was the first food in which umami was clearly recognized. In the test kitchen, we've used kombu to deepen the flavor of vegetable soups (try steeping a 4-inch piece in your next batch of lentil soup) and tomato sauces. Kombu can be stored indefinitely.

Beef Broth/Stock
FLAVOR FORTIFIER

Beef broth is rich in umami-enhancing compounds, but beef stock goes a step further: It also derives its flavor from the bones. The flavor of beef broth is so intense that we often dilute it with water or chicken broth, which is lower in glutamates. Our favorite commercial beef broth is Rachael Ray Stock-in-a-Box All-Natural Beef Flavored Stock.

**PAN-ROASTED PORK TENDERLOIN
WITH TOMATOES AND CAPERS**

LEMON RISOTTO WITH CHICKEN AND SWISS CHARD

RUSTIC CHORIZO, TOMATO, AND SPINACH SOUP

ROASTED TROUT WITH WHITE BEAN SALAD

LEMON RISOTTO WITH CHICKEN AND SWISS CHARD Serves 4

☑ **WHY THIS RECIPE WORKS:** Giving the rice a head start in the microwave speeds up the cooking and lets us make risotto with less stirring.

- 4 cups chicken broth
- 1 cup Arborio rice
- 4 tablespoons unsalted butter
- 4 (6- to 8-ounce) boneless, skinless chicken breasts, trimmed and cut into 1-inch pieces
    Salt and pepper
- 1 onion, chopped fine
- 4 garlic cloves, minced
- 12 ounces Swiss chard, stems chopped fine, leaves sliced into ½-inch-wide strips
- 2 ounces Parmesan cheese, grated (1 cup)
- 2 teaspoons grated lemon zest plus 3 tablespoons juice

1. Combine 3 cups broth, rice, and 1 tablespoon butter in large bowl. Microwave, covered, until most of liquid is absorbed, 12 to 14 minutes.

2. Pat chicken dry with paper towels and season with salt and pepper. Melt 2 tablespoons butter in large Dutch oven over medium heat. Add onion and cook until just browned, about 5 minutes. Add garlic and cook until fragrant, about 30 seconds. Add chicken and cook, stirring occasionally, until no longer pink, about 5 minutes. Stir in chard and cook until leaves begin to wilt, about 30 seconds.

3. Add parcooked rice and remaining 1 cup broth to pot and cook, stirring constantly, until rice is almost tender, 4 to 6 minutes. Off heat, stir in Parmesan, lemon zest and juice, and remaining 1 tablespoon butter. Season with salt and pepper to taste. Serve.

PAN-ROASTED PORK TENDERLOIN WITH TOMATOES AND CAPERS Serves 4

☑ **WHY THIS RECIPE WORKS:** Capers, tomatoes, and thyme add lots of flavor to quick-cooking pork tenderloin.

- 2 (12- to 16-ounce) pork tenderloins, trimmed
    Salt and pepper
- 3 tablespoons vegetable oil
- 1 onion, chopped fine
- 2 tablespoons tomato paste
- 4 garlic cloves, minced
- 2 teaspoons minced fresh thyme
- 1 (14.5-ounce) can diced tomatoes
- 1 cup chicken broth
- 1 tablespoon capers, rinsed

1. Adjust oven rack to middle position and heat oven to 475 degrees. Pat pork dry with paper towels and season with salt and pepper. Heat 1 tablespoon oil in 12-inch skillet over medium-high heat until just smoking. Add pork and cook until well browned on 1 side, about 5 minutes. Flip pork, transfer skillet to oven, and roast until pork registers 145 degrees, 5 to 7 minutes. Transfer pork to carving board, tent with aluminum foil, and let rest while preparing sauce.

2. Return now-empty skillet to medium-high heat (skillet handle will be hot). Add remaining 2 tablespoons oil, onion, and ½ teaspoon salt and cook until onion is just beginning to soften, about 2 minutes. Stir in tomato paste, garlic, and thyme and cook until rust-colored and fragrant, about 2 minutes. Stir in tomatoes and their juice and broth; bring to boil. Reduce heat to medium-low and simmer until thickened, 5 to 7 minutes. Off heat, stir in capers. Season with salt and pepper to taste. Cut pork into ½-inch-thick slices, transfer to platter, and pour sauce over top. Serve.

ROASTED TROUT WITH WHITE BEAN SALAD Serves 4

☑ **WHY THIS RECIPE WORKS:** A preheated baking sheet helps crisp the fish's skin. While the trout cooks, we make a quick salad using canned beans.

- 4 (6- to 8-ounce) boneless, butterflied whole trout
    Salt and pepper
- ½ cup olive oil, plus extra for drizzling
- 2 (15-ounce) cans cannellini beans, rinsed
- 2 shallots, minced
- ¼ cup chopped fresh parsley
- ¼ cup lemon juice (2 lemons)
- 2 tablespoons capers, rinsed and chopped
- 4 teaspoons minced fresh rosemary
- 2 garlic cloves, minced

1. Adjust oven rack to middle position, place rimmed baking sheet on rack, and heat oven to 450 degrees. Pat trout dry with paper towels and season with salt and pepper. Add ¼ cup oil to hot sheet, tilting to coat evenly, and return to oven for 4 minutes. Carefully place trout skin side down on sheet and cook until opaque and cooked through, 7 to 9 minutes. Transfer trout to platter.

2. Meanwhile, combine beans, shallots, parsley, lemon juice, capers, rosemary, garlic, and remaining ¼ cup oil in bowl. Season with salt and pepper to taste. Serve bean salad with trout, drizzled with extra oil.

TEST KITCHEN NOTE: We use cannellini beans for this salad, but any canned small white beans will work.

RUSTIC CHORIZO, TOMATO, AND SPINACH SOUP Serves 4

☑ **WHY THIS RECIPE WORKS:** Chorizo sausage provides a meaty, smoky base for this soup. We add the spinach at the end to preserve its fresh taste.

- 2 tablespoons olive oil
- 8 ounces Spanish-style chorizo sausage, sliced ¼ inch thick
- 1 onion, chopped
    Salt and pepper
- 4 garlic cloves, minced
- ½ teaspoon ground cumin
- 1 (28-ounce) can diced tomatoes
- 3 cups chicken broth
- 8 ounces (8 cups) baby spinach
- 1 teaspoon sherry vinegar

1. Heat oil in Dutch oven over medium heat until shimmering. Add chorizo and cook until beginning to brown, about 5 minutes. Add onion and ¾ teaspoon salt and cook until softened, about 5 minutes. Add garlic, cumin, and ¼ teaspoon pepper and cook until fragrant, about 30 seconds. Add tomatoes and their juice and broth and bring to boil.

2. Stir in spinach and cook, covered, until spinach is wilted and tender, about 2 minutes. Stir in vinegar. Season with salt and pepper to taste. Serve.

TEST KITCHEN NOTE: Be sure to use dry-cured Spanish-style chorizo for this recipe and not the fresh, Mexican variety.

SKILLET SAUSAGE AND MUSHROOM PENNE

PORK CUTLETS WITH SWEET POTATOES
AND MAPLE PAN SAUCE

ARUGULA SALAD WITH STEAK TIPS
AND GORGONZOLA

CHICKEN BANH MI

PORK CUTLETS WITH SWEET POTATOES AND MAPLE PAN SAUCE Serves 4

✓ **WHY THIS RECIPE WORKS:** We start the sweet potatoes in the microwave and then finish them in the skillet that we used to brown the pork.

- 2 pounds sweet potatoes, peeled and cut into ½-inch pieces
- ¼ cup vegetable oil
  Salt and pepper
- 2 teaspoons garam masala
- 2 teaspoons ground cumin
- 8 (3-ounce) boneless pork cutlets, ¼ inch thick, trimmed
- 4 garlic cloves, sliced thin
- ½ cup maple syrup
- 2 tablespoons Dijon mustard
- 2 tablespoons cider vinegar

1. Combine potatoes, 2 tablespoons oil, ½ teaspoon salt, and ½ teaspoon pepper in large bowl. Cover and microwave until potatoes are nearly tender, about 7 minutes; set aside.

2. Meanwhile, combine garam masala, cumin, 1 teaspoon salt, and ½ teaspoon pepper in bowl. Pat cutlets dry with paper towels and season with spice mixture. Heat 1 tablespoon oil in 12-inch nonstick skillet over medium-high heat until shimmering. Add 4 cutlets to skillet and cook until well browned and cooked through, about 2 minutes per side. Transfer to plate and tent with aluminum foil. Repeat with remaining 1 tablespoon oil and remaining 4 cutlets.

3. Add potatoes and garlic to now-empty skillet and cook over medium heat until browned and tender, about 5 minutes; transfer to platter. Add maple syrup, mustard, vinegar, and any accumulated pork juices to now-empty skillet and simmer over medium heat until thickened, about 2 minutes. Transfer cutlets to platter with potatoes and pour sauce over top. Serve.

SKILLET SAUSAGE AND MUSHROOM PENNE Serves 4

✓ **WHY THIS RECIPE WORKS:** Cooking the pasta right in the sauce infuses it with flavor and restricts the cooking to one pan.

- 12 ounces sweet Italian sausage, casings removed
- 4 ounces white mushrooms, trimmed and quartered
- 2¼ cups chicken broth
- 1 (14.5-ounce) can diced tomatoes
- 12 ounces (3¾ cups) penne
- ¾ cup heavy cream
- 2 ounces Parmesan cheese, grated (1 cup), plus extra for serving
  Salt and pepper

1. Cook sausage in 12-inch nonstick skillet over medium-high heat, breaking up pieces with spoon, until no longer pink, about 5 minutes. Add mushrooms and cook until beginning to brown, about 4 minutes. Transfer sausage-mushroom mixture to bowl.

2. Return now-empty skillet to medium-high heat and add broth, tomatoes and their juice, pasta, and cream and bring to boil. Reduce heat to medium-low, cover, and simmer, stirring frequently, until pasta is al dente, about 15 minutes.

3. Stir sausage-mushroom mixture and ½ cup Parmesan into pasta. Season with salt and pepper to taste. Top with remaining ½ cup Parmesan, cover skillet, and remove from heat until cheese is melted, about 5 minutes. Serve, passing extra Parmesan separately.

TEST KITCHEN NOTE: You can use hot Italian sausage instead of sweet.

CHICKEN BANH MI Serves 4

✓ **WHY THIS RECIPE WORKS:** To make this Vietnamese-style sandwich, we quickly pickle carrots and cucumber in lime juice and fish sauce and season a rotisserie chicken with the same flavors. Sriracha mayonnaise gives the sandwich a spicy kick.

- 2 carrots, peeled and shredded
- ½ cucumber, peeled, halved lengthwise, seeded, and sliced thin
- 1 teaspoon grated lime zest plus 5 tablespoons juice (3 limes)
- ¼ cup fish sauce
- 3 tablespoons packed dark brown sugar
- 1 (2½-pound) rotisserie chicken, skin and bones discarded, meat shredded into bite-size pieces (3 cups)
- ½ cup mayonnaise
- 5 teaspoons Sriracha sauce
- 4 (8-inch) sub rolls, split lengthwise and toasted
- ½ cup fresh cilantro leaves

1. Combine carrots, cucumber, 2 tablespoons lime juice, and 1 tablespoon fish sauce in bowl and let sit for 15 minutes. Combine sugar, remaining 3 tablespoons lime juice, and remaining 3 tablespoons fish sauce in large bowl and stir until sugar is dissolved. Add chicken and toss to coat. Whisk mayonnaise, Sriracha, and lime zest together in separate bowl.

2. Spread mayonnaise mixture on roll bottoms. Divide chicken mixture among rolls and top with pickled vegetables (leaving liquid in bowl), cilantro, and roll tops. Serve.

TEST KITCHEN NOTE: Shred the carrots on the large holes of a box grater. Our favorite Sriracha is Huy Fong Sriracha Hot Chili Sauce.

ARUGULA SALAD WITH STEAK TIPS AND GORGONZOLA Serves 4

✓ **WHY THIS RECIPE WORKS:** Dressing spicy arugula with a simple vinaigrette and fortifying it with tender steak tips makes for a quick and elegant dinner salad.

- 1 pound sirloin steak tips, trimmed
  Salt and pepper
- 2 tablespoons plus ¼ cup olive oil
- 1 shallot, minced
- 2 tablespoons cider vinegar
- 2 garlic cloves, minced
- 1 teaspoon Dijon mustard
- 1 teaspoon honey
- 12 ounces (12 cups) baby arugula
- 6 ounces Gorgonzola cheese, crumbled (1½ cups)

1. Pat steak dry with paper towels and season with salt and pepper. Heat 2 tablespoons oil in 12-inch nonstick skillet over medium-high heat until just smoking. Cook steak until well browned all over and temperature registers 125 degrees, 8 to 10 minutes. Transfer to plate, tent loosely with aluminum foil, and let rest for 5 minutes.

2. Whisk shallot, vinegar, garlic, mustard, honey, ¼ teaspoon salt, and ¼ teaspoon pepper together in large bowl. Slowly whisk in remaining ¼ cup oil. Add arugula and Gorgonzola to vinaigrette and toss to combine. Season with salt and pepper to taste. Cut steak against grain into ¼-inch-thick slices. Divide salad among individual dinner plates and top with sliced steak. Serve.

TEST KITCHEN NOTE: You can substitute any blue cheese for the Gorgonzola.

Loaded Breakfast Sandwiches

The perfect egg sandwich starts with perfectly cooked eggs—but then it requires a bit of assembly know-how. BY REBECCAH MARSTERS

FOR BETTER OR for worse, eating on the go has become a part of modern American life. No portable breakfast is as satisfying as a breakfast sandwich: They're hot, filling, and—when done properly—really, really good. In fact, breakfast sandwiches are so good that they've become a popular sit-down morning meal in cafés, diners, schools, and home kitchens. But most of the versions I've tried have fallen short of this ideal with a disappointing combination of soggy bread, cold cheese, and rubbery eggs. I set out to develop an easy, tasty recipe for breakfast sandwiches that brought out their full potential.

When I flipped through cookbooks and magazines for inspiration, I was overwhelmed by my choices—omelet-style, fried, or scrambled eggs? Bacon, ham, sausage, or prosciutto? Cheese? As for the bread, recipes called for everything from bagels to brioche and from pumpernickel to pita. I dove in and prepared a handful of the most intriguing recipes. After a ton of cooking and eating, my tasters and I landed on the following components: sturdy English muffins, fried eggs (my tasters particularly loved their runny yolks), sharp cheddar, and bacon (but I made a note of other options for possible variations).

We have a tried-and-true technique for fried eggs in the test kitchen: Place a nonstick skillet over low heat for about 5 minutes to ensure that it's thoroughly heated, add butter, turn up the heat, and pour in the eggs all at once (cracking them into bowls first makes this easy). After 1 minute in a covered pan over medium-high heat and then another minute off the heat, still covered, the eggs have slightly runny yolks and perfectly set whites with crispy, browned edges. I needed to cook the bacon, too, so for convenience, I'd use the same pan. And since cooked eggs can't sit around, I'd fry the bacon first. As I removed the cooked bacon from the skillet, I realized two advantages of this order: First, I could fry the eggs in bacon fat instead of butter, and second, the pan was already hot, so preheating was unnecessary.

I had the eggs and bacon figured out,

Switch it up. Get our recipes for **All-American Breakfast Sandwiches** and **Ham and Gruyère Breakfast Sandwiches** at CooksCountry.com/jan14.

We toast the buttered English muffins under the broiler for convenience and speed.

so I moved on to the cheese. After placing each egg on a toasted English muffin bottom, I topped it with a slice of cheddar cheese and a few pieces of bacon. The sandwich tasted great, but the cheese didn't melt all the way and the bacon tumbled out after the first bite. The cheese needed more than the residual heat from the egg to fully melt. Happily, I found that if I layered the cheese over the eggs when the pan came off the heat, an extra minute or so rendered it molten and gooey (the eggs don't overcook because the cold cheese slows their cooking). Taking a cue from the test kitchen's grilled cheese technique, I switched to shredded cheddar cheese, which melts more evenly. I tried laying the bacon on the eggs before sprinkling

the cheese on top—this anchored the strips in place so that I could transfer the whole egg-bacon-cheese stack to the muffin, with everything staying put.

Speaking of the English muffins, I needed to find a more efficient way to toast them—standing over a toaster wasn't cutting it. The broiler was the way to go; I buttered the muffins and lined them up on a baking sheet. A few minutes under the heat made the insides crunchy and golden. The outsides of the muffins needed even less time—just enough to crisp them.

For freshness, I added a handful of baby spinach and a tomato slice to each sandwich. A good smear of hot sauce–enhanced mayo on the bottom of the muffin added richness, heat, and

moisture. These sandwiches were salty, tangy, crispy, and gooey all at the same time. A breakfast sandwich may be an ideal on-the-go meal, but this one was good enough to sit down for.

BACON AND CHEDDAR BREAKFAST SANDWICHES
Makes 4 sandwiches
Bays English Muffins are our favorite.

- 4   English muffins, split
- 3   tablespoons unsalted butter, softened
- ¼   cup mayonnaise
- 1   teaspoon hot sauce
- 4   large eggs
     Salt and pepper
- 6   slices bacon
- 4   ounces sharp cheddar cheese, shredded (1 cup)
- 1½ ounces (1½ cups) baby spinach
- 4   thin tomato slices

1. Adjust oven rack 5 inches from broiler element and heat broiler. Spread insides of muffins evenly with butter and arrange split side up on rimmed baking sheet. Combine mayonnaise and hot sauce in bowl; set aside. Crack 2 eggs into small bowl and season with salt and pepper. Repeat with remaining 2 eggs and second small bowl.

2. Cook bacon in 12-inch nonstick skillet over medium heat until crispy, 7 to 9 minutes; transfer to paper towel–lined plate. When cool enough to handle, break each slice in half.

3. Broil muffins until golden brown, 2 to 4 minutes, rotating sheet halfway through broiling. Flip muffins and broil until just crisp on second side, 1 to 2 minutes; set aside while cooking eggs.

4. Pour off all but 1 tablespoon fat from skillet and heat over medium-high heat until shimmering. Working quickly, pour 1 bowl of eggs in 1 side of pan and second bowl of eggs in other side. Cover and cook for 1 minute.

5. Working quickly, top each egg with 3 pieces of bacon and ¼ cup cheddar. Cover pan, remove from heat, and let stand until cheddar is melted and egg whites are cooked through, about 2 minutes.

6. Spread mayonnaise mixture on muffin bottoms and place 1 bacon-and-cheese-topped egg on each. Divide spinach evenly among sandwiches, then top with tomato slices and muffin tops. Serve.

Spiced Pork Pie

Unless your ancestors were French Canadian, *tourtière* just may be the most delicious Christmas tradition you've never heard of. BY SARAH GABRIEL

TOURTIÈRE IS A spiced pork pie that French Canadians eat at Christmas as part of a post–midnight mass feast. French Canadians who immigrated to New England to work in the mills in the 19th century are thought to have brought the pie with them, which is why it shows up in places like Lowell, Massachusetts, and Woonsocket, Rhode Island, former textile mill towns with large French Canadian populations. However tourtière made its way across the border, a hearty pie of warm-spiced pork in buttery, flaky pastry is a Christmas dinner that everyone can get behind. In fact, a friend who grew up eating this dish practically got weepy when telling me how good it is.

After a bit of recipe research, I began to understand the differences in style and technique that would set the parameters for my first few batches. Tourtière is always a double-crust pie flavored with warm spices, but many of the other details were up for debate: Should I use potato? If yes, should I dice or mash it? Did I need a starch like flour or cornstarch to bind the filling? Or bread crumbs? Should I use pork alone or combine it with beef, or veal? Heck, there were recipes for tourtière made with everything from moose meat to pigeon. The crust options ranged nearly as widely. The moose meat and game birds were out of the question, but the only way to settle the remaining debates was to eat some pie. I grabbed a rolling pin and got started.

After we had worked our way through a tasting of six different pies, I had a good idea about how to proceed: For the filling, pork's mild sweetness edged out the combinations of meats, plus one meat was easier. But the fillings with pork were a little dry and crumbly; obviously, I'd need to fix that. Sautéed onion and garlic were easily voted in, while tomatoes (an unusual inclusion) were just as easily voted out. We found cinnamon, allspice, and nutmeg pleasantly warm, musky, and complex, and a pie that included 2 cups of mashed potato held together best.

After a few tries incorporating these choices, I thought that I had the flavor of the filling pretty well calibrated. I sautéed two chopped onions in butter, stirred in the spices, and then added the meat. I cooked the mixture until the

This savory pork pie is spiced with cloves, allspice, cinnamon, and nutmeg.

pork had lost its pinkness, at which point I stirred in 2 cups of mashed potato. I let the mixture cool since I had found that warm filling makes the crust greasy. I lined a pie plate with our favorite store-bought crust, loaded it with the cooled filling, crimped on the top crust, and baked the pie on the lowest oven rack to get good browning on the bottom crust.

When it was done, I rounded up some tasters, including Gilles, our television

crew's sound engineer—he's a Quebec native and Rhode Island resident who grew up with the dish. The verdict? The spice was almost right but needed a little more punch, the filling was too potato-y, and, as in the earlier versions, the meat had cooked—or rather overcooked—into tough, rubbery pellets. Clearly I still had some work to do.

The meat was both the main ingredient and the main problem, so I started

there. None of the recipes that I'd found put raw meat in the pastry crust, and when I tried it as a solution to overcooking, I could see why: The meat baked into a solid slab, like a meatloaf in a pastry shell, which was definitely not true to the dish. For safety, I had to cook the meat completely before letting it cool and putting it in the pie, and then I had to bake the pie long enough to cook the crust, so less cooking wasn't an option.

What I needed was a way to tenderize the meat despite all the cooking—and cooking at the relatively high temperature needed to brown a crust at that.

Luckily, this isn't the first time that we've seen this problem in the test kitchen: In previous dishes, we've used baking soda to tenderize sliced or ground meat. Cribbing from one of those recipes, I dissolved ¾ teaspoon of baking soda and some salt in a couple of tablespoons of water, and then I mixed the solution with the ground pork and let it sit for about 20 minutes. I cooked the filling and gave it a taste—so far so good. But would it survive being baked into the pie? It did. Unfortunately, though, now that the meat was tender, the mashed potato made the whole assemblage mushy.

Some of the first pies that I had baked used diced potato; one used grated. I'd gone with mashed because they bound the crumbly meat, but now that the meat was moist and tender, it was worth retesting the other options. I made three more pies, one each with mashed, diced, and grated potato. At the same time, I cut down on the amount of potato that I'd been using. I cooked both the diced and the grated potato in chicken broth until tender and then added the ground raw meat right to the mixture; since I'd worked so hard to avoid overcooking it, I didn't brown it first.

The mashed potato was again pasty. And Gilles, the Quebecois audio engineer, frowned disapprovingly at the prominent chunks of diced potato. But the shreds of grated potato worked beautifully, keeping the meat in place as I sliced. Also, the grated potato had sloughed off enough starch during cooking to thicken the broth and the meat's juices, giving the impression that the pie was moistened with a bit of gravy. At Gilles's urging, I added a pinch of ground cloves. I had just the right texture and warm, spicy flavor; it was time to tackle the crust.

Luckily, I had a recipe in mind. A couple of years back, while working on our recipe for Moravian Chicken Pie, a colleague developed a tender, flaky, and easy to handle pie dough with sour cream and egg that I suspected might be exactly the thing for my tourtière. It was. I put together one last pie using that dough recipe, and it drew raves from everybody, Canadian and otherwise. The tourtière was warming, stick-to-your-ribs food so delicious and surprising that I'm struggling for words to adequately capture it (maybe the French have some?). Within hours, people around the office who had never said a word about their heritage were chewing my ear off about French Canadian grandmothers. I figured that it was safe to put away my rolling pin and call it a day.

Tourtière, for the Uninitiated

This pie traditionally includes meat, potato, and warm spices in a flaky crust. Ours works within that tradition but takes it up a notch.

RICH, EASY CRUST
We include sour cream and an egg in our dough for tender texture and great flavor.

THICK, COHESIVE FILLING
We peel and shred russet potatoes and cook them in chicken stock, adding the ground meat to the resulting starchy sauce.

WARM SPICES
Tourtière uses unusual spices for a savory pie—cinnamon, allspice, nutmeg, and cloves.

TOURTIÈRE Serves 8

Plan ahead: Both the pie dough and the filling need to chill for an hour or more before the pie can be assembled and baked. If time is short, use store-bought dough. Shred the potatoes on the large holes of a box grater just before cooking. Don't soak the shreds in water or their starch will wash away and the filling won't thicken properly. To cool the filling quickly, chill it in a large baking dish. Eat the pie when it's just slightly warm.

FILLING

    Salt and pepper
¾ teaspoon baking soda
2   tablespoons water
2   pounds ground pork
2   tablespoons unsalted butter
2   onions, chopped fine
3   garlic cloves, minced
1   teaspoon minced fresh thyme
¼   teaspoon ground allspice
¼   teaspoon ground cinnamon
¼   teaspoon ground nutmeg
    Pinch ground cloves
3   cups chicken broth
12 ounces russet potatoes, peeled and shredded

CRUST

½   cup sour cream, chilled
1   large egg, lightly beaten
2½ cups (12½ ounces) all-purpose flour
½   teaspoon salt
12 tablespoons unsalted butter, cut into ½-inch pieces and chilled

1   large egg yolk lightly beaten with 2 tablespoons water

1. FOR THE FILLING: Dissolve 1¼ teaspoons salt and baking soda in water in medium bowl. Add pork and knead with your hands until thoroughly combined. Set aside until needed, at least 20 minutes.

2. Meanwhile, melt butter in Dutch oven over medium-high heat. Add onions and ¼ teaspoon salt and cook, stirring occasionally, until browned,

7 to 9 minutes. Add garlic, thyme, allspice, cinnamon, nutmeg, cloves, and 1 teaspoon pepper and cook until fragrant, about 1 minute. Add broth and potatoes, scraping up any browned bits, and bring to boil. Reduce heat to medium and simmer, stirring often, until potatoes are tender and rubber spatula leaves trail when dragged across bottom of pot, 15 to 20 minutes.

3. Add pork to pot, breaking up pieces with spoon, and cook until no longer pink, about 10 minutes. Transfer filling to 13 by 9-inch baking dish and refrigerate, uncovered, stirring occasionally, until completely cool, about 1 hour. (Cooled filling can be refrigerated, covered, for up to 24 hours before assembling pie.)

4. FOR THE CRUST: Combine sour cream and egg in bowl. Process flour and salt in food processor until combined, about 3 seconds. Add butter and pulse until only pea-size pieces remain, about 10 pulses. Add half of sour cream mixture and pulse until combined, about 5 pulses. Add remaining sour cream mixture and pulse until dough begins to form, about 10 pulses.

5. Transfer mixture to lightly floured counter and knead briefly until dough comes together. Divide dough in half and form each half into 6-inch disk. Wrap disks tightly in plastic wrap and refrigerate for 1 hour. Let chilled dough sit on counter to soften slightly, about 10 minutes, before rolling.

6. Adjust oven rack to lowest position and heat oven to 450 degrees. Roll 1 disk of dough into 12-inch circle on lightly floured counter. Loosely roll dough around rolling pin and gently unroll it onto 9-inch pie plate, letting excess dough hang over edge. Ease dough into plate by gently lifting edge of dough with your hand while pressing into plate bottom with your other hand. Wrap dough-lined pie plate loosely in plastic and refrigerate until dough is firm, about 30 minutes. Trim overhang to ½ inch beyond lip of pie plate.

7. Pour filling into dough-lined pie plate. Roll other disk of dough into 12-inch circle on lightly floured counter. Loosely roll dough around rolling pin and gently unroll it onto filling. Trim overhang to ½ inch beyond lip of pie plate. Pinch edges of top and bottom crusts firmly together. Tuck overhang under itself; folded edge should be flush with edge of pie plate. Crimp dough evenly around edge of pie plate using your fingers. (If dough gets too soft to work with, refrigerate pie for 10 minutes, then continue.)

8. Cut four 1-inch slits in top of dough. Brush surface with egg wash. Bake until edges are light brown, about 15 minutes. Reduce oven temperature to 375 degrees and continue to bake until crust is deep golden brown and liquid bubbles up through vents, 15 to 20 minutes longer. Let pie cool on wire rack for 2 hours before serving.

TO MAKE AHEAD

Wrapped dough can be refrigerated for up to 2 days or frozen for up to 1 month. If frozen, let dough thaw completely on counter before rolling. Assembled pie (without egg wash) can be refrigerated for up to 24 hours before brushing with egg wash and baking.

TEST KITCHEN DISCOVERY
Not Just for Baking
Most of the time baking soda lightens cakes, cookies, and pancakes, ensuring that they rise. It has a different function for our *tourtière*: We mix the ground raw pork with a little water, salt, and baking soda to keep the meat tender despite relatively long cooking.

SURPRISE FIND
Baking soda helps tenderize the meat.

Christmas Cookie Contest

We received submissions from 30 states and four countries, including India and Taiwan. The whole world loves cookies.

We've had many years of practice, but this job never gets any easier: picking just a single grand-prize winner and six finalists from among the hundreds of delectable recipes you send us.

DULCE DE LECHE AND CINNAMON SANDWICH COOKIES

Karen Cope, Minneapolis, Minn.

Recently, Cope has gone from strength to strength in the kitchen; she told us that four other items that she baked won blue ribbons at the Minnesota State Fair this past summer.

Makes 24 sandwich cookies

COOKIES

- 2 cups (10 ounces) all-purpose flour
- 1 teaspoon baking soda
- ½ teaspoon salt
- ½ teaspoon ground anise
- 16 tablespoons unsalted butter, softened
- 1 cup (7 ounces) sugar, plus ½ cup for rolling
- 1 large egg
- 1 teaspoon vanilla extract
- 1 teaspoon ground cinnamon

FILLING

- 1 tablespoon unsalted butter
- ½ teaspoon ground cinnamon
- ½ teaspoon ground anise
- 1½ cups dulce de leche

1. FOR THE COOKIES: Adjust oven rack to middle position and heat oven to 350 degrees. Line baking sheet with parchment paper. Combine flour, baking soda, salt, and anise in bowl.

2. Using stand mixer fitted with paddle, beat butter and 1 cup sugar on medium-high speed until pale and fluffy, about 3 minutes. Add egg and vanilla and beat until combined. Reduce speed to low and add flour mixture in 3 additions until just combined, scraping down bowl as needed.

3. Combine cinnamon and remaining ½ cup sugar in shallow dish and set aside. Working with 2 teaspoons dough at a time, roll into 16 balls and space them 2 inches apart on prepared sheet. Bake until edges are firm, 10 to 12 minutes, rotating sheet halfway through baking. Let cookies cool on sheet for 1 minute, place in cinnamon sugar, and turn to coat evenly. Transfer cookies to wire rack and let cool completely, about 30 minutes. Repeat twice more with remaining dough, letting baking sheet cool between batches.

4. FOR THE FILLING: Melt butter in small saucepan over medium heat. Whisk in cinnamon and anise and cook until fragrant, about 1 minute. Off heat, stir in dulce de leche until incorporated. Spread 1½ teaspoons filling on bottoms (flat sides) of each of 24 cookies. Top with remaining cookies to form sandwiches. (Cookies can be stored at room temperature for up to 3 days.)

$1,000 grand-prize winner

KEY INGREDIENT **Dulce de Leche**

Dulce de leche is a South American caramel made by slowly heating sweetened milk (or sometimes condensed milk, coconut milk, or goat's milk; if the last, it's called *cajeta*). In Latin America, dulce de leche, sometimes translated as "milk jam," is used in many sweets or simply spread on toast or pancakes. It reached the United States in a big way more than a decade ago when Häagen-Dazs used it for a new ice cream flavor. Look for dulce de leche in the international or baking aisle of your grocery store.

SWEET AND MILKY

BLACK CHERRY AND CHOCOLATE LINZERTORTE COOKIES

Kim Van Dunk, Caldwell, N.J.

Every Christmas when she was a child, Van Dunk baked sandwich cookies with her grandmother, filling most with jelly and a few with chocolate. As an adult, Van Dunk got the idea to combine the two flavors into a single fantastic cookie.

Makes 24 sandwich cookies

Plan ahead: The dough needs to chill before baking. You will need one 2½-inch and one 1-inch round cookie cutter. If you don't have superfine sugar, you can use granulated sugar processed for 30 seconds in a food processor.

2⅓ cups (11⅔ ounces) all-purpose flour	2 large eggs
1 teaspoon baking powder	½ teaspoon almond extract
½ teaspoon salt	1 cup (6 ounces) bittersweet
½ teaspoon ground cinnamon	chocolate chips
12 tablespoons unsalted butter, softened	1 cup black cherry preserves
1 cup (7 ounces) superfine sugar	Confectioners' sugar

1. Combine flour, baking powder, salt, and cinnamon in medium bowl. Using stand mixer fitted with paddle, beat butter and superfine sugar on medium-high speed until pale and fluffy, about 3 minutes. Add eggs, one at a time, and almond extract and beat until combined. Reduce speed to low and add flour mixture in 3 additions until just combined, scraping down bowl as needed. Divide dough in half. Form each half into 5-inch disk, wrap tightly in plastic wrap, and refrigerate for 1 hour.

2. Adjust oven racks to upper-middle and lower-middle positions and heat oven to 375 degrees. Line 2 baking sheets with parchment paper. Let chilled dough soften on counter for 10 minutes. Roll 1 disk of dough into 13-inch circle, about ⅛ inch thick, on lightly floured counter. Using 2½-inch cookie cutter, cut out 24 rounds, rerolling dough scraps just once. Space cookies ½ inch apart on prepared sheets. Bake until edges are lightly browned, about 7 minutes, switching and rotating sheets halfway through baking. Let cookies cool on sheets for 5 minutes, then transfer to wire rack. Let sheets cool.

3. Roll out second dough disk into 13-inch circle, about ⅛ inch thick. Using 2½-inch cookie cutter, cut out 24 rounds. Using 1-inch cookie cutter, cut circle from center of each cookie. Reroll any dough scraps, including circle cutouts, just once. Space cookies ½ inch apart on prepared sheets. Bake until edges are lightly browned, about 7 minutes, switching and rotating sheets halfway through baking. Let cookies cool on sheets for 5 minutes, then transfer to wire rack.

4. Microwave chocolate chips in bowl at 50 percent power, stirring occasionally, until melted, 2 to 4 minutes. Spread chocolate on bottoms (flat sides) of cookies without cutouts and let stand until chocolate is set, about 5 minutes. Spread 2 teaspoons preserves on chocolate on each cookie. Top with cutout cookies to form sandwiches. Sift confectioners' sugar over cookies just before serving. (Cookies can be stored at room temperature for up to 3 days.)

PRETZEL AND POTATO CHIP COOKIES WITH CARAMEL FROSTING

Patricia Harmon, Baden, Pa.

Harmon was familiar with potato chip cookies when she created her cookie. If crushed chips in cookies are good, she reasoned, chips plus pretzels would be even better, right? (Yes, right.) The caramel frosting kicks them up another notch.

Makes 24 cookies

Use a small, offset spatula to spread the frosting on the cookies.

COOKIES

12	tablespoons unsalted butter, softened
½	cup (3½ ounces) granulated sugar, plus ¼ cup for rolling
1	teaspoon vanilla extract
⅛	teaspoon salt
1½	cups (7½ ounces) all-purpose flour
2	ounces potato chips, crushed (⅔ cup)
¾	ounce mini pretzels, crushed (¼ cup)

FROSTING

½	cup packed (3½ ounces) light brown sugar
¼	cup heavy cream
3	tablespoons unsalted butter
	Pinch salt
½	teaspoon vanilla extract
1	cup (4 ounces) confectioners' sugar
¼	cup pecans, toasted and chopped fine

1. FOR THE COOKIES: Adjust oven rack to middle position and heat oven to 350 degrees. Line 2 baking sheets with parchment paper. Using stand mixer fitted with paddle, beat butter, ½ cup sugar, vanilla, and salt on medium-high speed until pale and fluffy, about 3 minutes. Reduce speed to low and add flour in 3 additions, scraping down bowl as needed. Stir in potato chips and pretzels.

2. Place remaining ¼ cup sugar in shallow dish. Working with 1 heaping tablespoon dough at a time, roll into 24 balls. Roll balls in sugar to coat and space them 2 inches apart on prepared sheets. Press dough to ¼-inch thickness using bottom of greased measuring cup.

3. Bake cookies, 1 sheet at a time, until set and edges are golden, about 15 minutes, rotating sheets halfway through baking. Let cookies cool on sheets for 5 minutes, then transfer to wire rack. Let cookies cool completely before frosting.

4. FOR THE FROSTING: Bring brown sugar, cream, butter, and salt to boil in medium saucepan over medium heat. Remove from heat and stir in vanilla. Transfer to bowl and let cool completely, about 20 minutes. Whisk in confectioners' sugar. Spread 1 teaspoon frosting on tops of each cookie. Sprinkle cookies with pecans and let stand until frosting is set, about 30 minutes. (Cookies can be stored at room temperature for up to 3 days.)

HAZELNUT ESPRESSO TRUFFLE COOKIES

Cindy Beberman, Orland Park, Ill.

Beberman was inspired to develop this recipe by the description of an "unforget-table" cookie that her sister enjoyed while traveling in Italy. Baking, says Beberman, is "one of life's great pleasures."

Makes 30 sandwich cookies

Both the dough and the filling need to chill. If you don't have superfine sugar, you can use granulated sugar processed for 30 seconds in a food processor. Use a thin spatula to help move these thin cookies from the counter to the baking sheets. To quickly cool the baking sheets between batches, run them under cold water.

2½	cups (12½ ounces) all-purpose flour	1	large egg plus 1 large yolk
1	cup hazelnuts, toasted, skinned, and finely ground	4	teaspoons instant espresso powder
½	teaspoon salt	2	teaspoons vanilla extract
½	teaspoon baking powder	¾	cup heavy cream
16	tablespoons unsalted butter, softened	3	cups (18 ounces) bittersweet chocolate chips
1¼	cups (8¾ ounces) superfine sugar		

1. Whisk flour, hazelnuts, salt, and baking powder together in medium bowl. Using stand mixer fitted with paddle, beat butter and sugar on medium-high speed until pale and fluffy, about 3 minutes. Add egg and yolk, one at a time, espresso powder, and vanilla and beat until combined. Reduce speed to low and add flour mixture in 3 additions until just combined, scraping down bowl as needed. Divide dough in half. Form each half into 5-inch disk, wrap tightly in plastic wrap, and refrigerate for 1 hour.

2. Adjust oven racks to upper-middle and lower-middle positions and heat oven to 375 degrees. Line 2 baking sheets with parchment paper. Let chilled dough soften on counter for 10 minutes. Roll 1 disk of dough into 14-inch circle, about ⅛ inch thick, on lightly floured counter. Using 2¼-inch cookie cutter, cut out 30 rounds, rerolling scraps just once. Space cookies ½ inch apart on prepared sheets. Bake until edges are slightly browned, about 7 minutes, switching and rotating sheets halfway through baking. Let cookies cool on sheets for 5 minutes, then transfer to wire rack. Repeat with second disk of dough and cooled sheets. Let cookies cool completely before frosting.

3. Heat cream in small saucepan over medium heat until simmering. Place 1¾ cups chocolate chips in medium bowl. Pour hot cream over chocolate chips; cover with aluminum foil and let sit for 5 minutes. Whisk chocolate mixture until smooth. Refrigerate chocolate ganache, uncovered, stirring occasionally, until thickened, about 40 minutes.

4. Using small metal spatula, spread 2 teaspoons ganache on bottoms of each of 30 cookies. Top with remaining cookies to form sandwiches. Microwave remaining 1¼ cups chocolate chips in bowl at 50 percent power, stirring occasionally, until melted, 2 to 4 minutes. Drizzle chocolate over cookies and let set, about 30 minutes, before serving. (Cookies can be stored at room temperature for up to 3 days.)

ALMOND-SCENTED MIXED DRIED FRUIT BITES

Barbara Estabrook, Rhinelander, Wis.

Estabrook turned fruitcake into a cookie, switching from the usual glacéed fruit to dried fruit, which she soaks in amaretto before adding to the batter. She says that apple juice or cider can be used as the soaking liquid instead of the amaretto.

Makes 24 cookies

This recipe calls for mini muffin tins. You can also use foil (not paper) liners without the muffin tin. Place the liners at least 1 inch apart on a rimmed baking sheet.

½	cup dried apple slices, chopped	⅛	teaspoon ground ginger
½	cup dried figs, stemmed and chopped	5	tablespoons unsalted butter, softened
⅓	cup dried cherries, chopped	½	cup packed (3½ ounces) dark brown sugar
⅓	cup golden raisins	2	large eggs
⅓	cup amaretto or other almond liqueur	2	tablespoons orange marmalade
2	tablespoons water	¼	teaspoon almond extract
½	cup (2½ ounces) all-purpose flour	⅔	cup mixed almonds, walnuts, and pecans, chopped coarse
¼	teaspoon ground cinnamon		Confectioners' sugar
⅛	teaspoon ground allspice		
⅛	teaspoon ground nutmeg		

1. Adjust oven rack to middle position and heat oven to 300 degrees. Line two 12-cup, or one 24-cup, mini muffin tin(s) with paper or foil liners. Combine apples, figs, cherries, raisins, ¼ cup amaretto, and water in small saucepan over medium heat and bring to simmer. Immediately remove from heat and let steep for 15 minutes. Strain through fine-mesh strainer, discarding liquid.

2. Combine flour, cinnamon, allspice, nutmeg, and ginger in bowl. Using stand mixer fitted with paddle, beat butter and brown sugar on medium-high speed until pale and fluffy, 2 to 3 minutes. Add eggs, one at a time, marmalade, and almond extract and beat until combined. Reduce speed to low and add half of flour mixture. Add nuts, fruit, and remaining flour mixture and mix until just combined, scraping down bowl as needed. Give batter final stir by hand. Fill each muffin cup with 2 tablespoons batter.

3. Bake for 15 minutes, then reduce oven temperature to 275 degrees. Continue to bake cookies until firm and toothpick inserted in center comes out clean, 15 to 20 minutes, rotating muffin tin(s) halfway through baking. Brush cookies with remaining 4 teaspoons amaretto while still hot. Let cool completely in muffin tin(s). Dust with confectioners' sugar just before serving. (Cookies can be stored at room temperature for up to 3 days.)

finalist

APPLE PIE CUTIE COOKIES
Amiee Deitz, Tualatin, Ore.

Deitz says that her family eats these cookies year-round but likes them best at holiday time because "they scream cinnamon, nutmeg, and all the holiday spices."

Makes 24 cookies

Deitz uses a round cookie cutter to stamp out the dough. But we found it easier to cut it into squares with a chef's knife—plus, there were no wasted trimmings. Plan ahead because both the dough and the filling need to chill.

PASTRY

- 2¼ cups (11¼ ounces) all-purpose flour
- 13 tablespoons unsalted butter, cut into ¼-inch pieces and frozen for 15 minutes
- 3½ tablespoons granulated sugar
- 1 teaspoon salt
- 4½ tablespoons ice water, plus extra as needed
- 1 teaspoon ground cinnamon
- 1 large egg, lightly beaten

FILLING

- ¼ cup water
- 1 teaspoon cornstarch
- 2 tablespoons unsalted butter
- 1½ pounds Granny Smith apples, peeled, cored, and cut into ¼-inch pieces
- ¼ cup packed (1¾ ounces) light brown sugar
- 1 teaspoon ground cinnamon
- ¼ teaspoon ground nutmeg
- ¼ teaspoon salt

1. FOR THE PASTRY: Using stand mixer fitted with paddle, mix flour, butter, 1½ teaspoons sugar, and salt and beat on low speed until mixture resembles coarse meal, about 3 minutes. Add ice water and mix until dough begins to come together, about 1 minute, adding extra water, 1 tablespoon at a time, as needed. Divide dough in half. Shape each half into 4-inch square, wrap tightly in plastic wrap, and refrigerate for 1 hour. Combine cinnamon and remaining 3 tablespoons sugar in small bowl; set aside.

2. FOR THE FILLING: Combine water and cornstarch in small bowl. Melt butter in 12-inch skillet over medium-high heat. Add apples and cook, stirring occasionally, until beginning to soften, about 5 minutes. Stir in sugar, cinnamon, nutmeg, and salt and cook until fragrant, about 30 seconds. Stir in cornstarch mixture and cook, stirring frequently, until sauce thickens, 1 to 2 minutes. Transfer to bowl and let cool completely, about 30 minutes.

3. Adjust oven rack to middle position and heat oven to 350 degrees. Line 2 baking sheets with parchment paper. Roll 1 square of dough into 12 by 8-inch rectangle, ¼ inch thick, on lightly floured counter. Spread evenly with apple mixture.

4. Roll remaining dough into 12 by 8-inch rectangle, ¼ inch thick. Using fluted pastry wheel, cut dough into sixteen 12 by ½-inch strips. Arrange dough strips diagonally in lattice pattern over filling, trimming as needed.

5. Cut into twenty-four 2-inch squares, brush tops with egg, and sprinkle with cinnamon sugar. Space cookies 1 inch apart on prepared sheets. Bake cookies, 1 sheet at a time, until golden, 30 to 35 minutes, rotating sheets halfway through baking; refrigerate second sheet while first is baking. Let cookies cool completely on sheets. (Cookies can be stored at room temperature for up to 2 days.)

WHITE CHOCOLATE–DULCE DE LECHE SHORTBREAD
Marisa Raponi, Vaughan, Ontario, Canada

Raponi says that this cookie resulted from good mother-daughter teamwork. The pair combined ideas on how best to dress up shortbread. The method for making the dough couldn't be easier: Raponi simply puts all the ingredients in the mixer at once and hits "start."

Makes 48 cookies

White chocolate can seize easily; take care not to overheat it. A rasp grater is our favorite tool for zesting oranges (and other citrus). Look for dulce de leche in the international or baking aisle of your grocery store.

- ¾ cup almonds, ground fine
- ¾ cup (5¼ ounces) sugar
- 4 cups (20 ounces) all-purpose flour
- 24 tablespoons (3 sticks) unsalted butter, cut into ½-inch pieces
- 1½ tablespoons grated orange zest
- 2 teaspoons vanilla extract
- 2 teaspoons almond extract
- 1 large egg white, lightly beaten
- 4 ounces white chocolate, chopped fine
- ½ cup dulce de leche

1. Adjust oven racks to upper-middle and lower-middle positions and heat oven to 350 degrees. Line 2 baking sheets with parchment paper. Combine almonds and ¼ cup sugar in small bowl; set aside.

2. Using stand mixer fitted with paddle, mix flour, butter, orange zest, vanilla, almond extract, and remaining ½ cup sugar on low speed until dough forms, about 4 minutes. Divide dough into 3 equal pieces.

3. Working with 1 piece at a time, roll dough into 12 by 8-inch rectangle on lightly floured counter. Brush dough with one-third of egg white, then sprinkle with one-third of almond mixture. Using fluted pastry wheel, cut dough into sixteen 3 by 2-inch rectangles. Repeat with remaining dough pieces, egg white, and almond mixture.

4. Space cookies ½ inch apart on prepared sheets, 12 cookies per sheet. Bake until golden around edges, 15 to 20 minutes, switching and rotating sheets halfway through baking. Let cookies cool on sheets for 5 minutes, then transfer to wire rack. Let cookies cool completely before frosting. Repeat with remaining dough and cooled sheets.

5. Microwave chocolate in bowl at 50 percent power, stirring occasionally, until melted, 1½ to 2 minutes. Using fork, drizzle chocolate over cookies. Microwave dulce de leche until pourable, about 30 seconds. Drizzle over cookies. Let chocolate and dulce de leche set, about 30 minutes, before serving. (Cookies can be stored at room temperature for up to 1 week.)

finalist

Cooking Class How to Cook with Dried Beans

Granted, cooking dried beans takes time, so you need to plan ahead. But creamy, flavorful beans are well worth the (mostly hands-off) wait. Our techniques yield perfect soup, and much more.

BY REBECCAH MARSTERS

Hearty White Bean Soup is just one of hundreds of ways to take good advantage of dried beans.

HEARTY WHITE BEAN SOUP
Serves 8

You can substitute collard greens or kale for the Swiss chard. In place of the cannellini beans, you can use any small white bean, such as great Northern or navy beans. Cooking times for all dried beans can vary depending on the age of the beans; taste the simmering beans often for doneness.

Salt and pepper
1 pound (2½ cups) dried cannellini beans, picked over and rinsed
6 slices bacon, chopped fine
1 pound Swiss chard, stems chopped, leaves sliced ½ inch thick
1 onion, chopped
2 celery ribs, cut into ½-inch pieces
2 carrots, peeled and cut into ½-inch pieces
8 garlic cloves, minced
4 cups chicken broth
2 bay leaves
1 sprig fresh rosemary
1 (14.5-ounce) can diced tomatoes

1. Dissolve 3 tablespoons salt in 4 quarts cold water in large container. Add beans and soak at room temperature for at least 8 hours or up to 24 hours. Drain and rinse well.

2. Adjust oven rack to lower-middle position and heat oven to 250 degrees. Cook bacon in Dutch oven over medium heat until crispy, 6 to 8 minutes. Using slotted spoon, transfer bacon to paper towel–lined plate. Pour off all but 1 tablespoon fat from pot.

3. Return now-empty pot to medium heat and add Swiss chard stems, onion, celery, and carrots. Cook, stirring occasionally, until vegetables are softened and lightly browned, 10 to 12 minutes. Add garlic and cook until fragrant, about 30 seconds. Stir in broth, 3 cups water, bay leaves, rosemary sprig, and soaked beans. Increase heat to high and bring to boil. Cover pot, transfer to oven, and cook until beans are almost tender (very center of beans will still be firm), 45 minutes to 1 hour.

4. Remove pot from oven and stir in Swiss chard leaves and tomatoes and their juice. Cover pot, return to oven, and continue to cook until beans are fully tender, 30 to 40 minutes. Discard bay leaves and rosemary sprig. Season with salt and pepper to taste. Stir in reserved bacon. Serve.

> ▶ We often cook dried beans in chicken broth. To read our chicken broth taste test, visit **CooksCountry. com/chickenbroth.**

STEP BY STEP Perfect Bean Soup

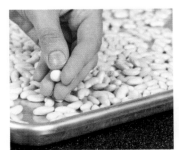

1. SORT AND RINSE
Pick through the beans for any pebbles or debris and rinse the beans.
WHY? Bags of beans often contain foreign matter that you don't want ending up in your soup.

2. BRINE BEANS
Dissolve salt in cold water, add the rinsed beans, and soak them for 8 to 24 hours.
WHY? An overnight soak starts hydrating the beans to reduce cooking time.

3. COOK BACON
Sauté the diced bacon until it's crispy and then set it aside.
WHY? The bacon fat gives the soup a savory, smoky base flavor.

4. SAUTÉ AROMATICS
Cook the vegetables in the bacon fat until they're softened and browned.
WHY? The browned vegetables will add a layer of flavor to the soup. We add the Swiss chard stems now so they can soften.

5. ADD LIQUID AND BEANS
Add the chicken broth, water, brined and rinsed beans, bay leaves, and rosemary sprig to the pot.
WHY? The beans need to be cooked in plenty of liquid to fully soften, and the chicken broth will make the soup taste better.

Core Techniques

TEST KITCHEN TIPS FOR ANY DRIED BEAN RECIPE

Sort Beans

Bags of dried beans sometimes contain small stones and other debris, so pick through the beans before cooking. Rinse the beans in a colander. Then, spread them out on a large white plate or baking sheet so you can easily spot (and discard) any detritus.

Brine Beans

Soaking beans overnight is standard procedure; brining them is even better. The salt in the brine seasons the beans and softens their skins. As the beans sit in the salty solution, the sodium ions in the salt replace some of the calcium and magnesium ions in the bean skins. Sodium ions weaken pectin, the glue that holds the cells together and strengthens the cell walls, so more water can penetrate, resulting in softer bean skins. Our ratio here—3 tablespoons of salt and 4 quarts of water for 1 pound of dried beans—will work for most bean varieties and recipes (lentils, however, do not require soaking). Refrigerate drained, brined beans in a zipper-lock bag for up to four days or freeze them for several weeks.

Beware of (Too Much) Acid

If the cooking liquid is too acidic, even hours of cooking won't soften dried beans. A low pH (higher acid) strengthens the pectin in beans, making them tougher; a very low pH prevents them from cooking. Although we found in tests that it takes a lot of acid to cause a problem, to be safe, we wait until beans are almost tender before adding acidic ingredients, like the canned tomatoes in our Hearty White Bean Soup.

Easy Does It

Cooking dried beans at a rolling boil can tear the skins and cause them to fall apart. Instead, once the beans and liquid come to a boil, we reduce the heat to maintain a slow, steady simmer. Baking beans, as we do here, is even more foolproof. A low oven—we opt for 250 degrees—coaxes the beans to tenderness.

Essential Gear

Dutch Oven

This recipe relies on a heavy Dutch oven with a tight-fitting lid. These pots are adept at simmering soups and sauces, frying chicken, and much more. They move smoothly from stovetop to oven, and they retain and conduct heat effectively. With cast-iron versions, we look for an enamel coating for easy cleaning and to prevent off-flavors.

**LE CREUSET
7¼-QUART ROUND FRENCH OVEN**
Our all-around favorite.

**LODGE COLOR ENAMEL
6-QUART DUTCH OVEN**
Our Best Buy.

Dried Bean FAQs

What if I don't have time to soak the beans overnight?
An overnight brine produces the creamiest beans, but if you're rushed you can do a quick soak: Bring the beans, salt, and water to a boil; turn off the heat; cover; and let them sit for an hour before draining and proceeding with the recipe. You can also simmer the beans in 3 quarts of water with 1 tablespoon of baking soda for 20 minutes; drain and rinse them well before proceeding.

Doesn't salting during cooking toughen the beans?
No. In fact, our brining method—we salt before we so much as turn on the stove—does the opposite, helping soften bean skins. The conventional wisdom—no salting while cooking—is wrong.

Why didn't my beans ever soften?
If your beans were soaked and then cooked for a long time (without acidic ingredients) yet still never softened, your beans were just too old or your water was too hard.

Why are beans hard to digest?
Beans contain small chains of carbohydrates called oligosaccharides that are hard to break down and digest and can cause gas. Presoaking and precooking beans removes some of these carbohydrates so may help eliminate digestive troubles.

6. BRING TO BOIL
Turn the burner to high and bring the mixture to a boil.
WHY? We cook the soup in the oven at a slow simmer, but first bringing the liquid to a boil on the stovetop jump-starts the cooking.

7. COVER AND BAKE
Put the covered pot in a 250-degree oven and cook for 45 minutes to 1 hour.
WHY? A low oven cooks the beans slowly and gently.

8. ADD TOMATOES
Remove the pot from the oven and stir in the Swiss chard leaves and tomatoes.
WHY? Added too soon, the acidic tomatoes can prevent dried beans from fully softening. We add the delicate leafy greens late in the cooking, too.

9. CONTINUE TO COOK
Return the pot to the oven for another 30 to 40 minutes.
WHY? In the remaining time, the beans will finish cooking, the greens will soften, and the flavors will meld.

10. ADD BACON AND SERVE
Season the soup with salt and pepper, stir in the bacon, and enjoy.
WHY? Adding the bacon at the end prevents it from becoming soggy during the long cooking time.

Obviously, it's easier to avoid batch-browning the beef before it goes into the cooker. But how do you compensate for the lost flavor that browning provides? BY SARAH GABRIEL

SOME DISHES ARE so perfectly suited to the slow cooker that it's almost a wonder we make them any other way. Beef stew—which requires hours of gentle, covered cooking—is at the very top of that list. Looking for a new angle on what the slow cooker does best, I collected recipes for daube Provençal, a French beef stew usually featuring the Mediterranean flavors of red wine, tomatoes, orange, and olives.

Right away I noticed a problem in translating the recipe for the slow cooker. Most recipes for this stew call for creating the deeply flavored gravy by taking a full bottle of red wine and simmering it uncovered until its volume has been reduced by one-third or more. Since very little evaporation takes place in the slow cooker thanks to the lid, I'd definitely need to cook down the wine before putting it in the cooker.

With that in mind, I started out by dealing with the meat. In the test kitchen, we like to buy a chuck-eye roast and cut it into cubes so that we know exactly what we're getting and can control the trimming and sizing—it's a little bit of extra work that's totally worth the effort. I seasoned and browned the meat in oil in a skillet in two batches and transferred it to the cooker. Then I browned chopped onion in the skillet and added garlic, herbes de Provence, tomato paste (which contributes color, flavor, and body), and flour to thicken. I stirred in 3 cups of wine and simmered until it reduced by about a third. I stirred the reduced wine mixture in with the meat in the cooker, along with some diced tomatoes, carrots, chicken broth, a teaspoon of grated orange zest, and chopped kalamata olives.

Soy sauce, extra tomato, and reduced wine give our unbrowned beef deep flavor.

After 6 hours on high, the meat was perfectly tender, the sauce velvety and just thick enough. Unfortunately, the orange zest had turned the stew sour and the olives tasted oddly metallic. These problems were easy to fix: I used strips of zest rather than grated for mellower orange flavor, and I added the chopped olives just before serving to avoid the odd taste that they can acquire through long cooking. These adjustments left me with a truly delicious stew

that had a nice balance of beefy and bright—but it was an awful lot of work to brown both the meat (in batches—ugh) and the onions before it all went in the cooker. Could I find an easier way?

I made the stew again, skipping the meat-browning step and starting by sautéing the onions in oil. This time the stew was thinner because I hadn't cooked any of the liquid out of the meat, and the flavor was, unsurprisingly, a bit wimpy due to the lack of browning. In the test kitchen, we often boost the meaty flavor of dishes with ingredients that are high in glutamates, the chemical compounds responsible for *umami*. I made another batch of stew, this time upping the amount of umami-rich tomato paste and cooking down the wine nearly to a paste. The consistency was back to where I wanted it and the flavor was much improved, but my stew still needed more backbone. Soy sauce—which the test kitchen uses with some frequency to boost meaty flavor in all manner of dishes—was the right fix here. After a few tests, I figured out the best way to use it: Trading ¼ cup of

broth for an equal amount of soy sauce added the depth that I was looking for.

With this new variation on my old favorite, I'll be eating twice as much slow-cooker beef stew this winter.

SLOW-COOKER MEDITERRANEAN BEEF STEW Serves 6 to 8

Salting the beef first gives the salt time to penetrate. Remove the zest strips from the orange using a vegetable peeler, being careful to leave the bitter white pith behind.

- 1 (4-pound) boneless beef chuck-eye roast, trimmed and cut into 1½-inch pieces
  Salt and pepper
- 2 tablespoons olive oil
- 3 onions, chopped fine
- ⅓ cup tomato paste
- 6 garlic cloves, minced
- 1 tablespoon packed brown sugar
- 2 teaspoons herbes de Provence
- ⅓ cup all-purpose flour
- 3 cups red wine
- 1½ pounds carrots, peeled and sliced ½ inch thick
- 1 (14.5-ounce) can diced tomatoes, drained
- 1 cup chicken broth
- ¼ cup soy sauce
- 3 (2-inch) strips orange zest
- ⅓ cup pitted kalamata olives, chopped fine

1. Season beef with salt and pepper; set aside. Heat oil in 12-inch nonstick skillet over medium-high heat until shimmering. Add onions, tomato paste, garlic, sugar, herbes de Provence, 2 teaspoons salt, and 1 teaspoon pepper and cook until onions are softened, 8 to 10 minutes.

2. Stir in flour and cook for 1 minute. Slowly whisk in wine and bring to simmer. Cook until sauce is consistency of ketchup and spatula leaves trail when dragged across bottom of skillet, about 15 minutes. Transfer to slow cooker.

3. Transfer beef to slow cooker and stir in carrots, tomatoes, broth, soy sauce, and orange zest. Cover and cook until beef is tender, 5 to 7 hours on high or 9 to 11 hours on low. Let beef sit, uncovered, for 10 minutes. Using spoon, skim any fat from surface of stew; discard orange zest. Stir in olives. Season with salt and pepper to taste. Serve.

Adding Mediterranean Flair

Even the most ardent fans of beef stew need to mix up the flavors every once in a while. While a splash of red wine is a common stew ingredient, our Mediterranean-inspired recipe starts with 3 full cups. It's also flavored with fragrant orange zest; kalamata olives; and herbes de Provence, a blend that includes rosemary, sage, fennel seeds, lavender, thyme, and marjoram.

PLANE TICKET
These ingredients transport beef stew to the Mediterranean.

Too often, stuffed mushrooms are either leathery or rubbery. We found the way to tender, flavorful stuffed mushrooms that you'd actually want to eat. BY NICK IVERSON

ATTEND ENOUGH HOLIDAY parties and you'll eventually run into stuffed button mushrooms. The encounter may not be happy, as they're often leathery caps with bland fillings. Recently, as I was politely declining yet another mushroom, I decided to revisit the recipe. I felt sure that I could make meaty, tender, and flavorful stuffed mushrooms, an hors d'oeuvre actually worth eating.

Fortunately, I had a head start. Several years back, we made a big discovery about stuffed mushrooms. Most recipes call for simply stuffing the raw caps and then baking the filled mushrooms for about a half-hour. Because mushrooms contain a lot of water, the hors d'oeuvre turns out soggy. In a misguided attempt to eliminate the moisture, some recipes call for cooking the stuffed mushrooms to death. After much experimentation, we were able to produce meaty caps with intense mushroom flavor by roasting the caps without stuffing first. We start gill side up, roasting at 425 degrees until the caps are nicely caramelized and their juice is released, about 20 minutes, and then we flip the mushrooms for the last 10 minutes to let the juice escape. At that point, we stuff the roasted caps and bake them for just a few minutes more.

There are almost as many stuffing possibilities as there are recipes. They run the gamut from bread crumbs, cream cheese, or chopped spinach to ground meat. But instead of looking for other things to

stuff the mushrooms with, I turned to an item I had right at hand: the mushroom stems. I stole the method from French duxelles, a classic mushroom stuffing: I chopped the stems in the food processor with shallot and garlic. I then sautéed the mixture, letting the mushroom juice come out and evaporate. I added white wine and let it, too, nearly evaporate, and then I stirred in thyme and lemon juice.

By the time the stuffing was done, the caps were cool enough to stuff, and after 5 minutes in the oven, they were ready to taste. Whoops—a hitch. The stuffing tumbled out as soon as we bit in—the last thing you want when you're wearing your favorite party clothes. I made a new batch, this time adding grated Parmesan cheese, which bound the filling and, a bonus, contributed good flavor, too.

Judging by the speed with which they disappeared, these mushrooms would never have to learn how to handle rejection. And they were so easy to make that I developed four variations.

STUFFED MUSHROOMS WITH PARMESAN AND THYME
Makes 24 stuffed mushrooms

24   large white mushrooms (1¾ to 2 inches in diameter), stems removed and reserved
¼   cup olive oil
     Salt and pepper
1   small shallot, minced
2   garlic cloves, minced
¼   cup dry white wine
1   ounce Parmesan cheese, grated (½ cup)
1   teaspoon minced fresh thyme
1   teaspoon lemon juice

1. Adjust oven rack to middle position and heat oven to 425 degrees. Line rimmed baking sheet with aluminum foil. Toss mushroom caps with 2 tablespoons oil, ¼ teaspoon salt, and ⅛ teaspoon pepper in large bowl. Arrange caps gill side up on prepared sheet and roast until juice is released, about 20 minutes. Flip caps and roast until well browned, about 10 minutes; set aside.

2. Meanwhile, pulse reserved stems, shallot, garlic, and ⅛ teaspoon pepper in food processor until finely chopped, 10 to 14 pulses. Heat remaining 2 tablespoons oil in 8-inch nonstick skillet over medium heat until shimmering. Add

stem mixture to skillet and cook until golden brown and moisture has evaporated, about 5 minutes. Add wine and cook until nearly evaporated and mixture thickens slightly, about 1 minute. Transfer to bowl and let cool slightly, about 5 minutes. Stir in Parmesan, thyme, and lemon juice. Season with salt and pepper to taste.

3. Flip caps gill side up. Divide stuffing evenly among caps. (Stuffed caps can be refrigerated for 1 day; increase baking time to 10 to 15 minutes.) Return caps to oven and bake until stuffing is heated through, 5 to 7 minutes. Serve.

STUFFED MUSHROOMS WITH CHORIZO AND MANCHEGO
In step 2, before adding stem mixture, cook 1½ ounces Spanish-style chorizo sausage, cut into ¼-inch pieces, in skillet until lightly browned, about 2 minutes. Proceed with remainder of step 2, substituting ¼ cup shredded Manchego cheese for Parmesan; 2 tablespoons chopped fresh parsley for thyme; and sherry vinegar for lemon juice. Add ½ teaspoon paprika to cooked stuffing.

STUFFED MUSHROOMS WITH BACON AND BLUE CHEESE
In step 2, omit oil and cook 2 slices finely chopped bacon in skillet (before adding stem mixture) until crispy, about 5 minutes. Proceed with remainder of step 2, substituting ¼ cup crumbled blue cheese for Parmesan; 2 tablespoons chopped fresh chives for thyme; and cider vinegar for lemon juice.

STUFFED MUSHROOMS WITH CHEDDAR, FENNEL, AND SAGE
Substitute ¼ cup shredded sharp cheddar cheese for Parmesan; ½ teaspoon fennel seeds and ½ teaspoon dried sage for thyme; and malt vinegar for lemon juice. Add ¼ teaspoon red pepper flakes to cooked stuffing.

STUFFED MUSHROOMS WITH OLIVES AND GOAT CHEESE
Substitute ¼ cup crumbled goat cheese for Parmesan; 1 teaspoon chopped fresh oregano for thyme; and red wine vinegar for lemon juice. Add 3 tablespoons chopped pitted kalamata olives to cooked stuffing.

The filling is made from shallot, garlic, Parmesan, and the sautéed mushroom stems.

TEST KITCHEN DISCOVERY
Most stuffed mushroom recipes call for stuffing raw mushrooms, which works if you like watery filling and spongy mushrooms. We prevent those by roasting the mushroom caps before stuffing them.

Cooking for Two Chicken and Dumplings

They say that less is more. Could we make less stew with less effort but wind up with more flavor?

BY SARAH GABRIEL

CHICKEN AND DUMPLINGS is a perfect warm-you-up winter stew. Most recipes feed six or so, but if you don't eat the dish right away, any leftover dumplings get soggy and start to disintegrate. I wanted a recipe tailored for two for the nights when that's how many are at the table.

The test kitchen already has a few chicken and dumplings recipes that feed about six. One calls for a whole chicken, while another calls for bone-in, skin-on parts, and the third goes with boneless, skinless breasts. All three use flour, salt, baking powder, and cream for the dumplings. The whole chicken recipe didn't make sense for two, so I tried the others. I won't bore you with the details of the bone-in recipe, but while it was delicious, it also created too many hoops to jump through for two servings. The second recipe, made with boneless, skinless chicken breasts, was slightly simpler; still, cooking and shredding the chicken required a tedious into-the-pot (for poaching), out-of-the-pot (for shredding), back-into-the-pot (to finish the filling) routine. Could I downsize the effort as well as the batch size?

Starting with the simpler boneless chicken recipe, I did some quick division to reduce the yield and, in hopes of nixing the in-and-out gymnastics

▶ Does the brand of sherry you cook with really matter? Yes, it does. Read our sherry tasting at CooksCountry.com/sherrytasting.

with the chicken, cut the meat into chunks before starting. I built the stew by sautéing the onion and carrots, adding flour, and then stirring in sherry, chicken broth, and cream. Once the stew was simmering, I introduced the diced chicken. When the chicken was done, I stirred in frozen peas and spooned out the dumpling batter; then I covered the pot. When the dumplings were finished, about 10 minutes later, the stew was boiling hot, so I let it cool a little before I called my coworkers to try it. The consistency and seasoning were right, but the peas were squishy and olive green, and the meat was way overcooked.

The cut-up boneless, skinless chicken breasts had made the stew easier and quicker, but they were too easy to overcook. Larger pieces would cook more slowly, but since they wouldn't be bite-size, I'd be back to the put-your-chicken-in, take-your-chicken-out hokeypokey. Not ready to give up on the pared-down method of starting with cut-up chicken, I traded the breast meat for diced boneless, skinless thighs. The meat was cooked through after simmering for about 15 minutes, so I scooped in the dumpling dough. This time, I let the dumplings cook partway before sprinkling the frozen peas around them, replacing the cover, and simmering everything 5 minutes longer. Once again, I let the stew sit uncovered for a few minutes to cool while I gathered bowls and spoons and summoned tasters.

Now, the meat was tender and still moist, the broth flavorful, and the peas perfectly cooked. I could have called it quits, but there was one last nagging detail. When I scaled down the original recipe, I ended up needing so little cream—a little in the filling, more in the dumpling batter—that I had started to wonder if I needed it at all. I tried the recipe once more, skipping the cream in the filling, and was pleasantly surprised to find the flavor brighter and more chicken-y. Next, I replaced the cream in the dumplings with broth plus a tablespoon of melted butter (to keep the tenderness lent by cream's fat). This switch delivered dumplings with deeper seasoning and a subtly meaty flavor.

My recipe was smaller, but the flavor was bigger.

Stock Two Ways

Sure, you'd expect us to use chicken stock (or broth) as the base of the stew for chicken and dumplings. But did you ever think we'd use it in the dumplings, too? Surprise. Replacing the usual cream with just a little stock gives us more deeply seasoned dumplings with a subtle meaty flavor.

TEST KITCHEN FAVORITE Swanson Chicken Stock.

Chopped boneless chicken thighs add meaty flavor fast.

CHICKEN AND DUMPLINGS FOR TWO

Make the dumplings just before adding them to the stew.

STEW
- 2 tablespoons unsalted butter
- 2 carrots, peeled and sliced ¼ inch thick
- 1 small onion, chopped fine
- 1 garlic clove, minced
- ½ teaspoon minced fresh thyme Salt and pepper
- 1 tablespoon all-purpose flour
- ¼ cup dry sherry
- 2 cups chicken broth
- 1 pound boneless, skinless chicken thighs, trimmed and cut into 1-inch pieces
- ⅓ cup frozen peas

DUMPLINGS
- ½ cup (2½ ounces) all-purpose flour
- 1 teaspoon baking powder
- ¼ teaspoon salt
- ¼ cup chicken broth
- 1 tablespoon unsalted butter, melted

1. FOR THE STEW: Melt butter in medium saucepan over medium-high heat. Add carrots and onion and cook until lightly browned, 5 to 8 minutes. Add garlic, thyme, ½ teaspoon salt, and ½ teaspoon pepper and cook until fragrant, about 30 seconds. Add flour and cook, stirring, for 1 minute. Stir in sherry, scraping up any browned bits, and cook until nearly dry, about 1 minute. Slowly stir in broth and bring to boil. Add chicken, reduce heat to medium-low, cover, and simmer until chicken is cooked through and tender, about 15 minutes.

2. FOR THE DUMPLINGS: Combine flour, baking powder, and salt in bowl. Stir in broth and melted butter until just incorporated.

3. Season stew with salt and pepper to taste. Increase heat to medium. Using 2 spoons, drop eight 1-inch dumplings into stew about 1 inch apart. Cover and simmer for 5 minutes. Sprinkle peas around dumplings, cover, and cook 5 minutes longer. Remove from heat and let cool slightly, uncovered, about 10 minutes. Serve.

Recipe Makeover Meatballs and Marinara

What's the secret to hearty, tasty meatballs that don't weigh you down? BY CRISTIN WALSH

MEATBALLS IN MARINARA have been a staple weeknight meal for me ever since I was a little kid, which is why I was so taken aback when I recently learned that a big bowl can contain a whopping 47 grams of fat and 830 calories, even without the pasta. Was there a way to lighten them without sacrificing flavor?

There are plenty of reduced-fat and low-calorie recipes for meatballs and marinara, but after preparing a handful of them, we agreed that none could hold a candle to the original. Many of these recipes simply swapped out the beef for ground turkey or chicken, but they made dull meatballs that lacked beefiness. More creative recipes tried replacing a portion of the ground beef with things like bulgur wheat, rice, or oatmeal, but the resulting meatballs were bland and spongy or mushy. The most promising recipe used finely chopped mushrooms, and though this recipe made meatballs that were wet instead of moist, the idea to harness mushrooms' meaty flavor held promise.

The test kitchen has a great meatballs and marinara recipe, so I started there. It combines ground beef, a white bread and milk mixture called a panade (which helps keep the meatballs moist), sautéed onion, eggs, parsley, garlic, and salt. We roll the mixture into balls and sauté them in oil to get a flavorful browned crust before finishing the meatballs in marinara sauce. The sauce is straightforward: Sauté onions and garlic; stir in tomato paste; add red wine and reduce; and then add crushed tomatoes, simmer, and stir in basil and cheese at the end. This recipe is really, really good.

I made a few obvious adjustments before I got to the mushrooms. First, I replaced the 80 percent lean beef with 90 percent lean and used just egg whites, no yolks. Moving on to the mushrooms, I started by replacing half of the ground beef with mushrooms that I ground in the food processor. No good. The moisture in the mushrooms made the meatballs soggy. I tried sautéing the ground mushrooms with the onion to cook out some of the water, but it took almost 30 minutes. To speed things up, I turned to the microwave. After 5 minutes in the microwave, a whirl in the food processor, and a quick sauté with the onion, my mushrooms were ready to go. I mixed the mush-

room-onion mixture with the other meatball ingredients, shaped 12 meatballs, and opted to bake them to avoid the oil that I'd need to sauté them. After a few tests, I found that baking them for about 15 minutes in a 475-degree oven gave me great browning (the meatballs would finish cooking in the sauce to allow the flavors to meld). The texture was right, but the flavor needed a little goosing.

To bump it up, I added soy sauce—which has a high concentration of meaty glutamates—and replaced the milk in the panade with savory (and naturally lower-fat) chicken broth. This new batch of meatballs was full-flavored. As for the sauce, I knew that I'd have to cut back on the wine and cheese to meet my nutritional goals. In the end, after several tests, I halved the cheese (from ½ to ¼ cup) and lost the wine in favor of more chicken broth. This meatballs and marinara recipe is as healthy as it is tasty.

REDUCED-FAT MEATBALLS AND MARINARA Serves 4

This recipe makes enough to sauce 1 pound of pasta.

MEATBALLS
- 12 ounces cremini or white mushrooms, trimmed
- 1 slice hearty white sandwich bread, torn into pieces
- 2½ tablespoons chicken broth
- 1 teaspoon olive oil
- ½ onion, chopped fine
- 2 garlic cloves, minced
- ¼ teaspoon dried oregano
- 12 ounces 90 percent lean ground beef
- ¼ cup chopped fresh parsley
- 1 large egg white
- 1½ teaspoons soy sauce
- ¾ teaspoon salt
- ¼ teaspoon pepper

MARINARA
- 1 teaspoon olive oil
- 1 onion, chopped fine
- 1 teaspoon salt
- ⅓ cup tomato paste
- 4 garlic cloves, minced
- ½ teaspoon dried oregano
- ⅛ teaspoon red pepper flakes
- 2 (28-ounce) cans crushed tomatoes
- ¾ cup chicken broth
- ¼ cup grated Parmesan cheese
- ¼ cup chopped fresh basil

Ground mushrooms replace half of the ground meat, cutting fat but keeping meaty flavor.

1. FOR THE MEATBALLS: Adjust oven rack to upper-middle position and heat oven to 475 degrees. Line rimmed baking sheet with aluminum foil and spray with vegetable oil spray. Microwave mushrooms in covered bowl until liquid is released, about 5 minutes. Strain mushrooms through colander, transfer to food processor, and process until finely ground, about 30 seconds. Return mushrooms to now-empty bowl; set aside. Add bread and broth to now-empty processor and process until paste forms, about 30 seconds. Transfer bread mixture to large bowl; set aside.

2. Heat oil in Dutch oven over medium-high heat until just smoking. Add onion and mushrooms and cook, stirring occasionally, until browned bits form on bottom of pot, 6 to 8 minutes. Stir in garlic and oregano and cook until fragrant, about 30 seconds. Add to bowl with bread mixture. Add beef, parsley, egg white, soy sauce, salt, and pepper and knead with your hands until combined. Using ¼-cup dry measuring cup, divide mixture into 12 portions, shape into meatballs, and place on prepared sheet. Bake until well browned, about 15 minutes.

3. FOR THE MARINARA: Meanwhile, heat oil in now-empty pot over medium

heat until shimmering. Add onion and salt and cook until beginning to brown, 5 to 7 minutes. Add tomato paste, garlic, oregano, and pepper flakes and cook until rust-colored and fragrant, about 1 minute. Stir in tomatoes and broth and bring to boil. Reduce heat to medium-low, cover with lid slightly ajar, and simmer until sauce is no longer watery, 20 to 30 minutes.

4. Add meatballs to sauce and simmer, uncovered, for 15 minutes. Stir Parmesan and basil into sauce. Serve. (Meatballs and sauce can be refrigerated for up to 3 days or frozen for up to 1 month.)

Equipment Review Roasting Pans

We went looking for a model that we'd want to use all the time, not just twice a year. BY AMY GRAVES

A HANDSOME, HEAVY-DUTY roasting pan bearing a big holiday roast—what could be more iconic? But twice-a-year employment for an item that can cost $300 (or more) never made any sense to us, which is why we were glad to find the reasonably priced Calphalon Contemporary Stainless Roasting Pan with Rack ($99.99). This sturdy, roomy workhorse impressed us with even browning and an ability to withstand high-heat searing on the stovetop. Luckily, Calphalon hasn't changed a thing about the pan since we discovered it in 2006, not even the price.

So why are we fixing what ain't broke? Cookware companies are constantly coming out with new roasting pans. Our search turned up six other contenders, costing $18 and up, including a $200 model that we tested to see if spending more meant better performance. Materials ranged from all aluminum to enamel-coated steel, plain stainless steel, a tri-ply construction of stainless steel sandwiching a core of aluminum. All models were at least 12 inches wide and 16 inches long and came with racks.

We started by roasting 2 pounds of potatoes coated in olive oil in each pan to see which materials browned evenly. Plain stainless steel was the worst, leaving spuds at the center pale while those at the edges overbrowned. Thin, enamel-coated steel pans weren't much better. Pans of stainless steel plus aluminum distributed the heat more evenly across their surfaces; most browned well. As for the all-aluminum pan, its dark surface browned evenly but very quickly: Its contents were deeply golden brown (the potatoes were perfect) in half of the time that the other pans took.

These results were repeated when we seared pork loins in the pans over a medium-high flame on the stovetop: The thin stainless-steel model buckled and burned, blackening the pan surface. We tried again over lower heat, but that didn't get a very nice sear on the meat. One enamel-coated steel pan fared even worse, blackening and making a popping noise as its enamel cracked and a few pieces of enamel fell off. (We got a second copy of this pan and lowered the flame, which helped.) And after their interiors blackened, these two pans were impossible to get completely clean; the rest cleaned up easily. Though tri-ply pans were heavier to maneuver, they heated steadily on the stovetop, never warping or buckling, leaving golden-brown crusts on the pork—ditto the all-aluminum pan.

Moving the pans was about more than weight. Large, easy to grip handles made a difference, as did pan shape. One sizable, boxy pan was awkward and heavy—not fun when we had to pour out hot drippings. The enamel-coated steel pans were lightweight, but their handles, also enameled, were slippery and small. Pans with big handles facing upward gave us a sure grip with potholders and helped us transfer the pan steadily, whether it held 2 pounds of potatoes or a 19-pound turkey.

But hoisting pans laden with big birds pointed to another factor: how well the racks fit. Some were much more secure and snug than others. Racks much smaller than their corresponding pans lurched and slid when we moved the heavy turkey. One traveled nearly 6 inches with a bird and hot drippings.

Deglazing drippings in the pans made us appreciate those with flat, or nearly flat, bottoms rather than deep grooves.

And while the dark anodized surface of the aluminum pan yielded darker roasted bits, verging on scorched, the tri-ply pans' lighter finish provided golden-brown fond that worked perfectly for gravy. (We could also monitor browning more easily in lighter pans.)

We're sticking with the Calphalon Contemporary Stainless Roasting Pan with Rack. Whether roasting a turkey, browning potatoes, or searing a pork loin, it gave us great results. For an even more budget-friendly alternative, get our Best Buy, also by Calphalon.

	CRITERIA		TESTERS' NOTES

HIGHLY RECOMMENDED

CALPHALON Contemporary Stainless Roasting Pan with Rack
Model: LRS1805P **Price:** $99.99
Source: cookwareking.net
Dimensions: 16 by 13.5 in; 5 lb, 12.5 oz
Material: 18/10 stainless steel surrounding aluminum core; dishwasher-safe

| Performance | ★★★ |
| Design and Handling | ★★★ |

This reasonably priced pan wins again. The tri-ply construction made it sturdy and reliable for stovetop searing and delivered even, consistent browning. The handles were roomy and secure, even with potholders. The U-shaped rack was slightly loose in the pan—a minor drawback.

RECOMMENDED

CUISINART MultiClad Pro Stainless 16" Roasting Pan with Rack
Model: MCP117-16BR **Price:** $129.95
Source: cutleryandmore.com
Dimensions: 16 by 12.25 in; 6 lb, 9 oz
Material: Stainless steel surrounding aluminum core; dishwasher-safe

| Performance | ★★★ |
| Design and Handling | ★★ ½ |

This pan vied closely with our winner, searing pork loin nicely without buckling or burning and putting an even, golden-brown crust on potatoes. It held a 19-pound turkey easily and its flat bottom aided deglazing. The rack fit snugly, but its handles line up with the pan's, making it tricky for unloading—our sole quibble.

CALPHALON Commercial Hard-Anodized Roasting Pan with Nonstick Rack
Model: GR1805P **Price:** $59.99
Source: cooking.com
Dimensions: 16.5 by 13 in; 3 lb, 8 oz
Material: Anodized aluminum; not dishwasher-safe

BEST BUY

| Performance | ★★ ½ |
| Design and Handling | ★★ ½ |

A great choice at about half of the price of our winner. This anodized aluminum pan browned potatoes quickly and made dark fond (so we had to watch it closely). It withstood stovetop heat without buckling, and its completely flat bottom was great for deglazing. The only drawback: Its handles flare inward and got in the way when we flipped the turkey (our method for ensuring even roasting).

RECOMMENDED WITH RESERVATIONS

LE CREUSET 17" x 13¾" Roasting Set
Model: SSC8512-40P **Price:** $199.99
Dimensions: 17 by 13.75 in; 7 lb, 3 oz
Material: Stainless steel surrounding aluminum core; dishwasher-safe

| Performance | ★★★ |
| Design and Handling | ★ |

Though it browned evenly and made great fond, this pricey pan was big, heavy, and boxy, making it awkward and tricky for pouring off drippings. Its rack slid in every direction as we moved the pan—scary when laden with hot drippings and a 19-pound turkey. For athletic cooks only.

NOT RECOMMENDED

CUISINART Chef's Classic 16" Roasting Pan with Rack
Model: 7117-16UR **Price:** $61.29
Dimensions: 16.75 by 13 in; 3 lb, 8 oz
Material: Stainless steel; dishwasher-safe

| Performance | ★ |
| Design and Handling | ★ ½ |

This all-steel pan was hotter on the edges and cooler in the middle, browning potatoes unevenly and rendering little fond from roasting turkey. It was roomy but so flimsy that we could twist it with our hands, and it blackened on the stovetop in no time flat.

GRANITE-WARE Open Rectangle Roaster with Non-Stick V-Rack
Model: 0564 **Price:** $17.48
Dimensions: 18.5 by 12 in; 1 lb, 15 oz
Material: Enamel on steel; dishwasher-safe

| Performance | ★ ½ |
| Design and Handling | ★ |

Potatoes came out striped from the bottom's raised grooves and overbrowned around the pan's edges. The grooves got in the way when we deglazed. The pan withstood stovetop use only if we kept the flame at medium-low. Its handles were small and slippery, and its too-small V-shaped rack slid. A 19-pound turkey would not fit.

RACHAEL RAY 16.5 Inch Roaster with Rack
Model: 54929 **Price:** $49.99
Dimensions: 16.5 by 12.5 in; 3 lb, 12 oz
Material: Enamel on steel; not dishwasher-safe

| Performance | ★ ½ |
| Design and Handling | ★ |

This thin, lightweight pan buckled on the stove, and enamel pieces sheared off. (A replacement pan held up better.) Channels on the bottom impeded gravy making and left stripes on potatoes. The pan's low enamel handles were impossible to grab—testers dropped the pan twice. Potatoes roasted unevenly, and fond from turkey was too dark.

Taste Test Bread Crumbs

Two styles of bread crumbs and seven determined contenders. The battle for big crunch and good grip was on. BY HANNAH CROWLEY AND TAIZETH SIERRA

ONCE UPON A TIME, if you went to the grocery store for bread crumbs, there wasn't much choice—often just that ubiquitous cardboard can full of crumbs the texture of fine sand. So for years, when we called for bread crumbs in the test kitchen, we told you how to make them yourself. But in 2006, we tried panko, Japanese-style bread crumbs. They were just becoming more widely available in the United States, and we discovered that we really liked them. Since then, we've often relied on them in our recipes. Fast-forward seven years and panko is everywhere in the States; many companies now make these crumbs. We decided to examine the new products and, while we were at it, revisit traditional bread crumbs. Since the competition is fiercer, maybe the traditional crumbs had upped their game.

Good bread crumbs should be mildly wheaty but otherwise neutral in flavor. What really matters is that they be ultracrunchy and have excellent coating abilities. We gathered seven best-selling national bread-crumb products—five panko and two traditional—and put them in the ring in an East-meets-West bread-crumb battle royal. Before we tell you the outcome, you may be wondering how the two differ: Traditional bread crumbs are made from loaves of bread that are baked in an oven, dried, and crumbled; for panko, the loaves are typically cooked by electric current. Raw dough is placed on metal plates that conduct the current through the dough, zapping it into pale white loaves (the crust never colors). These loaves, too, are dried, and then they're broken into big, jagged crumbs, which are quickly toasted in a high-heat oven.

Generally speaking, panko is made from flour, sweetener, yeast, salt, and sometimes fat. Traditional bread crumbs have a similar set of ingredients but contain more preservatives and may use potato, oat, corn, or rice flours.

We tasted our lineup deep-fried as a coating for chicken nuggets, shallow-fried as a coating for pork cutlets, and baked as a coating for chicken breasts. We had a blowout: The panko delivered craggy texture and excellent crunch, crushing the traditional crumbs. By contrast, the traditional crumbs failed to adhere tightly to the food and made soppy, wan, soggy coatings. One panko product in particular aced each test. Wondering what made it so exceptional,

we went back into the kitchen to examine the size of the crumbs.

If traditional bread crumbs were too fine, some of the panko crumbs, we discovered, were too large. While our leading contender had excellent coverage, some of the other panko brands had such big crumbs that they left gaps and clung shaggily, like coconut flakes. We sifted each panko product. The leading product contained 75 percent medium crumbs and 25 percent small crumbs, a texture about halfway between typical panko and traditional crumbs. The other pankos had a much higher percentage of larger crumbs, roughly 89 to 92 percent.

Next, we coated raw chicken cutlets with each product and weighed them, first naked and then coated. The cutlet coated with our leading contender took on 3 to 6 percent more bread crumbs by weight than any other brand. The more bread crumbs that adhere the better the coverage, thus, ultimately, the crunchier the item you're cooking. Our winner's combination of small and medium-size particles hit the sweet spot: small enough for great coverage and big enough for crunch, yet not so big that the crumbs sloughed off.

The largest crumbs turned out to have a second drawback: fat and steam absorption. Hot fried food will absorb any oil left on its surface and can become greasy, while any steam trapped inside the fried casing will be absorbed by the crust, turning it soggy. Three of the panko brands—as it happens, the biggest and flakiest—yielded greasy or soggy chicken nuggets. Was there a correlation? We weighed 1 cup of each brand and found that the largest crumbs were also the lightest. We discovered that the large, light crumbs are dotted with tiny air pockets, which pull in more oil and steam than denser crusts. Our winning brand, densest of all the pankos but still less dense than traditional bread crumbs, struck the optimal balance for crispy, not greasy, chicken nuggets.

Our front-runner faced one more hurdle: the meatball test. Yes, this product was a champ when it came to coating, but bread crumbs serve a different function in meatball recipes; they are mixed with milk to make a panade, which is what keeps meatballs moist and tender. We made batches of meatballs with our leading brand and with the better of the two traditional bread crumbs. Because panko is so much

fluffier, we measured by weight. (Be careful substituting panko for regular crumbs, and vice versa; volumes and weight vary greatly from product to product.) The panko eked out a win.

So which is best—East or West? Strictly speaking, the Western-style crumbs failed. But though our top pick is in the panko style, it nonetheless

struck an East-West balance between the large, crispy flakes of panko and the small, dense ones of traditional Western-style crumbs. It provided maximum coating, tender binding, and ultimate crunch. Ian's Panko Breadcrumbs, Original Style came in first the last time we tested panko, and it took the prize this time, as well.

HIGHLY RECOMMENDED		TASTERS' NOTES
IAN'S Panko Breadcrumbs, Original Style **Price:** $4.69 for 9 oz (52 cents per oz) **Particle size:** 75 percent large, 25 percent small **Density:** 85 g per cup		Although the competition has grown, Ian's—our previous favorite—won again. The crumbs were "crunchy" and "substantial," with particles big enough to stay crispy yet on the smaller end of the panko spectrum. The medium grain "allows for an even coating" and "great cling factor."
RECOMMENDED		
KIKKOMAN Panko Japanese Style Bread Crumbs **Price:** $1.99 for 8 oz (25 cents per oz) **Particle size:** 92 percent large, 8 percent small **Density:** 63 g per cup		Tasters liked these bread crumbs for their "good neutral flavor," "slight" sweetness, and "big" crunch. As one taster put it, "Holy crunch, Batman!" But the large and porous crumbs sometimes absorbed too much oil, making "greasy" chicken nuggets.
PROGRESSO Panko Crispy Bread Crumbs, Plain **Price:** $2.99 for 8 oz (37 cents per oz) **Particle size:** 86 percent large, 14 percent small **Density:** 67 g per cup		These bread crumbs "tasted fresh, not stale," our tasters said, and had a "definite crunch" from "big," "chunky" particles. A few tasters faulted them for ho-hum adhesion, but overall they were passable: "Didn't knock my socks off but seemed like a workhorse."
4C Bread Crumbs Japanese Style Panko, Plain **Price:** $2.19 for 8 oz (27 cents per oz) **Particle size:** 89 percent large, 11 percent small **Density:** 63 g per cup		These bread crumbs were "a little yeasty, like fresh bread," with a "crispy, crunchy, and jagged" bite. They were serviceable, but their larger particle size meant that they produced greasier food and left bare spots on meat.
DYNASTY Panko Japanese-Style Bread Crumbs **Price:** $2.95 for 8 oz (37 cents per oz) **Particle size:** 92 percent large, 8 percent small **Density:** 50 g per cup		These bread crumbs reminded tasters of "lightly toasted toast"; they were a "pleasant" complement to chicken. They were crispy and "super-light," but with the largest crumb size of all the products we tested, the crumbs were sometimes soggy, and they coated unevenly.
NOT RECOMMENDED		
4C Bread Crumbs, Plain **Price:** $2.99 for 24 oz (12 cents per oz) **Particle size:** 100 percent small **Density:** 90 g per cup		These traditional-style "sandy" bread crumbs were too small for proper crunch. They stuck together to form a limp crust, which then failed to stick to the chicken nuggets. Among the seven products we tasted, only this one elicited complaints about the salt; this product has five times the sodium per gram as our winning product.
PROGRESSO Bread Crumbs, Plain **Price:** $3.29 for 24 oz (14 cents per oz) **Particle size:** 100 percent small **Density:** 112 g per cup		Tasters likened these traditional-style bread crumbs to cardboard, describing them as "musty" and "dusty." They made a "powdery" coating that "separated from the nuggets" and was soggy in some spots yet "way too sandy and grainy" in others. In sum, "needs more crunch and cling."

Looking for a Recipe

Have you lost a recipe you treasure? Ask a reader. While you're at it, answer a reader. Post queries and finds at **CooksCountry.com/magazine**; click on **Looking for a Recipe** (or write to Looking for a Recipe, *Cook's Country*, P.O. Box 470739, Brookline, MA 02447). We'll share all your submissions online and one recipe on this page; please include your name and mailing address.

DEVILED HAM SPREAD

Makes about 2 cups
Lucille Klopfer, Arlington, Mass.

"As a kid, I loved the stuff in the paper-wrapped can with the devil on it. Now I prefer to make my own. It's easy, and my whole family likes it as much as I do." Starting with thinly sliced ham ensures the proper texture. Serve the spread on crackers or rye toasts or in a sandwich. Using softened butter is key.

- 12 ounces thinly sliced deli Black Forest ham, torn into ½-inch pieces
- 4 tablespoons unsalted butter, softened
- 5 tablespoons mayonnaise
- 3 tablespoons Dijon mustard
- 2 tablespoons sweet pickle relish
- ½ teaspoon pepper
- ¼ teaspoon cayenne pepper
- ¼ teaspoon ground allspice

1. Pulse ham in food processor until coarsely chopped, about 12 pulses. Add butter and pulse until incorporated and ham is finely chopped, about 10 pulses.
2. Transfer mixture to bowl and stir in mayonnaise, mustard, relish, pepper, cayenne, and allspice until thoroughly combined. Cover and refrigerate for at least 30 minutes before serving. (Spread will keep, refrigerated, for up to 3 days.)

Poor Man's Lobster
Tim Perry, Franklin, Mass.

Years ago, a fisherman buddy of mine made me what he called "poor man's lobster." It was actually made with chunks of halibut fillet. He said he learned the recipe while working as a deckhand on a fishing boat in Alaska. I love lobster, but I had to admit, his recipe was delicious. Has anybody ever heard of this, and does anyone know how to make it?

FIND THE ROOSTER!

A tiny version of this rooster has been hidden in the pages of this issue. Write us with its location and we'll enter you in a random drawing. The first correct entry drawn will win our winning roasting pan (see page 30), and each of the next five will receive a free one-year subscription to *Cook's Country*. To enter visit **CooksCountry.com/rooster** by January 31, 2014, or write to Rooster DJ14, *Cook's Country*, P.O. Box 470739, Brookline, MA 02447. Include your name and address. **Laurel Peakman** of Fairhope, Ala., found the rooster on page 6 in the August/September issue and our winning small slow cooker.

WEB EXTRAS

Free for 4 months online at CooksCountry.com

All-American Breakfast Sandwiches
Broiler-Safe Baking Dishes Testing
Chicken Broth Tasting
Classic Cheddar Cheese Ball
Ham and Gruyère Breakfast Sandwiches
Sherry Tasting
Simpler Shrimp Bisque
Yellow Layer Cake

READ US ON iPAD.

Download the *Cook's Country* app for iPad and start a free trial subscription or purchase a single issue of the magazine. All issues are enhanced with full-color Cooking Mode slide shows that provide step-by-step instructions for completing recipes, plus expanded reviews and ratings. Go to **CooksCountry.com/app** to download our app through iTunes.

 Follow us on **Twitter**
twitter.com/TestKitchen

 Find us on **Facebook**
facebook.com/CooksCountry

U.S. POSTAL SERVICE STATEMENT OF OWNERSHIP, MANAGEMENT AND CIRCULATION

1. Publication Title: Cook's Country; 2. Publication No. 1552-1990; 3. Filing Date: 9/24/13; 4. Issue Frequency: Dec/Jan, Feb/Mar, Apr/May, Jun/Jul, Aug/Sep, Oct/Nov; 5. No. of Issues Published Annually: 6; 6. Annual Subscription Price: $35.70; 7. Complete Mailing Address of Known Office of Publication: 17 Station Street, Brookline, MA 02445; 8. Complete Mailing Address of Headquarters or General Business Office of Publisher: 17 Station Street, Brookline, MA 02445; 9. Full Names and Complete Mailing Address of Publisher, Editor and Managing Editor: Publisher: Christopher Kimball, 17 Station Street, Brookline, MA 02445; Editor: Jack Bishop, 17 Station Street, Brookline, MA 02445; Managing Editor: Scott Kathan, 17 Station Street, Brookline, MA 02445; 10. Owner: Boston Common Press Limited Partnership, Christopher Kimball, 17 Station Street, Brookline, MA 02445; 11. Known Bondholders, Mortgagees, and Other Securities: None; 12. Tax Status: Has Not Changed During Preceding 12 Months; 13. Publication Title: Cook's Country; 14. Issue Date for Circulation Data Below: August/September 2013; 15a. Total Number of Copies: 383,639 (Aug/Sep 2013: 398,133); b. Paid Circulation: (1) Mailed Outside-County Paid Subscriptions Stated on PS Form 3541: 293,480 (Aug/Sep 2013: 305,192); (2) Mailed In-County Paid Subscriptions Stated on PS Form 3541: 0 (Aug/Sep 2013: 0); (3) Paid Distribution Outside the Mails Including Sales Through Dealers and Carriers, Street Vendors, Counter Sales, and Other Paid Distribution Outside the USPS: 25,282 (Aug/Sep 2013: 23,990); (4) Paid Distribution by Other Classes of Mail Through the USPS: 0 (Aug/Sep 2013: 0); c. Total Paid Distribution: 318,762 (Aug/Sep 2013: 329,182); d. Free or Nominal Rate Distribution: (1) Free or Nominal Rate Outside-County Copies Included on PS Form 3541: 2,153 (Aug/Sep 2013: 2,359); (2) Free or Nominal Rate In-County Copies Included on Form PS 3541: 0 (Aug/Sep 2013: 0); (3) Free or Nominal Rate Copies Mailed at Other Classes Through the USPS: 0 (Aug/Sep 2013: 0); (4) Free or Nominal Rate Distribution Outside the Mail: 515 (Aug/Sep 2013: 515); e. Total Free or Nominal Rate Distribution: 2,668 (Aug/Sep 2013: 2,874); f. Total Distribution: 321,429 (Aug/Sep 2013: 332,056); g. Copies Not Distributed: 62,210 (Aug/Sep 2013: 66,077); h. Total: 383,639 (Aug/Sep 2013: 398,133); i. Percent Paid: 99.17% (Aug/Sep 2013: 99.13%).

Bananas Foster Cake

Even without the classic dessert's trademark flambé, this spin-off made with yellow layer cake, rum-soaked bananas, and rum buttercream is a showstopper.

To make this cake, you will need:

- ¾ cup dark rum
- ½ cup packed (3½ ounces) dark brown sugar
     Salt
- 2 tablespoons unsalted butter, chilled, plus 20 tablespoons (2½ sticks) softened
- 4 ripe bananas
- ⅛ teaspoon ground cinnamon
- 2½ cups (10 ounces) confectioners' sugar
- 1 teaspoon vanilla extract
- 3 (8-inch) yellow cake layers*

FOR THE CARAMEL: Cook ½ cup rum, brown sugar, and pinch salt in 10-inch skillet over medium-low heat, stirring frequently, until spatula leaves 2-second trail when dragged through sauce, 7 to 10 minutes. Remove caramel from heat. Whisk 3 tablespoons caramel and 2 tablespoons chilled butter together in small bowl until combined; set aside and let cool completely.

FOR THE FILLING: Peel and cut 2 bananas into ¼-inch-thick slices. Add sliced bananas and cinnamon to remaining warm caramel in skillet, and stir gently to combine. Set aside and let cool completely.

FOR THE FROSTING: Using stand mixer fitted with whisk, mix remaining 20 tablespoons softened butter and ⅛ teaspoon salt on medium-low speed until smooth, about 10 seconds. Slowly add confectioners' sugar and continue to mix until smooth, about 2 minutes. Add remaining ¼ cup rum and vanilla and mix until incorporated, about 1 minute, scraping down bowl as needed. Increase speed to medium-high and whip frosting until light and fluffy, about 5 minutes.

TO ASSEMBLE: Place 1 cake layer on cake plate or pedestal. Spread half of banana filling over cake. Top with second cake layer and remaining filling. Top with final cake layer and frost top and sides of cake. Just before serving, peel and cut remaining 2 bananas into ¼-inch-thick slices and shingle around top edge of cake. Pour reserved caramel-butter mixture over bananas, allowing excess to drip down sides of cake. Serve.

▶ *Go to CooksCountry.com for our **Yellow Layer Cake** recipe.

Inside This Issue

Chicken Baked in Foil 10

Spinach Gratin for a Crowd 6

Prime Rib and Vegetables 4

Stuffed Mushrooms 27

Pork Chop Casserole 14

Dulce de Leche Cookies 20

Melting Potatoes 7

Chicken with Vinegar Sauce 15

Chicken and Dumplings for Two 28

Apple Pie Cutie Cookies 23

Mediterranean Beef Stew 26

Charleston Shrimp Perloo 12

Breakfast Sandwiches 17

Cherry-Chocolate Linzer Cookies 21

Pork with Tomatoes and Capers RC

White Chocolate Shortbread 23

Chicken Banh Mi RC

Spiced Pork Pie 18

Lighter Meatballs and Marinara 29

Mixed Dried Fruit Bites 22

Red Chimichurri Sauce 5

Hazelnut Espresso Cookies 22

Rustic Chorizo Soup RC

Pretzel and Potato Chip Cookies 21

Sausage and Mushroom Penne R